Peoples
of All Nations

VOLUME FOUR

Frontispiece—Vol. IV

ITALY

See page 2992

PEOPLES OF ALL NATIONS

Their Life Today and
the Story of their Past

By Our Foremost Writers of
Travel Anthropology & History

Illustrated with upwards of 5000
Photographs, numerous Colour
Plates, and 150 Maps

Edited by

J. A. Hammerton

VOLUME IV

Pages 2353-3120

Georgia to Italy

Published at THE FLEETWAY HOUSE London E.C.

VOLUME FOUR

TABLE OF CONTENTS

Descriptive and Historical Chapters

GEORGIA. *Henry W. Nevinson* .. 2353
GERMANY I. *William Harbutt Dawson* 2371
  „ II. „ „ 2453
GREECE I. *Hamilton Fyfe* 2465
  „ II. *A. D. Innes* 2531
GUATEMALA I. *F. H. Hamilton* .. 2537
  „ II. *Percy F. Martin* .. 2555
HAITI I. *H. Hesketh Prichard* .. 2559
  „ II. *Percy F. Martin* .. 2573
HAWAII. *Richard Curle* 2577
HEJAZ I. *Edmund Candler* 2595
  „ II. *D. G. Hogarth* .. 2616
HONDURAS I. *Percy F. Martin* .. 2621
  „ II. „ „ .. 2630

HUNGARY I. *F. H. Hamilton* 2633
  „ II. *A. D. Innes* 2684
ICELAND. *R. Pape Cowl* 2689
INDIA I. *Sir Valentine Chirol* .. 2705
  „ II. „ „ .. 2867
IRAK I. *Edmund Candler* 2883
  „ II. *A. D. Innes* 2917
IRELAND I. *Milton Kelly* 2923
  „ II. *Stephen Gwynn* .. 2969
ITALY I. *Hamilton Fyfe* 2979
  „ II. *Edward Hutton* 3099
  „ III. *L. J. S. Wood* 3109

List of Colour Plates

Facing page
GERMANY : Forest Maiden 2384
GREECE : Belles of the Border .. 2480
HUNGARY : Peasant Bridal Couple .. 2640
Page
INDIA : Elephant at Bengal Gathering 2737
  Calcutta Shrine-Keeper .. 2738
  Ivory Carver 2739
  Wife of a Gurkha Fighting Man 2740
  Fruit Vender 2741
  Maratha Warrior 2742
  Arab Dancing Horse .. 2743

Page
INDIA : Nautch Group 2744
  Indian Dancing Women .. 2841
  Colourful Group 2842
  Nautch Girl 2843
  Executioner of Rewah .. 2844
  Men of the Northern Marches 2845
  Women of Kashmir 2846
  Children of North Kashmir.. 2847
  Officers of the Indian Army.. 2848
Facing page
ITALY : Ragazzi of the Campagna .. 2986
  Beauty from the Abruzzi .. 3040

Pages in Photogravure

NEW SCENES IN GERMANY
  Wendish Girls of the Spree-
    wald 2401
  Busy Market-place of Worms 2402
  Lofty Dome of Berlin .. 2403
  Peasants of the Bavarian
    Highlands 2404
  Stuttgart Sabbath Dress .. 2405
  In a Forest of Charlotten-
    burg 2406
  Nature Study by a Stream 2407
  Bridal " schappel " of Sankt
    Georgien 2408
  Bückeburg Bridal Attire .. 2409
  Women of the Nördlingen
    District 2410
  Roman Catholic Funeral
    Procession 2411
  Gift of the Bavarian Bride's
    Father 2412
  Girls of Sankt Georgien .. 2413
  In a Village of the Rhine .. 2414
  Rhenish Labourer 2415
  St. Goarshausen's " Castle
    Crag " 2416

GREEKS OF TO-DAY
  On the Summit of Parnassus 2497
  Near the Tomb of Leonidas 2498
  In the Fertile Valley of
    Sparta 2499
  Greek Villagers Dancing .. 2500
  At the Village Oven .. 2500
  Traditional Dance of the
    Greeks 2501
  Khani on the Road to
    Sparta 2501
  Monk of S. George .. 2502
  On the Balcony of the
    Monastery of S. George 2503
  Rocks of Parnassus .. 2504

Domed Well of Gastouri .. 2505
Priests' Home at Zemenon 2506
Refectory of the Megaspe-
  leon 2507
Weaving at Andritsena .. 2508
In the Porch of his Dwelling 2508
In the Cloister of S.
  Stephen's 2509
Monastery of the Holy
  Trinity 2509
Treading out the Grain .. 2510
Villagers of Zemenon .. 2511
Greek from Kastoria .. 2512

MAGYARS IN RICH ATTIRE
  Peasant Lads of Mezökövesd 2641
  En Route to Market .. 2642
  Women of a Lowland Village 2643
  Hungarian Gypsies .. 2644
  Old Beggar of Hungary .. 2645
  Handiwork of a Hungarian
    Housewife 2646
  Unique but Effective Head-
    dress 2647
  Boy and Girl of Csömör .. 2648
  Sturdy of Frame 2649
  Lowly Magyar Couple .. 2650
  Baby's Embroidered Bolster 2651
  Headman of a Cowherd
    Station 2652
  Cowherds of the Hortobágy
    Plain 2653
  Dancing the Csárdás .. 2654
  Matyók Peasants 2655
  Town-bred Daughters of
    Hungary 2656

ITALIANS OF TO-DAY
  Devout Fisherfolks' Wooden
    Shrine 2993
  Scuola di San Marco .. 2994
  Narrow Waterway of Venice 2995

Venetian Vegetable Merchant 2996
Starting on his Last Voyage 2997
Flower Girl of the Eternal
  City 2998
Preservers of the Papal
  Peace 2999
Monastery of Monte Oliveto
  Maggiore 3000
In Aosta Cathedral .. 3001
With Heart at Peace .. 3002
Colonnade of S. Peter's .. 3003
Roman of the Campagna .. 3004
Roman Flower-girl .. 3005
Rimini's Triumphal Arch .. 3006
Campanile of Giotto .. 3007
Straw-plaiting in Fiesole .. 3008

ITALIAN HARMONIES
  In the Shadow of Mount Etna 3057
  Sicilian Grandsire and His
    Son's Son 3058
  Sicilian Darby and Joan .. 3059
  In a Hospice for the Aged
    Poor 3060
  Children of Sunny Sicily .. 3061
  Benedictine Monks of
    Catania 3062
  Sacro Eremo of Camaldoli.. 3063
  Laundry Day in Omegna .. 3064
  Isle of San Guilio .. 3065
  By Lake Maggiore 3066
  Simple Scene on Maggiore.. 3066
  The Garden of Lombardy .. 3067
  The Glories of Como .. 3067
  Watching for Tunny Fish .. 3068
  Istrian Peasants Church-
    ward Bound 3069
  Old Town of San Remo .. 3070
  Celebrating the Nativity of
    the Virgin 3071
  Monks of Savoca 3072

Photographs in the Text

GEORGIA

Housewife's Daily Task ..	2354
Where Women Work ..	2355
Woman of a Handsome Race	2356
Veteran of a Mountain State	2356
After their Morning Tub ..	2357
Descendants of the Golden Horde	2358
In a Georgian Glade ..	2359
Replenishing their Cellars ..	2360
Fetching the Day's Water..	2361
Ploughing in the Caucasus..	2361
Descendant of a Hardy Race	2362
Member of the Aristocracy	2363
Sons of the Mountain Peasantry	2364
Youth, Manhood, and Old Age	2365
Haymaking in the Mountains	2366
Ease and Luxury ..	2367
Riders of the Plains ..	2368
Bred to Arms ..	2369
Garb of his Ancestors ..	2369

GERMANY

Group of Peasant Women..	2370
Two Little Maids ..	2372
Part of the Daily Routine..	2373
Filigree Nimbus ..	2374
Homely but Comely ..	2375
Baptismal Procession ..	2376
In the Bosom of her Family	2377
Dancing in the Streets ..	2378
Historic Headgear of Bavarian Brides ..	2379
At the Village Spring ..	2380
Toil-worn Women Land Workers	2381
Fantastic Feminine Finery	2382
Gretchen of the Black Forest	2383
Hat Style from Gutach ..	2384
Cutting Turnip Radishes ..	2385
Scene in the Reichstag ..	2386
Outside the Reichstag ..	2387
Young Germania Passes By	2388
Inspection of War Veterans	2389
Berlin at its Busiest and Best	2390
In the Heart of Berlin ..	2391
In a Glass Factory ..	2392
Working for Humanity ..	2393
Commercial Activity ..	2394
Leipzig's Advertisement Parade	2395
Adherents of King Carnival	2396
Secure in Mother-love ..	2397
On the Road to Church ..	2398
Pleasure Combined With Business	2399
Wendish Peasant Funeral..	2399
In the School of Nature ..	2418
At the Drawing Lesson ..	2418
School in the Pine Forests..	2419
Charlottenburg Forest School	2419
Little Berliners' Hearty Appetite	2420
After-dinner Task ..	2420
Leisurely Pursuit of Learning	2421
Training in Perspective Drawing	2422
Teaching Cleanliness ..	2424
In the Maternity Ward ..	2425
Weighing Young Germany	2425
In a Beer Garden ..	2426
Healthy Homesteads ..	2427
Villagers of Hesse-Nassau..	2428
Old-time Simplicity ..	2429
Instruction in Cheesemaking	2430
Filling the Moulds ..	2430
The Finished Cheeses ..	2431
Dry-salting the Cheeses ..	2431
Where Nicest Accuracy is Needed	2432
In the Works at Siemensstadt	2433
Preparing Tobacco for Drying	2434

Hanging up the Leaves ..	2435
Peeling Osiers ..	2436
Osiers Laid Out to Dry ..	2436
Making Wicker Chairs ..	2437
Bargaining for Baskets ..	2437
Old-fashioned Rural Costume	2438
Jungingen Costumes ..	2438
At the Ulm Festival ..	2439
Before the Board of Examiners	2439
Peasant Bride and Bridegroom	2440
Starched Sobriety ..	2441
After the Flax Harvest ..	2442
" Weave the Warp " ..	2442
In a Land of Legend ..	2443
Square in Munich ..	2444
Main Street of Frankfort ..	2446
Corner of Dresden ..	2448
Nuremberg Market Place ..	2448
Ulm Market Place ..	2450
Where Schiller Dwelt ..	2450
At the Savings Bank ..	2452
Before the Rathaus..	2461

GREECE

In the Streets of Nauplia ..	2464
Musical Greek Gypsies ..	2466
At the Fountain ..	2467
Captain of a Comitadji Band	2468
Youthful Patriots ..	2469
Soldiers of Picked Corps ..	2470
Sentry at the Royal Palace	2471
Theseum at Athens..	2472
Splendid in Ruin ..	2473
Narrow Byway of Canea ..	2474
Business Corner of Candia..	2475
Hostages to Fortune ..	2476
Monks of the Greek Church	2477
Men of Thebes ..	2478
Evzonoi Scouts on Patrol ..	2479
A Roast of Lamb ..	2480
" Look at the Pretty Camera " ..	2481
City of Athens ..	2482
Dancing a Pas de Quatre ..	2483
At Patras Port ..	2484
The Village Laundry ..	2485
Modern Exquisite ..	2486
Greeks of To-day ..	2487
Trail to the Sea ..	2488
Ingenuity on the Road ..	2489
Peasant at her Loom ..	2490
Making Ready the Fields ..	2491
Cows in the Corn ..	2492
Amid Broad Acres ..	2492
When the Reapers' Work is Done	2493
Pitching the Corn ..	2493
Threshing with a Fork ..	2494
Sifting and Winnowing ..	2494
Pretty Marriage Custom ..	2495
Bright Plumage in the Cyclades	2496
Feminine Dignity Personified	2513
Glimpse of Sunny Corfu ..	2514
Corfu Sickle Shop ..	2515
Greek Peasant Lying in State	2516
" A Grazing Flock " ..	2517
Macedonian Manhood ..	2518
In a Marble Quarry ..	2519
Pulpit Among the Tombs ..	2520
Priest of a Fanatical Sect..	2521
Jewish Women at the Kippaw	2522
Hanadji at the Hebrew Cemetery	2523
Relic of Moslem Rule ..	2524
Prosperity and Poverty ..	2525
Dignity and Impudence ..	2526
Peasant Girls Make Merry..	2526
Industry in the Vardar Valley	2527
Greek Ceramic Ware ..	2528
Thessalonian Women in Gala Attire	2529
Sturdy Fisher Folk.. ..	2530

GUATEMALA

Inhabitants of the Coban District	2536
The Rising Generation ..	2538
Marketing Indian Wares ..	2539
Stricken City of Guatemala	2540
Ruins in Antigua	2541
Mule Train	2542
Luscious Fruits for the Thirsty	2543
Test of Strength ..	2544
Woman with Avocados ..	2545
Chicle-gum Collectors' Camp	2546
Guatemala Indian Villagers	2548
Monolith of Quirigua ..	2550
Descendants of Maya Stock	2551
Mixcan Beauty ..	2553
Group of Coffee-pickers ..	2554

HAITI

Advertisement and Display	2558
Haitian Folk	2560
Riverside Laundry	2561
Town Fountain at Port au Prince	2562
Looking Down the Main Street	2562
In the Cathedral Square ..	2563
Chatter and Commerce ..	2564
Principal Street in the Capital	2565
Threshold of Voodoo Temple	2566
Laundry Work as a Penitential Task ..	2567
" Where Black Rules White "	2568
Sorting Coffee Beans ..	2569
Officialdom in Uniform ..	2570
Ex-President as Admiral ..	2570
Architectural Eyesore ..	2571
Enjoying the " Royal Diversion "	2572
Native Traders ..	2574
That Piccaninny Smile ..	2575

HAWAII

Musicians and Dancing Girls	2576
Flower-wreathed Coquetry	2577
Preparations for Gargantuan Banquet	2578
Pounding Taro Root ..	2579
Hawaiian Family	2580
Eating Poi	2581
Rider of the Waves.. ..	2582
Diana Goes Riding	2583
Hawaiian Feast	2584
Hauling in their Seine ..	2585
Eligible Dancing Men ..	2586
Preliminary Movement of a Dance	2587
Waiting their Turn to Dance	2588
" Beauty Fair in her Flower "	2589
Under the Oriel of the West	2590
Bringing Ashore their Catch	2591
Two Dusky Sirens	2591
Family Happiness	2592

HEJAZ

With Hands Upraised in Prayer	2594
Hussein, First King of Hejaz	2596
Venders of Holy Water ..	2597
Mecca's Great Mosque ..	2598
Pilgrims Performing the Wukuf	2599
At the " Durbar of God " ..	2600
Kneading Dough for Bread	2601
Parade of the Arab Army..	2602
Homeward Bound from the Well	2604
Impenetrably Veiled ..	2605
Pilgrim Encampment ..	2606
Jeddah's Unpaved Streets..	2608
Emir Feisal's Bodyguard ..	2609
Beduins Bound for the Town	2610
Negro Architecture in Hejaz	2612
Warriors of the Desert ..	2613
Deputy to the Emir ..	2614
Temporal Activity in Medina	2615

HONDURAS
Smashed Arches at Teguci-
  galpa 2620
Spanning a Slumbering
  Stream 2622
Honduran Home 2623
In a Town of the Hinterland 2624
Winding over the Hills .. 2625
Five Men in a Boat.. .. 2625
At Either End of Four Gen-
  erations 2626
Sunday Market at Amapala 2627
Artillery at Practice Man-
  oeuvres 2628

HUNGARY
Aspirants for Cupid s Fav-
  ours 2632
Vestal Virgin of Hungary .. 2633
Linked by Sweet Symbolism 2634
Woman at the Well .. 2635
Feminine Confidence .. 2636
After Church Service .. 2637
Lord or Henchman ? .. 2638
In the Hungarian Highlands 2638
Cooperation in Jelly-making 2639
Young Matron of Mez -
  k vesd 2640
Bridal Pair from Sark z .. 2657
Mending a Family Cauldron 2658
Vagabond Sons of Hungary 2659
Moneyed Members of Wan-
  dering Tribe 2660
Family Trio.. 2661
Evening Meal at a Prairie
  Station 2662
Cowherds' Leisure Hour .. 2663
Geese of the Hortobágy
  Fisherman 2664
Preparations for Fishing .. 2665
Home-made Fishing Tackle 2666
Paying his Respects .. 2667
Budapest's Flower Market.. 2668
Shopping Day in Debreczen 2669
Brave Hearts and Strong .. 2670
Under the Greenwood Tree 2671
Hungarian Pedlar 2672
Woman of Many Arts .. 2673
Religious Procession .. 2674
Representatives of the Army 2675
Sunday Morning Scene .. 2676
Two Strings to his Bow .. 2677
Six Merry Schoolboys .. 2678
Graceful Girlhood 2679
" Ring a Ring o' Roses " .. 2679
Goosegirl Driving her Flock 2680
Ponderous Wooden Loom.. 2681
Conservative Spirits .. 2682
Handsome Peasant Handi-
  work 2683
Open-air Mothers' Meeting 2688
Three Generations 2688

ICELAND
Star of the North 2689
Hair to Advantage Dressed 2690
Fair Mother and Daughters 2691
Acres of Codfish 2692
Where Nature Supplies Hot
  Water 2693
Anchorage under Misty
  Mountains 2694
Shoreboats in the Harbour 2695
Winter in Reykjavik .. 2697
The Icelanders' Oven .. 2697
Milkmaid on her Morning
  Round 2698
On the Rock-walled Post-
  road 2699
Bringing back their Hay .. 2700
Mail Caravan 2702

INDIA
Buddha's Holiest Place .. 2704
Trinkets to Outwit Evil .. 2705
Insignia of their Calling .. 2706
Men of Naga Tribe in War
  Trim 2707
Veteran Abor Archer .. 2708
Gravity and Wisdom .. 2709
Content with the Warmth
  of the Sun 2710
Representative of Abor Vil-
  lage 2711

In the Abor Jungle 2712
Abor Grace Undraped .. 2713
Simple Village Life.. .. 2714
Miri Nagas 2715
Arrival of the " Big Six " .. 2716
Smiling Beauty of the Wilds 2717
In Full Warpaint 2718
Param's Headman 2719
Rough-rider of Baluchistan 2720
Forest Bowman of the Hills 2721
How Hook-swinging is Done 2722
Superstition's Willing Victim 2722
Hook-swinging in Madras .. 2723
Winnowing the Grain .. 2724
Blue-blooded Son of India.. 2725
Wayfarers of Baluchistan .. 2726
State Elephants of Baroda.. 2727
India's Magic Mango Tree.. 2728
Charming the Folded Snake 2729
Privileged Animal of Hin-
  duism 2730
Carrying Plough and Harrow 2731
Method of Irrigation .. 2731
Shrine of the Sacred Cobra 2732
Masks and Trumpets .. 2733
Scene at the Burning Ghats 2734
Performing the Last Rites.. 2734
Burning the Funeral Pyre.. 2735
In the Kingdom of Shades.. 2735
Bridge of Bengal 2746
Weighing Rice in Bengal .. 2747
Feasting off Banana Leaves 2747
In a Native Bazaar.. .. 2748
Hindu Laundry 2749
Venerable Chieftain of Sind 2750
Raising Water for the Land 2751
Lured from the Hills .. 2752
Fresh Vegetables for Visitors 2753
Bombay Dock 2754
Drying-ground of an Odori-
  ferous Industry .. 2755
Fishing-nets on the Way to
  Pickle 2756
Riding the Indian Waters.. 2757
Ritualistic Bathing.. .. 2758
An Open-air Bath 2758
Separating Grain from Chaff 2759
Cleaning the Grain .. 2759
Deccan Jazz Band 2760
Coppersmith of Karachi .. 2761
On the Steps of a Mosque .. 2762
At the Feet of the Idol .. 2763
Beauty of Udaipur City .. 2764
Votaress of the Jain Religion 2765
Glimpse of Animal Life .. 2766
Strolling Menagerie.. .. 2767
Swift and Sinuous Cruelty.. 2767
Donkey and Dhobi 2768
Jogging Along the Highway 2768
Well - matched Carriage
  Camels 2769
Out for an Airing 2769
Much-Moneyed Man of India 2770
Pious Pilgrim with Holy
  Water 2771
Asceticism Carried to Ex-
  tremes 2772
Two Cheerful Captives .. 2773
In Quest of Righteousness.. 2773
One of a Company of Saints 2774
Making a Merry Noise .. 2775
Woman Water-Carrier .. 2776
Transporting Barrels of Beer 2777
By Srinagar's Turbid Stream 2778
Travelling by Ekka.. .. 2779
State Barge of a Maharaja.. 2780
Leisured Beauty of Kashmir 2781
Toda Ladies 2782
Family Reunion 2783
Herdsmen and Agriculturists 2784
Members of an International
  Brotherhood 2785
Pariahs at Home 2786
Tamil Schoolboys 2787
Where Charlatanism Flour-
  ishes 2788
Monotonous Task 2789
Fixing Date of Rice Harvest 2790
Faithful Service 2791
Irrepressible Mendicity .. 2791
True Devotion at Worship 2792
Bright-eyed Dancing Girls.. 2793

Great Mosque of Delhi .. 2794
Courtyard of the Jama
  Masjid 2795
Lingait Funeral Ceremonies 2796
Young Victims of Leprosy.. 2797
In Unstable Equilibrium .. 2798
Poised upon a Living Arch.. 2799
Acrobat's Balancing Feat .. 2800
Interested Criticism of Ton-
  sorial Art 2801
Practising her Handicraft .. 2802
Sawyers at Work 2803
Happy-go-lucky Child Vag-
  rant 2804
Small Aspirants to Know-
  ledge 2805
Wanderers in the Himalayas 2806
Fourfooted " Jack-of-all-
  Trades " 2807
" Patience of the Labouring
  Ox " 2807
Amid the Solitudes.. .. 2808
Inflated River-craft .. 2809
Punjabi's Travelling Com-
  panion 2810
Pahari Woman Stone-
  breaker 2811
Priestly Mendicants .. 2812
Sociable Sprites of the Pas-
  tures 2813
Bullocks' Cumbersome Bur-
  den 2814
Ascetics in Silent Meditation 2815
Returning from the Annual
  Outing 2816
Making Funeral Pots .. 2817
Asset to India's Rural
  Regions 2818
Mechanism for Drawing
  Water 2819
Religious Instruction in
  Progress 2820
Cooling Draught from Pun-
  jabi Bhisti 2821
Ash-smeared Fakirs .. 2822
Following a Black Profession 2823
Sikh Priest 2823
Worshipping in the Great
  Mosque 2824
Hardy Ascetic at Benares.. 2825
Saintliness with Snake-like
  Halo 2826
Hindu Penitents 2827
About to Perform the Daily
  Cult 2827
Phodong Lama and At-
  tendant 2828
Lamaist Priests of Sikkim.. 2829
Oriental Sage 2830
Sikkim Village Headmen .. 2831
Unostentatious Dignity .. 2831
Costumed for the Devil
  Dance 2832
Procession of Red Lamas .. 2833
Pomp and Circumstance .. 2834
Lepcha Factory Girls .. 2835
Family of Sikkim Bhotias.. 2836
Professional Performers .. 2837
Mendicancy in the Name of
  Vishnu 2838
Dispensing Strong Waters.. 2839
Pious Publicity 2850
Fakirs of India 2851
Bare Feet and Red-hot Cin-
  ders 2851
Humble Naha Dwelling .. 2852
Low-caste Indians' Home .. 2852
Potter at Work 2853
Nearing Completion .. 2853
Sacred City of Hardwar .. 2855
Godliness Dependant on
  Cleanliness 2856
River Baptism 2857
Hindu Pilgrims Forgathered 2858
Printing Works near Poona 2859
Girl Members of the Aris-
  tocracy 2860
In a Lucknow Bazaar .. 2861
" Creeping Like Snail " .. 2862
Indian Confinement Hut .. 2863
Survivals of Prehistoric Man 2864
At Archery Practice .. 2864

7*

Group of Andamanese .. 2865
Enjoying Dance and Song.. 2866
Tripping Toes 2866
Devotion's Every Grace
 Displayed 2870
A Job for a Crane 2871
Hawkers of the Himalayas 2872
Papier Mâché Merchant .. 2875

IRAK
By the River's Brim .. 2882
An Arab Aristocrat.. .. 2883
Amara Gold and Silversmith 2884
Beating out the Gold .. 2885
Jewess of Bagdad 2886
Dark Eyes of Araby .. 2887
Dinner and Devotion .. 2888
Peace in a Backwater .. 2889
Drawers of Water 2890
Arab Shoemakers of Bagdad 2891
Market by the Mosque .. 2892
Their Lawful Occasions .. 2893
The Bridge of Boats .. 2894
A Bagdad Bazaar 2895
Descendants of Nomad Stock 2895
Beduin of the Inner Desert 2896
Deft Fingers and Prehensile
 Toes 2897
Paddling Canoes 2898
Quaint Basket Boats .. 2899
Fresh Fruit and Vegetables 2900
Tinsmith's Shop 2901
Bearded Weaver of Bagdad 2902
Warp and Weft 2903
Outside a Café 2904
Caravanserai of Kerbela .. 2905
Wayside Barber of Irak .. 2906
Man with Two Trades .. 2907
To Heights of Learning Bred 2908
Arabic Witchery Unveiled.. 2908
In the Fast of Ramadan .. 2909
Carnage Self - wrought at
 Hilla 2909
In a Grove of Date Palms .. 2910
Gathering the Fruits of the
 Earth 2911
Treading Down the Dates .. 2911
Activity on Ashar Creek .. 2912
Western Devices 2913
Pride of Pottery 2914
Semi-final Stage 2914
Earthenware Factory .. 2915
Last Stage of All 2915
A Human Air Pump .. 2916
Floating Made Easy .. 2916
On Tigris Stream 2916
Professional Scribe 2918
Lordly Indolence 2919

IRELAND
Barefoot Beauty 2922
Ulster Linen Factory Girls 2924
Off to the Races 2925
Dáil Eireann 2926
Ulster's Cabinet in Conclave 2927
At the Ratification of the
 Treaty 2927
Barges on the Liffey .. 2928
Blessing the Irish Tricolour 2929
Shedding the Archiepiscopal
 Blessing 2929
Procession of Orangemen .. 2930
Smiling and Pensive Shyness 2932
Ould Pat 2933
With Petticoat over · her
 Head 2934
Connemara Cabin 2935
Irish Schoolboys in Petti-
 coats 2936
Irish Jaunting-car 2937
Burning Seaweed for Kelp.. 2938
Two Ragged Kelp-burners.. 2939
Stacking Sods of Peat .. 2940
Hauling Cut Peat Home .. 2941
When the Load is Welcome 2942
An Old-fashioned Wheel .. 2943
Awaiting a Bite 2945
Waiting for the Doctor .. 2946
Maternal Pride 2947
Ninety-seven and Three .. 2948
In the Dress of the Straw
 Boys 2949
Fishermen of Inishmaan .. 2950
Where Simple Inventions
 Suffice 2952

An Illicit Still 2953
Sampling their Potheen .. 2953
Last Journey to a Long
 Home 2954
Young Ireland 2956
Off to Galway Market .. 2957
The Day's Work Done .. 2958
Friendship and Contentment 2960
Little Pitchers 2961
Six Little Pigs go to Market 2962
Smoking the Pipe of Re-
 membrance 2964
Funeral Procession on Inish-
 maan 2965
Coracles of West Ireland .. 2966
Home-made Footgear .. 2967
Wending her Homeward
 Way 2968
Three Fishers of Aran .. 2972
Looking Pleasant 2974
Not so Old as her Cloak .. 2976

ITALY
Venice, Queen of the Adriatic 2978
Debutante from Calabria .. 2979
The Passing of a Pontiff of
 Rome 2980
His Holiness Pope Pius XI. 2981
Women Fascisti on Parade 2982
An Inspection of Patriots .. 2982
Stalwarts of the Police .. 2983
Privates of the Bersaglieri.. 2984
Italian Dragoons 2985
Fruitful Corner of the Plain 2986
Professional Letter-writers 2988
On a Road to Rome .. 2989
Triumph Immortalised in
 Stone 2989
Oil and Wine Shop.. .. 2990
Workgirls of Naples .. 2991
Popular Open-air Restaurant 2991
Grizzled Fisherman of
 Salerno 2992
Artless Neapolitan Child-
 hood 3009
Bay of Naples 3010
Inexhaustible Match of the
 Neapolitan 3011
Garish Neapolitan Life .. 3012
Mothers' Meeting 3013
Favourite Haunt of Palermo 3014
Makers of Macaroni .. 3015
Inmate of the Certosa Mon-
 astery 3016
Franciscan Friars 3017
Florentine Brother of Mercy 3018
Bearing a Dead Brother .. 3019
Honouring the Holy Virgin 3020
Comely Peasant Maidens .. 3021
On the Quayside of Palermo 3022
Day of Religious Rejoicing 3023
Taormina's Market Place .. 3024
Business, Duty, and Gossip 3025
Sicilian Cottage Home .. 3026
Piping in Honour of the
 Madonna 3027
Almond Blossom in Sicily .. 3028
Unconventional Sicily .. 3029
Toy Beast of Burden .. 3030
Hirsute Paying Guests .. 3030
Priestly Dignity 3031
Sicilian Mountaineer .. 3032
Transport in Sicily 3033
The Evening Hour 3034
Story-teller of Catania .. 3035
Running Liquid Sulphur
 into Moulds 3036
Dumping-place for Sulphur 3036
Weighing Bags of Sulphur.. 3037
Loading a Steamer 3037
Pulping Sicilian Tomatoes.. 3038
Cooking Tomato Pulp .. 3038
Sorting the Fruit 3039
Tomato Sauce before Tin-
 ning 3039
Gathering Fruit from Prickly
 Pear 3040
Hardy Young Couple .. 3041
Sardinian Grace and Gen-
 tility 3042
Sunlight and Shade.. .. 3043
Returning from Market .. 3044

Glinting Copper and Gleam-
 ing Tin 3045
Scions of a Sturdy Stock .. 3046
Confidence and Affection .. 3047
Heart of Modern Venice .. 3048
Feeding the Feathered Flock 3049
Dark-eyed Daughter of
 Venice 3050
Midday Refreshment .. 3051
Water-front near Ducal
 Palace 3051
Simple Folks of Burano .. 3052
Revered Industry of Murano 3053
Venetian Hearse-Boat .. 3054
Fragrant Flowers for Sale .. 3055
Old Seaman of Capri .. 3056
Sugared Drinks for the
 Thirsty 3073
Modena's Medieval Master-
 piece 3074
Paduan Market Place .. 3075
Piazza delle Erbe 3076
Fractising the Tarantella .. 3077
Nuns of Convent near
 Perueia 3078
Good Samaritans of the Alps 3079
Quayside of Trieste.. .. 3080
Glimpse of the Grand Canal 3081
Istria's Historic Seaport .. 3082
Country Road near Pola .. 3082
Wayside Scene in Istria .. 3083
Istrian Land Labourer .. 3083
Healthy Specimens of
 Womanhood 3084
Braving the Boisterous
 Breeze 3085
Giant Blocks of Marble .. 3086
Transporting Marble to
 the Quay 3086
Fishing-smack from Pola .. 3087
Waters of Lake Como .. 3088
Brightly Gleaming Banners 3089
Goatherds of Southern Italy 3090
Busy By-street 3091
Representatives of Slavonic
 Race 3092
Fisher Folk of Naples .. 3093
Roadside Siesta 3094
Istrian Piety and Propriety 3095
Bordighera's Roman Gate-
 way 3096
Gossip in Old San Remo .. 3097
Ruins of the Forum
 Romanum 3098
Model Farm Premises .. 3103
Pastorale Piper of Capri .. 3104

ITALIAN COLONIES
The Waterman's Knock .. 3108
Valour Enhanced by Dis-
 cipline 3110
Spiritual Guides 3111
Blacks and Whites in Con-
 ference 3112
Young Maids of Italy .. 3113
Libyan Dancing Girl .. 3113
From Tripoli's Tower .. 3114
Modesty Stealing to the
 Mosque 3115
Swarthy Charms 3116
Helmet and Mask 3117
Jewish Nuptials 3118
Parliament at Benghazi .. 3119

List of Maps

Georgia 2353
Germany 2455
Greece 2533
Guatemala 2555
Haiti 2573
Hawaii 2593
Hejaz 2616
Honduras 2630
Hungary 2685
Iceland 2703
India 2869
Irak 2917
Ireland 2969
Italy 3101
Libya 3109
Eritrea and Italian Somaliland 3120

Georgia

The Ancient People of Trans-Caucasia

By Henry W. Nevinson

Author of " The Dawn in Russia "

IT is difficult to define the exact limits of Georgia, for since the treacherous invasion of the country by Soviet Russians, Armenians, and Turks in the March of 1921, the independence of the Georgians has been again overthrown and their territory absorbed within the nominal boundaries of Russia.

Before the Great War the Province of Georgia, or Trans-Caucasia, included all the vast valley lying between the range of the Caucasus (which runs for about 900 miles from the Black Sea to the Caspian) and the range of Anti-Caucasus, which culminates in Mount Ararat. Its capital was Tiflis, its ports Batum and Poti on the Black Sea, and Baku on the Caspian ; its connexion with Persia and Armenian or Kurdish Turkey ran through the southern town of Erivan, and near to Erivan stood the town and monastery of Etchmiadzin, the centre of the Armenian Church.

In former times the frontiers of the Georgian kingdom extended even beyond these limits, but the delegates of the Democratic Republic (established in May, 1918, and confirmed by the Constituent Assembly in March, 1919) claimed a much reduced territory from the Supreme Council in Paris, which gave the Georgian Republic " de facto recognition " in January, 1920, and " de jure recognition " in January, 1921.

We will keep to the frontiers then laid down, excluding the so-called Republics of Azerbaijan, with its capital at Baku, and of Armenia, with its capital at Erivan. Georgia proper will then be included within a line drawn from a point on the Black Sea, just

south of Tuapse, along the central summits of the Caucasus, over the two giant peaks of Elbruz and Kazbek (both over 18,000 feet), to a point about half-way down the mountain barrier of Daghestan, the home of the Moslem Lesghians.

The line then turns sharply south till it reaches the junction of the fertile Alaksan valley with the river Kura on its way from Tiflis to the Araxes and Caspian Sea. Then it follows the right or south bank of the Kura westward, and leaving the Kura below Tiflis, it runs almost due west across the Tiflis-Erivan railway, excludes Alexandropol, the junction for Kars, but includes Akhalkalaki and Ardahan, and so reaches the coast of the Black Sea just west of Riza, and about thirty miles east of Trebizond.

Within those frontiers is included a population of some three and a half or four million people, nearly ninety per cent. of whom are of pure Georgian stock. Their country is of singular beauty, fertility, and richness in minerals. The temperature ranges from perpetual snow down to sub-tropical heat. The land is always well watered by streams from both mountain ranges. The Rion

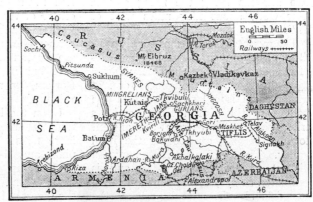

GEORGIA AND ITS PEOPLE

GEORGIAN HOUSEWIFE AT HER DAILY TASK

The Georgian love of finery can be seen in the gay materials from which this housewife's garments are made. Kneeling by her oven, she is engaged in baking thin, pancake-like chupatties of flour and water. The oven is merely a hole in the ground, in the centre of which is a wood fire; this supplies heat to the sloping sides, against which the bread is baked

Photo, Major W. J. P. Rodd

(ancient Phasis) with its tributaries draining into the Black Sea, and the Kura with its tributaries draining into the Caspian, form the chief river systems, the watershed between the two systems being the rising ground near Gori, about fifty miles west of Tiflis.

The mountain formations supply very little coal, but considerable quantities of copper and iron. The chief mineral wealth consists in manganese ore, of which there is a large deposit in the valleys of the Kvirili River and its tributaries, not far from the ancient town of Kutais, overlooking the Rion valley. The ore is distributed over a district of 400 square miles, and is estimated at 200,000,000 tons available. It exists also in several parts of the country. Oil has been occasionally tapped within the limits of Georgia proper, and I have seen prospectors at work for it at the head of the Alaksan valley, and in the neighbourhood of Batum. But hitherto it has not been found in such quantities as at the great centre of the oil district around Baku. Large numbers of "mineral" or medicinal springs, both hot and cold, are scattered over the country, the best known being in the district of Borjom, near the top of the Kura valley.

Upon the lower slopes of the mountains (about 3,000 to 4,000 feet) are large forests of oak, beech, chestnut, pine and boxwood. Rhododendrons flourish up to nearly 10,000 feet. Oranges and lemons grow freely along the coast of the Black Sea. Under cultivation there is great abundance of maize, the principal food of the peasants. Barley, wheat, cotton, rice, and tea are also grown, and before the war there was an increasing trade in Georgian tobacco, usually exported as Turkish. There was also considerable trade in silk, fruit, cheese, timber, liquorice, wool, and skins. But one of the chief products was wine.

In the Alaksan valley at vintage the whole country seems to run with wine. The grapes are squeezed in primitive presses, cleaned with boughs of yew, and the juice run off into huge earthenware vats sunk in the ground, and big enough to hold a man, for when fermentation is finished and the wine drawn off a man gets into the vat to clean it out. The wine is usually poured into tarred buffalo skins, which are laid upon narrow wooden carts and driven slowly along the mountain roads,

WHERE WOMEN WORK AND MEN ARE IDLE
The numerous races that inhabit Georgia share the laziness that is characteristic of the Oriental, many men spending their days in idleness, while their womenfolk do the work of house and field. Content to sit and meditate in their picturesque rags, these Georgians sometimes do not stir from their home all day, except, perhaps, for a short walk in the cool of the evening

Photo, Major W. J. P. Rodd

joggling as they go. In 1913 Georgia produced 32,000,000 gallons of wine, about a third of which was exported to Russia. But much was also sent to France to serve as "body" for "Burgundy" and "Bordeaux."

Before 1900 three-quarters of the export and import trade was done with England, but after that date until the war Germany rapidly forged ahead, so that in 1913 she held 65 per cent., and the British trade had dropped to 7 per cent., though the greater part of the shipping entering Batum was still

WOMAN OF A HANDSOME RACE
One of a hardy, liberty-loving people, this gaily-clad Georgian shares the national hatred of meanness, and is ever hospitality itself, believing in the proverbial saying : " A guest— a man from God "
Photo, Major W. J. P. Rodd

British, the German and other goods being chiefly carried in British bottoms. For passengers from Europe (Marseilles) France ran the best line of steamers.

In the high mountains a beautiful ibex (tur) may still be found, and the wild bison occurs. Bears are frequent, living chiefly upon the wild grape, varied with an occasional kid. Wild boar, reindeer, and antelopes exist in the forests, and along the banks of the Phasis (Rion), from which they take their name, are large quantities of pheasants, always marked, I think, with the white ring round the neck, as seen in recent English breeds. Before the war the price of a pheasant in the

VETERAN OF A MOUNTAIN STATE
Despite a brief spell of independence, his country is still under alien control, but with heart nothing daunted he continues to cherish the hope that Georgia will one day free herself from the tyrannous Russian yoke
Photo, Mrs. W. G. Wilson

"THINGS OF RAGS AND PATCHES": AFTER THEIR MORNING TUB

These black-haired, smiling Georgian girls, in their gowns of brightly-coloured Manchester cotton, and with their " shining morning faces," have just returned from their morning bath in the river, and are now busy washing their clothes. Though patched and torn, their simple dresses are gaily patterned and picturesque, forming bright spots of colour in a drab landscape

Photo, Major W. J. P. Rodd

country towns near the Rion was 25 kopeks (about sixpence). The number of domesticated cattle and sheep in the country was estimated at 12,000,000 head.

The name " Georgian " is said to be derived from a Persian word "Gurg," and Persian influence is easily traced in much of Georgian art. The people's own original name was Khartli, but the Russians call them Groussians. All Georgians still speak the same language, which, I believe, has not hitherto been traced to any other relationship, though some scholars, such as Rawlinson, Lenormant, Michel Tzarethcli, and

others connect it with Sumerian-Babylonian. Georgians remain one stock, though divided into several clans, according to district, such as the Gurians, the Mingrelians, the Imerethians, and the Svanes.

Upon the slopes of the higher mountains relics of almost pre-historic tribes are found, like strata left by the tides of successive invasions from Asia, and driven up to the least habitable regions.

Here and there, especially in the parts of Georgia east of Tiflis, one comes upon colonies of Molokans, the Russian Quaker sect, so called because they drink milk in Lent ; and one finds

DESCENDANTS OF THE GOLDEN HORDE EN FÊTE

These small Tartar children have donned their best clothes in honour of a national holiday. Bright colours are dear to the heart of the people of the Caucasus, and the scarlet velvet caps of this quintet of girls are gaily decorated with gold braid or beads. The name Golden Horde was given to a branch of the Kiptchak Tartars who invaded Europe in the thirteenth century

Photo, Florence Farmborough

MUSICAL INTERLUDE IN A GEORGIAN GLADE

Seated on the pile of timber he has been cutting, this Georgian peasant snatches a few minutes'
rest from his labour, and whiles away the time with a tune on his bagpipe. One of the most ancient
forms of musical instrument, the bagpipe is in great favour among the people of the Caucasus,
few of whom lack musical ability

also colonies of Germans who migrated from Swabia early in the nineteenth century because they were told the end of the world was at hand, and it would be well to be in Jerusalem when the time came. They moved slowly, and as nothing catastrophic occurred, and the agents whom they sent forward reported ill of life in the Holy City, they remained upon lands allotted them, and constructed typical German villages, cultivated their fields in the German manner, and still retained their German tongue and literature, though they speak Russian, and sometimes Georgian as well. At one time there were large settlements also of the Russian sect of Doukhobors, or Spirit-wrestlers, but owing to the persecution under Nicholas II., nearly all of them were emigrated to Canada at the end of the nineteenth century. In the mountains dwell tribes called the Ingoosh, especially along the route of the old Georgian military road —improved by the Russian Government in 1865—from Vladikavkas (Fortress of the Caucasus) to the ancient Georgian capital of Mtskhet, only a short distance west of Tiflis. These Ingoosh tribes are reported to live by brigandage, but I came through them undisturbed in 1906, though the military road was at that time declared closed and un-protected owing to revolution.

The Georgians proper are a finely-formed and remarkably intelligent

REPLENISHING THE CELLARS OF A GEORGIAN TAVERN
These men are just delivering at a village tavern a consignment of wine from the vineyards of Kakhetia, whence comes some of Georgia's choicest vintage. Wine is the common drink of all classes, and at vintage-time the country is running with it. The wine is usually stored in tarred buffalo-skins, three legs of which are sewn up, the fourth, which is tied, serving as a spout
Photo, Mrs. W. G. Wilson

people. They have a passion for education, and before the Bolshevist invasion of 1921 possessed in almost every village libraries of Georgian and other literature, which the Russian invaders at once destroyed. At Tiflis they had a great college or university, built by the Georgian Princes, or land-owners ; for when the Russian Tsars annexed the country, contrary to their formal treaty early in the nineteenth century, they granted the title of Kneaz, or Prince, to the chief land-owners, and it usually happened that a Prince owned about thirty acres.

Owing to the difficulty of the language and script, little is known of Georgian literature outside the country, though some German scholars have studied it ; and Marjory Wardrop, sister to Oliver Wardrop—himself a Georgian scholar and British High Commissioner in Trans-Caucasia, 1919-1920—translated "The Hermit," a poem written on an ancient Kazbek shrine by Prince Ilia Chavchavadze (born 1837). The most famous Georgian classic is "The Man in the Panther's Skin" (Vepkhvis Tkaosani), written during the reign of the great Queen Tamara, about the time of the English Richard I. Towards the end of the seventeenth century Prince Sulkhan, one of the great Orbeliani family, said to have originated from China, wrote an excellent account of a "Journey through Europe" in Georgian, collected the Georgian folk-lore—he was personally acquainted with La Fontaine—and compiled a Georgian dictionary of 25,000 words.

Church architecture is mainly tradi-tional, the type being best represented by the ancient monastery of Gelati, in the mountains above Kutais. It was

FETCHING THE DAY'S WATER SUPPLY FROM A CAUCASIAN RIVER

Though water is laid on in a more or less civilized manner in the larger towns, elsewhere in Georgia the methods of supply are still very elementary. This well designed bridge, strongly built in order to resist recurring floods, witnesses daily the filling up and removing of barrels of water which are drawn by bullocks or, sometimes, by mountain ponies

Photo, Mrs. W. G. Wilson

PLOUGHING IN THE PASSES OF THE CAUCASUS

This handsome Georgian boy is ploughing near the great military road over the Caucasus Mountains. The oxen on whose yoke he is sitting are only two in a team of a dozen which two boy companions help him to control. Some of these ploughs require ten pairs of oxen to draw, and seven men to guide them—a great expenditure of energy with but poor result

Photo, Maynard Owen Williams

STALWART DESCENDANT OF A HARDY MOUNTAIN RACE

With his faithful companion at his feet, this young Georgian stands outside his wooden dwelling. The large, sleeveless cloak, known as a *bourka*, that he wears flung over the left shoulder, is of thick black felt made from goat or horse hair, and serves not only as a useful waterproof for rainy days, but also as a warm blanket when the nights are cold

Photo, Mrs. W. G. Wilson

MEMBER OF THE GEORGIAN ARISTOCRACY

Until comparatively recent times, the feudal system existed in Georgia, and the peasant classes were ruled by petty princes.   Blue blood still runs in the veins of many landowners, and this prince is representative of the aristocracy of his country.   The goat's-hair cloak and astrakhan cap that he wears are characteristic of the Georgian, who is never without his dagger, except when in European clothes

built, probably upon an older foundation, in the latter part of the eleventh century, at the time of David the Restorer. The cone-shaped tops to the towers are distinctively Georgian, and though the Byzantine influence is evident, a Georgian church can always be recognized by its resemblance to traditional type. The sacred painting is traditional also, but it is hardly to be distinguished from Byzantine. The famous Iberian Virgin, now at Mount Athos, was a Georgian work—said to be of the seventh century—but the copy of it under one of the Kremlin gates in Moscow is so Byzantine in character that Russian worshippers regard it only as the most sacred of their icons.

In point of doctrine there is no real difference between the Orthodox Russian or Greek Church and the Georgian ; but the Georgians claim ecclesiastic independence, with control of their own church property, and their Church suffered much persecution and pillage at the hands of the Russian Government up to the Russian revolution. And it suffered under Bolshevist domination, though for different reasons.

Georgian houses are built of rough stone or baked mud, and usually provided with large wooden balconies round the first floor. The roofs are generally red tile, of the wavy shape common throughout the Near East. Often the houses in the richer districts, as in the Alaksan valley, are of great beauty, and sometimes traces of Persian occupation are seen in relics of harem screens before windows, and in brilliant glazed tiles built into the walls. Besides architecture and sacred icons there is little native art, except the work in silver and steel.

Fine daggers and swords of tempered steel, with sheaths of chased silver, were made in Vladikavkaz up to the Great War, and the daggers were part of the equipment of Caucasian soldiers, as well as of ordinary peasants. A very

YOUNG SONS OF GEORGIA'S MOUNTAIN PEASANTRY

Wearing the astrakhan caps that are the Georgian national headdress, these lads are sitting by the great military road which traverses the largest pass through the chain of the Caucasus. Kazbek, near by, is one of several villages to be found in the wider parts of the pass of Dariel, and takes its name from that of a great family that once owned the countryside

Photo, Maynard Owen Williams

YOUTH, MANHOOD, AND OLD AGE OF THE GEORGIAN RANK AND FILE

More than 2000 years ago the Georgians were a free people. Conquered by Alexander the Great, they again became independent on his death in 323 B.C., and their kingdom attained the zenith of its prosperity about 1200. After the annexation to Russia in 1801 the national spirit of enterprise virtually disappeared from Georgia, but the people, though still hard pressed by foreign rule, are gradually working their way towards light and liberty

Photo, Major W. J. P. Rodd

beautiful kind of silver belt or girdle was also made, and was worn by many Georgian women. But perhaps the very best metal work was done by the Moslem Lesghians of Daghestan and the mountains no longer included in Georgia.

The Georgian men usually wear an astrakhan cap called Papakh, and in winter a huge, sleeveless cloak of shaggy wool, called Bourka. When it is not very cold they wear a long coat or jacket (Tcherkeska) of rough wool, and underneath a linen or cotton tunic, loose trousers and leggings. The chest before the Great War was usually adorned with copious rows of cartridges, and a dagger was hung at the girdle. The women wear a similar Tcherkeska, skirts, and silver chains and buckles across the bodice. Their most peculiar article of dress is a stiff band of velvet round the head, holding in place a large white veil, two long false curls being attached to the velvet band. This adornment is a recognized object of sale in most Georgian shops or general stores.

At marriages large white veils, often of fine lace, are hung over the head, false curls and all. Widows and the mothers of babies who have died wear white veils without any ornament. At weddings, usually held just after the vintage, the bride's cart or phaeton is preceded by a cavalcade of her male relations, who ride desperately to and fro, galloping their horses up and down the steepest ravines, perhaps a faint reminder of the ancient marriage by capture. They represent the defending force. In front of the cart walks a "merryman," holding a long skewer in either hand, with bits of bread on one skewer and fragments of cooked meat on the other. At his side is a friend with a dripping wine-skin, and every passer-by receives a bit of bread and meat and a sup of wine in honour of the bride.

Then come the musicians with the bagpipes (Zurna), mandoline, and drum. The music is of that quavering, nasal, and minor kind common throughout the Near and Middle East, and usual even in India. Probably it is Persian in origin. It continues, with dancing, outside the church during the ceremony, and then the procession conducts the bride and bridegroom to their house, where the husband lifts the wife over the threshold in accordance with tradition common in other countries as well as in ancient Rome.

Near Signakh, a mountain town, overlooking the Alaksan valley in the district of Kakhetia, stands an ancient convent covering part of the holy Nina's remains (the Saint who first brought Christianity to the Caucasus, probably in the fourth

WRESTING A MEAGRE HAY CROP FROM A RUGGED SOIL

The inhabitants of this little Caucasian village of Gergeti, which is half-way up the Kazbek, called by the Georgians Ice Mountain, eke out a precarious living from their toil in the fields. Their flat-topped houses, like those of many of these mountain communities, are built so that the roof of one forms a front yard for the house above

Photo, Maynard Owen Williams

EASE AND LUXURY IN THE CAUCASUS

Surrounded by brightly-coloured rugs and hangings of rich Caucasian silks, this dark-eyed daughter of the mountains reclines at ease on her cushioned divan. A cultured woman of European education, she yet clings to the costume of her people, comprising a silken coat which covers loose trousers gracefully caught in at the ankles, and a scarlet velvet cap, richly ornamented with pearls

Photo, Florence Farmborough

century). The rest of her relics are now in a village church in Belgium, but I do not know how they came there. It is a place of peculiar veneration, but hardly less frequented is the white church of Allaverdi in the valley below. For about vintage-time a kind of Feast of Reason is held there, and all sects or religions and enemies of every kind may meet as under a Truce of God and drink wine together.

The word Allaverdi is said to mean God the Giver, and probably refers to the divine bounty of harvest and vintage, but Oliver Wardrop traced it to the memory of great assistance given by Tartars to the Georgians in one of their many wars against the Persian invaders. At all events the word has now passed into the Georgian language, and is the cheerful cry when at banquets they call upon the stranger to empty a goblet at one draught. For the country, as I have said, overflows with wine, though to be sure the more temperate sometimes drink the fermented mare's milk called Koumiss.

It must not be supposed, however, that life in the Caucasus, even before the Bolshevist invasion, was all milk and honey and wine. In the higher mountains life was wretchedly poor, the cattle and sheep and a little maize or rye bread being the only food. In the mountain inns or rest houses I have often found nothing at all to eat or drink, and have slept upon slightly slanted shelves of board with six or eight men lying in a row beside me— no covering or warmth of any kind.

The Georgians, especially in the region of Guria, which lies westward towards the Black Sea, are peculiarly capable of self-government. This was proved during the brief period of freedom from Russian rule (1904-1906),

RIDERS OF THE PLAINS AND HUNTERS OF THE HILLS: A HALT ON THE ROAD

Renowned throughout the world for their wonderful horsemanship, the Circassians well deserve their fame. It is said that they can ride before they can walk, and certainly the management of horses appears to be an instinct with the young Circassian, who is, indeed, bred to the saddle from his earliest years. These riders can perform many marvellous feats in the saddle, such as mounting a racing horse and standing erect at full gallop, and the Circassian's horse, being singularly surefooted, is especially bred for its ability to traverse the perilous paths of the Caucasus

when the Russian Government was too much occupied with the disastrous war with Japan, and Georgia declared her independence. The Gurian peasants live in isolated farms, but they combined into communes, elected their own councils, boycotted all Russian authorities, organized all their public works, and summoned transgressors before public meetings of the commune, where guilt was decided by vote, and the punishment (usually in the form of boycott) was duly allotted. It was of this experiment that Tolstoy wrote to a friend in the country:

What is happening in Guria is an event of immense importance. Tell the Gurians there is an old man who for twenty years has been ceaselessly repeating that all the evils of humanity are due to the fact that men are always expecting to find some external aid with which to organize their lives, and when they see that the authorities do not aid them,

THE GARB OF HIS ANCESTORS
The chief feature of this ceremonial costume, the " kuladja," which is now only seen at public festivals in Georgia, is the gold or silver dagger, which gives an added touch of richness to the crimson velvet jacket
Photo, N. M. Kirtashirli

BRED TO ARMS FROM INFANCY
This small Circassian lad is a miniature replica of his father, his white parade uniform being complete in every detail, with tiny dagger, cartridge-cases, and fittings and trimmings of Caucasian silver
Photo, Florence Farmborough

and do not create order, they begin to accuse them, to condemn them, to revolt against them. What should be done is exactly what the Gurians are doing—to organize life in such a manner that there should be no need for any authority.

Such being the character of the people, it is all the more lamentable that after their brief periods of freedom (in 1904-1906 and 1918-1921) they should again have fallen under the oppressive domination of the Russian hordes and the peculiarly arbitrary and centralised form of Soviet government.

GROUP OF GERMAN PEASANT WOMEN ADORNED WITH THE MANIFOLD FALLALS OF BLACK FOREST FASHION

The German Black Forest has a two-fold attraction, its picturesque scenery and its picturesque peasantry. Scarcely a valley but has its own peculiar charm of landscape, and scarcely a village but has its own variety of peasant dress. A native of the Black Forest may be easily recognized by his costume, and there are certain districts where the distinctive headdress seen above, composed of a high coronet of beads, is worn by every village girl .

Photo, Underwood Press Service

Germany

I. A Land of Many Races & Social Contrasts

By William Harbutt Dawson.

Author of "The German Empire, 1867-1914," etc.

GERMANY presents the utmost variety alike of physical, racial, and social characteristics, and a faithful description of the land and its people must be sparing of sweeping generalisations. As to its population in particular, it is to be remembered that the German nation, as we know it to-day, is an amalgam of many tribes and tribal combinations, each one with its own history and traditions, habits and customs, dialects and institutions. All that can be attempted in a summary survey, therefore, is such a picture as will bring into relief the essential facts of the collective life and character, special treatment being reserved for certain of the leading political divisions and tribes.

In physical conformation Germany falls into two great divisions, known as Upper Germany and Lower Germany respectively, the former consisting of a southern zone of highland, broadly stretching across the whole country from the Ardennes and the Vosges Mountains in the west to the extreme east, bordering on Bohemia and Austria, and a vast plain running northward of this highland to the seaboard.

Region of Mountain and Forest

The highland starts with a chain of hills and mountains of medium height—the Rhenish Slate Mountains, Westerwald, Hunsrück, Taunus, the Thuringian Forest, the Harz Mountains, the Erzgebirge or Ore Mountains between Saxony and Bohemia, and the Riesengebirge or Giant Mountains, between Prussian Silesia and the same group; while beyond stretches a high plateau flanked by the Odenwald, the Black Forest, and the Bavarian and Austrian Alps. The highest elevation is reached by the Schneekoppe in the Giant Mountains,

rising 5,260 feet above sea level. Very characteristic of this hilly region are the large number and extent of its forests.

The special features of the lowland of the north are the extensive lake regions of Holstein, Mecklenburg, Pomerania, and East Prussia (the Masurian district), the great area of its cultivated and uncultivated moorland and sandy plain, and an abundance of forest, as in the south.

Lovely Lakes and Waterways

A moist climate and the configuration of its surface have made Germany a land of rivers, ranging from the great waterways of commercial intercourse to hundreds of minor streams of all degrees of economic and local importance. All the large rivers run north, the Rhine, Weser, and Elbe flowing into the North Sea, and the Oder and Vistula into the Baltic; the Danube, it is true, has its rise in Germany (in the Black Forest), but though fed by several tributaries which pass exclusively through German territory, the greater part of its navigable bed lies in Austria, Hungary, and Rumania. The lakes of the north have already been mentioned. In the south are Lake Constance, of which Germany is a co-proprietor, the lovely lakes of Bavaria, ranging in size from some eighty square miles downwards, and a series of picturesque little lakes embedded in the hills of the Black Forest. The country is also exceptionally rich in mineral springs.

Along the coasts of the North and Baltic Seas lie a number of islands, mostly of small area, and some for that reason uninhabited. The largest is Rügen, which, like Heligoland, Norderney, Juist, Borkum, and other islands, has enjoyed great popularity as a holiday resort. Lying off the Baltic are several

The division of Upper and Lower Germany named above marks just as clear a distinction in language and dialects, as well as in habits, customs, and modes of thought, as exists between Scotsmen and English, or in England between north-country-men and southerners. As to language, the German of Lower Germany speaks on the whole with a softer intonation, while the Upper German, together with a certain harshness, has a greater range of tone. It is a seeming paradox that while the north claims to be the present home of High German speech, it is also the home of Low German, or Plattdeutsch, a vernacular of which the stories of Fritz Reuter, the Mecklenburger, are the literary classics.

North Germany claims to be Old Germany, for the south was peopled by migration from the north. Of the many Germanic tribes of history only the liberty-loving Saxons, occupying the flat lands of the north-west between the Rhine and the Harz Mountains, and the hardy Frisians, who inhabit the coast land of Oldenburg and North-west Schleswig, with many of the islands in the North Sea, can be said to hold their original territories. The Franks, on the other hand, spread from the Lower Rhine to the Middle Rhine and the Main, while the Slavic east of Germany was settled by various tribes, chief among them the Saxons, Franks, and Thuringians. Physically, the Low Saxon represents the ancient German type, as characterised by blond hair, light skin, and blue eyes, features which occur less commonly the more south one goes, until the pronounced brunette

TWO LITTLE MAIDS FROM SCHOOL

Along the dusty country road of a Black Forest district they are wending their way homeward from the Volksschule. On the morrow they will eagerly retrace their steps, for children of Germany seldom, if ever, need driving to school

Photo, C. Uchter Knox

large freshwater haffs or lagoons, cut off from the sea by narrow strips of land, pierced at a single point by the outflowing water.

The Prussian province of Holstein is perhaps the part of Germany which, in its general physical features and its climate, as influenced by the contiguity of the sea, most reminds the Englishman of his native land. There he finds the same undulating country, the same forms of cultivation, the same breeds of cattle as at home, with the hedges which the Angles introduced into England in distant ages. Similarly Bremen, rare in Germany as a town of single-family houses, approaches most nearly to the type of the English town.

type of Swabia and Bavaria is reached. Tall figures with long and narrow faces —the latter, too, typically Germanic— are characteristic of the north-west and the south-east, while in the south-west and also in the Slavic districts of the north-east a shorter build and the broad type of face predominate.

Some of the outstanding characteristics of the dominant tribes may be conveniently noted here. The Low Saxon is a man of strong and independent character, somewhat heavy, reserved, not very approachable, never the first to make advances, and inclined to suspicion and distrust. He has, however, all the old combativeness and strong sense of right, and these dispose him easily to be litigious. His is not a bright and sanguine temperament, for the atmosphere of the lowland, with its large share of cloud and fog, encourages moodiness and taciturnity. His essentially prosaic character, however, is redeemed by a rich, dry humour, and he is a man who can joke with utter immobility of features. He is given to proverbs, embodying much rude mother wit, as, for example, " Everything with measure, as the tailor said when he struck his wife dead with a yard stick." The Low Saxons have a strong practical sense,

PART OF THE DAILY ROUTINE OF THE BLACK FOREST HOUSEWIFE

Many a peasant wife and mother of a family takes it not at all amiss that she must spend the greater part of the day in hoeing, digging, or planting in the fields, and in South Germany, where nature is especially kind to her children, the conditions of life are much happier and more agreeable than those attending the rough-and-ready existence of the land workers in East Germany

Photo, O. Uchter Knox

FILIGREE NIMBUS OF RUSTIC REFINEMENT

The diversity of headgear prevailing among the peasantry of the Black Forest, the Bavarian Highlands, and the Spree Forest, is even more pronounced than the variety of dress. In the Black Forest virtually every valley possesses distinctive fashions of its own, and this frail hat of delicate lace-work surmounting the fresh face of a village maiden is undeniably attractive

HOMELY BUT COMELY PEASANT PAIR OF THE BLACK FOREST

The German peasant woman is accustomed to agricultural work from childhood; energetic, sturdy, and robust, she makes a very fitting mate for the peasant proprietor. The costumes of this newly-wed pair from Schapbach are lacking in all ostentatious display, but the "schappel," or chaplet, composed of coloured glass balls and beads, is a never-failing feature of the bridal attire

Photo, Georg Haeckel

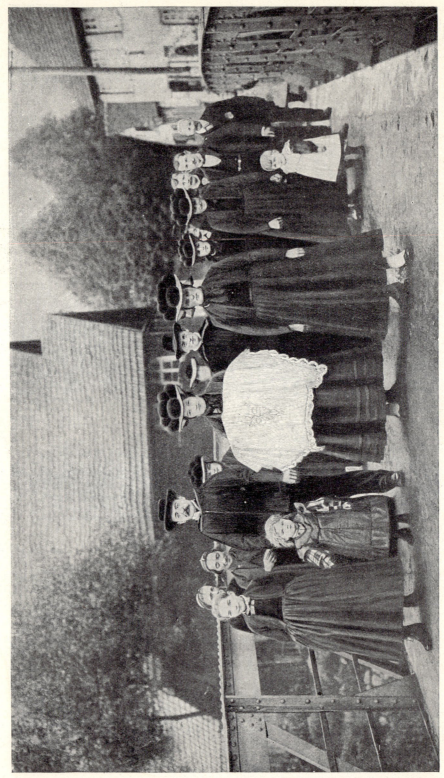

BAPTISMAL PROCESSION IN THE BLACK FOREST: THE PROUD PARENTS ACCOMPANIED BY RELATIVES AND FRIENDS

Personal taste in dress is an unnecessary quality in many a district of the Black Forest, where one style of costume and hat so far becomes law as to banish from the feminine mind all fastidious notions regarding fashions. The desire to outshine a neighbour in richness or originality of dress finds no home in the heart of these women ; one and all, rich and poor, adhere to the regulation attire, and wear it cheerfully and with pride on all occasions

MATERFAMILIAS OF MUNICH IN THE BOSOM OF HER FAMILY

When quite tiny tots German children are taught the elements of obedience, and so soon as they can walk, these small people—models of good behaviour—are admitted to many of the social gatherings of the grown-ups. The " Kinderstube " (children's room) is generally a delightful apartment, large and airy, and containing a wealth of enchanting nursery books and beautiful fantastic toys

and have produced many travellers and scientists, but their tastes do not specially lie in the direction of poetry and art.

The Frisians are people of tough fibre, both physically and in character ; they are very conservative in their habits and institutions, keep apart from their neighbours, and are greatly given to intermarriage, so that there are whole villages of relations. They are not musical—an old saying runs, "Frisia non cantat"—nor are they a poetical people.

Keeping still to the north we must note the cleavage made by the Elbe, which separates the old Saxon land on the west from the Slavic territories peopled and civilized by Saxons and other tribes. In this eastern region is the true home of the Prussians, the most virile of the modern German stocks, though of Slavic origin and allied to the Baltic-Lithuanian races.

Taking them collectively, the Prussians are a strong, gifted, and strenuous people. Without the imagination and vivacity of the Gaul, as represented by the people of the Rhine-

land, or the intellectuality and the fine instinct for culture which mark the Swabian, they are the master-minds of Germany in all that belongs to material civilization. In everything that lends itself to system, and finds in system its most perfect expression, the Prussians excel. Pre-eminently their capacity and strength lie in practical affairs rather than in those of the mind and spirit, and herein they are as Romans to the Greeks of Württemberg in the south. Thus they have never excelled in political government, which has to do with men, but have brought municipal government, which is concerned with things, to a degree of efficiency hardly equalled elsewhere.

Behind German enterprise and success in commerce and industry, in the organization of the powerful syndicates and trade federations, and in the great transport systems which have played so large a part in the industrialisation of Germany, are Prussian ideas and energy. Prussia has proved itself, indeed, the great driving force in the life of modern

Germany; whether without its influence Germany would have been something better it is impossible to say, but unquestionably she would have been something fundamentally different. For good or ill the States of the Republic are still yoked to this powerful leader, who, whatever his faults, never fails to pull his full weight, and where he goes they will be bound to follow.

The chief tribes of Central Germany are the Franks of the Middle Rhine and the Main region, and the Thuringians. The Franks are the most versatile, alert, and vivacious of all the German tribes. They are poetical, romantic, with pronounced aesthetic leanings and artistic tastes. They are also remarkably affable and decidedly a " likeable " people, easy to get on with. The Thuringians are a good-humoured, lively, and fairly energetic people, sentimental and musical, polite to the stranger, and easily contented. They are somewhat lacking in self-reliance and staying power, and are open to outside influence, but they are very industrious.

To the south are the Alemanni or Swabians and the Bavarians. The former inhabit the upper reaches of the Rhine, Neckar, and Danube, and are represented by the States of Baden and Württemberg. Like the Slavs of the east, the dark Swabians, in whom is a strong Celtic strain, are a people of more pliable nature than either the Saxons or the Franks, but they surpass both in intellectual qualities.

The Bavarians inhabit portions of the Upper Rhine, Neckar, and Main

LOCAL COLOUR DANCING IN THE STREETS OF REICHENHALL

Bad Reichenhall, in the heart of the Bavarian salt region, is famous for its saline baths and ozonised air and is much resorted to by sufferers from lung trouble and rheumatism. Annually in July the anniversary of the opening of the pump-room and baths which have brought prosperity to the town is celebrated by a popular festival in which the peasantry appear in national costume

regions, the high plateau lying east of the Swabian Jura, and the northern parts of the Alpine chain rising from this plateau. They are a people of strongly-marked individuality, though not as attractive as any of their neighbours. They are shrewd, keen at a bargain, yet cautious to a degree that indisposes them to undertake great adventures readily ;

west, as imposed by the Treaty of Versailles, its area has been reduced by some 27,000 square miles, with about six and a half million inhabitants, and as a result of this curtailment and of the losses caused by the war its population is now estimated at about sixty millions.

Until 1918 the Confederation consisted of twenty-five federated States

HISTORICAL HEADGEAR OF BAVARIAN BRIDES

These gay young couples from Effeltrich in Bavaria are resplendent in their nuptial finery. The brides' costumes are rich in gold embroidery, and the headdress, which from olden times has formed the chief attraction of Bavarian bridal attire, is massed with beads and trinkets. Even in modern times this costume is a costly one, and centuries ago it represented a fortune

always they have an eye to the main chance, and they act up to the motto, " Nothing for nothing." They are not without a certain capacity for affability, but they are slow to make friendships, and are very self-contained. Two of their traits—among the rural classes in particular—are unchanging attachment to their Church and loyalty to the dynasty.

Before the Great War the German Empire—known as the German Realm since the deposition of the imperial house—had an area of 208,780 square miles and a population of about sixty-eight millions. By the re-arrangement of its frontiers in the east, north, and

of which four were kingdoms—Prussia, Saxony, Bavaria, and Württemberg—six grand duchies, five duchies, seven principalities, and three free cities. Alsace-Lorraine occupied a special position as an Imperial Territory, though in late years it had enjoyed in most matters the political status of a federal State. In the revolution which followed the Great War all the Sovereigns, who, as Bismarck once said, in a fit of bad humour, " had lighted upon Germany like a swarm of bees," were deposed, where they did not abdicate and efface themselves voluntarily ; republicanism everywhere took the place of monarchy ; and while the confederation was

JUVENILE GREETINGS AT THE VILLAGE SPRING

Trim and neat in their quaint costumes the young girls of Sankt Georgien in the Black Forest are as careful of their deportment as they are of their personal appearance. The high-spirited rowdyism apparent in many peasant districts is almost unknown among these simple country-folk, and young and old possess an old-fashioned primness of manner outrivalled only by the sobriety of their dress.

Photo, Georg Haeckel

TOIL-WORN WOMEN LAND WORKERS OF EAST PRUSSIA

In the country districts of East Prussia the conditions of life of the poor are far from congenial.
Women take a large share in outdoor labour and are often terribly overworked in the fields. They
follow the plough, thresh the corn, and do much work which in former times fell to the men. Nevertheless, they are surprisingly contented with their lot and usually cheerful and good-tempered

Photo, Georg Haeckel

FANTASTIC FEMININE FINERY AT A MARRIAGE FEAST IN THE BLACK FOREST

Although the modern nuptial headdress might prove more becoming to these women of Villingen than the massive beaded "schappel," their taste in head millinery is still swayed by the traditional customs of a past era ; and the modern suits of the men form a contrast to the gay raiment of the womenfolk. Through the decorated portal bearing the greeting " Hearty Welcome," the guests will now pass to the reception, preparations for which have been going on for days beforehand

preserved, it, too, was re-organized on a republican basis, with a constitution which in theory is probably the most democratic in the world, though its practical success and chances of permanence remain still to be proved.

Since then there have been further political readjustments in the form of inter-State amalgamations, affecting the petty duodecimo States of Central Germany, of which seven have combined under the name Thuringia, while one (Coburg) has been absorbed in Bavaria, with the result that the federal territories now number eighteen — viz., Anhalt, Baden, Bavaria, Brunswick, Bremen (Free City), Hamburg (Free City), Hesse, Lippe, Lübeck (Free City), Mecklenburg-Schwerin, Mecklenburg-Strelitz, Oldenburg, Prussia, Saxony, Schaumburg-Lippe, Thuringia, Waldeck, and Württemberg.

At the census of 1910 61.6 per cent. of the inhabitants belonged to the Protestant and 36.7 per cent. to the Roman Catholic faith, one per cent. being Jewish. The transference of Alsace-Lorraine and the Polish districts have altered this ratio in favour of the Protestants, who now form about 65 per cent. of the population.

It is a fact that, even now, half a century after the triumph of national unity, the particularist spirit is still strong, though taking less egoistic and obstructive forms than before. For it must not be forgotten that earlier than the political consciousness of the Germans as a unified nation, and appealing more strongly to popular sentiment, is their tribal consciousness.

The German has two fatherlands and, in effect, two nationalities, and his attachment to Empire or Realm has none of the intimacy and tenderness, deeply-rooted in tribal instincts and traditions, which bind him, as Saxon, Bavarian, Swabian, and the rest, to his native State, which is his true

GRETCHEN OF THE BLACK FOREST
Dainty and demure is this young girl of Schapbach, in the Kinzig Valley, so trimly dressed in one of the multifarious costumes which the peasants of the Black Forest—no matter what their standing—loyally persist in wearing
Photo, Georg Haeckel

homeland. The passionate love of the Germans for their "narrower fatherlands" is the motif of much of their beautiful lyrical and narrative poetry.

Modern Germany may be dated conveniently from the war of 1870 and the great economic developments which immediately followed. The struggle, unlike the war with Austria four years

HAT STYLE FROM GUTACH, BLACK FOREST

The severity of her Puritanical garb is somewhat tempered by the quaint hat loaded with heavy pompons which are coloured bright red for the unmarried girl and sombre black when the wearer is to be a married woman

Photo, Georg Haeckel

Germany leaped into the front rank of industrial countries.

The close attention which had been given for the better part of a century to public education, and during later decades to scientific research and technical instruction, had yielded a rich harvest in the shape of a skilled army of technical directors, chemists, craftsmen, and artisans, who were now ready to man the factories and workshops which sprang up in the great centres of population and of natural resources. Germany's situation in the centre of the Continent, while it exposed her to special dangers, had the advantage that it made it easier for her people to throw out their energies in all directions by sea and land, and this they have done in increasing measure for half a century.

There is still, however, an Old Germany as well as this Germany of a now closed era of expansion and prosperity. The traveller, passing through the larger towns, is apt to regard the country as painfully new. Nevertheless, a fairer land, perpetuating the traditions and spirit of forgotten centuries, will meet his view if he but take the pains to seek it. It may be seen at its best in such survivals of medieval life as Hildesheim, Brunswick, Lübeck, Nuremberg, Goslar, Marienburg, Wismar, and Ulm, and in architectural memorials lingering in odd corners of the " old towns " of cities and towns which have taken a new life— in Hamburg, Bremen, Frankfort-on-Main, and Breslau, for example. Old Germany may be seen also in many a small, slow-going market town of the

before, saw all the German tribes united, fighting together under one supreme military command for an inspiring end—the assertion once for all of a common German nationhood. The effect of the struggle, for Germany so successful, was to liberate a vast store of enthusiasm and energy.

Within two decades old Germany and its life had been revolutionised in all directions. Ancient cities and towns were extended and rebuilt on an ambitious scale, not always in the best taste. The passion for building and rebuilding, with the dispersal of the £200,000,000 of indemnity, gave an immense impetus to production and manufacture, and at a single bound

GERMANY: FOREST MAIDEN IN HER SUNDAY FROCK

Traditional feminine costume in the Black Forest is set off by a high scarlet hat. On Sundays
this peasant girl takes her finery from the wardrobe where, all the week, it has lain in lavender

Photo, Georg Haeckel

centre and the south, lying off the track of modern progress, in quiet villages hidden away in the valleys of the Rhine and of Bavaria, and still untouched by the hand of the improver, in the moat-surrounded manor-houses of Westphalia, and nowhere more than in the picturesque peasant settlements of Thuringia, Bavaria, Baden, and Württemberg, where life pursues its even course to-day just as three centuries ago, before the Thirty Years War desolated the German lands and arrested the advance of civilization for generations.

What interests men most to-day, however, is the Germany that specially counts in the world's life, its work and employments, and the character of

DEFT ARTISTRY LENDS GRACE TO SIMPLE TASKS

In her pretty peasant costume, leisurely methods of work, and general air of contentment, this country girl is an embodiment of rural Bavaria, wherein her lot is cast—a fair region of the old Germany of medieval times. To her prosaic occupation of cutting turnip radishes she imparts the graceful art that helps to sweeten all the toils of human life

Photo, Georg Haeckel

SCENE IN THE REICHSTAG DURING THE CELEBRATION OF THE THIRD ANNIVERSARY OF THE GERMAN REPUBLIC

In August, 1919, the Constitution of the German Republic was established at the Weimar National Assembly, and the photograph reproduced above shows the celebration of the third anniversary of the Republic in progress in the Parliament House, Berlin. Handsomely, though not extravagantly decorated, the Reichstag presented a striking scene; the devices emblematic of the imperial regime were absent from their places over the doorway, where now a great eagle towers above the Republican slogan: "Unity, Justice, and Liberty"

its people. Before she became an industrial country Germany was a land of triumphant agriculture, able to produce all the corn needed to feed her people, with a little over for her neighbours. Agriculture in its many forms is still the mainstay of national prosperity, though no longer the main pursuit of the population, as of old, though over half of the population (51.2 per cent. in 1910) lives in rural townlets (2,000 to 5,000 (Prussia), Neckar (Baden and Württemberg), and Main (Hesse and Bavaria), and other parts of the country, with fruit trees numbered by the hundred million. Characteristic of Central and South Germany is the custom of planting fruit trees—chiefly apple, plum, and cherry—along the highways and byways. The local treasuries benefit by this characteristic device for making the most of the land. The usual plan

WHERE THE "VOX POPULI" OF GERMANY FINDS READY AUDIENCE
On the occasion of the celebration of the third anniversary of the Republic a vast throng gathered before the Reichstag in Berlin, the stately building erected "To the German people," where President Ebert and the members had assembled. The members are elected for four years by universal, equal, direct, and secret votes of male and female voters, on the proportional system

inhabitants) and rural communes (under 2,000 inhabitants). Before the Great War some thirty-five million acres were under grain of all kinds, but the cessions of territory have greatly reduced the extent and production of the national granary, and Germany will need to import far more than the old proportion of one-fourth or one-fifth of her food corn.

To the crops of grain must be added the rich produce of the vineyards of the valleys of the Rhine (Prussia and Baden), Moselle, Saar, Lahn, and Ahr is to farm the fruit trees yearly to the highest bidder.

Germany is still the home of a large and thriving independent peasantry and a country which offers good prospects to small owners and cultivators. In 1907 her $78\frac{1}{2}$ million acres of agriculturally employed land were divided into no fewer than five and three-quarter million holdings. It is not implied that large proprietors are rare, or are seriously threatened with extinction. The large estate is localised, however, and small

YOUNG GERMANIA PASSES BY DURING A CHURCH FESTIVAL IN BERLIN

These small folk are evidently no more averse to the publicity afforded by the camera than their sisters of other lands. The smiling throng, flower crowned and tricked out in their best, make an attractive picture as they patter obediently over the rough cobbles. Those who wear them are evidently pleased with the effect of their white boots, and each is conscious of looking bright and happy in a pretty frock. The tiny ones who bring up the rear are enlivening the dull stones with posies scattered from their be-ribboned baskets. In Germany the charm added to ceremonial occasions by the presence of children is fully realized

PRESIDENTIAL INSPECTION OF A COMPANY OF WAR VETERANS ON THE ANNIVERSARY OF THE REPUBLIC

Herr Friedrich Ebert, President of the new Germany, making, on the third anniversary of the Republic's inception, a round of inspection of a special company. Hat in hand, and followed by a civilian official in frock coat and also bare-headed, he closely scans the silent ranks, drawn up so stiffly upon their hard-paved parade ground. In the background the crowd congregated under the trees, above which the State banner droops and clings to its tall flag-staff, surveys with acute interest the representatives of civil administration and military authority inspecting these picked men of the Republic

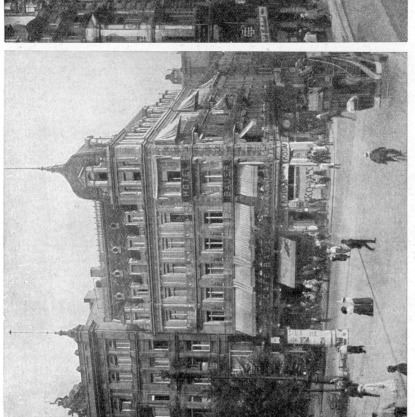

BERLIN AT ITS BUSIEST AND BEST: UNTER DEN LINDEN AND THE LEIPZIGERSTRASSE

In the spacious avenue, Unter den Linden, which runs from the Brandenburg Gate eastward to the monument of Frederick the Great, Berlin possesses perhaps the finest modern thoroughfare of any European capital city. Nearly two-thirds of a mile in length, 198 feet wide, and planted with rows of lime trees, it is a glorious boulevard with its most animated point here where it crosses the busy Friedrichstrasse. To the south of Unter den Linden and parallel with it runs the Leipzigerstrasse, shown here on the right

Photos, Donald McLeish

and medium holdings are the rule in most parts of the country.

The most backward agrarian districts occur in the Mecklenburgs and the east of Prussia, the homes of the great " latifundia." These unwieldy estates are an impediment in the way of

was abolished in Prussia, yet the retarding influence of feudalism still survives. It is a fact which carries its own condemnation of the economic and political pressure which has so long rested on the rural east of Prussia that great poverty and a relatively low standard of morality

HUMAN ACTIVITY HUMS IN THE PULSING HEART OF BERLIN

At the west end of the Leipzigerstrasse, one of Berlin's chief arteries of traffic, lies the square known as the Potsdamerplatz. Several palatial modern buildings look down upon this busy centre of life and movement, where the din of passing vehicles is seldom hushed, and the electric cars—the chief mode of transport for the Berliner, communication by which is so splendidly organized—glide over its spacious surface in ceaseless procession

Photo, Donald McLeish

scientific agriculture and a drag upon social progress ; they are not managed on rational principles, and they have prevented the creation of intelligent, healthy, and independent peasant communities, such as are found elsewhere. Far happier is the state of things which prevails in Westphalia, at the other end of the country, where even the farm labourer has a piece of land which he rents from his employer. Over a hundred years have passed since serfdom

characterise that region. A large part of Germany is given up to forest, partly of natural growth, but all systematically and commercially managed. The area under forest of all kinds—predominantly coniferous—exceeded in 1913 thirty-five and a half million acres, of which about one-third was held and worked by the States, one-fifth by municipal and other public bodies, and some 45 per cent. was in private hands. The State forestry service is an important department of the Civil Service, and admission to it entails severe specialised study and practical training.

In Germany the rivers and streams are harnessed, to a degree only equalled in Switzerland, not merely for the use of water-run mills and workshops of all kinds, such as are found in abundance in the forest districts, but for the generation of electrical current. Hence it is a common thing to find the villages and hamlets of a whole countryside, remote from towns, well and cheaply lighted by electricity. Domestic employment in what are called the "house" and "home" industries, affords a

livelihood to many thousands of people of both sexes and all ages in the hilly regions and outlying rural districts of Saxony, Silesia, Thuringia, Baden and Württemberg (the Black Forest), and Bavaria.

While agriculture thus occupies so important a position in Germany's economic and social life, more and more during the past forty years attention has been directed to industry. The occupation census of 1907 showed that while since 1882 the proportion of the occupied population engaged in agriculture and forestry decreased from 43.4 to 32.7 per cent., the proportion engaged in industry increased during that period from 33.7 to 37.2 per cent., and the proportion engaged in trade and transport from 8.3 to 11.6 per cent. The greatest displacement occurred in Prussia, the least in Württemberg.

The chief seats of industry are the Prussian provinces of Rhineland and Westphalia and Saxony, where the greatest agglomerations of population are found, the rate of density in Saxony in 1919 being 805 to the square mile, comparing with 318 for the whole country, but with 94 for Mecklenburg-Strelitz and 130 for Mecklenburg-Schwerin. The great iron and steel industries are located in the Westphalian Rhineland and Upper Silesia, but the engineering, electrical, and allied industries dependent upon them are carried on in a large number of other centres in Prussia, Saxony, Baden, Württemberg and Bavaria. There are large shipbuilding yards on the North and Baltic Seas, particularly at Hamburg,

AT WORK IN A GERMAN GLASS FACTORY

Germany has long been eminent for the manufacture of optical glass. To successful experiments in the famous Jena glassworks are due many of the methods in general use for the production of this delicate and most valuable material

Photo, Transocean

Bremen, Stettin, and Elbing. The chemical and dye industry, favoured by the possession of abundant raw materials, by long scientific research, and the capacity and will to put the results of this research to practical use, has grown to remarkable proportions. Its principal seats are several towns on the Rhine, Frankfort, and Berlin. The cotton industry is carried on in Saxony, Silesia, the Rhineland, and other parts of Prussia, the woollen industry in the Rhineland, and the worsted goods industry in Silesia and around Berlin ; linen is manufactured in Silesia and parts of Westphalia ; Saxony is the chief centre of the hosiery and lace manufactures, and Crefeld is the seat of the silk industry. Other important industries are the glass and porcelain, clock and watch, paper and paper-pulp, and small arms industries. Before the Great War about four-fifths of Germany's manufactures were consumed by the home market.

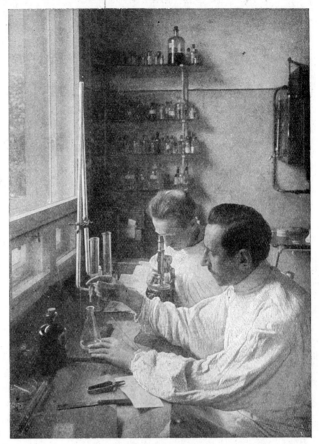

SCIENCE WORKING FOR HUMANITY

German scientists have long been to the fore in investigating the causes of diseases that still baffle prevention and cure. These men are working in the laboratory of the Institute for Cancer Research in Berlin

That the characteristics and the institutions of a people are in large measure the outcome of its history is a truism, but in the case of Germany the relation between the two has points of special interest. It is exemplified in a marked manner, for example, by some of the outstanding personal and domestic qualities of the German. To the former belong industry and efficiency. Before it achieved political unity in 1871 the German nation had to pass through a long and severe discipline. For centuries its history was a continuous record of tribal faction within, of war, and of oppression at the hands of foreign aggressors. Time after time its lands were invaded and laid desolate. The Thirty Years War, from 1618 to 1648, left a large part of the country a desert, and its population impoverished and ruined. No sooner had it recovered than there came the struggles which were forced upon the German rulers and tribes by Napoleon, culminating in the heroic War of Emancipation.

The national unity movement which followed developed under the jealous eyes of countries whose interest and policy it was to keep the German States apart, and three wars were fought before the Empire was re-established under the Hohenzollerns. Out of such searching ordeals as these nations must emerge either stronger or weaker, and the Germans emerged stronger. Since,

COMMERCIAL ACTIVITY OVER-BRIMMING IN LEIPZIG

Leipzig's great fairs have been important since the fifteenth century. The Jubilate fair lasts from the first Monday in March until the following Saturday week, and the Michaelmas fair begins on the last Sunday in August and continues for three weeks. During these periods the town is packed with German salesmen and with commercial visitors from all parts of the world, the activity in the Peterstrasse being particularly brisk

however, they had to fight for existence they became of necessity a military nation, and to such a people efficiency becomes instinctive.

Nature, too, has not been unduly lavish in her gifts to this country, in which over a large area agriculture has to battle with an austere climate, with short summers and severe winters, while its mineral resources are limited and very unequally distributed. While in the north and north-east there are

vast expanses of sandy land, which only with the greatest difficulty can be made to yield food for man and beast, stretching through Central Germany from the south-east to the north-west is the great chain of mountains and highland which has been mentioned, and here like-wise the struggle with nature is a ceaseless grind.

Even in the centres where great industries have been planted, serious obstacles have had to be overcome. The most highly-developed and successful of these is the iron and steel industry, yet it has had to contend with the disadvantage of inadequate supplies of native ore, for the most part of an inferior quality, and the fact that much of the necessary fuel lies at a distance from the furnaces and manufacturing plant. These and

LEIPZIG'S GREAT ADVERTISEMENT PARADE

Originally actual markets, Leipzig's fairs are now meetings for the exhibition of samples of German products. The sample weeks open with a parade from the Peterstrasse to the City Market Hall of cars and devices advertising German industries

YOUTHFUL ADHERENTS OF KING CARNIVAL KEEP OLD CUSTOMS ALIVE IN BRANDENBURG

Although North Germans generally take little part in the festivals common in other Continental countries before the beginning of Lent, yet carnival is observed with much jollification in Prussia. These young Brandenburgers are "going the rounds" from house to house, brandishing branches of birch and carrying stacks of buns fashioned in a particular shape which they exchange for gifts of money or apples. Some of the German customs may have a pagan origin, the little wheel-shaped cakes perhaps representing the sun and the branches of young birch the renewal of the earth as spring approaches.

HAPPY CHILDHOOD SECURE IN MOTHER-LOVE

Time was when the German " Hausfrau " could concern herself only with the four proverbial " K's " —Kinder, Küche, Kleider, Kirche (Children, Kitchen, Clothes, Church)—but her position has considerably changed in recent years. She now often shares the intellectual or business interests of her husband; but her devotion to her home remains unaltered, and German children, the centre of their mother's affection, have a wonderfully happy childhood

Photo, Florence Farmborough

other difficulties have called forth in a high degree the virtues of industry, courage, application, inventiveness, and enterprise, without which Germany might have remained one of the poorest of Continental countries instead of one of the most highly developed.

It is the same with the domestic characteristics which have given to German home life in all ages its high reputation—orderliness, thrift, frugality, and cohesion. Exposed to the harsh but stimulating regimen of poverty, the Germans were compelled to be provident, and to master the art of making a little go a long way. Still, as

in the time of Tacitus, the standard of family life in Germany is a high one. There, as elsewhere, the Great War has led to a certain weakening of household ties, and of parental control and discipline, yet in the homes of no country is life on the whole more healthy, in none are order and cleanliness more cultivated; and when it has been said that there are probably no better cared-for children in the world than those of the German working classes, let it be added that in no country is greater respect paid to the fifth commandment. All these things, likewise, make for and mean efficiency in national life. The German super-housewife is supposed to be found in Württemberg, where the instinct of cleanliness is so marked that it is jokingly said that the very milestones are washed every Saturday.

One of the few beneficent effects of the past political division of Germany has been the existence of so many courts and capitals, each of which has served in greater or less measure as a focus of culture and progress. With all their shortcomings and their disposition to pomposity, which was never shown so ridiculously as when they weakly aped the Grand Monarque and aspired to turn each of their " residences " into a little Paris or Versailles, many of these princes have nevertheless played an important part in the intellectual life and development of Germany. Potsdam, in the time of Frederick the Great; Weimar, in the time of Karl August; and Munich, in the time of King Maximilian, represented this side of court life at its best. But these courts and those of Stuttgart, Dresden, Karlsruhe, Brunswick, and many of the smaller

capitals, have at all times been centres of light and leading, radiating the refining influences of art and letters, music and the drama, throughout the States of whose life and welfare they were the natural guardians.

The independent courts and governments of the scores of States of Old Germany unquestionably created and maintained within these territories a higher general level of culture than would have been possible had the functions of government been exercised from a distant metropolis, whether Vienna or Berlin. It is also due to the spirit of particularism which the old State order has preserved that the over-centralization of government from which France suffers has been kept in check; that powerful stimuli to progress in the arts and sciences, the crafts and industries, have been operative in a multitude of different places; that many experimental centres have existed at which new theories in political and civil government could be tested and, if approved, applied; and that local

WENDISH WOMEN ON THE ROAD TO CHURCH.

Wendish women are strict conservatives in regard to dress, and many a German lady of high degree has made the journey to the beautiful Spreewald for the sole purpose of seeing her humbler sisters in their delightful old-fashioned costumes. On their marriage, Wendish girls generally possess a large stock of clothes, for they like to have many changes for every special occasion

Photo, Georg Haeckel

PLEASURE COMBINED WITH BUSINESS IN THE SPREEWALD

Every German can skate, the cold dry winters of northern Germany especially providing constant practice. This Wendish peasant is skating to market on the frozen roads in the Spreewald, a marshy district about fifty miles south-east of Berlin, so covered with a network of tributaries of the Spree that some of the villages are only accessible by water in summer, and over the ice in winter

SKATING AND SLEIGHING TO THE ICY VAULTS OF DEATH

To people unfamiliar with the conditions in the Spreewald a scene like this may appear grotesque— top-hatted mourners on skates drawing a sledge containing a flower-decked coffin, and the mourners skating mournfully behind. For the Wendish peasants themselves, however, skates are an integral part of winter footwear, and skating and sleighing are the only means of locomotion and transport

peculiarities in institutions and customs have been protected, and much that was good in the life and thought of old Germany has been preserved.

Certain political and social evils have, nevertheless, resulted from this particularism and the past exaggerated personal power of the Sovereigns. One of the former is the fact that Germany is a land of officials. From birth to death the German citizen is subjected to the well-meaning but often irritating attentions of an endless succession of bureaucrats of all degrees of importance and importunity, and he is allowed to do little himself which the State is able to do for him, though it may do it less well and wisely.

Bureaucracy Strangles Individuality

A mechanical efficiency in administration, for what it is worth, may be claimed for this drastic system of regimentation, but personal liberty is unduly restricted thereby, individuality and spontaneity are repressed, public spirit and private enterprise are discouraged, and the disposition which it creates to look to and depend on the " powers that be " in every situation of life does not make for the highest and strongest type of citizenship.

On the social side it is largely due to the multiplicity of courts, with their crowds of sycophants and hangers-on, that the system of titles and decorations has been developed to so ludicrous an extent in Germany. The higher branches of the nobility represent real distinction, and are not to be confounded with the futile " noblesse " which vaunts itself in several more easterly European countries ; and even the first step of the ladder of ennoblement, as connoted by the prefix von (represented by the French de), carries equal value in all the States.

Absurdities in Titles and Etiquette

It is chiefly in official and professional titles that abuse exists. Of these titles there is literally no end, and the observance of the recognized code of etiquette in relation to them, whether in verbal or epistolary intercourse, is a matter of solemn duty. The peculiar characteristic of Bavaria (as of Austria) in this respect is the abundance of its " councillors " (Raethe). The " councillor " of one sort or another, however, is common in every German State, and it is a social misdemeanour of the worst kind to omit to use this or any other title, wherever due. Sensible people hoped that the apparent triumph of democratic ideas, as evidenced by the institution of a Realm of Republics, would prove the death knell of these titular absurdities. Far from that having been the case, it is a common lament that the craze for titular distinctions has increased, and even spread to the servants' hall of the bureaucracy.

Reference has been made to certain distinguishing characteristics of the leading tribes, and it remains to speak more particularly of traits which are in some degree common to Germans in the mass. Every nation has temperamental qualities peculiar to itself—the product of all the various factors which have contributed to make up its civilization—race, climate, history, the pacific or violent course of its development as a community, social conditions, and the like. The German is often summarily spoken of as stolid and phlegmatic. So also is the Englishman. In each case only half the truth, or less, is told, for much of the stolidity and phlegm on both sides is only apparent and superficial.

Sterling Merits of the German

The average German, far from being stolid and cold, is singularly exuberant, and is pre-eminently a creature of feeling and impulse, though these traits are naturally found in various degrees in different tribes. Except in the west, however, he has little of the nervous sensitiveness of the French, and he may in general be described as a masculine character, in contrast to the essentially feminine characters of the races lying west and east of his country.

Every traveller judges as he sees, often judging wrongly, however, if he fails to see sufficiently and is lacking in sympathy. I would, at risk of

GERMANY: *New Scenes & Old Costumes*

Despite their loyalty to traditional costume the Wendish girls of the Spreewald do not despise the conveniences of modern mechanism

Photo, Georg Haeckel

*Beyond the busy market-place looms the Cathedral of Worms, the
ancient town where Luther made the vigorous defence of his doctrines*

*The lofty dome of Berlin's new Cathedral dominates the Lustgarten,
a quiet retreat where the leisured Teuton spends many happy hours*

Photo, Donald McLeish

Away among the hills in the Bavarian Highlands, costly medieval costumes are still in vogue with the peasantry of the olden school

2404

*Simplicity stamps the Sabbath dress of the rural folk near Stuttgart
with an attractiveness unequalled among other Württemberg peasants*

Photo, Kadell & Herbert

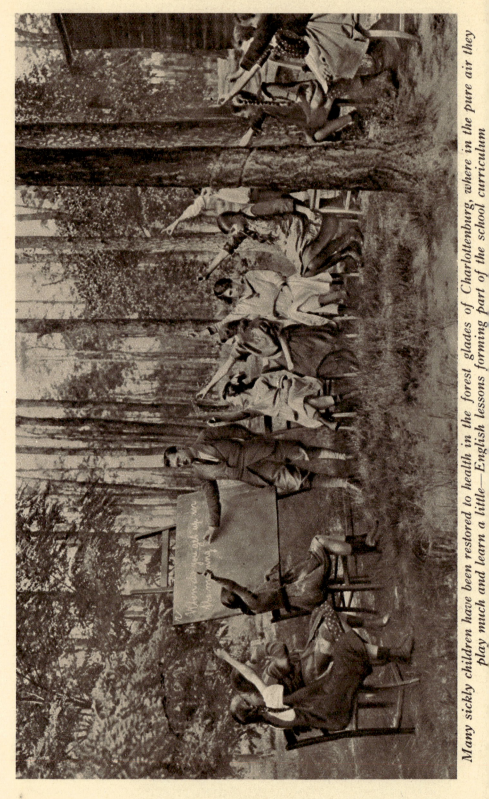

Many sickly children have been restored to health in the forest glades of Charlottenburg, where in the pure air they play much and learn a little—English lessons forming part of the school curriculum

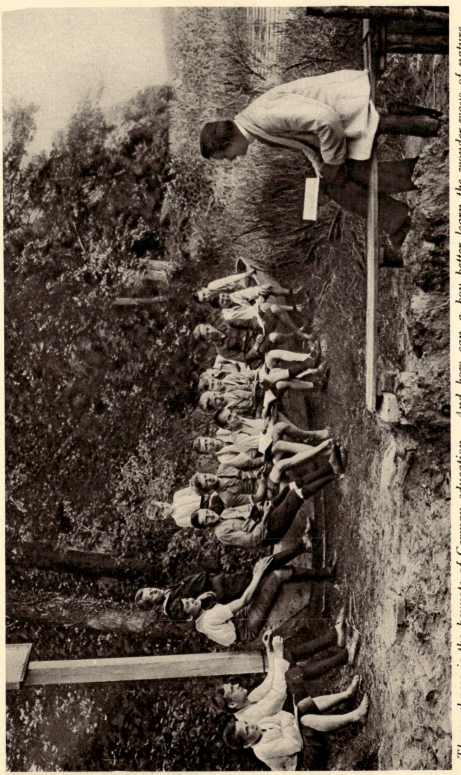

Thoroughness is the keynote of German education. And how can a boy better learn the wonder-ways of nature than by studying each aspect in her own garden, under shady bough and beside glancing stream?

*Sankt Georgien boasts divers styles of headgear, but none so proudly
worn as the rich bridal " schappel " of myriad-coloured glass balls*

Photo Georg Haeckel

Overmuch befrilled and beflowered, this maiden will be nothing loath to discard the heavy brocaded veneer of Bückeburg bridal attire

Photo, Georg Haeckel

The costumes of Bavaria are as diversified as the wild flowers that abound in its meadows, and the variegated finery of these women of the Nördlingen district, seen in colour, is strikingly picturesque

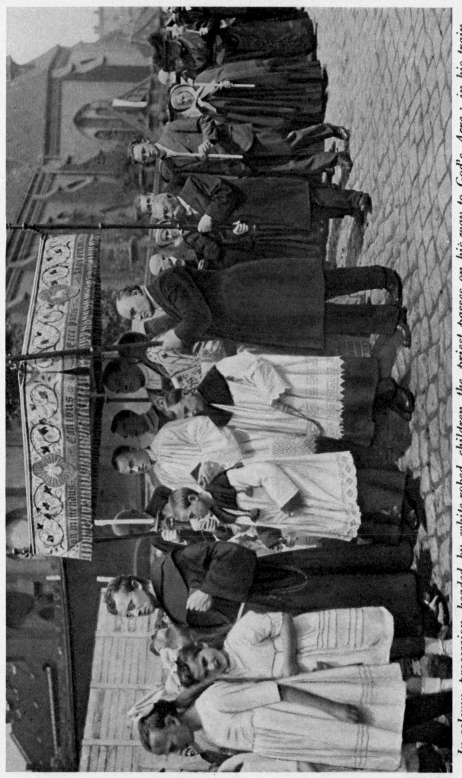

In solemn procession, headed by white-robed children, the priest passes on his way to God's Acre; in his train follow men and matrons anxious to pay reverence to a departed brother of the Church of Rome

*Useful, if not ornamental, is the gift of this Bavarian bride's father;
emblematic of the domestic felicity to attend her wedded life*

*Straw-plaiting was once a means of livelihood in the Black Forest,
now the Sankt Georgien girls plait more for pleasure than necessity*

Photo, Georg Haeckel

Youth is rife in this ancient, time-worn village of the Rhine, where the gay laughter of childhood is never hushed save at nightfall

Puffing at his meerschaum pipe the Rhenish labourer thoughtfully scans a poster that calls on his folk to support the Rhine Republic

Photo, Donald McLeish

*Above the small town of St. Goarshausen a " castle crag," imposing
in its scenic majesty, " frowns o'er the wide and winding Rhine "*

Photo, Donald McLeish

contradiction, call Germans in the mass —I have in mind, of course, the male part of them, for the female part would deserve a more discriminating character-isation—a bluff but hearty and kindly people. That as a nation they positively excel in the arts and " finesse " of social life need not be pretended, but all sorts of gifts and graces go to the making of an urbane and attractive character, and when you get to know them, the Germans invariably impress you by a sterling geniality for which no amount of superficial polish can be a substitute. For the most part they are distinctly sociable, hospitable, and generous, ready to help the stranger, and to entertain and give pleasure to their friends, though among them, as among other peoples, there often exists a tendency to mistake for generosity what is mere thoughtless prodigality.

Passion for Music and the Drama

The Germans are distinctly a pleasure-loving people, that description being understood in the best sense. The dreary doctrine that " man was made to mourn " finds little acceptance in their country. Music and the drama are their passions, and there is hardly a small town anywhere which is without its musical society or circle for the practical study of oratorio and other high-class music and the organization of concerts. It is creditable to the public spirit of the larger towns that generous municipal expenditure is bestowed upon theatres and concert-halls, as well as picture galleries and museums.

Most towns of any consequence not only own theatres, but run them, even at great cost, and it is indisputable that a higher level of dramatic taste is shown in a German town of the second or third rank than in the English metropolis, a fact which attests the serious place attached to the drama in Germany as a means not merely of recreation but of culture; while it is a notorious fact that Shakespeare, and even several modern English play-writers of repute, are oftener staged in Germany than in their native country. In the cultivation and satisfaction of the social side of life the public house of entertainment—be it hotel, or restaurant, inn, or coffee-house—takes a prominent part. This institution occupies in Germany a higher status than in England, and fulfils wider functions.

Social Function of the " Gasthof "

It is respectable and proper to go to a German hotel or restaurant at any time of the day or evening, not merely because the place itself is respectable and proper, but because it has a distinct social side, and because the idea of associating it with mere purposeless drinking and treating does not occur to the frequenters. In country towns and villages the little inn or " Gasthof " (guest-house) is the centre of social and public life, where parson and squire, doctor and lawyer, official and farmer, meet to eat and chat at the end of the day, sometimes in company with their womenfolk, or some of them.

In old-fashioned circles a meal is begun with a reciprocal " May the meal (" Mahlzeit ") do you good ! " and ended with a " May the meal be blessed ! " though elsewhere the double invocation is nowadays usually reduced to a chorus of perfunctory and slovenly " Mahlzeits ! " as the guests rise from the table. There is much intemperance in Germany, less, however, the result of beer and wine than of brandy drinking, but the bad reputation given to the Germans in this respect by Tacitus is no longer deserved.

General Talent for Oratory

The Germans are born orators, though as little prone to rhetorical rhapsodies as the English. They are excellent public speakers, and a strenuous poli-tician regards it as all in the day's work to bore parliament with a six-hours' speech. The clergy would as soon think of reading sermons as of preaching without gowns; and while there are university professors who use manu-script the majority lecture extem-poraneously, not always with the assist-ance of notes. Long ago I knew one who began his morning lecture before he had hung his hat upon the wall, and

ART STUDENTS BUSY IN THE SCHOOL OF NATURE

Seriously as children take their education in Germany, they can find pleasure in it, too, when the
modern methods of teaching there in vogue can take a whole class out into nature's pleasant places.
Here a lesson in drawing from nature is shown in progress, the subject a lovely mere in the grounds
of a stately mansion, the art master obviously as interested in the task as the boys themselves

SCHOOLBOYS WORKING AT THEIR DRAWING LESSON

German boys are usually steady and conscientious workers, although not often particularly brilliant.
The class seen above are drawing a sewing-machine which is placed on one of the desks in view of all.
Various parts of the mechanism have been drawn on the blackboard in the background.   Many of the
boys have their hair cropped close in true German fashion

Photo, Photothek, Berlin

WHERE DELICATE CHILDHOOD IS NURTURED IN MIND AND BODY

In the pine forests of Charlottenburg a forest school, or Waldschule, has been established which provides education for boys and girls of delicate constitution chosen from the elementary schools of Charlottenburg. Many children, living in poor, cramped houses, are eager to spend the summer days in these beautiful surroundings, where they receive sound moral and physical training

OPEN-AIR INSTRUCTION IN THE CHARLOTTENBURG FOREST SCHOOL

When the weather proves unkind the lessons take place under big shelters. From late spring to early autumn the young scholars go daily to the Waldschule, but lessons are not always de rigueur; the greater part of each day is passed in happy play on the sandy soil, and the more sickly children spend many hours resting on reclining chairs breathing in new vigour from the pure forest air

HEARTY APPETITES ENGENDERED BY LIFE IN THE OPEN AIR

In their bivouac under the trees of a public park these little Berliners are enjoying their midday meal. A holiday in the open gives them a greater appetite than usual, and meal-times are always awaited eagerly. The two flags standing at the entrance to one of the shelters show the tricolour of the new German Republic

AFTER-DINNER TASK AT A JUVENILE SUMMER HOLIDAY CAMP

The two long rows of troughs are lined by children who are spending their summer holidays in a country camp near Berlin. They have just finished their dinner, and are now washing their cups and plates under the supervision of two of their teachers. Suspended from the neck of the lightly-clad small boy on the right is his identification label

Photos, Otto Haeckel

kept up an uninterrupted flow of precise language until he had his hand upon the door-handle, preparatory to exit. And his subject was history, too.

In public places the German is apt to be loquacious and noisy. Anyone new to the spectacle of a discussion over beer and tobacco in a public restaurant would imagine that the heated talkers, all vociferating and gesticulating together, would at any moment be hurling chairs and glasses word) and depth, and also the vein of melancholy and pessimism which pervades so much exquisite German lyrical poetry. A less gracious trait is their intensely critical spirit, a characteristic which leads to contention and faction in political and to scepticism in religious life. A dogmatist by nature, the German has no patience with dogma ; a worshipper of systems, no system is yet safe against his attack. It follows that his intellect is stronger

LEISURELY PURSUIT OF LEARNING IN A FLOATING STUDY

" Keep a good student from his books, and it is wonderful ! " said Justice Shallow. If anything could accomplish the feat, one might suppose it would be floating on a placid mere in a steady boat, with a pleasant company of kindred souls. Yet these good students at Scharfenberg find their boat only a more convenient place for their work together, a silent study remote from possible interruption

at each other. Nothing of the kind ; they are simply engaged in the friendliest possible exchange of views about the quality of the beverage they are drinking or the merits of last night's performance at the theatre. A little less exuberance, a little more restraint and reserve, might be a useful addition to the many solid qualities of the German character.

One of the distinctive characteristics of the German races—for here they all agree—is their love of nature, with their marked susceptibility to natural influences and surroundings. This trait finds expression in the " inwardness " (to use Matthew Arnold's favourite on the destructive than the creative and constructive side, and strength of that kind is apt to be a source of danger to its possessor and of disadvantage to others. His enjoyment of humour is, perhaps, keener than is his sense of what is truly humorous, for here a certain delicacy and fineness of perception are lacking, as anyone will agree who compares the leading humorous journals of Germany with those of England.

Behind the important fact of manifold similarity in characteristics, however, lies the equally important fact of contrasts. The greatest of these are presented by north and south and by west and east respectively. It has been

PRACTICAL TRAINING IN PERSPECTIVE DRAWING: FIRST STUDIES FOR A HORSE AND CARRIAGE

German thoroughness in the groundwork of education is shown in this photograph of an art class drawing a "horse and carriage" in the school yard. A couple of trestles, a plank, and four hoops make the chassis of an admirable vehicle, while the body is suggested by half a dozen vertical rods connected at the top by horizontal rods. From this simple apparatus intelligent pupils can learn the perspective plan of the most elaborate coach they may desire to draw. A vaulting-horse supplies the model for a foreshortened steed, and a complacent lad represents the coachman

2422

said that the North German is marked pre-eminently by energy, strength, and tenacity of will, the spirit of enterprise, and capacity for practical affairs, but he does not excel either in the softer graces of character or in the finer expressions of culture. The poet Emmanuel Geibel, who was born in the north, but brought his art to maturity in the south, wrote :

For all I am and know the practical
    north I thank,
But it remained for the south to teach me
    the secret of form.

The South German claims that the south is the true cradle and home of German culture, and that the North German has borrowed from the south the best that he is and knows. The characteristics and the intellectual traditions of the south seem to favour this large claim. Personal traits in general are suaver and life more genial in the south than in the north. Where the North German is eager for success and prosperity, the South German, though not indifferent to these things, prefers his less strenuous life, lives more in the present, and is more satisfied with what the present has to offer.

Northern Grit and Southern Grace

The North German may be more self-reliant, more self-sufficient, and in his imperfect way more " finished-off " than the South German ; but the quiet unassertiveness of the latter, his self-possession, and his unostentatious assumption of superiority bear the unmistakable stamp of age, breeding, and race. Even the peasantry of the south, while they have all the hard-headedness of the northerner, seem to carry warmer hearts behind a rough exterior. It is hardly surprising that the South German shows little disposition to migrate to the north. Out of his tribal fatherland, in fact, he does not feel comfortable and at home.

Again, there is an equally fundamental difference between the west, with its early and Romanized civilization, and the east, with its later and lagging acceptance of modern ideas. The people of the Rhineland have much affinity, both physically and psychically, with the neighbouring French, while those of the agrarian east retain traits of the Slavic character which are hostile to progress.

Conservatism in Rural Districts

There is far more real character in the rural districts of any country than in the towns, where all the influences of modern life favour conventionality and tend to reduce mankind to a dead level of uniformity. Hence it is among the agricultural classes and the inhabitants of sequestered villages in the hilly regions and the forest zones that one must go for such relics as remain of old-time German folk life. There domestic architecture, a ruder dress, the manners, and the very physiognomy of the people attest a life and civilization left behind by the rush of modern days. Particularly marked is this detachment of rural Germany from the rest of the country in Roman Catholic districts, where conservative ways seem to be confirmed by religious sanctions.

The peasants' houses are substantially built, and, allowing for all sorts of modifications in different parts of the country, half-timbered structures predominate, in both the north and the south, the spaces between the framework being filled with brick and plaster. The older buildings in the north are thatched, while in the south small shingles, or " shakes," are often used as a roofing material.

General Plan of Rural Architecture

The commonest type of house, both in the Saxon districts of the northern lowland and the highland and forest districts of the south, is a large, solid, and plainly-constructed building, with high gables, in which domestic quarters, barns, stalls, and corn and fodder chambers are all brought under one roof. This building is entered by high central doors opening upon a wide passage. In the north the living-rooms are reached by a door at the end of this passage, while in front lie on both sides the chambers for livestock and stores. In the south this order is often reversed.

Again, while in the north the farm-houses usually stand alone, each surrounded by the fields going with it, in Bavaria the peasants tend more to live in villages, and have sometimes to go some distance to their fields. In Bavaria also, as in the Black Forest, all-timber houses are common as in Switzerland, often with a wooden gallery running round the exterior. Where wood is the principal building material the outer timbers are often carved with texts and proverbs expressive of the natural piety or mother wit of the original owners.

The alpine farm and other houses of Southern Bavaria belong to the most picturesque in the country.

It is on the occasion of the ever-popular church festivals and local holidays that rural life most assumes the guise and aspects of antiquity. It is then that the traditional costume—one of the oldest expressions of tribal and local patriotism and individuality—though worn, perhaps, by the older folk on Sundays and market-days, displays itself in all its amplitude and bravery. Much of the old-time dress exists

TEACHING THE YOUNG BERLINER CLEANLINESS
Every child in this Berlin school has a tooth-brush, a hair-brush, and comb contained in a case hung on a numbered peg. On arrival in the morning, after the midday meal, and again before leaving at night they have to brush their hair and cleanse their teeth. Thus they soon learn the value of personal cleanliness

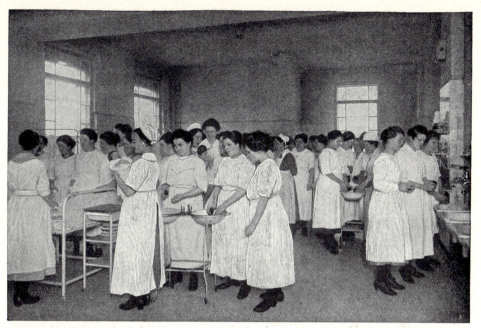

IN THE MATERNITY WARD OF A STATE MIDWIFERY SCHOOL

Midwifery as a profession for women was officially recognized and authorized in Germany long before it was properly regulated in Great Britain. German midwives are appointed by the State after thorough training in a State school of midwifery. They are given a certificate by the police which permits them to conduct confinements in a specified district, within which they must reside

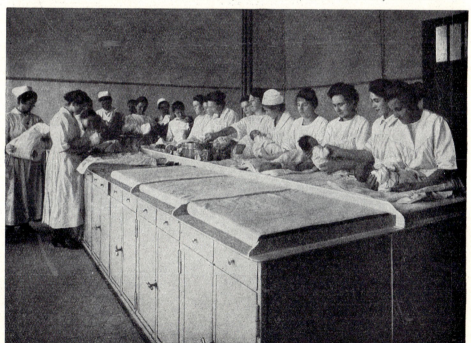

GIRL STUDENTS WEIGHING YOUNG GERMANY IN THE BALANCE

German thoroughness is admirably exemplified in the training provided for midwives. Large maternity wards are specially arranged for their instruction in practical obstetrics, and besides learning everything necessary to the mothers' welfare they are given a course in the practical care of the infants, washing and drying and dressing them, and keeping accurate daily records of their weight

Photos, Photothek, Berlin

STUDENTS' JOLLIFICATION IN A BEER GARDEN

Collegiate life of the kind rendered possible at Oxford and Cambridge by the existence of residential colleges with their separate foundations and customs is not known in Germany. There the bond of student comradeship, so valuable as a social influence, is knitted mainly by the institution of students' corps, companies of like-minded young men who meet together for social and intellectual intercourse and occasional merry-making

to-day only in the form of heirlooms treasured in wardrobes and chests, amid perfume of lavender and rosemary, or is known only as tradition, but in the more sequestered parts of the country, particularly in the agricultural States of the centre and the south, it is still common.

Thus distinctive costume is worn by men or oftener by women in Brunswick, the Prussian provinces of Westphalia, Hanover, and Pomerania, as well as the Spreewald and the island of Rügen, in Saxony (Lusatia), Altenburg, Hesse, and Schaumburg; and, further south, in Baden (particularly the Black Forest), the Bavarian highlands, and Württemberg.

Any summary description of peasant and rural costume is impossible owing to its great diversity, every tribal territory—and often each valley or countryside of the same State—having peculiarities of its own. Everywhere there are differences for each sex, not only in form, but in colour, decoration, the combinations in which these are used, and in material. There are also differences determined by the social position and age of the wearers, and, in the case of women, their married or single state.

One fundamental difference is the preference shown by the North German peasant for a plain dress of dark or modest hues, in contrast to the South German, who revels in gay colours and an abundance of ornament. The costume of the men usually comprises a smock, jacket, tunic, or long coat of cloth or velvet, with knee breeches of cloth or leather, showy stockings, and hat of felt or straw, or a cap. Girdles, collars, and neckerchiefs of special make may also belong to his festive attire. The women wear black or coloured frocks or skirts, with dainty bodices, kerchiefs, and aprons, but in all these the utmost variety exists, and still more in the headdress, the styles of which are endless. Both sexes pay special attention to their embroidery, which is usually many-coloured and of artistic workmanship, as well as to their buttons, clasps, brooches, and other ornamental jewelry, which is often of great age and value.

Here and there extravagances of attire are noticeable, like the huge hats, built up of tier on tier of pompons, worn by some of the peasant women of Baden, where the size of this embarrassing piece of headdress is an indication of social importance; but even such peculiarities are excused by

HEALTHY HOMESTEADS OF GERMAN LAND-LABOURERS
The conditions of rural life in Germany have been considerably ameliorated in latter times, thanks to the efforts expended by many building societies on the erection of better dwellings for the labouring class. These picturesque, half-timbered village homes in the vicinity of Hersfeld, a town in Hesse-Nassau, some 30 miles to the south of Cassel, certainly present a most inviting appearance. They are carefully re-whitened every spring

Photo, Georg Haeckel

RUSTIC ALLEGIANCE TO THE SABBATH: VILLAGERS OF HESSE-NASSAU ON THEIR WAY TO CHURCH

For the townfolk of Germany Sunday is the great day of the week; various places of amusement are open, and classical plays and well-known operas may be enjoyed for a mere trifle. The countryfolk spend their day of rest in simple, old-world fashion, and regularly every Sabbath day, in this quiet village near Ziegenhain, a leisurely procession makes its way to church. Specially noteworthy are the neat, short-skirted yet old fashioned costumes and modest manners of these peasant worshippers, among whom hobble many of the oldest women of the community

their long history. Until comparatively recently certain trade groups had their special costumes—that of the miners, for example—and the dress of the chimney-sweep is still very distinctive.

The country folk have their pleasures and occasions of social reunion like townspeople, these differing only in kind and quality. Dancing is, of course, a universal passion, and in the villages and hamlets, and on the

the countryside is a big marriage. A union between well-to-do peasant families in Bavaria may mean a whole week of jollity and junketing, in which good cheer is consumed in quantities so vast as to be incredible did not definite evidence on the subject exist.

A few oddities of rural custom may be taken at random. The ancient tribal rule of wife-buying has left a trace in a custom which prevails in

RUSTIC LIFE TAKING THE AIR IN OLD-TIME SIMPLICITY

This peasant woman looks as though she might be the eldest sister of the five strapping little maids rather than their mother. They are natives of Hesse-Nassau and live in a village watered by the River Schwalm, where, for the most part, superstition and ancient customs still retain a powerful hold over rural life and are particularly constant in encouraging the wearing of the delightful costumes of long ago

Photo, Georg Haeckel

isolated farms, it is indulged in whenever a pretext can be found or made. The "harvest home" is still a jovial festival, at which master and man meet convivially on a footing of equality.

Births, christenings, marriages, and deaths are all events of common interest, with which special observances, or customs, differing according to locality, are associated. The most festive event of the year in the life of

Hesse, Pomerania, and other parts, where the successful wooer confirms his betrothal by handing to the girl a gift in money. The occasion and formalities of this observance vary in different localities. In the Spree Forest it is customary to place in a coffin a comb, a piece of soap, and a rag, or alternatively some articles of which the deceased was fond—even to playing cards. In Pomerania a wife's love letters are

APPRENTICES RECEIVING INSTRUCTION IN CHEESE-MAKING

In the town of Wangen in the south of Württemberg near the Swiss frontier is a large cheese-making experimental factory. Run on the most modern lines the factory serves both as a school of instruction for apprentices and an experimental centre. In the above photograph a white-coated instructor is explaining to his class the uses of the huge cauldrons in which the ingredients are mixed

FILLING THE MOULDS WITH THE NEWLY-MADE SOFT CHEESE

In the moulding-room of the factory at Wangen large wooden frames are laid out on the tables. These frames are divided up into a series of compartments by cross partitions. The soft cheese is pressed with a wooden scoop into the moulds, where it will set hard. Care has to be exercised in filling the moulds evenly, and the experienced packer usually takes some time to reach efficiency

Photos, Photothek, Berlin

FINISHED CHEESES LAID ON SHELVES FOR MATURING

When the large round cheeses have been made they are taken into the maturing-room, where they are laid on wooden shelves and left to ripen. To assist in the forming of a firm crust the cheese is often smeared with salt water. The temperature of the room varies in degree according to the cheese that is made, but must be kept level

DRY-SALTING THE CHEESES TO HELP IN THEIR PRESERVATION

The workmen in the foreground are placing the round Tilsiter cheeses in their moulds for dry-salting. Throughout the making the greatest care has to be exercised in keeping the whey and other ingredients at the right temperature in the initial stages, for much of the success of the work depends on this. The workman holding the square wooden frame is dry-salting the soft cheese

Photos, Photothek, Berlin

buried with the husband, and with the wife her bridal wreath and ornaments. A coin is also placed under the tongue of the corpse by way of luck-money. In many localities the windows of the

WHERE NICEST ACCURACY IS NEEDED
Immense engineering works at Tegel, just north of Berlin, give employment to hundreds of hands. Here a couple of skilled workmen are shown measuring and adjusting a large model from which a cast will be taken

death chamber are opened in order that the spirit, figured as a bird, may take flight, and in Thuringia country folk will " tell it to the bees " when a death occurs in the house. The death watch or " wake " is also common, though observed more decorously than of old.

In the Harz, Bavaria, and elsewhere, the old customs incidental to mid-summer day and night are observed, including dancing round the Johannis (St. John) fire, in the course of which loving couples leap together

through the flames. Above all, the rites of Christmas-time are everywhere honoured with the old heartiness. There is also much superstition in rural Germany. Belief in witchcraft is common, and the farmer will still hide a piece of elder wood in stable and stall as a protection against evil influence.

It is to these districts, too, that we must go for the legendary lore which still retains so strong a hold upon the popular imagination. Germany is one of the favoured homes of saga and myth, and all sorts of stories, both wonderful and weird, have gathered round her mountains and valleys, her rivers and forests, most notably in the Harz, the Rhineland, Thuringia, Baden, and Württemberg, where the very atmosphere is saturated with the spirit of romance.

Some of the best known sagas have a distinctly historical background, and this is particularly the case with the Nibelungen saga associated with the Lower Rhine region, and enshrined in Wagner's "Ring" cyclus of operas— Rheingold, Walküre, Siegfried, and Götterdämmerung. Tannhäuser also is no mythical figure, but was one of the Minnesingers who contested at the Wartburg in medieval times. Myths gathered round him, however, and these Wagner wove into his well-known opera.

It will be remembered that the plot of " Tannhäuser " is fixed for the most part in Thuringia, and that a prominent place is given to the Hoerselberg there— the mythical Venusberg—a stretch of mountain near Eisenach. It was in the Hoerselberg that Tannhäuser disappeared to Venus. Similarly the

WIELDING AN ELECTRIC INSTRUMENT IN THE GREAT WORKS AT SIEMENSSTADT

The first discovery of Werner Siemens, the great German electrician, the coating of vessels with metal by electrical means, was the forerunner of numerous inventions. He helped to lay the Atlantic cable, invented the electro-dynamometer, and built and ran the first electric railway. He is largely responsible for the expansion of industrial electricity, and the entire civilized world is his debtor

Photo, Transocean

legend of the Kyffhäuser, which is likewise near Thuringia, relates to one of the most remarkable figures in German history—Barbarossa. The legend of Bishop Hatto and the mouse tower of the Rhine (opposite Bingen) similarly centres in a real historical figure, and the same may be said of the pied piper of Hameln (Browning in his poem uses the more rhythmical spelling Hamelin), near Hanover.

To quite another order of narrative belong such legends as that of the Lorelei maidens of the Rhine, who lured the river folk to their doom, the witches who danced on the "Hexentanzplatz" in the Harz Mountains on Walpurgis night, the flying horse of the "Rosstrappe," and the beautiful Princess Ilse, of which popular superstition speaks in the same locality, and the giant Rübezahl, of the Riesengebirge, or Giant Mountains. It was the habit of Rübezahl to do kind deeds to good people and to play tricks on bad ones. He excelled himself when, on one occasion, he turned a party of ill-conditioned wanderers into potatoes, carrots, and turnips.

The folk legends to which the Rübezahl story belongs are legion, and their themes cover the entire life of the over and under worlds, telling of the earth, sea, and firmament, of gods and heroes, of plants and animals, of all the mystic spirit dwellers of mountain and moor, forest and water, of giants and dwarfs, of gnomes and nymphs, of goblins, elves, and fairies. It is interesting to know that the so-called "fairy tales" (an inadequate translation of the German word "Märchen") associated with the names of the two Grimms were actually collected in various parts of Germany—for the most part in Hesse, in the neighbourhood of

GERMAN WOMEN PREPARING THE WEED THAT SOOTHES MANKIND

Tobacco cultivation is an important agricultural industry in Germany, a large proportion of the national demand being supplied from home sources. Speaking generally, the leaf is of medium size, and heavy, and is mainly used in the manufacture of cigars. This photograph shows women preparing the leaf for drying at a factory in the Uckermark region of Brandenburg

HANGING UP THE LEAVES IN A BRANDENBURG TOBACCO DRYING-SHED

As already explained and illustrated on page 1481 tobacco leaves are either gathered separately as they become ripe or the whole plant is cut when the middle leaves are almost ripe. In the former case the primed leaves, as they are called, are strung on string or wire and suspended as here shown between poles in well ventilated drying-sheds

which the brothers lived, but also in Swabia and in the north.

Reference may be made in passing to the great prominence given to forests and dwarfs in the Grimm collection of folk tales, as indeed in German folk-lore generally. To the Germans the forest is what the sea is to the English, in being the cradle of a hardy, virile, and independent race, but in addition it holds in Germany a singularly tender place in the popular imagination and affection, and the German poetry of the forest and woodland enshrines many of the gems of national literature. The spirit of the sea appeals to the blood of the English, but the spirit of the forest appeals to the hearts of the Germans.

The folk-tales in general are pervaded by a high moral tone. Invariably virtue triumphs and vice is undone, honesty rewarded and roguery punished; and if grief and disappointment, misfortune and suffering are permitted, it is only in order that in the end right may be vindicated and the eternal laws of compensation and retribution be asserted.

Among other strong features of German social life are its folk-songs, which must not be confused with the so-called " popular " songs that still represent the level of musical taste in far too many small English towns. These folk-songs are a faithful expression of the life and thought, the feelings and imagination, the joys and sorrows of the common people. The best known are songs of national heroes, of war and martial exploits, of famous episodes in national and tribal history, of mountain and valley, sea and river, forest and the chase, of vineyard and meadow, wine and women, home and homely people and virtues, love, its pain and solace, bird and beast, sunrise and sunset, and all the other manifold wonders and beauties of nature.

But whether grave or gay, lively or severe, whether they take the historical or epical, the didactic or amorous, the descriptive or reflective form, whether the humour be rough or delicate, always the songs are true to type, racy of the soil, faithful reflections of

FIRST STEPS IN THE CONSTRUCTION OF A WICKER CHAIR

Seated on a sunny bank beside a river the German wicker-worker and his youthful helper are entering on the first stage of their work. The supple twigs have been cut from the willow trees beside the water and are now being peeled of their outer husks. The workers hold the twigs in a firm, vertical position on a stump and peel them from top to bottom

PEELED OSIERS LAID OUT TO DRY ON A SUNNY BANK

Before the peeled willow twigs can be used in the construction of wickerwork articles they have to be well dried to remove the large quantities of sap which they contain. While the elder workman continues the peeling the young assistant is arranging the long, supple sticks in such a position that they will get the maximum of sunlight

Photos, Photothek, Berlin

MAKING WICKER CHAIRS IN A BAVARIAN FACTORY

Basket work is an easily learned industry and, properly organized on a commercial basis, is very lucrative. In the construction of wicker chairs, the seat is usually made first, and the wickerwork below and above it added next. The framework of the seat is of stout cane bent into a bow, to which long rods are fitted, the skeleton seat so formed being filled in by interwoven pliable osiers

BARGAINING FOR BASKETS IN A BERLIN STREET

The thrifty woman of Berlin is ever ready for a bargain, and welcomes the appearance in the streets of carts of country produce. A profusion of peasant wicker work is to be found in this travelling store, and the countrywoman on the left is here seen pointing out to the hesitating housewife the merits of a little fancy basket, which, with the rest of her stock, is home-made

Photos, Photothek, Berlin

LOYALTY OF WÜRTTEMBERG TO THE OLD-FASHIONED RURAL COSTUME

The older peasants of the sequestered German countryside show no inclination to adopt newfangled fashions, while the younger generation, having come into contact with modern life in the large towns, is not unwilling to exchange its traditional attire for the present-day unromantic clothing. These young couples are exhibiting at Ulm on Peasants' Day the old-time costumes of Württemberg

THE PARADE DAY OF THE GERMAN BAUER: JUNGINGEN COSTUMES

Many efforts are being made in Germany to encourage the use of the costumes of bygone years, and the grand parade of peasants at Ulm on a "Bauerntag" vividly testifies to the eagerness of the response of the country folk. All the surrounding districts are represented, and lads and lasses, each in his and her regulation garb, make a brave show in the streets of the fine old cathedral town

MUSICAL QUARTETTE FROM ELLWANGEN AT THE ULM FESTIVAL

They enjoy an honoured position at this fête, for a two-fold duty falls to their lot—they are there to be heard as well as to be seen. Grouped together, well apart from the crowd, they afford genuine entertainment by blowing lusty tunes on their wind instruments, and their répertoire is of a most select kind, as an unusually high standard of musical taste prevails among the German peasantry

BAVARIAN "BÄUERINNEN" BEFORE THE BOARD OF EXAMINERS

Special commendations are meted out to the deserving by a jury appointed to see that each of the districts represented has its costume complete in every minute detail. Even the footgear is rigorously examined ; and these peasant girls from the Bavarian highlands have obviously entered with light-hearted gaiety into the spirit of the festive occasion

PEASANT BRIDE AND BRIDEGROOM OF A HANOVERIAN DISTRICT, WITH THEIR CHOSEN ATTENDANTS

Weddings are celebrated with extraordinary fervour in some country places of Germany; not always, perhaps, so much from a religious point of view as from the fact that a marriage affords ample opportunity for the delights of a family festival. The young men and maidens, often attired as elaborately as the bride and bridegroom themselves, are the life of a wedding party, which inevitably terminates in joyous feasting and dancing

Photo, Georg Haeckel

STARCHED SOBRIETY IN THE SPREEWALD

Like some sculptured medieval figure she stands in her stone niche, the ancient portal of the village church providing an admirable setting for this young matron of the Spreewald, where the Wendish population still retains its original dialect and customs. The beauty of the Lower Spreewald, with wide expanses of deciduous trees, is in striking contrast to the flat pasture-land of the Upper Spreewald

Photo, Transocean

AFTER THE FLAX HARVEST IN WÜRTTEMBERG

One process in the preparation of flax is known as " scutching." In this the stems are passed through a rude mangle or press, and are then beaten in order to remove all traces of the woody core. The fibre is then tied up in bundles known as stricks, seen on the right, and is ready for the market. Although scutching mills are now very general, the process is still performed by hand in many places

"WEAVE THE WARP AND WEAVE THE WOOF"

The cottages of Germany are the birthplace of many of her industries, a number of which are still carried on by the peasantry of to-day. In the modest but speckless home of this newly-married couple of Mönchgut, in the island of Rügen, the loom at which they are at work is considered the most important piece of furniture

AT WORK IN A LAND OF LEGEND AND ROMANCE

About the month of August is a busy time of the year for the peasantry of many districts of the Black Forest, for then the flax has to be harvested and prepared for the looms. This old peasant is engaged in drawing the dried flax plants through a rippling comb in order to remove the immature seed before using the roller to break the straw

real experiences, often as old as tribal history. The words, too, are mated to music with a singular appositeness of melody. It may be noted that many of the old German popular airs have found their way into English hymnology, though this can be said of more than one of the students' drinking songs.

I recall also the stately and measured cadence of one old South German folk-song, set to the lyric beginning " Serenely rises now the moon " (" Gelassen steigt der Mond herauf,") which Brahms has taken as the theme of a movement in one of his beautiful sonatas. Of the same lineage, though belonging to a higher stage of development, are many of the songs of Schubert, Schumann, Franz, Loewe, and others, and not less the old songs and carols of the Christian faith, its festivals and saints, which are equally characteristic of German folk-life.

Although the German States are federated in the new Realm on the basis of parity, as they were in the old, five of them are naturally singled out from all the rest by size, population, and intrinsic importance. These are, in order of population, Prussia, Bavaria, Saxony, Württemberg, and Baden. These five States are represented in the Reichsrat, or Council of States of the Realm, by fifty of the sixty-six members of that body, and may be regarded as constituting a sort of informal Supreme Council. To what has been said about the tribal characteristics of these States must be added some reference to the countries themselves and their special features.

Baden: The Land of the Black Forest

COMPARABLE in size with Wales, Baden has a population in which the two great confessions are unequally represented, yet toleration has been the dominating note of its political and religious life in the past. Agriculturally it is a land of small proprietors and farmers, who cultivate their holdings in many ways. The main field crops are corn and potatoes, but the vine is extensively grown, and excellent vintages are produced in the Rhine and Neckar valleys. The tobacco plant is also cultivated on a large scale.

For a State of its small size Baden can boast many towns of interest. Karlsruhe, the capital, the focus of which is the grand ducal palace, has the quiet dignity of most German " residences," and the scoffer's common gibe, that intellectually its life is as dull as ditch-water, is only half true. Mannheim,

MARIENPLATZ: A SQUARE IN THE ARTISTIC METROPOLIS OF GERMANY

Munich, the capital of the Republic of Bavaria, has long been celebrated as an art centre, its rich art collection being the outstanding glory of the city. Merely an obscure village when Henry the Lion founded it in the twelfth century, it is now one of the best-built capitals of Europe. In the centre of the Marienplatz rises the column of the Madonna, erected by the Elector Maximilian I. in 1638

on the Rhine, more to the north, is the second capital of the State, and an important industrial and mercantile centre. The original town was built in chessboard fashion—in blocks of houses lying along straight streets intersected at regular intervals, and lettered in alphabetical order ; but modern Mannheim extends in all directions far beyond the old limits, and it has much fine architecture, both public and domestic.

Heidelberg, on the Neckar, near to the confluence of that river with the Rhine, is famous for its university, beloved of all German students of the " Gaudeamus " type, and its old castle, battered by the guns of an aggressive French king, yet beautiful in ruins. Lying at the foot of the Black Forest is the fine old university town of Freiburg, whose minster is one of the glories of South Germany. The country is also rich in mineral spas.

Baden shares with Württemberg the custody of one of the largest tracts of natural forest in Germany—the Schwarzwald, or Black Forest, which, beginning south of Karlsruhe, continues as far as the southern frontier near Freiburg. The dialect of the Black Forest is perhaps the most difficult of all German dialects to follow. The difficulty is not caused merely by its intonations or verbal inflections, but by the fact that it has a distinct vocabulary, which proves as puzzling to educated Germans as the racy colloquialisms of Cumberland and Westmorland to the English southerner.

Bavaria: An Agricultural Commonwealth

BAVARIA is somewhat smaller than Scotland, with a population exceeding that of Scotland and Wales. Its people belong overwhelmingly to the Roman Catholic faith, of whose interests, religious and political, it has ever claimed to be the special representative in Germany. No German State is so jealous of its rights, or so tenacious of its individuality as a political and social unit, as Bavaria. One may go further and say that none is so apt to magnify its importance and press its special interests in anything like the same degree. The special object of Bavarian antipathy is Prussia, and Prussia retaliates in kind. Bavaria dislikes Prussia because of its size, strength, and prosperity, and Prussia cannot forgive Bavaria for being so small, rustic, and easy-going. There is arrogance on both sides—on one side the arrogance of the " Haves," and on the other the arrogance of the "Have Nots."

More exclusively than those of any other of the major States—Mecklenburg-Schwerin excepted—Bavaria's inhabitants form an agricultural community. Besides its large production of grain it supplies most of the hops grown in Germany, and one of the most famous of its industries is beer-brewing. North German connoisseurs on the subject are ready to allow that such a thing as bad beer is not made in Bavaria, and the modest Bavarian acknowledges the compliment with the rejoinder that good beer cannot be made elsewhere. There is no doubt that the famous beer breweries of Munich and other Bavarian towns work with methods and materials which produce a very satisfying beverage.

The most enthusiastic devotees of Bavarian beer are the Bavarians themselves. One of their own proverbs says that a Bavarian would bear Purgatory itself if he could have his beer. In the middle of last century a revolution broke out in Munich because the price of beer was raised a farthing a litre, and it only subsided when the increase was struck off. But Bavaria can offer a finer draught than is distilled from the hop, for in the valleys of the upper Main the vine is grown with great success.

The Bavarians have a fine country, of which they may well be proud. Its mountain district is a foretaste of the greater grandeur of the Southern Alps, while the scenery of its lake district, situated south of the capital, is characterised by a ravishing softness and charm. The country is also rich in

SCENE IN THE OLD MAIN STREET OF FRANKFORT-ON-MAIN

The Zeil is the name of this busy thoroughfare, the principal street of Frankfort-on-Main, Goethe's birthplace and one of the most interesting, wealthy, and cosmopolitan of German cities. The Catherine Church, of which a glimpse is seen in the photograph, is famous as having been erected over the spot where the first Protestant sermon was preached early in the sixteenth century

towns of great interest. Among these Munich, the capital, easily carries the palm, for it is a veritable classic among cities, and its distinction is the merit of one man, King Max, whose life's ambition was, as he said, to make his capital so beautiful that to visit it alone would be worth a pilgrimage to Germany.

Then there is Nuremberg, more in the centre of the country. Known by school-boys as the place where the lead-pencils come from, this beautiful town appeals to the intellect and imagination as few other German towns do. The home of Dürer and Hans Sachs, it is a unique monument of the German renaissance.

Bamberg is a typical piece of old Bavaria, with whose ecclesiastical history it is intimately associated.

Augsburg, again, was the home of the famous commercial houses of Fugger and Welser, though its prosperity now depends upon its extensive machine works; while Ratisbon, or Regensburg, is a link connecting modern Germany with the ancient " Roman Empire of the German Nation," of whose Diet it was the seat.

Rural Bavaria is a country apart, living its old life in its own way, and heedless of the great world outside its narrow ambit. The "big peasant" (Grossbauer) thrives and grows fat by industry and frugality more than by regard for what he hears of scientific agriculture; the small proprietor holds his own without ever seeming to get " forrader," or greatly wanting to do; the farm labourer, with-out ambition, performs his daily trudge to and from his work like a machine. As part of the machinery which keeps the social system moving these rustic people fill a place which it would be ungrateful to disparage unduly. They also represent a static force in national life of decided value in these restless days.

A library of stories and dramas of rural life have been written in the uncouth vernacular of Bavaria. Before the Great War a company of peasant actors of the Tegern Lake district was accustomed to tour the country with plays of this kind. It may also be recalled that it was among a purely peasant community that the Passion Play of Oberammergau originated.

Prussia: The Predominant Partner

IT is at once the good and the bad fortune of the German Con-federation that its composition is so unbalanced owing to the dominating power of the major partner, Prussia. Even in its reduced proportions, Prussia still comprises about two-thirds of both the area and the population of the Realm, and the whole of Bavaria, Saxony, and Württemberg would go into three of its twelve provinces. Overwhelmingly its population is Protestant.

The country stretches half across northern Europe from the frontiers of France and Belgium to the new Polish State, while in the south it is bordered by Czechoslovakia, Austria, and Switzerland. The north-east and east form a vast sandy plain, given up to forest and corn and potato growing, and here is the home of the old feudalism and its offspring, the modern Junkers.

The north-west, a more or less hilly region, is the seat of some of Germany's greatest industries, coal-mining, iron and steel production, and the host of manufactures which depend thereon; in the south and south-west the vine and sugar-beet are grown on a large scale, while on the seaboard lives a hardy fisher folk which earns a pre-carious livelihood by scouring the North Sea and the Baltic.

Racially there is also great diversity; the strongest elements in the population are the Saxon, Frankish, Slavic, Celtic, and Frisian, but small racial remnants exist in the shape of the Wends of the Spree Forest and the Huguenots of Berlin, while in the far north-east there live many descendants of Scottish immigrants, still adhering to the old patronymics. The country has its full share of natural beauties and attractions, though its physical features do not run

ATTRACTIVE CORNER OF DRESDEN NEAR THE AUGUSTUS BRIDGE

The beautiful town of Dresden, the capital of Saxony, has long been noted for its porcelain and as an educational centre, especially for music and art; its museums of exceptional number being among the richest in the world. This photograph was taken from the Brühl Terrace, a promenade commanding a fine view of the river and possessing a handsome approach adorned with allegorical figures

THE MEDIEVAL GLORY OF NUREMBERG MARKET PLACE

Unrivalled in the abundance and beauty of its monuments of the German Renaissance, Nuremberg is also a leading industrial and commercial centre of South Germany. The picturesque market place is frequently bestrewn with the large, mushroom-shaped umbrellas of the market men, and is dominated on its east side by the beautiful fourteenth century Gothic Church of Our Lady

Photos, Transocean

to the sublime to the same degree as with Bavaria and the adjacent Austrian alpland. The Rhine and its valleys take pride of place, for here romance and scenic beauty commingle. Hard by is the Bergisches Land of Westphalia, picturesque still in spite of the process of industrialisation which its towns and villages have undergone. Still in the north is the sandy Sachsenwald, where Bismarck held court in his château of Friedrichsruh; nor must the famous Lüneburg Moor be forgotten, a region of far distances, long given up to solitude and silence, but now in part being slowly reclaimed.

To the south-west of this point lie the Harz Mountains, which, though not rising to any great height, except at the famous Brocken, are full of picturesque hill, valley, and river scenery, somewhat park-like in parts, but invested with irresistible charm. The Baltic coast has an appeal of its own, and to the westward it is lined with villages, quaint and trim, which are specially frequented by Berlin families in summer, while out to sea the chalk cliffs of the island of Rügen recall those of Dover.

In the south of the country, in Silesia, rise the Giant Mountains, broken on all sides into beautiful valleys, in which river and woodland combine to create the perfect landscape. A scenic peculiarity of Prussia is the Spreewald, south-east of Berlin. It is a rural region intersected in all directions by the river Spree and its feeders, insomuch that communication between the villages has to be maintained by boats of light draught. This Rural Venice, as it is called, is one of the last remaining seats of the ancient Wendish tribe, and its inhabitants still preserve their old customs, costume, and language.

Of the towns of Prussia the old are of incomparably greater interest than the new. For the modern town is a mechanical, conventional creation, displaying little good taste and no imagination—a thing of utility and convenience, but never of beauty. In this respect Berlin is typical, on a large scale, of modern North German towns in general.

Prussia is comparatively poor in medieval towns of the type common in Central and South Germany, but Hildesheim, Marienburg, and Danzig (as much now as before its severance) are the pride of Prussia and of all Germany. All the three remaining Free Cities of Germany—Hamburg and Bremen on the North Sea and Lübeck on the Baltic—adjoin Prussian territory. They are fine old cities, enriched with beautiful memorials of their commercial and maritime history.

Saxony: The Industrial Hub of Germany

THOUGH the fifth of the German States in area, Saxony is the third in population. In area it compares with Yorkshire, but its population somewhat exceeds that of the English county, though less than that of Scotland. Saxony is the hub of industrial Germany, just as Rhineland-Westphalia is the hub of industrial Prussia. Its industries are of the most varied character, but the principal are lignite and ore mining, and large manufactures of textile machinery and hosiery, though the famous porcelain manufactory of Meissen should not be overlooked. The great majority of the inhabitants are Protestants, but much of their Protestantism is of a negative kind, for, saturated with Socialist doctrines as Saxony has been for well-nigh half a century, unbelief is rife in the population to a remarkable degree.

The general standard of life of the Saxons is tolerably high, for the industrial workers of the towns earn well and spend freely. It is only in the hilly regions, like the Ore Mountains, the most densely populated mountain region in Germany, where the scanty largesse of agriculture has to be supplemented by the produce of home craftsmanship of various kinds, that anything like grinding poverty exists. Saxony has always been progressive in educational

OLD-WORLD ARCHITECTURE IN A CORNER OF ULM MARKET PLACE

The ancient town of Ulm, mentioned as early as 854, lies on the left bank of the Danube, and has belonged to Württemberg since 1810. The fine fountain, known as the Fischkasten, dates back to the fifteenth century. Many historic buildings embellish the old-fashioned streets, and the Protestant Minster, with its lofty tower, is, next to Cologne Cathedral, the largest Gothic Church in Germany

THE HOUSE WHERE SCHILLER DWELT IN "GERMAN ATHENS"

The name Weimar recalls memories of the great men of Germany whose presence graced the town during the reign of Duke Charles Augustus. Goethe, Schiller, Herder, and Wieland are among the celebrated men of letters who took up their residence in Weimar at the invitation of this liberal patron of literature, and whose fame won for the old town the title of the "German Athens"

matters, and its system of technical schools is one of the most comprehensive and efficient in Germany.

Of Saxon towns Dresden has a traditional attraction for English people and Americans, large numbers of whom had their permanent homes there before the war, with the result that English schools were numerous. No more beautiful city exists in Germany, for if Munich has a dignity and witchery of its own, Dresden exerts on all who know it a subtle charm, and an attachment once formed for it never diminishes. Saxony's most populous town, however, is not the capital, but Leipzig, finely built, the principal centre of the German publishing and book trade, and the seat of a university and of the Supreme Court of Justice.

Württemberg: A Picturesque Home of Romance

THE third State in the Realm in size, Württemberg may be compared in area and in number of population to Wales, with whose people its inhabitants have temperamental similarities. It is a pleasant hill country, running down to the northern shore of Lake Constance, and peopled by rough-tongued but genial Swabians. They have the round heads of the old alpine kind of Celt, and their emotional natures, alert minds, and sagacity make them a very important element in German life. Like the " canny Scot " and the penetrative Welshman, the Swabian is never far away when a good thing is going.

The Württembergers have been fighters and makers of history for many centuries, and their country is a veritable home of romance. There is hardly a good hill in the little country without a castle, or the mouldered ruins of one. On the Hohenstaufen height fought and flourished the family that gave to the Holy Roman Empire the line of emperors who split and ruined Germany and dissolved Italy by aiming at universal dominion. But the Hohenstaufens at least had the characteristic Württemberg versatility, and made their courts in southern Italy and Sicily radiating centres of a new literature and a new knowledge. But with the same torch that lightened Europe they burnt her. Then on the Zollern hill, with its limestone precipices and strangely reconstructed castle, was rocked the cradle of the Hohenzollern line, brilliant and unstable, which has likewise fallen on evil days.

But the Swabian has applied his genius in other than military ways. Always he has shown a strong bent towards research, inquiry, and philosophy. Albertus Magnus and Paracelsus were Swabians, and when the country was but a small duchy, half covered with forest and containing perhaps half a million people, it produced a remarkable succession of thinkers of the stamp of Kepler, Hegel, and Schelling, and poets like Schiller, Wieland, and Uhland.

A traditional preoccupation with religion led the Swabians to give early welcome to the Reformation, and this trait has encouraged a tendency to mysticism and sectarianism. It may be said of this remarkable stock that it has proved the principal leaven of thought, emotion, and imagination in the strong Germanic world. For good and for evil it has been the edge of the German sword in its ages of glory, and the wings of the German mind in its periods of soaring splendour.

Nearly half of the working class are peasants, whose fathers won the land they work, and parcelled it out among their children, until one-third of the good soil of the country consists of holdings of two and a half acres or less. The system of small properties has told strongly upon the character of the people. They were always hard-working, but stimulated by the fierce pride of ownership, they have developed a perfect passion for toil and become labourers of the most strenuous kind, impervious to modern ideas such as the eight-hour day and the Saturday half-holiday.

GLIMPSE INTO A DEPARTMENT AT THE SAVINGS BANK, A PUBLIC INSTITUTION IN THE CAPITAL OF THE GERMAN REPUBLIC

On October 1, 1920, the fifteen savings banks established on an independent footing in the various suburbs of Berlin, were merged, together with their entire wealth and liabilities, into the Savings Bank of the City of Berlin. This colossal establishment, which has been in existence one hundred years already, has now nearly two million depositors and, owing to the union with the neighbouring institutions, can claim to be the largest savings bank in the world

Germany

II. Through Federation & Empire to Republic

By William Harbutt Dawson

Author of "The German Empire, 1867-1914," etc.

THE Germans are an offshoot of the Teutonic stock, which on the dispersal of the Aryan family followed the Celts in their wanderings westward from Asia. The German tribes had come in conflict with the Roman power before the opening of the Christian era. Having towards the end of the second century B.C. subdued the Celts who had gathered on the northern and western confines of Italy, the Romans struck against harder rock when they found their farther progress barred by the tribe of the Cimbri. That collision was for Rome disastrous, for Papirius Carbo and his army met with signal defeat near the site of Klagenfurt (113 B.C.).

Flushed with victory the Cimbri pushed westward through Gaul as far as Spain, devastating the country through which they passed. Returning north they were joined by another powerful German tribe, the Teutones, who had moved west from their settlements beyond the Elbe, and the allies planned the invasion of the Italian peninsula simultaneously from the west and the north. This adventure ended with complete disaster for both tribes, Marius defeating and decimating the Cimbri at Vercellae and the Teutones at Aquae Sextiae (Aix-en-Provence) in 101-2 B.C.

Germans in Conflict with Rome

The check thus given to the German invaders was only local. A little later the struggle was resumed in Gaul, where the warlike Suevi (Swabians) had obtained a foothold. Attacking Ariovistus, the duke (Herzog) of this tribe, in Upper Alsace, Julius Caesar drove him back across the Rhine. It is to the Suevi, still a semi-nomadic tribe, that Caesar specially refers in his account of the Germans, their personal qualities, habits and customs and institutions. In the north and east of Germany, however, Roman influence was still unestablished, and under Augustus and Tiberius attempts were made to enforce and consolidate it, but not without serious repulses. The worst of these occurred in A.D. 9, when Arminius, or Hermann, chief of the Cherusci, who had learned military science in Roman service, destroyed a Roman army under Quinctilius Varus, in the three days' battle of the Teutoburg Forest. Then jealousies and feuds among their chiefs

weakened the resistance of the tribes, and under Vespasian Rome's power was reasserted and extended.

Of Germany at the end of the first century of our era Tacitus has left a systematic study of the utmost value. He speaks of the German tribes as inhabiting at that time the regions between the Danube in the south, the Rhine in the west, the North Sea, and the Slavic regions in the east. He describes the country as covered by dense forests, varied by treacherous morasses, and mountains which yielded iron and also precious metals. Agriculture was systematically carried on, the commoner fruits were grown, the earlier system of common land was giving place to private ownership.

Tacitus's Study of Germany

The people lived in villages protected against outside enemies, and while the women tilled the fields the men went to the war and the hunt. Domestic and married life showed a high standard of order and morality; marriage was esteemed a sacred institution, women were honoured, and wives, though they worked hard, ruled in the home. Religion and religious rites, including sacrifice to the gods, were practised, though there was no formal priesthood.

Tacitus speaks of courage, truthfulness, chastity, and hospitality as specially characteristic of the Germans, though he also records their addiction to intemperance and gambling. Already class divisions had begun to show themselves in the social organization; there were freemen (enjoying full rights of citizenship) and in small numbers an estate of nobles; below them came a class of semi-free persons, the Liti, who might not hold land in fee simple and who paid taxes to the owner in chief; and at the bottom of the social scale came the slaves or serfs, prisoners of war or descendants of the same, who performed the more menial work and were exchangeable as chattels.

During the second century the conflict between the primitive culture of the German tribes and the highly organized State system represented by Rome seemed to have worn itself out, and before its close the greater part of Germany, as we know it, had passed under Roman influence. Victorious generals had divided the territory lying on the left bank of the

Rhine into the two administrative districts of Germania superior (prima) and Germania inferior (secunda). Rome had also multiplied her strongholds and camps both on the frontiers and in the interior, and these became the nuclei of towns. Among the most important of the early centres of Roman influence on and near the Rhine were Cologne, Aix-la-Chapelle (Aachen), Coblenz, Treves, Strasbourg, Mainz, Worms, and Spires; while of Roman settlements in the south, the principal were Ratisbon (Regensburg), Augsburg, Passau, Salzburg, and Vienna.

Development of the Federal Instinct

Throughout German history there has been a constant conflict between two strong tribal characteristics—the tendency towards union and fusion in the presence of common danger and the deeper-lying spirit of independence and separatism. Already the federal instinct showed itself. Roman power decayed and provincial administration fell into disorder under a series of weak rulers, and the German tribes, which had preserved their virile virtues even in dependence, reasserted themselves. More and more the tribes had sought strength by union, and Rome had now to contend no longer with isolated units but powerful confederacies.

Thus in the middle of the third century there is mention of the great confederacies of the Suevi, the Alemanni, the Saxons, and the Franks. Allied to the Suevi were the Lombards of the Lower Elbe, the Vandals of the Upper Elbe, the Hermanduri, who survived in the Thuringians, and the Burgundians, who had settled in the north-east and east of Germany, between the Oder and the Vistula. The Alemanni were the successors of the Suevic confederacy, and ultimately settled in the present Swabia.

Irruption of the Goths under Alaric

The Saxons, first mentioned by Ptolemy in the second century, appear late in the following century as a tribal confederacy, comprising the Angles, Cherusci, Chauci, Angrivarii, and other stocks, inhabiting the coastlands west of the Elbe and Weser, with the Frisii (Frisians) for neighbours. The Franks, who now come into prominence, were an amalgamation of many tribes settled in the Middle and Lower Rhine regions.

The strongest of these tribal confederacies was that of the Goths, a masterful race which had trekked from Scandinavia across the Baltic to the Vistula, and asserted possession as far as the Black Sea. Theodosius had divided the Roman empire into eastern and western divisions, and the latter was the scene of the great historical irruption of the barbarians.

Towards the end of the fourth century the Huns, a wild nomadic Mongolian tribe, broke into Europe and dispersed the Goths, who were driven westward and southward. An incursion of West Goths into Northern Italy followed. Led by their brilliant general Alaric, the invaders continued their victorious progress to the walls of Rome, which they occupied and plundered (409-10).

About the same time the East Goths occupied Southern Gaul and all Spain, except for the small part (Portugal) which had fallen to the Suevi; the Vandals set up a kingdom in North Africa; the Burgundians appropriated the Rhone valley; and the Bavarians, a new tribal confederacy, settled in Raetia. The power of Rome was paralysed by these convulsions, and the garrisons in north-west Germany and Britain were withdrawn. As a result of the barbarian invasions the empire lost the best of its western provinces.

Invasion of the Huns under Attila

Once more the Huns moved forward. Under their terrible king Attila, they broke out of the Lower Danube region and Hungary, and poured like a flood over Central Germany and into Gaul. A collision with the Roman power took place in 451 at Troyes, where, with the help of the West Goths and Franks, the Roman general Aetius defeated the invaders, but his army was too exhausted to follow up its success, and Attila was able to withdraw in safety. In the following year Attila again wreaked vengeance on Italy, but with his death in 453 the menace of the Huns came to an end.

In the fifth century German tribes were firmly settled in all those parts of modern Germany which had been brought under Roman rule. Eastern Germany, however, was still occupied by Slavic tribes, who had migrated to Europe later than the other Aryan peoples. The German tribes were pagans and still nominally barbarians, but unlike the fierce Huns, they were not bent on wanton and purposeless destruction. Their first necessity was to live, and to that end they needed land on which to settle. They took land wherever the pressure of tribal needs drove them, but having settled, they were willing to live harmoniously with the aboriginals.

Gradually relationships of some confidence were established with Rome; Germans were admitted into her citizenship and service, and even to rank and high office therein; more and more also her armies were recruited from the German tribes. Rome had stood for the harsh and unbending principle of uniformity, and this principle demanded the repression of nationality and the assertion of one citizenship and one law. Roman civilization, as reflected in systematic administration, an orderly communal life, and well-built towns, must have powerfully impressed the barbarians with the inferiority of their own rude customs and manners, and it suffered no abrupt and wholesale effacement at their hands. Rather they may be said to have overlaid it, as the streets and fora of the Eternal City itself were overlaid during successive centuries by new levels. It has been well

The first orderly State system created by the German tribes owed its existence to this stock, which was characterised by a strong spirit of cohesion and exceptional political instinct. A king of the Salian Franks, Clovis, grandson of Merovaeus, after whom the Merovingian dynasty was called, ranks as the founder of the Frankish empire, which at his death extended from the Rhine, Neckar, and Main to the Atlantic.

In 496, in fulfilment of a vow made before taking arms against the Alemanni,

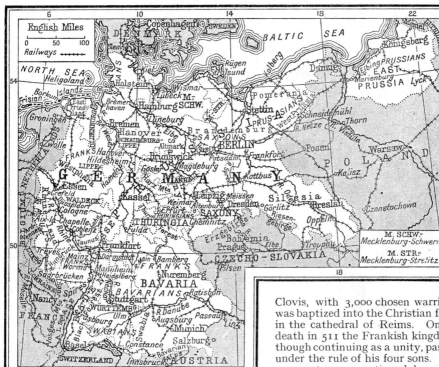

GERMANY AND ITS PEOPLES

Clovis, with 3,000 chosen warriors, was baptized into the Christian faith in the cathedral of Reims. On his death in 511 the Frankish kingdom, though continuing as a unity, passed under the rule of his four sons. His conquests were continued, however, and one of the earliest was the subjugation of the Thuringian realm in Central Germany, which was divided with the neighbouring Saxons, while Bavaria was appropriated later, and the Alemanni were also brought into complete dependence.

said by J. S. Brewer that what happened was " a change but not a complete transformation. What was dead was dead before the barbarians came ; what was alive lived on, and was now to enter into a new state of existence."

Of all the larger German tribes the Franks were the Romans' best neighbours, while the Saxons and Frisians most resented interference. The Franks were divided into the Ripuarian branch, settled on both banks of the Middle and Lower Rhine, and the Salian branch, at the mouth of the river and the adjoining seaboard. Not seldom they assisted the Romans to resist the encroachments even of other German tribes, though they were prone to aggression themselves when circumstances were favourable.

In the middle of the sixth, and again early in the seventh century, under Clovis the Great, the Frankish empire returned under a single rule. Practically the whole of the German tribes, with the exception of the Saxon and Frisian groups, had now been shepherded in the Frankish realm.

The civic organization of the Frankish State differed from that described by Tacitus. In particular there had been a change in the relations between the freemen and the semi-free, the Liti, or descendants of the aboriginals. Exposed to frequent obligation to military service, which kept them away for long periods from their farms, the former decreased in numbers and in fortune ; while the latter, upon whom military service did not impose a like penalty, rose to higher estate.

"Roman Empire of the German Nation "

The position of the freemen became worse when liability to military service was formally attached to the land. More and more, as this feudal relationship took definite shape, the poorer freemen lost their independence and became the virtual vassals of their landlords. The relations of State and Church had also changed. When the Frankish kings went over to Catholic Christianity they accepted the existing ecclesiastical system with its priesthood drawn from the original Latin-speaking population, as they found it. Nominally the Church was still dependent upon the Crown.

The halcyon era in the history of medieval Germany was the reign of Charlemagne (Charles the Great), son of Pepin the Short, lasting from 768 to 814. Charlemagne subdued in turn the Saxons, Wends, and Frisians, and extended Frankish rule until it comprised all the Germanic tribes with the exception of the Anglo-Saxons and the still pagan North-men of Scandinavia. Already the de facto successor of the Roman emperors, he received the imperial crown at the hands of Pope Leo III. in Rome on Christmas Day of the year 800. So it was that the institution of the " Roman Empire of the German Nation," so impressive to the imagination of the Middle Ages, yet so fantastic—half fact and half fiction—came into existence ; the truth being that more than a millenium was yet to pass before an empire of the German peoples could be created. Voltaire said truly that the Holy Roman Empire was neither holy, nor Roman, nor an empire.

Supremacy of Charlemagne

Charles had become the acknowledged head and protector of Roman Christen-dom, and for the present the Papacy itself owned allegiance to him. But the alliance between the secular power and the Church thus formed was to prove a disturbing and disintegrating factor in the later political life of Germany. Not long was the Papacy contented with a dependent relationship or even one of parity. Pope and Emperor claimed that they stood equally for unity and order ; each sought to establish peace on earth on the basis of authority, to be accepted on pain of forced submission ; each represented the grandiose ideal of a Christian World State. But the medieval world was not large enough for two despots ; one had to be supreme, and it remained to be seen which would prove the stronger.

While he was not slow to adopt Roman principles of government, short of doing violence to tribal customs and traditions, Charlemagne was pre-eminently a Teuton ruler, and under him the Frankish monarchy reached its highest develop-ment. The independent tribal duchies were abolished, so that the Emperor's sovereign position was now supreme. For purposes of administration the realm was divided as of old into districts or Gaus (Gauen), over which were counts, and these again into Hundreds, governed by centurions. The military system was developed further on the feudal principle, and the security of the frontiers was assured by the institution of Marks, or Marches, placed in the care of Margraves (Markgrafen), each being responsible for the defence of a given length of frontier.

Dawn of German National Existence

Within a generation the descendants of Charlemagne had divided his Empire five times. The principal division was that which resulted from the epoch-making Treaty of Verdun (843) which, by separating Germany from Gaul, marked the beginning of German national exist-ence. Though there was repeated reunion, the tribal spirit of independence, which Charlemagne had kept in check, revived and made steady headway ; while the Popes, taking advantage of the internal difficulties of the Empire, succeeded in magnifying their temporal power, gaining full control of Italy and claiming the right to confer the imperial title on whomsoever they would.

With the death of Louis the Child (911) the Carolingian dynasty ended, and eight years later the Saxon line succeeded in the person of Henry I. (the Fowler), one of the wisest and most progressive of German rulers, famous as the great town-builder. His son, Otto the Great, elected king at Aix-la-Chapelle (Aachen) by the acclaim of all the German tribes, ruled once more over an undivided empire as left by Charlemagne. Invited to Rome to protect Pope John XII. against Berengar II., he duly fulfilled that task, and received the imperial crown in reward (962). From that time dates the union of the Roman Empire with the German kingdom, whose rulers were required to receive the crown at the hands of the Popes. The double position imposed on these rulers heavy responsi-bilities, political and military, which were by no means to the advantage of Germany.

The Saxon was followed by the short-lived Franconian line of kings. Henry III., the second of the dynasty, consolidated his power, and by stern measures reformed the Papacy, which had fallen into abuse and discredit, deposing three Popes successively. Herein he rendered to the Church a great and urgent service, but events soon proved that in purifying the Papacy he strengthened it. Hildebrand, becoming Pope as Gregory VII., in 1073, made his great bid for temporal sovereignty in the decree asserting for the Church independence and immunity from lay interference. Henceforth neither the Emperor nor any temporal ruler was to have part or lot in the choice and investiture of the clergy.

This decision brought Henry IV. in antagonism with the Papacy, so long the faithful, and at times humble, ally of the temporal power. When he presumed to declare the Pope deposed, Gregory answered the challenge by citing him to appear in Rome to answer misdeeds alleged against him, and on his refusal excommunicated him (1076). The ban was only withdrawn when Henry, alarmed by the disaffection of the German princes, made a pilgrimage of submission to Canossa in the following winter. The dispute over the question of episcopal investiture remained open for nearly half a century, and was ultimately settled by the Concordat of Worms (1122), which made minor concessions to the Emperors, without essentially weakening the Papal claim.

The Empire Under the Hohenstaufens

The last of the Franconian line was Henry's son, under whom the first of the Crusades took place. Then Lothair II., the Saxon, ruled for twelve years (1125-1137), and the Hohenstaufen dynasty succeeded. On his deathbed Lothair had handed the imperial insignia to Duke Henry the Proud of Bavaria, then the most powerful prince in the Empire, for Saxony had passed into his hands, and in consequence Henry confidently hoped to succeed. But the tribes preferred a weak to a strong ruler, and their choice fell on Duke Conrad III. of Swabia, so initiating the bitter feud between the Guelph (Bavarian) and Ghibeline (Hohenstaufen) parties, which lasted until the close of the fifteenth century.

From Lothair, Albert the Bear, a Saxon noble, ancestor of the later Margraves of Brandenburg, received the Saxon Nordmark (later the Prussian Altmark), on the left bank of the Elbe, a foothold from which he quickly extended his jurisdiction and territories. Of the Hohenstaufens, who held the imperial dignity for 116 years, the most conspicuous was Frederick I., known as Barbarossa, or Red Beard (1152-90), around whose personality and deeds gathered much romantic legend, which is part of German folk-lore down to the present day. During his reign the relations between the Crown and the Papacy, which favoured the Bavarian claimants, assumed increasingly acute forms, but his domestic record in Germany was one of steady progress and prosperity.

Of outstanding events incidental to the Hohenstaufen era which were to prove important for the future of Germany may be named the ejection of the Wends from Northern Germany, henceforth colonised by Saxons, and the severance of Silesia from Poland, with its conversion into an independent duchy, which passed under German influence and culture. Now also we hear of the Teutonic knightly orders of S. John and the Temple, formed under the influence of the Crusades. These orders settled in districts like Brandenburg and the region lying eastward inhabited by Slavic tribes, and, following a persistent policy of more or less peaceful penetration, ultimately brought Eastern Prussia under German civilization and Hohenzollern rule.

Growth of Communal Institutions

In this later medieval period an important step forward was made in the development of civic and communal life and institutions. In every direction towns grew and prospered, often becoming autonomous communities. In particular, the old military settlements on the Rhine and other streams, which had suffered with the decay of Roman power, took a new life ; thriving ports rose on the seaboard and the larger rivers ; in the middle of the thirteenth century the powerful Hanseatic League of maritime and commercial towns began its career ; the arts and crafts rose in dignity and esteem ; and in this period were produced, under the combined influence of the Church and local patriotism, many of the most famous monuments of German ecclesiastical and municipal architecture.

Domination of the Hapsburgs

At the end of the Hohenstaufen period there followed an interregnum of twenty years during which the Empire was without a legal head, though the title was claimed and used by several rivals, one being Richard, Earl of Cornwall, brother of Henry III. of England. In 1273 Rudolf of Hapsburg was formally elected Emperor at Frankfort, owing his success largely to the influence exercised in his favour by Frederick III. of Hohenzollern, Burggraf of Nuremberg, head of a family which was destined to play a critical part in the later history both of Germany and the Hapsburg line. In the first half of the fifteenth century, with the election of Albrecht II. of Austria (1438) the imperial Crown passed permanently to the Hapsburg family. The election of the early Emperors was originally a very democratic proceeding. They were chosen by the tribes, every freeman having, theoretically, the right to vote, and the election took place in open-air assembly. In course of time the function was left to the higher secular and spiritual powers. By a decree known as the Golden Bull, issued by the Emperor Charles IV. in 1356, the method of electing the Emperor was amended, and the number of electoral princes was reduced to seven, three being ecclesiastical sovereigns (the Archbishops of Cologne, Mainz, and Treves), and four secular (the King of Bohemia, the Duke of Saxony, the Rhenish Palsgrave or Count Palatine, and the Margrave of Brandenburg). (Bavaria acquired electoral right in 1648, and Hanover in 1692.) Frankfort was fixed as the place of election and Aix-la-Chapelle (Aachen) as that of coronation.

Rise of the Hohenzollerns

A critical moment in the history of Germany came when the Hohenzollern family migrated from the south and took possession of the Mark of Brandenburg. Of this territory the Emperor Sigismund in 1411 made Burggraf Frederick VI. of Nuremberg governor. Several years later he came into full possession of the Mark and received the electoral title. Frederick inherited a neglected and undeveloped territory, plundered by a lawless nobility and demoralised by lax government, but by wise and strong administration he gave it a new life, and Brandenburg became the nucleus of a powerful State. At the imperial election of 1438 a Hohenzollern seemed to have a chance of the succession.

Charles V. and the Reformation

Of the later Emperors none recalled the glory of past ages—the time of Charlemagne, of Otto the Great, of Frederick Barbarossa—as did Charles V., King of Italy and Spain, who was elected in 1520. His reign synchronised with the Reformation, which inaugurated the modern epoch in German history. In the struggle with the Church, which began in 1517, the Emperor, jealous for the static principle of authority, championed the old faith. A time of violent storm and stress occurred in the political and religious life of Germany before a modus vivendi was reached by the two factions. This took the form of the Peace of Augsburg, concluded in 1555, which gave to the territorial rulers the right to accept or reject the reformed faith as the official religion of the State, such of their subjects as chose to be dissentients being allowed to seek freedom of conscience and worship elsewhere.

A disastrous legacy of the Reformation was the religious or confessional war which began in 1618 and, after lasting for thirty years, left the country impoverished and exhausted, its lands largely devastated, its rural economy destroyed, its towns decimated, and its civilization thrown back for generations. By the Peace of Westphalia (1648) the religious equality and rights of the German rulers as affirmed by the Peace of Augsburg were recognized, but right of conscience was still refused to the individual citizen. France secured portions of Alsace and was confirmed in the possession of several towns of Lorraine, already occupied by her in 1552, while Sweden received Western Pomerania, and the independence of Holland and Switzerland was affirmed.

The later history of the old German Empire is little more than a record of progressive senile decline, though it was still to drag on a feeble existence for a century and a half. The Empire's adversity was the opportunity of the territorial rulers, who more and more strengthened their independence and augmented their power at the expense of the Emperor, to whom little more than his title remained.

Brandenburg and the Great Elector

Conspicuous among the States which benefited by the slackening of imperial authority and the intrinsic feebleness of Austrian rule was Prussia. Step by step Brandenburg lengthened its cords and extended its stakes, until a petty margraviate grew into a powerful kingdom, able to challenge Austria's primacy. Within her own territories—the so-called "Hausmacht" of the Hapsburgs—Austria was sufficiently consolidated, but her position as head of the Empire was shaken.

Lacking effective defence, the Empire was exposed to menace from any enemy, either within or without, able to challenge its security. Thus it was that Louis XIV. of France (1643-1715), then the first of Continental rulers, made desperate efforts to establish a dominating influence in Germany, intriguing unscrupulously with faithless princes, some of whom accepted from him bribes and subsidies. The absolute monarchy of France found ready imitation at that time in Germany, where, in their petty courts, futile sycophants introduced the language with the manners and modes of France. By their unworthy mimicry of foreign ways, and their treason to the cause of nationality, these simulacra of kingship only deepened the humiliation which had befallen their country and increased the disaster which awaited it. In that critical time Germany was saved for the German nation by the will and effort of Frederick William, the Great Elector of Brandenburg (1640-88), then the most vigorous and also the most ambitious of her territorial Sovereigns. The duchy of Prussia had come to his house by marriage in 1618, and hereditary claims had extended its territories on the Rhine. Under this ruler the electorate made further progress. Recognizing that the strength of Prussia must rest on military efficiency, he created a strong standing army. He wrested Pomerania from Sweden, he got rid of the ancient Polish suzerainty over the duchy of Prussia, and finally consolidated his loosely held territories into a strong, organized State, which was to prove a " rocher de bronze " in the midst of a tumbling and crumbling Empire. He was the only German prince who seriously challenged and resisted the ambitions of Louis XIV.

After waging two wars of aggression against the Netherlands, Louis turned his attention to Germany, raiding and devastating the Palatinate, and annexing additional districts of Alsace and the Rhineland. Against such attacks the Empire was helpless, for it had no army of its own, and Austria cared only for her dynastic patrimony. The Great Elector stepped into the breach, and though he fought with wavering allies and only partial success, he did much to keep alive the spirit of patriotism and independence in the best part of the nation.

Creation of the Kingdom of Prussia

It was under his son and successor, Frederick I., that Brandenburg became the Kingdom of Prussia (1701). The grandson of this king, Frederick the Great, increased his realm by the seizure of Silesia after three campaigns against Austria. Later (1772) Frederick gained by his participation in the first partition of Poland, then a disorganized and ill-governed kingdom, the later province of West Prussia and the Netze region, while the remainder of the kingdom went to Russia and Austria, the prime movers in this act of spoliation. There was a second partition of the booty in 1793, and a third in 1795, as a result of which Prussia's share was increased.

When the French Revolution broke out, most of the German princes rallied to the support of the French Sovereign and the monarchical principle. It was a rash step, fateful to themselves and their peoples, who were far from approving it, for it secured for Germany the hostility first of the Republic, and later of Napoleon. German separatism never played so unworthy and unpatriotic a part as in the

succeeding wars with France. Saxony, Bavaria, Württemberg, and Baden openly allied themselves to Napoleon, and the rulers of the first three of these States accepted the royal status at his hand. In spite of the coalitions formed against France the rulers of Prussia and Austria succumbed, and Napoleon assigned much of their territories to his relatives, his generals, and his German allies. The treaties of Campo Formio (1797), Rastatt (1798), Lunéville (1801), Pressburg (1805), Tilsit (1807), and Schönbrunn (1809), emphasised the accumulating measure of Austria's and Prussia's humiliation and ruin. On August 1, 1806, Napoleon, who was crowned Emperor of the French in 1804, and King of Italy in 1805, declared the Holy Roman Empire dissolved, and five days later, at his bidding, Francis II. —who had already assumed the title of hereditary Emperor of Austria—resigned the imperial office.

End of the Napoleonic Tyranny

For Germany, and Prussia in particular, the only redeeming event of that time was the succeeding War of Emancipation (1813-15), which evoked a striking outburst of patriotism, discounted only by the defection of those of the German States whose rulers enjoyed Napoleon's favour or pay. The fifth and strongest of the European Coalitions was the precursor of the " Battle of the Nations " at Leipzig, marking a final turn in Napoleon's fortunes. Beaten in this decisive struggle, Napoleon began his fighting retreat to France, followed closely by the victorious allies, who on March 31, 1814, entered Paris, where peace was signed in May, Napoleon being consigned to Elba.

Later in the same year the Vienna Congress for the resettlement of Europe opened, but while it was still deliberating Napoleon returned to France and resumed the war. It was a last attempt to re-establish himself, and it failed. With the allied victory of Waterloo (June 18, 1815), won by Wellington and Blücher, and Napoleon's exile to St. Helena, Europe had peace for nearly forty years.

Reorganization of Germany

By the second Treaty of Paris (November 20, 1815) France was deprived of all the territory which she had seized since 1790, including the left bank of the Rhine. The most important of the other territorial readjustments were the cession to Prussia of a portion of the kingdom of Saxony, the repartitioning of Poland among the three Powers concerned, the return of Lombardy and Venetia to Austria, and the assignment of the Rhenish Palatinate to Bavaria, and of East Friesland to Hanover, which now became a kingdom. An important part of the work of the Congress was the political reorganization of Germany. To this end there was created, by the Federal Act of June 8, 1815, the Germanic Confederation, consisting originally of thirty-nine sovereign States, chief among them the six kingdoms of Austria—in which was vested the presidency—Prussia, Hanover, Bavaria, Saxony, and Württemberg. The Kings of Denmark and the Netherlands were members in respect of fiefs in the old Empire.

Rivalry Between Austria and Prussia

The rivalry between Austria and Prussia for primacy which had begun in the old Empire was continued in the new Confederation. The Liberal forces in Germany had hoped that the superhuman efforts and sacrifices made by the peoples in the overthrow of the Napoleonic tyranny would be rewarded by national unity in the form of a democratic commonwealth more or less of the English type. They suffered a sore disappointment. The Germanic Confederation was no more than an alliance of Sovereigns for the maintenance of the old political status; the Act constituting it made no mention of the nation. Even the stipulation of the Federal Act requiring the Sovereigns to introduce representative bodies was perfidiously ignored by most of them for nearly forty years, and it is significant that the causes of both popular government and national unity found clearer comprehension and stronger sympathy in the small States than the larger.

Bismarck the Empire-Maker

Prussia, which might at that time have acquired the intellectual leadership of Germany, was content to be the tool of Metternich and the reaction. Dominated by the two Great Powers the Imperial Diet for a generation practically concentrated its attention upon the repression of democratic movements and the Liberal spirit wherever manifested. The French revolution of February, 1848, caused repercussions across the Rhine, and in their fear the rulers made large promises, but no sooner had the danger of the moment passed away than these promises were again ignored. A constitution for all Germany was, indeed, drawn up by a national parliament, held at Frankfort, and the imperial crown was formally offered to the Prussian King, but only to be refused. It was a sign that a sterner discipline still awaited the German nation.

While, however, the political organization of Germany was thus postponed, her material prosperity advanced. Industry underwent great development; the railway system was introduced; the old inter-State Customs barriers were broken down; practical free trade was established with foreign countries; there was talk of a navy and the need for colonies; and already the foundations of a great economic future were laid.

It was due to Otto von Bismarck, who became Minister President and Foreign Minister of William I. in 1862, that Prussia finally attained the dominant position in Germany which history had marked out for her. Convinced that neither Prussia nor Germany could truly realize herself until Austria had been extruded, he worked for this end by the aid of all the resources of a statecraft as audacious as it was unscrupulous. First seeking to strengthen Prussia's maritime position by dispossessing Denmark of the Elbe duchies of Schleswig and Holstein at the end of a war arbitrarily forced upon her (1864), he adroitly made the joint occupation of the territories by Prussia and Austria the pretext for a quarrel, into which he drew Prussia's ally by affronts and aggravations whose object was as clear as their effect was certain.

Confederation of the Northern States

On the eve of hostilities Prussia declared the Germanic Confederation dissolved, and put forward a scheme for a new alliance of the German princes from which Austria was to be excluded. The ensuing Bohemian Campaign (June–July, 1866), was for Prussia a promenade militaire; within a week Austria lay at her rival's feet. The terms of peace imposed upon her were lenient, for Bismarck was concerned to make of Prussia's present enemy a future friend; he asked for no cession of territory, and was satisfied with the payment of the bare war expenses and Austria's withdrawal within her natural borders.

The war had led to a last display of the old spirit of tribal division, for while the majority of the smaller federal States joined Prussia, influenced more by fear than by enthusiasm for the promised reorganization of Germany, Saxony, Hanover, and electoral Hesse in the north, with Baden, Bavaria, Württemberg, and Hesse-Darmstadt in the south, sided with Austria. As a result of the war, Prussia appropriated both of the Elbe duchies, the kingdom of Hanover, the electorate of Hesse, part of Hesse-Darmstadt, and the free imperial city of Frankfort.

A confederation of the States north of the Main was now formed, with a liberal constitution, the southern States being for the present left to their own devices. It was a half-way house, a temporary resting-place on the way to complete national unity, and as such was described by

Bismarck, who never showed truer statesmanship than at that time, when he might have forced the reluctant States outside the ark to come in, but did not. It was an omen of progress, however, that in the first year of the Confederation there was created a Customs Parliament, consisting of the federal Diet enlarged by representatives of the southern States, empowered to enact a common fiscal policy for all Germany.

Apart from the lingering spirit of particularism, a further and more serious obstacle still blocked the way to the complete unification of Germany, and it was the antagonism of France. Louis Napoleon had watched the progress of the unity movement with growing jealousy and alarm, and by much and various futile intrigue had striven to counter it. Even yet he did not relinquish the hope of keeping the north and the south apart, the latter under the aegis of Austria, and with that end in view he cultivated the closest possible relations with the Emperor Francis Joseph and his late allies.

Determined to force matters to an issue Bismarck provoked a quarrel with France over the question of the Spanish succession, and, succeeding in his old device of putting his opponents in the wrong, he tempted Napoleon to a declaration of war (July, 1870). A supreme crisis in the history of the German nation found the whole of the tribes united under a common banner.

Totally unprepared for the encounter, mistaking paper soldiers for fighting battalions, and relying too confidently upon the strength of her emotions and a conviction of the justice of her cause, France invited defeat and sustained it. The penalty imposed upon her was the loss of Alsace-Lorraine, taken from the old Empire piecemeal in the three preceding centuries, and the payment of an indemnity of two hundred million pounds. On Jan. 18, 1871, in the Hall of Mirrors, at Versailles, the 170th anniversary of the creation of the Kingdom of Prussia, German unity, realized in a revived Empire, based on the principle of nationality, was proclaimed, and King William I. of Prussia elected by the federal Sovereigns as its head.

The history of Germany and its peoples from 1871 to the outbreak of the Great War in 1914 was one of steady advancement in material and, for at least half the time, in political power. The tribal spirit has never entirely disappeared, yet, subject always to an apparently irreconcilable incompatibility between north and south, the States, their rulers, and their populations have on the whole worked harmoniously together.

Prussia has never failed to press against her allies the advantages accruing to her in virtue of her larger population, amounting both before the war and still to a little over three-fifths of the whole, her greater military resources and wealth, and not least the prerogatives secured to her by the constitution : but however unpopular,

BEFORE THE RATHAUS IN A TOWN OF OLD GERMANY

Bonn, of which ancient city the above photograph shows the market place, stands upon the left bank of the Rhine some fifteen miles from Cologne. It is a residential town, famed as the birthplace of Beethoven and for its university. The scene presented here is a pleasant one, with the fine, tall buildings looking down upon the cobbled square across which the trams clank and rattle

from the political standpoint, Prussia may have proved as a predominant partner, there is no gainsaying the fact that the capacity, will power, and driving force native to the character of her people in every sphere were potent factors in the progress made by the entire Empire during the first four decades of peace.

Bismarck's Genius and Limitations

As Chancellor and Foreign Minister for just half of this period, Bismarck played a leading part in European politics, though never meddling in foreign questions without direct interest for his country. When in the early eighties he capitulated to the colonial movement, he did it under pressure of ardent pioneers of Empire, whose enthusiasm he did not share, and he was never convinced that the colonies were a sound investment ; while with the naval development which soon followed this departure he had no sympathy whatever. Rather his mind was set upon the consolidation of Germany as, in Metternich's phrase, " a saturated State " —a State fitly compacted together and finished once for all.

Germany's domestic progress, the development of her internal resources, both physical and intellectual, was his chief concern, and in its pursuit he laboured with single-minded devotion according to his lights. He was not equally wise in all the measures by which he sought to attain his ends, and he was invariably more successful on the material than the social and human side. The introduction of Customs tariffs for the protection of undeveloped industries and a threatened agriculture, the nationalisation of the Prussian railways, the promotion of great canal projects, and his workmen's insurance schemes are all measures which stand to his credit as evidences of far-sighted enterprise, attended by conspicuous success ; but his successive quarrels with the Roman Catholic Church, Social Democracy, and the Poles of Eastern Prussia, far from making for social peace and political stability, introduced elements of friction and bitterness into the national life which were productive of permanent harm.

Events Antecedent to the Great War

The broad lines of domestic policy laid down by Bismarck were followed by the later Chancellors, but with steadily diminishing independence of judgement and of action. Here the principal departure was in the prominence given to naval expansion. In foreign affairs the departures were more marked, and as time passed they became distinctly ominous. Although midway in his chancellorship Bismarck concluded an alliance with Austria-Hungary, he to the last held fast to the traditional tie with Russia. Under the third and last Emperor and his more tractable advisers the importance of maintaining this tie unimpaired was no longer recognized with the old clearness, and the special interests of Austria came more and more to govern German policy in relation to the south-east of Europe.

The inevitable effect was to undermine what Bismarck called " the good old relationship " between the Courts of Berlin and St. Petersburg, which had dated from the beginning of the nineteenth century, and to accentuate and bring into a fateful prominence the perennial Slavic problem. So it was that in the war which broke out in August, 1914, and of which the occasion, rather than the cause, was the murder of the heir apparent to the Hapsburg throne and his consort by Serbian conspirators, Germany and Austria-Hungary fought side by side, with Bulgaria and Turkey as their allies, against a powerful coalition of which Russia, France, Great Britain and Italy were the leading European members.

Establishment of the Republic

After lasting for more than four years, fortune oscillating strongly during its earlier stages, the struggle ended in the complete defeat of the Central Powers in Oct., 1918. By the ensuing Treaty of Versailles, concluded in June, 1919, Germany was required to pay a huge indemnity, and to cede to France Alsace-Lorraine, to Denmark part of North Schleswig, to Belgium several frontier districts, and to a revived Polish State the Polish portions of the Prussian monarchy ; the seaport of Danzig was made an independent State, and Memel was placed in the trusteeship of the League of Nations ; while the German colonies were transferred to Great Britain, France, and Japan under the League's mandates. For the present, and for a long time, Germany has altogether lost the position of primacy among the Continental Powers which she had occupied since 1870.

The close of the Great War coincided with a revolutionary movement, which, beginning in Hamburg in the north, spread like wildfire through the whole country, though only in a few of the States taking dangerously violent forms. Behind the movement was the entire force of social democracy, with the almost undivided support of the urban working classes, and also much sympathy from the down-trodden labourers of the rural districts. The middle classes and the aristocracy could only look on in stupefied amazement and alarm while the greatest political transformation in their country's history was consummated as by word of command.

Such of the rulers as were not summarily deposed abdicated voluntarily, and so far as they were concerned the transition from monarchy to republicanism was effected without bloodshed. The whole of the States duly adopted republican constitutions, and while the confederation was continued, even with the old name " Reich " (henceforth generally translated as Realm), it was on the same democratic basis.

The old Empire comprised twenty-five States, in addition to Alsace-Lorraine, which never received formal federal status. Owing to the amalgamation of seven of the small Thuringian States in one, with the name Thuringia, and the absorption of another of them by Bavaria, the number of the federal territories is now reduced to eighteen.

There is no doubt about the genuineness of the democratic order which has been established in Germany; it remains to be seen how far the model Republic will succeed in practice in a country with such strong monarchical traditions. The new constitutions are nowhere very popular outside the ranks of labour, though opinions differ widely in all classes as to the propriety of allowing some of the expelled rulers to return. It is probable that any early attempt to reinstate the old political order in States like Prussia and Saxony would be the signal for a great social convulsion. It is to Bavaria that the hopes of the monarchists are specially directed.

GERMANY: FACTS AND FIGURES

The Country

Comprises eighteen States: Anhalt, Baden, Bavaria, Brunswick, Bremen, Hamburg, Hesse, Lippe, Lübeck, Mecklenburg-Schwerin, Mecklenburg-Strelitz, Oldenburg, Prussia, Saxony, Schaumburg - Lippe, Thuringia, Waldeck, Württemberg. Total area about 181,780 square miles; population about 61,500,000. As a result of the Great War, the German realm lost in Europe about 27,000 square miles, and in population some 6,500,000 inhabitants, while the overseas possessions lost by the war had an area of about 1,000,000 square miles, and a population estimated at 15,000,000.

Government and Constitution

Republic, under constitution adopted by National Assembly of 423 members at Weimar, July 31, 1919, with a universal, equal, direct, and secret franchise of male and female voters on the proportional representation system. President elected for seven years. Legislature includes Reichsrat of 66 and Reichstag of 469 members, elected for four years.

Defence

Permanent Defence Force (Reichswehr), authorised establishment, 100,000; Public Safety Police (Sicherheitspolizei), armed and equipped, 150,000; Emergency Volunteers (Zeitfreiwilligen), 150,000; Civic Guards (Einwohnerwehr), 350,000. Navy includes six pre-Dreadnoughts, six light cruisers, twelve destroyers, with certain reserves without ammunition on board. Personnel of navy, 15,000, with 1,500 officers and warrant-officers.

Commerce and Industries

In 1920, the acreage and produce in metric tons of the chief crops were respectively as follows: Wheat, 3,453,185 and 2,255,055; rye, 13,313,117 and 4,971,800; barley, 3,996,155 and 1,799,713; oats, 8,109,180 and 4,870,126; potatoes, 6,149,680 and 28,248,765; beet, 817,435 and 7,964,024; hay, 13,721,665 and 23,669,144.

Fruit is largely grown and about 181,650 acres are devoted to vines. Forestry is extensive and scientific over a large area.

There are coal and iron mines in Prussia; silver and copper are mined in the Harz area; zinc is mined in Silesia, and coal, iron, and silver in Saxony.

The yield of the North Sea fisheries in 1920 was valued at 573,426,800 marks; of the Baltic fisheries 118,794,200 marks.

Principal industries include iron manufacture, steel, textiles, woollens, silk, potash, beetroot sugar, clocks and wooden ware, beer, and paper. Total exports to the United Kingdom in 1921 were valued at £20,549,999; imports from the United Kingdom, £17,831,748, the chief articles of export being hops, glass, dyes, cottons, woollens, clover and grass, machinery and toys.

The value of the mark of 100 pfennig normally 11¾d., or 20.43 to the £ sterling, was in November, 1922, about 27,650 to the £. In addition to local municipal issues, the paper money in circulation in January, 1922, was 122,496.7 million marks.

In 1913 Germany's total exports were valued at £509,965,000; imports, £560,335,800.

Communications

Of 35,919 miles of railway line, 34,689 belong to the State. Chief canals: The Hohenzollern, connecting Berlin and Hohensaaten, Rhein-Herne, and Ems-Weser. Length of telegraph lines, 144,150 miles; telephone lines, 91,326 miles.

Religion and Education

No State Church. In 1910, religious bodies included 39,991,420 Protestants, 23,821,453 Roman Catholics, 283,946 other Christian denominations, 615,020 Jews. Education is general, compulsory from the age of six to fourteen, and highly developed. Supplementary to the elementary schools is a system of secondary and continuation schools and gymnasia, which prepare pupils in a nine years' course for the universities and learned professions, and technical high schools, normal schools, agricultural high schools, and commercial schools. In addition to lyceums, there are twenty-three universities.

Chief Towns

Berlin, capital (population 1,779,000), Greater Berlin (3,801,230), Hamburg (985,780), Munich (630,700), Leipzig (604,380), Dresden (529,320), Cologne (633,900), Breslau (528,260), Frankfort-on-Main (433,000), Düsseldorf (407,338), Nüremberg (352,675), Hanover (310,430), Essen (439,250), Chemnitz (303,775), Stuttgart (309,197), Magdeburg (285,850), Bremen (257,920), Königsberg (260,890), Stettin (232,726), Duisburg (244,300), Dortmund (295,026), Kiel (205,330), Mannheim (229,570), Halle-on-Saale (182,320), Cassel (162,390), Altona (168,730), Gelsenkirchen (168,550), Elberfeld (157,200), Barmen (156,326), Augsburg (154,550), Aachen (145,750).

GREEK MANHOOD SWINGING DOWN THE STREETS OF NAUPLIA

It is among the peasantry that the finest type of Greek manhood is found, and these Arcadians marching down a street in Nauplia well exemplify the noble bearing ot the rural population. Straw hats are tending to replace the once universal red cap, but the short white kilt, or fustanella, is still the general wear, girt round by a gay sash and topped by a zouave jacket and full-sleeved shirt

Photo, C. Chichester

Greece

I. A Modern People Cast in Ancient Mould

By Hamilton Fyfe

Special Correspondent of "The Daily Mail"

IF, being in company with Greeks, you should have a mischievous desire to set them furiously by the ears, you have only to speak of the theory that the Hellenes of to-day (that is their name for themselves, the ancient name) are not the descendants of the Greeks of Hellas who left the world so rich a heritage of noble thought and noble emotion enshrined in their literature and architecture and sculpture.

This theory, elaborated by a German professor, is based upon the known fact that after the brightness of ancient Greece was dimmed four centuries before the birth of Christ, the land was over-run by tribes of Slav origin. According to the professor, these tribes exterminated and took the place of the ancient Greeks, becoming the ancestors of the Greeks of to-day, who should, therefore, be considered a Slav people.

Nowhere has the professor's hypothesis been treated as more than a possibility. In Greece it is considered an infamous slander. The Greeks will not allow any doubt to be thrown upon their direct descent from the Athenians and Spartans and the citizens of the other States which gave this small country so resounding a fame. And the probability is that they are right.

Succession from the Ancient Greeks

Certainly they are a mixed race. For so many centuries their land has been the home of people belonging to so many nationalities that this could not be otherwise. Yet it seems clear that the strain of Hellene blood persisted and was stronger than other strains. It was more lively than the Slav strain. It easily conquered such Turkish and other alien elements as were introduced during Turkey's long and evil rule over the Greeks.

It would be fantastic to suppose that the nation of to-day has a great deal in common with the Hellenes of the age of Pericles. But it appears to have enough resemblance to justify the belief of the modern Hellene that the mould has never been broken and thrown away, however much it may have been altered by the changing hand of Time.

True Democracy in Being

Since Greece was freed from Turkish domination in 1828 the likeness has become more noticeable. Liberty has allowed characteristics to shine out which were hidden by the pall of despotism. For example, the genuinely democratic sentiment of the Greeks has taken forms which recall ancient Greek history. They show no respect whatever for barriers of class or caste. Indeed, these can scarcely be said to exist. How could they exist in a country where a rich merchant will have brothers who are peasants, where a lawyer and a shepherd may be sons of the same father, where the man who drives pack-mules over the mountains may be closely related to a leading politician?

There is a healthy conviction among the Greeks that everyone is as good, socially, as anyone else. The artificial grades which divide men from one another, and give privileges to those who happen to have been born in old or wealthy families, are laughed at. The labourer who digs in your vineyard will shake hands with you when he says good-night. The boy who sells you a newspaper will tell you what he thinks about the political situation. The old woman who cooks for you will quickly leave your service unless your behaviour is what that of a gentleman should be towards a lady.

MUSICAL GREEK GYPSIES OF THE AETOLIAN PLAINS

Gypsies are known to have been among the inhabitants of the Morea in the fourteenth century and, at the present day, encampments of these dark-skinned nomads are not infrequently seen in some of the out-of-the-way districts of Greece. Despite their shiftless, vagabond life, their appearance causes no alarm ; brigandage among them is a thing of the past, and their peculiarities and eccentricities are tolerated with kindly indulgence

In England, where the feeling of class differences, of superiority and inferiority, has been bound up with the national life for so long, this kind of equality is scarcely possible yet. Even if those who have been brought up to believe themselves " superior " were ready for it, the labourers and the cooks and the newspaper-boys have only lately, and only in small numbers, begun to think of the possibility of any other relations between them and their employers than that which requires them to say " Sir " or " Ma'am," and to touch their caps and to suffer themselves to be spoken to in curt, masterful tones.

There are many Greeks who would prefer this relation ; they would like their money or their official positions to be recognized by some deference on the part of " the lower orders." But the lower orders will have none of it. They do not admit that they are " lower." The notion has probably never occurred to them. This is to be accounted for by the absence of any marked difference in manners and in speech between those Greeks who are well to do, and who follow "white-collar" occupations, and the mass of the people. The labourer sits down to dinner with you, and you find that his way of eating and drinking, his ease and courtesy, are like your own (perhaps a shade more correct and agreeable). The old cook is a lady in thought as well as in word ; to wound her sensitive feelings, to ignore her self-respect would, you recognize at once, be unpardonable. The newspaper-seller can express himself with fluent vigour, and his views are just as well worth hearing as those of anyone else.

That equality is surely very much in the ancient Athenian tradition. So is the interest which is taken by everybody in the Greek language, and the manner in which it is spoken and written. In the course of ages the tongue of Euripides and Plato has altered as all languages do. It has had words and expressions added to it from other languages. It has dropped a good deal of its rather complicated grammar. The result is a flexible, forcible speech. To those, however, who have their gaze fixed on the

GOSSIP AMONG THE PITCHER-FILLERS AT THE FOUNTAIN

Women work hard in Greece, and among their many household duties is the important one of filling the family pitchers. It is work that has its compensations, for in all lands the well, or the village pump, becomes a kind of central news exchange. Over this artistic fountain is an inscription recording that the philanthropist who had it erected did so at his own expense

Photo, E. Fowler

CAPTAIN OF A MACEDONIAN COMITADJI BAND

Native of one of the hill villages of Macedonia, he is a born fighter and an ill man to quarrel with.
The clothing of these people is all wool obtained from the hardy local sheep, and prepared and made
up at home. The boots are of pigskin taken from the wild mountain swine. A permanent article
of the men's decorative costume is a cummerbund, worn as a protection against malaria

Photo, H. B. Crook

YOUTHFUL PATRIOTS OF THE KINGDOM OF HELLAS

Merry-making is general in Greece on the occasion of a State holiday and usually finds expression in enthusiastic processions, of which waving banners and jubilant singing form the principal features; and the schoolboys, in fresh white fustanella, the linen kilt of Albania which has been virtually adopted as the Greek national costume, are well to the fore in vociferous acclamations of patriotism

past it seemed desirable that the older form of the Greek language should be brought back. Soon after the country became independent this movement was started. Gradually the older form came into use for written Greek, and was adopted by many people for common speech.

Yet the new form had its partisans too, and somewhere about the year 1900 the fight became furious. It was not waged merely with tongue and pen by philologists in academic quarters. There were individual combats, there were riots in Athens. Professors who enriched the language with new phrases were attacked, not only as bad scholars, but as bad patriots. A leading supporter of " new Greek " abused his opponents so scandalously that he threw a great deal of wavering sympathy on to their side.

The absurdity of this acrimonious controversy is emphasised by the fact that the " old Greek " which gained the day for the moment is not the Greek of the ancients. It is really very little

TRIO OF GREEK SOLDIERS OF A FAMOUS PICKED CORPS

The Evzonoi, selected by the Military Council, are a high class of soldier, and serve as the King's bodyguard. An evzonaki enjoys far greater prestige than the ordinary Greek soldier; his pay is higher, and his uniform more picturesque. He wears the fustanella, an elaborately embroidered zouave, a blue tassel on his fez, and blue tufts poised on the turned-up toes of his scarlet shoes

more "pure" than the new. There was no principle involved therefore, yet the excitement caused by the controversy could hardly have been more intense had it been proposed to abolish the Greek language altogether in favour of Esperanto. That illustrates the character of the modern Greek; his interests are literary to a surprising degree, just as were those of the ancient Hellenes.

It is hard to imagine an agitation being got up in England for a return to the English of Chaucer. Even "cranks" would scarcely be so cranky, according to the English standard, as that. It is quite impossible to suppose that, should such a movement be suggested, the general public would be found taking the faintest interest in it. The English language has changed since medieval times not less than Greek, but how many people care about it one way or the other? In Greece it is hardly an exaggeration to say that everybody cares. In controversies which in England only attract the attention of a few scholars every Greek feels bound to take a side. He may know little enough about the matter in dispute, but

SENTRY AT THE ROYAL PALACE, ATHENS

The overcoat donned in winter by the Evzonoi, who serve as the royal bodyguard, is of thick blue material, tightly drawn in at the waist by a belt, and pleated so as to stand out over the white kilt which is worn beneath

he must have an opinion, otherwise he would be false to his ancestry, unworthy to be reckoned "an educated man."

Curiosity is another trait which is found in the modern, as it was in the ancient, Greek. St. Paul's gibe at the Hellenes of his day, that they were always "seeking some new thing," might as justly be levelled at those of our own time. Nowhere are travellers asked a larger number of questions. They are everywhere met by the query: "Where are you from?" They must tell, if they want to be friendly, all about their own concerns and families, all about their business, all about other countries they have seen, and the state of the world at large. A crowd collects in Greece more quickly and with less urgent motive than in any other country. The people are determined not to miss anything. So if you bargain with a cabman, or ask the way, or stop to buy some street-hawker's wares, you are pretty certain to have several persons listening and looking on. They do this without giving offence, their interest is so natural, so childlike, so ingenuously sympathetic and friendly.

way to be kind. Hospitality is to them not merely a duty (as it is all over the East), but a sincere delight.

The idea prevailing among Western nations that the Greeks are always on the look-out for a " slim " deal, that they are grasping and unscrupulous, masters of low cunning, is certainly a false idea so far as the people of Greece

GOLDEN GLORY OF OLD GREECE: THE THESEUM AT ATHENS

Although probably not the temple originally erected by Cimon over the bones of Theseus, this wonderful monument of Greek architecture is universally known as the Theseum. Almost perfect externally—an exquisite but empty shell—the beautifully proportioned edifice, with rather slender Doric columns, is of Pentelic marble stained by the weather of more than twenty-three hundred years to a lovely golden hue

Photo, Keystone View Co.

Indeed, a Greek's notion of being friendly is to tell you his affairs and to listen while you tell him yours. If you refuse, he is puzzled as well as annoyed. He cannot understand why you should object. He begins to think that you must have something to conceal. Travelling in Greece enriches those who are wise enough to take people as they find them with a vast number of pleasant acquaintanceships. Rarely does one come across a Greek who is not anxious to be helpful. They go out of their

are concerned. Outside their own country some of them may have given cause for such condemnation. But in their own country they are not less, but rather more, honest than other nations. Far from trying to make all they can out of the traveller in Greece, the country people often refuse to accept anything for help they have given.

In the towns shopkeepers habitually ask far more for their wares than the wares are worth: far more than they expect to get for them. But this is

SPLENDID IN RUIN: THE TEMPLE OF THE OLYMPIAN ZEUS

Fifteen huge Corinthian columns of Pentelic marble are virtually all that remains of the superb temple which the Emperor Hadrian consecrated to the Olympian Zeus. The ruins stand on a much earlier substructure raised where the watercourses of the upper town of Athens found an outlet. Hence the old legend that Deucalion founded the temple in gratitude for the disappearance here of the last waters of the Flood

Photo, Keystone View Co.

2473

NARROW BYWAY OF CANEA: CHIEF SEAPORT AND CAPITAL TOWN OF "THE GREAT GREEK ISLAND"

The island of Crete in the Mediterranean became a part of the Hellenic Kingdom in 1914. Although celebrated in antiquity for its laws, it figures little in Greek history, but Greek mythology made it the scene of many of the adventures of the gods and heroes. The native islanders are a handsome people, and the martial bearing of the young Cretan on the left stamps him at once as a soldier. Crete has given many thousands of her sons to the army of the mother country

BUSY-BODIES, BARGAIN-HUNTERS, AND BEASTS OF BURDEN IN A BUSINESS CORNER OF CANDIA

One of the "hundred cities" ascribed by Homer to Crete, Candia, rebuilt by the Saracens in the ninth century, acquired such great prosperity under the Venetians in medieval times as the chief city and capital, that Crete was called in the official language of Venice the "island of Candia," which designation may still be noted in modern maps. Although now superseded by Canea as the political capital, Candia retains much of its ancient importance and carries on a thriving trade in oil, soap, and wine

Photo, C. Chichester

HOSTAGES TO FORTUNE: GREEK PEASANT WITH HIS WIFE AND CHILDREN

Taken generally, the Greeks are a hard-working people, the most laborious of the peasantry being found in the Peloponnese. All hands in a family take part in the agricultural work, starting off early in the morning, with the father leading his donkeys laden with all the necessary gear and the younger children, while the mother trudges behind with the last baby slung over her hip. Though conditions are hard, the Greek peasants manage to make a decent if modest living, and

MONKS OF THE GREEK CHURCH CARRYING MUCH-PRIZED VOLUMES OF THE LITURGY

Their Orthodox Church is still dear to the hearts of the Greek peasantry, and the monasteries, of which there are not a few, play their own special part in keeping the Faith a vital thing. The monks are often better read than the priests, and the hospitality dispensed at the monasteries is generous and cordial to the stranger seeking shelter there. Here is seen a group of these holy men clad in their gorgeously embroidered vestments, and holding copies of their precious Liturgy, of which the bindings are encrusted with jewels and adorned with beautiful devices

MEN OF THEBES, THE HOME OF NUMBERLESS LEGENDS

In the bright sunshine these white-haired Thebans are strolling leisurely about the hills which surround
modern Thebes, a little country town situated on the Cadmeia or Acropolis of the ancient city. Their
garments are chiefly home-made, but the gradual introduction of modern European clothing is spoiling
both the picturesqueness of the native costume and the admirable industry of the native character

Photo, Underwood Press Service

PICKED EVZONOI SCOUTS ON PATROL IN THE WOODS

First-rate shots and trained from boyhood in the woodcraft and other arts that make the successful mountain fighter, these Evzonoi are scouting in thickly timbered country. They need to know how to take advantage of every scrap of cover, for their white fustanella, breeches, and leggings make conspicuous targets. Yet they prefer their traditional uniform to any modern, less visible service dress

the practice of shopkeepers all over the East. It is no more than the opening move in the game of bargaining. The West is impatient with this system of doing business, calls it foolish and a waste of time. There is something to be said for it, nevertheless. In lands where trade is loosely organized there are no regular or standard prices. Bargaining is a means of arriving at a price which is fair to buyer and seller alike. It is the only means available.

I have seen Greek shopkeepers open their eyes wide and raise their brows in astonishment at an Englishman in a rage at being asked twice or three times the worth of some article exposed for sale. They could not make out why he lost his temper. He, for his part, could not make out why there were no fixed prices. It is the custom of sensible people in foreign countries to accommodate themselves to local customs, whatever they may be.

Where there does exist dishonesty is in political life, but who is to throw the first stone at Greece on that count? The same plan of filling up all public employments with supporters of the party which has managed to secure a majority is followed in the United States. The consequence is that opinion must very often be influenced by personal interest. Further, the public service suffers, and the time of ministers is largely occupied by considering the

SAVOURY ODOURS FROM A ROAST OF LAMB

It has been said that what beer is to the German, or water to the teetotaller, so is lamb to the Greek. Thus, at Athens, the hungry pedestrian may suddenly be confronted in the manner shown with a prospective meal in the cooking. The fearsome array of meat-hooks ranged above no doubt marks the site of former good joints that are no more

Photo, C. Chichester

GREECE: BELLES OF THE BORDER IN RICH ARRAY

Astonishing opulence of gold embroidery, silver craftsmanship, and delicate needlework enhances the splendour of their Macedonian costume, in which bold colours are blended with rare artistic skill

Photo, L. G. Popo}}

"LOOK AT THE PRETTY CAMERA!"

A happy picture of a promising young Greek with his mother. One sees how universal is the ancient cult of infant worship. His majesty the babe, seated on his throne, which seems somewhat massive for so slight a burden, is being begged in vain to turn his gaze to the lens. However, there is evidently something much more interesting just outside the picture

claims of their supporters to some reward for their assistance. Government employment is coveted by a vast number of the half-educated who will not soil their hands with useful work, preferring the lazy life of a public office or of some local official post.

Ministers themselves are more honest in Greece than in most of the countries in the south-east of Europe. But they are obliged to let a good deal of corruption go on without attempting to stop it. And though they may be personally upright, their policies are often shaped by the mere desire to "turn the other fellows out" and take their places. The party game is played as fiercely in Greece as in any country with a democratic form of government. The Greek system gives the people the whole power in the State. There is no hereditary ruling class. There is only one house of Parliament, though there is a nominated Council of State which can revise legislation. Yet the government of the country is notoriously defective, both in vigour and in good sense. This is not due to the failure of the nation to interest itself in political issues. No people is more given to talking politics. They vote with enthusiasm at all elections, and they can explain why they voted this way or that. Most of them believe they would be quite capable of running the machine of government if it were entrusted to

ATHENS: THE GREAT CITY OF THE AEGEAN SHORE SEEN FROM MOUNT LYCABETTUS

The Acropolis or citadel, the square craggy rock seen on the right, was the earliest seat of the Athenian kings, and at a later period was devoted solely to the gods. It is said to be unrivalled in its unique combination of natural grandeur, of artistic grace, and of sublime historical associations. Mount Lycabettus commands a magnificent panorama of the great plain of Attica where noble, built and clothed in beauty, lies "Athens, the eye of Greece, mother of arts and eloquence."

MERRY-MAKERS ON A NATIONAL HOLIDAY DANCING A PAS DE QUATRE BEFORE APPRECIATIVE SPECTATORS

Holidays are numerous in Greece, comprising days enjoined to be observed as holy by the Greek Church, and anniversaries of events of national importance. The festivals are celebrated with very innocent jollification, the wine-drinking being seldom carried to excess, and the amusement consisting for the most part of dancing. These men are engaged in the Albanian Fling, a lively dance for three or four persons, one of whom executes spectacular leaps and flourishes

Photo, E. Fowler

them. Yet the action that results from all the talk is pitifully meagre.

All foreigners who have lived in the country for any time see that, if the fervour and energy which are put into politics were to be devoted to agriculture and industry and trade, the Greeks would be a prosperous people. They might do far more to attract visitors to their historic and beautiful land. They might make things easier for the traveller who takes pleasure in " the glory that was Greece," as well as in her mountains and valleys, and blue, laughing waters which have not changed since they were celebrated by poets four centuries before the birth of Christ. To see where the Olympic games were held, and where the Oracle of Delphi delivered its mysterious pronouncements is sheer delight to every mind which can enjoy both natural beauty and historic interest.

For a visit to Olympia you can land on a rocky and desolate coast at a little port named Katakolo, where, if it be autumn, you will probably see the quayside piled high with currants for export. Currants are the produce of Greece which go most into the outer world. They are delicious to eat fresh, and in their dried state they sweeten puddings and cakes for millions who have never troubled to wonder what they are.

From the port a panting little train passes from the desolate region into a rich and rolling pasture-land, a land of plentiful crops as well as fat herbage. After arriving at a station in the midst of nowhere, a short walk through a sun-baked village takes one to the spot where victory in contest of speed or strength could make men famous all through Ancient Greece.

No more beautiful site could have been found. Two rivers twist their silver courses through the valley, which is closed in by wooded slopes, the foot-hills of the mighty ranges that edge the horizon. Here on the greensward, among the ruins of the pavilions and dressing-rooms, one can picture the scenes which once filled the valley with shouts of encouragement and triumph. One can imagine the packed rows of eager faces watching the games. One can see the strained looks on the

AT PATRAS PORT: CURRANT WINE BY THE HOGSHEAD

Overlooking the Gulf to which it has given the name, Patras, last survivor of Achaea's twelve cities, is a town of the Peloponnese, and stands upon its north-west coast. Wine is one of the many exports, and here are seen barrels and casks ready for the holds of the ships that are waiting to carry them to other lands

THE VILLAGE LAUNDRY IN FULL SWING

Here there is no whirring machinery to deal with the week's washing. More simple but no less thorough and effective methods are in force, for though soap is not used the clothes are repeatedly douched with water and dashed against the hard paving till they are spotless and ready for drying. The petrol can strikes a modern note in this scene of antiquated method

Photo, E. Fowler

features of the runners, the graceful swing of the disk-thrower, the wary eye of the wrestler, the proud lift of the winners' heads as they were decorated with the olive wreath.

Here was the holy place of that worship of bodily beauty and strength which has never been revived. Here the conception of the god-like was derived directly from the human at its best. What was the Hermes of Praxiteles, which is the jewel of the pleasant little museum at Olympia, but a perfectly-developed athlete, no doubt a competitor in the games somewhere about 500 B.C.? Little did the boy think he was posing as model for a statue that, 2,500 years later, would still be reckoned one of the noblest in the world.

I am not sure, though, that my most vividly enduring memories of Olympia do not cluster round a shepherd lad who, sitting under a tree to shade himself from the hot noonday sun, piped to his sheep a plaintive lay with all the melancholy of the East in its gentle cadences. Here was one of the charms

of Greek life outside the towns. It has altered scarcely at all since classical times.

For Delphi the landing-place is Itea. We landed there in hot sunshine well before nine o'clock, our pinnace cleaving a glassy surface of deepest blue. On shore mules and donkeys—you paid your money and took your choice—were waiting, and we began to mount at once through olive groves, then up stony slopes tufted with brown and green, and showing here and there the pink autumn crocus or the delicate purple of cyclamen. At the half-way village we refreshed ourselves with Turkish delight, brought out by the smiling landlord of a roadside inn. Then on again, still upwards, till a glorious valley opened out before us and we could see the hillside where stood the precinct of the Oracle famous throughout the ancient world.

The very stones of the Sacred Way which we had followed were trodden by the feet of all who came to ask for counsel. The very pillars we could touch supported the treasuries into

MODERN EXQUISITE AND AN ARCH'S ANCIENT GRANDEUR

The average Greek is of medium height and normally of a cheerful temperament. His dress varies somewhat according to his district, but the chief features of the national costume are the white pleated fustanella, gold-embroidered vest, tassel-tipped shoes, and the leathern belt from which usually depend the yataghan and tobacco-pouch

Photo, C. Uchter Knox

GREEKS OF TO-DAY STANDING WHERE ANCIENT HOPLITES TROD

Military service is obligatory in Greece, and liability to serve commences from the twentieth year and lasts for no fewer than thirty-one years. If illiterate, the conscript is taught to read and write, and must learn the Greek language if he speaks only Albanian. During his two years' compulsory service in the active army he may continue to exercise his trade, but not for his own benefit

Photo, Publishers' Photo Service

ROUGH TRANSPORT IN THE CYCLADES: THE TRAIL TO THE SEA

The track from the vineyards in the isle of Santorin is broken and stony, but the long train of sure-footed donkeys swings safely down the steep. Each with its two-fold burden of brimming casks, filled with the vintage of the hills, files down to the port below. Then, his task accomplished, the driver can turn his weary team home again to a well-earned supper and a good night's rest

Photo, C. Chichester

which they poured their gifts. This exquisite spot, overshadowed by Mount Parnassus, and moistened by the cool, clear waters of the Castalian spring, was once thronged by suppliants who had made the pilgrimage from the uttermost parts of the earth, as the Greeks knew it. Now it has become once more a magnet for voyagers from all lands, thanks to the French excavators whose skilful spadework has laid the foundations of the temple and treasuries bare. Still can be seen the holes in the rock where stood the tripod of the Oracle, though alas! the divine vapour rises no more, to be interpreted by Apollo's priestess.

Still, however, is the god of music worshipped by the dwellers at Delphi. Among the string of asses laden with wine-skins which passed unceasingly along the road by the side of our al fresco luncheon-place, driven by stalwart petticoated men, or by girls with distaffs in their hands, there came two pipers and a performer on the drum. Wonderful music they made for us—elemental, passionate, now yearning in a minor key, now triumphant with shrill ecstasy, while the booming of the drum supplied a harmonious background of accompaniment for the arabesques and convolutions of the pipe melody.

Sitting in concert-halls, listening to some solemn quartette or sonata, with an audience that seemed to find the occasion one of unspeakable melancholy, I have often thought of the inspiring effect of those primitive airs filling the golden air of afternoon on that delicious hillside.

A night's steaming from Itea brings one to Corinth. Only those who have looked upon it can understand how blue the Gulf of Corinth is. It is so blue that it leaves off being blue and becomes purple. The Greeks called it the "wine-dark sea," and they were right. If it were not so distant and so difficult to reach, many dangerously beautiful rivals to Nice and Mentone and Monte Carlo might spring up along the shores of this indescribably lovely coast.

Corinth itself is laid out in the American style, in blocks, every street straight, every angle a right angle. Yet how entirely non-modern it is in everything else! Shops with open fronts and

INGENUITY SURMOUNTS THE MONOTONY OF THE OPEN ROAD

For sheer novelty the sight of this Greek maiden engaged with distaff and spindle while in the saddle would be hard to equal, but confident in the sure-footedness of her mount, and in its obedience to the voice of her companion, she beguiles the golden hours of noonday with an industry long famed among the women of Greece. The scene is a hill road near Delphi

Photo, C. Chichester

WHERE THE HOMESTEAD IS THE FACTORY: A PEASANT AT HER LOOM

With the products of Lancashire at the disposal of so many countries it would perhaps seem strange that anyone should spend long hours learning and practising the delicate operation here portrayed. Yet this home industry is quite a live one in parts of Greece, and the finished article is more useful than would be thought possible in view of the home-made appearance of the machinery

Photo, E. Fowler

dark interiors where work and bargaining go on in the desultory Greek way. No streets in the English sense of the word, just roads, and monstrously bad roads, most of them. I felt like writing a Third Epistle to the Corinthians, exhorting them to put their highways into better repair. Driving to Acro-Corinth (the citadel) we thought more than once that the earth was quaking beneath our wheels.

But Acro-Corinth would be worth a much more desperate adventure. A magnificent reward awaited us at the summit of this steep rock, crowned with Venetian and Turkish forts in ruins. One way we looked over the plain, patched with red squares of currant-bearing soil, which stood out from the whitey-grey of the more stony earth which forms innumerable ledges of tableland supported by sheer cliffs of rock. In the other direction lay the Aegean Sea, separated from the blue gulf by a strip of land which from that height looks very narrow. Salamis and Aegina could be seen when the heat-haze lifted ; Athens, too, on a clear day. And all around are mountains— from violet Hymettus and snow-capped Parnassus to the hills of the Peloponnese —shimmering in the sunshine and flooding the soul of the beholder with joy and deep content.

A narrow canal cuts the strip of land between the waters; thence to Piraeus or to Phalerum Bay is only a short run. The bay is pleasanter than the crowded, smelly harbour of Piraeus, and an electric train, smartly managed, takes you to Athens in a very little while.

For many travellers Athens means simply the Acropolis, the most perfect relic of the finest architecture the world has known, a group of half-ruined temples which would tell us what the Ancient Greeks were if nothing else of their work remained. Sun-steeped, majestic, those marble columns, as they glow against a sapphire sky, seem to be giving out the stored-up golden light of twenty-five centuries. They make the Acropolis one of the glories of the human race. It alone, with the theatre of Dionysos, would well repay the journey to Athens.

But there is interest in the modern city, too. To begin with, there are the Athenians. Sit outside one of the cafés in Constitution Square on a fine evening, when the bootblacks and newspaper-sellers are fighting for custom, and the sellers of pistachio nuts, picture post-cards, sweet-scented flowers, and collar-studs, press their wares upon you. Here you very soon notice one way in which the Athenians seem to have changed very little. It was neglect of practical citizenship that ruined them in classical times. Listen to what a Greek newspaper said a few years ago: " If we were to print articles on Greek commerce, on the development of the country's resources, the replanting of its bare mountains, the improvement of its material condition, we should sell about fifty copies a day. When we give the latest rumours of an impending political crisis, the probabilities of a dissolution of Parliament, or the chances

MAKING READY THE FIELDS FOR THE WORK OF THE SOWER

The ground is stony and weed-grown beneath the hills, and the fruits of the earth are only gleaned after much toil and struggle with nature's unkindness. Yet the soil usually yields rich harvests despite the fact that modern theories of agriculture make but slow progress. He is sure of future rewards as behind the plodding team the ploughboy drives his lonely furrow

Photo, Henry Riley

COWS IN THE CORN: ELEMENTARY AGRICULTURE IN HELLAS

The unenclosed fields give a spaciousness to the landscape, over which the winds can blow full and free and help the sun to dry the corn. It is for this that the patient peasant is driving her yoke, the simple implement on which she sits turning over the stalks to expose a fresh surface to the air. The task is long and wearisome, and not every farm can afford oxen

CROWN OF THE YEAR AMID BROAD ACRES

As in most other branches of agriculture, the operation of gathering in the year's harvest in Greece is conducted by simple methods and with rude implements that have stood the testing of many a year's cultivation. The process, then, is a somewhat protracted one, but the Greek peasant finds that so far it not only supplies his country's needs, but leaves also a surplus for export

Photos, E. Fowler

WHEN THE REAPERS' WORK IS DONE

A rich yield from the well sown land is here being transported from the fields to the windmills whose giant sails, whirled by the lusty wind to turn the great mill-stone, the upper on the nether, will grind it to flour. The donkeys doing duty as farm wagons appear to bear their loads with patience, though the foremost seems to feel that this is the last straw and is proceeding to eat it

GREEK PEASANTRY PITCHING THE CORN

Greece is mainly an agricultural country, and although her economic life depends practically on the products of the soil only one-fifth of the total area is cultivable. To a large extent the land is in the hands of peasant proprietors, and the conditions of agricultural life, differing greatly in the various regions, are for the most part very backward, due chiefly to the dryness of the Greek climate

Photos, E. Fowler

2493

"NO LABOUR NO BREAD": THRESHING CORN WITH A FORK

Nothing could better illustrate the antiquated methods with which the Greek agricultural peasant is satisfied than this photograph of a woman threshing. The formidable fork with which she shakes the corn out of the ear before further sifting it in her huge sieve entails deplorable waste of physical energy as well as of good grain. In wide districts of the country no use whatever is made of machinery

SIFTING GRAIN AND WINNOWING THE CHAFF WITH A FAN

Even when they are placed in their way the Greek peasants are singularly slow to make use of modern inventions. These women are separating the corn from the husk by the simple process of sifting it through a large sieve while a man stands by with a winnowing fan made of twigs. It is virtually in Thessaly only that reaping and threshing machines are used

Photos, E. Fowler

PRETTY MARRIAGE CUSTOM IN MACEDONIA

Weddings in Macedonia are made an occasion for much feasting and festivity. A great feature is made of the wedding breakfast, in the course of which a certain ritual is observed. For instance, it is the custom for the bride to wait upon her guests. In this particular case she presented each of the company with decorated kerchiefs, the finest specimens going to the more honoured among the party

Photo, H. B. Crook

of a compact between two party leaders, our circulation goes up by leaps and bounds."

The results of this absorption in the political game of Ins and Outs, instead of in the material fruits of good citizenship, can be seen in the course of a stroll through the city. In Constitution

BRIGHT PLUMAGE IN THE CYCLADES
The peasants' baggy breeches are usually bright blue, the sleeveless vest is navy blue or red, and the cap a fisher's stocking-cap. To strangers it is a constant marvel how the heelless slippers are kept upon the shuffling feet
Photo, Henry Riley

the prisons, notice how the chief industries are in foreign hands, and your illusion will be quickly dispelled.

Not that the visitor of discretion need wish the old bazaar to be abolished or the old workshops to be brought up to date. They are to him a joy far transcending the plate-glass windows of the Hodos Hermou. Come into the Street of the Smiths at dusk. It is a lurid fantasy of dim interiors, lit by the flickering red glow of forge fires playing on swarthy faces, while mysterious figures flit about in dark recesses. Every shop has a different picture to show you. Here the fitful blaze of the embers blown into flame is reflected from the burnished surface of immense copper pans. There a Vulcan beats out a ploughshare. This smith is fashioning a lamp of traditional pattern ; that one is making keys. Not one smithy fails to charm the eye. Not one but would drive a painter to despair.

Scarcely less interesting is the Street of the Leather-workers and Boot-sellers. From the open-fronted booths dart forth the dark-skinned salesmen, many wearing the red fez and some, perhaps, the national fustanella (a kilted skirt), and all asking for their wares several times as much as the purchaser need pay.

Shopping can therefore be made an amusing pastime in Athens. Quite other emotions are aroused by visiting a prison. Passing through a narrow street close to the remnants of the ancient meeting-place of the city, you may see hands thrust out of a latticed opening, very little above the level of

Square, of which one side is filled by the white palace of the sovereign and the other sides by fine handsome hotels and shops, while its graceful grove of vivid green pepper trees forms the pleasantest of shady boulevards ; in the principal thoroughfares, Hermes and Stadium Streets, you might fancy the Greek capital a flourishing modern town. Plunge into the poorer quarters, visit

GREEKS OF TO-DAY
'Mid Vistas of Long Ago

From the now treeless summit of Parnassus, once sacred to Apollo and the Muses, shepherds watch the rising sun dispel the mists of morning

Photos, except that on page 2512, Fred. Boissonnas

Orchards of peaches, mulberries, and pomegranates grow over the site of ancient Sparta, and to-day fair Lacedaemonian maidens watch their cattle and sheep browsing near the tomb of immortal Leonidas.

Through the undulating, fertile valley of Sparta, watered by the silvern Eurotas, the goatherd leads his flock towards the sublime mountain mass of Taygetus, the very sanctuary of the Spartans of old

Hand-in-hand, Greek villagers dance in the golden evenings, bearded men in white kilts, and women in swaying robes of many colours

At conical village ovens like this, resembling gigantic ant-hills, Greek peasant women bake their bread, watched by interested children

Many of the Greek traditional dances suggest some ancient sacred significance, the linked chain winding with an almost solemn rhythm

Poor though it is, this khani on the road to Sparta gives the traveller opportunity for a glass of wine, while his ass has a bite of food

*Monasteries serve as inns to travellers in Greece, and this monk of
S. George's stands like mine host of the S. George and the Dragon*

*The monastery of S. George stands high on the forested Dourdouvana,
and from its balconies the inmates look down upon the Lake of Pheneus*

Storms, drought, and greedy goats have stripped Parnassus of all its
verdure, and the bare rocks now are shelter for shepherds and brigands

This domed well of Gastouri, Corfu, where Hera-like women fill their graceful pitchers, marks the stream where Nausicaa befriended Ulysses

2505

Cultured simplicity marks the home life of the priests at Zemenon—a low table, some painted coffers, and a small shrine furnishing the roughcast-walled sitting-room open to the woodwork of the roof

Once the richest, as it is still the most important, monastery in Greece, the Megaspeleon, in Achaea, has plentiful stores of wine to cheer the hearts of the monks gathered in their long, vaulted refectory

Her loom set in a sunny corner of her bare apartment, the good wife weaves at Andritsena, in Messenia, while her skirted spouse looks on

From the porch of his low, tiled dwelling the veteran looks out on Zemenon set in a fold of the hills and girt with olives and cypresses

In the cloister of S. Stephen's monks meditate undisturbed, for their monastery on the Meteora is inaccessible save by lowered ladder or rope

By means of this windlass the monks in the monastery of the Holy Trinity haul up in nets food and visitors to their sanctuary in mid-air

As they drive their horses and asses abreast over the corn to tread out the grain, the Nemean peasants make a humble presentment of the chariot races held on these same plains twenty-three centuries ago

Along the white track the villagers of Zemenon file home in the peaceful evening hour, bearded priests leading the train of white-clad men and full-robed, hooded women and children

Greek, from the neighbourhood of Kastoria, she carries well the rich decorative costume found on both sides of the Macedonian border

Photo, L. G. Popoff

2512

the pavement. Passers-by cheerfully tell you these are the hands of prisoners, and that if you want to see the prison you have only to apply at the gate round the corner. A few coins put into the palm of the gate-keeper make admission easy. You enter a paved enclosure with cages on either side.

Cages they are actually. Behind the bars a press of prisoners seek with loud cries and outstretched arms to attract your attention. Those who are awaiting trial and those who are serving sentences are all mixed up together. One poor wretch to whom I spoke said he had been in that miserable place four months, and had not yet been tried. He had not even a bed to lie on. Another, a German, capped this by protesting that he had been there for eight months. When I said that this could hardly be possible, a friend living in Athens assured me that such detentions of accused persons were nothing out of the way. It often took a year, he said, for an ordinary police-court case to get itself settled.

It is true there is no prison discipline, no restraint upon liberty except the bars of the cage. Within their narrow quarters the prisoners can move about and occupy themselves as they please. They get no exercise. What many of them do is to make knick-knacks to sell to visitors. The food supplied to them is of the poorest quality, so they are glad to earn money which will buy them something from outside. They can have anything they like brought in to them. Their conditions are, in short, very much like those of the debtors who

FEMININE DIGNITY PERSONIFIED

Her home is in the hilly region near the Isthmus of Corinth, and her strong frame and fine carriage indicate characteristics common to many of the country people of Greece : pride and independence, and the sobriety and temperance born of thrift

Photo, C. Chichester

were confined in the Marshalsea and other debt prisons in London in Charles Dickens's time, except that there was, of course, no cage for the prisoners whose plight he described.

One thing, and one only, there is to be said in favour of the Greek system. It may strike us as being unworthy of a country calling itself civilized. But if those prisoners were given the choice between the conditions under which they exist and those which are to be found in English prisons, they would nearly all of them choose to go on as

GLIMPSE OF SUNNY CORFU, NAMESAKE AND CAPITAL OF THE ISLAND, AND ITS OLD VENETIAN FORTIFICATIONS

Thrown by the glare into chequered contrasts of black and white, the market place is astir with the eager business of barter and bargaining. On all sides the venders are at their well-stocked booths while the itinerant merchantman with his piled barrow scorns the shade's advantage. Above, the fortalice frowns upon the unheeding throng, for Corfu has known warlike days. As late as 1915 the Serbian army found refuge here. The boy with his laden basket, the poodle, well shaved against the heat, and the citizens who pass the time of day are evidently enjoying the balsamy weather.

ALL THE LATEST IN AGRICULTURAL AND HORTICULTURAL CUTLERY

This old inhabitant of Corfu is about to make a purchase at the sickle shop where cutting implements for use in field and garden are for sale ; sickles predominate, and pruning knives and saws are to be found in varying sizes and styles. On account of its shape the island of Corfu was sometimes called Drepane, or the Sickle, as it describes a curve the convexity of which is towards the west

they are. They would be healthier in an English gaol. They would not be liable to be kept waiting for months before they were put on trial. But the solitude, the cleanliness, the inhuman regularity and order, would cause them worse sufferings than any they endure under their own system. Each country must follow its own sentiment in such a matter as this. Each must be allowed to know best what arrangements suit the national temperament. To suppose that what is best for one is best for all peoples is the mark of a small and inexperienced mind.

One sight in Athens stirred my indignation more than the hollow cheeks and piteous pleading hands in the prison. This was a cage on wheels being trundled round, literally chockfull

LAST SCENE OF ALL IN A LIFE DRAMA: A GREEK PEASANT LYING IN STATE

Some of the customs attending death and burial in Greece are distinctly curious. The dead, dressed in their best clothes and shod for their long journey to the other world, lie in state and are carried in unclosed coffins to the church. This exposure of the corpse until the actual moment of interment was originally ordained by Solon as a deterrent of foul play. In some remote districts there is a strange custom of disinterring the bones after a few years, sewing them up in embroidered sacks and depositing them in an ossuary near the church

"A GRAZING FLOCK—THE SENSE OF PEACE—THE LONG, SWEET SILENCE—THIS IS GREECE"

There is an indefinable something about the country places of Greece which seems to envelop each landscape with a soft, poetical glamour. In this quiet scene the shepherd, crook in hand, is gathering his flocks together preparatory to guiding them to a fresh pasturage; and they are alert to their master's voice, which reaches to a great distance, and come from heights a mile away in response to his cries. The small stream on the right, trickling down the parched bed of the river Galika, will, on the advent of storms to the scrub-covered mountain-chain, become a raging torrent which, reaching from bank to bank, will sweep all before it

Photo. Dr. H. A. Fawcett

2517

MACEDONIAN MANHOOD WITH FINE MILITARY SWAGGER

Comparatively few Macedonians are admitted to the Greek Army in comparison with the number of recruits from other parts of the kingdom. Yet they are good fighting material, sturdy of physique, as shown by this fine photograph of one Macedonian soldier in the Greek service, and possessed of a good local knowledge of the conditions prevailing in the difficult country of their birth

Photo. Dr. H. A. Fawcett

of dogs for sale. The poor beasts were several layers thick. They struggled and trampled one another down, fighting for air and breath, and a small crowd of street urchins, thinking the opportunity too good to be lost, were teasing them with sticks and jeering at their discomfort.

For that cruelty there was no excuse. Impossible to plead that the dogs could like this manner of being offered for sale better than the humane comfort tables sit smart cavalry officers, politicians, business men, and family parties (for café life in Athens has a pleasantly domestic side to it) who might be found in any capital. But this is only the veneer; this is the centre of fashionable life. In Harmony Square, at the other end of Stadium Street, in any of the popular quarters, a very different concourse can be seen. Here ordinary European clothes are almost the exception. The variety of

WORKERS AT LEISURE IN A GREEK MARBLE QUARRY

Used all over the world wherever there is ornamental building, quantities of many-coloured marble are ever in demand, and for many hundreds of years some of the finest has been exported from Greece. From Mount Pentelicus in Attica came the material in which the celebrated Elgin Marbles, removed from the Parthenon at Athens to the British Museum, were executed

and spacious kennels of the Dogs' Home in England. Geographically, Greece is in Europe, but as long as brutalities like that are practised openly without causing disgust she belongs in Asia.

Such callousness is Oriental. So is the slackness of method which accounts for the lack in Greece of good government, both national and local. Yet with the Orientalism is mixed a surface civilization which deceives a great many people. The cafés in Constitution Square might be in Munich or Naples. At the dress provides an ever-changing kaleidoscope of colour and bravery.

There swaggers a soldier of the royal bodyguard in starched, white, pleated petticoat, with a tasseled cap of liberty on his head. There an Albanian cuts a dash in divided skirt and zouave jacket of screaming blue, crowned by a fur cap or a deftly-twisted black silk handkerchief. Behind him comes a stalwart farmer from Boeotia. Notice his rough, white flannel coat with monk's hood. The sleeves hang down the back, for he prefers to treat it as a loose cloak, and a fine free figure he makes in it. The national shoe, with the toe curving upward, and its ball of white or coloured fluff attached to this, is seen everywhere.

The roads are little better than they were under the Turks. The principal streets are paved and lighted, but in the rest the wayfarer must grope and plunge as best he can. The outlying parts of the city consist of heaps of builders' rubbish dumped on waste spaces, with here and there little staring jerry-built houses, which seem to call upon the glorious relics of antiquity to fall upon and crush them.

If we want to make acquaintance with Greeks of the best type, we must go into the country. Everywhere it is the peasants who cultivate the land and those who earn their bread by the sweat of their brows in other manual occupations who compel respect and liking, though it is too often the noisy and restless town-folk who are accepted as representatives of the national spirit. The Greek on the land, or engaged in the sponge-fishing industry or minding flocks of sheep, is a finer fellow both in

JEWISH PREACHER'S PULPIT AMONG THE TOMBS AT SALONICA

In the sun's brightness stands the Hanadji, or chief rabbi, speaking comfortable words to the company around the graves. Silhouetted against the desolation of the waste ground behind and with the dead all round, their leader is exhorting the pious crowd who have come to honour their fathers' burial place. And here, away from the town's restlessness, the departed can rest in peace

Photo, Dr. H. A. Fawcett

VENERABLE HIGH PRIEST OF A FANATICAL SECT OF ISLAM

As he walks the cloisters of the old mosque on the hills outside the walls of Salonica, his stern face, beneath the flower pot-shaped hat of camel hair, speaks of great mystic power. He is the High Priest of the few remaining members of the Macedonian branch of Dancing Dervishes, and his confraternity, known as the Mevlevi sect, is held in much higher estimation than that of the Howling Dervishes

Photo, Dr. H. A. Fawcett

body and in character than the Greek who has lost his noble bearing and his simplicity by living in a town. Unfortunately, the prospects for the peasant are so untempting that very large numbers emigrate, mostly to the United States, but a good many to South Africa.

In the richest agricultural district of Greece, the plain of Thessaly, the owners of land do well, but the cultivators can win little more than a bare existence. On some of the islands, which make up so large a part of the territory of the Greeks, there is a good living to be made by growing oranges and lemons, and the islanders in general seem to be better off than the country-people on the mainland. Here the cottages are mostly built of mud, usually one-storeyed, and often without

glass windows, though they have shutters to close the house up at night. It is common to find animals, chiefly pigs, sleeping under the roof with the family. If the house has two storeys, they are kept in the lower one. If no upper part exists, then they have an enclosure walled off.

As a rule, the peasants' cottages are fairly clean. They are a self-respecting folk and bring up their children carefully. Holy pictures of saints or of the Blessed Virgin are always prominent objects on the walls and are saluted as the inhabitants pass out or come in.

The Greek Orthodox Church follows a ritual very much like that of the Russian Church. The priests wear full beards and high black hats, with a brim at the top instead of round the head of the wearer. They are as a class

JEWISH WOMEN AT THE KIPPAW

The Sephardim, as the particular branch of Jewry located at Salonica is termed, have adopted a somewhat specialized form of costume. Of the two women seen in the photograph, the one on the right is wearing the " Capitana," a peculiar headdress edged with fur. Behind stand the tombs of the cemetery, the scene of so many mournful gatherings

Photo, Dr. H. A. Fawcett

THE HANADJI AT THE HEBREW CEMETERY IN SALONICA

The Kippaw is an annual ceremony of mourning for their dead observed by the Jews of this region. On the appointed day the women flock to the cemetery, and going to the tombs of their relatives, shed tears and utter loud cries as they wait for the Hanadji to come and read his prayers. Pebbles are left on the tombs by visitors as a mark of respect

Photo, Dr. H. A. Fawcett

ignorant and very poor. They live on the payments which are made to them for the ceremonies they perform—baptism, marriage, extreme unction and burials—and on the Easter offerings of their parishioners. They are bound to marry unless they enter a monastery, where they need take no thought for the morrow, since their livelihood is secure so long as they behave themselves. Both monks and parish priests are usually of the peasant class, and the latter supports himself and his family by cultivating his patch of land. They are neither of them much respected, though if they become bishops they are treated with reverence, even men kissing their hands and asking for their blessing.

Yet the mass of Greeks, though they do not pay much heed to their clergy, are particular about obeying the ordinances of the Church. They keep not only the six-weeks' Lenten fast, but three other long periods of abstinence from meat, fish, eggs, oil, butter, and cheese. All that they have left to live upon during the fasts are bread, vegetables, fruit, olives (which help to make up for the lack of oil), and some kinds of very coarse fish which are exempted from the prohibition. Possibly it is the severe rule of fasting which makes the Greek so small an eater at all times. They seldom taste meat in the country, and consider a piece of bread with a few figs or olives quite a sufficient meal. Though they drink wine, generally home-made and tasting strongly of resin, they mix it with water all through the warm weather, and drunkenness is very rare.

Their ways of amusing themselves are simple and mostly in the open air. The public holidays are either national or religious by origin. They still

the politicians did not spoil the effect of his valour. A country where officers of the General Staff are changed whenever a new Ministry takes office cannot in the ordinary way expect to make war with much success. It was because the people were determined to beat the Turk and because the whole army was

RELIC OF FORMER MOSLEM RULE IN SALONICA

The soothing plash of the fountain sparkling in the sun affords welcome relief from the glare of torrid skies, and tempts the young generation from their play to rest in the cool of the courtyard. This ancient shrine of Allah wears a decrepit look with the grass springing up betwixt the cobbles and the lichen creeping on the stones all chipped and worn with time's passing

Photo, Dr. H. A. Fawcett

celebrate the day on which their War of Independence began with passionate and sincere enthusiasm. They are not merely word-of-mouth patriots.

This was shown clearly when Greeks flocked homewards from all parts of the world when the country went to war with Turkey in 1912, and in that war the Greek soldier wiped out the shame of the poor showing made against the Turks in 1897. He fought bravely and obstinately, and for once

filled with the spirit of victory that they won their battles in 1912 ; the same was true of their victory over Bulgaria in 1913.

The Greek navy is not a serious force when considered in relation to the naval power of the big States. But it has a fine seafaring population to draw upon for its sailors, most of whom come from the islands. Very beautiful those islands are,

Lily on lily, that o'erlace the sea,

as Browning pictured them. More

PROSPERITY AND POVERTY AT THE PORTALS OF A SALONICA MOSQUE

After the conquest of Macedonia the Turks converted the Greek churches into mosques, and the Eski Djuma, or Old Assembly, an interesting basilica said to date from the fifth century, acquired its name from having been the first church to be transformed in Salonica. The young Turks are of the more prosperous community, while the woman and children belong to Salonica's homeless population

Photo, Dr. H. A. Fawcett

DIGNITY AND IMPUDENCE OUTSIDE A VILLAGE INN

Fine, even dignified, fellow though he is after a rugged fashion, there is an air of squalor about this Macedonian peasant swathed round his head with a turban, round his middle with a cummerbund, and round his legs with loose bandages. For him and for his ramshackle ox-wagon the chubby little urchin in most voluminous breeches seems to entertain no very great respect

MAKING MERRY TO THE JINGLE OF A MYRIAD GLITTERING COINS

The complicated way in which they have joined hands adds to the striking appearance of this group of Greek peasant girls. Each vies with the other to produce the most dazzling costume, and this latter helps to cheer both themselves and their swains at the rustic gatherings for which they don these vivid garments with their coin corselets which glitter in the sunlight as they walk

MACEDONIAN INDUSTRY IN THE VARDAR VALLEY

Although water is precious, and the peasants are none too clean in their personal habits, the Macedonian housewife has to deal with a fairly heavy laundry. Winter and summer these countryfolk wear an enormous quantity of clothing, for the disturbed conditions of the country compel them to protect their possessions, even to the extent of carrying their entire wardrobe on their backs

Photo, Dr. H. A. Fawcett

MODERN CERAMIC WARE FROM THE GREEK ISLANDS ON THE WHARF AT SALONICA

The Greeks were famous in the earliest days for their fine pottery, which they ornamented with artistic designs and pictures. Handsome and varied as are their vases of the present day, the productions of antiquity far excelled those of modern times both in beauty of design and in grace of outline. In ancient Athens it was customary to present vases, sometimes containing some of the precious olive oil for which the district was then famed, as prizes for sports and games

beautiful, perhaps, from the water than when one lands upon them. Their very names, Chios, Naxos, Andros, Milo (or Melos), are an inspiration, and on a sunny day one can see through the clear transparency of windless air every feature of them, their little white towns and even lonely houses, their light-towers and olive-woods and cypress-groves, in unexpected sharpness of detail.

Greece might be a prosperous and contented land if it were not for politics. It is politics which sows distrust among the people, prevents them from pulling together for long at a time. It is politics which fills their imagination with misty hopes of a Greek Empire instead of fixing their minds upon doing the work that's nearest, and deludes them into embarking upon all manner of

THESSALONIAN WOMEN OF THE TWENTIETH CENTURY IN GALA ATTIRE
Salonica is notable for the handsomely decorated and embroidered costumes worn by its feminine population. The coins so lavishly displayed about their heads, necks, and waists are mostly family heirlooms, and innumerable strings of them, often interspersed with modern Turkish coins, are regarded as an essential feature of festive raiment
Photo, Underwood Press Service

The people of the islands are often of noble stature and fearless bearing. But they must have hard work to scrape a living out of the soil which covers scantily the underlying rock. They are also the victims of most unconscionable taxation. The speculators who buy the right of collecting the taxes fleece them without shame or fear. The rulers who ought to stop this are too busy with their political game to interfere.

visionary enterprises. The pity of it is that in a population of politicians so few individuals have emerged with any genius for statesmanship, and none with sufficient personal influence to persuade all these zealous partisans to concentrate their energy first of all upon the single purpose of fusing themselves into a united people, making the most of their many advantages to secure happiness and prosperity at home and confidence and respect abroad

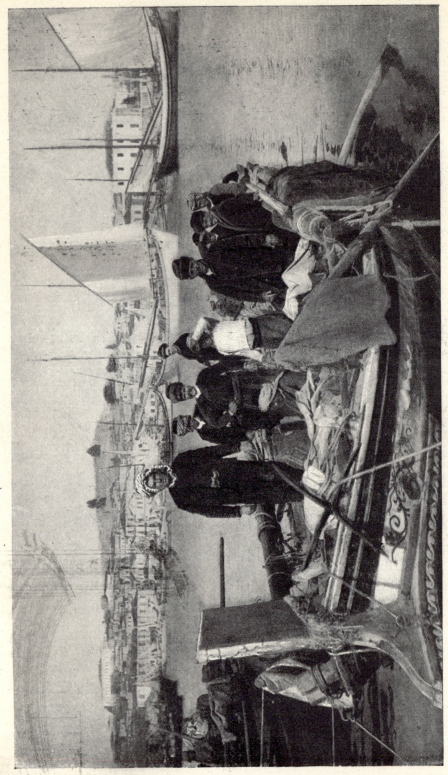

STURDY FISHER FOLK OF ANCIENT MITYLENE AND THEIR STOUT CRAFT

The old port of ancient Lesbos, home of Sappho and Alcaeus, still keeps its charm. The white houses cluster on the hill and straggle by the quayside where the multitudinous shipping finds safe mooring. It is from here that many of the olives, destined for the table of the gourmet, are shipped, and here, too, the boats lade their holds with skins. Pleasant it is in the chief harbour of this small gem of the Aegean, with the sun on the white sails, and where the reflections of the long masts

Greece

II. The Hellenes & their Wonderful History

By A. D. Innes, M.A.

Author of " History of England and The British Empire "

THE recorded history of the Greeks is older than that of any other nationality in Europe. Three hundred years ago, Greek-speaking peoples dominated more of the Balkan Peninsula than is included in the Hellenic Kingdom of the twentieth century, the isles of the Aegean Sea, and perhaps a part of the littoral of Asia Minor. For three thousand years Greek has been at least the dominant language of the whole of that area; and the speech of M. Venizelos to-day is visibly the speech in which Homer sang before the legendary she-wolf suckled the founder of Rome, differing from it little more than does modern English from Chaucer's.

When just six hundred years had passed out of those three thousand, the Greeks were triumphing in the first of their mighty achievements in the cause of human progress; they had saved the Western world from the domination of Orientalism; they had shattered the fleets and armies of the Persian Great King who held himself Lord of the World, in battles whose very names are the trumpet notes of liberty, at Marathon and Salamis, at Plataea and Himera, all in twelve short years.

Greece in its Golden Age

In the next century and a half they had raised temples of beauty unmatched; their sculptors had carved in marble and ivory and gold the most majestic and the most exquisite statuary ever seen. Great already in poetry through the Homeric epics, they had created the glories of the Athenian drama; histories, too, unrivalled in their kind. They had produced orators whose speeches remain models to this day, philosophers in both kinds, the scientific and the inspired, the twin monarchs of intellectualism, to one or other of whom, to Aristotle or to Plato, the most profound intelligences in Europe still own allegiance. And then in ten years more they had sent toppling the vast Eastern empire which they had so splendidly challenged before, and extended their ascendancy to the Oxus and the Sutlej and the cataracts of the Nile. The old military triumphs over enormous odds had been repeated not on European but on Asiatic soil.

Yet the Greeks did not politically master the world, because there was not and never had been a Greek nation. The Hellene, the Greek-speaker, who knew his Homer as the Briton has known his Bible, counted all Hellenes as kinsmen, and all others, till he met the Roman, as " barbarians." He did not count the kinsman as a friend, but for the most part as a rival of whom he was bitterly jealous. The geographical formation of the peninsula, of the islands, and of the coast of Asia Minor, had fostered the establishment, in every valley and every harbour, of a community mainly rural or partly maritime with a central city, separated but not cut off from other communities, each of which developed as a unit, only occasionally combining with or dominating its neighbours; each full of an intense political and intellectual life, but also of a not less intense consciousness of its own individuality.

A Thousand Years of Chequered Glory

Only the stress of the Persian menace had forced them to unity for a brief hour; when the menace had passed they fell to internecine feuds and struggles which were only a shade fiercer than the strifes of political factions within each State. For five and twenty years at the end of the fifth century oligarchic Sparta, the militarist State, strove for ascendancy with democratic Athens, the maritime State. Sparta defeated her rival, but could not hold her leadership securely; and the Greeks were again only combined rather than united when, after another half-century, Macedon—a tribal, not a city State, far larger than the rest but behind them in culture—established her supremacy, and Alexander led the Greek armies to the overthrow of Darius.

Alexander's empire broke up on his death. The Hellenic culture was spread over western Asia, but only superficially, and Macedon for a little more than a century retained her domination over Hellas, the Hellenes whom the Romans called Graeci (Greeks). But the time had come when all other Powers were to fall before the might of the Imperial Republic of Rome, into which, in the course of the second century B.C., all Greece was absorbed. Greece it remained, Greek not Roman, but the political liberty of its cities was gone for ever.

The Imperial Republic became the Roman Empire of the Caesars. But its centre of gravity began to sway eastwards, and early in the fourth century A.D. the city of Constantine on the Bosporus became Rome's rival as the seat of the Caesars. By the end of the fifth century the Caesar at Constantinople had ceased to rule over the Western world ; he was the head of an empire more Greek perhaps than Oriental, but more Oriental than Roman, and called according to taste the Eastern, Greek, or Byzantine Empire, which through many vicissitudes and many amputations remained alive until Mohammed II., the Conqueror, gave it the coup de grâce in 1453.

Moslem Subjugation of the Hellene

But the " Greek Empire " had not been Greece. Constantinople, from its first founding had been Greek, and had been the headquarters of Hellenism, of Hellenic Christianity, of Hellenic culture, through the centuries when the West had forgotten them. Other peoples, however, had swarmed into the Balkan Peninsula ; Slavs had absorbed a great part of it and set up the Serbian kingdom ; Bulgars had conquered and blended with Slavs and set up the Bulgarian kingdom ; Thrace and Macedonia had become composite of all races ; but all these regions, at the best, had never been more than half Hellene.

The real Hellas had been the southern portion of the peninsula ; and whatever the extent to which this had been penetrated, or as some would say permeated, or even swamped by the influx of " barbarians," it remained, along with the islands, Greek in tradition and sentiment and language. And this Greece had fallen under the sway of the Turk long before the crescent waved above the city of Constantine. The capture of the imperial city only set the seal on the enslavement of the Hellene to the Moslem. Hellene, Bulgar, and Serb had been dominated in the course of the preceding century, and only the fastnesses of Albania still defied subjugation, and Albania had never been genuinely Greek.

Reawakening of the National Spirit

Government, in the Turk's view, has two objects, the provision of revenue and of fighting forces by the infidel subject for the Moslem master. But even the worst of governments must be in the hands of administrators. In the centuries during which the Turks and the renegade Europeans who counted as Turks were the masters, they found in the Greeks particularly useful servants for running the business of administration ; and at the same time they took their toll of Greek children to be bred as Moslems and trained as soldiers in the famous corps of Janissaries, while taxation and extortion kept material progress down to a minimum. The Greek was a slave, but he accommodated himself to his slavery ; and the

Turk who would not be at the trouble of governing him left his multitudinous communities to govern themselves as best they could. The Greek clung to his " Orthodox " Christianity, and somewhere in the bottom of his soul preserved the consciousness of Hellenism, of a once glorious past, and some dim vision of a Phoenix-like rebirth. But for, more than three centuries he remained passive under the yoke.

Then, at the end of the eighteenth century, the spirit began to stir. The vision of the past and of the future became more vivid. The Western world was snapping its old bonds ; very soon Bonaparte was forging for his own ends that weapon of the Nationalist Idea which was presently to be turned to his own overthrow. The people who had once been the foremost champions of liberty were sure of the sympathies of the liberty-loving West. The sons of the Orthodox Church would have the goodwill of their Orthodox brethren in Russia. The time was at hand when they should again fling off the Oriental yoke, when the Christian should break free from bondage to the Moslem ; more than that, when the Greek should reign again in the imperial city, once his own, but now for centuries desecrated by the outer barbarian.

Outbreak of the War of Independence

The Greek had hardly realized that some three-fourths of European Turkey had no love for him, and that he was quite definitely an alien—and an unpopular alien—in Serbia and Bulgaria and the Trans-Danube. Greeks might be Hospodars, civil governors, and occupy most administrative posts where Christians could conveniently be employed, in the provinces of the Turkish Empire ; but the influence they already exercised only made the rest of the subject populations the more jealous of them.

Europe resettled itself at the Vienna Congress. The settlement ignored all that is meant by Nationalism, and, while it rendered ill-service to Constitutionalism, practically asserted in its strongest form the divine right of hereditary autocracy. Whatever sympathy might be looked for from intellectuals, from religious sentiment, or from doctrinaire liberalism, would have to be discounted by the fear of " the Revolution " which dominated every monarchy and every ministry in Europe. But Greek patriots overrated the favourable forces, and underrated those which were antagonistic.

The weakness of the Turkish system was emphasised when the Albanian Ali Pasha practically defied the Porte and assumed the authority of an independent prince. To crush him the Government had to withdraw its troops almost entirely from the classic land of the Greeks, the peninsula south of Thessaly and Epirus. The patriots had prepared their plans. They persuaded themselves that they had the Tsar Alexander at their backs. In 1821 they raised the standard of revolt, and the Greek War of Independence began.

The attempt to raise the northern Slavs under Greek leadership, with Greek dominion as the end in view, was a disastrous failure. The Tsar repudiated all association with the insurgents; the " Holy Alliance " saw in the rising a revolutionary rebellion against lawful albeit Moslem authority; the Western Powers were bound by the doctrine of non-intervention. So far the governments, though the Greeks had the entire sympathy of the peoples. Apart from the volunteers who were allowed to join them, and rendered them valuable service, they had to fight for their own hand without direct interference from abroad.

The rising collapsed at once in the north; in the south and in the islands it followed a different course. Wholesale massacres were perpetrated on both sides; victory for either still seemed remote when Sultan Mahmud called in the aid of the Pasha of Egypt. The time had come when Canning in England saw his way to take joint action with Russia to stop the war. The Egyptian intervention was checkmated when the allied fleets sank the Egyptian fleet in the Bay of Navarino (1827).

But almost at that moment Canning died; the control of British policy passed into the hands of the Duke of Wellington, who would have nothing to say to intervention in any shape, but with the further effect that Russia was left with practically a free hand. And the result of this again was the Treaty of Adrianople in 1829, which established Greece as an autonomous State, though it embraced only the continental territory south of Thessaly and Epirus, together with the Aegean islands called the Cyclades. In 1832 the pressure of the Powers procured the complete independence of the new kingdom of the Hellenes, with the Bavarian

GREECE, SHOWING THE BOUNDARIES OF 1913 AND 1920

Prince Otto as its monarch. The Greeks had fought valiantly, but their most successful leaders were men who had learnt the art of war mainly in the school of piracy and brigandage; law and order as understood in the West or in the three European empires were unknown to them. The government now presented to them was that of an alien bureaucracy quite incapable of understanding the people over whom it had to rule. King Otto's Bavarian counsellors at the outset, and King Otto himself when he took the government into his own hands (he was seventeen when he ascended the throne, and his rule began as a regency), failed completely to discharge the functions of government.

First Attempts at Constitutional Government

At the end of ten years of mismanagement Otto was forced by popular insurrection to grant a constitution, providing for what was intended to be parliamentary government on a democratic franchise. But even then the parliament never got to business. Innumerable parties only combined to turn out successive ministries which achieved nothing. Under the Ottoman regime the Greeks had possessed the germs of local self-government, out of which a democratic central government might have been carefully developed; but they were given instead the correct forms of Western democracy without having had the training to give them practical effectiveness. Real direction and government still remained in abeyance.

Friction, Faction, and Restless Ambition

Moreover, Greece remained dissatisfied, because the delimitation of her kingdom was wholly artificial. A line drawn between Turkey and Greece, from the Gulf of Arta to the Gulf of Volo, meant nothing. Traditionally, at least, Thessaly and Epirus and Macedon, too, were Hellenic. The whole Aegean was Hellenic, but only the Cyclades were in the Hellenic kingdom. The Ionian islands on the west had been a British protectorate since 1815. No one could deny that aspirations extending over Thessaly and Epirus were from a nationalist point of view legitimate, but there was no promise that they would be satisfied. When the Greeks tried to take advantage of the embroilments of the Crimean War, they were firmly and unanimously repressed by the Powers.

The Bavarian monarchy came to an ignominious end in 1862. In effect Otto was turned out, and removed himself and his belongings to less agitating surroundings; and after the Greeks had made various abortive offers of the vacant throne, it was accepted, with the approval of the Powers and under treaty, by young Prince William George of Denmark, who reigned for fifty years as King George, and brought with him the Ionian Islands as a coronation gift from Britain.

A new constitution, with a single democratically elected assembly to which ministers were theoretically responsible, still failed to teach the Greeks that their business was to organize and develop the resources of the kingdom and, till that was done, to restrain their territorial ambitions, however legitimate. Their restlessness kept out of the country the foreign capital of which it was in dire need, and arrested its economic progress. They got the Plain of Thessaly, however, out of the great Balkan imbroglio which culminated in the Berlin Treaty. Under the precarious ascendancy of a statesman, Tricoupis, real progress was made in the years between 1882 and 1895, but even then a rival politician, Delyannis, succeeded at intervals in spoiling what Tricoupis had half accomplished but was never allowed to complete.

Balkan Imbroglios and the Great War

Of the Hellenic lands which lay outside the kingdom, none was more eager for incorporation than the island of Crete. In 1897 the islanders rose against the Turkish domination under which they still lay, and declared their union with Greece. The Greeks went to their help; the Powers intervened, suppressed the fighting, turned the Greeks out, and took the island under European protection. The Greek Chauvinists declared war on Turkey, were soundly beaten, and paid the penalty in a rectification of the Thessalian frontier much to Turkey's advantage. The one point gained, if it was a gain, was the appointment by the Powers of George, the younger of the Greek princes, as High Commissioner of Crete. In 1905 the islanders again proclaimed the Union, but again failed to achieve their purpose—this time without any attempt at Greek intervention. Prince George resigned. But their failure transferred to Greece their leader Venizelos; at last she had a statesman to guide her—if she would follow him.

In 1908 Austria annexed Bosnia, and Bulgaria proclaimed her independence. Again Greece would have sought expansion, but again she was snubbed by the Powers. It was at this point that Venizelos was taken into the counsels of King George, with most beneficial effect; not least because the new minister saw that in a league of the Balkan States, and an agreed adjustment of their various claims, lay the best hope for all of them. Broadly speaking, the liberation of Macedonia, with its mixed population and its partition, offered the crucial problem. In 1912 the Balkan League had come into being, the treaties being secret. The League meant to act for itself with or without the approval of the Powers. In October, the Balkan War broke out.

The League was decisively successful in its military and naval operations, the latter being the care of the Greeks. But while they had comparatively little to do with the land-fighting, it was the Greek troops which occupied Salonica, the Aegean port which was the common object of desire for all three, Greece, Serbia, and Bulgaria—for Serbia partly because the Powers explicitly refused her access to the Adriatic. The Powers once more intervened to adjust the fruits of a victory much more complete than had been anticipated. The adjustment was viewed with extreme dissatisfaction by all the Balkan States, and most of all by Bulgaria.

While Greece and Serbia arrived at an accord, the League was broken up by Bulgaria's attempt to take from the others by force of arms the conquests to which she considered herself entitled. In the second Balkan War of 1913, which ensued, she was beaten. She had not deserved and did not meet with generous treatment from her former allies, though Venizelos would have conceded more than Greek popular opinion permitted. Greece retained her Macedonian ports. But the treaty of Bukarest left Bulgaria angry, embittered, and intensely dissatisfied. The Serbo-Greek alliance remained.

King George had already in the same year been succeeded by King Constantine, who had won a wide popularity through the recent successes of the Greek forces. The influence of Venizelos waned. When the Great War broke out he failed to carry with him the king, whose wife was a Hohenzollern. When Bulgaria fell upon the flank of hard-pressed Serbia, Constantine repudiated the treaty obligations and deserted his ally; but he was constrained to admit the troops of the Entente to Salonica at the same time that he dismissed Venizelos.

Greek opinion was violently divided, but the ultimate recovery of the Venizelists enabled Greece to claim at the end of the war the rewards that would have been hers had she taken the side of the Entente wholeheartedly from the beginning. She was awarded all that any but the ultra-Hellenists had ever dreamed of claiming for her, including Thrace and Smyrna in Asia Minor. But her desertion of Venizelos and the recall of King Constantine plunged her into more ambitious schemes, which developed into a Turkish war, of which the disastrous result was that by the autumn of 1922 the Greeks had been swept altogether out of Asia Minor, and were compelled to evacuate Eastern Thrace.

King Constantine abdicated for a second time in September, 1922, in favour of his son George, who assumed the title of George II. In November, Gounaris, a former prime minister, together with four other ex-ministers and General Hadjianestis, were found guilty of treason by a revolutionary court-martial and shot. A conference met at Lausanne, in December, to settle the boundary between Turkey and Greece, and to decide other questions which arose out of the Greek débâcle in Asia Minor.

GREECE : FACTS AND FIGURES

The Country
Lies south of the Balkan Peninsula, with a long coast line to the Aegean and Ionian Seas, and includes a large number of islands, among them Crete. Before the Great War the area totalled 41,933 square miles, and the population estimated at nearly 5,000,000.

Government and Constitution
Limited monarchy, with legislative chamber or Boulé, of 184 representatives, elected for four years by manhood suffrage, and, since 1911, a Council of State. The Constitution of 1864, vesting legislative power in the Chamber, was modified by re-establishment of a Council of State in 1911.

Defence
Military service compulsory and universal from the age of twenty, and lasts for thirty-one years, the normal period of active service being three years for cavalry, and two years for infantry, with twenty-one years in the first and eight years in the second series of the reserve. The navy is in progress of reorganization.

Commerce and Industries
Agriculture is the chief industry, and land is largely in the hands of peasant proprietors. Principal crops are wheat, maize, barley, vines, currants, oats, tobacco, cotton. Olives, nuts, figs, oranges, lemons, and rice are also grown. Leading industrial products include olive-oil, wine, textiles, leather, soap, and cotton. Great variety of mineral deposits. Total imports in 1921, £66,944,776; exports, £32,679,647. There is a mercantile marine of nearly 2,000 sailing vessels. About 1,470 miles of railway, 10,560 miles of telegraph lines, and 7,740 miles of telephone lines. A canal of about four miles runs across the Isthmus of Corinth.

Religion and Education
State religion that of the Greek Orthodox Church, but liberty is granted to all other sects. Education compulsory between ages of six and twelve years; cost borne by State About 6,800 primary schools, 76 high schools, 425 middle schools, 2 agricultural schools, a trade and industrial academy, government commercial schools, and two universities, the National and the Capodistria. The ministry of education is charged with the service of antiquities.

Chief Towns
Athens (capital—population 300,700), Salonica (170,190), Piraeus (133,480), Patras (52,130), Volo (30,060), Corfu (27,080), Candia (24,690), Canea (23,930), Kavala (22,960), Larissa (20,700), Kalamata (20,590).

GENIAL INHABITANTS OF THE COBAN DISTRICT OF GUATEMALA
Hospitality and good nature have long been outstanding features of the Coban Indians; and the writings of Las Casas, the Spanish " Protector of the Indians," bear witness not only to the good order of the native government in those early days, but also to the fact that the people were " more religious by nature and less given to abominable sacrifices than any other people in the whole of the Indies "

Photo, Brown Bros.

Guatemala

I. Indians & Half-Castes of Central America

By F. H. Hamilton

Writer and Traveller

THE peoples of Central America, that narrow neck of land which lies between Mexico and South America, washed by the Pacific and Atlantic both, are commonly held to be less advanced in civilization than the other Spanish-Indian races. Nor is that common belief unjustified. "La gente mas bruto del mundo español," was how a Spanish critic described them to the writer, and the odd thing is that it is these peoples who have succeeded to two of the most advanced civilizations of the western hemisphere—those of the Aztecs and the Mayas.

In each of the five Central American Republics — Guatemala, Nicaragua, Costa Rica, Honduras, and Salvador— there is a very large proportion of Indians and half-breeds among the inhabitants, while in some there are a great many negroes. The number of " white " people is almost negligible. There is no really enlightened or organized public opinion.

That revolutions have been fewer in number of late is due to the refusal of Europe and the United States to find any more money either for loans to, or for enterprises in, the Spanish-American countries as long as they were so continually disturbed. The politicians now find they can do better by maintaining law and order.

President Barrío's Statesmanlike Vision

It would be unfair, however, to deny that some among them are ambitious for the Republics as well as for themselves. In Guatemala, for example, an effort has been made to convince the people of the value and dignity of education. Every year in October the Festival of Minerva is celebrated. All schools take part in this; the parents of the boys and girls are invited also.

It was President Justo Rufino Barríos who gave his country the impetus towards education of which this festival is a lonely relic. He was a man of Indian origin, a native of the same valley on the border between Mexico and Guatemala as that in which Porfirio Diaz, the great Mexican President, was born. Himself uneducated until he had reached almost to man's estate, Barríos saw that the beginning of progress for the Republic must be the development of intelligence in the people. He established schools and made all parents whom he could reach send their children to be taught. He would not allow doctors to practise unless they were qualified. He came near to abolishing drunkenness, the curse of the natives, by wise regulation of the drink trade.

Land of Perpetual Summer

When he drove the monks and nuns out of the country and cut down the powers which the Church had exercised for so long, he made an effort to introduce some form of Protestantism. He first invited the Church of England to send missionaries among his people. This invitation was declined, on account of the " disturbed state of the country." Then President Barríos made the acquaintance in the United States of a Presbyterian minister and encouraged him to start a mission ; it never had much success. The law of Sunday rest, however, remained in force for a good while ; its effect has not altogether disappeared yet.

The staple crop, coffee, requires a climate neither tropical nor mountainous; while bananas, rubber, and mahogany, other exports which have been gaining in importance for a number of years past, flourish only in the hot and swampy coast regions. The climate of the

RISING GENERATION OF GUATEMALA

Children, dogs, chickens, and pigs form to a great extent the main "live stock" of every small Guatemalan village. The children are particularly sociable and cluster round the stranger, chattering and gesticulating like a flock of lively brown sparrows

news. One soon grows accustomed to this, however—so accustomed that one finds it difficult to drop the habit when one comes away !

Years ago someone said of Guatemala City that it was oppressed by the memory of the disasters that befell the two capitals which went before it and apprehensive that some day it might be overwhelmed also ; a catastrophe which came, sure enough, at Christmas, 1917, and laid a large part of the city in ruins, taking heavy toll of the hapless citizens. The first city built by the Spaniards in this neighbourhood was dedicated to "Saint James the Gentleman." Less than twenty years after it had been begun an appalling catastrophe wiped it out. For three days rain fell in torrents. On the fourth day there was a terrific wind, with thunder and lightning of alarming violence. In the night which followed the earth rocked so that it was impossible to stand. The terrified inhabitants rushed out of their houses, only to be swept away by a flood of water, carrying with it sand and ashes, which came from one of the two volcanoes close by. This was in consequence named Agua (water), and in order to escape a repetition of its evil activity, the rebuilding of the city was started three miles away.

In the course of nearly two and a half centuries Antigua Guatemala had become the chief centre of learning, wealth, religion, and the arts in the whole of Spanish America. Then its doom fell upon it. There was a convulsion below the surface of the earth ; instead of bursting into eruption the volcano

high plateau which lies between the two oceans is pleasant and healthy. The weather is for the most part like that of a fine European summer.

The educated Guatemalan has courteous and agreeable manners ; he is kindly and hospitable, and in appearance entirely European. His insistence upon shaking hands a great many times is at first apt to be rather disconcerting. He does this, not only at meeting and at parting, but also as an acknowledgment of polite inquiries after his health and that of his family, as congratulation if you say a good thing, as condolence in the event of your telling him bad

shuddered with awful violence; the earth quaked, and the second Guatemala City lay ruined. There the massive blocks of stone, the pillars and arches of its fifty churches, remain for visitors to marvel at; there can be seen the convents and monasteries attached to them, some with cells for as many as five hundred women or men. The surroundings are of delicious beauty, and the place is still inhabited. If one asked inhabitants whether they were not afraid to live so near the volcano, they replied: "Oh, no, señor, it has been blessed by a priest! There is no harm in it now." The writer has not had an opportunity of gathering their opinions on the efficacy of the blessing since the fatal Christmastide of 1917; but no doubt the matter of that earthquake has been satisfactorily explained to the intelligence of the Guatemaltecos.

The city is well worth a visit, if only for the sake of the journeys up to it from the Atlantic and down from it to the Pacific on the principal railway of the Republic. Starting from Puerto Barríos, a new port which already does a brisk trade in fruit, timber, and rubber, the train climbs first through tropical forests and jungle, then among waving palms and orange groves, and so into a highland region of pines and firs. The capital is reached in twelve hours or so.

On the way down towards the Pacific the line runs through fields of sugar-cane; the traveller's eye is delighted by masses of magnolia bloom and every kind of cactus; and if he is lucky, he will see alligators sunning themselves on the river banks. At the stations Indians surround the carriage windows, offering fruit, eggs, and sometimes cooked chickens at ridiculously small prices. Land which has been cleared and

SHADY CORNER FOR THE MARKETING OF INDIAN WARES

There are many "early birds" among the Indian population of Guatemala, who, with the dawn, make their appearance in the towns laden with marketable goods, and ply their trade in pottery, fresh fruits, vegetables, and sweetmeats. Bargaining is a recognized feature of each sale, and as there are no fixed prices, goods may often be secured for less than half the figure demanded

STRICKEN CITY OF GUATEMALA DURING A VOLCANIC VISITATION

The third City of Guatemala grew up on a site held to be immune from earthquakes, and in splendour and size far exceeded the former capitals. The Church of the Recollección, seen above, was partially ruined in December, 1917, but the final and most terrific shock of Jan. 3, 1918, completed the work of destruction, and the twin towers and the massive pediment between crumbled into a heap of debris

Photo, American Field Museum of Chicago

RUINS IN ANTIGUA GUATEMALA THAT ATTEST ITS FORMER SPLENDOUR

Three times, and each time in a different location, has the capital of Guatemala been devastated by earthquakes. The second city flourished for more than two hundred years, but was completely ruined by the earthquake shocks of 1773. Many of the survivors refused to leave their shattered homes, and under the name of Antigua Guatemala the place has been inhabited down to the present time

Photo, Percy F. Martin

MULE TRAIN TOILING OVER THE RUGGED GUATEMALAN HILLSIDES

Sound animals are scarce and expensive in Guatemala, but the mule, no matter what his condition, is invaluable as the pack-animal of the traveller, for this wise beast can scramble up the rough hillsides, or slide down the perilously steep and slippery mountain-paths with remarkable surefooted-ness. In the rear of the long mule trains are the muleteers, or arrieros, their loud, harsh voices awakening echoes in the silent valleys

planted with cacao, used for making chocolate and cocoa, may be noticed here and there ; this is a new industry, and one which promises excellent results.

For a long time the cochineal insect was a source of wealth to Guatemala. This feeds on the nopal cacti, and when the leaves have been dried the tiny creatures can be scraped off. They are then either baked or boiled, to make either blue or red dye ; but aniline dyes soon supplanted all others, and now cochineal dyes are used only by the Indians. The fibre sashes which the women wear on their tight skirts of cotton are of a brilliant scarlet ; their blouses, their only upper garment, worn next to the skin, are embroidered with crimson and purple thread. They make their whole costume themselves, unless they live near a town. Even their sandals are of home manufacture.

Very pretty and graceful the young women look, with their hair in braids and their lissom figures, and their dark faces lit up by modest, friendly smiles.

Beauty in girls is highly prized, whether they are white or half-white or Indian. Photographers thrive not only upon vanity but upon the sale of their portraits of good-looking women. The Spanish women spoil their faces by the amount of thick powder and other "aids to beauty" which they plaster on to them. Americans

LUSCIOUS FRUITS FOR THE HOT AND THIRSTY

In Guatemala there is a continual movement of vegetable and fruit carriers to and fro between the villages and towns. The produce of the former are brought, mainly by Indians, to the markets in light wooden crates called "cacastes." These are either borne by hand or pannier-wise on the patient backs of donkeys or mules, and a lively trade is done

WHERE MUSCULAR STRENGTH IS TESTED

Vegetables, fruits, and other village produce are chiefly borne to the townsfolk on the sturdy backs of the Indian carriers, the weight of the often heavy load being distributed by a broad band passed round their foreheads

baby tied round her hips and a heavy load on her head stepping out briskly and feeling no fatigue at all. The men carry their loads on the back in a basket, with a band round their foreheads to distribute the weight. They are so used to a burden that often when they return home with empty baskets they will put stones in to make them feel properly balanced. All that they wear as a rule is a pair of scanty trousers, more like short drawers. The nearest that President Barríos ever came to provoking a revolution was when he issued orders that everyone should wear what he considered to be "proper clothes."

In general, the Indians, who make up more than half of the two million population, are an honest, hard-working, orderly folk, contented with very little in the way of food and household possessions. Their looks are melancholy; they do not seem to have forgotten the hideous cruelties of the Spaniards in the sixteenth century. Yet they are fond of excitement and love noise. They celebrate the festivals of the Roman Catholic Church with enthusiasm, and always end up with a display of fireworks.

make a joke of it, saying that if you kiss one you risk lead poisoning. A Swiss lady who kept a school for the girls of the " best families " in Guatemala City tried hard to break her pupils of this disfiguring habit. No boarders were allowed to have any " make-up " in their possession, and the principal used to wait outside in the morning with a basin of water, a sponge, and a towel to clean up the girls who came by the day.

The Indians are surprisingly strong, women as well as men. They can keep up a pace of six miles an hour, and it is common enough to see a mother with a

The study of the native races of Guatemala is in part the study of Mexico and Yucatan, as the chief aboriginal tribes and the national cultures were common to the territories named. But the subject is a complicated and a highly-specialised one when we range beyond the three main nations of the Aztecs, the Toltecs, and the Mayas, the last-named being in many respects the

GUATEMALAN WOMAN WITH AVOCADOS OR ALLIGATOR PEARS

Although the upper classes of Guatemala come within the influence of foreign fashions, the humbler folk remain true to their native dress, which, as far as the women are concerned, is often very attractive with its bright colours and embroidery on blouse or vest. The country abounds in tropical fruits and flowers, many specimens of the former being unknown in the more northerly countries of America

CHICLE-GUM COLLECTORS CAMPED IN THE TROPICAL FOREST OF GUATEMALA

An increasingly important source of revenue to Guatemala is the gum resin of the naseberry tree, achras sapota, from which the chicle- or chewing-gum, so popular in the United States, is mostly made. The tree, somewhat similar to the indiarubber tree, exudes a milky sap during the rainy season, and this is collected by workers known as chicle-bleeders, who live in camps in the bush, oxidised, melted in a crude oven, and made up into bales for export. The chicle camps, erected

most interesting for their curious resemblances to the ancient Egyptians in certain of their customs. There are numerous tribal differences among the Guatemalans of to-day, and although the whole of the Indians may be regarded as in a state of degeneracy contrasted with that of their ancient vigour and achievement, it is possible to trace among them some of the outstanding characteristics of the powerful tribes of the past, such as the Quichés and the Cachiquels, the two dominant native races at the time of Alvarado's conquest of the country.

Since the Spanish conquest there has been no very noticeable fusion among the aborigines, although each of the great native cultures has completely passed away, the natives of to-day being, on the whole, a spiritless people who provoke no great curiosity as to their origins, while the intermingling of Spanish, Indian, and negro blood has produced a great variety of types, to each of which a distinguishing name is given.

Illuminating Glimpses of the Indians

While much has been written about the ancient cultures of Mexico and Yucatan, little attention has been given to the Guatemalan, possibly because of its close relationship to these others. Indeed, the life of Guatemala has exercised the attention of very few investigators ; but there is the notable exception of the work by Mrs. and Mr. A. P. Maudslay, entitled " A Glimpse at Guatemala," in which these able archæologists give a most interesting record of their experiences in the country, and offer what is probably the best study of its past history and present-day life that has appeared in the English language. Although their expedition was archæological in its purpose, both Mr. and Mrs. Maudslay had an observant eye for the life of the people, and their admirable work records many lively incidents. From Mrs. Maudslay's description of Santo Tomas we take the following vivid picture of a scene which will serve to show how the Indians still contrive to retain some of their ancient superstitions even though they are nominally within the pale of the Roman Catholic Church.

" Santo Tomas boasts of no inn, but we found something to eat at a dirty little house, where we were attended to by an old crone, who spoke no language intelligible to us. After breakfast we strolled into the picturesque plaza, bright with the gala costumes of the Indians. The women wore heavy chains of beads and coins round their necks, and were clothed in the most elaborately embroidered huipils we had as yet seen. Almost every man carried a blue or brown-striped rug on his shoulder, and some queerly-dressed old men wandered amongst the crowd, with distaff in hand, spinning woollen thread.

Native Indifference to Indian Customs

" A grand fiesta was in progress in the church—probably a preparation for ' Candelaria,' which falls on February 2 —to which, as usual, the Ladinos appeared to be supremely indifferent ; indeed, they never seem to trouble themselves about the customs of the race so nearly allied to them, and look down on the Indians as inferiors, only fit to be human beasts of burden. It is useless to ask them what an Indian ceremony may mean ; the only answer one gets is, ' No se, señora, es costumbre de los Indios.' Even Gorgonio, whom I delight to look upon as an exception to the rule, on this occasion showed no desire to enlighten my curiosity, so we mounted the steps and entered the great bare church to learn as much as we could for ourselves.

Praying Round a Cross of Flowers

" At the top of the stone steps in front of the open church-door a large pile of wood-ashes smouldered and flickered faintly in the sunlight ; the man who tended this fire every now and then threw on the embers small pieces of copal, which scented the air with its heavy perfumed smoke, while around the fire groups of women knelt to pray before entering the building. We found the interior to be charmingly decorated with flowers. The floor had first been strewn with fragrant pine-needles, and

GUATEMALA INDIAN VILLAGERS PLACIDLY CONTENT IN THEIR THATCHED HUTS AND LINHAYS

An Indian village is a harmony in brown; the small, square, brown houses with brown thatch, nestle comfortably on dull brown earth-banks, or are poised securely on hard brown rocks; the striped huipils, or cotton blouses, of the women, and the coloured handkerchiefs bound round the heads of the men standing out in pleasing relief against this tawny background. The houses are usually built of rough stones, held together by a framework of sticks, and thatched with grass

on this carpet the flowers were arranged in the shape of a huge cross, extending almost the whole length of the church. In some parts the lines were traced in green and coloured leaves, and filled up with scattered rose-petals ; in others with clusters of all the flowers that could be found in bloom, edged with little groups of lighted candles. Picturesquely dressed Indians, singly or in couples, were dragging themselves on their knees the whole length of the cross, stopping at intervals to repeat prayers. No priest officiated, and none but Indians were in the least interested in the service, if such it could be called.

" As we were leaving the church we stopped to watch a funeral procession coming across the plaza. The men ascended the church steps, carrying the ugly black catafalque on their shoulders, but to our surprise, instead of entering the church with their burden they turned the catafalque round three times in front of the fire where the copal was burning, fired off a rocket, and then went away again. While this ceremony was being rapidly performed the friends and relations of the dead man stood some distance away in the plaza crying and weeping loudly."

Universal Use of Rockets

To Mrs. Maudslay we are also indebted for a note on another Guatemalan characteristic which is probably more marked in the Spanish countries of Central America than in the Southern continent. " To anyone not already used to the ways of the Spanish peasantry one of the first things that strikes one as curious in Central America is this constant firing of rockets in the daytime. No ceremony is complete until the swish and report of a rocket have been heard. The pilgrim when he reaches his native village fires a rocket to announce his arrival. It is the expression of joy at a fiesta, and it is the last rite necessary for the repose of the dead."

Another glimpse of the queer customs obtaining in some of the Indian towns is given in Mrs. Maudslay's account of a visit to San Antonio on the shores of Lake Atitlán. " After arranging our camp-beds," she writes, " and ordering our supper from the estar co, we stroll d about the town to see the sights. While we were enjoying the lovely view and watching the changing lights upon the water, a procession of Indians, clad in their black, sack-like garments, came towards us. It was headed by the alcalde with his staff of office, who was followed by his alguacils and mayores, each carrying a long white stick.

Crying the Orders for the Week

" They stopped at house after house, apparently giving some directions to the inmates, and as they passed us the alcalde civilly wished us ' buenas noches ' ; then a little farther on they halted, and an alguacil, clambering up a wall, stood on the top, and in a loud, clear voice, which seemed to travel up the hillsides, called out the instructions for the work to be put in hand on the morrow, and repeated the municipal orders for the week. After a moment's pause he was answered by a voice far away in the distance, then by another in an opposite quarter of the town, and when all was quiet again the Indians ceremoniously bade one another good-night, and the procession dispersed. This, we learnt, is the usual custom on a Sunday night, and in the stillness of the fading daylight it was a curious and impressive ceremony."

Yet another impression of Indian life from the same graphic pen touches the religious observances of the Indians, and it may be allowed to stand without comment as an example of their " progress " from the medieval ages in which they lived their own national and municipal life with a primitive religious and social system which had served them not inefficiently until the coming of the Spaniard :

When the Indian Pilgrims Come Home

" While we were at Panajachél, a matter of especial interest presented itself to us in the curious ceremonies of the Indian pilgrims returning from Esquipulas. Our room looked out on the plaza, which in the morning always afforded a few picturesque groups of

MYSTERY MONOLITH OF THE PRIMEVAL FORESTS OF QUIRIGUA

This remarkable carved obelisk was discovered among the ancient ruins of Quirigua, together with many other monuments of great architectural merit, the origin of which is still shrouded in mystery. The sides of the monoliths, which number over a dozen, are covered with hieroglyphs and picture-writings, a complete deciphering of which would solve many great problems of Maya civilization

Photo, Alfred P. Maudslay

DUSKY DESCENDANTS OF THE ANCIENT MAYA STOCK

The Indians of Guatemala comprise many interesting types, and their costumes and several of their customs vary considerably in the different villages. For the most part, they are a religious people and participate in their numerous Church festivals with whole-hearted devotion; the ritual and formality attending the functions of the Church of Rome having become almost a part of their daily life

market women, but was almost deserted by noon ; then, as evening approached, little companies of pilgrims, bending under their burdens, filed into the town, and as night fell the plaza was lit up by numerous small fires, around which the pilgrims gathered for their supper. This important meal ended, they began their religious functions by laying down petates (mats) in front of the cacastes which had already been arranged in a line across the plaza. Then each man produced from his cargo a small wooden box, usually glazed on one side, containing the image of a saint, and these were arranged in a row against the cacastes, between lighted candles, the place of honour in the middle being assigned to a box containing a figure of the Black Christ.

Evening Service in the Market Place

" When these arrangements were completed, the Indians, who were dressed in long black woollen garments, with long white veils fastened to their black straw hats, prostrated themselves in turn before each shrine, and crawled along from one to the other on hands and knees, laying the forehead in the dust, offering up their prayers to each saint, and kissing the box which contained its image. These acts of devotion were several times repeated, and then grouping themselves on their knees before the shrine of the Black Christ, and led by one of their number, who seemed to have some sort of authority over them, they all chanted the quaint hymn we had so often heard in the early watches of the morning. After singing for nearly half an hour they withdrew to their fires, rolled themselves in their blankets, and were soon fast asleep."

Spanish Destruction of Indian Civilization

In beautifying life and making it easier the Spaniards have taught the natives relatively little. Before the conquest the Central American Indians had worked up to a high pitch of civilization. Their arts and crafts were marked by taste as well as skill, showing some affinity with those of the Chinese to whom the original Guatemalans are in some degree related. They practised a religion based on the teaching of a sacred book, which gave an account of the Creation not unlike that which is contained in the first chapter of Genesis. All their beliefs, arts, industries were swept away by the invaders. If the story of what the Spaniards did had not been told by one of themselves, the Dominican monk, Las Casas, who did not share the current delusion that God had put the Indians there for the white men to torture and kill, it would be scarcely possible to persuade oneself that such barbarities could have been committed.

When Guatemala declared itself free and independent in 1821, it abolished slavery at once. For a time it seemed to be on the way to develop upon gradual democratic lines. The priests, however, soon stirred up trouble, as they did in Mexico, with which country Guatemala was for a short time united. In 1844 a Liberal president was driven from office by a savage, ignorant Indian, Rafael Carrera, who persuaded people that he was the Angel Raphael, and who ruled them for nearly a quarter of a century by cruel and despotic methods. Thus from the very start of independence the energy which should have been put into educating the nation and giving it sound institutions was spent on struggling for power by means of civil war.

German Influence in Guatemala

Up to the beginning of the twentieth century the United Kingdom did more trade with the Guatemalans than any other country. Since then the United States have taken first place, and until 1914 the Germans were ahead of the English by a good deal. Although the educated Guatemalan likes to be thought Parisian in his appearance and way of living, he admires German thoroughness and industry. The army was trained by German officers on German lines, and compulsory service was introduced after the German model, that is to say, service which is compulsory upon the poor, but from which the rich can manage to escape, in the last resort, by buying themselves off. The Guatemala coffee fincas were mostly owned by Germans before the Great War, and still remain largely in their hands.

Cultivation is easy and crops are abundant, if they are sensibly chosen. There is one enemy of the cultivator, though, which will have to be got under, that is the ant. In columns from three to four yards wide masses of ants travel through the country, destroying all that lies in their way. The only consolation the farmer has, after they have passed and left his season's work ruined, is that they destroy all other pests. At their approach cockroaches rush about in terror, seeking to hide from them. They exterminate centipedes and even scorpions.

Spiders show ingenuity in escaping the ants. There is one species which has eight rather long legs. It keeps its body above the ants by balancing, now on five legs, now on four, some-

MIXCAN BEAUTY AMID THE PALMS

This girl, with her loose-sleeved embroidered dress, hails from Mixco, a small town some eight miles from what was Guatemala city. Here the traveller finds steep paved streets with rough native houses climbing up the hill, and the inhabitants largely gained their living as bakers, washerwomen, and purveyors to the capital that perished in the earthquake of 1917-18

times on three, picking them up as the ants come near them, doing a kind of dance in which it can frequently find safety. Green-leaf locusts roll themselves up and let the ants pass over them as if they were really leaves.

To meet an ant-drive is an interesting incident of travel in Guatemala. There is magnificent scenery, too, to make the way pleasant, and the ruins of Antigua Guatemala are full of interest for the searcher into the glories of the past. But in general, travelling in Guatemala, except by rail, is not to be recommended for pleasure. The roads, excepting those round the capital, are all

bad. Mule coaches of ancient pattern are the vehicles used.

Considerable attention has been given to the railways of this part of Central America, and in 1912 the International Railway of that name was incorporated, representing a consolidation of the Guatemala Railway, 195 miles, the Occidental Railway, 51 miles, the Ocos Railway, 22 miles, and the Guatemala Central Railway, 139 miles. This company received subsidies from the Governments both of Salvador and Guatemala, and the latter may purchase the lines at a price to be decided by arbitration after the year 2002.

MERRY GROUP OF COFFEE-PICKERS DURING A PAUSE IN THEIR WORK

Coffee is one of Guatemala's leading products, and trees and bushes of this plant, that yields a fragrant drink for thousands all over the globe, are a decided feature of the landscape with their bright red berries. The crop is often gathered by Indians who may be seen at their work laughing and singing, as who would not in this pleasant clime? Above is a gathering of cheerful workers who were evidently quite agreeable to having their photographs taken. Some of the smaller members

Guatemala

II. Its Spanish Rulers & Later Dictators

By Percy F. Martin, F.R.G.S.

Author of " El Salvador," etc.

WITH a superficial area of 48,290 square miles Guatemala is among the most mountainous of the Central American States, its highest ranges reaching to 7,000 feet above sea-level. Among its bristling array of volcanoes, Fuégo (fire), with a disastrous record of eruptions, stands 12,577 feet, while the neighbouring crater, Agua (water), destroyed the earliest Spanish capital of Guatemala (1541), and contributed again in several subsequent eruptions (1863, 1874, and 1917) to demolish the capital.

The climate of Guatemala differs little from that of the neighbouring States, being almost fully tropical ; which is equivalent to saying that it is warm and generally healthy except on the coast, where it is malarial. There are, however, temperate and cool zones, while in the uplands snow occasionally falls. As its Indian name signifies—" a land covered with trees "— Guatemala is thickly wooded, possessing a rich flora and fauna. Much of the country's natural wealth exists in its as yet untouched forests, abounding in mahogany, estimated to cover an area of 1,300,000 acres. A belt of country extending from the coast-range of mountains on the western frontier, near the Pacific, across the Sierra Madre to the coast-range of the Caribbean slope, comprises a highly-mineralised territory which might, one day, yield valuable treasure in metals.

When, in 1522, Pedro de Alvarado, the Spanish adventurer and lieutenant of Hernando Cortés, at the age of twenty-seven, landed in Guatemala, he had already had some experience of dealing with the natives of Yucután (Mexico), whom he had massacred or cruelly enslaved. Thus he was quite ready to deal with the equally fierce and untractable Guatemalans, especially as he had been provided by his chief with an ample

force. Merciless severity finally subdued opposition, and Spanish administration, introduced with little further difficulty, was forcibly maintained for nearly three hundred years. In 1821 the general revolt of the Spanish dominions against the Crown, then worn by Ferdinand VII., freed Guatemala, among other Latin-American Crown Colonies, from its long-endured servitude.

What is now known as " Guatemala " forms but a very small part of the original colony bearing that name, which, under the Spanish dominion, stretched over nearly two-thirds of South America. Upon breaking loose from Spain, Guatemala formed one of the Central American countries, then joined in a Federal Union ; but this combination did not last very long. Breaking up in 1827 into independent Republics, Guatemala, like its neighbours, chose its own executive : the earliest proved members of a long line of tyrants or dictators—sometimes both— who succeeded in keeping the country in a state of continual war, both internecine and with its neighbours. The first constitution (1822) was discarded, being replaced by a second in 1845, and by a third in 1851, while amendments and alterations to the adopted enactment have since taken place at various periods (1885, 1887, and 1889).

The President whose rule endured the longest was Rafael Carrera. Elected in 1840, he succeeded in forcibly maintaining his position as life executive, or dictator, ruling until 1865, just a few years longer than Estrada Cabréra, of whom more later. The next significant administration was brought about by the triumph of the Liberal Party (which had played a very active rôle in Guatemalan political history) and the expulsion of the Jesuits from the country. Successive presidents, notably General Justo Rufino Barríos.

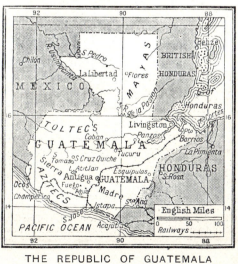

THE REPUBLIC OF GUATEMALA

followed in the same direction, the Church being disestablished during his period of office (1873-85), which ended only with his death on the battlefield.

A veritable stormy petrel, Barríos endeavoured unsuccessfully to bring about a combination of the five Central American States of which he was to be supreme head; and, in order to convert others to his way of thinking, he invaded Salvador but was compelled to defend his own frontiers against Nicaragua and Costa Rica. He was succeeded in 1886 by General Manuel Barillas, who established much-desired peace between the conflicting States. His successor, General José Maria Reina Barríos, elected in 1892 and again in 1897, was assassinated February 8, 1898, and Manuel Estrada Cabréra was elected (September 9) Acting-President.

Peaceful Penetration by Germany

At this time German influence commenced to make itself felt in Guatemala, as it had already done in Nicaragua and Salvador. A large number of agricultural and banking concessions fell into Teutonic hands, and prospered apace. A certain Herr Kilhauer was granted a concession to establish an agricultural bank which proved the forerunner of a number of other affiliated monetary and mortgage institutions. Some exist under different names to-day.

During the war in 1906 between Guatemala and Salvador, the troops of the former State were charged with crimes similar to those alleged by the Allies against certain German and Austrian officers during the Great War—that is with having killed their Honduran prisoners as soon as they were captured. All the Central American States subscribed—as did Germany—to the Hague Convention of 1899, so that this barbarous act created intense hostility and evoked speedy reprisals. Later on in the same year (July 20), the three States of Honduras, Guatemala, and Salvador signed the six articles of what is known as the " Marblehead " Pact (arranged on board the United States warship of that name).

Successive Plots and Counter Plots

Fresh internal discontent then commenced to assert itself ; the stern rule of Provisional-President Estrada Cabréra created a number of enemies among the landed classes, and the flight of a number of influential political opponents to the safe refuge afforded in the United States and Mexico enabled them to maintain a vigorous crusade against the authority of the Executive. Plots were hatched and guided by prominent Guatemalans such as Dr. France, General M. S. Barillas,

Emilio de León, J. Ramón Calena, etc., and the Cabréra régime found itself assailed in many different directions.

In August, 1907, there was a serious attempt to assassinate the President by means of a mine, laid in the street (no more than 120 feet from the American Legation) along which the chief magistrate was accustomed to take his morning drive. Although Cabréra escaped, his Chief-of-Army, General Orellana, was wounded. Nineteen persons supposed to have been concerned in the plot, including members of some of the best families, were executed, notwithstanding strong personal appeals made to the President for clemency by the British Minister, Sir Lionel Carden, and other foreign diplomats.

A few months before, General Barillas, while in Mexico City, had been assassinated. Of this crime President Estrada Cabréra was declared to have been the instigator, just as, later on, he was suspected of having been the cause of the assassination of Manuel Enrique Araujo, President of Salvador (April, 1913), while two other Guatemalans, General José María Lima and Colonel Orofie Bone, were publicly accused of carrying out the deed. As a consequence, diplomatic relations between Mexico and Guatemala were severed, the usual petty indignities to each other's flags being perpetrated. An even greater danger threatened the poorer classes of the people, by reason of a serious famine, which the poverty of the Government could do little to alleviate. At the end of 1908, virulent smallpox also broke out, and soon assumed alarming proportions, the death-rate proving exceptionally heavy.

International Relations and Finance

The frequent quarrels between Guatemala, Honduras, Salvador, and Nicaragua again came to a head that year (1908), when the Central American Peace Court, sitting at Cartágo, Costa Rica, was established for the purpose of settling those and other disputes. The court was afterwards made permanent, the late Andrew Carnegie having contributed a sum of $100,000 (£20,000) towards the provision of a suitable building, which, however, was subsequently destroyed by an earthquake.

In February, 1910, the boundary convention concluded between Guatemala and Honduras (March 1, 1895) was extended for a further period of two years, while on December 8, 1911, it was again prolonged until March 1, 1914.

Elected full Constitutional President for the first time, March, 1911, Estrada Cabréra (who in previous years had himself been an active revolutionary, working from New Orleans), in violation of the constitutional law, retained after his term had expired the executive chair year after year by organizing his own re-election. He ruled until March, 1920, when he was forcibly deposed, imprisoned, and succeeded, as Provisional President, by Carlos Herrera.

Notwithstanding the virtual reign of terror that had endured during Cabréra's long and oppressive rule, he undoubtedly effected much for the cause of education, up till then greatly neglected; he increased the number of schools in one year by 250, and their complement of pupils by 7,020.

In the summer of 1911 an attempt was made by an American financial coterie, known as the "American Mining and Development Syndicate" (headed by Mr. A. E. Spriggs), to obtain control of the entire economic resources of the Republic. This effort, encouraged by the Executive and a complacent Congress, would no doubt have succeeded but for the energetic protests of other countries, particularly the United States, whose Government strongly disapproved of the project, which inter alia comprised exclusive rights to all the waterways, railways, telegraphs, and telephones in Guatemala in return for the " promise " of ten per cent. of the profits earned.

In 1912 the British Government, after exemplary patience, decided to compel Guatemala to settle her long-standing indebtedness; thanks to the devoted services and unfailing tact of Sir Lionel E. G. Carden (H.B.M. Minister to Guatemala and other Central American States), an agreement was brought about, but nothing was actually paid. Guatemala's foreign indebtedness at this time (default had existed for over thirteen years) amounted to £1,482,800, without arrears of unpaid interest.

In May, 1913, therefore, the British cruiser Aeolus was sent to Puerto Barríos (Guatemala) to support the British Minister in his efforts to obtain a definite preliminary payment upon the Guatemalan Four per Cent. External Debt. In the month of June a satisfactory agreement was entered into, and the first actual payment was made, while subsequent remittances from time to time have been unfailingly received, sometimes before actually due. To-day, with accumulated interest, and allowing for the amount that has since been redeemed, the debt stands at £1,940,643.

Towards the end of December, 1917, Guatemala City was visited by a series of earthquake shocks which, continuing throughout January, 1918, caused a large number of deaths and serious damage to property, over 125,000 people being rendered homeless.

After the deposition, April 14, 1920, of President Cabréra, new elections took place (August), when Carlos Herrera, Provisional President of the Republic, was confirmed in the Executive Chair by a large majority of votes to serve for the customary term of four years. But in March, 1922, he was succeeded by General José María Orellana.

Guatemala, Salvador, and Honduras agreed, on September 15, 1921, to form a Central American Federation. By its constitution, Tegucigalpa was to be the capital, there were to be two legislative chambers, and the Federal Council was to be inaugurated on February 1, 1922. But Guatemala and Salvador withdrew.

GUATEMALA : FACTS AND FIGURES

The Country

In Central America, Guatemala lies south and east of Mexico, and is bounded south by the Pacific, east by British Honduras, the Gulf of Honduras, Salvador, and Honduras. Area about 48,290 square miles. Population estimated at 2,003,580, about 60 per cent. pure Indians.

Government and Constitution

Republic under constitution of 1879, modified 1885, 1887, 1889, 1903, by which legislative power is vested in National Assembly and Council of State. Members of the Assembly, one for every 20,000 inhabitants, are elected for four years under universal suffrage. Council of State consists of thirteen members elected by the Assembly or appointed by the President. President is elected for six years.

Defence

Military service compulsory between the ages of eighteen and fifty. Army when mobilised numbers about 85,500 officers and men ; reserve, 40,500.

Commerce and Industries

Soil fertile. Chief crops are coffee and sugar. Rice, maize, bananas, beans, wheat, and potatoes also grown. Important trade in mahogany, dyewoods, and gum ; cattle breeding extensive ; mining little developed. Total imports (cotton, foodstuffs, linen, hemp, jute, paper, corn, steel, leather) in 1920, £2,908,940 ; exports (coffee, rubber, timber, hides, bananas, sugar), £3,720,581.

Few good roads ; railways about 400 miles ; 4,500 miles of telegraph lines, and 416 miles of telephone lines. Metric system in force. Currency of paper, nickel, and copper ; the dollar or peso of 100 centavos of nominal value of 4s.

Religion and Education

Education free and compulsory between the ages of six and fourteen. Government schools in 1920 numbered 1,334. University of Guatemala opened 1918. There are schools for arts and handicrafts and a national Conservatoire of music. Roman Catholicism prevalent, but there is complete religious toleration.

Chief Towns

Guatemala (capital—population before earthquake, December 1917—January 1918, 90,000), Quezaltenango (28,940), Coban (30,770), Totonicapam (28,300).

ADVERTISEMENT AND DISPLAY ON THE HARBOUR FRONT AT PORT AU PRINCE

Utensils of every shape, sort, and size are here for sale grouped in crowded plenty round the dusky saleswoman. The cluster of capacious urns in the background have an air of amplitude in their their well-rounded outlines, and were designed to hold generous quantities. The construction of all this motley assemblage of household wares is simple and utilitarian, though it will be noticed that such ornamentation as has been attempted is varied in its execution. Shaded by her large-brimmed hat, this Haitian woman hopes to attract the undecided customer as well by her welcoming smile as by the soundness of her goods

Haiti

I. Life in the First of the Negro Republics

By H. Hesketh Prichard

Author of " Where Black Rules White "

SINCE the American occupation there have been many changes in Haiti, but the character of the people remains the same.

Haitian life is grafted upon French life, and one of the aims of every real Haitian is to visit Paris. There can be no doubt, even while criticising in the friendliest spirit, that the Haitian negro is too French—he is apt to overdo it. This refers, of course, to the town-dweller. In the country districts the peasants are altogether superior and, besides, there are among them no professional or moneyed classes, such as lawyers and politicians ; all work for their living, and gain it from the soil itself.

To say that the Haitian is greatly attached to his independence would be true, yet in all but name this independence is a thing of the past. There is always, and always has been, in Haiti a certain amount of rebellion, and since the American occupation certain individuals calling themselves " cacos " have taken to the hills and set authority at defiance. They have not been very successful and, according to the author of " Roving Through the West Indies," six thousand cacos have been got rid of, whereas the American casualties have numbered four. It is said that cacoism is now dying out, as, indeed, it must die out.

Honesty Bred by Responsibility

If we consider the character of the Haitian, we find the most curious inconsistencies. Let us take the case of the Government courier. He is simply a negro employed in some minor Government work, such as sweeping out the Post Office or carrying sacks of coffee to the Custom House. From time to time it is necessary, or was a few years ago, to send large sums of money by the lonely forest track which lies between Jacmel and Port au Prince. This money was confided to the care of the courier, the small Government servant to whom I have referred. In private life this man may have had the most elementary ideas of honesty, but the moment the courier felt his responsibility he became a new man, and it is a fact that in all the years in which that lonely mountain road was used not once was there a theft by a courier of the money entrusted to him. This throws a peculiar and gracious light upon the Haitian character.

Autocratic General Officers

Again, let us consider the peasant of the interior of Haiti. Quite different from the town-dweller, the vociferous wharfside negro, this peasant is a man entirely reliable. In wandering through the interior of the country I have stopped at various villages, and have had to ask for shelter for the night. Never once would my hosts, however poor they might be, allow me to pay for my entertainment. On departing it was usual to make some present, but it had to be given as from man to man, and was considered in no way as a substitute for payment for the night's lodging.

Of course, in considering these rural districts one must realize that people living there dwelt in the ever-present shadow of punishment of the most violent kind. I remember once entering a village where there was a newly filled grave. A man had been shot that afternoon by the orders of the General de la Place et de la Commune. A cow had been stolen, and suspicion fell upon this unfortunate individual. Whether or not he was guilty I do not know—there seemed to be considerable doubt upon the point—but he had been shot, and an example made. One of the natives told me that for many months there would be no fear of stealing in that village.

The general of a village possessed, when I travelled in Haiti, the absolute right of life and death, although he was nominally subject to the President and Council in Port au Prince. Certainly, in any consideration of Haitian life one must not overlook these high-handed rural generals who for years have had so tremendous an influence upon the character of their countrymen. From

them sprang several Presidents. There was Johannis Merisier, a coal-black negro ruling in the Jacmel district, who afterwards made a bold and successful bid for power. This man could neither read nor write, but he succeeded in carrying on his business very well, for what one man wrote he called another man to read, and woe betide the writer who tried to play him a trick !

As to the personal life and character of these autocrats, they were much mixed up in politics, and most of them were polygamists, having two or three and sometimes more wives. They received

HAITIAN FOLK WHO FOSTER PRIMITIVE TENDENCIES

Of the total population of Haiti, the first of the negro republics, about ninety per cent. is black ; the remainder consists chiefly of mulattoes, descendants of the former French settlers, and Europeans. If all accounts be true, the peasantry of the rural districts—despite more than a century of self-government—seem to show a deteriorating tendency, even to the point of savagery

very little pay, and that very irregularly. I believe £140 was the full pay of a general of division and honorary aide-de-camp to the President. This they never received, but their hands were heavy upon the people over whom they ruled, and the various villagers were put to work for them. Still, with all their faults, it was they and the people who groaned under their tyranny who made up the real character of rural Haiti.

In the towns things, as I have said, were different, for while the rural general was a man possessing real power, and was usually the only general in his district, each town possessed perhaps a couple of hundred generals, only a few of whom had any power at all. The rest possessed the rank and nothing more. It appears from an old consular report that at one time there were 6,500 generals in Haiti, 7,000 regimental officers, and 6,500 privates. This state of things is very typical of the country. The rank of general has been spread broadcast by the various Presidents. It is given as a reward for services rendered to the State; in fact, it is perfectly true to say that no Haitian who has not attained the rank of general has even begun to prosper in the Black Republic.

This is one of the strongest characteristics of the Haitian race. They love display, they love uniforms, they love gold lace. The Haitian politician, though often a general, is not invariably so. He may be a lawyer, but he is one of the few persons who dress their parts as politicians. Even in that torrid atmosphere he wears an enamelled straw hat, a frock coat, and black trousers, and his life is one very full of adventure.

A politician in Haiti in the days before the American occupation might go to bed a minister and wake up to find that bed surrounded by a number of troops, himself borne off to the dreadful prison, where he might spend the next year or two manacled to a wall, still in his incongruous garb of straw

RIVERSIDE LAUNDRY IN HAITI
The difficulties and discomforts of her task, the uncongenial stones on which she squats, and the somewhat limited capabilities of this method of cleaning clothes do not for a moment daunt the quiet determination of the laundress

hat and frock coat. In fact, visiting the prisons of Haiti I have seen several such, the frock coat and pink straw hat much the worse for wear, and the political prisoner at the end of his chain begging for the filthy food which was brought to the prison gates.

One thing certainly has an influence on Haitian life, and that is the excellent rum which is made in the country. In old days there used to be a little hotel in Port au Prince. This was the only hotel in the town. It was surrounded by windows with wooden slats, through

TOWN FOUNTAIN AT PORT AU PRINCE

It must surely be a pleasing thought that under the sun-baked cobbles of this tropical thoroughfare cool water finds its way from the cold depths of the earth to bubble and flow from the refreshing fount. Languid ladies taking their siesta in the noonday heat must find this a restful spot as they gaze across their shaded balconies down into the silent street

LOOKING DOWN THE MAIN STREET IN A PORT OF HAITI

Port au Prince has witnessed some wild doings, though this scene seems peaceful enough, with few people about, scanty traffic, and a suggestion in the look of the place that one need not hurry here. But on the site of these houses pirates of the Spanish Main and buccaneers from the Tortugas have sworn and swaggered, fought and roared and drunk, and ogled the dark-skinned Haitian girls

HOMELY SCENE IN THE CATHEDRAL SQUARE OF PORT AU PRINCE

Among the principal buildings of Port au Prince are the wooden palace, the cathedral, and the Senate House. On the open sunlit space before the cathedral much business is transacted, and the coloured cottons of the negro women, the bright fabrics with which the stalls are hung, and the many-hued wares impart a pleasing impression as of a maze of sunshine, colour, and movement

RIOT OF CHATTER AND COMMERCE UNDER THE VERTICAL RAYS OF THE SUN IN PORT AU PRINCE

It may be safely said that Haiti is not excelled by any other country in the world where richness and variety of vegetable produce are concerned. All tropical trees and plants appear in perfection, and even the vegetables and fruits of more temperate climes are successfully grown in the Haitian highlands. In these surroundings, where kindly nature does more than her share, it is not surprising that the people, almost all pure-blooded negroes, should be endowed with indolence and ignorance

curious little balls of wool, or red rags, or some unsavoury mixture in a bottle, to be hung in the thatch of his victim's dwelling. The negroes show great fear of these outward signs of the hand of the Voodoo priest, many of them being willing to walk round great distances in order to avoid passing by spots where such uncanny things are said to have been placed.

Haiti, while it is savage, has at the town of Port au Prince a certain number of newspapers, though most of them have had chequered careers, and have appeared under many different titles when, as often happens, they have been suppressed. They generally contain a single sheet of news, about the size of the London " Evening Standard." It is hard to believe that any of them has a circulation much in excess of one hundred copies, and how they succeed in paying their way will always be a mystery. It is a curious fact that the

LAUNDRY WORK AS A PENITENTIAL TASK FOR HAITIAN EVILDOERS
There is little suggestion of the courtyard of a gaol in this scene, with the clean clothes and linen hanging on the lines and the women at the wheels of their mangles. Only the watcher in the turret at the angle of the yard beneath the tall palm tree, and the tall warder, with a revolver at his hip, show that this is a house of detention for wrongdoers

best-known newspaper of twenty years ago was edited by the consul of the Republic of Liberia, the only other Black Republic in the world, who was then accredited to Haiti. No doubt the fact of his official position saved the enterprising editor from some of the difficulties under which his contemporaries worked. No newspaper which has not the benefit of a State subsidy can flourish in the Black Republic, and should any editor publish anything but very colourless views, he is at once dragged off to prison.

Haiti has always been a hot-blooded republic, and the number of revolutions is legion. Of the first seventeen of her Presidents, only one died in power, all the rest were assassinated, exiled, or sought safety in flight.

The Haitian dislikes the white man, and as you wander about the streets you can always hear the word " blanc " hissed after you. But much as he dislikes the white man, he dislikes the yellow man more. No doubt many politicians have come to the front solely owing to their black skins. The best class of men therefore do not go into politics, which is left almost entirely to the ultra-negro element.

The Haitian law is founded upon the Code Napoléon, and a great deal could be written concerning justice as it is interpreted in Haiti. The judges are, of course, black, and can generally be bribed—indeed, I have never been in a country where bribery is so rife as in Haiti. Almost everybody is bribable, even the highest officials, and you could not get anything done unless you gave way to the universal custom.

In her wars with the Dominican Republic, which occupies the other half

PEACEFUL DEMOCRATS OF THE LAND "WHERE BLACK RULES WHITE"
Haiti has suffered continually from internal dissensions and quarrels, and the history of both Haiti and Santo Domingo is summed up in the words " a patchwork of revolutions." Sanguinary insurrections are now practically a thing of the past, but the black citizens are still jealously suspicious of the mulattoes, the aristocracy of the Republic, and the relations between them are not amicable
Photo, Publishers' Photo Service

SORTING COFFEE BEANS FOR EXPORT

The industrious figure with bright striped turban and loose, baggy garments, brown shanks and shoeless feet, is only one of many seated all around and diligently absorbed in their important task. For these natives are examining the beans spread before them lest damaged ones or foreign matter should be passed and so spoil the market value of the whole

of the island, Haiti has invariably been beaten, and the Dominican frontier has been pushed ever forward. The country which was under the French the richest and the most fertile of the West Indies, has sunk back into forest. In the interior of Haiti you may wander through plantations long since ruined, where the coffee bean grows wild, and you may see the ruins of many a fine dwelling of some old French planter. The Haitian does not like grand houses, he is much happier sitting under a shelter of banana leaves than in the grand halls of the ruined castle of La Ferrière, which looks out over Cap Haitien in the north.

When I was travelling in Haiti there were still to be found in the out-of-the-way districts some of the jewels which were seized from the old French colonists. One day a negro offered me a diamond brooch, for which he asked, if I remember rightly, fifty Haitian dollars, which was the equivalent of about £3. I was induced to buy it, and one or two other ornaments, and on my return to England was surprised to find them genuine, and worth considerably more than I gave for them. But the Syrian pedlars have now invaded Haiti, and there is no chance that they have left anything of this nature behind them. Throughout the whole of Haiti they wander with their packs and cheap ornaments. The first of them to come probably made a fortune.

The Haitian negroes enjoyed their freedom in Haiti for over one hundred years. They started with a made country, out of which they drove the French. They had therefore the benefit of a running civilization of the highest kind. But what has happened since?

OFFICIALDOM IN UNIFORM
Haiti is remarkable for its uniforms, and here
we have General Zephirin, Commander of the
Commune of Hinche, in full regimentals

may hold for Haiti, who knows?
But when all has been said that
can be said against them the fact
remains that they are a kindly people;
to my stay among them I look back not
without pleasure.

As I have said, they are very much
attached to their independence. A
phrase often used in the papers was,
"In Haiti alone a man may show a
black face without receiving upon it a
buffet!" But I think the days of
Haitian independence are over, and the

EX-PRESIDENT AS ADMIRAL
Antoine Simon, who fought through revolution to the Presidency of Haiti, only to be
broken in 1911 by the same drastic force

The country has been allowed to fall
back into tangled forest, and not one-
twentieth of its great natural wealth
has been exploited. What the future

ARCHITECTURAL EYESORE IN MEMORY OF A HAITIAN PRESIDENT

General Hippolite, to whose memory this arch was raised, was the victorious leader in the civil war of 1888-89, his opponent being General Légitime. He became President in the latter year, and kept his office with an absolute authority till his death in 1896. The inscription beneath the clock and the words " Paix " and " Travail " on either tower indicate the veneration felt for his name

history of those hundred years and more when it is weighed in the balance will be found wanting.

The Haitian people have all the desire to do great things in this world for themselves and for their country, but they have not the necessary character to succeed in bringing their imaginations to the definite facts of life. Many things are begun—few are finished. They seem to be cursed with the spirit of ineffectuality, and thereby destined to fall into the power of the white man. The treaty with the United States ratified in November, 1915, by the Haitian Congress, entailing a virtual protectorate by the former nation, suggests that this has come to pass already.

GUARDIANS OF THE PEACE FROM TWO COUNTRIES ENJOY THE "ROYAL DIVERSION"

Cock-fighting is still a very popular form of amusement in Haiti, though prohibited in many other parts of the world. Here two birds of the fighting breed are being matched by a couple of the American marines who help to enforce law and order in the Republic. The judge of the contest presides in his chair, ready to award the victory when one of the feathered opponents has sufficiently maimed its adversary. Among the other spectators are several of the Haitian police

Haiti

II. Stormy History of the Black Republic

By Percy F. Martin, F.R.G.S.

Author of "Through Five Republics of South America," etc.

OCCUPYING the western part of the large island of Haiti, or San Domingo, one of the four islands of the Greater Antilles, lying in the Caribbean Sea between Cuba and Porto Rico, the Republic of Haiti, since 1915-16 virtually an American Protectorate, has nearly twice the population, although little more than one-half the area, of its eastern neighbour, the Dominican Republic.

The name Haiti, meaning mountainous, was given to the island by its original inhabitants, the Caribs. It was altered in the fifteenth century, by Columbus, to Hispañola, or Hispaniola, later to Saint Domingue, and then Santo Domingo, after the chief port; but the old name was revived early in the nineteenth century, and is now generally applied to the western, and that of Santo Domingo to the eastern, section of the island.

The physical characteristics of both States are the same, but the climate of Haiti, if anything, is more tropical, owing to the preponderance of lowlands. In Santo Domingo the mountainous country favours a better temperature.

Probably Haiti, of all the Latin-American Republics, has had the most stormy career. For close upon one hundred years this State has proved a cause of anxiety, not alone to its immediate neighbour, but to the adjacent American continent. When discovered by Columbus in 1492, the island was divided into five States, or Cacicats, continually warring with one another. The Spaniards put an end to this state of affairs by slaughtering one-half of the population, replacing them by negroes from Africa, and enslaving the other half. Until 1630 the conquerors enjoyed possession undisturbed; but in that year French buccaneers and free-booters, descending upon the island, practically

secured the country, which they named Saint Domingue.

Upon the outbreak of the French Revolution (1789), the population, now become multi-coloured by reason of inter-breeding between the original Indians, negroes, Spanish, and French, revolted. The National Assembly in Paris granted them independent rights, which caused friction between the people and the colóns (French landlords). They called the English to their aid, and the latter at the end of 1793 took possession of part of the island. There were then English, French, and Spanish settlements; but a fresh outbreak of the emancipated people, led by Toussaint l'Ouverture, himself a slave, brought about the expulsion of both Spaniards and English; the French remained in possession.

The National Government in France appointed l'Ouverture governor of the island, but he was deposed by Napoleon I. In 1801 General Leclerc, appointed governor, arrested l'Ouverture, and sent him in custody to France, where he died in prison. Again the people rose, and the French were finally expelled from the island. The Haitians proclaimed their independence on January 1, 1804, when slavery was abolished for the first time in this part of the world. In 1822 the Spanish part of the island came under the administration of Haiti, but in 1844 separation took place, and the Spaniards established an independent government, known to-day as Santo Domingo, or the Dominican Republic.

Since then Haiti has known hardly one year's political peace; one President, Hippolite, only has served a full term, others having either fled or else been murdered.

During the administrations of Lecomte, Tancrède Auguste, and Michel Oreste,

THE REPUBLIC OF HAITI

NATIVE TRADERS AT PORT AU PRINCE

Though they take their shopping as seriously as other folk, these Haitians convey an impression of unhurried progress as they pass from stall to stall, and there is ample leisure to stop and be included in the photograph. A saunter down the market has for them possibilities of gossip and meeting neighbours, and an easy indolence is supplied by the tropic heat and surroundings

demands were made by European Powers for payment of the Republic's foreign debt; France and Germany were only deterred from taking forcible possession by threats of the Monroe Doctrine. With a view to the protection of American nationals, the United States landed troops in 1907.

Germany made efforts to take control of Haiti, but again Mr. Roosevelt, as in the case of Santo Domingo, intervened. In the following year President Nord Alexis was deposed and took refuge on board a French training-ship, General Légitime being his successor. United States cruisers took part in the proceedings, a dispatch-boat also being ordered to Haitian waters. In the same

year a revolution against General Légitime broke out, the minister, General Lecomte, and several other prominent officials participating. Légitime fled to London, July, 1911.

Foreign Legations made requests to their Governments for the dispatch of warships to Haiti, the cruiser Bremen arriving to protect German interests. The French Consul was seriously wounded. In August, General Cincinnatus Lecomte triumphed, became President, and the same month was recognized by the United States. Within a few days, however, Lecomte was burned to death in his palace, from an explosion in an adjacent powder-magazine, while at the same time

350 other people were killed. Vice-President Tancrède Auguste succeeded, but at once was confronted with a revolution headed by General Saint Just.

Auguste succeeded in maintaining his position until 1913, when he suddenly died, presumably from poison. Thereafter, Generals Oreste Zamor, Davilmar Théodore and Bordas struggled for supremacy, Théodore being killed in battle near the frontier. Meanwhile Germany, Great Britain, the United States, and France presented ultimatums relating to claims for damages. The British claim was for $62,000 compensation, due to an Englishman whose saw-mill had been destroyed. The cruiser Suffolk, sent to Port au Prince, brought about a speedy settlement. The claims, however, occasioned further popular disturbances, which came to a head in January, 1915.

President Théodore's government was replaced by that of General Vilbrun Guillaume. In July following an infuriated mob removed Guillaume from the French Consulate (where he had sought refuge), and shot him in front of the building. As a result of the continuance of political disturbances, the United States took practical possession of the country (August, 1915), Mr. Lansing officially referring to Haiti as a " protectorate." In the following year a treaty was ratified with the country; by the terms of this Haiti gave up control of its finances and police, as well as its political independence. This treaty proved a serious blow to German influence, which until then had secured the greater share of the import and export trade of the country.

Oppressive administrative measures caused fresh dissatisfaction, the Americans finding it necessary to assert their authority by sheer brute force. Towards the end of 1920, outbreaks were threatened, certain acts of brutality being proved against American marines. So

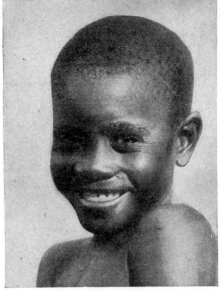

THAT PICCANINNY SMILE

The laughter of the younger generation in Haiti is usually infectious, for the sunshine keeps them jolly. This young fellow is one big smile

serious were some allegations considered that the Secretary of State (Mr. Daniells) was compelled to order an official investigation. Brigadier-General Barnett, former Commandant of Marine Corps, admitted that " unlawful and indiscriminate killing of natives by American marines had occurred," and Lieutenant H. T. Exshaw, who was held officially responsible, was declared " insane." In May, 1921, three Haitian delegates arrived at Washington to present a memorial to President Harding accusing Americans of having perpetrated a long series of atrocities, and demanding their withdrawal from Haiti.

HAITI : FACTS AND FIGURES

The Country

Comprises western part of island of Haiti, West Indies. Western coastline greatly indented by Bay of Gonaïves, which lies between two mountainous peninsulas. Includes several islands, the chief of which are La Gonave, Tortuga, and La Vache. Rivers include the Artibonite, Grand Ause, and Trois Rivières. Principal ports, Port au Prince, Port de la Paix, Gonaïves, Jacmel, St. Marc, Cape Haitien, Jérémie, Aux Cayes, Miragoane. Area about 10,204 square miles ; population about 2,500,000, mainly negroes.

Official language, French. Religion, Roman Catholicism. Armed constabulary of 110 officers and 2,688 N.C.O.'s and men, instituted 1916, with coastguard service attached. Reserve troops, 19,128 men.

Constitution

Republic under constitution of June 12, 1908. President elected for four years. Legislative power vested in Chamber of Deputies chosen for two years by popular vote, one member for each 60,000 inhabitants ; and Senate of fifteen members chosen for six years. U.S.A. protectorate established November, 1915.

Commerce and Industries

Chief products coffee, cocoa, cotton, tobacco, logwood, sugar. Industries mainly agricultural. Undeveloped mineral resources include gold, silver, copper, iron, antimony, tin, sulphur, coal, kaolin, nickel, gypsum, limestone, porphyry. Imports 1919-20, 27,398,411 dollars ; exports 18,990,032 dollars. Nominal value of dollar 4s. About 64 miles of railway, telegraph lines 124 miles.

Chief Towns

Port au Prince, capital (population 120,000), Cap Haitien (15,000), Jacmel (20,000), Aux Cayes (15,000), Gonaïves (8,000), Port de la Paix (5,000).

MUSICIANS AND DANCING-GIRLS OF THE HAWAIIAN ISLANDS IN STARRED AND STRIPED RAIMENT

The Hawaiian or Sandwich group, in the North Pacific, consists of eight inhabited and several small uninhabited islands. The aboriginal Hawaiians are said to belong to the Malayo-Polynesian race. A handsome, pleasure-loving people, they, like their kinsmen of the South Sea Islands, delight to deck themselves in garlands of bright flowers and feathers, but the better class are beginning to ape European fashions, and much of their simple attractiveness is disappearing

Hawaii

I. Pleasure-Loving Islanders of the North Pacific

By Richard Curle

Author of "Into the East," "Wanderings : a Book of Travel and Reminiscence," etc.

THE Hawaiian Islands, which now rank as a territory of the United States of America, are a chain of eight inhabited and several uninhabited islands lying just within the northern tropics of the Pacific Ocean. The inhabited islands stretch for a distance of 380 miles, but if the un-inhabited islands, which have no value save for guano deposits and shark-fishing grounds, are included, that distance is increased by several hundred miles. Honolulu, the capital town, is about 2,100 miles from San Francisco.

The total area of the inhabited islands is 6,651 square miles, divided as follows : Hawaii, 4,210 square miles; Maui, 728 ; Oahu, 600 ; Kauai, 547 ; Molokai, 261 ; Lauai, 139 ; Niihau, 97 ; Kahoolawe, 69. The islands are all of volcanic origin and contain forty volcanic peaks. The greatest volcano — indeed, the greatest volcano in the world—is that of Mauna Loa (Great Mountain), in Hawaii, which is 13,760 feet high, with a base circumference of 75 miles. It erupted a dozen times between 1832 and 1907. Actually the highest peak in the islands is that of Mauna Kea (White Mountain), in

FLOWER-WREATHED COQUETRY

Their love for flowers is the Hawaiians' most engaging characteristic. Every girl wreathes her pretty head with living blossoms and wears great ropes of them on neck and bosom

Photo, R. M. Clutterbuck

Hawaii, which reaches to 13,805 feet. The upper surface of the mountains, which is hidden in snow, is one huge mass of lava, and they contain great caves, caused by lava flows, whose crust formed quickly, 60 feet to 80 feet in height and sometimes several miles in length.

The pure-bred Hawaiians (often called Kanakas in the past), a race of almost copper-coloured people, with brown or black hair, which is straight or curly, and with very large eyes, are fast dying out. There were probably about 250,000 of them at the time of Captain Cook's discovery (the navigator's own estimate was as high as 400,000), but the census of 1832 put the number at 130,000, the census of 1878 at 44,000, the census of 1900 at 30,000, and the census of 1920 at 23,700. The reasons for this decline are various. The Hawaiian mothers, up to recent times, took little care of their children, the islands have been ravaged by small-pox and measles, leprosy has claimed many victims since it was introduced from China in 1853, and drink and venereal diseases have also decimated the population. But it must be

PREPARATIONS FOR A GARGANTUAN BANQUET

Luaus are a favourite form of social entertainment among the Hawaiians—general feasts to which all the participants contribute some of the comestibles. Pigs roasted whole are a standing dish on these occasions, and a native chef and his assistant are here shown cooking one camp-wise on hot stones over a fire made in an earth oven. These luaus are usually gluttonous orgies

Photo, R. M. Clutterbuck

remembered that the natives have inter-married freely with Europeans and other races, and that while the Hawaiian death-rate is the largest in the islands, the part-Hawaiian birth-rate is also the largest. In 1878 there were only 3,420 part-Hawaiians, in 1920 there were 18,000. If the Hawaiian strain is to survive it will be in a mixed form. The total population of the islands is now about 260,000, of which Oahu with 124,000, Hawaii with 65,000, Maui with 36,000, and Kauai with 29,000, are by far the most populous. A strange conglomeration of races inhabits the islands, which have become, indeed, very cosmopolitan. Apart from the Hawaiians and part-Hawaiians, there are, among others, about 80,000 Japanese, 27,000 Portuguese, 23,000 Chinese, 21,000 Filipinos, 10,000 Americans, 5,500 Porto Ricans, and 2,500 Spaniards.

It is remarkable, considering this, how distinct the Hawaiians have kept their national customs, and how deeply they have impressed what one may call their national personality upon the whole modern life of the group. They are a gay, thriftless, amiable, and pleasure-loving people, who blend very well with other races. The higher class Hawaiians have become Europeanised in many ways, especially in the matter of clothes and social usages, but even they are tenacious of their own heritage.

There is a natural streak of poetry in the Hawaiians, and this finds an outlet in their love of flowers—they have a passion for decorating themselves and their guests with leis or wreaths of flowers—and in their love of dancing and music. In fact, the hula, as the native dance-festival is called, is one of the chief national pleasures. Both sexes are passionately fond of riding and bathing. They play many games, throwing into the performance of them all the exuberance of their buoyant natures. Wrestling, surf-riding, spear-throwing, a kind of bowls played with stone disks, and hill-gliding are some of their principal delights. This last game calls for special comment. A smooth track, either of cobblestones or dry grass, is made down the side of a steep hill for a distance of perhaps half a mile, and the Hawaiians shoot down it face forward on a sledge set on hard-wood runners twelve to fourteen feet long, two to three inches deep, and placed some four inches apart. It is an exciting sport and rouses them to the utmost pitch of enthusiasm.

On all their games they gamble recklessly, both men and women being quite ready to wager everything they possess. This proclivity of theirs for gambling has caused much distress and is a national failing.

The Hawaiians of the poorer class are largely employed on sugar and other plantations. The native dwellings are constructed of wood, or are mere huts thatched on the sides and top with grass. Most of the cooking is done outside. Their favourite dish is poi, which is called " one finger " when thick, and " two finger " when thin. Poi is made from the taro root boiled till soft and then pounded up and mixed

with water, and allowed to ferment for a few days. They are also very fond of pork, raw or cooked fish, sweet potatoes, and fruits. In olden days one of their chief delicacies was a special breed of dog fed exclusively on poi. The natives still delight in luaus, or feasts, for which different people provide different things, and after which no participator is fit for any work for some days. The tables are spread with fern leaves, and such dishes as poi, fish wrapped in sweet ti leaves and cooked in underground ovens (or imus), pigs roasted whole, a thick flavouring paste made of pounded kukui nuts, yams, bread-fruit, etc., are consumed in vast quantities.

As for clothing, the women, who still do much of the work, wear the holoka, a loose garment with sleeves, reaching from the neck to the feet. On their heads they wear coloured handkerchiefs or straw hats. Long ago the general wear was bark cloth made from the paper-mulberry and dyed in various colours. The Hawaiian language is musically

KANAKAS POUNDING TARO ROOT FOR MAKING POI

What macaroni is to the Italian poi is to the Hawaiian, a favourite and a staple food. It is prepared by boiling until soft the large tuberous rootstock of the taro plant which is rich in starchy matters, pounding it, mixing it with water, and allowing it to ferment. It is called " two finger " or " one finger " according to whether it is made thick or thin

HAWAIIAN FAMILY GATHERED TOGETHER FOR DINNER

Their dwelling is a somewhat unsubstantial hut with walls and roof of thatch, and their domestic equipment, like their wardrobe, is scanty. But they are a well-favoured and contented family party who obviously enjoy and thrive upon their frugal fare of poi eaten as it is cooked, picnic fashion in the open air, and a kind of natural grace distinguishes both their manner and their manners

Photo, Underwood Press Service

soft and seems strangely suited to the psychology of the people. The Hawaiian character has, indeed, something child-like about it that is very charming. When work stops at four in the afternoon the Hawaiians begin to taste the full flavour of existence. They are a histrionic race, and this love of the dramatic finds vent in their liking to present tableaux from their legendary history. Life is to them a light-hearted affair, and the beauty of their islands and their climate is reflected in their attitude towards the world.

Very little is known authentically of the early history of the Hawaiian Islands before Captain Cook discovered them in 1778. He called them the Sandwich Islands, after John Montagu, fourth Earl of Sandwich, then First Lord of the Admiralty, and that is their alternative name to this day. Although Captain Cook was killed in Kealakekua Bay, Hawaii, in the following year, his industry had already discovered much about the customs of the islanders. The old Hawaiians, who were true Polynesians and probably migrated to

HAWAIIAN MISS HORNER EATING HER FAVOURITE POI

Fingers were made before forks, and are still preferred to any other implement by the Hawaiians for the purpose of eating poi. The agreeable flavour of this national dish is indicated by the gratified smile of this lady who has just pulled out a mouthful from her generous helping, while its nutritive value is attested by the very ample proportions of her still youthful figure

Photo, R. M. Clutterbuck

HAWAIIAN RIDER OF THE WAVES AND HIS SURF-BOARD

Hawaiians take to the water from infancy as naturally as young ducks, and throughout life are devoted to bathing and sporting in the sea. Surf-riding is a favourite pastime of natives of both sexes and all ages. Swimming out beyond the break of the waves they get on to their surf-boards and balancing themselves with astonishing skill are brought in on the rollers shouting and laughing

Photo, R. M. Clutterbuck

DIANA GOES RIDING IN DIVIDED SKIRTS

Conventional decorum could suggest no fairer compromise between breeches and riding-habit than is effected by this Hawaiian lady who, while riding astride conceals both legs within such flowing drapery. The wreaths around her own and her horse's neck are evidence of her native love of floral decoration, and she betrays truly feminine consciousness of the attractive picture she makes in the dappled light

WHERE GOOD DIGESTION WAITS ON APPETITE, AND HEALTH ON BOTH

Hospitality is comparatively inexpensive for the pleasure-loving Hawaiians since it is the custom for all the guests to contribute something to the banquet provided for the common enjoyment. The cloth, of matting, is spread on the ground and decorated with fern leaves, and the menu includes enormous quantities of poi, fish cooked in sweet ti leaves, pigs roasted whole, and preparations of nuts, yams, and bread-fruit. After a luau, the guests are often incapacitated for work for several days

Photo, R. M. Clutterbuck

LONGSHOREMEN HAULING IN THEIR SEINE ON CORAL-BOUND HAWAII

Fish abound round the shores of the Hawaiian Islands, and besides being taken at sea are kept in artificial ponds in the coral bays. They include species remarkable for the brilliance of their colouring, and provide an important part of the food supply of the population. These fishermen well exhibit the latitude of custom in respect of men's dress in Hawaii, some of them wearing a costume of coat and trousers with collar and tie, while others are virtually naked

Photo, R. M. Clutterbuck

ELIGIBLE DANCING MEN OF HAWAII IN CORRECT MASCULINE BALL COSTUME

Draped from waist to ankle in skirts of bark cloth and with frayed palm leaves twisted round their neck and thrust into their girdle, these mature Kanakas are participating in the hula dance, of which the women, like the men, of these enchanting islands never tire. A theatrically appropriate background for the evolutions of the dance is provided by the tropical ferns and palms, with flowers rioting everywhere, filling the place with heady fragrance and dazzling the eye with colour

Hawaii in the tenth century, were a pleasant and superior race as Captain Cook found them—his murder at their hands was almost in the nature of a deplorable accident—but their religion and taboos were attended with hideous cruelty.

Religion required human sacrifices, and the breaking of taboos, which were often trivial—for example, women were not allowed to eat bananas, coconuts, pork, turtle, and certain kinds of fish—was followed by death. But there were

chiefs, who were much superior in physique to the ordinary people, were divided into three classes. The first consisted of the royal family and its connexions, the second of the hereditary governors of islands and other such exalted officers, the third of village headmen, rulers of districts, and so on.

When Captain Cook arrived it seems that the islands were split up into three kingdoms—Hawaii, Oahu, and Maui. King Kamehameha of Hawaii (1736-1819) conquered the other two kingdoms

PRELIMINARY MOVEMENT OF A HAWAIIAN DANCE

The island of Hawaii offers a variety of colourful amusement, but none so whole-heartedly enjoyed as the dance. Clothed chiefly in flowers and foliage, with anklets, necklets, and wreaths of living sweet-smelling blossoms, the native women sway gracefully to and fro, their seductive dances being well in keeping with the enchantment of the idyllic surroundings

Photo, R. M. Clutterbuck

in Hawaii two cities of refuge, where murderers and taboo-breakers were safe, and to which old people and children used to retire during war-time. The Hawaiians believed in a second soul and in ghosts. They had four principal gods—besides many lesser ones—and those were: Kane, father of men and founder of the world; Kanaloa, his brother; Ku, the cruel one; and Lono, to whom the annual New Year games were dedicated.

The form of government was an absolute monarchy—it was death for a common man to stand even at the mention of the king's name—and the

and became king of the whole group. He made two Americans his advisers, encouraged foreign trade, grew rich, and consolidated his position. His son, Kamehameha II., was a friendly, mild-mannered man, but he had not the energy of his father, and he and his wife died from measles during a visit to England in 1825. It was during his reign, in 1820, that American missionaries started their work in the islands, and it is curious to note that in 1825 the Ten Commandments were acknowledged as the basis of Hawaiian law.

Kamehameha III. ruled from 1825 till 1854. A constitution was promulgated

"DANCING'S A TOUCHSTONE THAT TRUE BEAUTY TRIES"

Dancing, music, and flowers are the three things dearest to the heart of the Hawaiians, and all three are gratified in the hula or native dance. These girls are waiting to take their place in the dance. Their costume, of grass and leaves and blossoms, displays their shapely limbs yet suggests nothing of immodesty, but rather the elusive beauty that belongs to water nymphs and dryads

Photo, R. M. Clutterbuck

in 1840 and the legislature met for the first time in 1845. A new constitution was promulgated in 1852. Kamehameha IV. ruled from 1854 till 1863, and his brother, Kamehameha V., from 1863 till 1872. A third constitution was promulgated in 1864. Lunalilo, a grandson of Kamehameha I., reigned from 1872 till 1874, and he was succeeded by Kalakana, who longed to enlarge his dignity and sought to obtain the primacy of the Pacific.

A queer sort of visionary, Walter M. Gibson, was his Prime Minister from 1882 till 1887, and the discontent of the islanders precipitated itself into a revolution during the latter year through the discovery that the king had accepted two bribes of $75,000 and $80,000 for the assignment of an opium licence. This revolution was successful:

"BEAUTY FAIR IN HER FLOWER"

The bounteous kind of handsomeness possessed by Hawaiian women generally is well exemplified in this native belle, together with the intelligence and the mildness of temper that make her people the most likeable of all the Polynesians

the king signed a proper constitution and dismissed his unpopular minister. However, it was not long before he was again intriguing, and it was perhaps fortunate that he died in San Francisco, whither he had gone for his health, in 1891.

He was succeeded by his sister, Liliuokalani, who foolishly attempted to force another constitution on her people. The Americans stepped in to save the lives and property of American subjects, and a Republic was declared in January, 1895, over which Sandford P. Dole became President. He was the only President Hawaii ever had, for on Aug. 12, 1898, the islands were formally annexed to the United States. Since then peace has taken the place of turmoil, and it may safely be said that few more successful attempts at colonising have been achieved than the government of the Hawaiian Islands

by the United States. The first sight of the Hawaiian Islands from the sea gives one no true idea of their deep appeal. There is something desolate in the view of these immense mountains descending sharp to the water's edge and tipped with snow or clouds. But inland there is enchanting and ever-changing beauty, and there are wonderful scents of stephanotis, ginger, and plumaria. The rocks are covered with creepers; flowering shrubs, such as hibiscus, abound; waterfalls are numerous; and view upon view opens out with majestic loveliness and exotic splendour.

Hawaii itself, although it has no town bigger than Hilo with its 10,000 inhabitants, is not only by far the largest of the islands, but by far the most attractive. It offers endless variety of scene and almost endless variety of climate. Its volcanoes are among the wonders of the world—the crater of Kilauea, for instance, has a circumference of eight miles—and when the lava is flowing there are sights, more especially in the dark, of inexpressible strangeness and beauty. The lava will spout up in fountains a thousand feet high and will flow in streams, sometimes a mile and a half wide, at a speed of ten miles an hour.

In Kapiolani Park, Honolulu possesses a fine open space of 125 acres, where flowering trees and palms may be seen to exquisite advantage.

The Hawaiian Islands possess practically no indigenous mammals, and they are also singularly free from snakes, but they have wonderful birds in their forests and wonderful fish around their shores and in their coral bays. The most

HAWAII UNDER THE PAINTED ORIEL OF THE WEST

Over the wind-ruffled water, for a moment lightened by the last rays of the sun ere advancing clouds bring with them the dusk of night, the lonely boatman plies his solitary paddle. The frail outrigger skims the surface to where, beyond the palm-fringed strand, lights gleam and wink from the windows. The last bird flutters to roost, somewhere a brown girl softly laughs, and from the distance comes the throb and cry of a eukalele

These will spread out, gradually forming pools and lakes, over which gleams and spurts of fire play mysteriously in the night.

Honolulu, the capital town in Oahu, is an up-to-date city of 83,000 people, with electric tramways and modern buildings. It lies along the shore on a level strip of land about a mile broad and seven miles long, and extends back into five valleys amid hills that rise to nearly 4,000 feet. Private gardens line the streets and the houses have each their vine-clad verandas, called canais, which are almost more used for living in than the houses themselves.

famous birds are probably the mamo, now very rare and seldom found outside of Mauna Loa, and the iiwi, a song bird. It was from these two birds respectively that the royal cloaks of yellow feathers, tipped with scarlet feathers—of which examples may be seen in the British Museum—were made. Such coats are now of fabulous value. There are in the islands no fewer than three hundred varieties of land-snail and five hundred varieties of beetle, eighty per cent. of which last are unknown elsewhere. As for plants there are something like a thousand species, including seventy kinds of seaweed, which the natives use

BRINGING ASHORE THE HARVEST OF THE BLUE PACIFIC

The long roll of the ground swell aids the Hawaiian fisherman to beach his well-laden outrigger. The waves that can sweep and tower and crash like charging cavalry upon these sun-lit sands are here but gentle helpmates to these swarthy toilers of the sea with their bronze skins agleam with the wet. Soon the shore will bear glinting heaps of silver fish, and the catcher will get his due

TWO DUSKY SIRENS OF THE HONOLULU SHORE

Steel guitars with six wires and smaller four-stringed eukaleles are the best known of Hawaiian musical instruments. The photograph shows a form of duet with the first. One player plucks out the melody while the other, holding her instrument across her knees and pressing down the wires with a steel bar, thrums an accompaniment. A plectrum will be noticed on the thumb of the accompanist

Photos, R. M. Clutterbuck

FAMILY HAPPINESS SHELTERED IN HOUSES THAT LOOK LIKE HAYSTACKS

Grass huts like this are tending to disappear from the Hawaiian Islands, and are now found only in out-of-the-way places. Poor though these homes are there is little squalor about them, for all the cooking is done outside, so that no fireplace is needed indoors, and all the meals are taken in the open air. Thus the hut is virtually only the family dormitory, sufficiently ventilated by the doorless aperture at one end

Photo: P. M. Gutterbuch

as a relish. The forests contain many varieties of trees. The islands are not rich in minerals, though they contain deposits of pumice, sulphur, gypsum, and alum, and it is from agriculture that they have grown prosperous. Certain crops do remarkably well, and, indeed, sugar, which is the main crop (it was first planted there in 1835), yields from thirty to forty tons an acre, which is a world's record. Coffee, tobacco, rice, and sisal of fine quality are also grown, and bananas are even reared amid the lava of the hill-sides. Pineapple cultivation and the canning of pines have made great progress. The tins for the canning are made locally, and one factory is in a position to turn out 100,000 tins in an hour.

Under the monarchy a complicated system of land tenure prevailed throughout the islands, but this has been simplified and brought more into line with modern requirements. There are 1,850,000 acres of private lands, 876,000 acres of Crown lands, and 830,000 acres of Government lands. The islands have been made accessible by many fine roads, and in the four principal ones there are, besides, 350 miles of railway. There are also 650 miles of sugar plantation railway.

The Hawaiian islanders are outwardly, at least, the most adaptive of people, and it is that, added to their natural intelligence and mildness, which has enabled them to accept civilization with so good a grace. They are a tolerant people, and so long as they are permitted to enjoy their island-life without undue interference they are, perhaps, rather indifferent about abstract ideas on liberty. This they own quite sufficiently in fact not to bother endlessly about it in theory.

They are a finely built race—many of the women in particular are handsome in a large, bounteous sort of way—and their zest for life is keen. They belong to the happy races of the earth, and existence has been made easy for them through the natural richness of the soil and the sea. If, as a body, they have neither the intelligence nor the vigour of the Maoris, a people of Polynesian stock in New Zealand, they are nevertheless far ahead of most Polynesians. Indeed, if we regard life mainly as an experiment in enjoyment, the Hawaiians must be ranked among the most favoured peoples on this planet.

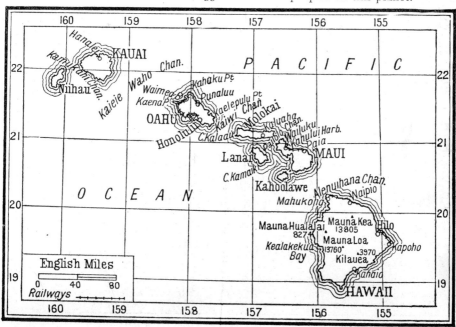

THE UNITED STATES TERRITORY OF HAWAII

WITH HANDS UPRAISED IN PRAYER THE CONGREGATION FACE THE HOLY KAABA IN MECCA'S MOSQUE

Ritual is developed to the highest point of elaboration in the Mahomedan religion, and every attitude and every gesture in the ceremonial is strictly prescribed. This is almost equally true of social observances in daily life, and the fact explains the enormous difficulties that beset the non-Moslem who would seek to penetrate into Mecca and Medina and set foot within the great Mosque. Detection would entail instant death, for honour and reward await any Moslem who discovers an infidel within the Holy Places

Hejaz

I. Life in the Holy Places of Islam

By Edmund Candler

Author of "The Mantle of the East"

THE Arabs speak of their country as El Jezireh, or "the Island," a word that also denotes a peninsula. As a matter of fact, Arabia is in everything, save in the strict geographic sense of the word, an island, for the northern deserts cut it off from commerce with the outside world. It is a country difficult of access to the stranger on all sides, by reason of its inhospitable approaches. Large areas are unmapped and unexplored. The southern desert, the Ruba el khali, as the Arabs call it, or "Abode of Emptiness," interposes such a barrier of uncompromising sterility between the coast and the interior that there is no record of it ever having been traversed by man. Broadly speaking, the whole of Arabia is almost rainless and niggard of vegetation, and contains no perennial streams, only the wadis (valleys, gulleys or ravines) fertilised by intermittent torrents and dry for the greater part of the year.

A Vast "Abode of Emptiness"

The desert is generally hilly or undulating. A journey across the peninsula will take one over gravelly plains, wide stretches of deep sand forced by wind pressure into high billows and hummocks that loom like mountains in the mirage; soft dune country, and patches of hard fissured lava or scoriae overlaying mountains and plain. The rare oases of Central Arabia are found in the wadi basins where there is ground water, or in land which receives a precarious drainage from mountain chains. Oman in the east and Yemen in the south, which receive a certain precipitation from the monsoon, alone have sufficient periodic rains, while in the "Empty Abode" the rainfall does not amount to more than an inch in five years. An image of the desolation of the peninsula may be conveyed statistically in the statement that it is a country of a million and a half square miles, which only contains five inland settlements important enough to fall within the category of towns.

Mysterious Mecca's Infinite Lure

Mecca and Medina, the Holy Cities of Islam, Sanaa, the headquarters of the Imam of Yemen, and Hail and Riadh, the capitals of Ibn Raschid and Ibn Saad, the kings of northern and southern Nejd, these are cities of romance which most travellers have dreamed of entering, but in which few have set foot. The physical barriers to a journey in Arabia are considerable, yet they are small beside the social, religious, and political exclusiveness of the town-bred Arab and the Beduin's cult of brigandage and assassination. Mecca and Medina are fanatically guarded, yet they have been penetrated by more Europeans than Sanaa, Riadh and Hail, though the command of the Prophet that no unbeliever should set foot in the sacred territory has been interpreted by his followers in its strictest and most literal sense. Mecca, to employ the Mahomedan word, is "haram," a term which first implies "unlawfulness," and then in the natural sequence of associations "sanctuary." To visit it at least once in a lifetime is the sacred obligation of every Moslem; for the Kafir, or infidel, to be detected within the precincts means death at the hands of the faithful.

Thus Mecca has become the pivot and focus of Islam. The city prescribes the physical and spiritual orientation of every Moslem. Millions of heads are bowed towards it at the hour of prayer. The dead are buried with their feet towards the Holy City, ready to

HUSSEIN, FIRST KING OF HEJAZ

Of Arabian princely blood, Grand Sherif of Mecca and hereditary custodian of the Holy Cities of Mecca and Medina, Hussein Ibn Ali proclaimed the independence of Hejaz and assumed the title of king in 1916

So to the European Mecca has become the supreme adventure of travel. To the fascination of the desert is added the greater fascination of the perilous transgression of bounds. The Arab proverb, " Voyaging is Victory," is often quoted by pilgrims on the road. To the unbeliever who accompanies them at the risk of his life the saying is more than a pious commonplace. For in the company of the faithful he must keep a vigilant watch on himself. Any lapse of ritual, whether in social or religious observance, as in drinking a glass of water, in greeting a wayfarer or in gesture or attitude during prayer, would be certain to arouse suspicion. Islam is as much a free-masonry as a religion, and the prescribed ceremonial of the daily routine is not easy to acquire. There are certain distinctive habits, formalities, and peculiarities of dress by which Moslems know one another. Then there is always the danger of being recognized by pilgrims who may have known one at other times and in other scenes. The Moslem who discovers the infidel in the Holy Places merits honour and reward, whereas one detected in conniving at the sacrilege would be likely to receive short shrift.

To few Europeans has it fallen to be carried along with the tide of humanity that is borne every year in the annual pilgrimage to Mecca. There is no record of a professed unbeliever who has entered the city, and it is quite certain that if any have entered none has returned. To the European who is not a Mahomedan two ways only are open :

spring up facing the Prophet at the first note of the trump of doom. It has lent such an inflection of body and spirit to the faithful that we in the West, in conceiving a pilgrimage, borrow from it our metonymic headlines and speak, quite reverently, of the Mecca of golfers, or gourmets or gamblers, though we never speak of the Jerusalem, the Benares, or the Budh Gaya of folk who are drawn irresistibly by any magnet. The influence of Mecca in the mere physical orientation of humanity is second only to the Pole Star.

he must profess Islam or go disguised. The first way is easy, but there is little glamour in it, and none of the challenge, the demand for courage and resourcefulness which lends the adventure its appeal. The pilgrim would find himself a despised renegade, allowed to move among the faithful on sufferance, spied upon, the object of suspicion and contempt.

To travel in disguise as a Moslem and take the extreme risk—assassination in the case of exposure—is the adventurous course. Not more than a dozen Europeans, apart from born Moslems or apostates, have been known to reach Mecca during the last hundred years, of whom four were Englishmen. Of these only Sir Richard Burton and Major A. J. B. Wavell have left any record of their experiences. Burton's " Pilgrimage to Meccah and Medinah " is the classic of travel in the Hejaz. Wavell's modest narrative " A Modern Pilgrim in Mecca " records an equally daring

journey. It is a tale carelessly told, as publication was an afterthought. Nevertheless, it glows with colour and human interest. Burton travelled alone, Wavell with two Moslem confederates, a Mombasa Swahili and a Europeanised Arab of Aleppo domiciled in Berlin. The Hejaz is the most dangerous and difficult point by which a European can enter Arabia. The system of espionage is an effective barrier to all who have not learnt to impersonate an Oriental on an Oriental stage. The Asiatic is inquisitive, and one must avoid the risk of meeting pilgrims from the country to which one is supposed to belong. It is best to appear as a vagabond. In Egypt, Burton chose the part of a wandering Dervish, a character assumed by Moslems of all ranks, ages, and creeds, and, what is more, one to which much remissness in ceremony and politeness is forgiven. But before leaving for the Hejaz he abandoned the Dervish's

VENDERS OF HOLY WATER FROM HAGAR'S WELL
Mahomedan tradition says that it was at the well Zem-Zem that Hagar drew water for Ishmael, and that later the well was covered up and only rediscovered by Mahomet's grandfather. Now enclosed in a vaulted building within the Mosque at Mecca, its tepid waters are credited with healing powers. They are also supposed to choke Christians, while washing away the sins of true believers

MECCA'S GREAT MOSQUE, THE HOLIEST SPOT ON EARTH IN MOSLEM EYES

The famous Mosque at Mecca is a great rectangular space, open to the sky and surrounded with colonnades. In the centre stands the cube-shaped structure known as the Kaaba, covered with the annually renewed Kisweh, or curtain of black silk brocade with a legend composed of extracts from the Koran embroidered in gold around it. Adjoining the Kaaba is the enclosed well of Zem-Zem. The pilgrims walk or run round the Kaaba seven times, reciting prayers, and, at the end of each

PILGRIMS PERFORMING THE WUKUF: "STANDING ON" MOUNT ARAFAT TO LISTEN TO THE SERMON

On the eighth, ninth, and tenth days of the Hadj the pilgrims pay the ceremonial visit to Mount Arafat which earns for them the title of Hadj or Hadji. Mounted and on foot, and followed by baggage animals, the white-robed host, often numbering half a million, streams to the Mount of Mercy. Here on the ninth day they "stand," listen to a sermon, and pray till sunset, returning on the following day for another "stand," after which they ceremonially "stone the devils,"—pillars marking the spots once occupied by the idols which Mahomet destroyed

PIOUS MOSLEMS GATHERED AT THE "DURBAR OF GOD"

Immensely impressive is the spectacle of the vast congregations that assemble for worship in the Mosque at Mecca. Clothed in white ihrams, they face the Kaaba in the centre of the Mosque, and led by an imam, bend and sway in prayer, kneel and rise with him, and with one impulse bow to the ground, every brow pressed to the marble flags that pave the courtyard

gown, though not the character of vagrant. Wavell, who described himself as one Ali bin Muhammad, a subject of Zanzibar, ran greater risk of detection in adopting for his country a district in which he was known. More than once he felt he was on the point of being unmasked. He describes how at Mina three Mombasa Swahilis, who he believed would have denounced him, looked straight into his tent, but were blinded by the morning sun falling directly on their eyes, and so passed on without

suspicion. No rehearsing of one's part is a safeguard against accidents like these. The traveller may be a born actor and a competent Orientalist, but to be at home in the character he has adopted he must know how to mix freely with Moslems, to attend ceremonies in and out of the mosque, to accept and return hospitality and salutations, to finger his rosary and adjust his dress without making mistakes. One cannot learn to pass inconspicuously among Moslems without making Moslem acquaintances and friends, and this means, however disciplined or observant or vigilant one may be, that there is always the danger of discovery through recognition. Both Burton and Wavell changed their identity on the road, but with embarrassing consequences that pursued them throughout the journey. "Bazaar rumours," as Burton observed, "fly quicker and hit harder than newspaper paragraphs."

The perils of the spurious Hadj are probably greater to-day than ever they were. A new danger has arisen since Burton's time through the system of attaching special guides to pilgrims of different nationalities. These "muto-wifs," as they are called, regard travellers from their own particular provinces as their prey, study their dialects and idiosyncracies, and know a great deal too much about their pedigrees, antecedents and connexions. Like all

WOMEN OF HEJAZ KNEADING DOUGH FOR BREAD

They seem amused by the photographer's interest in their occupation—woman's work from imme-morial times, and so dignified by importance and association that it has given the very word " lady " to the English language. The bread these women are making is unleavened , a simple mixture of coarsely-ground grain moistened with water and kneaded by hand and baked in a crude oven

SECULAR POWER DISPLAYED IN MECCA KEEPS IN CHECK EBULLITIONS OF RELIGIOUS ZEAL

While the Koran contains precise regulations as to the conduct of pilgrims, and the Meccan chiefs have provided for a suspension of tribal feuds during the three months of pilgrimage, as well as for the perpetual interdiction of bloodshed within their own precincts, the influx of so vast a number of religious fanatics inevitably puts a heavy responsibility on those in charge of law and order in the holy city. Demonstration of force often prevents necessity for its use, and parades of the Arab army in the streets of Mecca are a constant feature of the annual spectacle

exploiters of pilgrims, they are singularly adhesive and difficult to shake off. Yet to go the round of the Holy Places in their company means encountering the very folk it is most essential to avoid.

The modern European pilgrim to Mecca or Medina would do well to hit on some stratagem to dissociate himself from the "mutowifs." The safest plan, perhaps, would be to discover a place of derivation which one shared with no one else. The Arabs and Turks are so abysmally ignorant of geography that a pilgrim might invent a language and country for himself, and gain admission to Mecca as the subject of a kingdom that did not exist. The language difficulty, as a matter of fact, is not so great as is generally supposed. It is the least of the obstacles to be overcome. Owing to the multitudinous dialects of Arabic, and the number of communities scattered all over Asia and Africa, who call themselves Arabs, but have no claim to the title, peculiarities in accent excite little attention. The Hadj is cosmopolitan in its confusion of tongues.

By Train or Caravan to Mecca

Mecca and Medina lie in the province of the Hejaz, that narrow strip of territory in the west of Arabia bordering the Red Sea. In Turkish maps it is painted green, the Prophet's colour, though why green should be the symbolic hue of the brown and tawny wildernesses that make up nine-tenths of the territory of Islam it is difficult to say. The Hejaz is only less barren than the "Abode of Emptiness," for the monsoon current does not penetrate so far north as Jeddah. Mecca is a fire-pit. It is completely shut in by hills, and its bare and rocky background, which precludes any breeze, retains and reflects the heat all night. Rain only falls once or twice a year, and then in torrential downfalls, which sometimes flood the city to the depth of several feet and inundate the Mosque.

The Hejaz railway takes the bulk of the pilgrims now as far as the terminus at Medina, a journey of four days, though many of the pious and conservative

Moslems of the old school still march all the way under the Emir-el-Haj, the commander of the pilgrimage. The Egyptian caravan passes by Sinai and Midian to Yembu, and thence to Mecca or Medina. The Bagdad caravan leaves the Euphrates at Najaf or Samawah, and crosses the desert to the oasis of Hail, and thence to Medina. An alternative route is by Koweit on the Persian Gulf through Qasim. Wavell arrived at Medina by the Hejaz railway from Damascus, Burton by caravan from Yembu, whither he sailed in a pilgrim boat from Suez.

Medina and the Prophet's Tomb

Thus both travellers began the Hadj at Medina, which to the stranger is the more dangerous city of the two. During the pilgrimage season the risk of exposure is less in Mecca, where the crowd is so packed that anyone with a fair knowledge of Arabic and Moslem ceremonial stands a good chance of passing unnoticed. Less than a third of the pilgrims go on to Medina, as a visit to the Prophet's tomb, though meritorious, is not essential in the Hadj. The Medani, consequently, is more suspicious and inquisitive, the mutowifs of the city are more difficult to evade. Moreover, at Medina there would be less chance of escape after detection on account of the greater distance to the sea.

Outer Barbarians Who Live by Plunder

The Beduins of the Hejaz are notoriously the most predatory cutthroats in Arabia. They have little commerce with the towns, which are independent of them, and subsist almost exclusively on plunder; manual labour they consider degrading. The pilgrims have reason to hate and fear them, and to the town-bred Arab they are "outer barbarians." They hang on the skirts of caravans and pick off stragglers, sniping them at two or three hundred yards, and, when they make a hit, galloping in to plunder their victim. Even the short journey of 55 miles from Jeddah to Mecca is insecure in spite of the protecting blockhouses with their armed garrisons at frequent intervals

HOMEWARD BOUND FROM THE WELL

Though not beautiful, she has grace of figure developed by the Eastern custom of carrying water vessels upon her head, and not to be hidden by the sombre draperies that envelop her from head to foot

display nothing of their ancestral qualities except " greed of gain, revengefulness, pugnacity, and a frantic kind of bravery, displayed on rare occasions."

These Beduins are not good Mahomedans. Only in extremities are they known to pray. Nor is it religious fanaticism that makes them hostile to foreigners so much as fear of political penetration. Also the intrusion of the infidel in their forbidden Holy Places touches their pride. The first Beduin who caught sight of the Frank's hat, Burton remarked, would not deem himself a man if he did not drive a bullet through the wearer's head. They are always looking out for spies. To be seen sketching is to run the risk of assassination. They regard pen and paper with the greatest suspicion. Burton was nearly betrayed by a sextant. He used to cut up his sketches into squares, number them, and hide them in the tin canisters that carried his medicines.

Rarely does a Hadj return from the pilgrimage without some story of an encounter with the Beduins. The Turkish garrison, when the Hejaz was nominally a province of the Ottoman Empire, was never able to subdue the Arabs. When Burton

on the road. The train from Mecca to Medina is infested with thieves. The Hejazi Beduins are frankly plunderers, and murder is merely the preliminary to pillage. Of pure race, they have kept their blood unmixed for centuries and boast of their nobility, though they entered Medina, in 1853, the Yembu caravan with which he travelled was held up by the Beduins outside the city, and only permitted to proceed on condition that its escort of 200 horses retired to their barracks. His caravan was attacked again two marches before Mecca, and suffered many casualties. Wavell, fifty years later, entering Medina by the Hejaz railway, found the city in a state of siege; desultory fighting continued during the whole of his stay.

It is the lurking presence of the Beduins, the human fauna of the wilderness, haunting the rocks and wadis, and appearing as if by magic out of the arid level steppes to waylay the traveller, that lends Arabian travel its sense of danger and fascination. In solitary journeys the stimulus of the desert is even greater than with a caravan. It is with a feeling of awe and exhilaration that the traveller rides out of the last palm-fringed village into the illimitable desolation beyond. The sense of the desert is upon him, the embracing, soothing spirit of unconfinedness which breathes out of those boundless wastes, too real, too awful for monotony.

Folk living in green countries are apt to think of the desert as flat and featureless; in reality there is little sameness in it, and the monotony, such as it is, only stimulates the imagination with the sense of great distances overcome. Burton has noted in the desert how every slight modification of form or colour rivets observation. The senses are sharpened, and the perceptive faculties, prone to sleep over a confused shifting of scenery, act vigorously when excited by the capability of embracing each detail. And if there is any monotony in the scene it is dispelled by

ENIGMATIC WOMAN IMPENETRABLY VEILED
Amenities of life are few in the arid Hejaz and the discomforts many, even for the indigenous population. An occasional walk abroad can bring little in the way of recreation to the veiled women gliding along the torrid streets

the mirage. However colourless and flat the earth may be, there is always food for imagination in the air. Apart from the lurking Beduin, there is material in a day's journey in the desert for a thousand and one romances. A desert journey should be undertaken

DEVOUT PILGRIMS TO THE HOLY CITY ENCAMPED AT THE FOOT OF THE MOUNTAIN OF MERCY

Photography is very strictly prohibited in the Holy City, and infringement of this rule might involve grave penalties if discovered. Consequently, photographs of Mecca are exceptionally rare. This and the one on page 2602 were taken by an Indian officer, and have not been published elsewhere. The scene when the hosts of pilgrims from all parts of the world are encamped outside Mecca is astonishing, the plain, white with tents among the myriad crowd, swarming in early winter or spring. In summer the heat is insupportable. Happily, the Hadj is an ordeal prescribed for the pious Moslem only once in a lifetime. The pilgrimage must be performed in the first ten days of the last month in the Moslem lunar year; thus he can choose his season in the revolving cycle, the dates of the successive pilgrimages differing by about a month in our solar year. The Moslem, however, generally chooses his hour and year as the spirit moves him. He is not providently bound by seasons. The Hadj may fall in January or August, but the influx of pilgrims varies very little. In the summer the desert is a fiery furnace. The heat is staggering. The ground scorches one's feet. The sun, when it is strong, is the most relentless enemy that man can have. And in visiting the Holy Places the pilgrim must go uncovered. His back and head, if he is not a Beduin, will be raw and blistered from exposure to the sun.

The Supreme Moment in Moslem Life

When all the hardships, dangers, and difficulties of the journey are passed, and the pilgrim approaches Mecca or Medina, his imagination is overawed, his feelings are too strong for speech. He walks with his eyes, as the Arab says. A hush falls over the caravan. There is no longer any shouting, singing, or discharge of muskets. Soon he will be in the holy Presence, the mystery towards which he has turned his face five times daily at the hour of prayer throughout his life. " O Allah ! " he cries, as he approaches Medina. " This is the Haram (sanctuary) of the Prophet; make it to us a protection from hell-fire, and a refuge from eternal punishment. Oh, open the gates of thy mercy, and let us pass through them to the land of joy ! "

Medina is seen from afar, but Mecca lies in a deep and narrow valley, so completely hidden on the seaward side that the sudden revelation of it to the jaded and weary pilgrim must be the most dramatic moment of his life.

" O Allah ! " he cries at the first glimpse of the Mosque of the Prophet.

" Verily this is thy safeguard and thy sanctuary. Whosoever entereth it, he shall become secure."

Before entering the Haram, or the sacred circle, marked by pillars, that is drawn round Mecca, the pilgrim must discard his turban and sandals and put on the ihram, two cloths of soft pure white, the one worn round the waist, the other over the shoulders. This is the obligatory garb of the Hadj, and ensures that all enter God's house in a uniform spirit of humility, undistinguished by any mark or badge of rank or privilege. His first office is the tauf, or circumambulation of the Kaaba (Arabic, " Ka'bah ").

" The Most Sacred Spot on Earth "

The Kaaba, the Holy House in the centre of the Beyt Ullah, or House of Ullah, is to the Moslems the most sacred spot on earth, the kibla, or pivotal point, to which every worshipper turns when praying. It has made Mecca the navel of the world, the parent city, the mother of towns. The Kaaba was an object of veneration in pre-Islamic days. According to the Arab legend it was built by Adam in the likeness of a house he had seen in Paradise before the fall. It was rebuilt after the Flood by Abraham and Ishmael and reconsecrated to the service of the true God. Afterwards the Meccans became idol-worshippers, until Mahomet conveyed to them the message of Islam and purified their temple of its abominations.

Satisfaction of the Desire of the Heart

The first sight of the Kaaba evokes awe and wonder and ecstasy and tears; the thought of it kindles an inward flame in men's hearts in distant parts of the earth. In the pilgrims' fancy, the rustling of the Kisweh is the beating of angels' wings. They cling, weeping, to the curtain, and press their hearts and lips to the stone. The Moslem standing at prayer in some far country, head erect, and eyes fixed raptly on the horizon, is gazing Meccawards; his vision penetrates mountains, deserts, cities, forest trees, the curvature of the ocean, obstacles through which devout eyes

JEDDAH'S UNPAVED STREETS PARCHED BY A PITILESS SUN

Except to the pilgrims landing there on their way to Mecca, Jeddah is an uninspiring town. Rectangular balconies and windows break the monotony of the walls—often of rough coral—of the houses of the Arab population. The houses are set flush to the narrow winding streets lying between the better built sea frontage and the very mean outer suburbs occupied by negroes and Somalis

cleave a vista of faith to where at the end gleams the black and golden-banded pall of the Kaaba calling the faithful to the Durbar of God.

The pilgrim walks or runs round the Kaaba seven times, repeating the prescribed prayers, generally hand in hand with the inevitable "mutowif," and at the end of every circuit kissing the Black Stone; or if the crowd is too packed to approach it, he raises his hands to his ears and exclaims: "In the name of Allah, and Allah is omnipotent!" and kisses his fingers. This ceremony of the tauf is repeated every day during the first seven days of the Hadj. After it, the pilgrim drinks of the holy well of Zem-Zem, and feeds the pigeons of the Mosque, and performs the ceremony called El Sai, or the running seven times between the sacred hills of Safa and Marwah, quoting lengthily from the Koran and abundant in praise of Allah. This is a ritual of expiation. The rest of the day is filled with praying or attending sermons in the Prophet's Mosque, or visiting the holy sites in the neighbourhood of the city.

The great Mosque containing the Kaaba is the parent mosque, the model for the world of Islam. The inspiration is of the desert, conceived and inspired by illimitable horizons, designed for the expansion of the soul. It is in large open spaces, in broad and clean courts, in the bright light of the sun, that man appeals with the greatest sincerity to God. The Mosque is free of lurking mystery, dark images, oblique symbols, tortuous designs. It is " grand and simple, the expression of a single sublime idea."

Friday prayer in the Beyt Ullah is the most impressive scene. The uniform white of the pilgrims' ihrams covers the courtyard and the cloisters, but not, as in every other mosque in the world, in parallel straight lines governed by the kibla, or point of direction ; for the Kaaba alone, being the object to which they turn, has no kibla, and the pious form circles round it instead of the usual straight lines with their faces turned towards Mecca. As the imam

BLACK STALWARTS OF EMIR FEISAL'S BODYGUARD

With their bright blades flashing in the sun, as if keen to carve their master's foes, this ferocious-looking pair have apparently stipulated that a military pose is the only one to which they will consent. The scene is Akabah, a town of Arabia standing near the top of the gulf of the same name that forms the north-east arm of the Red Sea, and on the ancient pilgrim route from Egypt to Mecca

BEDUINS BOUND FOR THE TOWN FROM THE MOUNTAINS AND DESERT OF HEJAZ

Treeless hills and brown and tawny regions of wilderness broken by small and infrequent areas of vegetation are the dominant features of the landscape of the almost rainless Hejaz. And the people are as unfriendly to strangers as their arid land. These Beduins are on their way to Akabah from the interior of the country. Their purpose is peaceable enough, but every man has his gun and other weapons, and not even armed garrisons at blockhouses along the road can

mounts the pulpit the multitude are hushed in expectation, there is a little stir and agitation, freshets moving on the surface of the great human tide, the pious preface to the rhythmic swell. The imam is kneeling, arms dropped to the knee, eyes fixed on the earth, back fervently inclined, still as a chrysalis and as informed with the winged spirit. Up again, head erect, arms folded on the breast, eyes fixed raptly on the Kaaba, and as he leads the prayer and bends and sways and kneels, and stands erect and awed, or bowed in the presence of God, the others bend and sway with him, moved with one rhythmic impulse, perfectly attuned, body and soul, in the Prophet's inspired discipline of supplication.

Rhythmic Impulse of Religious Exaltation

Then, when the sermon ends, and he calls the takbir, the sea of white bodies rises with one impulse, thousands of white backs, like serried breakers, poised to fall. As the cry goes up from the pulpit the crests sway forward as one ; then, at a word, they rise again and sink to earth, every brow pressed to the marble of the flags, not a head to be seen in that vast multitude, only the white loin cloths and the soles of the feet. At the moment when the forehead is pressed to the earth, not a sound, save the cooing of Allah's pigeons, breaks the silence of the Mosque. Again the word is spoken, and a reanimating thrill pulses through the multitude. They rise with a solemn stir and rustle of muslin and clink of weapons, like ghosts in their winding-sheets at the trump of doom. The moment the prayer is finished there is a rush to the Kaaba, the ceremony of the tauf is repeated amid a din of pious shouts and exclamations that may be heard in the mountains around.

The eighth, ninth, and tenth days of the pilgrimage are taken up with the visit to Arafat. This is the most obligatory of all the ceremonies, " the true pilgrimage," and it is the observance of it that earns the pilgrim the title of Hadj. In addition to the pilgrims, every able-bodied citizen of Mecca, from the Grand Sherif downwards, takes the road. Burton and Wavell have described the crush. Between sunrise and ten in the morning at least half a million white-robed pilgrims, bareheaded, barefooted, half of them mounted and followed by a train of baggage animals, crowd the road and narrow defiles between Mecca and Muna. The roar of the great column is like a breaking sea, and the dust spreads for miles over the surrounding country.

Confusion after " The True Pilgrimage "

The ninth day is the ceremony of Wukuf, or " standing " on Mount Arafat, when the pilgrims listen to the sermon and weep and pray until sunset, and then decamp and return hastily to Muna, the half-way station. This is the hour of the greatest confusion. " Like the hurry from Arafat " is an Arab proverb which conjures up a scene of struggling and swarming humanity. Litters are crushed, pedestrians trampled, camels and asses overthrown, the pilgrims attack one another with sticks and knives.

On the morning of the tenth day there is another " stand " at Arafat, followed by the ceremony of the " stoning of the devils." The great, the lesser, and the middle devils are pillars marking the position of the pre-Islamic idols which were destroyed by the Prophet, and the rite of lapidation symbolises the Moslem's contempt for heathen gods.

Flight after Stoning the Devils

Here the press of pilgrims struggling like drowning men to approach as near as possible to the devils is so packed that a man might walk over their heads. Among them are " horsemen with rearing chargers, Beduins on wild camels, and grandees on mules with out-runners, breaking a way by assault and battery." A goat or a sheep is sacrificed after " the throwing." Then follows " the flight "—the return post-haste from Muna to Mecca in the midst of indescribable confusion. The tauf and the sai are repeated, once more the pilgrim kisses the Black Stone, and then, shaved and in secular dress, returns

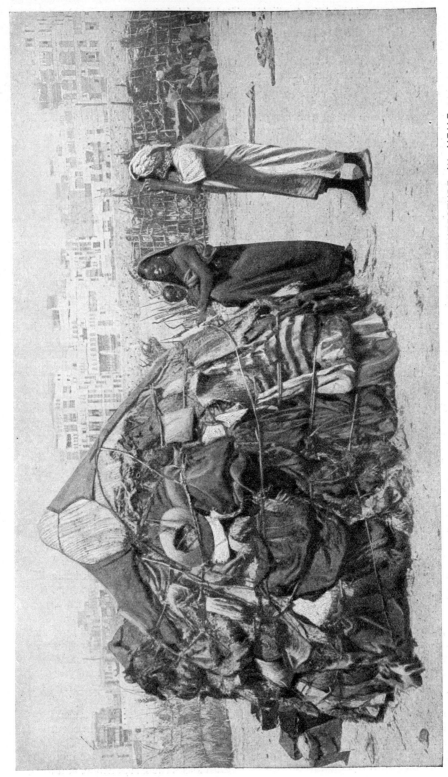

RAGS AND ROPES IN LIEU OF BRICKS AND MORTAR: NEGRO ARCHITECTURE IN HEJAZ

It would be difficult to imagine anything more unsavoury as a dwelling-place than the kind of beehive hut found in the negro villages near Jeddah. It consists of a mass of old felt, sacking, and rags of any and every description—this specimen even including an old hat among its components—lashed together with ropes. Verminous, dark, and airless, its only conceivable redeeming quality is its imperviousness to the solar rays due to the thickness of its textile substance

FIERCE WARRIORS OF THE DESERT WHO OWN ALLEGIANCE TO THE KING OF HEJAZ

Hejazi Beduins have a very definite reputation among travellers who have become acquainted with them. They are the most predatory cutthroats in Arabia, frankly plunderers with whom murder is merely a preliminary to pillage. While they boast of their pure lineage, they are not good Mahomedans, and, in turn, are a turbulent and troublesome element in the population. The Beduins here photographed have come to have audience with the Emir at Akabah

ARAB SHEIKH REPRESENTING THE EMIR

This is the Sheikh Youssef in his office of deputy to the Emir.
Seated in a portable collapsible chair of European origin, he
deigns for a moment to raise to the camera his eyes—those
watchful eyes of the East

high hill on the palm-trees of Medina, when his eyes will rest on the four glittering minarets and the green dome of the Prophet's tomb, when he will enter and pray even where the Prophet himself stood and prayed, saying: "One prayer in this, my mosque, is more helpful than a thousand elsewhere!"

The Hujra, the chamber in which Mahomet lies beside Abu-Bekr and Oman, the first two Caliphs, is hidden from the world by dark-green curtains, but, according to tradition, illuminated by a blinding supernatural light. Near the curtain on the north side is the tomb of Fatima, the Prophet's daughter. The garden she planted is outside. All the places consecrated by association with the Prophet's daily life are pointed out to the pilgrim who, as he drifts round ecstatically with the "mutowif," is filled with a great exaltation of spirit. The more emotional burst into tears and frantically kiss the railings of the Hujra, or fall in a swoon at the foot of the curtain. The imagination is more affected than at the Kaaba itself.

Arabia is little changed since the days of the Prophet, and Islam is less overlaid with superstitious accretions than other faiths. The people and the religion are much what they were twelve hundred years ago. The Mecca pilgrimage must be more like a translation from a dream to a reality than is possible in lands where materialism and progress have dulled the instinct of veneration. In Arabia the spirit of religious tradition colours every hour of the people's daily life.

before dark to Mecca for the day of the great feast. He may stay, if piety prompts him, for "the three days of the drying flesh," though this is no part of the obligatory ritual. The Hadj is completed.

Not more than a quarter of the pilgrims who appear at Arafat go on to Medina, though the Masjid-el-Nabawi, the Prophet's Mosque, is, after the Kaaba, the most venerable sanctuary of Islam. If the degree of merit is less in a visit to the Moslem Holy Sepulchre, the degree of ecstasy is even higher, and every devout Mussulman dreams of the day when he will gaze from a

TEMPORAL ACTIVITY IN ISLAM'S SECOND HOLY CITY

Quintessentially Arabian both in architecture and in atmosphere is Medina, the city that ranks next to
Mecca in sanctity in Moslem eyes, and, like Mecca, is forbidden to the "infidel." Down this main street,
flanked on both sides by shops crammed with wares of every kind, the devout Moslems pass on their way
to the sacrosanct Mosque that enshrines the tomb of the Prophet

Photo, M. Gervais-Courtellemont

Hejaz

II. From the Prophet Mahomet to King Hussein

By D. G. Hogarth, C.M.G., D.Litt.

Author of "The Penetration of Arabia," etc.

HEJAZ is the name generally given to the undelimited section of the Red Sea slope of the Arabian Peninsula which lies north of Yemen. Hali Point is considered its southern limit. On the north, Khaibar was the old limit of the domain of its sherifial princes ; but the district is now understood to extend up to Akabah and Maan.

It has no known history before about the date of the birth of Mahomet the Prophet, in or about 570 A.D. At that epoch Mecca, an old sanctuary and market of polytheistic tribesmen, had grown recently into a town through settlement successively by Yemenites (Khuthaa) and Koreish ; the last perhaps hailed from the Euphrates and introduced Allah and an Abrahamic tradition.

This commercially-minded tribe supported polytheism, seeing that the more gods—not excepting, it is said, the Byzantine Virgin—that could be settled round the Black Stone the more popular would be resort to its sanctuary. To promote this affluence and secure some safety for their caravan trade with Syria and Persia, the Meccan chiefs procured a suspension of tribal feuds during the month of annual pilgrimage and the perpetual interdiction of bloodshed within their own precinct.

The rest of Arabia, however, was not all pagan. In the east and centre a barbaric Christianity, derived through the Byzantine and Persian client-states of Ghassan and Hira, was professed ; much of the south-west was Abyssinian Christian or Judaized ; and Jews (or Judaized Aramaeans) were strong in north Hejaz and not unknown in Mecca.

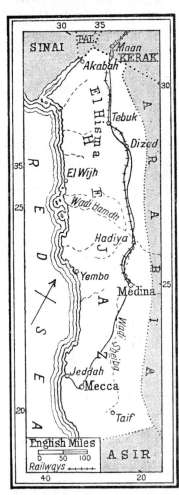

THE KINGDOM OF HEJAZ

See also map of Arabia, p. 192

Their influence, and that of other monotheists of Nejd and elsewhere, acted powerfully on a certain Meccan, Mahomet, born about A.D. 570, of the Hashimite clan of the Koreish. When he was sent, like other youths of family, with caravans to Ghassan and Syria, he realized that the kingdom of this world was to worshippers of a single god. His temperament, his sojourning in deserts, and, perhaps, an epileptic tendency made him see visions, from which state, having married money and had long leisure for meditation, he emerged before he was forty, convinced of a divine mission to make Allah even as Jehovah, and exalt his own native city as the focus of a common worship.

He began, about the year 610, with a single ally, Abu-Bekr, to sap the established polytheism by proselytising among the poor. After four years he had perverted more than a hundred families, and a sect crystallised round a small nucleus of better-class citizens, which men abused as the "Hanif" or the "Muslim," and so often threatened that presently the bulk of it fled to Christian Abyssinia, greatly to the chagrin of the Meccan chiefs. After failure to obtain delivery of these refugees, the religious conservatives of the city, fearful for their trade and the popularity of their sanctuary, took strong measures, outlawing and segregating the Muslamin during two years. But as this quarantine did not stop the disease, a compromise was effected.

This Mahomet soon disowned, and his preaching began to attract Arabs from without, notably certain Khasraj tribesmen of Yathrib in north Hejaz, who were seeking help in a local quarrel. The Meccan chiefs saw nothing for it but murder, whatever the consequence of blood-feud; but Mahomet slipped away into the waste and made his way to Yathrib on September 20, 622. That city was henceforward to be known as el-Medina, and this dates the era of Hejira or Flight.

Medina was small and barbarous despite its Yemenite tribes and its many Jews, but as it commanded Meccan trade routes to the north, Mahomet's enemies were gravely disturbed. At first, for lack of funds and prestige, he made little way in the place, the Jews refusing to accept him into the company of the Prophets. He could organize no more than occasional raids on small caravans, in one of which a Meccan protégé was killed during the sacred month. Early in 623, failure to ambush a large caravan, led by the Koreishite chief, Abu Sufian, ended in Mahomet and a few hundred believers colliding at Badr, where the Medina road emerges to the coast from the hills, with a more numerous force, sent to the caravan's support. The prayer-discipline kept the Muslamin in rank, while the enemy's cavalry and camelry wore itself out on the sands, and in a single day Mahomet became an acknowledged Prophet and a temporal King, able to put his faithful into the high places of Medina and deal at will with its Jews.

Rise of Mahomet's Star

The Meccans now made their effort. Marching three hundred miles to Medina itself, they skirted the walls on the west to meet Mahomet and his levy in the gardens under Mount Uhud. A doubtful day ended in the dispersal of the Muslamin and the wounding of their Prophet. Hearing he was dead, Abu Sufian, who desired no war with the city, drew off, only to learn too late that Mahomet was challenging again. Twice more the Meccans tried to finish with him, but their last expedition, in 627, failing to pass the Khandak, a low breastwork or trench covering the east of Medina, suffered too severely. Five years of such failure had served to exalt the Prophet's star in all Arabia. He had exterminated the Medinese Jews; he had won over the Beduins on the Meccan roads; and he judged it time to test feeling in Mecca by appearing, a would-be pilgrim, without its walls. Though he might not enter the city, he wrung a promise of a ten years' truce out of the disheartened chiefs, and went back well content. Fighting men now flocked to his banner, and the problem of feeding the lusts of their bodies and souls made him look round for non-believers to mulct. The last of the Jews at Khaibar served for a turn, but Mahomet foresaw a moment when no more satisfaction might be got from barren Arabia. Therefore, he sent out a famous notice of his intention to attack all the provinces on its borders, failing their ransom by confession of his creed and tributary submission.

Pilgrim, Conqueror, and Prophet

Meanwhile, another season of pilgrimage impending, he rode to Mecca again with a doubled following, entered the city, and during three days ostentatiously honoured its ancient shrine. Civic opinion slid ever more rapidly towards his side. Leaders in war, like Khalid el-Walid, followed his return to Medina, and when a twelve-month later he was again before Mecca with ten thousand riders, the city was at his mercy to order as he would by fusing its traditional observances with his own tenets. He had still to reckon with Beduin enmity outside, but a supreme victory at Hunain (probably near Wadi Safra and Badr) ended that danger; also, he had still to combat the hostility of Mecca's rival, Taif, but with this he compromised after an abortive siege. Later in that year, 630, he could muster thirty thousand men for a raid up the Syrian road, designed to wash out a serious check suffered a twelvemonth earlier in Ghassan. The season after his return saw his apogee. Embassies from all Arabia beset his mean hut, and he made his last pilgrimage unarmed. But his health was failing; campaigning, excitement, sensual indulgence, had sapped his vigour, and when fever attacked him on his return from Mecca in May, 632, he succumbed.

His army was camped outside the town, and as soon as the disputed succession was assured to Abu-Bekr, the Caliph thought well to dispatch it to the trans-Jordan country, as the Prophet had intended. Other soldiers, however, had to be found, for on news of Mahomet's death almost all the peninsula abjured Islam. Flying columns, reinforced late in the year by the returned army of Syria, restored the situation with astonishing ease, no serious resistance being met with except in Wadi Hanifa of Nejd.

Christendom Routed in the Holy Land

The re-entry into Medina of all these fighting zealots raised the old problem more acutely—how should they be satisfied?—and Abu-Bekr was compelled to the far-reaching plan of a permanent northern war on the marches of Syria and Mesopotamia. The bulk of the army was drafted off in three divisions towards Palestine, while a single column went north-eastward, followed by Khalid, to pick up Beduins and try its luck on the Euphrates. Abu-Bekr lived to hear, a year later, that, having carried the outposts of the Byzantine and Persian

Empires, both armies were unlikely to be seen again for long enough. Dying in August, 634, he left the sequel on the knees of Omar.

The second Caliph encouraged perseverance in the campaign by reinforcing both armies. The Syrian had been taken over by Khalid, who drove an imperial force out of Galilee and occupied Damascus, but had to withdraw again to better ground to wait the main attack of Byzantium. The final shock was delivered in August, 636, in the Yarmuk plain below the Lake of Gennesaret, on a day of torrid, sand-laden storm, and the army of Christendom recoiled a wreck. The emperor, who had waited at Antioch, repassed the Taurus, and, but for one abortive effort, left Syria to the Arabs.

Omar Master of Arab-speaking Asia

On the Euphrates four years of guerrilla war roused Yezdegird, Sassanian king of Ctesiphon, to restore Hira and end the trouble. The first objective attained, his general, Rustum, sat down, in 637, at Qadesiya to force Saad el-Waggas, the Muslim leader, to disperse his army or fight. The latter waited for Syrian reinforcements, and for such another day as had favoured the faith on the Yarmuk. Then he swooped on the Persian camp with the same catastrophic success. Fugitives, whom he chased to the Tigris, scared the Sassanian out of his capital, and two years later Yezdegird abandoned Mesopotamia for Iran. By 639 virtually all Asia that is Arab-speaking to-day obeyed Omar.

The Caliph laboured to control the uncontrollable and to bind to their poor place of origin men who were finding richer homes and founding greater States, and he did succeed in imposing canons of social, though not political, uniformity on all Muslim territories. He it was who provided for the committal of God's revealed words to an unalterable form, though the Koran was not actually ready before his murder in 644. He it was also who, using judiciously other remembered words and the daily example of the Prophet in life, confirmed to believers everywhere common social pre-eminence, without life being rendered intolerable for the unbelieving.

Schism, Sedition, and Strife

But more he could not do. Political control of the empire from Medina was impossible, as the invasion of Egypt by Amr el-As, in 639, without leave of his Caliph, sufficiently demonstrated. Under a third and weaker successor, Othman, disintegration quickened. Mesopotamia, Iran, and even a great part of Arabia began to dissent on spiritual not less than material grounds. Millions of new-made Muslamin, naturally incarnationist, who felt God's sanction of their faith and state weakening with each successor to the Caliphate, called for a leader of more immediate divine authority to stay the secularisation of Islam.

Ali, the Prophet's son-in-law, had been named (so they believed against the hostile witness of Ayesha) by the God-inspired lips. His sons, who were of the blood and adepts in the esoteric law, would provide a way for all flesh to God. When Othman tried to counter sedition by imposing on all provinces the rule of Meccan Koreishites, his days and those of the Medinese Empire were numbered. Men from Irak and Egypt slew him in his house in 656, and Ali, after a stiff struggle, came into his own.

The fourth—Legitimists hold him the first—Caliph made good in Arabia, Egypt, and even Irak, but not in Syria, where ruled the strongest of Othman's Meccans, Moawiya, son of old Abu Sufian. Ali left Medina to inaugurate Muslim civil war, but failing against Moawiya at Siffin, on the Euphrates, he accepted an arbitration inconsistent with his own claim to exclusive legitimacy. The Syrian governor assumed the Caliphate, and Ali died at Kufa in 660, by the hands of disappointed vindicators of his divine right.

Rise of the Grand Sherifate of Mecca

For about a generation Hejaz held out against the secular Caliphate established by Moawiya in Syria in 660 ; but by 692 its opposition was worn out. It passed peaceably to the Abbasid Caliphs ; but, remaining at heart attached to the line of Ali, it needed to be alternately chastised and cajoled. Haroun al-Rashid, in particular, did his utmost to conciliate its Holy Cities, but they were treated as provincial. Like the rest of the peninsula, Hejaz fell under the Carmathians, and in 928 suffered at their hands the loss of the Black Stone of the Kaaba. A sherifal family of Nejd then seized Mecca, and set up a private tyranny in the city about 950 ; but the Fatimite Caliph of Egypt expelled it and introduced, in 966, the Mussa sherifs, who are regarded as the first legitimate princes of Mecca.

Thus in schism and under heretical domination began the Grand Sherifate of Mecca, destined for two centuries to be a scourge of the pilgrimage. A show of orthodoxy and consideration for the Muslim community was not assured again until Saladin and his Turco-Syrians, having captured Yemen, gripped Hejaz between their twin forces in South Arabia and in Syria. The result was an abasement of the Sherifate, from which Qatadah, of a new house of Ali's kin, redeemed it about 1200. His dynasty, generally respectful of Egypt, but careful to rest on a nearer alliance with the Zeidi heretics of Yemen, contrived to recover practical independence and keep it till, in the fifteenth century, the later Mameluke Sultans took steps, in the interest of the common faith, to mediatise the custody of its spiritual centre. Unconsciously they prepared a way for stronger Turks than themselves—the victorious Osmanlis, who passed over their bodies to take Hejaz without a struggle in 1517.

The Sherifial dynasty, however, continued without interruption, and its history throughout the sixteenth, seventeenth, and eighteenth centuries tells of persistent efforts to recover practical independence and establish a lasting hegemony over the Beduin tribes of western Nejd and the oasis of Qasim. This aim was virtually achieved by about 1750, and the half century following this date is looked back to now as the Golden Age of the Sherifate. It was closed by the Wahabite invasion of 1803, which led after a few years to an occupation of the country by Mehemet Ali, Viceroy of Egypt. He did not withdraw till 1840. After a few years of anarchy the Turks succeeded in imposing their control again on the Holy Cities. They experienced constant trouble with the Abadilah family of Sherifs, which Mehemet Ali had preferred to the throne, and in 1838 ships of Great Britain and France had to intervene with their guns at Jeddah to repress an anti-Turk movement. By the 'eighties local power in Hejaz had passed entirely from the Emir to the Vali of Mecca.

The revolutions of 1908-9 at the heart of the Ottoman Empire weakened its hold in Arabia. A new Emir of Mecca, Hussein, treated his masters with growing contumely, and Abdul Aziz es-Saud, heir of the Wahabite Emirs, who had turned the Rashids out of Riadh and Qasim in 1902, fell on Hasa, in 1913. When the Turks embarked in the European War further revolts were to be expected. In Yemen they increased their holding by invasion of the Aden Protectorate. But in Hejaz Emir Hussein was not to be staved off, once he had seen how Arab nationalism was dealt with in Syria, and learned that a Turkish Expeditionary Force was to traverse his country.

Supported by British supplies, he rose in June, 1916, and in little more than three months freed all south Hejaz; but he could make no impression on the well-supplied garrison of Medina, nor on its railway communications, till his son, Feisal, moved up the coast early in 1917 to operate first from El Wijh and finally from Akabah. Neither Medina nor Maan, however, was taken in the end by his arms. Allenby's advance, in September, 1918, emptied the last, and the terms of the Armistice tardily compelled, in January, 1919, the surrender of the first.

Meanwhile, in 1916, Hussein had proclaimed himself king of Hejaz, aspiring to be single lord of all the Arabs. The unreality of his power, however, was exposed, as soon as his European helpers and the Turks had withdrawn, by the Emir of Riadh, strengthened by a recent revival of Wahabite fervour among certain of his subjects calling themselves Brethren (Akhwan). He captured Taif in 1920, and would have had Mecca, like his forefathers, but for his fear of the British, whom he wished as allies but had done little to help in the war.

Unsettled conditions continued in 1921-22. Towards the close of the former year fighting took place between the forces of the Sultan of Nejd and Ibn Rashid, resulting in the surrender of the latter's capital and the capture of Taif, sixty miles south-east of Mecca, thus threatening the position of King Hussein. The rule of the latter, by no means secure, was only possible owing to the subsidy granted by the British Government to the neighbouring Arab chieftain Sultan Ibn Saud of Nejd. In addition, both the King of Hejaz and the Imam of Yemen are subsidised, pending development of their territory under British auspices.

HEJAZ: FACTS AND FIGURES

The Country

Lies for nearly 700 miles along east coast of Red Sea, stretching about 200 miles inland, from Akabah on the north to Asir on the south, with the emirate of Nejd and the Great Nefud and Great Arabian Deserts on the east. Includes territories of the Zahran, Ghamid, and Bisha tribes. Armies in 1918 numbered 40,000 men.

Government

Free and independent kingdom since 1916 when, under the Grand Sherif of Mecca, it threw off Turkish allegiance and the Sherif, also known as Emir Hussein Ibn Ali, assumed the title King of Hejaz, to whom Great Britain grants a subsidy. By the Treaty of Sèvres, August 10, 1920, the loss by Turkey of her Arab territories was confirmed, including that of Hejaz.

Products

Area barren or semi-barren, chief crop being dates, grown especially in Medina oasis. Small quantity of hides, wool and gum exported. Chief source of wealth derived from annual pilgrimage to Mecca.

Communications

Hejaz railway, from Medina to Damascus, about 1,105 miles, constructed 1901-8.

Chief Towns

Mecca, capital (population 70,000), Medina (10,000), Yembo, and Taif. Jeddah is the chief port of the country, and in addition to its importance as the place of entry of pilgrims going to the Holy Cities of Mecca and Medina, has a large trade in carpets, hides, coffee, mother-of-pearl, etc., with a population of 25,000.

SMASHED ARCHES AT TEGUCIGALPA IN THE CHOLUTECA'S FLOODED PATH TO THE SEA

Anxiously crowding the forlorn-looking ends of the broken bridge, the unfortunate people are waiting under their umbrellas until communication is once more established by means of a hawser. The force and drive of the fierce volume of angry water may be gauged by a glance at the difference in the level of the river on each side of the arches. Through these the torrent pours and whirls, trying still to demolish this barrier in its course, and surging and eddying to gain its freedom

Honduras

I. Its Mixed Peoples & Their Pursuits

By Percy F. Martin, F.R.G.S.

Author of "El Salvador of the Twentieth Century," etc.

CLAIMING an area of 46,250 square miles, Honduras measures about 375 miles in length by 125 miles in width; much of this territory is mountainous or malarial, and, therefore, commercially unprofitable. The northern and north-eastern boundaries are formed by the beautiful Gulf of Honduras and the Caribbean Sea, while on the south-west and west stretch the Pacific Ocean and the neighbouring States of El Salvador and Guatemala. Ranges of mountains, rising tier upon tier, distinguish all three countries alike; but, fortunately for Honduras, the number of its volcanoes is considerably less, and such craters as exist are—and long have been —quiescent.

Comparatively few members of the Central American chain of volcanoes are of the type with which fierce eruptions are commonly associated, and the fertility of the soil on their flanks and slopes—due to the high percentage of soda and potash contained in volcanic dust—tempts agriculturists to remain even in a neighbourhood that again and again has been devastated— as has been the case in El Salvador and Jamaica. Happily, hitherto, Honduras has escaped such experiences.

Magnificent, Forested Mountain Heights

The highest of the mountain peaks is a little under 10,000 feet; but there are many that soar above 5,000 feet, while nearly all are thickly clothed with closely-growing forest and dense undergrowth, which take on a rich, deep green in the bright sunlight, imparting a charming aspect as one approaches from the sea. Close to the frontier of Nicaragua one sees the magnificent Jutigalpa, Camasca, and Tompocente ranges, all forming part of the immense Antillean system. But there are also two subterranean ridges stretching across the Caribbean Sea between Honduras and the Sierra Maestra range in Cuba and from Cape Gracias á Dios to Jamaica. No doubt at one remote period the great banks of the western Caribbean formed projections of land connecting Central America with Jamaica—and possibly Cuba.

Natural Beauties of a Sun-Blest Land

Many and bountiful rivers, like the Choluteca, the Patuca, and the Ulua, and the Chamelicón, León, Aguan, and Tristo; large lakes such as Caratasca — really a lagoon—and Yojoa, twenty-six miles long by eight miles wide; fertile plateaux and valleys—the Plain of Comayagua stretches forty miles in length—a wealth of fauna and flora such as can be found in few other countries of the world, are among the natural attractions of this sun-blest land, supplying "all the world's bravery that delights the eye."

The Republic likewise has many excellent ports, the chief one being Amapala on the Pacific; Puerto Cortés and Omoa are on the Gulf of Honduras; La Ceiba, Trujillo, and Roatan on the Caribbean. But Amapala alone offers good anchorage; the others are merely open roadsteads, passengers and goods being taken ashore in surf-boats and lighters. Inland transport is still principally conducted on horse or mule-back. Of railroads—practically all on the Caribbean side—there are fewer than 400 miles in operation.

What sort of people inhabit this region? Where was their original home? How came they to form part of the inhabitants of Central America? Upon these questions authorities differ —as authorities will—though each may base his belief upon reason or experience. The present race, where they are not

WHERE THE BROAD HIGHWAY SPANS A SLUMBERING STREAM
Mighty are the piers that uphold this fine bridge, its parapets white in the sun, and the solidity seems unwarranted by the placidity of the river, still enough, despite the shallows, to reflect the arches above. The scene would be very different after the rains, with the flood-water boiling round these stout supports and filling the stony channel. Nor could the oxherd so lightly lead his cattle to water

Spanish, are the offspring of the Caribs, a savage tribe having its original habitat at the headwaters of the Xingen and other southern affluents of the far-away Amazon in Brazil.

Certain it is that the Caribs did not come from the North American Indians, as some writers have boldly declared; but, migrating to the Guianas, they spread from that region to Venezuela, thence north to the Indies, Nicaragua, and Honduras. Remnants or descendants of these primitive people —primitive no longer—may still be found scattered between Central America and Central Brazil. Possessing no kind of political or social adherence, they nevertheless present a sort of kinship which rests entirely on their common speech—a highly polysynthetic stock language represented by a considerable number of extremely divergent branches and dialects.

Travellers penetrating far into the interior of Honduras have found the inhabitants outside the towns and villages a reserved and restless people, somewhat suspicious of all foreigners, and fearful even of their native rulers. Unlike the conditions prevailing in the neighbouring State of El Salvador, social and political power in Honduras is largely free from the dictates of any middle class. "Hacendados" and "estanciéros"—owners of plantations and cattle-ranches — exercise little influence over the common people; on the other hand, the number of lawyers, bankers, doctors, engineers, journalists and other professional men carry considerable weight, especially among the great mass of people below them.

Physically the natives of Honduras are not unattractive. Some are even handsome. Many of the men are well-built, extremely robust, and stand above normal height; even those inhabiting the malarial coasts display little evidence of ravage by fever. The tribal men have long, narrow faces, slightly oblique eyes, well-shaped noses, and straight, black, usually very dirty hair. In colour their skins are reddish-brown, seldom remarkable for cleanliness. The tribal women are less noticeable for physical allurement; they are and always have been the drudges of their men-folk, and bear upon their tired features, and in the neglect of their apparel and person, strong evidence of the hard lives that they lead and the burdens that they must bear to the last days of their colourless lives.

But natives of Honduras, like those of other Spanish colonies in South and Central America, have never been slaves. The Viceroys, fulfilling instructions from the Crown in Madrid, were ever solicitous about the welfare of the conquered races. Enslavement was prohibited. The Indians were legally recognized and treated, at least nominally, as subjects of the Crown. This was designed to protect them against exploitation and oppression, while restraining them from any relapse into the ways of barbarism. But in Honduras, as in all other Spanish-American colonies, through disregard of these pious instructions, the lot of the natives was often a hard one.

The Hondurans are not a fecund race. The population, to-day approximating 600,000 (it was 350,000 in 1861), increases slowly, although large families are not infrequently met with. On the other hand, infantile mortality is large, arising to a considerable degree from neglect and infantile disease.

As in most Latin States, families are closely allied by marriage. Among the wealthier classes young girls are kept under strict surveillance, and marriage is only arranged by consent of the parents. While young men and women are not supposed to go out together without a chaperon, traditional barriers of this character are fast disappearing. The " new woman " is making her appearance here as elsewhere, and with the spread of female education she is likely to become a permanent institution.

As parents, the Hondurans are an affectionate race, not always displaying, however, that intelligence in the training of the infantile mind or in controlling

FAMILY PHOTOGRAPHY AND A HONDURAN HOME
From the father and his elder sons down through stages of graduated growth to the last baby held up above the older heads by the mother standing unassumingly at the back, all the family circle are here on view. As may be imagined, the housing accommodation is not luxurious, and there is not much danger of feeling lonely within the restricted confines of these sun-cracked walls

Photo, F. J. Youngblood

the juvenile propensity for mischief that more advanced nations adopt. From the age of two to six the peasant children are allowed to run almost wild, and a merry life they contrive to lead. Then they become enlisted among the working members of the family, and usually take to the innovation willingly enough. Domestic life is intimate, not to say crowded.

Spanish America, and family life is, for the most part, beautifully portrayed, offering, indeed, in certain respects a marked contrast to that of other nations. The women of Spanish origin consider that they have done their part when they have made their well-ordered houses a pleasant abode for their men-folk and their children. As house-keepers, home-makers, wives and

IN A TOWN OF THE HINTERLAND OF HONDURAS

San Pedro Sula, a place of some eight thousand inhabitants, stands upon the railway from Puerto Cortés to La Pimienta. Above is a photograph of its main street, and a pleasing aspect of the scene is the presence of a border of trees, which give the muddy thoroughfare, rut-worn with the passing of many wheels, an air almost of a boulevard

It is quite a common occurrence to find several generations abiding peace-fully and patiently, amid much in-convenience, under the same roof; married and single members of the family often occupy the same room, the oldest member—grandfather or great-grandfather—being much deferred to, and as a rule, governing his little circle with a despotic but tolerant hand. Indeed, parental authority is greatly respected in this country, as throughout

mothers, the women of South and Central America have little to learn from their European sisters.

No doubt in their original state the native races wore skins. The Caribs knew little and cared less about the weaving of threads for clothing, but purchased, by bargaining their own produce, such materials as came their way in the course of trading. To-day the people are industrious. The usual type of costume, except in the towns,

solemnity. The Hondurans have been reproached by certain writers with being a lazy and indolent race, but although few are " blessed with the horny hands of toil," they are far from that. In common with the other five States constituting the Central American Republics, the people of Honduras are ten per cent. white, fifty per cent. Indians, and the remainder mestizo or negro. The lower classes are composed of numerous tribes with varying customs, and no doubt a certain proportion of them obey the latent instinct of hatred for physical labour. But consider the climate under which they live—the intense heat, the

SUNDAY MARKET IN THE ISLAND PORT OF AMAPALA

On Tigre Island, in the blue Bay of Fonseca, stands this town with its free port and sheltered road-stead, where the visiting ships find safe anchorage. Above is seen the crowded market, a native woman chewing a cigar and a buyer mopping his heated brow. There is an export trade in silver, coffee, and hides, and steamers call from New York

BATTERY OF HONDURAS ARTILLERY AT PRACTICE MANOEUVRES NEAR LA ISLA

Artillery practice is one of the most stirring of military manoeuvres, and these Honduran gunners are determined to lack nothing in verve and smartness. Unlimbered in the rear, the guns are man-handled into line, a non-commissioned officer marking the position that each is to occupy. In the background, an officer with his orderly stands watching the operation, and all that indicates that this is only practice and not the real thing is the presence of some civilians on the left front

ever-present malaria (on the coasts), and the slight incentive to active work by reason of the prodigality of food products, both natural and cultivated, around them. In their disinclination to indulge in continuous toil these people differ in no respect from other Indian races living in a land whose soil and climate remove much of the necessity of manual toil.

Labour in Central America generally is independent and proud, feeling little necessity to solicit the patronage of capital. On the contrary, capital, in the person of the contractor and cultivator, has often to solicit the aid of labour. The pernicious preaching of alien labour agitators, however, has penetrated to Honduras, especially at the ports. Unpleasant and usually unprofitable disputes have occurred of recent years. In August, 1920, it was necessary for the United States to despatch the gunboat Sacramento to La Ceiba to quell the fierce revolt of labourers in progress there.

Labour, Politics, and Amusements

Something like 600,000 bushels of maize are grown annually, chiefly in the Departments of Copán, Gracias and Santa Barbara. Millions of bananas are cultivated and exported; wheat, sugar, rice and tobacco, coconuts, lemons and oranges; sarsaparilla, indigo and other dyes and spices are planted; and altogether, through the energies of the working-classes over £650,000 worth of produce is reaped annually, while the Republic records a total annual export worth nearly £2,000,000.

Like most Latin Americans, the Hondurans devote much of their attention to politics. Recognizing the effect that a good or a bad government may have upon individual as well as collective prosperity, every voter—and all citizens over 21 years of age, or over 18 years if married, and who can read and write, have a vote—goes conscientiously to the poll. That they are not always allowed to exercise their privileges when they get there, finding preventive bayonets more plentiful than ballot-boxes, must be admitted.

Located on the river Choluteca, 114 miles distant from the port of Amapala and 207 miles from Puerto Cortés, Tegucigalpa, the capital, 3,500 feet above sea level, must be reached by a tediously long but well-constructed highway. The city is neither picturesque nor beautiful—some might even regard it as distinctly prosaic—but it is fairly comfortable, notwithstanding its subtropical climate and average temperature of 74 degrees, its narrow streets and some 40,000 (mostly noisy) inhabitants. Of amusements there are few; the main native attraction in the absence of the popular bull-ring (which the people are too impecunious to afford) is the cock-pit; some of the most valuable game-cocks are bred in Tegucigalpa.

Great Possibilities for Cattle Raising

Where wealth has been accumulated or acquired—and it is found chiefly concentrated among the old Spanish families established for centuries upon the same domains—it has been created by cattle-raising. No tropical or subtropical country possesses better natural facilities for pastoral pursuits than Honduras. With cheap grazing lands, abundant if somewhat erratic labour, salubrious climate and luxuriant vegetation, combined with an exceptional wealth of river, lake and spring water, this favoured Republic might easily rival Argentina or Uruguay in the number and quality of horned cattle that it could rear. And yet in Honduras to-day there are probably fewer than 500,000 head.

One of the most notable features of Honduran forests is the extraordinary number of mahogany trees, veritable giants, growing prolifically and in regiments, practically untouched by the axe, notwithstanding the millions of potential capital that they represent in marketable state. Known botanically as Swietenia Mahagoni, this beautiful tree attains a height of 100 feet or more, and grows to an immense girth. Sound throughout, no better wood could be found for the manufacture of furniture.

Honduras

II. The Story of the Central American Buffer State

By Percy F. Martin, F.R.G.S.

Author of " Through Five Republics of South America," etc.

HONDURAS, among other countries of the New World, owes its discovery to the Genoese traveller Cristóbal Colón (Christopher Columbus). Sailing along the coast to Cape Gracias à Dios, on a certain day in August, 1502, upon his fourth and last voyage, and accompanied by his brother Bartoloméo, the intrepid explorer landed on these shores, to find the natives unexpectedly friendly, but curious. After formally annexing the country in the name of his Sovereigns, Ferdinand V. and Isabella, Columbus returned to Spain, only to die there, a poor and discredited man, four years later.

The dispatch of Hernando Cortés and his hosts followed. They speedily conquered the country, their colonising progress being accompanied, however, by few

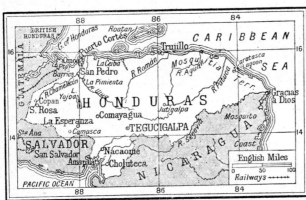

THE REPUBLIC OF HONDURAS

of the customary Spanish brutalities. The fact that there survive to-day numerous pure-blooded descendants of the original inhabitants testifies to the comparative mildness of the conquerors' methods. But their progress was not without difficulties. Writing to Ferdinand's successor, Emperor Charles V., on September 23, 1526, Cortés observed : " I can assure your Majesty that even the horses, led as they were by hand and without their riders over the tops of the hills, sank to their girths in the mire!"

Once free from the bondage of the Spanish vice-royalty—with its perpetual exactions, abuses, cruelties, and injustice —the Hondurans found themselves handicapped by their poverty, and confronted by fresh problems arising from the changed conditions. Independence has been described—was it not by Napoleon ? —as " a rocky island, like honour, without a beach." The Hondurans soon found that it had its responsibilities as well as its privileges, and self-reliance its drawbacks.

At no time has the small State produced any leader or patriot like Miranda or Sucre, of Venezuela ; Bolívar, the Washington of South America ; San Martín, the great general of Argentina ; Artigas, of Uruguay ; O'Higgins, of Chile ; or Morélos, of Mexico. But Morazán is still a name famous in Central American history. He it was who led the successful revolt in the nineteenth century against Spain, and although in the end he personally failed to maintain his influence, he failed gloriously.

Honduras' political history proved comparatively uneventful until the struggle for freedom from Spain in 1821. Released from that domination, Honduras joined the Mexican Confederation, but broke away in 1823. Remaining in the Central American Federation, which followed, till 1839, the people formed themselves into an independent and separate State ; some twenty years later (November, 1859), Great Britain ceded to them the Bay Islands and, later on, helped to finance their governments. After many tentative forms of administration, the first Constitution was adopted in 1848 ; the second in 1865 ; the third in 1880 ; and the fourth, now in existence, in 1894. The capital was likewise changed from Comayagua to Tegucigalpa.

For years past Honduras has been— and for years to come seems destined to remain—the buffer-State between El Salvador, Guatemala, and Nicaragua, fated by geographical propinquity to sustain the shock of the rivalries, racial as well as political, of these quarrelsome neighbours. The unicameral Congress sits for sixty days, a period which may be extended forty days at its own discretion or that of the President of the Republic. He may also convene the Assembly in extraordinary session.

HONDURAS & ITS STORY

In 1860 a filibustering expedition under William Walker, an American of Scottish descent, landed at Trujillo from the United States and attacked Honduras, as Nicaragua had been attacked some years earlier (1855), the latter people being compelled to elect him President. This second expedition proved the last; Walker, surrendering to the British, was tried and executed by his enemies. In 1906 Honduras and El Salvador went to war with Guatemala, while revolutions occurred between 1910-11. Boundary questions with its neighbours led to war on many other occasions. In 1911 King Alphonso XIII. of Spain settled one controversy with Nicaragua, and another with Guatemala two years later. President Dávila, obliged to resign in 1911, was succeeded, by Francisco Bertran (1913 and 1916), and by General Bonilla, a former Executive and refugee in the United States. A far-reaching treaty with the Northern Republic was signed November, 1913.

Several times Honduras has attempted to become a member of a Central American Union, as a safeguard against North American aggression, but no settlement has been reached. One further effort in this direction is being organized under the auspices of a "Central American Federation." The important commercial treaty entered into with Great Britain on January 21, 1887, was "denounced" in October, 1909, and came to an end in 1910. Although determined efforts were made by the British Minister (the late Sir Lionel Carden) to renew and improve the treaty, opposition by the United States Government prevented it.

Yellow fever raged in 1912 and 1919, when the Gracias and Cordona revolutions, among others, occurred, but were speedily suppressed. The British destroyer Constance took an effective part. Armed conflicts again ensued between Honduras and Nicaragua, August, 1918, and following months, while trouble threatened with Germany, the President placing an embargo on German lighters and interning their owners. General Rafael López Gutiérrez, a former revolutionary, became Executive in 1920. His opponent—Alberto Membreno, also a former president (he died February, 1921)—had caused popular risings, both United States and British warships again intervening. Fresh revolts broke out (February, 1920), martial law being proclaimed.

In August labour troubles arose, and the U.S. gunboat Sacramento landed troops at La Ceiba. In November, the presidents of Honduras, Nicaragua, and El Salvador met at Amapala, and in January, 1921, a diplomatic mission from Costa Rica visited Honduras. On June 5, 1921, was signed the Pact of Union with El Salvador and Guatemala. The finances of the States for 1919-20 fell into low condition, the public accounts showing a deficiency of 1,082,000 pesos, the total outstanding foreign debt (in arrear for nearly fifty years) now exceeding £27,800,000; the home debt reaches 3,556,000 pesos. In March, 1920, the British Controlled Oilfields, Limited, were granted by Congress a concession for oil over territory approximating 30,000 square miles.

HONDURAS: FACTS AND FIGURES

The Country

Bounded north by the Gulf of Honduras and Caribbean Sea, south by Nicaragua, Pacific Ocean, and Salvador, and west by Guatemala. Area about 46,250 square miles; population in 1921, 637,114, chiefly Indians, with an admixture of Spanish blood, and on the north a large number of negroes. Includes 17 departments and largely unexplored territory of La Mosquitia.

Government and Constitution

Republic under charter of October, 1894. Legislative power vested in Congress of forty-two members, one per 10,000 inhabitants, chosen by popular vote for four years, and Council of five ministers; President nominated and elected by popular vote for four years.

Defence

Universal service in regular army from age of twenty-one to thirty-five; reserves from age of thirty-five to forty. Total force 77,611, of which 21,505 in reserves.

Commerce and Industries

Chief products: Bananas, coconuts, coffee, tobacco, sugar, indigo, vegetables, yucca, wood, cereals. Castor-oil plant cultivated. Rubber production is decreasing. Straw hats and cigars made for export. About 500,000 head of cattle. Minerals include gold, silver, copper, lead, zinc, iron, antimony. Exports, 1920-1921, totalled £1,357,147; imports, £4,180,675. Silver peso normally one-half of American dollar.

Communications

Mules and ox-carts general for travelling and transport. Between 400-500 miles of railways. Telegraph lines 4,663 miles; telephone lines, 877 miles.

Religion and Education

Prevailing religion, Roman Catholic, but without State aid; all creeds guaranteed freedom. Education free, secular, and compulsory, from age of seven to fifteen. Over 900 schools; Central University, Central Institute for secondary instruction, and a military and automobile school at Tegucigalpa; school of jurisprudence at Comayagua.

Chief Towns

Tegucigalpa, capital (population, about 40,000), La Esperanza (11,450), Santa Rosa (10,570), Choluteca (8,060), Nacaome (8,150), San Pedro Sula (7,800), Comayagua (3,000).

YOUTHFUL ASPIRANTS FOR THE FAVOURS OF CUPID

A quaint vintage custom is observed in the Baja district of Southern Hungary. On certain days the unmarried women and girls, carrying vases of flowers and cooking utensils, go into the fields to prepare a meal for the men-workers. The flowers and fruit are presented, and if a man fancies a particular girl he hands her a large lump of sugarloaf as a token of their betrothal

Photo. Kankovszky, Budapest

Hungary

I. Magyars & Tziganes of To-Day

By F. H. Hamilton

Writer and Traveller

ALONE among the nations of Europe the Hungarians, or as they prefer to be called, the Magyars, have kept up the structure of medieval society, or rather the structure of society into which that of the Middle Ages developed. What rural England was in the eighteenth century, when it was described for us by Addison, in his Sir Roger de Coverley essays in the "Spectator," Hungary still is to-day. There is the same dependence upon agriculture. There is the same separation of classes, which does not prevent the magnate or the squire from being on excellent terms with the farmers and peasants. There is the same simplicity of outlook upon life.

The Magyar magnates, it is true, have been influenced ("corrupted," the purists say) by their life in Vienna, by their habit of travel, by the readiness with which they pick up foreign, especially English, ways. But the class next to them, the lesser nobility, what we may call the squires or the county families, have been mostly too poor to change their traditional mode of living. They have maintained the feudal aspect of social relations. Originally all who owned land were "nobles," and helped to put armies into the field by sending one or more knights at the king's call, or by contributing to the outfit of one. In return for this service they were excused from the payment of taxes, and they enjoyed this exemption up to 1848, a curious relic of bygone feudalism. In that year the squires determined to surrender their privilege, but the magnates would not give it up until it was taken from them.

Nor have the magnates yet abandoned the wearing of their traditional costumes, which make them look as if they were going to a fancy dress ball in some family costume kept carefully in an old chest with lavender and rosemary. These are, of course, kept for ceremonial occasions; but there is no disposition to fall in with the general disposition elsewhere to regard such finery as antiquated, and to leave dressing-up to children. It was partly because the Austro-Hungarian Foreign Minister in 1914 was known to the world by a photograph taken in his Magyar magnate's dress that the world refused to take him seriously, and instinctively

VESTAL VIRGIN OF HUNGARY

On the eve of marriage, clothed thus in spotless raiment, she is expected, by custom, to spend a day and night before the village altar worshipping the Holy Virgin

Photo, Kankovszky, Budapest

sympathised with Serbia in the quarrel over the murder of the Archduke Ferdinand. Any kind of uniform is dear to the Magyar mind. No such variety of military equipment was ever seen to compare with that which amused the visitor to Budapest during the early years of Admiral Horthy's "reign." It seemed as if every officer one met must have designed his own kit, and tried to outdo all the rest in elegance and originality.

Next to the squires come the members of the professional class, very few in number, the business men, not more numerous, and the shopkeepers in the towns. This section is made up largely of Jews, and the feeling between Magyars and Jews, which had improved during the period before the Great War, has become dangerously bitter again. There is in the country a long and evil record of persecution. Not until the end of the eighteenth century were Jews admitted to the right of voting, and then they were subjected in many places to an odious form of derision. An Imperial decree allowed them to

SWEETHEARTS LINKED BY SWEET SYMBOLISM

Large lumps of sugarloaf are displayed in the window of a girl-vintager's house in the Baja district on the Danube to signify the fact that she has become engaged. These sweet emblems of affection are not usually removed from view until the marriage has been celebrated, and the arrival of the rustic lover at his lady's home would indicate that the course of their true love is running smoothly

Photo, Kankovszky, Budapest

THE WOMAN AT THE WELL, A FAVOURITE TRYSTING-PLACE

In a hamlet not far distant from Kalocsa this well is the most popular of institutions. In the dryest of seasons its waters never fail, for, as in many a Danube region, the supply is drawn from that grand old river which, to some extent, makes up for Hungary's lack of seaboard. If this wooden wheel could speak, it would relate countless happy stories of rustic lovers

Photo, Kankovszky, Budapest .

take German names in place of their own Hebrew names. Very many were ticketed with their nicknames, often opprobrious, given them by their Magyar neighbours. Thus one would be called Redhead, and another the Fire-extinguisher, and another the Knocker. These and many such surnames exist to this day, perhaps altered in spelling, but recalling the time when the Jew was an object of contempt and derision.

The revival of these feelings, with fear added, is due partly to the capture of commerce by the Jews, partly to the bitter resentment aroused by the short Bolshevist experiment in Hungary, which was directed mainly by Jewish revolutionaries. Since there existed no middle class when the country began to come within the orbit of the European trade system, and since the nobles would have nothing to do with trade, the Jews had it all their own way. They took to business with alacrity, and soon had pretty well all of it in their hands. This turned the aristocracy against them, and they naturally struggled against this ill-will by making the most of the power which money gave them. They went into politics, their influence became noticeable everywhere.

Most of those who have made the art, learning, and science of Hungary known outside its borders have belonged to this race. They have the lowest

FEMININE CONFIDENCE FLAUNTING IN FROCKS AND FRILLS

She comes down the steps with a splendid swagger, born of proud consciousness that her frock is proof against the criticism of any envious woman, and that her face and figure will compel the admiration of any man. Physically not unlike a Turk, this woman is of the semi-Oriental Hungarian aboriginal stock, and belongs to the district of Sarköz, about fifty miles from the junction of the Danube and the Drave

PAUSING FOR FRIENDLY CONVERSE AFTER CHURCH SERVICE

After attending church these Hungarian women, in their voluminous black garb, find it pleasing to relax a little and chat together before wending their several ways back to home. Perhaps they are discussing the sermon, and the little girl in white stands listening to the enlightened opinions of her elders. The façade of the building from which they have just emerged can be seen in the background

Photo, Kankovszky, Budapest

the Red Terror. The White Terror which followed was just as bloodthirsty, but it was regarded as a justifiable reprisal.

Under the reign of Admiral Horthy the small landowners controlled Parliament, and "Christian Nationalists" held the greater number of Cabinet offices. Admiral Horthy had all the simplicity of the Magyar squire, therefore he seemed to this class to be well qualified to rule. His conceptions of

LORD OR HENCHMAN?
With his manly, upright figure, energetic appearance and handsome costume, he might well pass for the Mayor of Debreczen, whose worthy coachman he happens to be
Photo, A. W. Cutler

IN THE HUNGARIAN HIGHLANDS
Barefoot she wanders at will on the verdant hillside, her fingers never at rest. In simple guise, Hungary has cherished many an ancient industry
Photo, Florence Farmborough

percentage of illiterates among them, the Evangelical Protestants coming close after, with the Roman Catholics some distance behind, and the Orthodox (Eastern Church) out of the running. It is unfortunate that "Christian" should in Hungary mean anti-Jewish, for although the Jews are only about five per cent. of the nation, they include half the doctors, engineers, and lawyers. The "Christian" parties proclaim their hostility to liberty of speech and the Press; they favour the policy of the heavy hand upon all who advocate change. These are the views which triumphed as the result of the excesses of

COOPERATION IN JELLY MAKING AT CZINKOTA

They are making plum jelly, an almost universal task in Hungarian villages in the autumn, husband and wife taking turns at stirring the jelly, which must be kept up continuously for twenty-four hours. At first sight the husband seems to be wearing the petticoats which his wife might have donned with advantage, but in fact they are trousers cut very wide and loose

Photo, A. W. Cutler

politics were childish. He would declare, for example, that he was in favour of a free Press, and then go on instantly to say that "of course anyone who published anything hurtful to the country must be severely punished." That kind of "freedom" seemed right to the minds of the peasants as well as to those of the squires. The peasants supported Horthy, therefore, and opposed the return of the ex-Emperor

YOUNG MATRON OF MEZÖKÖVESD
On her head is a floral coronet, the symbol of the newly-married woman, which tradition decrees that each wife must wear for a year after marriage
Photo, A. W. Cutler

Karl Hapsburg because the revolution had given them land and because they grudged the money spent on keeping up an Imperial Court.

This shows that the Hungarians are "realists" in political affairs; they think more of their interests than of traditions. Half the nation belongs to the Roman Catholic Church, and that Church would have been glad to see the Hapsburgs in power again. But the peasants shook their heads shrewdly, and without their support no attempt at restoration could be anything but a failure. Calvinism is fairly strong, and perhaps the sturdy independence which that faith fosters has had some effect even upon those who remain in the Catholic fold. It is not practised gloomily, it puts no ban upon enjoyment. If it did that, it could never have gained any hold upon the cheerful Magyars. After Sunday services there are village dances; these take place even under the church walls, and the pastors raise no indignant protest.

The Magyar capital, as the town of Debreczen (Debreschen) is called, is also known as "Rome of the Calvinists," and here is the centre of the Reformed religion. This is in truth a "city of the plain." You drive straight out of it on to the vast dusty level puszta, three hundred square miles of it the finest pasture in Europe, where countless cattle and sheep and horses are raised, not to mention pigs and chickens. With immense wheat and maize fields as well, Hungary can do far more than support itself in the way of food. Everywhere the bread is fine and white, butter abounds, meat is cheap; only in the slums of Budapest does one see anything like oppressive poverty.

The cowboys, the shepherds, the horse-breeders, are all of them worth study. They have their own customs and costumes, their own traditions and methods of life. The coats they wear are of rough sheepskin, worn with the fleece inside as soon as the cold weather begins. They spend most of their time in the open, but slip off whenever they can to the inns of the plain to eat and drink by the warmth of a fire, and to make love to the first woman they come across. The Magyar is a great lover, he makes an art of courtship. Much as they admire the English, the Hungarians cannot understand what they

HUNGARY: PEASANT COUPLE IN BRIDAL ARRAY

Reminiscent of a past era are many practices attending Hungarian nuptials, and especially dear to the heart of the peasantry is the elaborate wedding garb with its tinselled and flowery headgear

Photo, A. W. Cutler

RURAL HUNGARY
Magyars In Rich Attire

These are no young priests in costly ecclesiastical vestments, but mere peasant lads of Mezökövesd in their ordinary Sunday garments

Photo, A. W. Cutler

En route to market these Hungarian housewives indulge in a confidential chat ; the geese half suspect that it closely concerns them

Photo, A. W. Cutler

Peacefully they pass their days in a sequestered village of the Hungarian Lowlands, recking nothing of the weal and woe of urban life

Photo, A. W. Cutler

Their country is the world, Hungary a chosen home. Of rare beauty the gypsy lass is versed in every wile liable to distract the heart of man

Photo, A. W. Cutler

By means of the crudely-fashioned crucifix and his supplicatory lament, this crafty old beggar of Hungary harvests many a coveted coin

Photo, A. W. Cutler

An Hungarian wife's industry is well illustrated in the family wardrobe. Her rich embroideries on aprons and shirts give to these home-made garments an impression brilliant in the extreme

Photo A W Cutler

Unique but effective is this headdress, with a cone-shaped basketwork structure enveloped in a florid silken kerchief, but fashion-mongers are unknown in Mezőkövesd, the home of these stately young dames

Photo, A. W. Cutler

This boy and girl of Csömör display their Slovak origin in their distinctive attire and attitude, characteristic of an old Slav dance

2648

Sturdy of frame and serene of face, she is an embodiment of the robust rural scenery adjoining Lake Balaton where her lines are set

Photo, Underwood Press Service

*A lowly Magyar couple, but in their rustic romance a medieval
princess bidding her lover godspeed as he sets forth on knight-errantry*

*The embroidered bolster of this Mezőkövesd baby is a fantastic garden
of silken blossoms reared by the Matyó mother's patient skill*

Headman of one of the cowherd stations on the Hortobägy Plain, he is looked up to as a demi-god by his company of lively young herdsmen

Photo, A. W. Cutler

Far from the world dwells King Cowherd ; his palace—a rude reed-shelter, his kingdom—the infinite expanse of the great Hortobágy Plain

Photo, A. W. Cutler

Full of animation and colour is this courtyard of a Magyar peasant home, where to the lusty acclamation of small maidens a big sister shyly treads the mazy steps of the Csárdás, the Hungarian national dance

Pedigree peasants are numerous among the Matyók people, many of whom can trace their families back to the 13th century. In their houses and resplendent costumes ancestral influence still holds its own

On the occasion of a fancy-dress dance, the well-to-do, town-bred daughters of Hungary delight to discard prevailing modes and to don the costumes worn by their lowly-born sisters in the remote countryside

call the coldness of the Anglo-Saxon. They themselves are temperamentally inflammable, they slide from one great passion into another with rapturous delight. This helps to explain their delight in music. Nowhere else does the "concord of sweet sounds" have so palpable and so complete an influence. Nowhere else could one imagine a Prime Minister dancing by himself to the strains of a Tzigane band for hours on end. That was a practice of Count Tisza's; no one thought it in the least odd.

Where the Tziganes, or Gypsies, came from exactly is matter of dispute still. They are certainly of East Indian origin, and they seem to have made their appearance in Hungary some 400 years ago. They wandered about, making music for a living, and they have gone on doing that ever since. If you see a band of them in a fashionable restaurant in

BRIDAL PAIR FROM THE SARKÖZ DISTRICT
There are still in Hungary some racial reminders of the days of Turkish invasion in the shape of a semi-Oriental strain which persists in this particular region. The crinoline is a feature of the bridal attire

the capital, they look clean and smart in their evening clothes; though the leader, who both leads and plays the violin, will probably have long hair with a good deal of oil in its curly blackness. Hire a company to play in a private room or, better still, go to a Tzigane village, and you will see what they are like in their natural state. The children are lovely little ragamuffins; their black eyes glitter with an unearthly fascination, their black curls enforce the charm, their dusky limbs are perfectly formed and can be seen to perfection, since their clothing is of the scantiest. Until they are between twenty and thirty the Tziganes, men and women both, keep something of the beauty of their childhood. Then it fades rapidly into

an unlovely decay. They live in a state of indescribable dirt, ignorance, laziness and contentment. They are thieves by profession as well as musicians, though it is only fair to them to admit that they have begun lately to take up more creditable ways of gaining their livelihood than begging, telling fortunes, and picking up any trifles that come within reach of their long, lithe, olive-coloured hands.

Though there are less than half a million of these strangers in Hungary, they have done a great deal to make the country famous. It is by Hungarian music that Hungary is chiefly known throughout the world, and it is the Tziganes who have given it a world-wide popularity. There seems to have been always a musical strain in the

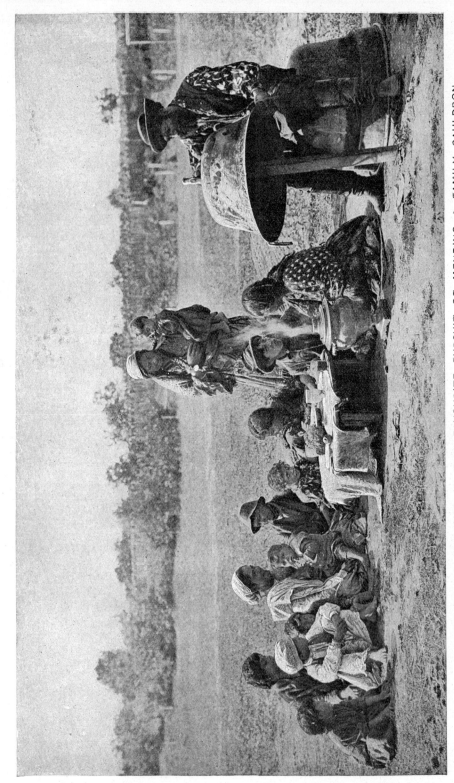

GYPSY PATERFAMILIAS ENGAGED IN THE FAVOURITE PURSUIT OF MENDING A FAMILY CAULDRON

The gypsies are believed to have come over to Europe early in the Middle Ages, and their appearance and the structure of their language would prove them to be undoubtedly of East Indian origin. Like all their kinsfolk, the Hungarian gypsies seem to have a horror of a sedentary life, and are ever on the move. The men, when they care to work, show great skill as tinkers and metal-workers, and as menders of the large iron pots used in the making of preserves, of which Hungarians are very fond

VAGABOND SONS OF HUNGARY WHOSE MUSICAL CAPABILITIES HAVE BROUGHT FAME TO THEIR FOSTER-COUNTRY

Through the wandering gypsies of the fourteenth century, dance music became popular in Hungary. Greatly sought after at weddings and special functions of the lower classes, the Hungarian gypsy bands also found entrance into the palatial homes of the nobles and the wealthy, and their popularity has never decreased. Dominic Kálmán, who acquired great fame in the sixteenth century as a violinist, was one of these gypsy nomads

Photo, A. W. Cutler

Magyar temperament. The instruments with which the people of the Great Plain beguile their long hours have a very long ancestry. The tilinko (flute), which the shepherd or the cowboy will pull out and play when he feels joyful or melancholy, and the lute, which is played in the villages to-day, were used in very early times. The violin was, however, probably introduced by the gypsies, and that is the instrument which has done everything to carry Hungarian music into all lands.

It is the alternation of wild, reckless delight with slow, sad, thoughtful, measured cadences that gives the czárdás or inn dances their fascination, and these effects could be obtained from no orchestral combination save strings. As one listens to them one is inclined to think that the violin was invented for such contrasts, and that it ought to be used for Tzigane music alone. Upon the Magyars this music has a positively intoxicating influence. There is some beat in their blood

MONEYED MEMBERS OF A TRIBE OF THE WANDERING FOOT

The climate and fertile lowlands of Hungary are especially congenial to the gypsy, and many of these vagrants amass much wealth from their diversified pursuits in this country. They are all extremely fond of gaudy colours and glittering ornaments. The big silver buttons displayed on the man's coat weigh several ounces each, and can be purchased from him only at a fabulous price

Photo, A. W. Cutler

FAMILY TRIO ARRAYED IN ITS BRIGHTEST AND BEST

The vivid colouring of many of Hungary's wonderful costumes relieves the monotony of more than one drab town thoroughfare. In the country, where these bright hues accord so well with the clearness of the atmosphere and the beauty of the landscape, they are particularly gratifying to the eye. The Mezökövesd mother stands second to none in her skilful blending of lively colours

Photo, A. W. Cutler

which responds to it ; it has a meaning for them which can be but dimly discerned by other nationalities. This is symptomatic of a more elemental nature than any which can be found among the peoples of Europe farther west.

Hungary is the gateway of the East. Beneath a veneer of Western civilization and convenience one comes quickly to the essential Eastern character below. The Magyars are like the Arabs—they are never insignificant. Tall and graceful in figure, moving with an indolent ease, they would rather ride than walk (which is true of the Arabs again), they would prefer wasting time elegantly, if that were possible in all seasons, to working hard. In the short

summer this is utterly impossible for those who work the land. From sunrise to sunset they must labour—that is to say, from between three and four in the morning until after eight at night. After this effort they seem exhausted, nor can one be surprised at that. Yet they are never too tired to welcome strangers. Hospitality is another of their Eastern characteristics.

In all countries where the distances between towns, even between villages, are considerable, and where there are very few inns that travellers can rely upon, there is a readiness to receive guests in private homes. In Hungary the word " readiness " does not sufficiently describe that kindly desire to be

THE EVENING MEAL AT A PRAIRIE STATION OF THE HUNGARIAN COWHERD ON THE HORTOBÁGY PLAIN

The great plain of the Hungarian lowlands is the heart of Hungary and the home of the genuine Magyar herdsmen. There are three varieties of herdsmen who live on this vast flat land, which, like a calm ocean, stretches away into infinity—the horseherd, the cowherd, and the shepherd. The stations of the cowherd, or gulyás, are dotted at wide intervals about the plain, and the life lived in these solitary domiciles is simple and primitive in the extreme

Photo, A. W. Cutler

LEISURE HOUR OF THE HUNGARIAN COWHERD

Glimpses of modern civilization find their way now and then into the remote solitudes of the Hortobágy Plain, and while the cattle are housed in the byres, the cowboys gather round the gramophone and, with rapt attention, listen to Hungarian songs sung by famous artistes in far-away cities, rumours of which float across to these lonely prairie-dwellers like fairy-tales from another world

Photo, A. W. Cutler

of service to the foreigner which is so universal and so pleasant to recollect. The Magyar regards hospitality not merely as a duty, but as a pleasure; he is an enthusiastic host, the best he has is put at the stranger's disposal; he considers no expense or trouble too great for the foreigner's entertainment.

The salutation so common, " Ista hozott " (God has brought you here), is a literal expression of the feeling in a Magyar heart when a guest presents himself. If it be summer, staying in Hungarian homes, whether they are nobles' castles or squires' manor-houses or peasants' farms, is delightful. In cold weather the closed windows and the rooms filled with smoke may be found uncomfortable. Not even the sacred duties of a host can overcome the Hungarian dislike of open windows and fear of fresh air. It may be, also, that the eating and drinking will be too plentiful for those who are not accustomed to such profusion. The cleanliness which is found among all true Magyars will, however, be most comforting, and will make up for any shortcomings in other directions.

Mr. Foster Bovill, in his valuable study of " Hungary and the Hungarians," tells how he was struck by

GEESE THAT LAY THE GOLDEN EGGS FOR THE HUMBLE HORTOBÁGY FISHERMAN

This tumble-down home, made of adobe and thatched with reeds and straw, is one of many situated on the borders of the Hortobágy river, the serpentine stream that meanders over the surface of the plain of the same name, on which vast expanse of flat country—300 square miles—great herds of cattle have their grazing-ground. This fisherman takes much pride in his family of geese, which are allowed to wander daily about the plain under the vigilant care of a young goosegirl

Photo, A. W. Cutler

PREPARATIONS FOR A FISHING EXPEDITION DISPLAYED ON A BANK OF THE HORTOBÁGY RIVER

Preparations are begun some days before the expedition, for the fisherman knows that success depends largely on the condition of his nets and traps. He is a man of many trades, and ekes out a by no means unpleasant subsistence manufacturing brooms, plaiting mats, and making baskets of rushes and osiers. Sobriety and honesty mark his uneventful days. The spirit of the Hungarian lowlands is his spirit; the same absolute straightness and the same taciturnity characterise both

Photo, A. W. Cutler

two features of an institution specially for young offenders which he visited some years ago in the town of Kassa. These two things were " the daily use of the tooth-brush and the neat folding of the clothes every night." The Magyars are a clean folk, like the Finns, to whom they are related, both being descended from Asiatic stock, as may be seen in both countries by the prevalence of slightly oblique eyes and eyebrows, with cheekbones set rather high. They have not, however, cut themselves loose yet from their Oriental character, as the Finns have done.

Among the higher aristocracy the outward habits of life are those of the West. Knowledge of French, English, and German is usual. English clothes are worn by the men. It is enough to label anything in a shop-window " English " to make it popular at once. Many of the oldest and richest Hungarian families have been well known and warmly liked in England for a great many years past. They have been familiar figures on English racecourses, for they are as fond of horses and of racing as the British aristocracy in whose country houses they used to be regular guests. But their ideas, when they are at home, are not those of the twentieth century. Duelling, which has died out almost everywhere else, killed by commonsense and ridicule, is still a custom of Hungarian nobles. There is an Anti-Duelling League, and there is a law which makes the duel technically illegal ; but it is not by any means rigidly enforced.

With a mentality which can tolerate such an anachronism as this, the Magyar aristocrats could hardly be expected to hold other than antiquated views

HOME-MADE FISHING TACKLE OF THE HUNGARIAN PEASANT

Parallel to the Bakony Forest lies Lake Balaton, Hungary's largest lake, some fifty miles in length and ten miles in width. It is a shallow lake, its depths not exceeding thirteen feet, is fed by springs, and has its outlet to the Danube by the Sio. Here the fisherman reaps a moderate harvest of fish, and in the surrounding marshy shorelands may collect many eggs and young wild fowl

Photo, Underwood Press Service

PAYING HIS RESPECTS AT THE PARENTAL PORTAL

Courtesy, that charming characteristic of the Hungarian, is eloquently portrayed in this photograph, where a gallant of some ten summers is seen kissing the hand of a juvenile guest with all the grace of a courtier.   The hand of a lady is usually kissed on arrival and departure, and this custom is observed even among the children, just as in the matter of dress young and old wear similar fashions

Photo, A. W. Cutler

as to the relation of landlord and tenant. For a long period there was a steady drain of peasants to the United States, the number rising sometimes as high as 150,000 a year. The people in the country are better off than they were, but the process of breaking up the huge estates of the magnates is still regarded as a step essential to the contentment of the people.

With feudal notions about land-holding went a wide and unfortunate gulf between capital and labour. More than four-fifths of the working population are engaged in farming ; the remainder, who sought their living in the towns, had a hard and hungry time to go through in the early days of Hungary's industrial development. This only began about the last decade of

BUDAPEST AND ITS GREAT MARKET OF FLOWERS

An Hungarian institution—affecting numbers of people—is responsible for a great display of floral beauty every year at the market place of the capital. On All Saints' Day, Nov. 1, crowds throng this fine tree-grown square, and the baskets are emptied of their beautiful contents. Then those who have lost loved ones make their way to the cemeteries, which break forth in wreaths and garlands, while, when night comes, special illuminations light up the macabre scene

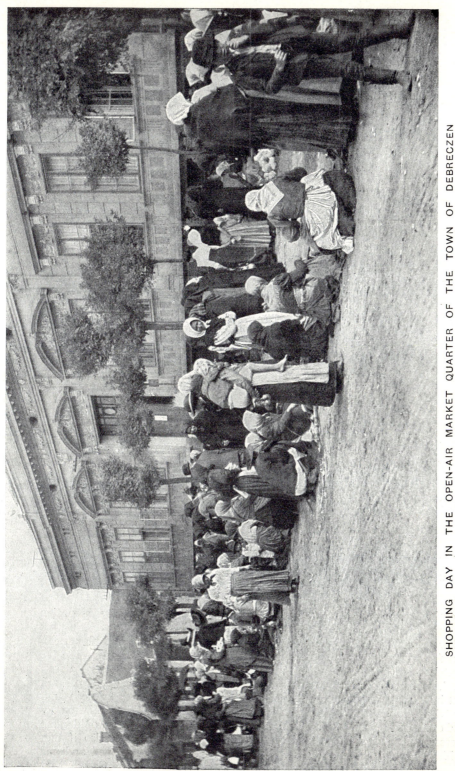

SHOPPING DAY IN THE OPEN-AIR MARKET QUARTER OF THE TOWN OF DEBRECZEN

Those who buy and sell here have learnt to dispense with stalls for the wares and are content to inspect and display goods on the ground. Chickens are the principal kind of stock on sale in this particular street, and the long lines of women who are vending them sit facing each other while the public walks between. The woman carrying a child on her back is a beggar who hopes to arouse for herself and her burden the sympathy of the spending crowd

Photo, A. W. Cutler

BRAVE HEARTS AND STRONG

A happy sunlit scene is this where man and wife—simple Hungarian country folk—with glad hearts and faces work side by side in the fruitful fields. Little is necessary to satisfy their wants ; they are contented with their lot, and never despair, even when the soil in its intractability fails to yield the crop which shall secure for them a meagre subsistence

Photo, A. W. Cutler

the nineteenth century. Until then the Hungarians had depended largely upon other countries, chiefly upon Austria, for factory products. Their own industries were of the small home-worker kind, sufficient for a sparse population, but inadequate when the country began to fill up. Between the beginning and end of the nineteenth century the nation increased from six millions to sixteen.

If the natural course had been followed, and Hungarian manufactures had been taken in hand as they were in other countries by a native-born middle-class, it is probable that the workers would have had better treatment. For there is in the Magyar nature a kindliness and a sense of comradeship which keep relations surprisingly sweet between magnate or squire and the children of the soil. These qualities would come into play in the factories also if they had been built and equipped and managed by natives. But the Government, seeing, perhaps, that the Magyars were neither inclined nor fitted for such enterprises, did all it could to encourage foreigners to start them. Then it soon had to intervene to protect the workers. As early as 1891 an Insurance Fund was established by law, which gave sick pay, provided doctoring and medicine, with confinement allowances for married women, and a sum to pay funeral expenses in case of death. To this fund both employers and employed were bound to subscribe. It was not until many years later, the Hungarians are fond of pointing out, that such insurance was introduced in England.

Since the Great War, all who can use their hands have been better off in Hungary than those who depended on their brains for their livelihood. The disastrous drop in the purchasing power of the currency reduced many who had

been in easy circumstances to poverty, which made it difficult for them even to exist. All who subsisted on fixed incomes from investments or house property, all who lived on pensions, all who were engaged in teaching, all who did clerical work of the simpler kind, found that sums which had served to keep them in comfort before scarcely enabled them to pay for a poor lodging and for just enough food to keep them alive.

This has been a damaging blow to the recently formed middle class, especially to the Magyar element in it, which has not proved itself so ingenious as the Jewish element in discovering ways of escape from utter ruin. All who possess land and can cultivate it are prosperous, all who can undertake manual labour are pretty sure of a good

HUNGARIAN BEGGARS RESTING UNDER THE GREENWOOD TREE

The hedge-side makes a welcome resting-place, and the woman sucks consolation from her huge pipe, with a glance between puffs at her lord and master as he munches the few tomatoes he has managed to get. Her dress is a medley of oddments ; his boots seem, so to speak, on their last legs. They have chosen the tramps' road and find in it consolations for its penalties

Photo, A. W. Cutler

"WAITING ON BUSINESS": HUNGARIAN PEDLAR

His gaunt, familiar figure is often seen outside the central station of Budapest, where he may be heard expounding the fine qualities of his thousand and one gimcracks which make appeal to the eyes of the passing pedestrians. Judging from his trim appearance he is doing well, and the neat, symmetrical knee-patches would suggest that a thrifty housewife exists not far off in the background

Photo, A. W. Cutler

KALOCSA WOMAN OF MANY ARTS AND CRAFTS

A pleasant-mannered people, the peasants of Kalocsa have many admirable attributes, and their hospitality is specially noteworthy. During the summer months some of the women find employment in the surrounding country places, where they undertake manual labour in the fields; in winter, however, home industry occupies their days, and much of their beautiful handiwork is produced

Photo, Kankovszky, Budapest

HUNGARIAN ROMAN CATHOLIC PRIMATE TAKING PART IN A RELIGIOUS PROCESSION.

There are many legally recognized religions in Hungary, including the Roman and the Greek Catholic, the Evangelical, the Greek-Oriental, the Gregorian-Armenian, the Baptist, the Jewish, and the Mahomedan religions. Among these there is perfect equality, each being independent in the administration of its own affairs. The Hungarian State prides itself on the fact that religious toleration is one of its fundamental principles.

wage; the stratum of the population from which the intellectual workers have to be drawn suffers severely, and finds it exceedingly difficult to educate the younger generation to take up and carry on the torch of enlightenment.

This is really a much more serious matter than the transfer of certain territories which were under Hungarian rule to Czechoslovakia, Yugo-Slavia, and Rumania. The Magyars deeply resent what they call the " loss " of most of their mountainous regions. This is, however, scarcely more than a sentimental grievance, whereas the weakening of the intellectual life of their country would be a catastrophe very hard to repair.

While they were united with the Austrians under the Hapsburg Crown, a great deal was done in Hungary by Austrian initiative for the benefit of the people, especially in education. There was an excellent chain of schools for teaching trades, which included all kinds of carpentering and heavy metal work, with lighter occupations such as basket-making, toy-making, clock-making, woodcarving, and, for girls, needlework and lace. Already in this and in other educational directions a lowering of standard is noticeable.

In general the Magyars have not the same sense of order and skill in management that the Austrians possess. This is forcibly impressed on those who take the steamers which make the delightful voyage down the Danube from Passau, in Bavaria, through Linz and Vienna to Budapest. Those which are in the hands of Austrian managers are admirably clean, and all things are well arranged for the comfort of passengers.

In the boats under Hungarian control there is an Oriental disregard of punctuality, convenience, tidiness, regularity. The saloon is filled all day long; those passengers who have had their meal must be forcibly ejected to make room for others still unfed; there is a close, smoky atmosphere; the stewards rush about, getting more and more damp and dishevelled, and, instead of arriving at the advertised

RESPLENDENT REPRESENTATIVES OF THE HUNGARIAN ARMY
On the occasion of an important State or Church holiday, Hungary musters all her bravest and best to assist in the wide-spread celebrations, and the brilliancy of the cortège may be judged from this photograph. So picturesque is the national dress, that the Hungarian nobleman never fails to attract universal attention at ceremonial functions in foreign Courts

SUNDAY MORNING SCENE AT THE VILLAGE CHURCH

A colourful day is the Sabbath day in Mezökövesd, when the feminine population arrays itself in its best and brightest garments. In the wide skirts which swing from side to side in graceful folds as they walk, in the tight bodices, and with their neatly-coiffured heads, the girls resemble gaudy humming-birds as they flit about in the open, preparatory to attending divine service in the church

Photo, A. W. Cutler

hour, the steamers reach Budapest late at night, when there is a fierce rush for the few cabs on the quay, and a stream of disappointed and wearied people seeking their hotels in the darkness on foot.

Yet it is worth arriving by night to enjoy the beauty of Budapest after the lights have come out on the hillside of Buda, and all that is commonplace by day has been transformed into a fairy dream. Pest is the new city on the flat right bank; it has grown very quickly, has over a million inhabitants, and covers a very large area, for the reason that the building of houses, offices, or shops with more than two

storeys has been begun only within quite recent years. It is not a city that leaves on the visitor's mind memories of any vivid sort. It has none of the mingled beauty and impressiveness of Vienna. Some of its public buildings are large and ambitious in design, but none of them has any outstanding architectural merit. The streets are agreeably wide, and there are many good shops; but they are scattered amid others which are poor in appearance, so the general effect is not striking.

The best streets in this respect are down towards the Promenade, or Corso, along the river bank, where the most fashionable cafés and restaurants are grouped, and where chairs are set out row behind row in warm weather, to be filled by those who do not care to stroll up and down the roadway along which no traffic is allowed at any time of day or night. When a military band is playing in the afternoon, or when the Tzigane orchestras are performing in the cafés at night, this is a very pleasant place in which to walk and to meet acquaintances. The Park of Budapest is at the extreme end of the city, so it is little used for social purposes. The Corso is convenient and admirably adapted for the sitting and strolling of those who wish to see and be seen.

In the capital the women are mostly of a rather opulent, Oriental type—those, at any rate, who are most in evidence. You have to go into the country to see the pure Magyar charm of feature and complexion. On the Corso there is more to admire in the way of dress than of beauty, so far as

the women are concerned. There is as much smartness here as in Vienna, though not quite the same impeccable taste. The men are well-set-up and mostly good-looking; they like to fancy they look like Englishmen, but their quick, excitable way of talking prevents the illusion from lasting long. They even call their cafés " kavehaz " in Budapest, under the impression that this is how coffee-house should be pronounced. Very fine rooms these places have, with innumerable newspapers and magazines, and seats outside on terraces, and all kinds of refreshing temptations as well as delicious Hungarian coffee.

At a certain time in autumn almost everyone has before him a huge slice of red pumpkin, iced and running with juice, as welcome an aid to getting through a hot day as could be imagined. And the days in autumn are hot, lovely, mellow days, that prolong the summer till October. Then there is a pause

TWO GAILY DECORATED STRINGS TO HIS BOW

The Hungarian Slovak has a natural inclination to agriculture and the breeding of cattle. He is by choice a herdsman or tiller of the ground, and by dint of hard work seldom fails to reap a plenteous harvest from the soil. These peasants of Csömör, near Budapest, although Magyarised, are of Slovak descent, and their distinctive raiment is not the least apparent of their racial characteristics

Photo, Kankovszky, Budapest

before winter begins in earnest. In Budapest there is not generally a long or severe spell of cold weather, but on the Plain there are snow and ice in plenty, and all over the country people are glad when the spring begins and the sun shines with power again, which it does early in the year.

Summer or winter, spring or autumn, the sight of Buda by night is a perpetual joy. Opposite Pest the older town climbs up a steep hill, with the ruins of

world. There are waters of some value, too, on the Margaret Island, which lies in the Danube a little lower down and provides the people of Budapest with a place of entertainment something like the Wurstel-Prater in Vienna. It is a pretty spot on a summer evening, and those who prefer quiet to the insistent orchestras and the chatter of the crowd can find it easily by strolling a short way under the dusky trees. From here or from any part of the Pest

SIX MERRY SCHOOLBOYS SEATED IN A ROW

Hungary ranks high where charitable institutions are concerned, especially those connected with child-welfare. The State is the " over-parent " of every boy and girl born within its borders, and expends much anxious thought in its efforts to maintain health and happiness among the children. The jovial expressions of these small boys, so neatly clad and wearing the characteristic apron of the peasantry, would argue well for the parental care

Photo, A. W. Cutler

a citadel on the top. Here for a century and a half the flag of the Crescent floated, and the Turks were in possession of most of the country until, in 1686, they were for ever driven out. Buda had been a city long before that. The Romans found a Celtic settlement there and turned it into an important place. There are still traces of an arena that held 20,000 spectators, of a theatre for 8,000, of temples and baths.

The rock was famous for its medicinal waters, which are still bottled here to-day. That called after the warrior Janos Hunyadi is known all over the

bank the myriad lights of Buda look exquisitely beautiful. The uninteresting royal palace on the hill can only be seen now as a pattern of gold dots on a cloth of black velvet. The modern ugly houses which have been allowed to deface the prospect by day are merely twinkling groups of yellow stars. The bridges which join the two parts of the city, the old and the new, have their chains of light reflected in the stream. The little steamboats which ferry passengers across and up and down move like constellations dropped from the sky. Thus the

GRACEFUL GIRLHOOD IN SUNNY HUNGARY

They are members of the peasant community of Kalocsa, a cathedral city and seat of a Roman Catholic archbishop, situated in the vicinity of the Danube, nearly seventy miles to the south of Budapest. Although not great churchgoers, the utterance of religious sayings comes very naturally to them, and in passing the time of day they often adopt some pious phrase as an appropriate salutation

"RING A RING O' ROSES" IN WIDE SWAYING SKIRTS

A peculiarly proud carriage and a graceful swinging gait are characteristics of these Hungarian women, who are descendants of a semi-Oriental stock. Often very beautiful in face and figure, the attractiveness of their appearance is enhanced by their traditional attire, which, seen in the full glory of its harmonious colouring, imparts an impression not lightly obliterated from the memory

Photos, Kankovszky, Budapest

HUNGARIAN GOOSEGIRL DRIVING HER FLOCK TO THEIR LAST DESTINATION: THE MARKET PLACE OF DEBRECZEN

Situated on a slight elevation above the sandy plain of the north Alföld is Debreczen, one of the most truly Hungarian towns in the country. Possessed of a famous historical past, the town, sometimes called the Protestant "Rome," played an important part on the side of the Reformation, and was the Hungarian headquarters of Calvinism. It is now one of the largest provincial towns in Hungary, with a very high level of intellectual life and important industrial concerns

Photo, A. W. Cutler

2680

PONDEROUS WOODEN LOOM OF HUNGARY

Even in olden times the industries of the Magyars embellished many a palace and castle, and their pottery, embroidery, carpets, and ornamental leather-work were renowned in many large European towns. Constant struggles with overwhelming enemy forces greatly impeded industrial progress, . but several of the artistic industries were preserved and developed in the homes of the peasantry

Photo, A. W. Cutler

situation of Budapest lends it a charm which never stales.

For some the city has attractions of a different order. It has the reputation of being the gayest capital in Europe, the term "gay" being used in a technical sense and implying vicious. That is probably quite an undeserved epithet. There is, however, one line of "gaiety" in which the Hungarian city is perhaps pre-eminent. If you want to lose money by gambling, you can do it here with the utmost ease. Every kind of facility is offered. There are magnificent card-playing establishments in which the company is aristocratic and the play high. Among the

magnates this passion is very common, and stories are told of fortunes being wrecked over the green tables, and men leaving the rooms in the morning light beggars who the night before were rich.

If you feel that you would soon be out of your financial depth in such society, there is a wide choice of less distinguished gambling saloons. Or, supposing cards do not tempt you, you can get all the excitement you want by taking lottery tickets. Not only is there a State lottery for big prizes, but all sorts of private enterprises solicit your attention, most of them connected with charity, some even with religion. Churches have been built out of the

CONSERVATIVE PEASANTS WHO CLING TO ANCESTRAL CUSTOMS

Mezökövesd, a market town of considerable importance, is inhabited by a people called " Matyók,"
a branch of the Palocz race. The peculiar tucks seen at the dress-waist of the woman on the right are
stiffened with cardboard and covered with black velvet. As a small child she dressed in similar
fashion, and if she lives to be a centenarian this queer style may still be seen on her

Photo, A. W. Cutler

proceeds of this form of gambling.
Hospitals, schools, institutions for the
relief of poverty and misfortune see
nothing incongruous in raising funds by
such means. Nor does there seem to
be any reason why, if people will " have
a flutter," they should not benefit some
useful object instead of enriching private
individuals. It will be long before the
Magyars are cured of the idea that they
are more likely to make a good living
by the purchase of lottery tickets than
by steady work. It will be long before
the gambling mania can be shaken off.
It goes with their careless optimism,
their apologists say ; with their love of
taking chances ; with their simplicity of

character. Traces of the same simplicity
may be seen in the obligation upon all
Hungarian subjects to belong, or to say
that they belong, to some religious body.
The State has long been the paymaster of
all ministers of religion, Roman Catholic,
Protestant, and Jewish alike. The
funds for this purpose are provided by
a personal tax which no one is allowed
to evade. Everyone must call himself
something and pay his tax to whichever
body he has chosen, even though he
never attends a place of worship at all.
The system seems to work well enough ;
it ensures, at any rate, religious equality.

There is less need in Hungary than in
Britain for the upkeep of philanthropic

HANDSOME HANDIWORK OF THE HUNGARIAN PEASANTRY

Hungary abounds in natural beauties, and her rivers and lakes, her highlands and lowlands contribute their full share to the fascinating scenery. In her people, too, a great love of beauty prevails, and in the lowliest peasant home artistic skill is displayed in the fine embroideries on handspun garments and sheepskins and the decorative designs on the earthenware household utensils

Photo, A. W. Cutler

institutions by voluntary effort. The State does a great deal in this direction, and does it handsomely. Children are looked after with especial good sense and care. Machinery exists which is a long way ahead of that in England for protecting them from cruel or even harmfully thoughtless treatment on their parents' part. There are kindly homes for those who have lost their parents or have had to be taken from them ; all who are in any way handicapped for the race of life are helped. In the wise handling of young people who have drifted into crime Hungary's plan could hardly be bettered. Thus you find a mixture, sometimes

puzzling, sometimes irritating, always interesting, of old-fashioned prejudices and customs with ideas of advanced progress. Many of these ideas they owe, it must be remembered, to the Austrians; but they are hardly likely now to let them go, for the Magyar is anxious to stand well with the rest of the world.

Hungarian patriotism finds expression in the literature of the country, notably in the works of Nicholas Zrinyi (1618-64), who wrote the national epic; and George Bessenyei (1747-1811), the herald of a literary awakening; while among Hungarian writers of fiction Sigismund Kemény (1814-77) and Maurus Jokai (1825-1904) won wide fame.

Hungary

II. A Thousand Years of Magyar History

By A. D. Innes, M.A.

Lecturer and Examiner in History and Literature

HUNGARY, formerly a portion of the Dual Monarchy or " ramshackle empire " familiarly known as Austria, is to-day an independent State, whose boundaries, as a consequence of the Great War, have been defined upon a nationalist basis, and encircle it between Yugo-Slavia on the south, Teutonic Austria un the west, Czechoslovakia on the north, and an expanded Rumania on the east. The dominant race in Hungary, the Magyars, are of a stock entirely different from that of any of the encircling States. Its area corresponds but roughly to that of the historical Hungarian kingdom which generally extended over territories now assigned to other nationalities.

The area itself has been occupied by the Magyar people for something over 1,000 years. The popular inclination to connect the name of Hungary with the Huns is entirely erroneous. It is a corruption of " Ugrian," the title by which the Magyar invaders were originally known.

Turbulent Waves of Invasion

Apart from Trajan's military colony in Dacia, which was the beginning of Rumania, the Roman power never effectively penetrated beyond the Danube; nor did the barbarian tribes—presumably Slavonic—who were in normal occupation develop any organized attack on the Roman marches. In the third and fourth centuries, however, Goths from the north were making Hungary their base for threatening the Danube line, ejecting or dominating the Slavs. The fifth century saw the terrific incursion of the migrating Mongolian hosts of Attila and his Huns, who, however, vanished into space after Attila's death, and were heard of no more.

Slavs surged in again, only to be again subjugated in the seventh and eighth centuries by the Avars, of the miscellaneous central-Asiatic stock. The power of the Avars was broken by Charlemagne. Like the Huns, they disappeared, and once more a Slavonic power was being organized when, at the end of the ninth century, it was shattered by the Tartar Magyars, the Ugrians or Hungarians who, led by their mighty if somewhat mythical Khan Arpad, took permanent possession of the country and gave it their name.

The terms Mongolian, Tartar, and Turk are used, it may be remarked, for lack of any adequately distinctive titles of the far from homogeneous stocks from Central Asia which successively flooded into Europe by way of south Russia ; stocks concerning which the only definite statement that can be made is that while they differed from each other materially, all were primarily nomadic hordes and none were Aryan.

Magyars Masters of the Land

From the days of Arpad the Magyars were the masters of Hungary. For a time they threatened the Western Empire, but in the middle of the tenth century met their decisive overthrow at the hands of Otto the Great. From that time they ceased to be a menace to the West, accepted Christianity, and at a later stage became a bulwark of Christendom against Mongol and Turk, both before and after the final downfall of the Byzantine Empire. In fact, with their Christianising under their Khan or King Geza, they began, so to speak, to become good Europeans. Geza's son, S. Stephen, or Stephen the Great, was the very remarkable ruler (997-1038) who raised the Hungarian kingdom from barbarism to civilization. He was not only zealous in the spreading of Christianity and of Western ideas by the foreigners whose presence he encouraged ; he imitated the system which Charlemagne had initiated in his empire of dividing his own kingdom under " counts," who were not hereditary rulers but royal officials. He could not, however, overcome the established conditions which made the Magyars proper a ruling caste, and kept the rest of the population in a subject position.

Decay of the Arpad Dynasty

Under Stephen's successors (after an interval), Ladislas and Coloman (1077-1116), the borders of the Magyar kingdom were considerably extended, and its government was admirably conducted. But the later kings of the Arpad line degenerated ; the effective power passed into the hands of the greater Magyar nobles, whose position had become hereditary. The disintegration was checked by King Bela IV. (thirteenth century) after Hungary had been devastated by the last great Mongol or Tartar deluge; but the ruin wrought thereby had been too destructive. The last of the Arpads could not maintain their authority, and at the beginning of the fourteenth century the crown of Hungary was bestowed on a foreign dynasty— a branch of the Angevin house which had recently been established in the kingdom of Naples.

Charles Robert and his son Louis (1303-82), rulers of great ability, restored a strong and stable government on Western lines, the lines of French feudalism, developing the control of the crown over the great nobles, and the growth of the towns and of commerce, while they relied largely upon the aid of Italian and other foreign ministers. The royal family became closely associated with that of Poland, and from 1370 the two crowns were actually for a time united. During this period, however, the Ottoman Turks were beginning to establish themselves in the Balkan peninsula, and on the other hand the Angevin dynasty was weakened by the succession (1382) of Louis' two daughters to the crowns of Poland and Hungary respectively.

The marriage of one established the Jagellon dynasty in Poland; that of the other made Sigismund, best known in the West as a very unsatisfactory emperor, a very efficient King of Hungary. Single-handed, and with no support from the West, he held up the advance of the Turks under Amurath, or Murad II., and established the great fortress of Belgrade, which, as long as it remained in Christian possession, was more than a thorn in the side of the Ottoman. But Sigismund, dying in 1437, was succeeded by his daughter's husband, Albert of Austria, who died two years later, to leave a disputed succession between his posthumous son Ladislas and Ladislas King of Poland, to whom the Hungarian nobles offered the crown.

During the troubled years which followed, the defence of Hungary against the Turk devolved upon the hero Janos Hunyadi, a gentleman of the southern marches who had risen to authority by sheer force of character and ability. His military achievements wrung from the Ottoman the peace of Szeged (1444), to which the de facto king Ladislas having assented, immediately broke. Ladislas was then killed in an overwhelming defeat at Varna, and Hunyadi, obviously the necessary man, was elected " governor " of Hungary. Before he died, in 1456, the Moslem tide was stemmed, though it had submerged Constantinople, and two years later Hunyadi's son Matthias " Corvinus " was unanimously elected king of Hungary on the death of the still youthful Ladislas " Posthumus."

The reign of Matthias was the most brilliant period of Hungarian history. On every side the young king's arms triumphed. In his father's day the Hapsburgs, as the guardians of young Ladislas, and the Bohemians, whose crown he also inherited from his father, had occupied the western and northern

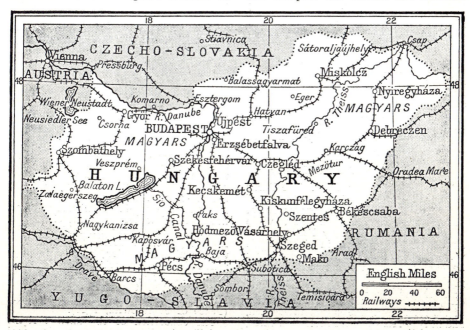

THE MAGYAR STATE OF HUNGARY

provinces of the Hungarian kingdom. Matthias drove both of them out, beat off the Turks, and organized not only a regular army under his own control, but also a great Danube flotilla. His troops and his very able finance ministers enabled him at once to present an invincible front to enemies on all sides, to restore an irresistible royal authority, to re-establish order and law, to rule with stern but unerring justice, and to revive the material prosperity of his kingdom; though, despite his own vigorous efforts for the development of intellectual culture, it barely touched the nobles, and was practically restricted to the greater clerics and a few of the minor gentry.

Days of Glory under Matthias

He was working for great ends under difficulties which would have overwhelmed any less masterful personality, and though in his later years he was probably the most powerful potentate in Europe, the brief glory of Hungary was destined to prompt decay when his strong hand was withdrawn. His young heir was unable to retain his grip on the reins. The Magyar nobles wanted a king who would be their puppet, not their master, and in 1490 they elected the weak Ladislas of Bohemia, who promptly confirmed all their privileges and cancelled most of the salutary legislation of the great Matthias.

Chaos followed. The nobles acted after the fashion of the baronage of England in the nightmare reign of King Stephen. Each did what was right in his own eyes; together they made laws for the oppression of the peasantry. A fierce peasant rising in 1514 was brutally stamped out, like that in Germany a decade later, and the peasants were reduced to a condition of abject serfdom from which they never recovered. Ladislas died in 1516, and was succeeded by a child. The chaos grew worse. In 1521 the Turks captured Belgrade. Five years later they annihilated at Mohacs the hastily-summoned Hungarian levies.

Defeat and Partition of Hungary

The young king was killed. The Turks retired after devastating a quarter of Hungary. John Zapolya, governor of Transylvania, was elected king, while the crown was claimed by Ferdinand of Austria (later emperor) in right of his wife, the dead king's sister. In effect Zapolya retained the crown by ceding a third of the kingdom to Ferdinand. There was some recovery, but Zapolya died, Ferdinand challenged the election of his infant son, the sultan intervened, and in 1547 Hungary was divided in three, the Turk annexing the biggest share

wedged in between the Hapsburg and Transylvanian dominions on the west and east respectively, Ferdinand being nominal suzerain of the " Prince " of Transylvania.

In the eyes of successive Hapsburgs, who became, in fact though not in form, hereditary emperors, their Hungarian kingdom was merely an unremunerative but inconveniently necessary buffer between Vienna and the Turk. They ruled from Vienna, and the Magyars were held in a wretched depression. Both here and in Transylvania Protestantism was prevalent; the Turks disregarded it, and the first Hapsburgs were tolerant. But the day of toleration passed. In the years immediately preceding and following the close of the century there were fierce persecutions and wars in which Magyar patriotism and Protestantism were in some degree identified. The temporary triumph of the imperialists, ruthlessly used and grossly abused, was reversed, and by the peace of Vienna (1606) Transylvania became in effect an independent Magyar State, the nominally elective " kingdom of Hungary " remaining practically an appanage of the Hapsburgs. Throughout the Thirty Years War (1618-48), Transylvania, under its vigorous princes Gabriel Bethlen and George Rakoczy, was a thorn in the side of the imperialists. In the kingdom of Hungary, on the other hand, the Magyars were held in a state of repression as, at best, potential rebels throughout the seventeenth century by their German rulers, who practically crushed out Protestantism.

Hapsburgs Succeed to the Turks

In the third quarter of the century Magyar rebellion was headed by Tökölyi and stimulated the Turkish attack on Austria developed by the Kuprili Wazirs. Vienna was saved by the intervention of the great Pole, John Sobieski (1683). Prince Eugene's victory at Zenta (1697) and the resultant peace of Karlowitz (1699) expelled the Turks from all but a fraction of their possessions in Hungary; but though the Turks were expelled, the Magyars were more completely than ever reduced to subjection and repression by the Vienna government, and the struggle had again incorporated Transylvania with the rest of Hungary. Nevertheless, Magyarism was in continuous revolt during the first decade of the eighteenth century, and actually extorted from the Hapsburgs, embarrassed by the war of the Spanish succession, a formal recognition of the " ancient rights and liberties " of the Magyars. Another Turkish war finally cleared the Turks out of the Hungarian territories still held by them (Peace of Passarowitz, 1718).

The concession of the ancient rights and liberties did not mean constitutional independence, but it introduced a new atmosphere of comparative liberality on the part of the Hapsburgs and acquiescence on the part of the Magyars, which was accentuated by Hungarian loyalty to Maria Theresa in the war of the Austrian succession (1740-48). The queen and her sons, Joseph II. and Leopold II., were typical enlightened despots, who ruled with paternal benevolence but without allowing their subjects more than a consultative voice in the government. Hungary enjoyed a long reign of law, order, justice, and administrative reform, under which her prosperity recovered.

The Magyar nobility and gentry were treated with favour, and were not excluded from official positions. As a consequence, Hungary remained loyal through the great French wars (1792-1815). There, as elsewhere, however, the wars were accompanied by the infiltration of Liberal ideas and a renascence of Nationalist sentiment, not only among Magyars, but also among the subordinate Slav populations of the south. Such doctrines, however, had little chance of active expression under the rule of Metternich, who directed the Austrian government under Francis II. and his successor, Ferdinand. Nevertheless, both Liberalism and Nationalism, inspired by Széchenyi, Deák, and the perfervid Louis Kossuth, were already assuming a prominence in the diets alarming to the Vienna authorities, when, in 1848, all Europe was flung into violent perturbations by a common revolutionary eruption.

Metternich fled. The imperial government, menaced everywhere with revolt—in Italy, in Bohemia, in Hungary, by Liberalism in Vienna itself—made immense concessions. But the Hungarian extremists, headed by Kossuth, went too far even for the moderate liberals, demanding complete independence. The government took heart; the rebels, successful at first, were crushed by the aid of the Russian Tsar. In the Austrian empire, as elsewhere, the reaction triumphed over the revolution, and exacted the penalty from Hungary with vindictive brutality.

Even then the results might have been very different but for the innate age-long hostility between Austria's Slav and Magyar subjects. The structure of the Austrian empire was desperately unstable ; it was becoming obvious that concessions must be made to the diverse nationalities of which it was composed. The Italian and Prussian wars of 1859 and 1866 gave the finishing touches, and in 1867 the system known as the Dual Monarchy was established.

That system practically made the Austrian emperor also the constitutional king of Hungary, while it gave to the Magyars a position on an equal footing with the Germans in the councils of the united empire. It lasted till the final catastrophe of 1918, when that empire was disintegrated into its component parts, and Hungary became a separate Magyar state, shorn of its Slavonic provinces.

HUNGARY : FACTS AND FIGURES

The Country

New European State, bounded by Austria, Czechoslovakia, Yugo-Slavia, and Rumania. Area, 35,654 square miles ; population, 1921, 7,840,830, of which 83 per cent. are Magyars.

Government

Monarchy, under a regent, elected by National Assembly on March 23, 1920, when a government order was issued that the official title of the ministry was " Royal Hungarian Ministry." Representative bodies for communes, those for towns elected for six years with life officials. The counties and cities with communal rights are independent municipalities, with councils modelled on the representative bodies of the communes.

Defence

Armed forces include National Army of 35,000, with voluntary enlistment for twelve years, six of which have to be with the colours ; 12,000 police, 12,000 gendarmerie, and 4,500 customs guards, each with minimum of six years' service.

Commerce and Industries

Chief industry, agriculture. Soil, fertile. Products : Wheat, rye, barley, oats, maize, tobacco, sugar, grapes, coal, wine, lignite, rock salt, and precious metals. Cattle industry considerable. Milling, distilling, manufacture of sugar, hemp, flax, leather, textiles, iron and steel works carried on. Area under forest, 1,357,438 acres. Total imports in 1916 estimated at about £80,500,000 ; exports, £66,250,000. Unit of currency the kronen, normally 24.02 to the £, but quoted in December, 1922, at 10,000-11,000 to the £.

Communications

Railways, 4,372 miles, of which 1,858 State-owned ; telegraphs, 5,800 miles ; navigable rivers, 687 miles.

Religion and Education

All religions tolerated, but greater number of Magyars are Roman Catholics, with, however, large Protestant minority. Elementary education compulsory between ages of six to twelve years. In addition to extended facilities for secondary education, there are four State-maintained Universities.

Chief Towns

Budapest, capital (1,184,600), Szeged (109,890), Debreczen (103,200), Kecskemét (72,760), Hód-mezo-Vásárhely (60,850), Miskolcz (57,380), Ujpest (55,800), Kispest (50,200), Györ (50,000).

OPEN-AIR HUNGARIAN MOTHERS' MEETING IN PROGRESS

The Matyó women of Mezökövesd have a strange custom of " bolstering " their babies-in-arms.   These. immense pillows are of the softest down, covered with bright material often gorgeously decorated with fancy patterns in coloured silks and cottons.   The young mother on the left seems fully aware that her person and pillow bear eloquent witness to her artistic taste and nimble fingers

Photo, A. W. Cutler

THREE GENERATIONS OF A MAGYAR PEASANT FAMILY

Hungary is one of the healthiest countries in Europe, and the Magyars are accounted as one of the handsomest races. Originally, they came from Central Asia, and, according to many a learned Orientalist, are of Turko-Tartar stock, mixed with the Finn-Ugrian branch of the Ural-Altaic family The Magyars are a proud, high-spirited, brave, and hospitable people, of tall and athletic frame

Iceland

A Cultured People of the Hardy North

By R. Pape Cowl

Writer on Icelandic History and Culture

APART from the important factors of origin and environment, perhaps the most powerful influences that have been at work in moulding a racial type in Iceland have been the spiritual unity and culture in which the generations of the Icelandic people have been linked together from the beginnings of the island's history.

The Icelanders, a thrifty, industrious, and enlightened community, inherited from their Norse ancestry the practical sense which has stood them in good stead in their hard battle for existence with the remorseless powers of nature. Yet, with their stern sense of realities, there is a visionary and romantic strain in the people, partly derived from communion with the solemn grandeurs of nature and partly from the Celtic infusion in their blood.

They have retained a contact with their past, and particularly with the past of their golden age, which is unique in the history of European peoples. They speak the language, in more than the literal sense, of the twelfth century, read the books of that age, and write

STAR OF THE NORTH

Beauty stamped with exceptional dignity is the heritage of this daughter of Iceland, whose fine bearing suggests that in her veins runs the blood of heroes sung in saga

their poetry in alliterative form. Their speech is the old Norse, the synthetic or inflexional language spoken a thousand years ago by all Scandinavian peoples. Even children can read without difficulty the still popular sagas of the twelfth century.

The composition of the sagas extended probably over one or two centuries, and most of them had been told and re-told for generations before they were first committed to writing. All alike are told with the supreme art of the story-teller who has seen, with the mind's eye, all he describes, and who can make us see with him and share the interest with which he himself follows the doings of his personages.

Iceland's population of 95,000 souls is thinly spread over a country considerably larger than Scotland or Ireland. There are about nine persons to every ten square miles, but as the interior is a high plateau, covered with barren mountains, glaciers, lava-fields, morasses, and desert wastes, the population is largely concentrated in the lowlands near the coasts. Nowhere, however, is the population

GLORIOUS HAIR TO ADVANTAGE DRESSED
Very long, fair hair is a chief beauty of the women of Iceland.
They wear it hanging in thick plaits, surmounted by a cap of dark
cloth with a long tail twisted into semblance of another plait

frieze, which is woven on the farms, the dress of the men is that ordinarily worn in Western Europe. The women, however, with few exceptions, are faithful to their national costume. Their ordinary dress (pey-suföt) consists of a jacket and skirt of dark material, a silver belt, a tasselled cap (húfa) and, out of doors, a shawl. The hair, often beautiful in colour and texture and of great profusion and length, is worn in plaits. The festival dress (upphlutur or skautbúningur) is of great antiquity. The skaut is a headdress of lawn, bound over the forehead with a band of gold. The bodice and skirt are most richly embroidered.

A few women have adopted "European" costume, which is said to be more comfortable, if less picturesque, than the national dress. The ordinary peysuföt is especially becoming when worn as a riding-habit; and to see, as one sometimes does, a company of ladies on ambling ponies is a vision that is strangely reminiscent of the Middle Ages. The trains of pack-horses one meets occasionally on road or bridle-path strike, too, the medieval note that is so insistent. There are, by the way, no railways in Iceland, and roads are few and hard to travel over in carriage or motor. The ordinary means of transit is on the backs of the sure-footed and friendly native ponies along bridle-tracks, where cairns point the way in winter, and where, here and there, is a Saeluhús to offer a welcome shelter to the traveller overtaken by storms.

The principal industries are sheep-farming and fishing, and in these more than sixty-five per cent. of the population

dense, except in the town of Reykjavik, the capital, which has 18,000 inhabitants —about one-fifth of the whole population.

The Icelander is generally of good stature, and of a strong rather than of a powerful frame. It is rarely that he runs to flesh; on the contrary, he is often lean, wiry, and weathered in his looks. Usually he is light-complexioned and fair-haired, but a combination of dark hair and blue or grey eyes is not uncommon. The men have strong or rugged features; the women are frequently gifted with physical beauty and refinement, but their greatest charm is perhaps a complexion of delectable freshness and delicacy.

Apart from the general use in the country districts of vadmál, a kind of

are directly engaged. The coasts are everywhere rich in bird life, and the waters teem with fish of great economic value. Iceland's mighty falls of water and hot springs are great potential sources of wealth as yet undeveloped, though a woollen mill, near Reykjavik, is operated by water-power, and has limitless supplies of hot water for the processes of manufacture and heating from a neighbouring hot spring.

With so small a population to so large a territory it may be surmised that there is more than enough work for every available pair of hands. The country priest is invariably a farmer also, and, may be, a postmaster. The schoolmaster in vacation lends a hand in harvesting the hay—Iceland's only crop—or pulls at an oar in a fishing-boat. The leading tragedian in the Repertoire Theatre is probably a bank manager when he is off the boards.

Yet Iceland finds a way to enable her most gifted sons to specialise in science, in literature, and in the arts. She has produced, even in periods of national depression, poets —some really great lyric poets—statesmen, and scholars. To-day drama, music, and landscape painting flourish; and Einar Jónsson, of Reykjavik, is one of the greatest living masters in the art of sculpture.

Reykjavik—an unpretentious but agreeable little capital—is picturesquely situated on Faxa Fiord, with green hills about it and a background of mountains and glaciers. The dwelling-houses are generally small and are built of wood with roofs of corrugated iron ; the public buildings are of stone or concrete. The social life of the capital, with its Parliament,

university, cathedral, and artistic circles, is charming in its naturalness and obvious sincerity. Manners are simple, and the people most kind and hospitable. Excellent coffee and pastries are offered at all times, and sometimes the national dish, skyr, or curds. In the winter dancing is fashionable, and the young people ever take delight in singing. Many can converse freely in Danish or English, and the general standard of education is high. Iceland is " dry," though it has been found necessary to re-admit Spanish wines.

The first authentic mention of the island is found in a work, " De Mensura Orbis Terrae," by an Irish monk, Dicuil, who relates (in 825) that he had conversed with monks who had visited the island of Thile, or Thule, which may almost certainly be identified with

FAIR MOTHER AND HER FAIRER DAUGHTERS
Warm and close family affection is a trait of all Scandinavian peoples. It is charmingly in evidence in this group of a sweet-faced Icelandic mother with her daughters, on whose countenances candour and confidence are written

ACRES OF COD-FISH LAID OUT TO DRY AT REYKJAVIK AFTER BEING SALTED

At first sight this might be mistaken for a snow-covered landscape, especially in view of the white-sprinkled mountains seen on the left. There is a keen wind blowing, fluttering the workers' skirts and stiffening the flag over the sheds. In reality it is a drying-ground, complete with light railway, for the prolific harvest of the Icelandic seas. The cod fisheries of these latitudes are among the most important in European waters. Of the whole population of the island, about 95,000, of whom nearly 18,000 live in Reykjavik, it is estimated that some 16,000 are engaged in the fisheries

SHOREBOATS IN THE WELCOME CALM OF REYKJAVIK'S FINE HARBOUR

Icelandic fishermen must be ranked among the boldest and most daring of all toilers of the sea. Their fishing-grounds are very stormy, and whereas the British and French fishermen who frequent them have large and stout vessels, the Icelanders, mainly from want of capital, use comparatively small open boats, though their fleet of fishing smacks is gradually being enlarged. Their disregard of danger is remarkable, unaffected by the very heavy toll of life exacted by the sea

Iceland. Dicuil's story is confirmed by the earliest Icelandic accounts of the Norse settlement in Iceland.

Naddoddur, sailing from Norway to the Faroe Islands in 870, was driven out of his course by storms and carried to a country unknown. He landed on the east coast, and gave to the country the name of Snaeland, or Snowland. The next visitor, Gardar Svavarsson, called it Gardarshólm, or Gardar's Island. Gardar was followed by Flóki of the Ravens, who, finding drift ice in one of the fiords, gave to the island its present name.

Men and Matters of the Sagas

The pioneers in the colonisation of Iceland were two brothers, Ingólfur Arnarson and Hjörleifur Hródarsson. They were followed from Norway by many Northmen of good family (874-930), and by others from the Norse Kingdoms in Ireland. Of the 312 names of the first settlers mentioned in the Landnámabók or the Book of Lots —the most detailed account of its origins that any people possesses— more than half are those of men from the British Isles. Many bore Celtic names.

In the saga period (930-1030), in which occurred most of the events that are recorded in the wonderful stories of the people (Íslendingasögur), the Icelanders established a Commonwealth that appears to have had its origin in a spontaneous movement among the leading men to provide a legal sanction for the existing local forms of government and to secure a uniform administration of a common code of laws through the island. The local Things, or parliaments, over which the great chiefs presided, became the model for the Althing, or general Court of Parliament, which was established in 930.

Order, Justice, and Prosperity

In the year 965 the whole island was divided into four Quarters or Provinces, each Quarter to have its own Court of Justice at the Althing. The Quarters were again each sub-divided into three jurisdictions (Thingsóknir). Each of the Quarters had its Quarter Thing,

and each of its sub-divisions had its Spring Thing. Suits begun in the Spring Thing might be carried to the Quarter Thing, and thence, if desired, to the Althing.

An important change was made at the same time in the constitution of the Althing. The Lögrjetta, or Court of Law, while retaining its deliberative and executive powers, was shorn of its judicial functions, which were distributed among four Courts representing the four Quarters. A Fifth Court, or Court of Appeal, was established in 1004 by the advice of the great lawyer, Njáll.

From the conclusion of the saga period (1030) down to the beginning of the Sturlunga period (1197), the people enjoyed the blessings of good government and public order. A literary period of extraordinary brilliance opened in 1117-1118, when for the first time the laws were written down in good Icelandic. Ari Thorgilsson (1067-1148) laid the foundation of Icelandic saga with a sketch of the island's history down to 1120. Ari is also believed to have collaborated with Kolskeggur the Sage in the composition of the original Landnámabók already referred to.

Norway's King and Iceland's Pawns

In the Sturlunga period (1197-1262), the Icelandic Commonwealth was rent and torn by the feuds of four great families, including the powerful Sturlungar. The great chiefs were devoid of patriotism, and often conspicuous for their vices. They appealed, when in difficulty, for assistance to King Haakon of Norway, and King Haakon astutely played off one chief against another. From acting as arbitrator in this way Haakon proceeded to appoint this or that chief as Jarl of Iceland, and more than one chief conspired with Haakon to bring Iceland under the rule of the kings of Norway. Ultimately Haakon, growing dissatisfied with the dilatoriness of Jarl Gissur, sent one of his own men to Iceland who compelled Gissur to take action in the interests of his master Haakon.

The Althing that assembled in 1262 agreed to a covenant (Gamli Sáttmáli)

HOARY WINTER SPREADS HIS BLEACHED MANTLE OVER REYKJAVIK

Street sounds, the wheels of heavy carts, plodding hoofs, and strolling footsteps, are all deadened by the muffling of the snow. At an upper window of the corner house on the right, by which a solitary lamp-post leans to the road, a girl looks down from behind the part-drawn curtain to watch the passers-by and the ponies at their provender, in Langavegur Street, a thoroughfare of the capital

VULCAN STOKES THE FURNACE FOR THE ICELANDER'S OVEN

Volcanic action in Iceland, destructive and desolating as it is, is not without some compensations. While no cereals can be grown there, and all the flour has to be imported, the surface of the earth is so hot in some places that the people are actually able to bake their bread in pails sunk in shallow holes dug in the ground with a spade

ICELANDIC MILKMAID ON HER MORNING ROUND

This is a fine sturdy pony standing so stockily for his photograph, and he can make light of his burden of buxom beauty with her heavy can of milk. She cares not for saddle or stirrups, for most of these island people are born to horseback, and her everyday costume amply serves the purpose of a riding-habit for this strapping Viking's daughter, with her long tresses shining in the breeze

MAKING HASTE SLOWLY ON THE ROCK-WALLED POST-ROAD

As might be expected, the best of Iceland's few roads are in the neighbourhood of Reykjavik, the capital. The eastern post-road runs thence for about sixty-two miles, and along it pony-drawn post-chaises of somewhat elementary construction carry passengers and mails. This photograph of a section of the road between Almannagja and Thingvellir well illustrates the volcanic formation of the island

ICELAND PONIES BRINGING BACK THEIR HAY GATHERED BENEATH HEKLA'S FIERY CREST

The frigid climate of this island forbids anything but a scant vegetation. The trees, birch, rowan, and willow, are stunted in their growth, heather and grass being the most common products of the earth. All inland transport is done on pony-back, and the huge loads borne by these sturdy little beasts testify their efficiency. The mass that rears its sombre height above them is Hekla, the volcano which from time to time vomits seas of molten lava to desolate the land

under which Iceland entered into a personal union with Norway. The King of Norway was to be represented by a Jarl, though, as a matter of fact, there was never again a Jarl in Iceland after the death of Gissur (1268). The Icelanders were to retain their ancient rights and laws. The Quarter Courts and the Court of Appeal were abolished, the judicial attributes of the Althing being transferred to the Lögrjetta, which now consisted of thirty-six members.

Under the Commonwealth the spirit of the Icelandic people had been remarkable for its sturdy independence and its power of initiative. Under the kings of Norway it drooped, though at times it could offer a stout resistance to the oppression of the foreign tax-gatherers to whom the kings, from 1354, leased out the revenues of the island. In 1388 Iceland passed with Norway under the rule of Denmark.

Danish Scorpions for Norwegian Whips

The yoke of Denmark proved to be heavier than had been that of Norway. The rights and privileges of the nation were filched one by one, till at last, in 1798, the last shred of independence disappeared with the abolition of the Althing. In the sixteenth century Lutheranism was imposed upon the island with the aid of Danish battle-ships, and the lands of the Church were transferred to the Danish Crown.

In 1662 the Danish Governor, Admiral Henrik Bjelke, coming with a battleship to Iceland, compelled the Icelanders to swear fealty to King Frederick III. and his dynasty. Two years previously the Danes had given absolute powers to their sovereign, but to impose absolutism on the Icelandic people was again a violation of the Covenant, the one constitutional link between Iceland and Denmark. The Icelanders, overawed by Bjelke, agreed to sign the document presented to them, but only after a clause had been introduced which confirmed them in the possession of their ancient rights and privileges.

Twenty years later (1680) the Danes began to enforce more rigorously the trade monopoly they had established in Iceland. In the fifteenth and sixteenth centuries the foreign commerce of the island had been in the hands of English traders, who were first attracted to Iceland by its fisheries. Later the competition of German and English merchants improved matters for the Icelanders, but ultimately the Danish kings stepped in and excluded both English and German merchants from the Icelandic trade. The foreign trade of Iceland was placed in the hands of Danish monopolists.

Ruin Wrought by Natural Forces

In 1783 volcanic eruptions were responsible, directly or indirectly, for the loss of 9,000 lives, and for the destruction of 11,000 cows, 27,000 horses, and 186,000 sheep. In the following year further destruction was caused by earthquakes. To such an ebb had the fortunes of the Icelandic people sunk in 1785 that the Danish Government decided to transport the whole surviving population to Denmark, and to re-settle it upon the moors of Jutland; but nothing came of this project.

The Icelanders are a tenacious breed, and deeply attached to their homeland. By the thirties of the nineteenth century they had recovered from the effects of the disasters that had befallen their land in the last quarter of the eighteenth century, and had initiated a national movement to recover their lost political and economic liberty. In spite of opposition from the Danish Governor, the Althing was restored in 1843, though it did not actually meet till 1845. A few years later it was strong enough to resist successfully an attempt on the part of Denmark to reduce the status of Iceland to that of a Danish province.

Union of Iceland and Denmark

From 1850 the political movement was guided by Jón Sigurdsson, one of the wisest statesmen that ever directed the destinies of a nation. Sigurdsson possessed all the qualities of a great political leader. He won the respect and trust of his adversaries, while he commanded in unstinted measure the love and devotion of his friends

CLARION NOTES PROCLAIM THE COMING OF THE MAIL CARAVAN OVER ICELAND'S PATHLESS PLAINS

There are no railways and few roads in Iceland, and in the remote parts of the country even bridle-paths are virtually non-existent. Thus communications and transport have to be effected on horseback. Iceland ponies are small and very hardy, and besides being thus indispensable to the islanders rank high among the exports. Intelligent and enlightened, great readers of books and newspapers, and avid of news of the outer world, the country people hear with delight the sound of the horn that announces the arrival of the mail caravan

and followers. Sigurdsson's first important success was gained in 1854, when the trade of Iceland was thrown open to the world, and this freedom of trade, won by Sigurdsson, laid the foundation of the great material prosperity that Iceland has since enjoyed.

The second great achievement of the Icelandic statesman was the winning of a Constitution in 1874. This constitution was imperfect from the Icelandic standpoint. An Icelander became Governor of Iceland, but, on the other hand, one of the Danish ministers acted as Minister for Iceland, and advised the King in matters relating to the island. This minister was in practice solely responsible in Icelandic affairs, and many Bills passed by the Althing were vetoed in Copenhagen. By an amendment of the Constitution in 1903 Iceland received a Prime Minister, who was to be an Icelander and to reside in Reykjavik. The Prime Minister was to be responsible to the Althing, and to be assisted by an executive consisting of a Secretary of State and three departmental chiefs. From 1904 the King never exercised his power of veto over Icelandic Bills.

The relations of Iceland and Denmark, notwithstanding, continued to be strained, till at last, in 1918, a Commission, sitting in Reykjavik, agreed upon the terms of a Treaty of Association between the two nations. The Danes, accepting the Icelandic contention that the Gamli Sáttmáli was a covenant between two equal and free peoples, agreed to acknowledge Iceland as a sovereign and independent State, united with Denmark by one King. Under the new Constitution the King of Iceland acts solely on the advice of his Icelandic ministers, who again are solely responsible to the Althing. The two nations cooperate in certain matters of mutual interest, but Iceland

has declared her neutrality in all wars in which Denmark may become engaged. The Treaty, if not previously renewed, will lapse in the year 1943.

Denmark in the past carried things with a high hand in Iceland, yet it would be difficult to find a parallel in the history of international relationships to the reasonableness and magnanimity that Denmark has displayed in her dealings with the Icelandic people from the days of Jon Sigurdsson onward. Till 1918 Denmark had paid to Iceland for many years interest on the computed value of the lands, etc., in Iceland confiscated to the

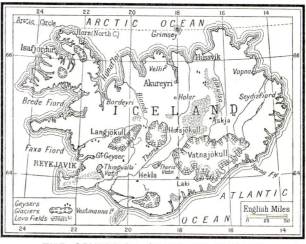

THE SOVEREIGN STATE OF ICELAND

Danish Crown centuries ago. The rate of interest was, no doubt, infinitesimal, but the acknowledgment of the debt was an act of justice rare, if not unique, in the history of nations.

The Icelandic people has passed through trials and tribulations, but to-day it may with truth be described as a happy and prosperous community, though, since the Great War, nouveaux riches and a proletariat have, unfortunately, emerged and present a sociological problem that is new and disquieting. The population has almost doubled within the last century, while the public revenue and external trade of the island have shown commensurate progress, the imports in 1918 totalling £2,259,235, and the exports £2,033,050.

BUDDH GAYA: BUDDHA'S HOLIEST PLACE

Over five hundred years before the birth of Christ there came into this world the "Light of Asia,"
Gautama Buddha, to whose name and memory a thousand wondrous shrines were to be raised.
This photograph was taken on one of the four terraces of the vast pagoda at Buddh Gaya, Bengal,
near where is the sacred Bo tree under which the holy one attained Nirvâna and his desire

Photo, F. Deaville Walker

India

I. Its Myriad Races, Beliefs, & Customs

By Sir Valentine Chirol

Author of "India Old and New," "Indian Unrest," etc.

In this comprehensive contribution the distinguished authority on India surveys that vast country and its infinitely varied peoples. Under the headings Bhutan, Burma, Ceylon, Nepal, the British Empire in Asia, and France : New Colonial Empire, will be found other articles on peoples and lands which, though connected with India, have claims under our editorial scheme to separate treatment

FOR a survey of the many peoples of India and of their many peculiar customs and beliefs there is no better starting-point than the extreme south, where the great peninsula tapers down to Cape Comorin, a few degrees north of the Equator. For it is there that all along the Malabar coast the great social and religious structure of Hinduism remains more than anywhere else intact, while in tropical forests and secluded mountain valleys the earliest aboriginal populations have survived, almost equally untouched by the successive waves of Aryan immigration in ancient times, of Mahomedan conquest in later ages, and in still more recent time of the less violent invasion of Western civilization.

Let us land at Quilon, an ancient coast town barely 100 miles north-west of Cape Comorin, in the state of Travancore, the largest and most important of the native states of Southern India. The Indian Ocean beats in eternal rhythm, now a mere murmur,

TRINKETS TO OUTWIT EVIL
Wearing numerous heavy earrings, this Garo woman believes that after death the devils who wait to devour her soul will fight instead for the rings, while she makes good her escape
Photo, the Rev. L. Barber

but during the monsoon a deafening roar of far-flung breakers, upon the coral reefs and golden sands of a long coast line, fringed in most places down to the water's edge with groves of coconut palms stretching far inland, which constitute one of the chief sources of the commercial and industrial wealth of this part of India.

From the uplands of the interior, where in the highest altitudes ebony, blackwood, teak, white cedar and sandalwood grow in dense primeval forests; over the lower slopes, where tea and coffee and pepper and cardamom and rubber are successfully cultivated; and then through miles of carefully irrigated paddyfields which yield the staple article of food of a rice-eating population, a stream descends and broadens into a beautiful lock, called by a Scotsman the Loch Lomond of Travancore, on which Quilon has led for centuries its sheltered existence.

Save for a few modern buildings in the European or semi-European style, it is a town

MANIPURIS CLOTHED IN THE INSIGNIA OF THEIR CALLING

As head boatmen of the Rajah of Manipur these finely-built men—natives of the Manipur state—enjoy a prestige above that of their ordinary brothers. Their handsome national costume has been donned on the occasion of the annual boat race, an event of much importance in the eyes of the Manipur population ; and their turbaned headdress is surmounted by egret plumage

Photo, Eleazar

of single storeyed tenements of sun-dried brick, for the better Quilonese classes, white or yellow-washed and with occasional daubs of colour and rudely painted designs to drive away maleficent spirits, while for the humbler folk it is a place of straggling shanties, sometimes of sun-dried mud, sometimes of grass matting and bamboo, dingy and odorous, but affording just enough shelter from blazing sunshine or from heavy downpours of rain in a climate of perennial summer heat.

Odorous, too, are the bazaars, long rows of open shops, each but a few feet deep and broad, in which, for the most part, in different quarters of the town, the venders of the same class of articles either of food or of clothing or of other simple necessities squat behind their wares in receipt of custom, serving their customers as they happen to come, with much bargaining, but with no apparent jealousy of their trade rivals on either side.

The crowds of purchasers come and go with the same listlessness, each usually returning day after day to the same vender, partly because the force of habit is indomitably strong in India, partly because the choice is limited by the deep dividing line of caste. Each recognized caste, as well as the "untouchables," who can even draw water only from the wells and tanks specially assigned to them, has its own quarter and its own bazaar, and each can be recognized by a caste-mark smeared on the forehead, or by distinct styles and materials of clothing, or by peculiarities of gait denoting in their several ways the high caste's pride of birth, and the abject humility of the despised "no-caste" man.

Northwards from Quilon, through the state of Travancore and the adjoining native state of Cochin, a great network of canals, often broadening out into lagoons separated only by narrow sand dunes from the Indian Ocean, affords the easiest means of communication and the most attractive mode of travel. A somewhat primitive houseboat, propelled to the modulated rhythm of weird but not unmelodious chants, which vary according to the stroke, by sturdy rowers whose dark brown skins glisten with oil in the sunshine, threads its way for the most part between coconut groves whose graceful fronds sometimes almost meet overhead, and now and again past populous villages where shoals of chocolate-coloured

MEN OF A MARAUDING NAGA TRIBE IN WAR TRIM

The generic term of Naga is given to a series of hill tribes in north-east India, distinguished as using no weapons but the javelin and dao, or billhook. Little is known of them save that they were early worshippers of the serpent, whence they derive their name, "Naga." Formerly inveterate marauders, their attitude towards the dwellers in the plains is less hostile now

Photo, Eleazar

VETERAN ARCHER TEACHING THE YOUNG ABOR HOW TO SHOOT

This is a village elder of one of the Mongoloid Abor tribes of the Assam border. He is giving an exhibition of his skill with the bow and arrow, and being an important personage, a gam, wears his outer coat of red Tibetan cloth, and his usual cane helmet is adorned with boars' tushes and red cotton waste. At his side is suspended a long Tibetan sword

Photo, Major-General D. Macintyre

GRAVITY AND WISDOM BETOKENED BY THE BEARD

Being of Mongoloid origin, most Abors are smooth-faced. These two gentlemen arrived with other headmen as a deputation to the Political Officer, and were photographed as being notable in respect of their beards, of which they were inordinately proud. And, indeed, throughout the ages the beard has been regarded as a symbol of manhood, strength, venerability, and wisdom

Photo, Major-General D. Macintyre

WRINKLED ELD CONTENT WITH THE WARMTH OF THE SUN AND A PIPE OF GOOD TOBACCO

On the whole, the Nagas of Assam are good to their old people, who mind the babies, tend the village fires, dry the chillies and bamboo shoots on mats, do a certain amount of weaving, and prepare the tobacco which all the people, of both sexes, smoke in great quantities. The old men need but a cloth to cover them and a tobacco bag, and discard all adornments ; but the old women cherish the brass rings worn in their hair, the earrings, heavy slabs of crystal which have distended their ear-lobes since girlhood, and their necklaces of shells and red cornelian.

REPRESENTATIVE OF AN ABOR VILLAGE ON HIS WAY TO DISCHARGE A FLOATING LIABILITY

The Abors of the low-lying lands are very skilful watermen, using dug-outs for fishing and passenger boats, and rafts for transport purposes by the river. On one of these rafts, most ingenious and simple constructions of bamboos lashed together, this man is bringing down the Dihang a live bullock which has been exacted from his village by the Political Officer as a fine for infraction of regulations. A voyage down the Dihang is a delightful experience owing to the grandeur of the scenery, but the journey up stream is arduous, and the frequent rapids are difficult to negotiate

Photo, Major-General D. Macintyre

IN THE ABOR JUNGLE—THE ORCHID-HUNTER'S PARADISE

For working in the fields and for travelling through the jungle—which they do with astonishing celerity—the Abor men wear nothing but a loin-cloth, for their shell necklaces and brass-disked shoulder-belts cannot be regarded as clothes. Their equipment includes a spear and sword, the latter with hilt and scabbard of bamboo, and a deerskin pouch to hold tobacco and pipe and various sundries

Photo, Major-General D. Macintyre

ABOR GRACE UNDRAPED IN THE SERVICE OF AGRICULTURE

She is discarding her blue-and-white striped loin-cloth before beginning work in the fields, and will toil clad only in her " boyup " or girdle of brass disks which every Abor girl wears from infancy until she first becomes a mother. This girl possesses an unusually large collection of blue and red beads, and her erect bearing is largely due to her practice of carrying loads on her head

Photo, Major-General D. Macintyre

SIMPLE VILLAGE LIFE HIGH UP ON THE NAGA HILLS

Naga villages are perched on hilltops for purposes of self-defence in tribal raids or feuds. Within the thatched, mat-walled houses the family sleep on planks set round the fireplace, often with a pig under the bed and fowls roosting in the rafters. Grain-pounders, implements, and baskets are kept in the entrance to the houses, and the cattle usually lie out in the middle of the street

Photo, Major-General D. Macintyre

children splash through the water, clapping their hands in welcome to the unwonted " white " travellers.

A small temple with many-armed deities roughly painted on the walls, and a young girl perhaps in a short, bright sari, with heavy anklets and bracelets and earrings and a nose-ring, too, beating the temple gong to attract the notice of the god, may mark the village as a Hindu village of some consequence. In another village, the whitewashed walls and belfry of a Christian church vaguely reminiscent of Southern Europe remind one that Christianity gained a footing in this part of India at an earlier date even

than the Portuguese, who were the first Europeans to land on its shores with intent to conquer. Elsewhere a mere stone, rudely shaped and daubed over with red paint, suffices for worship unto a more recent settlement of some jungle " no-caste " tribe.

Throughout this part of the Malabar coast, otherwise called the Malayalim country, from the language chiefly spoken by its inhabitants, the Nambudri Brahmin is the recognized lord of creation. For his lighter complexion shows him in most cases to be the lineal descendant of the Aryan immigrants who subdued the darker aboriginal races, and nowhere else in India does any Brahmin swagger along the road with quite such a sense of superiority. Has it not been said of him that " his person is holy, his directions are commands, his movements a procession, his meal is nectar—the holiest of human beings and the representative of God on earth " ?

As a matter of fact, his food is very simple, and consists chiefly of rice served on a plantain leaf or on a bell-metal plate, and by his wife, if no other men are present, though she never eats with him. Very simple, too, is his attire. The sacred thread of three strands, symbolising the primitive Hindu trinity, worn over his left shoulder, is of country-grown cotton, and so is his spotlessly white loin-cloth. The stripes on his forehead and chest, which denote his caste or his special form of worship, are laid on with sandal paste. He may wear amulets of gold or silver depending back and front from his neck, and his ears are pierced, though he seldom wears earrings. On his feet he may have wooden clogs, but never leather shoes, as all leather is regarded as " impure."

The house in which he lives is a square building enclosing several inner court-yards, into which the living-rooms open. One wing forms the zenana, strictly

MIRI NAGAS CHARGED WITH A MISSION OF APOLOGY

Wearing their meanest garments in token of humility, the four half-naked Miri Nagas in the front row have come from the Burma side of the Dikhu river to make their peace with the British Political Officer after punishment for a raid on some protected villages. The gentleman in the centre is an Ao Naga, who acts as intermediary, and wears his best embroidered cloth for the occasion

Photo, Major-General D. Macintyre

ARRIVAL OF THE "BIG SIX" FROM THE ABOR HILLS FOR A POLITICAL CONFERENCE

Theoretically, each Abor village is an independent community, although, owing to strength and man-power, a large village sometimes establishes a certain degree of authority over smaller and weaker neighbours. Feuds and fights are of constant occurrence, and life is punctuated with incidents in the Abor hills. The six gentlemen here shown are headmen from the lower hills, come down to interview the Political Officer. The imposing envelope held by one of them contains the political pass, a document which is highly prized as guaranteeing security from passers-by and neighbours

reserved for the women. The furniture is scanty, the beds are of coconut fibre, and the seats of plain wood, one of them, usually shaped like a tortoise, being reserved for devotional purposes. In the north-east corner of the enclosure is the go-sala, where oxen and cows are housed, and in the north-west corner is the sarhakkavu, or the "abode of snakes," equally sacred animals in the Nambudri Brahmin's eyes.

His religious exercises, which include daily ablutions, preferably in running water or in a natural reservoir, have to be performed at stated hours. They involve an elaborate ritual and take up a very large proportion of his time. The rest he devotes to the cares of his estate, to the paying and receiving of calls, such civilities being, of course, confined to his fellow caste-men, to a few permissible amusements, among them theatrical performances mostly of a quasi-religious character and of great antiquity, and to the more intimate pleasures of family life.

The number and variety of omens, good and bad, of which he has to take account when he sallies forth on the day's round of occupations, are as endless as those of the gods whom he has to invoke in order to confirm the auspicious and avert the inauspicious ones. Great, too, are the precautions which he must take to avoid pollution from proximity to fellow creatures of lower castes, who are forbidden to approach him beyond the precise number of paces fixed according to their lowliness in the descending scale of caste. So when he walks abroad he utters from time to time a curious

bellowing noise, which is the signal for the lower caste Hindu to remove himself out of the great man's way lest the latter's atmosphere should be defiled.

The writer once saw a well-dressed and well-to-do bunnia of the trading caste turn hurriedly back when more than half across a bridge at the sound of

SMILING BEAUTY OF THE WILDS
An acknowledged village belle, this Abor girl's youthful figure is muscularly developed by much arduous work. Like most Mongoloid peoples, the Abors smile in all circumstances
Photo, Major-General D. Macintyre

an approaching Brahmin, and in many parts of the country the common folk had trodden themselves a footpath through the fields, or across the jungle, to avoid these awkward meetings on the high road. And all this is done as a matter of course and without any sense of personal humiliation.

Religious holidays are frequent, and through the various stages of the

TUMLU NAGAS IN THE GLORY OF FULL WAR PAINT

Peculiar to the Tumlu Nagas is the bark waistbelt, drawn to such torturing tightness that the stomach often protrudes abnormally. The warrior's equipment includes a cane helmet, cowhide shield, spear, and dao or chopper. Only those who have taken part in a successful head-hunt may carry tufted spears. The boar's tushes worn on helmet and neck are highly prized as mascots

Photo, Major-General D. Macintyre

Nambudri Brahmin's life every festive or mournful occasion is marked by long and elaborate ceremonies, which make equally heavy calls on his time and on his purse. For if he is the lord of creation, he is himself the slave of his exalted station, of which he can never allow himself for a moment to forget the many engrossing obligations.

Next in importance to him, but greatly beneath him, comes the Nayar, with just as many curious customs peculiar to the Malayalim country. The Nayars, a handsome race whose regular features and whose complexion, though generally darker than that of the Nambudri Brahmin, also show traces of a mixed Aryan as well as

PARAM'S HEADMAN—THE VERY PINK OF COURTESY

Although generally rough and suspicious, some individual Abors have an amiable disposition and pleasing manners. " Quite a sahib," was the verdict passed upon this gam, or headman, of the village of Param, photographed in front of his thatched dwelling. The dogs here shown are excellent watch-dogs, and have good noses for sporting purposes. They are not infrequently killed and eaten

Photo, Major-General D. Macintyre

ROUGH-RIDER OF BALUCHISTAN'S WILD WASTES

Baluchistan is a country where horsemanship is rigorously put to the test. With its chaotic jumble of mud-coloured hills, its fertile valleys, upland plateaux, and one wide plain, it presents the rider with a varied landscape on which to display his skill as an equestrian. Horses and ponies are among the chief imports of Baluchistan, and come mostly from Afghanistan and Persia

Photo, E. Lindsay Young

Dravidian descent, were once a warrior caste, but they are now split up into many sub-castes, and have gradually exchanged the sword for the plough, and for such other peaceful avocations as their caste-laws allow. Polyandry, in the shape of several brothers sharing one wife, was formerly not uncommon, and accounts for the prevalence even to-day among them, and also among many Nambudri Brahmins, of the very ancient matriarchal system known as Manumakkathayam, under which descent is traced through the female line.

A male member of the family inherits, but he does so only as the son or grandson or other male next-of-kin of the senior female member of the family, i.e., a man's natural heir is not his son, or his grandson, or his brother's son or the descendant of a common male ancestor, but his sister's, or his sister's daughter's son, or some other descendant of a common female ancestress. Adoption, permissible in default of heirs through the female line, must be also of females through whose subsequent offspring the line of female descent may be carried on. The Maharaja of Travancore, who succeeded his uncle in 1885, and by special grace and payment of his own weight in gold was admitted to be half a Brahmin, had to adopt a sister, having none

FOREST BOWMAN OF THE HILLS IN CENTRAL INDIA

This wiry archer, with his body's weight "laid" to his well-stretched arc, is one of the Bhil tribe, a semi-savage people found mainly in Rajputana, the Central India Agency, and Bombay. They are a remnant of a Caucasian race, and owing to years of oppression took to the hills, where they became expert foresters. The archer's cummerbund serves both as sword-belt and quiver

HOW HOOK-SWINGING IS DONE
His back having been benumbed by blows
the flesh is pulled taut and with a quick
thrust two hooks are inserted just below the
shoulder blades
Photo, the Rev. J. H. Powell

or non-conjugal pleasure where she listeth. Many Nayars are attached by traditions of service to the household of Nambudri Brahmins who are believed to exercise not infrequently the same droit du seigneur, which was known in ancient France as droit de jambage, upon the prospective brides of their humbler retainers. To-day there are not a few Hindus in Southern India who owe their marked distinction,

of his own, in order that she might give him an heir. More indirectly, and indeed through an apparently inverse process, polyandry produced another strange practice also still very widely prevalent, namely, that of sham marriages, in which, with such pomp and ceremony as circumstances allow, and in the presence of a Brahmin to bless the ceremony, a boy bridegroom ties a tali, or marriage badge, round the neck of his appointed girl bride—or brides, as sometimes there are whole batches of brides to one bridegroom—receives a fee for his pains, and then departs after one or more days' feasting and merry-making, sometimes brought to a close by an equally sham form of divorce, without having had, or claiming even to have, the right to any intimacy with the girl, who also remains free to go her own way and seek conjugal

SUPERSTITION'S WILLING VICTIM
With the ropes by which he will be swung
crossed over his shoulders, the flower-
garlanded fanatic walks to the platform
where his self-sacrifice will be completed
Photo, the Rev. J. H. Powell

HOOK-SWINGING IN THE MADURA DISTRICT OF MADRAS IN HONOUR OF THE GODDESS MARI-AMMA

To an upright post a long cross-pole is pivoted in such a way that it can be either rotated or its ends raised and lowered. The ropes attached to the hooks are wound round the cross-pole, but not round the man's body, and supported only by the hooks he is raised clear of the platform seen in the lefthand picture. Two or three persons seated on a swing-board at the other end then shuffle round with their feet, so rotating the fanatic, his deliberately incurred agony lasting as long as ten minutes

Photos, the Rev. J. H. Powell

HARDY HUSBANDMEN OF NORTH-WEST INDIA WINNOWING THE GRAIN ON A NATIVE HOLDING

Like the Baluchis, the Brahuis are a mixture of Arab and Scythian stock and inhabit Baluchistan and parts of Sind. For the most part they are a stay-at-home people, much attached to their families, and although endowed with endurance and manliness and having all the makings of valuable soldiers, they find life in cantonments so distasteful that they return as soon as possible to their homes, where most of them have property in the shape of land or camels

Photo, V. S. Manley

physical and intellectual, to a Nambudri father and a Nayar mother. The Nayar maiden, striding along to fill her copper water vessel at the village well or at the river-bank, can be recognized as surely by her erect figure and delicate features as by the immaculate cleanliness of her tightly-wound white loin-cloth and the little white bodice which just covers her breasts, or by the spray of bright-coloured flowers jauntily stuck into the knot of raven hair which crowns her shapely head. Armlets and anklets are of relatively recent fashion with Nayar women, but all wear a peculiar neck ornament which used formerly more often than now to be shaped like the hood of a king-cobra.

Cleanliness ranks next to godliness with the Nayar men as well as women folk, and their once martial qualities still find an outlet in various sports and games in which shooting with bows and arrows as well as a rough form of boxing often play a prominent part. The Nayars have almost as many religious festivals and ceremonies of their own as the Nambudri Brahmins, and while to the latter they yield the road in all humility, they clear it for themselves as against all lower castes by a shout hardly less imperious than that of the Brahmins.

Yet it is on this same Malabar coast, where Hinduism has retained so many of its most archaic forms, that we find the principal seat of early Indian Christianity—far earlier than the contact established between India and Western Christendom across the highways of the ocean. Bishop Medlicott has written a learned work to prove that the Apostle Thomas must be regarded as no mere legendary evangelist of India, and that he may well have suffered martyrdom, as local tradition has it, near to the spot called San Thomé, just outside Madras, where the Portuguese erected the cathedral to his memory.

More sceptical investigators have played havoc with the pious bishop's arguments; but that Christianity had been imported into India from Western Asia by the sixth century there can be little doubt, nor that the first Christian

BLUE-BLOODED SON OF INDIA
Dignity stamps this native of Southern Baluchistan, and his coat of chocolate-brown, with its heavy gold embroidery, befits him well as the son of a local chieftain
Photo, Major W. J. P. Rodd

Church was established by Nestorians with bishops of the Chaldean or Syrian rite. Political vicissitudes and sectarian propaganda have in the course of time split up Indian Christians into many different churches. Some still adhere to the original forms of Eastern orthodoxy. Others, under Portuguese influence chiefly, and as the result of S. Francis Xavier's personal apostolate, have transferred their religious allegiance to the

WEATHERBEATEN WAYFARERS OF BALUCHISTAN

The soldiering days are over for these hoary-haired Baluchis, who have adopted the musical profession as a means by which they may glean a humble pittance to satisfy their daily needs. The life in their desert homes has been one long struggle against nature, and despite the hardships encountered during their wanderings, they ever present a cheery countenance to the world

Photo, V. S. Manley

See of Rome. In modern times the Protestant missionaries have made large numbers of converts all over India, for the most part from the depressed castes, often attracted chiefly by the prospect of social betterment. Of late years there have been mass conversions among those castes, which have confronted the missionary societies with difficult economic as well as spiritual problems. To-day there are almost four million Indian Christians, of whom the great majority are still in Southern India.

Kottayam, on one of the great lagoons through which one passes between Quilon and Cochin, is still the seat of the ancient Syrian rite, and in a crowded church, reputed to be itself of great antiquity under its outer coat of whitewash, the writer attended on a Sunday an elaborate service in which the rich robes of the officiating clergy, the long-drawn nasal chants, the overpowering smell of incense, the illuminated missals and the Byzantine stiffness of the sacred paintings on gold ground brought back recollections of similar scenes in the great Christian Churches of Western Asia.

One custom, however, obtained which was peculiar to India and connoted the enduring influence of Hinduism even on communities that had abjured its religious beliefs. The old caste prejudices survived, and the congregation was divided into separate pens. Those who could boast some admixture of European blood, mainly Portuguese, would never rub shoulders with their co-religionists of purely Indian descent. Nevertheless, Kottayam, with a population at least one-third Christian, and two large Syrian Christian schools besides more recent missionary schools, stands out conspicuously among the small towns of the Malayalim country as a clean and thriving little centre of progress and enlightenment.

Nor is Christianity the only alien religion which has been imported from ancient times into India on the Malabar coast. Cochin, one of the very first Portuguese settlements, visited by Vasco da Gama himself in 1502, and by S. Francis Xavier in 1530, is to-day the chief port of Malabar, on a backwater which forms a fine natural harbour several square miles in extent, but too shallow for modern steamers until works projected for deepening the bar have been completed.

The majority of the population are Indian Christians, but when one emerges from the maze of bamboos and coconut palms that both shelter and serve for the construction of the scanty huts in which the lower caste Hindus are herded together, he comes suddenly round a

STATE ELEPHANTS OF BARODA GAILY CAPARISONED

Nothing could out-vie the splendour with which these noble beasts are invested on state occasions. Their heads are painted with a variety of vivid pigments, and gorgeous ornaments depend from their bodies. In the foreground is the "Flag Elephant" belonging to the Gaekwar of Baroda, with its gold-plated howdah, paraded at a garden-party in honour of the Prince of Wales's visit during 1921-22

A charter which they still possess, engraved, like most title deeds of Malabar, on copper plates, dates back at any rate to about A.D. 700, and was conferred upon their ancestors by Hindu rulers of the time as a mark of special confidence and friendship. But the Jews no more than the Christians of India have altogether escaped the influence of the Hindu atmosphere in which they have lived for so many centuries. There are "white" Jews, who bear the stamp of excessive inter-breeding and who still hold socially aloof from the "black" Jews

corner into a few streets of a strangely different character. The houses of stone and brick are lofty and built in an Occidental style, though they bear on their doors and walls the stamp of poverty and sloth in the slimy moisture of tropical rains of which no attempt is apparently ever made to remove the disfiguring stains.

There is the same woe-begone look on the pale faces of their denizens and on their threadbare clothes, which equally show their kinship with the old-fashioned Ghettoes of Eastern Europe or Western Asia. It is the Jewish quarter of Cochin, the only Indian town except Bombay (where they are already scattering), in which the Jews have had a settlement of their own from times almost immemorial. At Cochin they claim to go back to the time of the dispersion.

INDIA'S MAGIC MANGO TREE

Squatting at the spectators' feet the conjurer puts a seed into a tin and pipes to it, as shown in the top photograph. Then, covering it with a cloth, he makes passes over it, sprinkles it, and reveals successively a branching twig and fruit-bearing tree

Photos, the Rev. J. H. Powell

CHARMING THE VENOM OF THE FOLDED SNAKE

The snake-charmer's outfit consists of a cobra, whose poison fangs are extracted, a mongoose—presumably to catch the snake if it escapes—and a wind instrument fashioned from a gourd. On hearing the notes of the pipe, sometimes accompanied by a tom-tom, the cobra raises its body from the basket, spreading its hood and swaying, withdrawing into the basket on the cessation of the strains

Photo, the Rev. J. H. Powell

whose forbears probably embraced Judaism at a time when the "white" Jews enjoyed some measure of territorial power under Hindu overlordship.

"White" Jews and "black" Jews have their separate synagogues and Rabbis, and live in different streets, but both testify to the tenacity of their common creed as well as to the tolerance of ancient Hindu rule before the first Portuguese invaders introduced into

and industry, from one of the steamers that ply daily between Ceylon and the mainland, and travel up to Madras by rail through a region very different from the Malayalim country.

With the exception of the small native state of Pudukkóttai it is not under indigenous rule, but under direct British administration, and forms part of the Presidency of Madras. It is inhabited by peoples of Dravidian

THE PRIVILEGED ANIMAL OF HINDUISM

The cow, taking advantage of its sacred rights as a symbol of bounteous nature, enjoys an undisturbed rest in a busy street of Calcutta. Both the bull and the cow are sacred animals to all Hindus, and in no circumstances will a Hindu eat beef in any form ; the slaughter of cattle, and even the sight of the flesh after dressing, hurts their religious feelings very deeply

Southern India with their political ambitions and sectarian fanaticism a new element of racial and religious distrust.

Not on the relatively narrow lowland between the Western Ghats and the Malabar coast are the chief cities of Southern India to be found, but on the much broader watershed of the Eastern Ghats towards the Coromandel coast, which from Cape Comorin trends northwards towards the Bay of Bengal. There we can land at Tuticorin, a thriving centre of modern commerce

descent, but they speak not Malayali but other Dravidian tongues, Tamil in the south, Telegu farther north. It is a more open country devoted mainly to food crops, among which rice and pulses are most conspicuous, while the best soils yield sugar-cane, tobacco, and " garden " crops.

It is a cattle country, too, and its various breeds of buffaloes are valued even more for their cows' milk than for the heavy ploughing and slow draught usefulness of the males. Most of the

RUSTIC HINDU CARRYING BOTH PLOUGH AND HARROW TO THE FIELDS

The influence of the splendid Colleges of Agriculture in India has by no means reached all the remote villages, for in this vast country where the varieties of soil and climate are manifold many experiments are necessary to ascertain how these varieties may be successfully dealt with. But the homely farmer in his native village carries on his simple methods of cultivating the soil in a truly conservative way

POPULAR SEE-SAW METHOD OF IRRIGATION IN INDIA

No great physical strength, but much patient endurance is required for the irrigation of these small fields, about twenty feet square, and this native agriculturist, though ripe in years, still feels equal to the arduous task. The wooden trough is pulled down into the pool till it fills, and a weight at the other end of the bamboo helps to lift it when full

Photos, the Rev. L. Barber

HINDU DEVOTEE PROSTRATING HIMSELF BEFORE A SHRINE OF THE SACRED COBRA

Despite their deep reverence for the snake, the Hindus have not yet become entirely reconciled to these creatures, but few would ever dream of molesting or killing them for fear of the supernatural powers they are thought to possess. The special sanctity of the cobra is due to the belief that its hood formed a canopy over Vishnu the Preserver, and on the whole, the snake is worshipped as an object of fear rather than of love. Hindus sometimes keep deadly snakes for years in their houses at the risk of their lives, yet no member of the family would dare to lay sacrilegious hands on the honoured inmate

MASKS AND TRUMPETS THAT GO BEFORE A PROCESSION OF LAMA DANCERS

The grotesque coverings that conceal the features of these leaders of the barbaric rout whose long shadows stripe the grass beneath the trumpets, indicate what is coming. The devil worship, that has gnawed its ugly way, like some insidious parasite, into the sonorous liturgy of Buddhism must needs find some forcible expression. This it has obtained in dances and ceremonies designed to placate the eldritch conceptions of the Oriental mentality—the evil spirits. And the adjuncts of these gruesome rites are as bizarre as their instigation, but are impressive, too, at this pageant in the Maidan at Calcutta

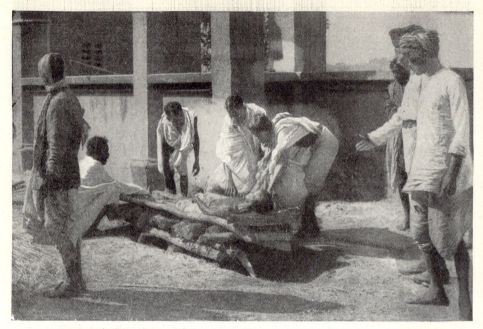

HINDU CREMATION: SCENE AT THE BURNING GHATS, CALCUTTA

The death of a Brahmin has always been associated with a number of indispensable ceremonies, and most Hindus observe many formalities on the death of their relations. The practice of cremation, carried to India by the early Aryans, still prevails, and the funeral pyre seen above, erected by the deceased's nearest of kin, is a common sight in the cremation-ground or burning ghats of Calcutta

PERFORMING THE LAST RITES FOR A HINDU BROTHER

The pyre erected, the corpse is placed upon it; then, in the sight of the mourners, who in tense attitudes are grouped around, the wood is piled over the body and set alight by the chief mourner. The Hindus have professional mourners who undertake to make the necessary lamentations and wailings, and sacred oil is poured on the body before and while the pyre is alight

Photos, Frank Scott

CHIEF MOURNERS WATCHING THE BURNING OF THE FUNERAL PYRE

The dead bodies are often carried to the cremation-ground exposed, but in some towns in India they are covered in a shroud while being burnt. Years ago, if the corpse was that of a man, the wife would throw herself on the burning pyre and be burnt with her husband rather than endure the shame of being a widow, for as such it was considered to be

IN THE KINGDOM OF SHADES AND SILENCE

The charred and smouldering funeral pyre is now deserted and the body consumed ; the ashes are then scattered in the river Hooghli, or in the great sacred river of India, the Ganges. After this, the mourners return home, thinking little of the body, but much of the spirit that has departed. " Death is only an incident in the long journey of the Hindu pilgrim "

Photos, Frank Scott

land is held by smallholders under the ryotwari system, in which there is, in theory at least, no intermediate landlord between the cultivator and the state. The villages and small townships resemble those of the Malabar coast, but native industries and even modern forms of industry have been more highly developed, and a larger part of the population has been attracted into cities which were famous long before Madras was founded as one of the earliest British settlements in India. Hinduism is not less supreme on the Coromandel than on the Malabar side, and wears outwardly an even statelier aspect.

Monumental Hindu Temples

This is the land of monumental temples, as imposing in their massive proportions as the temples of ancient Egypt, whose lofty pylons might have inspired the builders of the huge gopurams that tower above the main entrances to the great courtyards which enclose the innermost sanctuaries of Hinduism. On their massive walls, as well as in immensely long galleries, of which the mystery is enhanced by darkness, the deities of the Hindu pantheon, generally in their most terrifying forms—for it is the cult of Siva the Destroyer which usually prevails—are repeated thousands of times over in stone and marble, and sometimes in terra-cotta, and if they lack the majesty of the Egyptian Pharaohs, they doubtless make an even stronger appeal to the imagination of the Hindu worshippers whose minds are attuned to terror as the chief attribute of the many destructive manifestations of tropical nature which they personify.

Majestic Dravidian Architecture

This style of architecture, known as Dravidian, is peculiar to the south of India, and goes back to the eleventh and twelfth centuries, when Siva became the most popular of deities. It held its own in later centuries, when Vishnu grew to be a formidable, if friendly, rival. At Rameswaram, on an island which forms part of Adam's Bridge, the temple, dedicated in this instance to Rama, is built of a dark, hard limestone, and of black granite, fashioned in the doorways and ceilings into slabs forty feet long, and encloses an oblong area 1,000 feet long and two-thirds as broad, which is approached by a gateway 100 feet high.

One can wander for the best part of a mile through its broad and lofty galleries and pillared halls, lined with weird and monstrous figures, and still showing on the ceilings the faded glory of ancient paintings. The shaded avenues leading from the landing-place to the temple shelter, at frequent intervals, the different inns at which the thousands of pilgrims who flock during the year from all parts of India to Rameswaram are lodged and fed, according to their separate castes, by the Brahmins alone privileged to reside on the island.

Siva's Perfect Shrine at Tanjore

At Trichinopoly long flights of stairs and passages, cut in the living rock, with stone elephants eighteen feet high, and columns crowned with lions, and friezes of weird designs, lead up to the summit of the rock on which a famous Siva temple, with a huge silver-cased Nandi bull on a platform in front of it, looks down from a height of 230 feet on the city of over 100,000 inhabitants, most widely known perhaps to-day for the brand of cigars to which it has lent its name. Not only of very great antiquity, according to Hindu tradition, it frequently played an important part in the struggle of the British and the French for mastery in Southern India in the middle of the eighteenth century, and the bones of French and British soldiers lie peacefully at rest in its graveyards.

Tanjore boasts the most perfect as well as one of the oldest Dravidian temples. The vimana, or central tower, with its tiers upon tiers of carven deities, and the dome-shaped monolith which crowns it, is 200 feet high, and at the foot of it the gigantic bull sacred to Siva has been fashioned out of a

IMMEMORIAL INDIA
Its Colour & Magic

Resplendent in trappings of scarlet and gold, this majestic elephant makes an imposing appearance at Bengal's chief festive gatherings

Photo, the Rev. L. Barber

Outside the Kali Temple in Calcutta sits a shrine-keeper, the silvery voice of his bell persistently bidding passing pilgrims to prayer

Photo, F. Deaville Walker

2738

*Under his skilful hands the shapeless block of ivory is transformed
into the thousand and one delicate designs peculiar to Indian art*

Photo, Publishers' Photo Service

*The wife of a sturdy Gurkha fighting man, she is bent on bringing up
the small son in her arms to love and honour a soldier's calling*

" *Small profits and quick returns,*" *a system by which India's traders in tropical produce earn a fairly substantial subsistence*

Photo, Publishers' Photo Service

Possessing all the fighting qualities of a warrior, the Maratha nevertheless inherits the love of intrigue of his filibuster ancestors

Photo, H. S. Talbot

A singular exhibition of four-footed rhythmic grace is given by this superbly caparisoned Arab dancing horse of the Maharana of Udaipur

Photo, Herbert G. Ponting

The "pan supari" (betel-nut) parties of Hindu social life are invariably enlivened by musical divertissement, when with singing and dancing a Nautch group supplies the pièce de résistance—often of a dubious kind

Photo, S. R. Norton

single block of black granite over sixteen feet in length, brought from far-distant quarries, and anointed every day with oil by the attendant Brahmins, till it shines like burnished metal.

The pride of the place, however, is the shrine of Kartikkaya, the son of Siva and god of war, a relatively small casket of exquisitely wrought stonework, upon which Hindu sculptors have lavished all the phantasies of their religious imagination, but combined them with a delicate sense of beauty which they too often lack. It consists of a tower only fifty-five feet high, rising from a base forty-five feet square, but its graceful lines and perfect symmetry make it the most attractive piece of decorative architecture in the whole of southern India.

Madura's Awe-inspiring Temple

In the great temple of Madura, on the other hand, of much more recent construction—it does not date back farther in its present shape than the sixteenth century, and one of its towers, which was to have been loftier than those of any rival temple, has never been completed—the chief purpose of the architects has been to inspire awe and terror. The pillared galleries, with their endless vistas of forbidding deities and grimacing demons and fabulous animals looming out of dim and gloomy recesses, the canopied figures of gods and kings of heroic stature, even the great hall of 1,000 pillars—the number is no mere figure of speech—which is the central and amazing feature of the immense sanctuary, are almost as bewildering and terrifying a nightmare in the uncertain daylight that pierces them with occasional shafts of blinding sun-shine as in the obscurity of night, when only a few stationary lamps or the flare of processional torches fitfully illuminate a world infinitely remote from all our conceptions of the sublimely divine.

Conjeeveram, Coimbatore, Tirwalla, and indeed all the large towns possess their own temples, many on a scarcely less grandiose scale, and all laid out on approximately the same lines. In most of them there stands in one of the inner courtyards the huge wooden car with monstrous figures and devices carved on the sides in deep relief, on which the chief idols of the shrine are borne in solemn procession on great festivals, arrayed in all their barbaric splendour of gold and silver and priceless jewels, sometimes only within the temple enclosure, and sometimes abroad to pay visits to other kindred temples.

A Land of Perpetual Paradox

The carvings on these cars, like the paintings on many temple walls, and the groups of bright-eyed little girls playing about the sacred courtyards who are devoted from their childhood to a life of prostitution which service to the gods is held to redeem from shame, illustrate too frequently other popular aspects of Hinduism in which the worship of nature in its erotic tendencies, stimulated by well-known episodes of Hindu mythology, degenerates into rank obscenity.

Yet all these strange manifestations of the ancient religious and social life of the country have persevered for centuries through all the vicissitudes of Indian political history, and go on to-day side by side with as many and no less striking manifestations of the modern forms of government and of economic and industrial life, imported with British methods of administration, with railways and telegraphs and telephones, with steam and electricity, with the printing press, and the many other applied sciences of the West. In some respects, indeed, the latter have helped the former.

Brummagem Aids to Brahminism

Railways have swelled the crowds of pilgrims who flock to all the principal shrines of Hinduism from increasingly distant parts of India, cheap oleographs and postcards and little brass idols and other temple mementoes—often " made in England "—adorn thousands of Hindu homes, and vernacular news-papers provide the lesser Brahmins with inexhaustable materials for a pro-paganda carried from village to village, in which the manifold superiority of Hindu civilization over that of the West is instilled into the receptive minds of the simple ignorant masses who have forgotten the old days of their oppression in pre-British times.

Madras itself, a stately city spread along a golden stretch of surf-beaten coast, is entirely a creation of the British period. Its public buildings, as well as the chief residential quarters of the small European population, still abundantly illustrate the subdued luxury

marriage lines of one of Milton's daughters in the register of S. Mary's Church, the first English church ever built in India, nearly two and a half centuries ago. If it be a merely apocryphal tradition that S. Thomas suffered martyrdom on Dec. 21, A.D. 68, on the hill which the Portuguese named San Thomé, the church first erected on the site which his blood, shed by a Brahmin, is popularly supposed to have hallowed, has a remarkable cross above the altar, which a Nestorian inscription

ONE OF THE DIFFICULTIES OF DRIVING IN BENGAL

All roads are embankments in Bengal, and the country being flat floods very quickly when the rains come. Here a bridge has been washed away and a frail footbridge improvised ; the ground underneath is a veritable mire in the wet season, and if a loaded bullock-cart reaches this spot, its contents must be unloaded and carried over the bridge while the cart is dragged through the deep mud

Photo, the Rev. L. Barber

and spacious tastes of the East India Company days, and its leafy avenues still shelter many old-fashioned houses with deep verandas and lofty living-rooms, standing peacefully secluded in grounds sometimes sufficiently extensive for their modern occupants to lay out a nine-hole golf course within their own " compound."

Fort St. George contains many interesting relics of the times of stress and storm through which the original British settlement passed when France and England were striving for mastery, and none perhaps more curious than the

shows to go back to the beginning of the ninth century.

From the crowded Georgetown, formerly called Black Town, the indigenous population of about half a million altogether has gradually spread into many other scarcely less crowded quarters where Hinduism practises its weird religious rites in the recesses of great Dravidian temples, within earshot of the throbbing cotton-mill power-house, and the scream of passing trains, and the deep hooting of ocean-going steamers, and sometimes cheek by jowl with equally up-to-date cinemas. On

MEN WHO FEAR NOT THE FLEETING FEET OF TIME

Although many tons of rice have to be weighed by these Bengali natives, the scales they use are no bigger than those to be found in the shops. It is also no unusual sight to see men sitting down and cutting away at grass two or three inches high with a bowie-knife; a couple of hours' work will give them a pile large enough for a cow's meal

FEASTING OFF BANANA LEAVES IN A VILLAGE OF BENGAL

They dispense with plates and dishes, for the broad banana leaf furnishes them with all the utensils they require; and in a land where a man of inferior birth may not touch the vessels of a high-caste man, these unsoiled plates of nature's giving are specially welcome. All eat with the right hand and never touch any dish with the left, which is reserved for unclean work

Photos, the Rev. L. Barber

WAITING FOR THE CUSTOMER IN A NATIVE BAZAAR

There is a total lack of romance in Bengal, and the architecture is of the crudest. When the rest of India was building palaces and temples Bengal was jungle, and emerged from obscurity after the building age had passed. Tin roofs and mat walls form the bulk of the houses in this bazaar, where the natives market their wares on small squares of ground hired for that purpose

Photo, the Rev. L. Barber

MUSCLE AS A CLEANSING MEDIUM OF A HINDU LAUNDRY

Strength would seem to be the all-important factor in the laundry methods of this young native, and it was surely of him that Mark Twain was thinking when he wrote : " The queerest thing I saw in the East was a man smashing stones with a shirt-front ! " The truth of the proverb, " The washerman's brother is a tailor," is obviously incontestable in this instance

Photo, the Rev. L. Barber

VENERABLE CHIEFTAIN OF SIND AND HIS ATTENDANTS

Sind, a province of north-west India, is comprised in the governorship of Bombay. It is an arid country dependent on the Indus, and owing to a very scanty rainfall eighty per cent. of the cultivated area is irrigated. Karachi, the great wheat exporting port near the delta of the Indus, receives the bulk of its exports from the Punjab

Photo, Major W. J. P. Rodd

the same coast as Madras, but 100 miles farther south, the town of Pondicherri, divided by a canal into a " Ville Blanche " and a " Ville Noire," the one with the streets and shops and boulevards and the marine promenade of a small French Mediterranean town, and the other a straggling maze of lanes and hovels redeemed from squalor by the graceful fronds of palm trees bowing to the sea breeze, is the chief town of the largest of the half-dozen strips of territory with barely 150,000 souls, still under French rule in India.

A statue of Dupleix, who founded Pondicherri, and went near to founding a French Empire of India, looks out upon the ocean in which his ambitions foundered with France's failure to wrest sea-power from British hands.

Eight hundred miles across the sea, due east of the Madras Presidency, lie the two chief groups of scattered islands, Andaman and Nicobar, under direct British administration by the Government of India. The aborigines, with tufted black hair and sheeny black skins, are a race apart, as primitive as

RAISING COOL WATER FOR THE THIRSTY LAND

It is many years since grim necessity with her torrid skies first mothered the invention of irrigation systems in India. Perhaps the earliest form of machinery for this purpose was the " denkli," consisting of a pole with, at one end, a bucket, and, at the other, a counterpoise. Here a native stands on the pole at its point of balance, and, by movement to and fro, helps to raise and lower the bucket

LURED FROM THE HILLS TO TURN AN HONEST PENNY

Modest, quiet, and dignified, these women and children are inhabitants of the native villages built upon the spurs of the Western Ghats near Matheran. They come into that health resort to sell their produce, milk and vegetables, for which they find a ready market in the holiday season. Like all Eastern women they carry their burden easily on their heads, using no supporting hand

Photo, H. S. Talbot

FRESH VEGETABLES FOR VISITORS TO MATHERAN

Father of the boy and girl beside him, this scantily attired native has come, like the women shown on the opposite page, to sell some of his garden stuff in Matheran. Unlike their neighbours the Kathoris, who live in complete detachment, these villagers are not aborigines but are orderly people well disposed to the civilizing influences of the hill sanatorium established in their midst

Photo, H. S. Talbot

YOUNG HINDU FISHWIVES AND THE FAMOUS BOMBAY DUCK
From its name Bombay Duck would seem to the uninitiated to be an ornithological species. In reality it is a small eel-like fish, Harpodon nehereus, found in large quantities in the Indian and China seas. When newly caught it is brilliantly phosphorescent; in a salted and dried condition it is Bombay Duck, a delicacy eaten in a crumbled form as an accompaniment for curry

Photo, Harry Cox

the language they speak and the superstitions that cluster round the worship of their tribal and extremely human god Puluga. Children of nature, they are merry but quick-tempered, with little stability of character, but free from the grosser forms of vice, monogamous, and kindly to their womenfolk and children. The deeply indented coast, with its beautiful coral beds, and the narrow valleys confined between steep hills which rise to over 2,400 feet in the North Andaman, all clothed with a dense tropical vegetation, afford an immense variety of striking scenery. Amongst the many valuable products of the forests the padauk tree yields

exceptionally fine timber which, when polished, assumes a deep claret colour of unique quality. The islands, of which Port Blair is the capital, have been used hitherto by the Government of India as the chief penal settlement for criminals sentenced to long terms of transportation. But the system now stands condemned by a recent commission of inquiry.

The broken, forest-clad hill country that rises generally rather abruptly from the Malabar coast, and more gently from the Coromandel coast of the Madras Presidency, whence it stretches on into the wildest regions of the Central Provinces, has provided

ELEVATED DRYING-GROUND OF AN ODORIFEROUS INDUSTRY
Bombay Duck is the source of a considerable industry in many a village in the Bombay Presidency.
After each elongated " duck " has been more or less cleaned the drying process begins. For several
days the fish are hung on specially-constructed frames, and the offensive odour emanating from
this mass of fish exposed to the sun's hot rays pervades the whole atmosphere of the village

Photo, Harry Cox

for centuries some of the retreats
which still shelter the most ancient
and primitive of the Dravidian peoples
of India. They are for the most part
outside the pale of Hinduism, some,
however, just on the fringe. The
official census has invented for their
religions or superstitions the unsatisfactory name of Animism.

Rocks weirdly shaped by nature, or
stones rudely fashioned by their own
hands, strangely gnarled trees, roaring
waterfalls, or silent pools hidden in the
recesses of the hills, are the shrines at
which they worship the dread powers
and elements, vaguely personified and
mostly maleficent, that people the air

and the forests and the waters around
them. The chief cult which they have
in common with the highest castes
of Southern India is that of the snake-
god. To kill a snake is a deadly sin,
and in some parts of the Malayalim
country special groves are set apart as
sacred pleasances for snakes, with temples
to the serpent king and queen, and
thousands of granite images of snakes,
and special Brahmins in charge of them.

On the outskirts of even the humblest
jungle village a bowl of milk may often
be seen exposed under a sacred tree in
the hope that it will keep the dreaded
cobra at a safe distance from the
dwellings of men. Or, again, you may

FISHING-NETS ON THEIR WAY TO THE PRESERVING PICKLE

Most of the populace of the fishing villages of Western India are employed in the Bombay Duck industry. Men, women, and children all take a hand either in catching the fish, in curing it, or in making and mending the nets. After the nets have been used they are deposited in a certain pickle which is guaranteed to preserve them until such time as they are again required for use

Photo, Harry Cox

find an upright stone wreathed with flowers to propitiate the goddess of smallpox, or the goddess of some other fell disease that has lately decimated the neighbourhood, or, on the spot where a man-eating tiger has killed a villager, a flat stone with an impressionist representation of a tiger, which is supposed both to avert any further visits from the wild beast and to keep the spirit of its victim from haunting the village where he lived.

Ghosts are a constant terror to the simple folk of all creeds and castes, but to none more than to the Animist jungle folk. Even the highest Hindu castes, like the Nambudri Brahmin and the Nayor, have their magicians and soothsayers, but nowhere is the exorcist who can lay a ghost or disarm the evil eye and all other evil spells, or smell out a witch, quite so mighty a personage as in the primitive jungle where the gods and goddesses of the Hindu Pantheon are still unknown. He is its high priest.

Sometimes a whole tribe acquires a wide-spread reputation for the possession of exceptionally potent charms, like the Malayan caste in North Malabar, who are in great request far and near. On special occasions they enhance their prestige by prancing about in the disguise of hobby horses, or they personate demons and minor deities, wearing

RIDING THE INDIAN WATERS IN SEARCH OF BOMBAY DUCK

This is one of the fishing smacks built by the native fishermen, and although of a clumsy and primitive type it is admirably fitted for its allotted task. Bombay Duck is not restricted to the sea, being abundant in the rivers and estuaries of Bengal and Burma; it is exported principally from the west coast of India, Bombay being a centre of trade for the dried fish

Photo, Harry Cox

blood-red masks and pantomime helmets of plaited straw woven into terrifying designs, and bamboo hoops from which depends a rustling skirt of long streamers cut out of the banana leaf and dipped in blood.

For their incantations blood has to be drawn, sometimes from the exorcist's own arm, with which he smears his face, sometimes from animals, and especially from fowls, and he either himself sucks the blood of the victim from the neck of the decapitated bird, which he plunges, still quivering, into his mouth, or else he introduces it into the mouth of the patient to drive out the evil one by direct action.

Formerly human sacrifices were not uncommon, and the Madras Museum possesses a sacrificial post with a revolving wooden beam roughly fashioned in the shape of an elephant's head, to which the Khonds, who inhabit the hill tracts of Ganjam, in the north of the Madras Presidency, tied the human victim selected by their wizards. As soon as the beam began to whirl round the crowds rushed in and hacked off pieces of the still living flesh, which they carried away to bury in their fields to the accompaniment of a ghastly chant, as charms against bad harvests and other forms of ill-fortune. Buffaloes, monkeys, and goats became

RITUALISTIC BATHING IN THE SACRED RIVER GODAVARI

The numerous sacred spots with which India is thickly strewn are thronged at certain times of the year by pilgrims. Bathing in the waters of a sacred river is believed to be miraculously beneficent, and large crowds of pilgrims frequent the banks of those rivers which possess power and sanctity; with an eager reverence they dip themselves ceremoniously, each seriously intent on his eternal destiny

HE WON'T BE HAPPY UNTIL HE GETS OUT OF IT!

Not everyone enjoys an open-air bath! Although he is being washed in the Godavari, one of the holy rivers of India, this big boy looks far from pleased. His mother, determined to do her work thoroughly, has none too light a hand, and has used the stone, seen near the boy's left hand, instead of soap, which fact probably accounts for the unhappy expression on his face

Photos, Harry Cox

HUSBANDMEN OF KATHIAWAR SEPARATING GRAIN FROM CHAFF

Village life in Kathiawar, a province of the Bombay Presidency, has remained unchanged from very ancient times. The husbandmen are thrifty and industrious, irrigating and tilling their own fields and their common village lands laboriously. Close to every village is the village grain yard, into which the whole harvest of the village is brought to be threshed and winnowed and then measured and divided

CLEANING THE GRAIN IN A VILLAGE GRAIN YARD, KATHIAWAR

After the grain has been threshed, or rather trodden out by bullocks, the workers stand on high stools, as shown in the upper photograph, and winnow it by pouring it on to the ground from baskets, the wind carrying away the chaff. A period of still atmosphere causes much inconvenience. Finally, the grain is cleaned by being poured through sieves, as shown here

Photos, Major Meek

the usual substitutes for human victims when British law vetoed the more ancient practice, but the sacrifice of human beings still occasionally occurs, and the popular songs which recall the archaic rites still arouse a holy frenzy.

Some of the primitive tribes still live chiefly by hunting ; some on the sea-coast by fishing ; some by rudimentary agriculture and handicrafts ; some, resembling the English gypsies, pick up a miscellaneous livelihood. Many of them have their own language and dialects. They are often meat-eaters, have none of the Hindu scruples about forbidden food, and they bury their dead instead of burning them. Of those who are beginning to rise in the social scale as they come into contact with more modern conditions, characteristic instances are to be found in the Nilgiri Hills, in which the Madras Government spends the hot weather at Ootacamund

7,200 feet above the sea, on the edge of a great plateau of undulating downs.

The Badagas now devote themselves to agriculture, the Todas to cattle-breeding, and the Kotas have become artisans. A Badaga village, generally situated on a slight hilltop, consists of rows of dwellings under one continuous roof between cultivated fields, with a space in front of each house for drying and threshing grain, and stone kraals in which the cattle are kept. A sacred boulder, or an erect stone slab, occupies a central position in the village, and near it is a platform made of bricks and mud, on which the village elders squat at their ease in leisure hours to discuss their affairs and exchange gossip.

They are qualifying for inclusion in Hinduism, and have their own temples, at which goats are freely sacrificed, though in some places stone cromlechs of unknown origin are still held in chief

DECCAN JAZZ BAND READY FOR ACTION

Indian taste in music is peculiar, but is certainly worthy of a deeper study than it has yet secured. The large and weird instruments are constructed from most crude material, dried gourds being chiefly in request. The performers set to work with great solemnity, and are unwearied in their exertions to produce a wealth of sound. The toy panther on the floor is the talisman of this band

Photo, W. H. Sendall

COPPERSMITH OF KARACHI AT WORK OUTSIDE HIS SHOP

Many compliments are passed on the pots and pans of the Indian household, even the common vessels of earthenware being pleasing to the eye. The Hindu is exceedingly particular in his choice of brass and copper utensils, ordinary examples of which—despite an absence of ornamentation— are of a highly artistic outline ; this coppersmith is well versed in the most approved designs

Photo, Major W. J. P. Rodd

reverence. The men wear a long body-cloth, often striped with red and blue, and broad turbans, or quaint nightcaps of the brightest colour, while the women wear a white body-cloth with a white under-cloth tightly wrapped across the breasts and reaching to the knees, and on the head a white cloth folded like a cap. The men are branded on the shoulder and fore-arm, for this is believed to give them strength, and the women are copiously tattooed with rows of dots and stars on forehead, arms, and wrists. They are admirable cultivators, and many Badagas go off to work as gardeners in European houses as far even as Madras. The Todas lead a simple pastoral life, maintaining a large-horned race of semi-domesticated buffaloes, on whose milk and its products they largely depend. Their small hamlets consist of a few huts built of bent bamboos closely laid together and fastened with rattan, the hive-shaped roof being thatched and the two ends closed with solid planks of timber and a doorway cut through at one end. Each hamlet owns its own herd, which is driven every night into a circular enclosure surrounded by a loose stone wall, and has its own primitive dairy some distance away from the dwelling huts, with its own dairy priest and dairy temple, conspicuous for its tall, conical, thatched roof crowned with a large flat stone.

Polyandry still obtains among the Todas, a woman being often married to two or more brothers, and perhaps for that reason the men do all the work, even in the dairy, while the women, copiously tattooed, spend their time buttering and curling their glossy ringlets. Their ascendancy, which is certainly not due to any physical charm, for the men are far finer physically, is however declining with the restraints now placed upon female infanticide.

The Kotas, though looked down upon by both Badagas and Todas as meat-eaters and even carrion-eaters, and addicted to heavy bouts of drinking, are admittedly skilled artisans, black-smiths, tanners, potters, rope-makers, and even gold and silver smiths,

LOITERING IN THE SUNSHINE ON THE STEPS OF A MOSQUE

In this beautiful temple of worship, one of the many mosques of Central India, the artistry of the ancient Moguls can be traced. The massive construction of the pillars and walls speaks well for their architectural methods, and the building has suffered little since the days of that Mahomedan Tartar Empire when it was erected. Such a lovely spot naturally attracts many devotees of beauty

Photo, Major W. J. P. Rodd

AT THE FEET OF THE IDOL AS UNRESPONSIVE AS ITS STONE

Jainism, a form of the Hindu religion, is celebrated for the splendid building of its many temples. Here a Jain priest is seen bearing a humble sacrifice to lay before the giant toes of this mighty image, over sixty feet high, which for a thousand years has stood upon a hilltop near Belgola, Mysore, its dark mass silhouetted against the brilliant skies of Ind.

Photo, F. Deaville Walker

indispensable to the other hill tribes. But their physique is inferior, their huts more squalid, even their code of morality, if they have one, lower. They are polygamous, not polyandrous.

Their temples, consisting generally of two pent-shaped huts on a large square, walled about with loose stones, may be dedicated to Siva or to his consort, but they contain no images of the deities, and the chief god in whose honour they hold prolonged and uproarious festivals, with much drinking and indecent dancing, is a tribal god, sometimes personifying cholera, of which they stand in mortal dread.

North of the Nilgiri Hills one drops down suddenly into the large native state of Mysore, with nearly six million inhabitants, for half a century under direct British administration, but restored in 1881 to the ancient Hindu dynasty which had gone under in the days of the great Mahomedan adventurers, Haider Ali and Tippoo Sahib. To the wealth of its forests, in which the sandalwood tree, exploited mainly up to the Great War for the German perfumery

HIGHLY DECORATIVE BEAUTY OF UDAIPUR CITY

Udaipur, founded in 1568, is one of the most picturesque cities in India ; the beautiful granite and marble palace and the Juggernaut Temple in the Indo-Aryan style being its dominant features. No less attractive are the inhabitants of the city, and this dusky young mother with her bonnie boy astride her hip makes a charming picture against the magnificently-carved background

Photo, Frank Bailey

GENTLE VOTARESS OF THE GENTLE JAIN RELIGION

Speaking generally, the Jains are a rich community engaged in banking and wholesale commerce. They practise a strict morality, and so scrupulously regard the vital principle that, not content with being vegetarians, they strain all the water they drink through a cloth to avoid destruction of insects it might contain and sweep the ground before sitting down lest they should crush some immortal soul

Photo, Major Meek

market, and to that of its fertile agricultural districts, has been added within the last thirty years that of the great Kolar goldfields, equipped with every modern appliance and served by a railway line of their own, which have produced as much as nearly £2,000,000 worth of the precious metal in one year from their free-milling quartz veins.

Of the native states of India, Mysore is among the most progressive. There are still some primitive Animistic tribes

black magic are in very great request both for the recovery of stolen property and for the secret killing of enemies by cabalistic incantations. Too foul altogether for description are the rites by which both initiation into the art of black magic and its effective practice are accompanied.

Others, on the other hand, are more reputably employed as the guardians of village boundaries, of which they are supposed to have inherited an intimate

GLIMPSE OF ANIMAL LIFE WHILE TRAVELLING NEAR UDAIPUR
The wild woodland creatures of India keenly resent intrusion into their forest fastnesses, and the railway-lines have succeeded in driving them deeper into the jungle. But monkeys, with their insatiable curiosity, quickly grow accustomed to strange sights, and watch the trains go by, and even mount the platforms where they never fail to receive kindly attention at the hands of the passengers
Photo, Frank Bailey

in the jungles and the hills, and the population is for the most part of Dravidian origin, and speaks mostly Kanarese, which is another Dravidian tongue. Among the " untouchable " castes, shunned by all the higher caste Hindus, the Holeyas, as the Paraiyans, or Pariahs, of Mysore are called, who form one-tenth of the population, occupy the lowest place of all, though as devil-dancers those among them who are specially credited with a knowledge of

knowledge from the times when their forbears were mere serfs, sold and bought with the land, or chattels owned by the individual cultivators on whose estates they happened to be born. Their houses are mean thatched sheds, often merely partitioned off with a few coconut branches, and easily shifted, according to the needs of times and seasons. They are worshippers of devils and of ghosts, and eaters of unclean food, and the distance within which they may not

STROLLING MENAGERIE AND ITS TURBANED TRAINERS

All over the world a dancing bear or a performing monkey still attracts the attention of passers-by, and India has never lacked in respect of wayside entertainments. The two small simians with their bell-hung collars make an excellent advertisement as they bestride their hirsute mount, whose features are veiled in some apparatus of the show. The bear, too, has a smile for the camera

SWIFT AND SINUOUS CRUELTY BURNING IN THE PARD

Cheetahs, or hunting leopards, are natives of the Deccan, where they are trained for hunting the antelope. They are long-limbed, rough-haired animals, with blunt, only partially retractile claws. When loosed from the leash the cheetah springs on its prey with a swiftness exceeding that of any other mammal, and if it misses the kill seldom follows the quarry, but returns to its master

Photos, H. S. Talbot

DONKEY AND DHOBI ON THEIR HOMEWARD WAY

Indian donkeys are very small, and their life is an incessant round of hard work on food which they mostly have to find for themselves. At the end of the day's work their masters mount the patient little beasts, tucking up their legs, which otherwise would touch the ground, with a grotesque effect exemplified by this dhobi, or washerman, homeward bound

JOGGING ALONG THE HIGHWAY IN THE DUST AND HEAT

These are members of one of the numerous wandering tribes of India, their particular name being Banjaras. The small family seen here is pursuing its never-ending journey, slowly and painfully, along the parched road, the mother with her child astride the back of one of the ubiquitous bullocks that are used so extensively for so many purposes. The hump makes a good substitute for a saddle pommel

Photos, H. S. Talbot

WELL-MATCHED CARRIAGE CAMELS PLYING FOR HIRE

Camels supersede cattle for all agricultural operations in the Indus valley and in the sandy desert that stretches into Rajputana, and are extremely numerous in the Punjab. Broken to harness they make docile draught animals, and are constantly used for vehicles plying for hire. A well-matched pair, like that shown here, cut a very presentable figure in their own familiar environment

NATIVE LADIES OUT FOR AN AIRING IN A "RŬTH" AND PAIR

Varieties of the humped breed of cattle in India are numerous, some of them very fine, and Government does much to encourage and stimulate improvement of the indigenous breeds. Notable herds are found in Mysore, Gujarat, the Punjab, Madras, and in the Central Provinces, where there is a particularly high-class breed of trotting bullocks in great demand for wheeled carriages

Photos, H. S. Talbot

MUCH-MONEYED MAN OF INDIA

This spruce individual, with his trim beard and neat apparel, is a banker, and enjoys much prestige among the members of the community who support his profession

Photo, H. S. Talbot

yokes and buckets for raising water. But among both Holeyas and Madigas some are beginning to emerge out of the slough, either by their own industry and talent for money-making or thanks to the admirable work which is being done among them by Christian missionaries.

Altogether, in Mysore one leaves behind something of the stagnant atmosphere of the Dravidian south and notes a gradual transition to the more progressive atmosphere of Aryan India. Polygamy is rare. Polyandry and infanticide are rare also, and there are scarcely any remains of the ancient matriarchal system. The almost uniformly white garments of the extreme south make room for more varied colours; the women's sari, wrapped round the lower limbs and brought up over the shoulders, is usually of dark blue or dull red with yellow borders; and their tight-fitting bodices, which leave the arms, neck and throat and the middle bare, are often of a gay colour or adorned with gay trimmings. Their hair is picturesquely dressed, in different ways, according to their caste, and sometimes finished off with a spray of bright flowers or with gold and silver ornaments.

Among the well-to-do classes, rich silk from indigenous looms is worn instead of the cotton materials which the poorer classes can alone afford. Other signs of wealth are cumbrous silver anklets, as well as ear and nose rings, sometimes of gold and precious stones. Mysore, the capital of the state, has a large modern quarter, with government and public buildings, including the new palace of the Maharaja, more showy, perhaps, than beautiful; and Bangalore, with a British military station, is one of the most attractive of the semi-European towns of Southern India.

The Mahomedan population of Mysore is small—barely five per cent.—but the Hindus have not forgotten the days of Mahomedan domination from which the British freed them; and even if they were inclined to forget it, they have close to their own borders reminders of what it was and can still be. The narrow strip of territory between Mysore and

approach a Brahmin is 128 feet, which is the greatest prohibited distance for any " untouchable " caste.

Only slightly less abased are the Madigas, who are workers in leather, a profession held to be hopelessly " impure " by Hindus of the higher castes. They remove the carcasses of dead cattle and dress the hides to provide the villagers with thongs for their bullock

PIOUS PILGRIM RETURNING WITH THE HOLY WATER
Countless pilgrims flock yearly from distant parts of India to the river Ganges, the entire length of
which possesses sanctity and supernatural powers. On their return many treasure receptacles filled
with the sacred liquid, and their hearts are at rest, for having bathed in " Mother Ganga " at the
appointed season and with certain prayers they firmly believe that they are washed clean of their sins
Photo, H. S. Talbot

the Malabar coast is the home of the Moplas, or Mappillas, a Mahomedan community of over 800,000 souls, partly the descendants of Arab traders who settled from time to time on the coast, and partly of Hindus of the lower castes

ASCETICISM CARRIED TO EXTREMES
Held ever in the one position his arm has withered and the finger-nails have grown through the palm of his hand. It is for the advancement of his spiritual welfare that the Hindu ascetic thus mortifies his flesh
Photo, H. S. Talbot

more or less forcibly converted to Islam in the days of Tippoo Sahib.

Lawless and brave, they have always been notorious for their fanaticism, and there have been periodical outbreaks throughout the last century, sometimes directed against the British Government, but more frequently against their Hindu neighbours. None, however, has been so fierce and so widespread as the rising in the summer of 1921, which followed the pro-Turkish agitation engineered by Indian Mahomedan extremists. It was aimed originally at the British raj, and several Europeans were done to death at the outset, while the town of Calicut was for a short time in some danger.

But it soon took the shape of a ferocious campaign against the Hindus, with plunder, arson, and murder on a vast scale, and indescribable cruelties perpetrated upon Hindu men, women, and children when they refused to pronounce the Mahomedan confession of faith. Large bodies of troops had to be moved into the district, and owing to the very difficult character of the country and the dense forests specially adapted to guerrilla warfare, several months elapsed before the last Mopla bands were destroyed and order at last restored.

Not actually in Mysore territory, but in the adjoining district of the Madras Presidency, northeast of it on the banks of the Tungabhadra river, one of the chief tributaries of the Kistna, lie the mighty ruins of Vijayanagar, once the splendid capital of the last great Hindu kingdom of Southern India to be laid low by the flood of Mahomedan conquest. The site on which Vijayanagar, the " City of Victory " stood, is scarcely less wonderful than the ruins of the city itself, which once had a circumference of sixty miles.

As far as the eye can see, great masses of bare granite boulders have been piled

TWO CHEERFUL CAPTIVES IN TEMPORARY BONDAGE

Forcibly detained thus, the evil-doer has leisure to contemplate his imperfections, but whereas, in England, the delinquent usually had the stocks to himself, here the instrument is capable, if necessary, of accommodating a whole family. By only imprisoning one foot still more accommodation is gained,

PERPETUAL MOTION IN QUEST OF RIGHTEOUSNESS

Less painful than the self-mortification selected by the holy man shown on the opposite page, but more fatiguing, is the religious exercise practised by this Dhanukdhari fakir. He represents himself as in a state of perpetual motion, shuffling his feet and quivering when not walking, and never for an instant keeping still. How he contrives to sleep is a matter into which his admirers do not inquire too closely

Photos, H. S. Talbot

up as if by giants' hands into mountainous ridges, or stand poised one on the top of the other like cyclopean logging-stones, while even the level spaces between these natural scarps are encumbered with detached blocks of such colossal size that one of them has been fashioned into an uncouth but startling figure, some thirty feet high, of the Man-Lion incarnation of Vishnu.

It must have been no easy task to lay out a city for a population of many hundred thousand souls amidst such surroundings. Those granite bulwarks, however, served as natural defences to strengthen the sevenfold lines of wall which enclosed the inner city with the royal residence and the chief government buildings. To the north the city was protected by the Tungabhadra sweeping round the castellated hills of Anegundi, the parent fortress of Vijayanagar.

A large lake, artificially dammed for purposes of irrigation, covered the southern approach. It is difficult now to follow the exact plan of the city. Only one great street remains relatively intact, with a double line of stone-built mansions, mostly gutted and roofless, but showing an almost unbroken front of pillared and painted porticoes. These must have been the residences of the great nobles. The poorer quarters consisted largely of mud houses and mat huts, and have long since disappeared. Palm groves and mango trees still line the stone-revetted water-channels which once irrigated pleasure gardens and orchards.

Scattered over the whole area are the eloquent remains of palaces and temples. Neither Madura nor Tanjore can show a more splendid gopuram or pylon than that which rises to a height of over 160 feet at the north entrance of the great temple of Siva, still an object of pious pilgrimage from all parts of India. Nowhere has the sacred architecture of Hinduism found more characteristic expression than in the temples of Krishna and of Vitalaswami, with their terrific deities in dim, mysterious shrines, their pillared halls, their graceful columns, each crowned with the carved plantain-flower bracket, their weird avenues of hippogryphs

ONE OF A LARGE COMPANY OF SAINTS

Usually of Mahomedan origin, the Pirs are holy men, supported during life and venerated after death by Mahomedans and low-class Hindus alike. Rather a miscellaneous lot, they are found throughout India, this man's habitat being in Gwalior

Photo, H. S. Talbot

and other fabled monsters, and their endless processions of ceremonial elephants in bas-relief along the walls.

The "Zenana" palace and the "Ladies' Bath," the Council Room and the King's Throne, a lofty granite platform with sustaining walls on which legends from the Ramayana unfold themselves in storeyed relief, and, of more impressive dimensions than perhaps any other building, the massive domed elephant stables, afford each in its own style abundant evidence of the wealth and art lavished on their capital by successive rulers of Vijayanagar.

The iconoclastic zeal of the Mahomedan conquerors spared nothing in the final sack of the city. They mutilated every carven figure within their reach, just as they struck down every living "infidel" without mercy for age or sex. They made of the teeming city what it has been ever since, a solitude in which King Cobra reigns supreme. But the solitude merely enhances the pathos of so much departed greatness.

Vijayanagar was in its day not only the capital of a powerful state extending from sea to sea across the southern portion of the Indian peninsula from the Kistna down to Cape Comorin, but also the opulent emporium of a vast trade which ultimately came into touch through Goa with the whole Western world. "Its streets," says the Portuguese Barbosa, a cousin of Magellan, who travelled in India in the first decade of the sixteenth century, "are constantly filled with an innumerable crowd of all nations and creeds. There is an infinite trade in the city." Abdur Ruzzak visited it as ambassador from Persia in 1443, and words fail him to describe the splendour of the city, which "is such that the pupil of the eye has never seen a place like it, and the ear of intelligence has never been informed that there existed anything to equal it in the world." Not less dithyrambic is his account of one of the great Durbars which he attended during his residence at Court :—

In pursuance of orders issued by the King, the generals and principal personages

MAKING A MERRY NOISE

Music enters largely into Indian marriage ceremonies, and this trumpeter plays a prominent part in native wedding processions. In unaccustomed ears the fearsome instrument makes a most unholy din

Photo, H. S. Talbot

from all parts of the realm presented themselves at the palace. They brought with them a thousand elephants, which were covered with brilliant armour and with castles magnificently adorned. During three consecutive days the vast space of land magnificently decorated, in which the enormous elephants were congregated together, presented the

WOMAN WATER-CARRIER OF HYDERABAD

Grinding the grain is the chief employment of the women of India, and is regarded as a feminine occupation, but there are many tasks in which the men seldom lend a hand. Water-carrying is taken up by some women almost as a profession, but judging from the emaciated look of this woman the hard work is leaving its mark on her health—if not on her cheery disposition

Photo, T. A. Herbert

NOVEL METHOD OF TRANSPORTING BARRELS OF BEER

The huge cask supported on the heads of these Indian women contains beer for a British military canteen; a particularly awkward as well as heavy burden it would appear to be, but the women, nothing daunted, step briskly along the street. The heavier the load the quicker their pace, as though they believed that speed would assist them to make their task easier as well as shorter

Photo, T. A. Herbert.

appearance of the waves of the sea, or of that compact mass which will be assembled at the day of the resurrection.

Over this magnificent space were erected numerous pavilions to the height of three, four, and five storeys, covered from top to bottom with figures in relief. In the front of this place rose a palace with nine pavilions magnificently ornamented. In the ninth the King's throne was set up. The throne, which was of extraordinary size, was made of gold and enriched with precious stones of great value. Before the throne was a square cushion, on the edges of which were sewn three rows of pearls.

During the three days the King remained seated on this cushion. When the fête was ended I was introduced into the middle of four galleries, which were about ten ghez (twenty-one feet) both in length and breadth. The roof and the walls were entirely formed of plates of gold, enriched with precious stones. Each of these plates was as thick as the blade of a sword and was fastened with golden nails.

The glory of Vijayanagar endured for about two centuries, and came to an end when the Moslem Sultans of the Deccan finally composed their own bitter feuds in order to sweep down upon the decaying Hindu kingdom of the south, the prospect of unmeasured loot stimulating equally their religious zeal and their desire to avenge past defeats. Treachery and cruelty, almost unparalleled even in those days, marked this last campaign. The poor old king, Rama Raya—ninety-five years old according to Ferishtah—collected the Hindu hosts together to the number of 900,000 foot and 45,000 horse, with 2,000 elephants and 15,000 auxiliaries.

The clash of battle came on Jan. 23, 1565, near Talikot, to the south of the Kistna. At first fortune hesitated. Rama Raya descended from his litter to encourage his army, and seated himself in a conspicuous position " on a rich throne set with jewels, under a canopy of crimson velvet," with heaps of money all round him for the instant reward of conspicuous bravery. But all was of no avail. A furious charge of Mahomedan cavalry broke the Hindu centre. Rama Raya was captured and his head struck

GRASS-GROWN ROOFS BY SRINAGAR'S TURBID STREAM

From the windows of the houses and on their weedy roofs, from the crumbling banks of the wharf, in boats and canoes and from every coign of vantage, the townsfolk crowd to see the show, for it is not every day that the royal barge goes by. Still, the dwellers by the water have ever the changing surface of the Jhelum to call them to their windows

Photo, G. T. Bookless

TRAVELLING BY EKKA THROUGH THE HEIGHTS OF SRINAGAR

Throughout India the ekka is the ordinary vehicle in which the natives travel, and until recent times was in many places the only one available for Europeans. Two- or four-wheeled, and drawn by bullocks, or, as here, by horses, they are springless, uncomfortable carts in which the traveller sits where and how he can and possesses his soul in what patience he can command

Photo, Publishers' Photo Service

off, and raised on a long spear to be visible far and wide.

The Hindus broke and fled. The slaughter was terrific, and the plunder of the Hindu camp so great that " every private in the allied (Mahomedan) army became rich in gold, jewels, effects, tents, arms, horses, and slaves." Panic reigned in the defenceless capital, the royal family having no thought but to save themselves and their treasure by head-long flight. On the third day the Moslem conquerors stood within its walls, and for five months the work of slaughter and destruction went on which converted one of the greatest cities India has ever boasted into a

wilderness. Thus ended the last great Hindu kingdom of Indian history.

Most Hindus themselves have now forgotten the very names of the great Vijayanagar rulers, but at the gate of the splendid temple which they built the Brahmin goes on levying his toll from the pious pilgrims. One picture of Vijayanagar will remain always in the writer's memory. The hideous mono-lithic statue of the Ugra Narasimta incarnation stood out, doubly gigantic and terrific against the flaming back-ground of a stormy sunset, and a young peasant woman, herself little more than a child, with an infant son on her shoulder, stole up in fear and trembling

STATE BARGE OF A MAHARAJA ARRIVING AT KASHMIR'S ROYAL CAPITAL

Its many paddles sweeping and flashing with the muscular play of strong, brown arms, the royal craft steers its proud, unhesitating way. The river is the Jhelum, and flows through the vale of Kashmir, while on its banks are seen the houses of Srinagar, the capital, with their grass-grown roofs. The stream is spanned by native-built wooden bridges of curious appearance, and there is a royal palace, for once the Mogul Emperors had their hot-weather residence here. The place is further remarkable for two hills, the Throne of Solomon and the Hari Parbat, crowned by a temple and fort respectively

to lay her propitiatory mite of sweet-smelling wild flowers at the broken feet of the monstrous deity.

The greater part of the Vijayanagar Empire was divided after Talikot between the Mahomedan conquerors, but in the south some of the members of the royal house contrived to retain fragments of territory and a semblance of independence. It was a small raja, claiming descent from the rulers of Vijayanagar, who conveyed to the English in 1629, by a grant inscribed on a plate of gold, the site for the first fort and settlement, a few miles north of Madras, from which British power was to start forth to the conquest of the Indian Empire.

The desolate site of Vijayanagar is only divided by the Tungabhadra river from the great Mahomedan state of Hyderabad, a survival itself of one of the Mahomedan kingdoms which laid it low, and the Hindus who form the vast majority—nearly nine-tenths—of the subjects of the Nizam of Hyderabad know something of what Mahomedan domination meant in olden times in spite of certain restraints which the British overlordship places on the worst forms of Oriental despotism in even the most powerful of native states.

None is more powerful than Hyderabad. Its population equals that of Belgium and Holland combined, and its area is three times larger. Its public revenue is only about £4,000,000, but

LEISURED BEAUTY OF KASHMIR

Her father is a village headman near Srinagar, the capital of the mountainous and secluded native state of Kashmir, and his social status forbids her employment in the famous shawl industry which has its chief centre in the town

Photo, Col. W. B. Pearson

the Nizam's private wealth is untold, and at court and on his travels, as well as in the privacy of a zenana maintained on a scale which King Solomon himself would have envied, he keeps up in modern India all the traditions of Mahomedan despotism. He traces

TODA LADIES, WHOSE CHIEF GLORY IS THEIR HAIR

Seven yards of unbleached cotton cloth twisted negligently round their body is the only garment
of the Toda women, supplemented in cold weather by a brown woollen blanket bought at the native
bazaar but obviously of Bradford manufacture. The only real beauty of these women is their fine
and glossy hair, which they twist into ringlets with " curl papers " of dwarf palm-leaves

Photo, Mrs. Lynde

his descent from one of Aurungzebe's successful generals who brought the independent Mahomedan kingdoms of Central and Southern India under subjection to the Mogul Empire, but when that Empire fell into dissolution, his forbears threw off their allegiance to it, and ultimately entered into relations of permanent alliance with the British raj. The Nizam who succeeded in 1911, and upon whom the King-Emperor conferred the exceptional title of " His Most Exalted Highness," is not only the foremost but the most independent of the feudatory princes of India, and his ideas and methods of rulership are reputed to be sometimes very medieval, though great reforms were introduced on European lines by the two Salar Jangs into the administration of the state in the latter half of the nineteenth century,

and a certain number of European officials are employed at headquarters.

The population is mostly agricultural, and except in a few favoured regions the villages look more than usually poverty-stricken, often consisting merely of small mud houses roughly thatched or tiled, and in the case of the " untouchables," of whom there are a million and a half in the state, of miserable huts made of reeds and hurdles, plastered over with mud and cow-dung. Even among well-to-do Hindus so tenacious an institution as the joint family system breaks down after one generation under arbitrary and oppressive state exactions.

In the great capital city of nearly half a million inhabitants which gives its name to the state, Mahomedan ascendancy is naturally more in evidence than in the rural districts,

Four stately minarets, 180 feet high, rise in the middle of the city, whence four chief roads radiate to its outer walls, and more conspicuous than any of the numerous royal palaces is the Mecca Mosque, built entirely of stone and surmounted by two large domes, rising 100 feet above the arches of the roof. Almost all the great families of the state are, like the reigning dynasty, Mahomedan, and some of their palaces rival those of the Nizam himself for size and ornateness of architecture.

The Mahomedan population is apt to bear itself still with all the haughty pride of a ruling race, and on gala days the young nobles, richly attired and mounted on gaily caparisoned horses, monopolise the principal streets with prancing cavalcades, making the night as well as the day hideous with the chronic feu de joie of their picturesque carbines and pistols, more suitable, however, for such festive displays than for the stern business of modern warfare.

The ancient fortress of Golconda, on a ridge of bare granite only five miles west of the city, with a castellated wall three miles in circumference and eighty-seven well-preserved bastions, and the granite tombs of the old Kutb Shahi Sultans, may still recall to the Mahomedans of modern Hyderabad the days when Islam was supreme in India. But a British cantonment not much farther off in another direction is also there to remind them that the final responsibility for peace and order and tolerance rests now with the British raj. That is the meaning of the double-storeyed

FAMILY REUNION OF THREE GENERATIONS OF TODAS

Toda men wander far afield when grazing their cattle, and so are seldom at home. To celebrate the return of this head of a family his wife and daughters have donned their festal striped " chudders " and ranged themselves beside him while the aged grandmother smiles happily in the background. The thatched shanty with its fowl-house entrance appears rather small for so large a family party

Photo, Mrs. Lynde

HERDSMEN AND AGRICULTURISTS FORGATHER AT A WOODCUTTER'S SHELTER IN THE NILGIRI HILLS

A pastoral tribe in the Nilgiri hills, the Todas are simply herdsmen. The four men behind the women on the left well exemplify the hairiness of this tall brown people, whose conditions of life are very primitive. Their chief link with the outside world is the agricultural Badaga tribe, one of whom, in white robe and striped turban, is standing behind some Kanarese police officials on the right. The Badagas visit the bazaars to sell their produce and take back food and raiment for themselves and their Toda allies

barracks built for British troops at Secunderabad, where the broad shady avenues laid out with infinite care throughout the cantonment form a grateful oasis in a great steppe-like plateau, broken only with frequent outcrops of underlying rock, stark and scorched black by the sun.

American Civil War, has come to be known as the black cotton country; and there, too, we pass into a land inhabited by a race largely Aryan in descent, which has played within recent centuries a part in Indian history far more conspicuous than its mere numbers would suffice to explain.

MEMBERS OF AN INTERNATIONAL BROTHERHOOD

The great movement of the Boy Scouts is spreading rapidly in all quarters of the globe, English methods being adopted in many a foreign country where kindred organizations for boys have been started. In India great enthusiasm is aroused by this movement, one of the chief aims of which is to promote mutual goodwill and comradeship between the boys of the various nations of the world

Photo, F. Deaville Walker

The southern and eastern portions of Hyderabad state, and especially the wild forest tracts in the north-east, which border the Godavari and merge into the equally wild jungles of the Madras Circars and of the south-eastern districts of the Central Provinces, are chiefly inhabited by Dravidian races. But in the west and north-west the Deccan trap has formed great stretches of that wonderfully fertile black soil which, since the cultivation of cotton received a sudden impetus during the

We are on the threshold of Maharashtra, the homeland of the Marathas or Mahrattas, a hard-bitten people, by no means unworthy sons of the hard-bitten country produced by the peculiar cosmic convulsions which shaped this part of the Indian continent in the womb of Time.

Just within the north-west borders of Hyderabad state, the wall paintings of the rock caves of Ajanta have preserved a singularly vivid record of Buddhist piety and a high standard of art

PARIAHS AT HOME IN A VILLAGE NEAR MADRAS

Besides the four recognized classes or castes in India, there is a fifth-class man who has no caste, and therefore comes under the category of Out-caste or Pariah. Throughout India the Pariahs are looked upon with contempt and aversion, and are treated by other castes as slaves. Theirs is a hand-to-mouth existence, and they never know what the morrow will bring them

Photo, F. Deaville Walker

BOYS WHO ARE BLESSED WITH A BRIGHT MEMORY

The Tamils form the most civilized and energetic of the Dravidian peoples, and are certainly the most enterprising of the south Indian tribes. These Tamil school-lads, with their wooden slates and the marks of their god on their foreheads, meet with few difficulties at their lessons; the race is credited with an astounding memory, and possesses combined qualities of patience and politeness

Photo, F. Deaville Walker

2787

throughout the eight centuries, from 200 B.C. to A.D. 600, during which they were the abode of Buddhist anchorites, whose freshness and delicacy of expression seem to claim some spiritual and artistic kinship with the devout monks of the early Italian quattro cento.

Among the rock-temples of Ellora, only a few miles off, the great monolithic temple of Kailas, entirely isolated from the surrounding cliff, out of which a courtyard—for it has been hewn 154 feet wide by 276 feet long at the base—has stood, on the other hand, ever since the eighth century, as an imperishable monument to the enduring victory of Hinduism. In the large figures of Siva and Vishnu, and the gigantic columns and many subsidiary shrines of Ellora, all cut out of the living rock with almost cyclopean brutality, there is a note of triumph, which goes on resounding to the present day.

Intensely Hindu is the spirit, too, of Maharashtra. Mahomedan conquerors never extinguished it, though the splendid dome of the Gol Kumbaz over the tomb of Mahomed Adil Shah at Bijapur still dominates the Deccan tableland, just as the dome of S. Peter's dominates the Roman Campagna. But unlike S. Peter's, the Bijapur dome is an almost perfect hemisphere, raised above the four plain and lofty walls of an austere sepulchral shrine 136 feet square, and it encloses the largest domed space in the world.

Not all, however, of the Mahomedan buildings of Maharashtra are marked by the same stern simplicity, and even at Bijapur, itself built largely from the spoils of Vijayanagar—both names meaning "The City of Victory"—the Ibrahim Rauza and several other mosques betray Hindu influences in their more florid style of architecture and infinite wealth of ornamentation.

The Hindu temples of Maharashtra are themselves of a different order from those of Southern India. They have not the same majesty of size nor do they inspire the same sense of monstrous awe. Many of them are sacred to the usual great gods and goddesses, but the villagers prefer to worship at the more popular shrines of the playful Hanuman, the monkey-headed, or of the wise and good-natured Ganesh, the

WHERE CHARLATANISM FATTENS UPON SIMPLE CREDULITY
Quack doctors are not infrequently seen in the streets of India extolling their wares with successful effrontery to a credulous public. Many of these charlatans do a brisk trade in their quack medicines and panaceas, and travelling from place to place, never stopping to hear the result of their remedies, they invariably find the patrons and dupes in whom their hearts delight
Photo, F. Deaville Walker

MONOTONOUS TASK ENLIVENED BY MELODIOUS SONG

Mortar work in India is quite an attractive occupation. Round and round the bullocks travel, causing the great stone wheel to revolve which grinds the mortar, and their master alternately whips them and sings to them. He sings in a cheery, humdrum manner, the grating of the wheel his only accompaniment, but song relieves the monotony of labour, stimulating even the beasts

Photo, Norman Whittey

elephant-headed. Above all, the favourite god tends to assume with the Marathas a peculiarly national character, and his cult to be associated with that of national heroes. For the Marathas were imbued with a strong sense of local and racial nationalism long before there grew up in India the broader conception of an All-India nationalism. It was Sivaji, the great soldier and statesman and adventurer of the seventeenth century who first summoned his Marathas to revolt against Mahomedan domination, and it is not merely Maratha poetry and Maratha legends that connect with his deeds of prowess most of the hill-forts whose frowning walls, often still intact, crown many of the topmost crags of the Western Ghats.

The grim battlements of Pratabgarh— as stout as any of the English border castles—look down upon the valley where, meeting Afzul Khan for an unarmed parley, and ripping his bowels open with the steel "tiger-claw" concealed in the folds of his quilted

coat, he fell on the Bijapur Mahomedans and smote them hip and thigh.

Another of his mountain fastnesses he called Singarh, "the Lion's Den"— for was he not the lion of Maharashtra ? —and in a third called Raigarh, "the Royal Fort," he was crowned as king in 1674, and died in 1680. Satara, where his famous "tiger's claw" and his great sword, Jai Bhawani, are shown to the present day, lapsed to the British raj just before the Mutiny; but in Kolhapur, chief among the remaining native states of Maharashtra, the reigning Maharaja claims descent from the founder of the Maratha power.

Sivaji, like the Hindu kings of old, had a great Brahmin as his principal adviser and minister, and Poona, which became in later days under the Maratha Peishwas, the seat of Maratha government when the real power passed into the hands of the Brahmins, has remained under the British raj the cultural centre of Maharashtra, and, with all its excellent modern schools and colleges, a great

BRAHMIN WISDOM FIXING THE DATE OF THE RICE HARVEST FOR THE VILLAGE FARMERS

These are men of Yagatsukh in the Kulu Valley, one of the northern valleys of the Himalayas, engaged in the important ceremony of fixing the date on which the rice harvest is to begin. The Brahmin with the book in his hands has been called up from the Plains to settle the propitious date. The same man comes each year, and knows exactly the time that suits the district, but to keep up his reputation he goes through the minutest calculations before he arrives at his conclusions

Photo, R. Richardson

stronghold of Brahminical influence, while it shares with Mahábaleshwar, on the very crest of the Western Ghats, the distinction of serving as summer quarters for the Government of Bombay, and is from its strategic position the military capital of Western India.

From Parbati Hill, so called after a great temple dedicated to the consort of Siva, Poona is seen lying in the midst of an almost treeless plain, with the confused roofs of the crowded native city and the wide avenues and carefully-tended gardens of the European quarter embosomed in a broad belt of enclosed

IRREPRESSIBLE MENDICITY

Beggars constitute a regular professional class in India. The pertinacity with which they continue to demand alms is fully displayed by this ferocious-looking mendicant

Photo, Publishers' Photo Service

FAITHFUL SERVICE

European women resident in India have cause to bless the ayah, ladies' maid and nurse. Her devotion to her mistress and to her employers' children is perfect

Photo, H. S. Talbot

orchards and umbrageous groves. Old and new India live there side by side, commingling nowhere perhaps so effectively in the spirit as in the Servants of India Society, founded by one of Poona's most distinguished and enlightened sons, Mr. Gokhale, for the moral and social as well as political advancement of the Motherland, to whom its members dedicate their lives.

Impulsive and quick to respond to racial and religious emotions, the Marathas have many admirable

TRUE DEVOTION AT WORSHIP IN THE TEMPLE OF THE MIND

Seated on his prayer-stool, set close to the ground so as to afford no scope for machinations of the evil one, and armed with bell, book, and candle, this Brahmin devotee makes puja—act of worship —to his gods. With his right hand thrust into a black stocking-like glove he tells the beads within, free from observation, gravely intoning his ritual the while

Photo, Mrs. Lynde

qualities. Hard-working and frugal, theirs is a country beautiful indeed, and grand in many of its aspects ; often doomed to scarcity and famine when the rains fail to surmount the lofty barrier of the Western Ghats ; lightning-riven and scorched black by a pitiless sun ; and again with splendidly fertile tracts and gracious prospects, but always a divine inheritance set apart for the Maratha people by the gods themselves.

Each village is a little world of its own within the larger world of Maharashtra, where the daily round of the Hindu peasant's life can be seen at its very best. He rises at dawn, and after worshipping the household gods, he arouses the bullocks and oxen, stalled close to his own humble dwelling-house, and strolls off towards his fields, driving his oxen in front of him and carrying in a cloth the coarse cakes cooked and wrapped up for him overnight by his womenfolk, with an onion or some other spicy condiment to season his frugal breakfast ; and whether it be to plough or to sow or to reap, he works on with only short intervals for rest, till at midday the housewife, who has swept and garnished the mud floor of the house, cleaned the few metal or pottery utensils which constitute its modest equipment, drawn water at the village well, and ground from the handmill the necessary supply of flour for the day, sallies forth about noon with the meal for which the hungry husbandman is by that time more than ready.

The men collect together and partake of it in common, and after perhaps an hour's slumber return to another short spell of work, while the

women pick up the fragments and go home to make everything ready for the evening hours of leisure which crown the day's toil for men and women alike. Those are the hours when the rustic story-teller and the local bard earn unfailing applause and a few extra crumbs of food with tales from the great Hindu epics, or with legends of olden times when Sivaji plucked the hated Mahomedans by their beards, and Maratha horsemen swept across India to the famous Ditch of Calcutta and to the marble halls of the Great Mogul at Delhi.

On innumerable festival days, or when the agricultural season is slack, the whole village turns out, the men in clean white dhotis, and the women draped in their graceful saris of brownish-red or bluish-green edged with yellow,

BRIGHT-EYED DANCING GIRLS
Borne along in their decorative though not too comfortable carriage, these Nautch girls display all the smiling animation with which they are credited by Western imagination, unaware of the drab and seamy side of their life

STREET IN DELHI LEADING TO THE STEPS OF THE GREAT MOSQUE

Delhi, the capital of India since 1911, contains many notable structures, among the most beautiful of which is the Great Mosque, or Jama Masjid, erected by Shah Jehan in the middle of the seventeenth century, and said to be one of the finest buildings of its kind in India. Delhi is a prominent industrial centre, and is famous for the artistic productions of its native craftsmen

Photo, Major W. J. P. Rodd

and bangles of glass or metal on arms and ankles, to visit some popular shrine or to make merry at some neighbouring fair ; and wherever they go the state of the crops, the prospect for the next monsoon, the rise or fall of the few prices on which their livelihood depends, the good luck or the bad luck of their neighbours and their own will furnish never-failing themes of conversation and easy jest, while the keener spirits among them break out into boisterous song in honour of the gods that personify the ever present forces of nature all around them, and in celebration of the past and future destinies of their great sacrosanct homeland, Maharashtra.

Village life no doubt has its tragedies in Maharashtra, as elsewhere, and ghosts and witches, and rapacious money-lenders and almost equally rapacious Brahmins, may play havoc with many a tormented home, but nowhere else perhaps in India is the simple joie de vivre so widespread and so hearty.

From its westernmost edge this great basaltic plateau, which drains eastwards in much gentler slopes, drops down in a series of precipitous scarps into the Konkan, a relatively narrow strip of wildly broken and often heavily timbered country, which divides the Western Ghats from the Arabian Sea. Extremely fertile in some parts and covered with a luxuriant vegetation down to the sea shore, the Konkan is said to have been redeemed from the ocean by the gods themselves as a homeland for a party of shipwrecked Brahmins, the mystery of whose origin lingers unsolved to-day behind the grey eyes, almost unknown elsewhere in India, of the Chitpawan Brahmins who claim descent from them.

At the southern extremity of the Konkan lies Goa, once the prosperous capital of the Portuguese dominions in India, and the first great trading centre through which India was brought into contact with the West. Of old Goa there remains little but two large

churches with some subsidiary ecclesiastical buildings, the cathedral founded by Albuquerque, and the Bom Jesus, which still attracts Roman Catholic pilgrims even from Europe to worship at the splendid tomb of S. Francis Xavier ; and between them the spacious square in which the Holy Inquisition consigned its victims to the stake.

Was it the curse of the Inquisition or the pressure of changing economic conditions that caused its downfall ? Anyhow, its downfall was complete. The jungle has swallowed up its palaces, and dank grass has obliterated its once crowded thoroughfares. A new Goa

IMPRESSIVE SCENE IN THE COURTYARD OF THE JAMA MASJID, DELHI

The Great Mosque, one of the many majestic architectural glories of Delhi, has three domes of white marble, and two lofty minarets between which and the great entrance arch are graceful arcades surmounted by panelling in red sandstone and white marble. The crowded courtyard on the occasion of a Moslem festival is a sight not easily forgotten

Photo, Stanley R. Norton

CEREMONIAL OBSEQUIES ATTENDING THE DEATH OF A MAN OF THE SERVILE CLASS OF HINDU SOCIETY

The last ceremonies rendered to the dead by the Sudras, members of the fourth or servant class of Hindu, are accompanied by much formality. The toilet of the corpse receives special attention, and having been made as elegant as possible the dead man is placed in a sitting posture on an open litter or in a palanquin, splendidly decorated with garlands of flowers, banana leaves, and coloured cloths, and borne on the shoulders of men by poles to the funeral pyre

Photo F. Deaville Walker

PATHETIC YOUNG INDIAN VICTIMS OF THE IMMEMORIAL SCOURGE OF THE EAST

Practical Christianity shows itself nowhere to more advantage than in its work to alleviate the lot of the unfortunate victims of leprosy which is so common in the East. These young people are inmates of a large leper asylum at Perulia, in the Calcutta district. Already affected to some degree with the disease, they are kept apart from the adults, men and women, for whom the asylum was founded, and are carefully watched and treated, and meanwhile educated

Photo, Miss M. N. Tuck

IN UNSTABLE EQUILIBRIUM

Astonishing strength and agility are displayed by the native
acrobats who wander about India. Long practice, requiring no
little nerve and indifference to falls on the part of the assistant,
must have preceded perfection in this balancing feat

Photo, E. P. Giles

India, where ocean-going steamers unload their freights of passengers and merchandise from the Occident to be distributed all over India by the iron roads which in long loops and heavy gradients have carved their way up a northern gap in the Western Ghats.

Bombay — the Bay Beautiful, as the Portuguese aptly named it—is more than any other city of the British Indian Empire a microcosm of modern India, a fairy city, with the fine sweep of its bended coast and its splendid sea-front from Kolaba Point, thrusting out towards the famous lighthouse, to the firmly-planted heel of Malabar Hill, seven miles away, and its ancient islands quivering on the sunlit waters, and the jagged line of purple mountains which are the great staircase on to the Deccan tableland.

A matter-of-fact, very modern and bustling city, too, in which motors and motor lorries and taxis jostle the slow creaking country bullock cart and the ramshackle one-horse vehicle with its close-drawn shutters that conceal a veiled freight of purdah ladies ; even an ugly black city where the countless chimneys of cotton mills and factories blot out the blue sky with a thick pall of low-spreading smoke, and always a Babel-like city of many voices and many tongues in which all the ages and all the races, not of India alone, jostle one another in clamorous confusion.

Less picturesque than many others but more peculiar to Bombay, and indeed in no small degree its makers, are the

was built nearer the sea with an array of whitewashed public buildings, which make a show of Western gentility along the river bank. One of them, of more ambitious structure, is the residence of a high Portuguese official who continues to be styled "Governor-General of the Indies."

Bombay, once also a Portuguese settlement, is to-day what Goa might have been—the western gateway of

Parsees, barely 1,000,000 of them all told, descendants of Zoroastrian refugees from Mahomedan persecution in Persia some ten centuries ago, whose purer Aryan blood has made them on the whole more responsive than any Indo-Aryans to the influence of the West. The majority of the older generation may still be recognized by their shiny-black mitre-shaped headdress, and their priests are still always white-robed.

Tenacious of their ancient customs, gruesomely typified in the Towers of Silence on which, instead of burning or burying their dead, they expose them to be devoured by vultures lest mortal corruption should contaminate the sacred elements of fire, earth, and water, and above all of fire, which is the supreme object of their worship, the Parsee community stands apart in race and in religion. None can be of its

SINEWY LEANNESS POISED UPON A LIVING ARCH

Among the itinerant entertainers met with in India, the contortionist seems to be as popular as any. Men and boys are able to twist their bodies into the most extraordinary positions. They are, of course, trained to the business from earliest youth, and keep their joints extremely supple. A contributory cause of their flexibility may, perhaps, be the fact that they carry so very little flesh

Photo, Harry Cox

membership except by birth. But in all other respects they have thrown themselves whole-heartedly into the stream of modern life. They are essentially traders, and from small beginnings as petty shopkeepers and money-changers and retail traders, many of them have risen in the course of a few generations to be captains of commerce and industry and finance in the foremost commercial and industrial and financial city of India.

The Parsees were the first to appreciate the value of Western education and the first to combine with a more exclusive sense of communal pride in the achievements of their own peculiar race a broad sense of civic pride in

the greatness of Bombay. Their munificent donations and their educational and philanthropic institutions have been as conspicuous as the marble and stucco palaces which, not a few of them under the very shadow of their Towers of Silence, gratify the opulent tastes of a plutocracy whose social ambitions and public services have found an equal reward in the titles and distinctions conferred by Government on most of the leading Parsee families.

Bombay owes its prosperity in the first instance to British enterprise and to the British rule of law, and nowhere else in India have Hindus and Mahomedans also taken so active a share in its expansion, but the contribution made

BALANCING FEAT OF A WANDERING ACROBAT

These travelling shows of India proceed from place to place, taking their audience and their fortune as they come. Above is seen a troupe of peripatetic contortionists who, beside their ability to twist themselves into various astonishing attitudes, are also prepared to give a display of tight-rope walking. A chance meeting with a few Europeans, and the apparatus is soon erected

Photo, Harry Cox

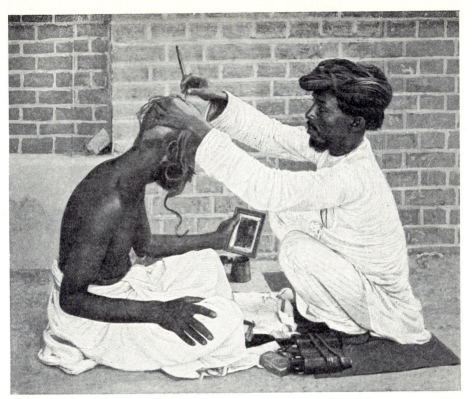

INTERESTED CRITICISM OF TONSORIAL ART

Highly esteemed among all visitors to the compound is the native barber, who retails the latest gossip from the bazaar while performing services indispensable to every self-respecting Hindu. Thoughtfully he supplies his patron with a mirror, wherein to watch the progress of operations down to their conclusion in a deft twist of the ends of the moustaches round the ears

Photo, Mrs. Lynde

to it by the intelligence and industry and public spirit of the Parsee community is in many ways unique. With a population of about one million, Bombay, originally built on a narrow tongue of land, hemmed in on two sides by the sea, is at last breaking across the boundaries within which its industrial growth and the constant influx of labour threatened it with intolerable congestion. Vast reclamation and extension works are giving it elbow-room to develop on ample lines not unworthy of the Manchester-cum-Liverpool of India.

North of Bombay the Marathas are soon left behind. Beyond Nasik, a sacred city on the Godavari river, itself only less sacred than the Ganges, and the great dividing line between Southern and Central India, we pass into Gujarat, with its own tongue and its own proverbially bucolic population, which the wild preachings of Gandhi, a native of Gujarat, roused only too successfully out of its bovine apathy.

Ahmadabad, the capital of Gujarat and second only to Bombay as a centre of the modern cotton industry, has this in common with Bijapur in Maharashtra, that it was once the seat of a splendid if short-lived Mahomedan dynasty, the Ahmad Shahi Sultans, who have bequeathed to it a wealth of peculiarly interesting monuments. It may even be of some interest to Englishmen that, to a saint with whom it has been sought to identify the English S. George, Mahomedan tradition ascribes the foundation of Ahmadabad.

The Arab historian, Firishta, describes Ahmadabad as in his day " the handsomest city in Hindustan, and perhaps in the world," and its monuments present the nearest approach to a fusion between Hindu and Mahomedan types

PRACTISING HER HANDICRAFT IN FULL PUBLIC VIEW

Sitting on the floor of a shop by the roadside, this woman artist decorates red lacquered furniture with designs in other colours, being engaged at the moment in lining some bedstead legs with yellow. The average Hindu artificer knows nothing of the vagaries of the " artistic temperament," and carries on his work in public with phlegmatic indifference to the criticism of casual onlookers

Photo, Mrs. Lynde

of architecture. That even the mosques bear evidence of Hindu rather than Mahomedan inspiration is probably due not merely to the ascendancy exercised over the Mahomedan conquerors by Hindu civilization in many ways superior to their own, but to the genius of a community that had acquired, and still to some extent retains, a monopoly of the building craft of Gujarat.

Jainism, originally a revolt against Hinduism, akin to Buddhism, and of about the same date, never rose to quite the same eminence, and perhaps for that reason was never so completely crushed out. There are still some four million Jains in India—simple, peace-loving folk, who carry their dread of taking away life in any form to such lengths that they will often wear a bit of muslin over their mouth lest they should destroy some minute insect by swallowing it, or, if they have to remove vermin from their person, will preserve them in a small box until they can safely throw them away, and for the most part prefer trade and craftsman-ship to agriculture because the plough may kill a worm.

The Jains have a tendency to revert to Hinduism, from which they never diverged quite so far as the disciples of Buddha, but they have their own Scriptures and their own literature, and their own temples in which they have developed their own style of architecture, and in Gujarat they attained before the Mahomedan invasion a considerable measure of political as well as cultural ascendancy.

So at Ahmadabad the craftsmen of the Jaina school worked for their Mahomedan conquerors as they had worked for their Hindu rajahs, and embodied in the mosque of Ahmad Shah, and, outside the city, in the octagonal tomb of Ganj Bahksh, the spiritual guide of Ahmad Shah, and, above all, in the exquisite mosque and tomb of Ranee Sepree the architectural genius already displayed in their earlier temples on Mount Abu and revived once more

in the great temple of Hathi Singh, built in the middle of the last century at a cost of one million sterling.

To the present day these master-builders possess, jealously locked away in iron-bound chests preserved for safe keeping in their temples, many ancient treatises on civil and religious architecture of which only a few have hitherto been published.

Eastward from Gujarat, the three great native states of Baroda, Indore, and Gwalior stretch far across Central India, and powerful Maratha rulers, Gaekwar, Holkar, and Scindia, have retained there large slices of the empire achieved by their ancestors a century and a half ago at the expense

ORIENTAL ANTIPATHY TO LABOUR-SAVING INVENTIONS

Oriental conservatism breeds complete indifference to advantages that might be secured by the adoption of new methods. Thus these sawyers adjust a ramshackle framework of poles lashed together with bits of rope, and prop the timber to be sawn up against it with stones. The entire apparatus has to be taken down and readjusted for every section of the block that is being sawn up

Photo, Harry Cox

HAPPY-GO-LUCKY CHILD VAGRANT

He is of the Brahui stock, and belongs to a nomadic tribe from
the highlands of Baluchistan, who, with an innate love of
liberty, wander at will, knowing no settled home or occupation

Photo, V. S. Manley

But it never forgets that
it owes its birth to the
gods themselves. When
Uma wedded Siva her
father slighted him, not
knowing who he was, for
the mighty god had wooed
and won her in the disguise
of a mere ascetic
mendicant.

Horrified at her father's
blunder, she made atone-
ment by casting herself
into the sacrificial fire,
which consumed her in
the presence of gods and
Brahmins. Hence she is
worshipped also as Sati,
the prototype of all the
pious Hindu widows who
have since then ascended
the funeral pyres of their
husbands in order to
accompany them into the
next world. So maddened
with grief was Siva when
he gathered up the remains
of his unfortunate consort
that he danced about with
them in a world-shaking
frenzy, and the scattered
bones fell to earth—here
an arm, a foot there, and
wherever they fell the
spot became sacred and a
temple sprang up in her
honour. One of her elbows
fell on the banks of the
Sipra at Ujjain, and few
shrines enjoy greater and
more ancient fame than the great temple
of Maha-Kal, consecrated to her worship
and to that of Siva.

Its wealth was fabulous when it
was looted and destroyed by Altamsh
and his Pathan hordes in 1235. The
present buildings are, for the most
part, not two hundred years old, and
remarkable chiefly for the insistency
with which the lingam and the bull, the
favourite symbols of Siva, repeat themselves in shrine after shrine.

Ujjain is one of the seven most sacred
cities of India, and while every year
it attracts large numbers of pilgrims, it

of the moribund Mogul Empire. But
the peoples they rule over are not
Marathas, and the army which tramps
every twelve years to Ujjain, and is
fed and entertained there for a whole
month by the Maharaja Scindia, presents a far stranger spectacle than
any of the Maratha armies which his
ancestors led forth to its conquest can
ever have presented.

At most times Ujjain is a quiet, old-
world little town with narrow, tortuous
streets and quaint native bazaars full
of varied wares and painted houses with
latticed windows and delicate woodwork.

holds in every twelfth year an extra-ordinary festival to which as many as three hundred thousand people flock from all parts. The peculiarity of this festival is that, in memory of the form which Siva assumed when he wooed Uma, it attracts a veritable army of sanyasis, or ascetics, sometimes as many as fifty thousand, whose sanctity is measured by their nudity.

Seldom, except at the great Jaganath (Juggernaut) festivals at Puri, is a larger congregation seen of weird figures, some clothed only with their long, unkempt hair; some with their bodies smeared all over with white chalk and the symbol of their favourite deity painted conspicuously on their foreheads; some displaying ugly sores or withered limbs as evidence of life-long mortification of the flesh; some moving with dreamy eyes and impassive features, as if lost already to this world's realities; some with frenzied eyes shouting and brandishing the instruments with which they profess to torture the flesh into subjection; some with sly, leering eyes and heavy, sensuous jowls affecting a certain coquetry in the ritualistic adorn-ment of their well-fed bodies—surely the strangest medley that the world can show of fanaticism, of harmless religious

SMALL ASPIRANTS TO KNOWLEDGE WITH THEIR BOOKS
Education is by no means compulsory in India, yet a growing number of natives are coming to realize its advantages. It is now possible for a poor lad to pass through the official schools, primary and secondary, and so to one of the universities, where a State scholarship may be obtained, enabling the holder to study in England. Above are seen five young hopefuls
Photo, Harry Cox

WANDERERS IN THE HIMALAYAN HEIGHTS

Way-worn and weary is this Tibetan mother, tramping with her strapping infant the rough Himalayan road. The Tibetans invariably carry their children slung in a shawl round their backs, while the Hindu woman carries her baby across the hip

Photo, Frank Scott

mania and of palpable imposture.

Just as untouched by modern life, and far more attractive, is the picture of Hindu chivalry which has survived in the large group of Rajput states that expand to the west and north-west right up to the valley of the Indus. The British power that spared the great Maratha states of Central India at the beginning of the nineteenth century held them from laying hands on Rajasthan when its rulers could have looked nowhere else for help.

A stern, stepmotherly country on the whole, this epic Rajasthan, this "land of kings among men"; an area larger than that of the whole of the British Islands; a not infertile soil wherever there is water to give life to it, but with infrequent streams, apt to run quickly dry and a very scanty rainfall; great stark plateaux with rocky outcrops, and towards the Indus a vast stretch of almost unbroken desert; sparsely populated, and the rare towns, built as they were for the most part as cities of refuge, at the foot of some impregnable hilltop crowned with the battlemented castle of the Rajput chief, lord, or overlord of the surrounding country.

Whence exactly this martial race of Rajputs came, though clearly of Aryan stock, and in what remote age, historians have not yet definitely established. But, as

FOURFOOTED "JACK-OF-ALL-TRADES" IN A NOVEL CAPACITY

At a very early age the Indian donkey has to work for its living, and its days are spent chiefly in carrying heavy weights in panniers for building or road-mending purposes. The monotonous and unusual task of treading corn must come as a god-send to these patient animals which, small of stature and badly fed, suffer not a little at the hands of their taskmasters

TESTING THE "PATIENCE OF THE LABOURING OX"

In an unceasing circle these oxen tread the corn in old-time fashion. A bell is often attached to one of the animals, its pleasant jingling inciting them to energetic movement, and the persuasive speech and well-timed blows of the master succeed in tiring the harassed beasts, thus fulfilling to a nicety the purpose of labour, for the wearied ox ever sets down his foot the more heavily

Photos, V. S. Manley

AMID THE SOLITUDES OF THE WORLD'S HIGH PLACES: GIGANTIC RAMPART OF HIMALAYAN HEIGHTS

The Himalayas, which contain the highest peaks in the world, rise from the plain of the Ganges in ranges generally parallel, forming a stupendous barrier between North India and the high plateau-land of Tibet. The numerous passes are crossed with difficulty, but the hill-tribes who dwell in the isolated security of these lofty altitudes have learnt the language of the mountains, and with their eagle eyes can trace among the rugged mist-laden peaks the unbeaten tracks which their feet may tread without fear

INFLATED RIVER-CRAFT OF THE HIMALAYAN HINDU

This curious canoe rides the waters of the river Sutlej. The "dreas," or "mussocks" as they are sometimes called, are inflated bullock skins, but are exceedingly light, and when afloat must be manipulated with care, as they are easily overturned. The native lies across the "drea," paddles with his hands, and steers with his feet. If there is a passenger, he sits astride the native

Photo, Frank Scott

becomes their claim to have descended from the sun and the moon, their prowess has filled for ten centuries many splendid pages of Indian history. The Pax Britannica has tempered the fierce clan jealousies and the strife of personal ambitions which made the Rajputs powerless to oppose a united front cither to Mahomedan or to Maratha invaders. But under the aegis of the British crown the Rajput states still represent a feudal stage of society resembling in many ways that which existed in the European Middle Ages.

Absorbed long ago into Hinduism, they seem to have adapted its caste system to their own tribal institutions, and if the Brahmin may sometimes be

NATIVE OF THE PUNJAB AND HIS TRAVELLING COMPANION

India has no lack of street entertainers; jugglers, acrobats, and numerous followers of charlatanism may be met with at every corner. The dancing-bear is a less common sight; this fine specimen was captured in the Himalayas, where such huge beasts abound, and now accompanies its captor on his wanderings, helping him, through ungainly antics or so-called dances, to earn an honest anna

Photo, Robert Chisham

PAHARI WOMAN ENGAGED IN A TOILSOME TASK

The wrinkled, careworn face of this Pahari, or hill-woman, speaks of a life of great hardship, and the occupation of stone-breaking must strain her old limbs to the utmost. No matter what the work, these hill-women, who always wear baggy trousers drawn in at the ankle, never discard their ornaments, which are regarded by young and old as an indispensable addition to their apparel

Photo, Frank Scott

PRIESTLY MENDICANTS OF THE SIMLA HIGHLANDS
The Brahmin, or priest, is the first of the four recognized classes of Hindus, and all priests are Brahmins, but all Brahmins are by no means priests. These three members of the priestly brother-hood, photographed in the hills near Simla, have exchanged their monotonous temple duties for the precarious life of the wanderer, but the orthodox take care that they never lack for food
Photo, Frank Scott

the real power behind the throne, the Rajput prince is revered and feared as the lord and father of his people, and he commands the unquestioning allegiance not only of the warrior caste that claims kinship with him, but of the agricultural caste that tills his land, and of the artisan castes in the towns and of the few primitive tribes that represent a survival of the aboriginal population.

The younger generation of Rajputs may have been educated at the Chiefs' Colleges at Ajmer or Indore, may speak English and play cricket, and, above all, polo, and shoot and go pig-sticking with the British sahibs, whom they know

how to treat as comrades without fear or favour. Some of them have larger political ambitions, and are playing a leading part in the new Council of Indian Princes at Delhi. Some have learnt to move so far with the times that they have introduced into their states a pale reflection of the latest democratic institutions of British India. But the greatest of them still stand in the old ways.

At Udaipur, the city of white marble palaces mirrored in azure lakes, the aged Maharana, whose ancestors refused to defile the bluest blood of Rajputana by giving their daughters into marriage with the Mogul Emperors in the prime of their power, sleeps on a low trestle bed of woven matting in a high turret chamber more like an armoury than a royal bed-room, with his sword at his side, and his men-at-arms in coats of mail keeping watch at the door, and his family Brahmin reciting sacred mantras at the household shrine.

He himself once a year officiates as the high priest of his own house at the ancestral temple of Mahadev, the great god Siva, built in a narrow defile, of which the gloom enhances the majesty of a solemn and unique ceremony. Few of his people can read or write; fewer still do not know by heart the romance of Prithvi Raja, who fell before the Mahomedans in 1192 at Talawari, the Flodden Field of Rajasthan, with the flower of Rajput chivalry, or the grim tragedy of Chitor, the ancient capital, when the beautiful Queen Padmani and all the ladies of the court, and all the wives of the fighters, " built up a vast funeral pyre in the centre of the city and passed, as in a chariot of fire, into

SOCIABLE SPRITES OF THE HIMALAYAN PASTURE-LANDS
These merry young people are tending livestock in the hills near Simla, and as children of the Paharis or hill people, their duties come quite naturally to them. They are very friendly towards strangers, always ready with a smiling welcome, and the dirty rags which cover many of these lithe young forms detract no whit from their general attractive appearance
Photo, Frank Scott

BROAD BACKS THAT PULL CUMBERSOME BURDENS

Trussed up securely in supports of twisted branches, enormous loads of grain or straw can be packed on the bullock-carts, and the docile Indian bullock draws them along the roads at a snail's pace with good-humoured placidity. Should he become stubborn and refuse to move, blows with a thick stick, and energetic tail-twistings, usually restore him to his normal equanimity

Photo, Frank Scott

the heavens," while the warriors, clad in the saffron robe of sacrifice even unto death, rushed headlong through the gates to snatch victory from the enemy's overwhelming hosts.

Behind a triple line of walls and bastions, the castle of Jodhpur, both palace and fort, stands in grim magnificence on an isolated rock 400 feet above the surrounding plain, mounting guard over the old walled city, pierced by six gates still studded with sharp iron spikes to protect them against the fury of the ramming elephants. Though Jaipur itself is a less ancient city, whose pink painted streets look rather garish save when they merge into a flood of sunset glow, the venerable Maharaja is among the most conservative of Rajput

princes, and still lives in the traditions that haunt the deserted palace of his forefathers at Amber.

Absolutely remote from the modern world is Bundi, perhaps the most picturesque of all the towns of Rajputana, in a gorge nearly surrounded by steep wooded heights, of which its narrow streets and many storeyed houses climb the lower slopes in crowded tiers. In the whole city the post-office is the one building that looks out of place. For it alone has notices printed in English, and a clock that marks the progress of time where time would otherwise seem to have stood still for the last two centuries at least.

Above the town the Maharaja's palace rises in a series of terraces and hanging gardens clinging to the mountain side ; and when his Highness was lying so dangerously ill that it was decided to summon expert advice, it was only after having run the gauntlet of half a dozen courtyards and halls and staircases, through crowds of resentful, murmuring courtiers and scowling men-at-arms, that the doctor, though known to be invested with all the authority of the Imperial Medical Service, was able to force his way to the ruler's private apartments, and then only after many mysterious consultations with terrified ladies whispering messages of persistent

delay from behind the purdah was he allowed access to his illustrious patient.

Fortunately, in his skilled hands, the Maharaja recovered speedily, and his gratitude took the no less characteristic shape of extending to his medical adviser the privilege hitherto never granted to a single non-Rajput of shooting a tiger in the Bundi jungles !

At Bikaner, on the fringe already of the great Thar desert, the Maharaja, better known to Englishmen than any other Rajput Prince, both as one of India's representatives at the Paris Peace Conference and as a right royal

GROUP OF HINDU ASCETICS SUNK IN SILENT MEDITATION

They belong to the great army of Indian fakirs, which term has come to include not only the vast numbers of wandering Mahomedan mendicants, but also Hindu, Sikh, and Jain religious devotees. They have renounced the world in order to attain perfection of soul, and the austerity of their ascetic life is such as to make them regarded in the eyes of the orthodox as men of much sanctity

Photo, Frank Scott

host in the modern palace of red sandstone and white marble, equipped with
every Western luxury which he, and
doubtless his guests, too, prefer to the
grim stateliness of the old fort, stands
for a new spirit of progress in methods
of state administration and governance
which few other Rajput states have yet
emulated.

Far beyond Bikaner, and a mere
oasis in the heart of the great desert,
Jaisalmir, a small poverty-stricken town
of barely 7,000 inhabitants, enclosed
within great fortified walls three miles
in circumference, is the last outpost of
Rajputana in a strangely inhospitable
land. The history of the rulers of
Jaisalmir is as grim as their barbaric
surroundings, or as the massively
buttressed and bastioned fort which
protects the straggling pile of buildings
that are the Maharaja's palace,
crowned by a huge umbrella of metal

on a stone shaft as the emblem of his
rude sovereignty.

Outside, and to the west of Rajputana
proper, two peninsulas washed by the
Arabian Sea—Kathiawar, which is split
up into 188 small native states, mostly
under Rajput rulers, and Cutch, " the
sea-coast land," whose Maharao is also
of Rajput descent—cut off the main part
of the Bombay Presidency from its
northern province of Sind and the
estuary of the Indus.

It was in Sind that, at the beginning
of the eighth century, an Arab expedition dispatched by the Caliph of
Bagdad first planted the standard of
Islam in India. Hence, among the
Mahomedans who form three-quarters
of the very sparse population, an
extravagantly disproportionate number
call themselves Sayyids and wear the
green turban as reputed descendants of
the Prophet. All still wear voluminous

RETURNING HOME FROM THE ANNUAL OUTING
The Fair held at Sultanpur is the event of the year in the simple lives of this Kulu man
and wife. Sturdy hill-folk, they care nothing for the hardships attending the long journey ; the
delights of the fair, meeting their friends, making their purchases, cause them to forget the
discomforts of the road and give them something to talk over for the rest of the year
Photo, R. Richardson

FUNERAL POTS FOR FOOD OFFERINGS TO THE DEPARTED

The Indian potter is usually an itinerant trader   Earthenware pots are slowly disappearing from the Hindu household, but continue to play important rôles in funeral ceremonies. While the vessels are new, in the potter's care, they may be handled with impunity, but once filled with water they may be used only by the person who filled them, or by members of his caste

Photo, V. S. Manley

white turbans, a loose shirt, and ample baggy trousers drawn in at the waist and ankles; while their womenfolk never venture abroad except in the long white burka which envelopes them from head to feet, with two open-work slits that just allow the eyes to see.

Easy-tempered, except when their fanaticism is aroused, the Sind Mahomedans are withal a lazy and swaggering, and often dissolute, race, without the virile qualities of their Baluch co-religionists, who, retaining all their tribal organizations under their own hereditary chiefs, have become under British overlordship the wardens of the northern marches of the Indian Empire from Gwattar, on the Persian Gulf, through Makran and Baluchistan to Quetta, the great British place of arms in a wilderness of stark and rugged mountains over against Kandahar and the western plains of Afghanistan.

Sind has the unpleasant reputation of registering the highest temperatures recorded in the whole of India during the torrid months of April, May, and June, before it receives its very scanty share of monsoon rains, and the tall wind-shafts erected on the flat house-roofs to catch the slightest puff of cooling wind constitute the most striking features of its inland towns.

Irrigation from the Indus is gradually extending the narrow margin of cultivation, and extensive harbour works, carried out at great cost and labour over a long series of years, have converted Karachi into the chief port of shipment from Sind, not only for local produce, but for the expanding harvests of the Punjab, now one of the great wheat-growing areas of the world.

For variety of interest, no other province of British India surpasses the Punjab, especially if we include in it the wild borderland detached from it for administrative purposes to form the new North-West Frontier Province. It is the historic land on the threshold of the rich alluvial plains of Upper India into which successive waves of invasion

MOST VALUABLE ASSET TO INDIA'S RURAL REGIONS

In their anxiety to obtain that most valued possession—a good well, many landowners engage in sinking operations with reckless energy, thereby making the frequent and fatal mistake of choosing an ill-advised spot, often with the result that the search has to be abandoned. At some Indian wells bullock labour raises the water; at others this old-fashioned hand method is followed

Photo, J. Fryer

have from times immemorial poured down from Central Asia. Time after time, during the last nine centuries, the northern passes, and notably the Khyber Pass from Kabul, have witnessed hungry hordes of Mahomedan conquerors stream through those rugged gates of the Punjab with the sword in one hand and the Koran in the other.

To the present day, the barren mountain fastnesses which are its best defences are tenanted by fierce Mahomedan tribesmen constantly straining at the British leash, which alone holds them back from adding a new chapter to the old story. Unlike the Baluch tribes on the borders of Sind, who are generally amenable to the authority of their acknowledged chiefs, each of the Pathan tribes on the Punjab border constitutes a little republic in which every tribesman can claim to have an equal voice. They transact their affairs of state in open jirgahs, or tribal assemblies, that are quite as likely to be carried away by the fanatical preaching of a holy Mullah as to listen to the more prudent counsels of their Maliks, or " elder statesmen."

All that the Raj demands from these unruly tribesmen is that, in return for the various subsidies allotted to them, without which indeed they would often starve, they should respect the Pax Britannica within certain narrowly prescribed limits ; and the combined tact and firmness of the British frontier officer is never put to a higher test than when he has to go out and meet one of these great tribal gatherings and compose, if possible, by friendly conference the many disputes which must constantly arise between the settled forms of government that prevail within British territory and the lawless conditions of a veritable No Man's Land.

Peshawar, now the capital of the North-West Frontier Province, has an evil reputation for turbulence, and in its picturesque bazaars one rubs shoulders with every type of cut-throat, not only from the hillside, but from Afghanistan and from the more distant regions of Central Asia which Bolshevism has once more plunged into utter chaos. But at Peshawar a British garrison upholds the British rule of law. Nine miles north of Peshawar, on the other hand, the British rule of law ceases, except immediately along the road which crosses the Khyber Pass into Afghanistan, and on either side extends the belt of "independent territory" which in varying breadth runs all along the North-West Frontier. Within this "independent territory" the tribes govern or misgovern themselves according to their own ancient customs.

As soon as the boundary of direct British administration is crossed, one enters into another world of social conditions, not indeed entirely lawless, but subject to such primitive laws as to be only one degree removed from mere savagery. For, if the frontier tribes can be restrained with difficulty from carrying

aggressive warfare into British territory, they must be left free to carry on their customary internecine warfare among themselves, and in the Afridi country every man is or may be his neighbour's deadly enemy.

Blood-feuds break out not only between different tribes, but still more frequently between different families within the same tribe. There is no limit to their duration and extension. Sometimes they divide one part of a village against another ; sometimes one half of a valley against the other. They may be carried on from father to son, or break out afresh after a long truce imposed by some common danger. So every man makes of his house a castle

INGENIOUS NATIVE MECHANISM FOR DRAWING WATER

This imposing earthwork manifests much inventive faculty on the part of the Hindu engineer. The water is drawn by hand, the receptacles being lowered into the well and when full raised by means of weights attached to the ends of the poles. A well with a plentiful water supply is of much assistance to a landowner, ensuring an independent irrigation of his land

Photo, J. Fryer

as stout for defence and as convenient for offence as his circumstances allow.

An Afridi village straggles therefore over a relatively extensive tract of always bleak and stony country, just capable of meagre cultivation. A stout mud wall carefully loopholed has to surround the enclosure in which the tribesman lives with his womenkind and such of his children as are not yet in a position to set up for themselves, and in the centre of the enclosure he builds a square tower, generally about twenty or twenty-five feet high, and if possible of stone plastered over with mud. If he is at war with his neighbours it is from the curtained gallery which runs round the upper storey of the tower that he keeps up a brisk or desultory fire upon them, according to his stock of ammunition, and if he is hard pressed, the tower is his last refuge, until either his friends relieve him, or his powder or his supply of water is exhausted, or his assailants, having burrowed under the ground, can pile up a big fire which burns or smokes him out.

Operations may not be always carried to such extreme lengths, and are in most cases prolonged rather than sanguinary, for however unrelenting his enmity may be the Afridi takes as few risks as he can. Quite a common sight, however, is a tribesman squatting hawk-eyed behind a rock to cover his family with his rifle while they are tilling his fields.

Yet all the time these untamed tribesmen, who have to carry on an equally hard fight to wring their daily bread out of an unfertile soil, have their own code of honour, from which they seldom depart. Nor are they altogether unamenable to discipline, for they enlist freely in the Frontier levies which have done good service in keeping peace on the borderland, and they pass with little apparent effort from surroundings in which they know no law that is not of their own making into the confinement of the barrack-room and the still more chafing confinement of its inexorable rules and regulations.

While he wears his uniform, the Afridi will resist even the call of a blood-feud unless he can obtain leave from his British officer to return for a few days to his village " on private and urgent family business." But when his term of

RELIGIOUS INSTRUCTION OF HINDU YOUTH IN PROGRESS

A large proportion of the Hindu lower-class children grows up with little or no systematic religious teaching, but the Brahmins are usually careful to teach their sons a few Sanskrit prayers, and if the religious instruction does not end there the children are placed under a guru, or professional religious teacher, whose services as father-confessor they often retain after they have grown up

Photo, J. Fryer

COOLING DRAUGHT FROM THE MUSSOCK OF A PUNJABI BHISTI

The bhisti, or water-man, is a familiar figure in India and follows the calling because it belonged to members of his family for generations before him. A conscientious worker, he has often shown considerable bravery under fire, and a fighting regiment once selected for the Victoria Cross a bhisti who had carried water to the thirsty and wounded during the thick of the battle

Photo, V. S. Manley

service has expired, he goes back with just as little effort to the dirt and squalor of his mud fort, and to the lawless social practices of his race. He carries just the same lawlessness even into the practice of his religion. He is a fierce Mahomedan, and, though he knows only the rudimentary elements of his faith, he is easily swayed by the itinerant Mullahs who know how to appeal to his fanaticism. Sometimes their appeal recoils on to their own heads.

There is in the Khyber Pass the tomb of a holy Mullah who ventured to express surprise that in that whole countryside he had not yet come across a single shrine raised to the memory of a dead saint. So the tribesmen promptly atoned for this deplorable deficiency by killing the worthy preacher and erecting over his remains a tomb worthy of his virtues and of their piety, at which they can worship as he ordained!

Fat and tempting indeed to these needy hillmen must be the plains of the Punjab, " the land of the five waters," as it is called from the Indus and its four great affluents, whose waters have been spread by great irrigation works over large areas of virgin but formerly unproductive soil, and almost uninhabited, but now supporting a large population, and bearing the finest wheat crops in India. The lines of social cleavage differ very widely from those in other parts of India. The Punjab bore the brunt of all the Mahomedan invasions from the north, and as late as the eighteenth century the Emperor Aurungzebe made his Hindu subjects feel the full weight of Mahomedan tyranny.

The majority of the population is Mahomedan, and the influence of Islam, which knows nothing of caste, has tended to loosen the bonds of caste among the Hindus, though, on the other hand, old Hindu customs still prevail among many of the Hindus converted to Islam. The latent hostility between the two communities is nevertheless

ASH-SMEARED FAKIRS WHO FLOURISH ON VILLAGE CREDULITY

Indian fakirs are of two kinds: the ascetic orders, which for the most part live in monasteries and have been compared to the Franciscans, and the wandering charlatans who live upon the superstitions of the villagers. The second type, as seen above, are of extremely unwholesome appearance, indescribably dirty, and have the unpleasing habit of daubing themselves with ashes

Photo, Frank Scott

still deep-seated, and apt to explode at any moment and on very slight provocation into open and riotous violence.

Though Mahomedan domination had to yield to British rule, its memories still persist, and are upheld by the martial qualities of the great fighting races, largely Mahomedan, which furnish to the present day, as was abundantly shown during the Great War, the largest relative quota of recruits for the Indian army.

More distinctly Aryan than perhaps any other type in India, the Punjabi is tall and spare, and his black hair and full black beard, which he often dyes red with henna when it begins to turn

grey, combine with his keen dark eyes to convey an impression of splendid virility. His complexion, sometimes almost as light as that of any European, is seldom darker than the deep olive brown of southern Italy or Greece. The peasantry, frugal and industrious as elsewhere, are more efficient because their physique is finer, while the urban and trading population, largely Hindu, is in comparison under-sized and weakly. But its intellectual superiority has become all the more marked with the diffusion, however slow, of modern education.

The Arya-Somaj movement directed towards the emancipation of Hinduism

FOLLOWING A BLACK PROFESSION

One of a party of charcoal carriers, he makes a living by daily bringing charcoal to Dalhousie Bazaar. He is usually as black as the coal in his well-worn wicker basket

Photo, W. L. Tapply

Hinduism. The son of a Sikh is not a Sikh until he has been admitted into the community through the ceremony of the pahul or baptism by steel and " the waters of life."

Theoretically, Sikhism is open to converts of any race or religion, but in practice the Sikhs, or Khalsa, the " elect," as they style themselves, are recruited from the peasantry of the Punjab. For the most part they are Jat Hindus, reputed to be of the same Scythian origin as the Rajputs. That the greater part of the community spring from a homogeneous stock might seem to be proved by the marked and distinctive physiognomy and bearing that differentiate the Sikh almost unmistakably from every other type.

The marks that distinguish the Sikh are only partly physical. One may recognize him also by certain definite insignia which he has adopted—tokens

SIKH PRIEST

He stands in bearded dignity before the Golden Temple at Amritsar. Round his turban is the quoit, at his side a knife, symbols of his martial race

Photo, Frank Scott

from the tyranny of caste and other superstitions, as well as towards the fulfilment of Indian national aspirations, has greater vitality to-day in the Punjab than the older religious reform movement of the Brahmo-Somaj has retained in Bengal. Especially noteworthy has been the impulse given by the Arya-Somaj to female education.

But to the deep lines of cleavage between Mahomedans and Hindus the Punjab adds yet a third which is peculiar to it. It is the home of the Sikhs. Amritsar is their chief city, and the Golden Temple, or Durbar Sahib, their chief shrine. The Sikhs are not a distinct race. Sikhism is a religion, and began as a religious revolt against

FOLLOWERS OF THE PROPHET OF ALLAH WORSHIPPING IN THE GREAT MOSQUE AT DELHI

Five times a day must the Mussulman make his prayers and centre his mind on Allah, and the sight of a Mahomedan praying alone is impressive in its matchless reverence and simplicity. Genuine devoutness and true worship likewise mark the public prayers in the mosques. The chief prayers of the service are composed of verses from the Koran, and during their recital the members of the congregation, with measured uniformity, rise, bow, kneel, and prostrate themselves as one man, presenting a spectacle of religious absorption which it would never occur to them could thus have been preserved by the camera of a daring infidel

HARDY ASCETIC AT BENARES PIOUSLY INDIFFERENT TO A COUCH OF NAILS

Many religious codes, and especially those of India, have advocated or enjoined the mortifying of the flesh and its resulting subjection to the spirit. All over this land of many faiths one may see yogis, fakirs, and all varieties of the mendicant religious, practising with every vigour what their leaders have preached. Marriage, speech, and cleanliness are among the popular renunciations, and in this photograph we have another example of self-suppression. Whatever may be said of other methods it is abundantly evident that this one has its points

Photo, A. H. Smith

which one quickly comes to associate with the martial bearing and proud consciousness of superiority that belong to membership of the Khalsa. These are not the badges prescribed by the founder of the sect, Guru Nanak, born in the neighbourhood of Lahore in 1469, to whose followers the name of Sikhs, or disciples, was given. Nanak's creed was not militant; his preaching was moral and religious only. Neither he nor his successors claimed godhead. His mission was to sweep away idolatry and intolerance, and his message was not addressed exclusively to Hindus,

SAINTLINESS WITH SNAKE-LIKE HALO

This fakir's chief concern is his hair which, with the addition of quantities of goat's hair, he twists into long ropes. Coiled round his head, as shown above, these form a kind of sun-resisting turban

Photos, Mrs. Lynde

though Mahomedans turned a deaf ear to it. There was nothing bigoted in his doctrine; no Mahomedan fanaticism, no Hindu asceticism.

In the seed sown by the mild and gentle Nanak none could have foreseen the growth of the fighting community that ruled the Punjab three centuries later under Ranjit Singh. Militant Sikhism grew out of persecution, but this was not until the tenth Guru, Govind Singh, had bestowed on his followers a distinct national existence and fired them

HINDU PENITENTS IN THE PURSUIT OF SPIRITUAL PERFECTION

As a follower of the doctrine of meditation the yogi, or holy man, in the foreground hopes to attain emancipation of his soul; another penitent qualifying for special favours in the hereafter is submitting to the self-inflicted punishment of remaining in a standing position for seven years, and is supported on a board suspended from a tree lest he should fall to the ground while asleep

Photo, Mrs. Lynde

SIVAITE PRIEST ABOUT TO PERFORM THE DAILY CULT AT A SHRINE

This priestly follower of Siva officiates daily at this small shrine and has charge of several temples dedicated to Kali, the consort of Siva, who, despite such a sinister symbol as her string of skulls, is loved, feared, and worshipped as the Great Hindu Mother, and among the Hindus is said to be excelled in popularity and importance only by Vishnu and Siva

Photo, F. Deaville Walker

PHODONG LAMA AND ATTENDANT WITH PRAYING-WHEELS

The hatted figure is the High Priest of Sikkim who, from his temple at Tumlong, played an important part in governing the province during the absences of the Maharaja. Praying-wheels, a feature of Lamaism, are seen in the hands of both figures. These, often made of copper, contain a prayer which is revolved by pulling a chain. Each revolution represents one repetition of the prayer

Photo, John Claude White

with the ambition to become an independent people.

It was Guru Govind who instituted the Khalsa, the commonwealth of the " Elect," and prescribed for them the insignia which distinguish the community to this day, the wearing of the kirpan or dagger and the steel bracelet on the wrist, the adoption of breeches in the place of the loin-cloth, and the wearing of the hair long, tied in a knot at the top of the head and secured by a comb. These are the distinguishing marks of the Sikh, but there is something more—an impress of character and prestige won by stern discipline.

It was Govind, too, who ordained that every Sikh should adopt the old Rajput title of Singh, or lion. IIe had the captain's eye for the value of tradition and prestige. Sikhism had been wrought to a white heat by the murder of the ninth Guru, Tegh Bahadur, Govind's father, at Delhi, and Guru Govind Singh stirred the religious passion of his followers until the movement gained something of the force and fervour of a crusade. The Sikh of that period was probably the nearest analogy to the Templar in the history of Hindustan.

Amritsar, "the pool of immortality," became the headquarters of the Sikhs

LAMAIST PRIESTS OF SIKKIM AND THEIR WONDROUS ROBES

Talung Monastery is the most sacred in all Sikkim, being packed with objects of veneration and antiquity. To this foundation these two Lamas belong, and the one on the left is wearing the rugen, a complicated adornment of apron and circlet, beautifully carved but gruesome in origin, for it is made from human bones. The cloak and hat of the other are of great age and value

Photo, John Claude White

ORIENTAL SAGE AND HIS EMBLEMS OF SANCTITY

From the domed skull, hairless with age, the narrow eyes look out with a kind of hard intolerance. This is Sherab Gyatsu, a Lama renowned for his sanctity and his learning, and before him are a praying-wheel and a sacred book

Photo, John Claude White

to the Granth Sahib, which is the Sikh Bible, displayed on a low stand beneath a canopy of silk within the temple whose golden roof and cupolas are reflected in the green water of an artificial lake. The Granthi, or priest in charge, sits behind the Book and receives the offerings of the faithful.

The ceremony is literally a Durbar, for the obeisance to the Granth was enjoined by Guru Govind himself, lest his people should be tempted to make of him an object of future idolatry. The Book, as the representative or vicar of the Gurus for all times to come, receives the homage which they would not permit to be paid to themselves.

To the north-west of the Punjab, beyond " the happy valley of Kashmir," itself 5,000 feet above sea-level, the Himalayas begin to rise in their incomparable majesty. Kashmir's picturesque ramshackle capital, Srinagar, is sometimes called the Venice of the East, with its lovely lakes and terraced Mogul gardens, and its wealth of orchards, apple and pear, almond and peach, and its fields of white and purple iris and all the flowers with which English people are familiar at home, and in the autumn the gorgeous red and gold of its giant chenars or plane trees and the pale gold of its stately avenues of poplars. Its lazy, good-tempered and singularly handsome people—the women especially sometimes quite fair—are mostly Mahomedans, but ruled over by an extremely orthodox Hindu Maharaja of Rajput descent who rigorously forbids the slaughter of kine within the state.

From the Woolar lake a solitary mountain road leads over two high passes of 12,000 and 14,000 feet up to the outposts of Empire at Gilgit and

in the latter half of the sixteenth century, and has been ever since the spiritual home of the fraternity and the focus of the long-drawn and sanguinary struggle with Islam.

Since British rule restored peace to the Punjab the Sikhs have been apt to fall back under the influence of Hinduism, and for the last sixty years it has been the Indian army more than anything else that has kept the spirit of the Khalsa alive in its splendid Sikh regiments. The Great War stimulated their old fighting instincts, and since the Armistice a great wave of unrest has swept over the community.

How powerful a force Sikhism still is anyone may observe for himself who stands on the marble causeway of the Durbar Sahib at Amritsar. All day long the worshippers—men, women, and children—file up to make their offering

"AT WHAT TIME YE HEAR THE SOUND OF THE SACKBUT, PSALTERY, DULCIMER, AND ALL KINDS OF MUSICK—"

Here we have a procession of Red Lamas, with full orchestral effects, shuffling round the Phodong, or Royal Monastery at Tumlong, Sikkim. In front droop long banners borne by acolytes, then come the thurifers with their smoking censers, closely followed by a boy helping to support the not inconsiderable instrument wielded by the man behind. If noise can be measured by the yard, then this man must be able to make the welkin more than ring

Photo, John Claude White

POMP AND CIRCUMSTANCE ATTEND A PRINCE OF SIKKIM AT DELHI DURBAR

When the native chiefs of India show themselves to the public gaze little is spared that will emphasise or assist the great presence. Mounted high in the swaying howdah we see Sidkyong Tulku, Maharaj Kumar of Sikkim, his father's chosen representative, about to take part in the great Elephant Procession at a Delhi Durbar. Orderlies in the military uniform of Sikkim and led by one of the headmen accompany the elephant, on whose wise and patient head squats the mahout

Photo, John Claude White

LEPCHA FACTORY GIRLS FROM THE CARPET WORKS AT GANGTOK

Among the activities of the Maharani of Sikkim was the establishment of the rug and carpet industry at her palace at Gangtok. Above are some of the hands employed, and a distinct Mongolian strain may be discerned in their faces. The patterns for their work were obtained from China and Tibet, while the luxuriant jungle supplied the dyes, the results yielded being delightful in the extreme. The smiles on the sallow countenances of this barefoot fifteen indicate a conscious pride in work well done and skill tastefully applied

Photo, John Claude White

ALL DRESSED UP FOR THE MAKING OF THEIR PORTRAIT

This, a family photograph of Sikkim Bhotias of Tibetan origin, displays paternal authority with its formidable whip, motherly piety with a praying-wheel, and juvenile obedience seated humbly beneath. Their gorgeous apparel proclaims this is a wealthy family, for the mother has turquoise earrings and the daughter a jewel-studded charm-box. They are of a patriarchal race, sons bringing their wives to live under the paternal roof

Photo, John Claude White

Hunza-Nagar, past the terrific precipices of Nanga Parbat, over 26,000 feet high, which towards the Indus drop almost sheer. Nanga Parbat is the western buttress of the succession of mighty Himalayan ranges which shut off North-Eastern India from the lofty and bleak plateau of Tibet.

Only the fringe of its vast ice-fields has been explored, and none of its highest peaks has yet been trodden by human feet. Scientific expeditions reconnoitred the approaches to Mount Everest (29,002 feet) in 1921, and nearly scaled its peak in 1922. The snow-line in the Himalayas begins much higher than in the more northerly European Alps—sometimes, on slopes with a southerly exposure and accessible to the warmer currents of air sweeping in from the Bay of Bengal, only at about 17,000 or 18,000 feet.

Though forests are seldom found above 12,000 feet, vegetation and even cultivation occur right up to the highest snow-line in sheltered valleys, tenanted by Buddhist monks, around whose old-world monasteries small weather-beaten villages draw a penurious living from the scanty fruits that can be wrung from the earth during the very short months when it is not buried in the

PROFESSIONAL PERFORMERS IN PUBLIC AND RELIGIOUS CEREMONIES

Dancers by profession, the Nautch girls take part in public performances and are employed within the precincts of some temples, especially in Southern India, where they assist in religious ceremonies. Their official duties are not confined merely to the dance, or to the service of the Indian divinities, and they enjoy a recognized freedom which the women of India generally do not envy

Photo, Frank Scott

MENDICANCY ADOPTED IN THE NAME OF VISHNU

The Vishnavite, a votary of Vishnu, is a beggar by profession. To beg for alms is considered not only his right, but also his duty. This mendicant is pursuing his begging to the accompaniment of music and singing; his instrument, the vina, is repeatedly mentioned in Hindu books as being played by the gods, who delighted to seek the soothing influence of its sweet melodies

snow. The people are Tibetans who have crossed over from the farther side of the "Roof of the World."

The rare and very high passes in the Himalayas are traversed even in summer only by hardy travellers and sure-footed yaks—a long-haired breed of oxen peculiar to those regions—and flocks of goats broken to carry light burdens on their backs. Familiar to most Anglo-Indians are the first stages at least of "the old Tibetan road" which starts from Simla, the summer headquarters of the Government of India, perched at an altitude of 7,000 to 8,000 feet on the foothills of the Himalayas. When Lord Amherst first pitched his camp there, a little less than a hundred years ago, he can never have pictured to himself the Simla of to-day, clinging for several miles in superimpending rows and terraces of public buildings and private residences to the sides and crest of a narrow wooded ridge, a health-resort, no doubt, and not lacking in beauty with its wonderful outlook on the eternal snows, but an overcrowded and supremely inconvenient site for a busy town of nearly 40,000 inhabitants which is for nearly half the year the administrative capital of India, and now the seat of Army Headquarters all the year round. Far finer is the approach to the central axis of the Himalayas from

Naini Tal, the summer quarters of the Government of the United Provinces, up the gorges of the Alaknanda Ganges to the principal head waters of the sacred river at Badrinath and Kedarnath, with their ice-bound shrines, to which thousands of Hindu pilgrims flock every year from the tropical far south and the sun-scorched plains of Upper India, men, women, and children often clad in nothing but their customary thin cotton garments, exposed to every inclemency of mountain weather and to every hardship of giddy mountain tracks and still more giddy rope-bridges across roaring torrents, dying often like flies from exposure and disease, but always sustained by their unwavering faith in the virtue of their long and arduous pilgrimage.

West of Nanda Devi, the highest peak (25,645 feet) wholly within British territory, the kingdom of Nepal extends for 500 miles along the southern slopes of the Himalayas at an elevation of between 4,000 and 5,000 feet. In subordinate alliance with the Government of India, and at the same time until recent years sending quinquennial tribute missions to Peking, but successful on the whole in maintaining their traditional policy of isolation and keeping their country free from any but the most restricted intercourse with all foreigners, the rulers of Nepal claim Rajput descent.

Of their, roughly, four million subjects nearly half profess Hinduism, and a slightly larger half Buddhism, now generally debased by the later incorporation of demon-worship and blood-sacrifices. The inhabitants speak for the most part dialects kindred to Tibetan, and their pagoda-shaped

DISPENSING STRONG WATERS IN A DRAM SHOP IN BENARES.

This drink shop in Benares has an indescribably pathetic air of poverty and squalor about it ; its trade, however, is a brisk one, and brings in an ample income to its proprietor who pays a Government tax of several thousand rupees per annum on the spirit sold. The drinking vessels in use in this establishment are little clay cups similar to the one seen on the " bar "

Photo, F. Deaville Walker

temples and the houses, and even the dress of the well-to-do classes, show the pervasive influence of China. The Gurkhas, among whom the Indian army recruits many of its best fighting regiments, have marked Mongolian features.

Majestic Beauty of Nature

Through the deep depression of the Chumbi valley between Sikkim and Bhutan, two native states in which rulers and peoples, language and customs are essentially Buddhist and Tibetan, lies the main road to Lhasa, the capital and Vatican of Tibet, from Darjeeling, the summer quarters of the Government of Bengal, whence the well-known Himalayan panorama includes the embattled peaks of Kinchinjunga, towering up into the skies in a seemingly unbroken sweep from the deep intervening valley of the Tista.

Through forests in which great tree-ferns and giant rhododendrons abound, and past terraced tea-gardens redeemed from the jungle, a little mountain railway drops down in incredible loops and gradients into the north-eastern plains of Bengal. Here, after sweeping down from Tibet through Assam, a small province of alluvial silt and fertile hill country with tea-gardens that rival those of the Darjeeling district and aboriginal or mixed Indo-Chinese tribes as primitive in their beliefs and superstitions as any of the hill tribes of Southern India, mingle the mighty waters of the Brahmaputra with the still mightier waters of the Ganges, to flow not merely in one great stream, sometimes ten miles broad, but in innumerable minor channels and narrow interlacing creeks between partially submerged islets of dense jungle and mangrove swamps into the Bay of Bengal.

Densely Populated Agricultural Land

But except in this aquatic fringe, where the Gangetic delta is still in process of formation, the greater part of Bengal is an alluvial plain of incomparable fertility. The province of Bengal, as at present constituted, no longer has the largest area, but it still has the largest population (47,549,350,

according to the preliminary census returns in 1921) of any province in India, exceeding that of the whole of the British Islands by a million, and in density per square mile almost equalling that of England and Belgium, though it is an almost entirely agricultural country.

Jute grown on a larger area than anywhere else in the world is commercially the most important crop, but rice is the most extensive, as it covers nearly three-quarters of the cultivated acreage, and only a long way behind follow other food-crops, such as cereals and oil-seeds, and pulses and sugar-cane. There are few trees except groves of bamboos and of mango, of areca and coconut palm, in which the scattered villages and homesteads of the people are almost buried.

Intellectual Quality of the Bengalis

The climate is humid, and for all but a couple of winter months intensely oppressive, and malaria is rampant. The most striking characteristic of Bengal is the racial homogeneity of the population, though almost equally divided between Hinduism and Mahomedanism, the latter slightly in excess. Bengali is the most widely spoken of all Indian languages, and has become almost a sign and bond of common nationhood between the forty or fifty millions who speak it.

Thanks very largely to the labours of learned missionaries in the early part of the nineteenth century, Bengali has developed singular literary qualities, which the Hindu Bengalis have brought to fine fruition. They are a quick-witted and imaginative people, who have often been the victims rather than the makers of history while successive tides of conquest have rolled over them through the ages. But during the last century they have been in the van of educational progress. For readiness to learn, for retentiveness of memory, for intellectual flexibility and for facile eloquence they have few rivals and no superiors in India.

It was in Calcutta, the one great city of Bengal, with a population now, including the suburbs, of a million and

Seldom is the poetry of movement displayed with more alluring charm
and harmony than in the seductive steps of the dances of Indian women

Boldly using colours of amazing brilliancy, the " gorgeous East "
dazzles many a Western eye with the splendour of its entertainments

Consecrated in youth to the service of a deity, the Nautch girl employs all the artifices of coquetry for the delectation of unspiritual man

Photo, Herbert G. Ponting

Clad in the prickly insignia of power, the grim form of the executioner of Rewah, Central India, strikes terror to the heart of his victims

Photo, Bourne & Shepherd

*To the belligerent proclivities of the Afridis and other Pathan
tribes is due the unending warfare in the northern Indian marches*

The bright garments of Kashmir women, be they poor or rich, never produce discord of colour, and are eloquent of a high artistic taste

Photo, Publishers' Photo Service

The Hindus of North Kashmir rank among the finest of Indian races,
and a singularly soft beauty stamps most of the women and children

Officers of the 15th Ludhiana Sikhs and of the 1st Brahmins, these stern-faced fighting men represent the Indian Army at its best

Photo, Bourne & Shepherd

a quarter, that Western education, when first imported a century ago into India, at once appealed to the higher classes among the Hindus, and even Brahmins responded to the new call. It was in Calcutta that were found the moving spirits of religious and social reform when Hinduism seemed to be seeking and finding enlightenment. The Bengalis were the first to take possession of the public offices, the bar, the press, and the teaching profession, and from Calcutta no less than from Bombay came the first impulse towards the political advancement of India which led to the foundation of the Indian National Congress.

Calcutta is to-day a great centre of Western industrial and commercial enterprise, and in the European quarters one has, more than anywhere else in India, the impression of a city which, if not actually European, differs only from the European type in the complexion and dress of its Oriental population and the architectural compromises imposed on European buildings by a tropical climate.

East & West Blend in Calcutta

The Marquess Wellesley built Government House in 1799, on the model of Kedleston Hall, in Derbyshire, and it is still the stateliest official residence in British India. Fort William, with Clive's ramparts and fosses, is still almost untouched, and with an ever-expanding Valhalla of bronze or marble governors and viceroys and commanders-in-chief, and, at the farther end, the white marble halls and domes of the Queen Victoria Memorial Hall—the one noble monument the British have built in India—at last nearing completion, the broad expanse of Calcutta's incomparable Maidan is, even more than London's parks, the green playfield and the vital lung of the whole city.

Along and behind Chauringhi there are still a few of the old-time mansions of Thackeray's " nabobs," with their deep, pillared verandas standing well off from the road, each with its garden " compound." But they are rapidly making room for " eligible residences,"

more opulent perhaps but more closely packed, or for huge blocks of residential flats, even less adapted to the climate. The great business quarter round Dalhousie Square has been steadily rebuilt on a scale of massive magnificence scarcely surpassed in the City of London, and many of the shops compare with those of London's West End.

Cosmopolitan Traffic by Road & River

The river, too, all along the Garden Reach and far below, is often almost as crowded as the Pool of London, with ocean-going steamers waiting to load or unload their cargoes, as well as with lumbering native sailing ships and the ferries that ply ceaselessly between the different quarters of the city on both banks of the Hooghli, whose devious channel runs through a long succession of dangerous quicksands, down to the Bay of Bengal, eighty miles distant. East and West mingle in the continuous roar of traffic in the busy streets ; and crowds gather nowhere more thickly than round the cinemas.

The East still prevails in the squalid suburb of Kali-Kata, with its popular temple sacred to Kali, the black goddess of destruction with a protruding blood-red tongue, who wears a necklace of human skulls and a belt of human hands and tongues and, holding in one of her many hands a severed human head, tramples underfoot the bleeding bodies of her victims.

Magnet of Western Education

But the most distinctive feature of Calcutta is its university, which numbers more students—some 26,000—than all the universities of Great Britain put together, and has produced not only an abundant harvest of real learning, but also, unfortunately, a lamentable crop of tares. In none of the other university cities of India has Western education yielded both better and worse results, because nowhere quite as much as in Bengal has the Indian developed such an avidity for Western education or for the fruits which it is supposed to yield, combined with so great a lack of educational

WHERE THE ALMIGHTY IS TRUSTED TO ENCOURAGE TRADE

These swarthy cloth merchants grouped outside their establishment are determined to leave nothing to chance.   Not only are they relying on the soundness of their wares and the subtlety of their salesmanship to tempt good trade, but, making doubly sure, they exhibit a board bearing the legend , " God Bless & Co.," in the hope that Heaven will take note of this pious publicity and be propitious

Photo, E. P. Giles

FAKIRS OF INDIA AND THEIR ASHEN COUNTENANCES

Forbidden by their religion to wash themselves or use water for purposes of cleanliness, the fakirs are addicted to rubbing themselves with ashes, which, as can be seen in the case of two among this group of dusky wanderers, has the effect, if not of entirely cleaning them, at least of considerably lightening their darkness. It will be noticed that one is reading to the company

Photo, Publishers' Photo Service

BARE FEET AND RED-HOT CINDERS AT A FESTIVAL IN MADRAS

Asceticism in India takes many strange forms. To cultivate a state of mind which has as its central fact indifference—indifference to the body and its needs, desires, and dislikes—is the end held in view, and to gain it, many are prepared to perform, with smiles, extraordinary feats of self-torture. These fire walkers wear garlands, and rings on their toes. Beneath the umbrellas is an altar

HOMELY TASKS BEFORE A HUMBLE MAHA DWELLING

In the Maratha country, a district of Western India, live the Mahas, a privileged class who, because of a service rendered to some emperor of yore, receive every morning a free dole of bread. Their business is to collect the revenue and carry Government messages from village to village. The figures on the wall of this small home, whose inmates are Christians, denote the census number

LOW-CASTE INDIANS' PATHETIC INDIFFERENCE TO COMFORT

A tiny yard to the left and a small chamber to the right complete this low-caste dwelling in North India. The family sleep behind the half-wall at the back, and the portable fireplace is the only furniture. All squatting on the bare floor, the veiled wife goes on sifting grain while her husband smokes his hookah and the children just do nothing

Photos, F. Deaville Walker

INDIAN POTTER AND AN EMBRYO SAMPLE OF HIS WORK

In the days when prehistoric man discovered that by revolving his rude lumps of clay he could bring every part of them in succession to his moulding, the art of pottery may be said to have had its real beginning. The wheel was the fundamental. Such an Indian potter as this obtains his clay from the riverside, kneads it to shape, and it is ready for turning

WORK NEARING COMPLETION UNDER THE POTTER'S THUMB

With his material on the table at the wheel's centre, the potter turns the whole with his foot and with deft fingers moulds the plastic clay to his needs. On the right is seen a pile of semi-cylindrical tiles for roofing. One shape yields two tiles and is divided before baking. Quantities of the yet undivided article are seen on either side the wheel

Photos, the Rev. J. H. Powell

perspective. Nowhere do students come up—many from the smallest towns and villages—more inadequately equipped, both intellectually and physically, or with greater illusions as to the real meaning of education, of which the passing of examinations as an open sesame to lucrative employment and to a higher social status too often seems to them the one supreme purpose. Their parents make pathetic sacrifices to maintain them at the university, though often on a pittance that barely keeps them from starvation ; they rush from one crowded lecture-room to another, they grind away at their text-books in ill-lighted, stuffy lodgings, for there is no collegiate life such as English universities afford, and most of the secondary schools, as well as colleges, are non-residential.

Mixed Fruits of the Tree of Learning

Deplorable under such conditions, which are morally and physically as well as intellectually deleterious, is the wastage of students who fall out at one or other stage of the university course, and still more deplorable the large proportion of those who persevere to the end to find themselves ultimately landed in a blind alley, merely to swell the ranks of a dangerous intellectual proletariat, unemployed and unemployable. Surprising, nevertheless, in such circumstances is the proportion of genuine success.

Across the Great Gangetic Plain

The problem is acute everywhere in India, but nowhere more acute than in Calcutta, where the Bengali student, whose slouching gait and greasy black hair and seldom over-clean dhoti wound untidily round his swarthy figure often earn for him as much derision as his comical flights of English rhetoric, and who yet when he cares can play football barefooted and bareheaded against sturdy British teams and sometimes defeat them, seems to embody all the defects and qualities of the Bengali character.

From Bengal the great Gangetic plain extends through the province of Bihar and Orissa and the United Provinces of Agra and Oudh, embracing a large part of Central India and merging in the north over an almost imperceptible water-shed into the plains of the Punjab, watered by the great affluents of the Indus. It is an almost unbroken plain, uniformly drab during the greater part of the year, but covered with a green mantle of rich harvest after the short seasons of rain have called forth its inexhaustible fertility. Drab also are its mud villages, and even the trees, which grow rarer with the greater dryness of the atmosphere at an increasing distance from the sea, are apt to assume the same drab colour under their coats of all-pervading dust.

In Bihar, where the people are racially akin to the Bengalis, and speak a kindred language, though there is little love lost between Biharis and Bengalis, and in the United Provinces, the most populous administrative unit (46,725,770) in India except Bengal, the Aryan and Dravidian types have intermingled in almost equal proportions and religion still constitutes the deepest line of cleavage.

Unceasing Battle of the Creeds

The Mahomedans form only one-fifth of the whole population, but the memories of Mahomedan domination and the often oppressive grip which the great Mahomedan landlords have retained in Oudh upon the cultivators, mostly Hindus, keep alive the old antagonism which still breaks out from time to time into violent and sanguinary feuds, especially during religious festivals and over the Mahomedan practice of cow-killing for sacrificial purposes, the most abominable of sacrileges in Hindu eyes. The battle of the creeds underlies the battle of the languages waged between Hindi, which is the language of the Hindus, and Urdu, the language of the camp, or Hindustani, which was a creation of the Mahomedan conquest.

The Gangetic basin was the cradle of ancient Indian civilization. There the earliest Hindu states grew to maturity and decayed. Though large cities are rare in any part of India, which has always been and still is a pre-eminently

EVERYDAY LIFE IN A STREET OF THE SACRED CITY OF HARDWAR

Although along its entire course the Ganges is sacred, there are three particular places where its
sanctity reaches a special degree; these are Hardwar, Allahabad, and Benares. At Hardwar, where
the river issues from the gorge at the foot of the majestic Himalayas, its waters are as pure as crystal,
and even its icy temperature is no hindrance to the bathing of multitudinous pilgrims

Photo, F. Deaville Walker

COMMONPLACE SCENE IN THE HOLY CITY OF INDIA, WHERE GODLINESS IS DEPENDENT UPON CLEANLINESS

Many Hindu temples look down upon the bathing ghats of Benares where bathers and washerfolk—men and women of all ages—may be seen at their ablutions. Besides the ritualistic bath the pilgrims, some of whom have saved up their annas for many months to enable them to undertake this religious holiday, must visit the temples and do "puja" to Siva, the great god Mahadev; and here their meagre savings rapidly disappear, a portion of them in consecrated offerings, but the bulk into the pockets of his priests.

RIVER BAPTISM WHEREBY MERITLESS MEN MAY BE SANCTIFIED IN HUNDREDS OF THOUSANDS

Benares has been a centre of holiness for many centuries, and records show that even five hundred years before the birth of Christianity it was a very ancient and a very sacred city. Religion may be termed a regular business in Benares, and its water front, bordered with fine temples and palaces, is lined with countless pilgrims praying and bathing in the Ganges, that mighty river of India, the waters of which are believed to cleanse the faithful from their sins

Photo, F. Deaville Walker

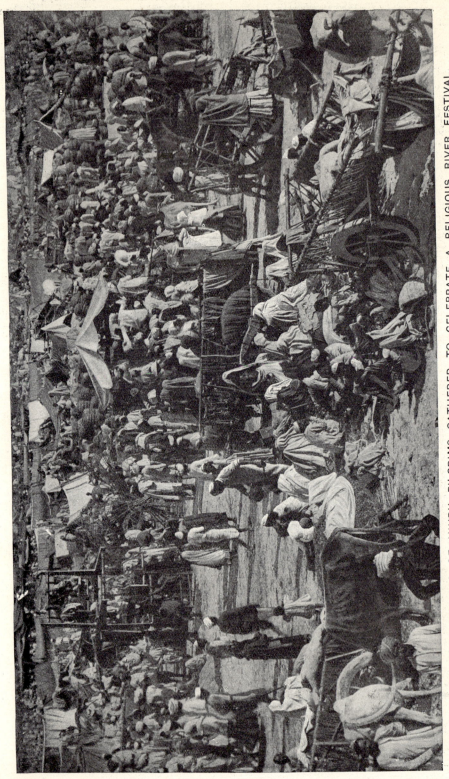

MASSED MULTITUDES OF HINDU PILGRIMS GATHERED TO CELEBRATE A RELIGIOUS RIVER FESTIVAL

No country fair could present a more vivid or interesting scene than the dry bed of the Ganges at Anupshahr during the great bathing festival held every November at the time of the full moon. Thousands of Hindus assemble near the sacred river, and religious ceremonies mingle with amusements, swings and big wheels being much in evidence, for although the pilgrims enter heart and soul into the solemnity of the occasion they nevertheless manage to enjoy all the pleasures of a social holiday

INDIAN WOMEN EMPLOYEES AT A PRINTING WORKS NEAR POONA

This is one of the branches of a refuge for Indian widows and friendless women established by the Christian widow of a wealthy Brahmin. There is employment for a thousand hands at these works. The entire process of composing, casting, printing, and binding is done by female labour, and even the care of the machines is entrusted to its charge. Several of the girl compositors learned to set up type in Greek and Hebrew, and printing is commonly done in several languages

Photo, F. Deaville Walker

agricultural country, containing altogether less than thirty towns of over 100,000 inhabitants, more than a third of these and the most historic are on or relatively near the Ganges.

Some fifty miles south of Patna, now the capital of Bihar and Orissa, where the ruins of Asoka's Pataliputra are buried under the silt of the Ganges, lies Buddh-Gaya, where a spreading Bodh (or Bo) tree is worshipped to-day by the

and its strange temples, and, far more impressive, the massive palaces erected by the great Hindu princes and noblemen from all parts of India, whose pious ambition is to die close to the purifying waters of the Ganges, the whole panorama, however, still dominated by the towering mosque and minarets which the Emperor Aurungzebe erected as a monument of Mahomedan mastery over an "idolatrous" people.

LITTLE GIRL MEMBERS OF THE INDIAN ARISTOCRACY
It is becoming more the custom for the women of the wealthier families to learn to read and write. Here are five Hindu girls who have been sent to the mission school at Khurja, some fifty miles from Delhi. As schoolgirls they are remarkable for wonderful silk garments and jewelry. Before them are their slates on which they have been inscribing Hindu characters
Photo. F. Deaville Walker

faithful as the same one under which the Buddha sat when he "found enlightenment," and a shrine divided now between Buddhists and Hindus is a hallowed goal of pilgrimage from the most remote parts of the Buddhist world, far away from the land which was the cradle of its faith.

Farther up, Benares, the most sacred of all Hindu cities, stretches along the Ganges its long line of ceremonial bathing ghats for the living, and burning ghats for the cremation of the dead,

The fort of Allahabad, which ranks as the second capital of the United Provinces, was built by the Emperor Akbar at the confluence of the Ganges and the Jumna, specially hallowed, according to Hindu tradition, by the accession of a supposed subterranean stream which is no other than the goddess of learning, Sarasvati herself, who escaped in a watery shape from the attack of furious demons in far Thanesvar down that invisible channel, and emerged beneath the temple of the Imperishable Banyan

SHOPPERS AND SHOPPING IN A BAZAAR OF LUCKNOW

Once the capital of the Nawabs of Oudh and celebrated for its siege in the Indian Mutiny, Lucknow is also famous for its buildings and minarets which, from a distance, show a crenellated line of architecture along the right bank of the Gumti river. On the wall of this booth, where two natives have paused in serving their customer, is the advertisement of a Norwich firm

"CREEPING LIKE SNAIL UNWILLINGLY TO SCHOOL"

There was probably small difficulty in persuading these two young Maratha scholars to delay for a moment their journey towards the ascent of Parnassus and "look pleasant" for a little while. On the slate are seen rows of Maratha characters such as are used in the Deccan, and the lads have worn their clothes as schoolboys will, for there are marked signs of wear and tear

Photo, Harry Cox

Tree which still owes to her its reputed immunity from decay.

At Cawnpore, now the greatest inland manufacturing centre in India, was enacted on the banks of the Ganges the most terrible tragedy among all the horrors of the Mutiny. At Lucknow, the degenerate kings of Oudh have bequeathed in their palaces and mosques equally degenerate monuments of Mahomedan art, which on the other hand has achieved its supreme triumph in the great fort at Agra, with its pearl mosque and palatial halls of fretted marble, and above all in the Taj Mahal, the unique shrine built by the Emperor Shah Jehan just three centuries ago as

a resting-place worthy of his beloved consort, the fair Mumtaz-Mahal.

Not on the banks of the Ganges, but on those of the Sutlej, one of the greatest of its tributaries, Imperial Delhi, now the capital of the British Indian Empire, embodies as no other Indian city does the whole history of India throughout the ages. The Kutb Minar, the splendid minaret overlooking the mosque called Kuwal-ul-Islam, "the Might of Islam," which the first Mahomedan conqueror to proclaim himself Emperor of Delhi erected six centuries ago, seems to dominate not only the modern city and the vast graveyard of fallen dynasties that surround

IGNORANT SUPERSTITION INCREASES THE SORROW OF TRAVAIL

For three weeks if the child is a boy, and for four if a girl, the Indian mother is ceremonially unclean, and in many homes confinement huts are put up in the yard for her accommodation. Here she must remain, touched by none of her relatives and tended only, as a rule, by an ignorant midwife. The humane woman emerging from this hovel is an English missionary nurse

Photo, Miss M. N. Tuck

it, but the great plain beyond, where the fate of India, and not of India alone, has so often been decided.

There were fought out the fierce conflicts of ancient Aryan races around which the poetic genius of India has woven the wonderful epos of the Mahabharata. The Purana Kilat, the fortress built by Humayun, covers the site, but has not obliterated the ancient name of Indrapat, the city founded by the Pandavas themselves after performing on the banks of the Jumna the great horse-sacrifice in token of their victorious claim to empire. On a mound beyond Indrapat stands the granite shaft of one of Asoka's pillars on which, with a

fine faith that the world has never yet justified, the great Buddhist Apostle-Emperor inscribed over 2000 years ago his edicts prohibiting the taking of life.

At the very feet of the Kutb Minar the celebrated iron pillar commemorates the victories of the "Sun of Power" and the Golden Age of Hinduism in the fifth and sixth centuries of our era. Spread on all sides are the monuments, some in ruins, some still splendidly intact, of the six centuries of Mahomedan domination, at times not without glory, but often sinking to the lowest depths of depravity and oppression.

The peerless hall of private audience with the famous inscription "If Paradise

SURVIVALS OF PREHISTORIC MAN IN THE ANDAMAN ISLANDS

Andamanese are specially interesting to the anthropologist as representing the last pure remnant of palaeolithic man. They are frizzy-haired, dark-skinned people, averaging four feet ten inches in height, and are a merry, good-humoured folk among themselves, living in extremely elementary conditions of civilization. They include about a dozen tribes, grouped into coast- and jungle-men

ANDAMANESE AT ARCHERY PRACTICE AT PORT BLAIR

Bows and arrows are used by the Andamanese for killing land animals and fish, and detachable harpoons in the pursuit of turtle and sharks. These natives are employed by the Port Blair authorities against the wild tribes who have a habit of killing the convicts settled on the land for the sake of the iron ring round their neck, which is useful for tipping arrows

Photos, Commander W. A. Usher

there be on the face of the earth, it is here, it is here, it is here," witnessed in turn the invasion of Nadir Shah, the Persian, who carried away the priceless peacock throne; of Ahmad Shah, the Afghan; of Maratha soldiers of fortune, and of Rohilla freebooters, who cruelly blinded the old Emperor Shah Alan, and usurped his power until Lord Lake delivered him in 1806 and brought peace once more to Delhi for half a century.

Then, on the historic Ridge, the tenacity and superior discipline of a small British and loyal native force during the three awful months of May, June, and July, 1857, kept the flag flying against everwhelming odds, until Nicholson stormed the walled city, and died the soldier's death, but broke the back of the Mutiny. It was on the plain of Delhi that the assumption by Queen Victoria of the Imperial title was solemnly proclaimed in 1878, and, with still greater pomp, King Edward's accession in 1903. There, again, in 1911, King George, the first of his line to visit his Indian Empire as King-Emperor, received in person the homage of its Princes and peoples, and restored Delhi to her former pride of place as its Imperial capital.

The latest but not the least of the great historic scenes enacted in Delhi was the opening on Feb. 6, 1921, by the Duke of Connaught, acting in the King-Emperor's name, of the new Indian Legislatures, created under the great charter of 1919, to set India on the road to Dominion self-government within the British Commonwealth of Nations.

PEOPLE TO WHOM CIVILIZATION MEANS EXTINCTION

Once an independent and formidable race, the Andamanese are now a sickly people dependent on the Government of India. Contact with civilization has proved disastrous to the aborigines, introducing diseases which have decimated them. The Government's one effort now is to keep alive such as remain and save the race from entire extinction

Photo, Sir Harry Johnston

LIGHT-HEARTED ABORIGINES ENJOYING DANCE AND SONG

Andamanese are devoted to dancing, in which they indulge for hours on end every night, besides on such ceremonial occasions as a meeting between tribes. Their dances consist in hopping on one foot and swinging the arms backwards and forwards to the time of a song kept up by one man, the women clapping their hands loudly and joining in the chorus

TRIPPING TOES KEEP TIME WITH STEADY TRAMPING FEET

Time for the dancers is often beaten on a dancing-board. This is a hollow piece of hard wood in the form of an ancient shield which is placed on the ground, hollow side downwards, and stamped on by one of the party who keeps it steady by placing a foot on the pointed end. Places are changed constantly during these performances

Photos, Commander W. A. Usher

India

II. The Tangled Skein of Its Age-Long Annals

By Sir Valentine Chirol

Author of "India Old and New," etc.

INDIA appears on a map of the world as only a small, lozenge-shaped projection from the huge continent of Asia. Shut off in the north from the rest of Asia by a natural barrier of difficult, and in many places impassable, mountain ranges, it stretches down between two seas into the Southern Ocean just north of the Equator, almost equidistant at its southernmost point from South Africa to the west and from Australia to the east.

Within an area of 1,802,657 square miles—not one twenty-fifth part of the land surface of the earth—it has a population of 320,000,000, or about one-fifth of the total population of the world and nearly three-quarters of the total population of the British Empire of which it forms part. To put it in another form, its population is about equal to that of the whole of Europe without Russia, about seven times that of Great Britain and Ireland, about forty times that of Canada, over fifty times that of the South African Union, and over sixty times that of Australia.

Its climate ranges from Alpine to tropical. Its natural resources are immense and varied, both above and beneath the surface of the earth; minerals and forests, pasture and agriculture. Its peoples, often very highly gifted, belong to many different races and creeds and complexions, and speak many absolutely different languages, and while they are for the most part in different and widely remote stages of social evolution, the vast majority share in a more or less highly developed form a peculiar civilization which reaches back to prehistoric times, and only a small but very influential minority have been brought in the last century into close contact and communion with Western civilization.

Physical Conformation of India

Geography is the key to history. In India, as in all other countries, the physical and climatic conditions govern in a great measure the beliefs and customs of the people and their social and political evolution—in India perhaps even more than elsewhere.

The Indian peninsula, in itself a sub-continent, with a coast-line of over 3,000 miles altogether, but without a single fine natural harbour suited to modern requirements, can be divided physically into three distinct zones : the Alpine or Himalayan

highlands, the great plains of Upper India fed by the Himalayan rivers, and the broken tableland of Central and Southern India, fed by its own river system.

The Himalayas, which separate India from Central Asia, are the highest mountains in the world. The loftiest peaks are roughly, about twice the height of the European Alps, and several thousand feet higher than the Andes, in South America.

It is from the eternal snows and the vast glacier fields of the northern and central Himalayas that descend the two great rivers and their almost equally great tributaries which irrigate, directly or through an elaborate system of irrigation canals, the immense plains of Upper India, formed of the silt deposited by them through countless ages.

River Systems of the Peninsula

The Indus is about 1,800 miles in length from its sources in Tibet on the northern face of the Himalayas down to the Delta through which its waters are discharged into the Western or Arabian Sea, a little south of Karachi. Its chief tributaries, the Jhelum, the Chenab, the Ravi, and the Sutlej, form with it the "Five Waters" from which the Punjab takes its name. The Ganges, though it falls short of the Indus in mere length—1,550 miles—is the greatest and ranks as the most sacred river of India, and with the Brahmaputra at last finds its way into the Bay of Bengal, either down the main waterbed, in places ten miles broad, or through innumerable minor channels intersecting the Gangetic Delta. In the great alluvial plains traversed and indeed formed by the Ganges are to be found the densest agricultural population and many of the great historic cities of India old and new.

In remote geological ages the whole of this Upper Indian basin of the Indus and the Ganges was at the bottom of the sea, and the tableland to the south of it was connected with the African Continent—a connexion of which traces survive to-day only in the few groups of islands such as the Laccadive and the Maldive, that still break the vast expanse of the Indian Ocean—and formed with it the great Gondwana Continent that has long since ceased to exist.

. The tableland, commonly known as the Deccan, which extends southwards of the great alluvial plains, still recalls visibly one of the great periods of convulsive travail through which the earth passed when, as can still be seen to-day, great masses of basaltic lava flowed in molten sheets over the country.

Diversity of Climatic Conditions

This portion of the Indian peninsula has its own system of mountains and rivers, far inferior in magnitude to the Himalayan system, but not less important in the influence which it has exercised on the ethnical and historical development of India. A dividing line is the Narbada river, flowing in a deep trough formed by the parallel ranges of the Vindhya and Satpura Hills. Farther south begins the great range known as the Western Ghats, which rises like a steep staircase (ghat) out of a generally narrow, intervening strip of foreshore from just north of Bombay down the Malabar Coast to the southernmost point of the peninsula at Cape Comorin and then curves back to form a similar but lesser range known as the Eastern Ghats above the Coromandel Coast.

The result of this formation is that the greater part of Central and Southern India consists of a broken plateau tilted down to the east from the crest of the western sea-wall. The Godavari, the Kistna, the Cauvery, to name only the most important rivers, all rise in the Western Ghats almost within sight of the Arabian Sea, but all flow down to the eastern coast of the tapering peninsula.

As diversified as its geological formation is the climate of a sub-continent which nearly touches at the extreme north the thirty-eighth degree of latitude, almost on a line with Yokohama, San Francisco, and Lisbon, and extends in the extreme south to just within eight degrees north of the Equator. It owes, however, its chief climatic variations not so much to the accident of latitude as to the remote forces of nature that govern its rainfall.

Prosperity Dependent on the Monsoon

The one wet season, without which the greater part of India would be a barren desert depends upon the south-western monsoon—the inflow of the great south-west trade winds, which are generated in Central Africa and drawn towards the Asiatic continent by the high-pressure belt prevailing in the winter months over Central Asia and North-East China. Absorbing on their way the moisture of a vast ocean expanse, they discharge it freely when they approach the Indian peninsula, dividing into two main currents that beat respectively on its western and eastern coast lines.

On the western coast the monsoon breaks against the solid and precipitous wall of the Western Ghats, exhausting a great part of its precious energies before

it has surmounted that barrier and can spread itself over more distant inland regions.

Along the eastern coast of India, where the monsoon is not so abruptly arrested, it distributes its moisture less unevenly over larger areas until it is held up in the gigantic cul-de-sac formed at the foot of the eastern Himalayas where the heaviest annual rainfall probably in the whole world occurs, measuring some 1,200 inches.

The average but very unequal rainfall for the whole of India is estimated at about 45 inches, and of that rainfall 90 per cent. is discharged during the three months of the south-west monsoon. . If this monsoon, uneven as is its distribution of moisture, were only constant and regular, India would have little to complain of, but in some years it is disastrously weak or unduly late or abnormally short in its duration, and then scarcity and famine with sickness in their wake afflict large areas which no system of irrigation can reach.

Monstrous Fauna of Prehistoric Times

The hot weather, in which the shade temperature over a large part of Upper India rises to between 120° and 130° in the daytime and for weeks falls very little lower even during the night, corresponds with the dry season par excellence, March, April, May, and early June, before the monsoon bursts. During all these months the sun pours down pitilessly from the deep blue vault of heaven. Then for a few days huge storm clouds begin to tower above the south-western horizon, dispersing at first into space, but ultimately discharging, amidst an almost continuous crash of thunder and lightning, an incredible volume of torrential rain upon the arid, sun-scorched earth, with the promise at last of some revivifying coolth to man and beast.

Before there was any navigation across the seas the Indian continent was practically closed against the rest of the world, except along its largely impassable northern frontier. As to the beginnings of the human race in India there is more conjecture than knowledge, but what we do know is that south of the great basin of the Indus and the Ganges, which can have had no attraction for man until he had learnt to till the soil, primitive races grew up in the wild jungle and mountain fastnesses who gradually asserted their right to existence against many formidable types of animal life of which only a few representatives have survived to the present day.

Of elephants, which are now tamed to play a majestic part in Indian State pageants or for other humbler and more utilitarian purposes, seventeen different types which existed in those remote ages are now virtually extinct. Tigers which the big game hunter has to track down to-day to their infrequent lairs, lions that have disappeared except in the wild districts of Kathiawar, leopards and panthers were as common as the huge herds of deer and antelope on which they preyed.

The crocodile, that may still be seen stretching twenty or thirty feet of scaled armour on the sandbanks of the lower Ganges, is almost the only survivor now of all the amphibious monsters that once peopled most of the Indian streams and swamps. Even more ubiquitous then than now was the whole venomous tribe of snakes and vipers that still help substantially to swell the Indian death-roll.

Through slow stages of evolution the dark-skinned races whom we call Dravidian gradually won through and spread northwards to the plains of Upper India in order to gather there the more abundant fruits of the earth which they had learnt to cultivate. Into those plains also descended in unknown prehistoric times tribes of Mongolian origin, and, somewhere between 2500 and 1500 B.C., other waves of migration from the vast reservoir of the

human race in Central Asia, representing already a higher type of civilization, with a much fairer complexion, flowed down into India through the easier passes and more open country stretching from the main Himalayan range towards the Arabian Sea. These were the tribes of various origin to whom the generic name of Aryan has been applied, and whose fusion with the earlier and probably indigenous population of India produced the Indian civilization of historic times.

Not till about the sixth century B.C. does India emerge into history, and only modern research has succeeded in unravelling to some extent the tangled skein of her annals for the next thousand years and more. In few countries of such great antiquity has so little of the work of man's hands survived to help the historian. We should, indeed, know nothing of the Indian civilization evolved during the ten, or perhaps twenty, centuries which elapsed between the great Aryan inflow into India and the actual beginning of Indian historic times were it not for the mass of more or less sacred literature in which later generations embodied oral traditions in divers forms, and so enabled us to

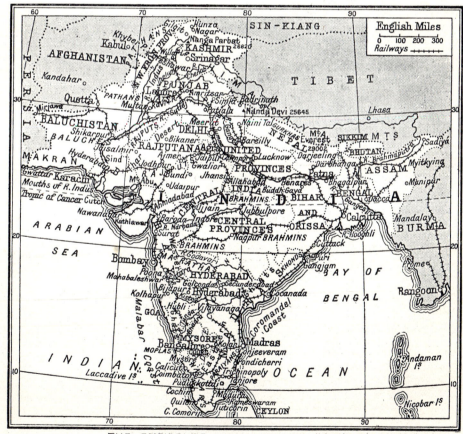

THE EMPIRE OF INDIA AND ITS PEOPLES

reconstitute a fairly faithful picture of the religious and social, and even political, conditions of that remote period which still largely shape Indian life to-day.

Out of the earliest worship of the forces of nature portrayed in the Vedic hymns at a time when the leaders of the Aryan tribes were warriors and bards, there grew up a vast religious system compounded of

DEVOTION'S EVERY GRACE DISPLAYED

With her bell to call the attention of the god and offerings spread before her, the pious Hindu woman squats on her carpet laid at the foot of the temple steps and tells over and over again the names of the gods as she slips her rosary beads through her fingers

Photo, Miss M. N. Tuck

polytheism and pantheism and abstruse philosophical speculations with which was linked up a still more unique social system.

Of the innumerable deities that people the Hindu Pantheon, Brahma was originally, perhaps, the one Supreme Being, but so supremely vague that there is only one temple to him now in the whole of India. Vishnu, the Preserver, is credited with ten different avatars or incarnations. Siva, the terrific Destroyer, is also the Creator. Indra is the national god of the Aryans; Rama and Krishna are the deified heroes of the later myths. Other favourites are Ganesh, the elephant-headed; Hanuman, the monkey-god; Lakhshmi, the consort of Vishnu and goddess of

prosperity; Kali, otherwise Durga, the consort of Siva, and no less terrific; Sita, the consort of Rama.

These, and the countless other gods and goddesses, local and tribal and vocational, beneficent or maleficent, sometimes merely sacred streams and trees and stones, have waxed and waned and gained and lost worshippers and undergone many strange transformations, while different schools of philosophy have in turn sought to probe the deeper mysteries of life and death, and to interpret for the elect the esoteric meaning of crude beliefs good enough for the vulgar masses. But far more enduring, far more universal than the popularity of deities or the teachings of philosophers, has been the hold upon countless generations of Hindus of the social system of Hinduism.

The keystone of that system is the unique institution of caste, and the ancient Sanskrit word "varna," which means colour, gives the clue to its origin and purpose. The Aryans who built up Hinduism were of a much lighter complexion than the earlier population with whom they came into contact. Compared with these, they were, in fact, in India the "white race" of those prehistoric ages in which they poured down into India and imposed their domination upon the darker and more primitive races by their superior civilization even more than by their superior equipment and skill in arms.

Supreme among them was the Aryan Brahmin who had the monopoly of religious lore and acted as the sacrificial intermediary between gods and man. He was the trusted adviser of kings, and the real power behind the throne, and he was also the law-giver.

To give a divine sanction to the institution of caste, it was taught that that of the Brahmins or priests, though they were not always or necessarily discharging what we should call the functions of priests, proceeded in the beginning of things from the brain of the supreme creator, Brahma; that the Kshatryas, or warrior caste, proceeded from his shoulders; that the Vaishyas, or caste of traders, including writers and medicine men, proceeded from his thighs; and that, far beneath these three, the Sudras, or the serving caste, proceeded from the deity's feet.

To the Brahmin, therefore, belonged the right to lay down for every Hindu the laws that prescribe how he shall be ushered into the world, what he shall eat and wear and do, with whom he shall sit at meals and have social intercourse, what manner of woman he shall marry, what his funeral rites are to be, and how his inheritance shall be disposed of.

In the course of time, each of the four great castes has been subdivided into innumerable sub-castes and septs, each with its own rigid rules, always under Brahmin supervision as to permissible food and dress and marriage and employment. Caste law has thus shut off all the component parts of Hindu society into a multitude of watertight compartments from which, strictly speaking, none can emerge in this life.

Even after death the Hindu has not done with caste. The most deep-rooted Hindu belief is the transmigration of souls, death signifying merely the re-birth of the soul into a new shape determined by its merits or demerits in the shape which it has just put off. That re-birth may be into the same, or into a higher or a lower caste, or even into some degraded human form outside the pale of the four recognized castes; or, worse still, into the yet more degraded shape of beast or bird or reptile.

Hence, for every Hindu the importance of early marriage, often contracted between mere infants, lest he should die childless with none to safeguard his re-birth. Hence, too, the inferior status of the Hindu woman, whose supreme function in life is to provide the indispensable son.

Besides the chief divisions of the four great Hindu castes which have split up, in the course of ages, all over India into innumerable minor sub-divisions, often due to differences of language, or to racial peculiarities, or to specialisation in trades or industries, or in various forms of manual labour, there remain, especially in Southern India and in the more remote parts of Central and North-Eastern India, many extremely primitive people whom the Hindu Aryan conquerors never displaced or assimilated, and who still lie beyond the pale of Hinduism.

Officially lumped together under one denomination as "the fifth caste," they are in reality of no caste, and as

SCORES OF COOLIES TOILING AT A JOB FOR A SINGLE CRANE

Machinery has by no means entirely replaced man-power in India, as may be seen from this photograph of a gang of " Bundanis " carrying a stone beam up to the top of a building in process of construction in Gwalior. As many as a hundred and twenty-eight men have been known to be harnessed to a single beam, the latter being slung by ropes from poles borne on the men's shoulders

Photo, H. S. Talbot

KEEN EYES FOR ANYTHING IN THE WAY OF A BARGAIN

Himalayan hillmen, they hawk native products among European visitors in Darjeeling. The elder
man has a couple of kukris under his arm—knives used for every purpose by the hill-tribes—and his
tunic very likely contains some cases of butterflies and a puppy or two. His companion is offering
one of the beautifully striped cotton cloths worn by the Lepchas and a Tibetan praying-wheel

Photo, the Rev. J. H. Powell

such, from the Hindu point of view, at the very bottom of the social ladder— " untouchable," because contact with them defiles a Hindu who belongs to a recognized caste, and consequently, subject to all manner of humiliating disabilities.

The laws of caste, which still to a great extent govern Hindu society to-day, though, in many non-essentials, and more rarely in essentials, they have yielded something to the exigencies of modern conditions of life or to the inroads of Western education, had not reached their full development at the time when India emerges for us from the twilight of legendary ages.

But the Aryan peoples had gradually passed, after many vicissitudes of peace and war, out of the primitive conditions of nomadic and pastoral life into the more settled stage of agricultural life, and separate polities had grown up under separate rulers with towns and cities in which artisans and all skilled craftsmen congregated, called into being by the expanding requirements of more settled forms of society. In 600 B.C. the most powerful states of which there is then for the first time some historical record, as might be expected, in the rich Gangetic plain.

Buddha's Challenge to Hinduism

It is one of the peculiarities of Hinduism that its origin cannot be associated with any single great teacher or prophet. It has no Moses and no Christ, no Confucius and no Mahomet, but it produced in the sixth century B.C. a great rebel known as Buddha, whose gospel was to dethrone Hinduism for a time over the greater part of India.

Buddhism, as preached by Buddha himself, was an appeal directed to all classes and to both sexes, and, as such, a direct challenge to Hinduism, with its rigid hierarchy of caste and the inferiority to which it relegated all women within its pale who failed to fulfil the functions assigned to them for the preservation of the continuity of caste.

The conflict between Buddhism, with the larger outlook on mankind which helped it to spread ultimately far beyond the confines of India, and Hinduism, with its narrower conception of human society limited to an Indo-Aryan nationhood, fills the pages of Indian history for a thousand years after Buddha.

One brief irruption of Europe into India occurred in the fourth century B.C., when Alexander the Great pushed his conquests through the northern passes down to the banks of the Indus. But so slight was the impression made by this wonderful episode on the life of India as a whole that no mention is made of it by a single Indian writer.

Of the few landmarks to guide us through the obscure maze of ancient Indian history, the most striking is the reign of the great Apostle-Emperor Asoka, in the middle of the third century B.C. He was fortunate enough to inherit a powerful state from his father and grandfather, and in the fourteenth year of his reign he became a Buddhist, and, forswearing war, resolved to apply the teachings of Buddha to the governance of his people.

Kanishka & Hinduism's Golden Age

Some of the laws which he then gave may be read to the present day carved into granite pillars and into the face of the living rock in many parts of India. No temporal sovereign has ever proclaimed himself as he did, a convinced prince of peace, or legislated so fully and exclusively for the spiritual and moral advancement of his people.

Before Asoka died, about 231 B.C., he had raised Buddhism to a position of supremacy in India which may well be compared with that of Christianity in Europe under Constantine. But with him the great Mauryian dynasty had spent itself, and Asoka's life-work fell to pieces almost as soon as he had passed away.

Buddhism henceforth succumbed slowly, and after a long period of obscurity, only for a short time broken by Kanishka in the extreme north, the next great landmark to emerge is the Gupta Empire, in the fourth or fifth centuries of our era, with which the Hindus still associate the " Golden Age " of India. It was certainly the golden age of Hinduism, and assured its final triumph over Buddhism when Vikramaditya, the Sun of Power, known in popular legend as Raja Bikram, held his court at Ujjain, a most ancient and sacred city of Central India, which became the centre of a great revival of Sanskrit, the language of the Hindu Scriptures.

Revival of Sanskrit Literature

Tradition has grouped round Rajah Bikram " the nine gems " of Sanskrit literature. Many of the oral traditions of Hinduism were reduced to writing; poetry was adapted to both sacred and profane uses, and astronomy and astrology, logic and philosophy were all cultivated by learned Brahmins to the greater glory of the system with which their ascendancy was bound up.

But the Gupta dynasty lived little longer than the greatest of its predecessors, and only after the long reign of terror which India endured during the invasion of the White Huns under Mihiragula, who was to India what Attila, at the head of another great horde of Hunnish invaders, had been to Europe a century before, does another great figure hold the stage for forty years (606-648)—King Harsha, who reduced to subjection almost the whole of Northern India from the Arabian Sea to the Bay of Bengal before he was twenty and paid at last solemn tribute to the departed glory of Buddhism.

Irruption of the Mahomedan Flood

Shortly after Harsha's death India relapsed once more into political chaos, and among glimpses that we get of successive kingdoms rising and falling in ceaseless rivalry, the most notable features are the steady penetration of Aryan influences into the Dravidian south, and the appearance of the Rajputs in Central and North-Western India. Around their origin have been woven epic legends, tracing back their pedigrees to sun and moon, and justified to the popular mind by their warlike prowess and fine chivalry; but fierce clan jealousies kept them divided, and no single state or federation of states existed in India capable of meeting the storm that was about to break upon her from the north.

Already in King Harsha's time Arab followers of the Prophet had crossed the sea from Arabia, the cradle of Islam, and got a foothold in Sind, in the remote north-west corner of the Indian peninsula. In the year 1001 the Mahomedan flood for the first time poured down into India from Central Asia through the northern passes, and in successive waves of increasing volume and force swept over the whole of India except the extreme south.

After a succession of at first merely devastating raids, the Mahomedan conquerors were firmly established at Delhi at the beginning of the thirteenth century. One ruler displaced another. Afghan, Turki, and Tartar dynasties rose and fell in a long-drawn sequence of cruelty and depravity; but all in turn knew how to strengthen and extend the power and glory of Islam, to which many splendid monuments reared by their hands still bear ample testimony.

Glory of the Mogul Empire

The irruption of Tamerlane, or Timur, and his Tartar horsemen, as meteoric as that of Alexander, but, unlike his, leaving behind it a fiery trail of savage destruction and bloodshed, shook the supremacy of Delhi and plunged all Northern India into a welter of anarchy in the closing years of the fourteenth century. But it did not arrest the progress of Islam.

While for another century Mahomedan soldiers of fortune carved out for themselves as they willed new kingdoms in which each enjoyed his brief period of magnificence, recalling in some ways the best and the worst of the Italian Renaissance in the same age, it was not till the middle of the sixteenth century that the great Emperor Akbar consummated the conquest of Hindustan undertaken by his grandfather, Baber, and gave to Mahomedan domination that stability and efficient centralization to which the Mogul Empire owes its great place in history.

Akbar attempted even the still more difficult task of welding India into a nation. He succeeded to some extent in composing the social differences between the Mahomedan conquerors and the conquered Hindus. He employed Hindus as his generals and ministers, and he sought matrimonial alliances with the most illustrious Rajput houses. But when he tried to achieve a religious fusion between Hinduism and Islam by founding an eclectic creed which was to make him head of the Church as well as of the State, even his genius failed.

Yet even before the foundations of the Mogul Empire were laid another and yet greater power was knocking, no longer at the land gates, but at the water gates of India. It came by sea from Europe. The Portuguese Vasco Da Gama had discovered the Cape route to India, and in 1502 established the first European settlement in India on the coast of Malabar.

Arrival of the " Merchant Venturers "

The conquest of Constantinople by the Turks, and the barrier established by the growth of powerful Mahomedan states against the old overland routes, over which Europe had maintained difficult but lucrative intercourse with the Orient, had driven Christendom to explore the uncharted ocean for new lines of communication. The Portuguese were the pioneers, and the Dutch and many others followed in their wake, among them the English, who were to outstay all their rivals.

In the year 1600, when Akbar's splendid reign was drawing to a close, one of the last acts of his great contemporary, the English Queen Elizabeth, granted to a group of London " merchant-venturers " a charter under which the East India Company rose to be the ruling power in India, and laid the foundations of the British Indian Empire.

The isolation of India from Europe, unbroken for nearly 2,000 years after Alexander's short-lived invasion, was at an end. The ocean ceased to be an insurmountable barrier to intercourse, and served, on the contrary, as a highway to promote it.

Unlike the great invaders from the north, who came to conquer, the English first appeared and settled on the far-flung shores of India as peaceful traders.

It was as suppliants for imperial favour and protection that the first embassy from the East India Company approached the Mogul throne at Delhi, and for 150 years the instructions laid down by the directors of the East India Company in London for the guidance of their agents in India imposed upon them complete abstention from any political interference in Indian internal affairs, and, above all, from warlike operations, which they regarded as incompatible with, and, indeed, ruinous to, their sole and only purpose, namely, the development of their lucrative trade with India.

From that policy they were ultimately forced to depart when the disintegration

at Plassey in 1757, made England the dominant power in a continent which, with the disruption of the Mogul Empire, was rapidly relapsing, as so often before, into anarchy. Two years later the grant of the Diwani to the East India Company by the titular Emperor of Delhi conferred for the first time upon a great trading corporation full rights of rulership over the wealthiest provinces of India—Bengal, Bihar, and Orissa. Until then the problems of administration had been relatively simple.

Very different became the position of the company as soon as it acquired actual

PAPIER MÂCHÉ MERCHANT AT HIS ACCOUNTS

Pressing and moulding pulped paper is an art that has long been practised in the East, Kashmir being especially celebrated for the production of artistic pen-tray work, small coloured boxes, and other fancy work. Swedish wood-pulp and waste paper are commonly used for the manufacture of the material, and the finished articles, such as are displayed here, are often noticeably intricate

Photo, Bourne & Shepherd

of the Mogul Empire, under Akbar's less worthy successors, began to plunge India into internal anarchy, and in the course of the great duel for sea-power between France and England which filled the eighteenth century, and was only terminated in favour of the English by the crowning victory of Trafalgar in 1805, the Indian Ocean and a great part of the Indian peninsula became one of the chief theatres of war between the two great European Powers.

The battle of Baxar, in 1764, even more decisive than Clive's great victory

dominion over large and wealthy tracts of country with a great indigenous population. At first it showed no clear perception of the duties involved in the exercise of its new rights, which were mainly applied to the amassing of wealth by the same means and through the same agencies as their native predecessors.

Grave injustice was often done to Clive, and still more to his great successor, Warren Hastings, in the wholesale denunciation of oppression and misgovernment in India with which Fox and Burke made, not only the House of

Commons, but the whole country, ring. For both Clive and Warren Hastings were no less conscious than Fox and Burke of the fearful shortcomings of a system which they had not created, but inherited, and of the need of drastic reforms, and it was indeed Warren Hastings who chiefly laid the foundations of the British Raj on a basis of justice and integrity and efficiency not unworthy of Britain's new destinies in India in cooperation with the best elements among the native population.

Parliamentary Control of the Company

What was, however, perfectly sound in the general attitude assumed by the British people towards Indian affairs was the instinctive recognition that the novel responsibilities assumed by the East India Company as rulers in India were greater than a trading corporation could safely be left to discharge uncontrolled, and that they must at least be shared by the State if the acquisition of vast and populous possessions was to redound to its honour as well as to its material prosperity.

Lord North's Regulating Act of 1773 was the first of the long series of enactments in which Parliament steadily asserted its authority over the East India Company and its agents in India until the Crown assumed direct sovereignty in 1858. Pitt's much more famous Government of India Act of 1784 placed the company itself under the effective control of the Crown by the establishment in London of a Board of Control over the Courts of Directors and Proprietors, of which the President was ultimately to develop into the Secretary of State for India. Henceforth, too, the renewal of the company's charter at intervals of twenty years was to afford an opportunity for revising from time to time both its relations to the Crown and its methods of government in India.

Rapid Expansion of British Dominion

British dominion in India meanwhile continued to expand with a rapidity which often outran the desires and the judgement of the agents of the company on the spot, and of British ministers at home. It expanded in obedience to the law which inevitably compels higher organisms to absorb lower ones. Outside the limits of British dominion the welter of confusion and strife continued to increase, and the only remedy was an extension of British authority, either in self-defence or quite as often in response to appeals from Indian populations or rulers, who were driven by their own necessities to seek protection under the one power capable of maintaining law and order. Thus the map of India assumed, partly by the direct annexation of large tracts of territory and partly by treaties with native rulers, the shape which it wears to-day.

Roughly, less than two-thirds of the total area of the Indian Empire with, however, more than three-quarters of the whole population, constitute British India under direct administration by the Government of India. The remainder consists of native states, numbering over six hundred, great and small, scattered over nearly the whole length and breadth of the continent, which continue to enjoy a large but varying measure of administrative autonomy under their own dynastic rulers.

Some of these native states compare in size and wealth with the smaller States of Europe; some only measure a few square miles with a few thousand inhabitants. Their relations with the paramount British power have been not inaptly described as relations of subordinate alliance, based upon treaties and engagements not altogether uniform, but all having this in common—namely, that the ruling chiefs and princes bind themselves to entertain no relations with any other but the paramount power, while the paramount power guarantees in perpetuity their special rights and privileges, subject to their loyalty to the British Crown and to reasonably good government.

Natives Admitted into Government

In British India every revision of the company's charter showed a great stride forward. In 1813 the company surrendered its trading monopoly as a first step towards the abrogation, twenty years later, of all its trading privileges. Then, finally rescued from the temptations which beset a commercial corporation, it was set free to devote itself as a mere instrument of government to the discharge of its immense responsibilities in a new spirit of trusteeship towards the vast population, alien in race and creed and social customs, committed to its care.

It was under the impulse of the great democratic movement which had brought the first British Parliament under the Reform Bill into being at Westminster that the company's charter was renewed in 1833, and gave a wide extension to a principle of policy which had never been formally enunciated before, though it had been tentatively carried into practice long before that date.

Indians had been employed in steadily increasing numbers in the company's service, and Warren Hastings had been the first to recognize the importance of promoting Indian education. But that Indians had any right to a share in the administration and government of their country had never yet been recognized, and the failure to recognize it was becoming a grievance which Parliament now for the first time admitted to be legitimate.

A Parliamentary Committee reported that their exclusion from a larger share in the executive government was not warranted on the score of their own incapacity for business or want of application or trustworthiness. Accordingly, when the charter was renewed, Parliament declared that " no native of the said Indian territories, nor any natural British-born subject of his Majesty resident therein, shall by reason only of his religion, place of birth, descent, colour, or any of them, be disabled from holding any place, office, or employment under the company."

The inevitable corollary of that declaration was the introduction of Western education into India, for which Macaulay pleaded successfully in his famous Minute of March, 1835. Indians could only be equipped for a larger share in the government of their own country by admitting them to full partnership in Western knowledge.

Effects of Western Education

Of the tremendous consequences which were to follow many Englishmen were doubtless only dimly conscious at the time, and even to-day there are many who seem unable to appreciate them. Some, however, of the greatest British administrators in India had a clearer vision. Sir Thomas Munro had already drawn up in 1824 a remarkable official Minute, in which he arrived at the conclusion that " if we pursue steadily the proper measures we shall in time so far improve the character of our Indian subjects as to enable them to govern and protect themselves."

India seemed at first to respond enthusiastically to the new call. Modern schools and colleges sprang up in all the great centres, partly under the impulse of Western missionaries and partly under the aegis of the State. Calcutta took the lead. Not a few high-caste Brahmins actually embraced Christianity, while others started religious movements to purge Hinduism of its grosser superstitions and bring Hindu philosophy into line with the best ideals of Western thought.

Except for an ill-starred war in Afghanistan and for the conquest of the Punjab, which was reluctantly carried out in order to break the aggressive power of the Sikh Confederacy, the two decades which followed the revision of the company's charter in 1833 were a period of peace and progress.

Lord Dalhousie, the last Governor-General to complete his term of service under the East India Company, regarded the introduction into India of the two great discoveries of applied science, which were just beginning to revolutionise the Western world—namely, railways and the telegraph, together with a unified postage —as instruments of progress no less potent than the universities about to be created or the extension of education to Indian women, then for the first time warmly advocated. But events were soon to show that he, like many other great Englishmen, had underrated the deep-seated forces of indigenous resistance which the rapid and forceful impact of the dynamic energies of the West was bound to provoke.

Horrors of the Indian Mutiny

Within a year of his departure from India his immediate successor, Lord Canning, was to witness the dire fulfilment of the strangely prophetic words uttered by him as he was leaving England : " I wish for a peaceful term of office. But I cannot forget that in the sky of India, serene as it is, a small cloud may arise. no larger than a man's hand, but which, growing larger and larger, may at last threaten to burst and overwhelm us with ruin."

After some faint preliminary rumblings the storm burst on May 10, 1857, when some native regiments mutinied and killed their officers in Meerut, and thence marched on Delhi and proclaimed as Emperor of Hindustan the feeble descendant of the Moguls who had been allowed to retain as king the outward trappings of sovereignty. The Mutiny spread by the end of the month to Lucknow, and the massacre of men, women, and children at Cawnpore after the surrender of the garrison on June 28 sent a thrill of horror throughout the world.

Forces of Reaction Over-Estimated

The struggle centred, however, on Delhi, where a small force of British and of loyal Indian troops kept the flag flying on the historic Ridge until reinforcements, chiefly from the Punjab, enabled Nicholson to storm the great walled city in September, paying with his own life the price of victory. The final relief of Lucknow was only achieved in March, 1858, and another year elapsed before the last embers of rebellion were stamped out. But from beginning to end the trouble was confined within a relatively small part of Upper and Central India.

A large part of the native army remained true to its salt ; no native state broke away from its allegiance ; the Mutiny remained a military movement and ostensibly a Mahomedan movement, though many Hindu regiments were as prompt to mutiny, and the brains of the movement were Hindu rather than Mahomedan. Such men as Nana Sahib and Tantia Topee relied upon the support of all the reactionary forces, Hindu as well as Mahomedan, and of all the personal enmities and selfish fears of vested interests among men of all classes and castes which the clash of Western civilization with the static civilization of India had inevitably provoked. But they relied upon them in vain.

Enhanced Prestige of the British Raj

The British Raj emerged from the struggle with increased prestige and authority, and if the East India Company disappeared it was only to make room for a closer and more visible association of India with the British Crown. The change was, however, one of form rather than of substance.

For the system of Indian Government remained, as before, one of paternal despotism to be tempered still by the control of Parliament. The Secretary of State for India in Council took the place of the old President of the Board of Control, and the Governor-General came to be designated as Viceroy. Twenty years later Queen Victoria assumed the title of Empress of India.

The Indian army was reorganized. It was never again allowed to have any artillery, and into the structure of the whole army, as well as into individual infantry and cavalry regiments, a more careful balance was introduced between different races and creeds.

No attempt was made to provide Indians with higher military education, or to fit them for promotion to the higher ranks of the army. Not only were all the higher executive and administrative posts in the army reserved for Europeans, but the British officers of native regiments, even to the youngest subaltern from home, held a superior rank to, and exercised unquestioned authority over, all the native regimental officers, who were in fact little more than glorified non-commissioned officers.

Material Development of the Country

How well the system worked on the whole in spite of its obvious limitations has been shown repeatedly in the close and gallant cooperation of the Indian and British armies in Egypt and the Sudan, in Afghanistan, China, and Tibet, and in the chronic frontier fighting on the turbulent north-west border, and last of all, on the battle-fields of France.

The one profound and deplorable change effected by the Mutiny was in the spirit that crept over the relations between the two races. Neither could bring itself entirely to forget the appalling excesses perpetrated on the one side and the stern repression practised on the other. The vision entertained by earlier British administrators of an India moving steadily on the lines of Western education and progress and equipped by Western education to govern and protect herself was indefinitely blurred.

With the growth of a great European bureaucracy required for the steady expansion of every branch of the administration to meet modern demands of efficiency, there was a tendency to concentrate on the material development of India. Roads and railways, posts and telegraphs, irrigation and other public works were pushed forward systematically, while education, though by no means neglected, was conducted somewhat mechanically and with an eye rather to quantity than quality of output.

The Indian demand for education never slackened, but its chief results were looked for in the examination rooms. In a curriculum from which the principle of religious neutrality scrupulously observed by the State excluded all influence on religious and moral training there was little scope for the formation of character.

Beginning of the Nationalist Movement

Few and reluctant were the attempts made to further Indian political education, or even to give Indians that larger share in the executive government of their country to which more than half a century earlier Parliament had recognized the legitimacy of their claim. Meanwhile, the actual number of Indians who had qualified or believed themselves to have qualified in British schools and colleges for employment in the public services was increasing steadily. Discontent increased equally steadily with disappointed expectations.

Racial feeling, which the Mutiny itself had done much to revive, received a fresh stimulus when in 1883, under Lord Ripon's Viceroyalty, a violent agitation among the European population in India, official and unofficial, proved powerful enough to defeat the intentions of a Viceroy known to be friendly to the Indian and the fate of the Ilbert Bill taught Indians the value of political agitation.

The immediate consequence was the foundation of the Indian National Congress in 1885 by a small group of educated Indians, many of whom had learned in England the lessons of English civic and political life, which they believed to be as essential to Indians as to Englishmen. But frowned on by the official world, it gradually assumed the airs of an irreconcilable Indian Parliament, in which a new school of extremist politicians ultimately ceased to disguise their hostility, not only to alien rule, but to many of the Western ideals for which the British Raj stood.

In the first years of the nineteenth century the prolonged and often successful resistance of two small South African Republics to the armed might of the British Empire, and the emergence of Japan as an Asiatic State capable of challenging and defeating a great European Power, had not only shaken the Indian's belief in the invincible superiority of the West, but had stimulated the consciousness of an Indian nationhood underlying all the differences and rivalries of Indian races and creeds, to which the National Congress had for the first time lent an outward appearance of reality. The great apostles of this new Indian Nationalism, confined originally to the Hindus, were Marathas, chiefly Brahmins, and the intelligentsia of Bengal.

In 1905 an administrative measure for dividing up into two provinces the huge province of Bengal, with 70,000,000 inhabitants, which had outgrown the capacity of a single provincial Government, was interpreted as a blow aimed at the nationalist movement in one of its principal strongholds. Against this partition of Bengal a violent and quite unprecedented agitation broke out and spread to other parts of India, and rapidly assumed the shape of a general revolt against the autocratic and bureaucratic methods of Indian Government, in which reactionary and revolutionary elements seemed to have joined hands. It was accompanied by an epidemic of political crimes, largely modelled on the doctrines and practice of Russian anarchism.

Kingship and the Coronation Durbar

Mr. John Morley (later Lord Morley) brought to the India Office, on the return of the Liberal Party to power at home at the end of 1906, his old convictions as Irish Secretary that repression might be a remedy for active disorders, but was no sufficient remedy for discontent rooted in national sentiment. The Indian Reforms which he embodied in the Indian Councils Act of 1909 gave Indians for the first time a voice in the executive Government by admitting an Indian to be a member of the Government of India, and appointing Indians to sit on the Secretary of State's Council in London, and they introduced the elective principle into Indian representation in the Legislative Councils. Their powers, however, remained purely consultative, and he himself repudiated all idea of laying the foundations of responsible Parliamentary Government in a country still in his opinion entirely unsuited for them.

King Edward VII. had paid, as Prince of Wales, the first Royal visit to the greatest Eastern dependency of the British Crown. King George V., while Prince of Wales, followed his example in visiting India, with the Princess, in 1905, and though by that time the first great wave of political unrest had begun to sweep over the country, he was received with no less demonstrative loyalty than his father had been thirty years before.

In 1911 India had for the first time an opportunity of welcoming the reigning Sovereigns, and the welcome given to them often assumed all the fervour of semi-divine worship which the Indians have been wont to pay, from times immemorial, to the majesty of kingship. The transfer of the seat of British Government in India from Calcutta to Delhi, announced at the splendid Durbar held by their Majesties in that historic city, together with a sweeping modification, amounting almost to a reversal, of Lord Curzon's partition of Bengal, made a profound appeal to Indian imagination as a manifestation of sovereignty not unworthy of Indian traditions.

India's Part in the Great War

On the other hand, an attempt on the life of the Viceroy, Lord Hardinge of Penshurst, just a year later, when he was making his State entry into Delhi as the new capital in which he was to take up his residence, and the continuance of lawlessness among the youth of Bengal, showed that extremism had not died out, while the satisfaction at first created by Lord Morley's reforms made room for a sense of disappointment at the small results which they in effect yielded. The Western educated classes were once more agitating for a further instalment of political concessions when the Great War broke out in August, 1914.

The magnificent response at once made to the call of the Empire by the princes and peoples of India in all the native states, as well as in every province under direct British administration, was so loud and so genuine that the voice of faction and even of extremism was hushed. A great thrill of legitimate pride went through India when the Indian army was dispatched straight to France to fight shoulder to shoulder with the Allies, and the British Prime Minister, then Mr. Asquith, gave expression to the admiration and gratitude of the British people by assuring India that in future the problems of Indian government would be approached from " a new angle of vision."

Failure of German-hatched Disaffection

New schemes of constitutional reform were conceived, but unfortunately too slowly and laboriously to satisfy the tremendous expectations aroused in India, not only by Mr. Asquith's promise but by the reiterated proclamation of the generous war aims of the Allied Powers fighting for freedom throughout the world. German plots to raise the standard of rebellion in India failed ignominiously, and a few sporadic disturbances, and notably an outbreak in the Punjab engineered by disaffected Sikhs, who had returned from Canada saturated with racial hatred, were promptly quelled.

Extremist Clamour for Home Rule

A series of unfortunate reverses in Mesopotamia, which was the seat of operations nearest to India, and the many vicissitudes and indefinite prolongation of the war in Europe tended, however, to produce a certain reaction of lassitude, while the long delay in producing any definite scheme of Indian reforms provoked renewed impatience among the politically-minded classes. A cry was raised for immediate Home Rule, and the Indian National Congress came to the front again with an imperious programme which fell little short of Home Rule, and was supported just as insistently by the All-India Moslem League. The Indian Mahomedans, who number over 66 millions or about one-fifth of the total population, had originally taken no part in political agitation nor concealed their dread of Hindu ascendancy. But among them, too, there gradually grew up a new school that professed to subordinate considerations of creed to the higher call of Indian Nationalism. Even when Turkey came into the Great War against the Allies the loyalty of the vast majority of Indian Mahomedans remained unshaken, but among the extremists there was a group that had been in contact with " the Young Turks " before the war and hardly concealed its sympathies and hopes when the German Emperor, " the friend of Islam," provoked a world conflict with the British Empire. This group had dominated the Moslem League and brought it into line with the Indian National Congress, now also controlled by the extremists faction.

Effect of the Montagu-Chelmsford Report

It was at this juncture that Mr. Montagu, who had just become Secretary of State for India, made on August 20, 1917, simultaneously with the Viceroy, Lord Chelmsford, in Simla, the solemn announcement on behalf of his Majesty's Government that the purpose of British policy was not only " the increasing association of Indians in every branch of the administration, but also the greatest development of self-governing institutions with a view to the progressive realization of responsible government in India as an integral part of the British Empire."

This was a momentous announcement, even though accompanied by reservations as to manner and rate of progress.

The Secretary of State shortly afterwards proceeded to India, and there drew up in conjunction with the Viceroy the exhaustive State Paper known as the Montagu-Chelmsford Report, which served as a basis for the great constitutional changes embodied in the Government of India Act, 1919.

This Act, designed to provide the first stage in the advancement of India from the position of a mere Dependency governed on more or less despotic lines to the status of a self-governing Dominion within the Empire, left the authority of the Supreme Government theoretically intact, and only conferred in the Provincial Governments a real measure of responsibility upon Indian Ministers placed directly in charge of certain specified branches of administration. A new distribution of powers and responsibilities between Indians and Europeans was thus inaugurated, and this system came to be known as Dyarchy.

At the same time a new All-Indian Legislature, consisting of a Council of State and an Indian Legislative Assembly, and Provincial Legislative Councils were established with Indian unofficial majorities elected on as wide a suffrage as the backwardness of the great mass of the Indian people allowed. The new Indian Legislatures, together with the introduction of a considerable proportion of Indians into the executive Councils of Government, both at Delhi and in the provinces, and the progressive Indianisation of the public services have in fact given Indians a measure of influence, even in the shaping of public policy, which goes far beyond the statutory powers technically conferred upon them by the Act of 1919.

Progress Towards Dominion Independence

This great reform scheme has nevertheless failed to arrest the growth of Indian unrest, itself partly an outcome of the great wave of political and social and economic unrest which has swept over the whole world as a consequence of the Great War. Disturbances of a very serious character broke out in India and especially in the Punjab in the spring of 1919, and their stern repression, notably at Amritsar, together with vehement propaganda among Indian Mahomedans in favour of Turkey, of whose name they had hardly heard before the Crimean War, gave the extremists an opportunity for starting against the Government the Non-Cooperation movement, of which Mr. Gandhi, regarded by his followers as saint and prophet and inspired leader, became the fanatical apostle.

It led to frequent rioting and bloodshed, even during the Prince of Wales's progress through India. But it has not affected the steady purpose of British statesmanship, solemnly re-affirmed when, on Feb. 9, 1921, the Duke of Connaught inaugurated the new All-Indian Legislature at Delhi in the King-Emperor's name, with a royal message in which his Majesty declared to India that she now had " the beginnings of swaraj (self-government) within my Empire, and the widest scope and ample opportunity for progress to the liberty which my other Dominions enjoy."

INDIA : FACTS AND FIGURES

The Country

Central peninsula of Southern Asia, divided into British administrations or provinces (Madras, Bombay, Bengal, United Provinces of Agra and Oudh, Punjab, Burma, Bihar and Orissa, Central Provinces and Berar, Assam, Delhi, North-West Frontier Province, Ajmer-Merwara, Coorg, Baluchistan, Andaman and Nicobar Islands), and feudatory or allied States (Manipur, Hyderabad, Mysore, Baroda, Central India Agency, Kashmir, Sikkim, Gwalior, Rajputana Agency, North-West Frontier, and a number of others). Area of British provinces (including Burma) 1,093,074 square miles ; population (1921), 247,138,396 ; area of States and agencies, 709,555 square miles ; population (1921), 71,936,736. Total area (including Burma) 1,802,657 square miles ; total population, 320,000,000, or about 177 to the square mile. Many different races speaking upwards of fifty languages.

Government

The King of Great Britain and Ireland is Emperor of India. Administration in England is entrusted to a Secretary of State, assisted by Council of not less than eight and not more than twelve members, whom he appoints for five years, one half of their number being persons who have served or resided ten years in India not more than five years previous to appointment.

In India supreme executive authority is vested in Governor-General (or Viceroy) in Council appointed by Crown, usually for five years. Legislature includes Governor-General ; Council of not more than sixty members, of whom not more than twenty are officials, elected for five years ; and Legislative Assembly of 144 members, appointed for three years, of whom twenty-six are official members, and 103 elected. President of Legislative Assembly appointed by Governor-General.

The eleven departments of Government are in charge of Governor-General's Executive Council, at least three of whom must have had ten years' service in India, and one be a barrister or pleader of not less than ten years' standing. At head of each department, except that of railways, is a secretary to the Governor-General in Council. Foreign and Political department is under immediate superintendence of the Governor-General. The administrations are under governors, lieutenant-governors, chief commissioners, or agents.

Governments of Bengal, Madras, Bombay, Bihar and Orissa, United Provinces, Punjab, Central Provinces, and Assam are based on a system of dyarchy, consisting of Governor-in-Council, and governor acting with ministers. Governor's Executive Council consists of not more than four members, one qualified by twelve years' public service in India.

Legislative Council consists of at least seventy per cent. elected members, and no more than twenty per cent. of official members appointed for three years. Provinces are usually sub-divided into divisions under commissioners, and these into districts, controlled by an executive officer. The Indian States are governed by the Indian princes, ministers, or councils under the control of the Supreme Government.

Defence

Military forces consist of British Regular Forces, paid by the Indian Exchequer, and Native Army, Auxiliary Force, and Imperial Service Troops, raised and maintained by Native States. Royal Air Force in India consists of eight squadrons, commanded by an Air-Commodore.

Industries and Commerce

Between twenty and twenty-five per cent. of the total area is under cultivation, nearly 225 millions being supported by agriculture. State irrigation works supply about twenty-five million acres. Chief among the industries, which employ over 35 millions, are spinning and weaving, and the tea industry, about 345 million pounds of tea having been produced in 1920-21. Minerals include coal, gold, petroleum, manganese ore, and salt; among other industries are silk-rearing and weaving, shawl and carpet-weaving, wood-carving and metal-working. Imports (merchandise), 1920-21, Rs. 347,13,89,522 ; exports (merchandise), Rs. 265,93,47,563. Rupee Rs. 10 to the £ ; prior to September, 1920, the rupee was valued at 1s. 4d.

Communications

Length of roads maintained by public authorities, about 206,330 miles ; navigable canals, 3,190 miles ; railways, 37,030 miles, of which 26,650 miles are State lines, 7,550 miles being worked by the State ; telegraph lines, 369,270 miles ; the telephone system is in the hands of the Post and Telegraph Department.

Religion and Education

Of the total population of India over 217,000,000 are Hindus ; Mahomedans, 66,000,000 ; Buddhists, 11,000,000 ; Animists, 10,000,000 ; Christians, 4,000,000 ; Sikhs, 3,000,000 ; Jains, 1,000,000. Parsees and Jews form a large proportion of the remainder.

There are six federal universities in India ; three unitary teaching and residential, two denominational, and two universities in Indian States. There are also over 200 colleges with 66,000 scholars ; 164,000 institutions for general education, with over 7,000,000 scholars ; 4,000 special schools, and over 34,000 private institutions. A system of State scholarships enables boys to pass from village schools to the universities and to study in the United Kingdom for two years or more.

Chief Towns

Calcutta, old capital (1,263,300) ; Bombay (1,172,950), Madras (522,950), Hyderabad (404,225), Rangoon (339,525), Delhi, capital (303,148), Lahore (279,560), Ahmedabad (274,200), Lucknow (243,555), Bangalore (238,110), Karachi (215,780), Cawnpore (213,045), Benares (199,495), Agra (185,945), Poona (176,670), Amritsar (160,410), Allahabad (155,970), Nagpur (149,520), Mandalay (147,430), Srinagar (141,630), Madura (138,895), Bareilly (127,940). Meerut (122,570), Jaipur (120,195), Patna (120,110).

EVENING PROMENADE BY THE RIVER'S BRIM BELOW BAGDAD

Even the native population find the climate of Bagdad very trying, the heat being so great that they have to sleep on the roof at night and take shelter in the underground serdab, or ventilated cellar, by day. In the cool of the late afternoon the foreshore of the Tigris provides a welcome promenade, where mothers can stroll and children play under the palm trees

Photo, Major W. J. P. Rodd

Irak

I. Arab Life in the New Mesopotamian State

By Edmund Candler, C.B.E.

Author of " The Long Road to Baghdad "

THERE is probably less variety of scenery in Irak—or, to give it its old name, Mesopotamia—than in any other country of the same extent. Arabia, at least, has the Yemen range and the Jebel Akhdar, green and grassy slopes rising 9,900 feet behind Muscat, but Mesopotamia contains no green valleys and tablelands save in the ranges that form the glacis of Persia and Kurdistan to the east and north. To the west and south the boundaries are desert and sea, and in the country east of the Euphrates and south of Basra the illimitable monotony is repeated that is so wearisome to the eye on the journey up the Tigris from Basra to Bagdad.

On entering the country from the sea the palm belt on the Shat-el-Arab, stretching from the Gulf to a few miles north of Kurna, where the Tigris and Euphrates meet, gives an impression of tropical fertility. According to the Moslem geographers of the twelfth century, the gardens of the Uballa Canal at Basra were held by the Arabs to be one of the four earthly paradises. Kurna is reputed by local legend to be the Garden of Eden, and a certain gnarled thorn bush is pointed out as " the tree of the knowledge of good and evil." In the eyes of the first desert dwellers this fringe of fertility would naturally have appeared paradisiacal. But it is an isolated zone, and does not stretch more than half a mile inland from the river bank. One passes out of the shade of the palms into the barren sand or baked clay which is Mesopotamia.

That the country was once rich and populous evidence abounds. North of Ctesiphon one can scarcely traverse a mile without discovering the site of some ancient city or town. Everywhere one comes across mounds strewn with fragments of vases, bricks, potsherds, and glazed tiles. The remains of ancient embankments which used to carry the fertilising irrigation channels to the fields are the only features on the desert horizon that the mirage can torture into hills. The bricks of Babylon bearing the stamp of Nebuchadrezzar (Nebuchadnezzar) or Sardanapalus, which were built into the walls of Hilla and Bagdad, represent but a single layer in the strata of ancient civilizations which the thirsty soil of the country has swallowed up. In Mesopotamia one is reminded every day that the territories subject to the Osmanli lie dead under his hand, that the

AN ARAB ARISTOCRAT

Beduins of the desert, of whom this man is one, are the old aristocracy of Irak's Arab population, disdainful of the degenerate ways of their settled riverain kinsmen

Photo, R. Gorbold

GOLD AND SILVERSMITH OF AMARA

Age's quiet dignity and the assurance given by years of fine and successful craftsmanship reveal themselves in the bearded countenance of this ancient of Amara. The town was wrested from the Turk by General Townshend in 1915

Photo, G. Wagstaff

palm clumps at intervals on the horizon. On the Tigris, a few miles above Kurna, one enters a treeless tract of swamp and desert with a thin belt of irrigated land beside the river. The villages resemble those of the Punjab or the North-West Frontier of India, the same sloping mud walls enclosing the courtyard, with the cow-dung cakes for fuel plastered against the walls to dry in the sun. The only brick-built habitation in the permanent villages is the house of the sheikh. Above Amara the reed huts of the Arab give place to goathair tents.

The settled Arab population of the cultivated delta of the Tigris and Euphrates are descendants of immigrants from the Arabian deserts. Physically, the adoption of the cultivator's life has improved them ; they are better nourished, stronger, heavier, taller men than the Beduins, and bigger in the bone, though by abandoning their nomad existence they have lost in honour and independence. The Beduin scorns them, and will not inter-marry with them. Yet, apart from the town-dweller, the old tribal organization remains, tribal law and customs hold good, and the blood-feud is still obligatory.

Many of the riverain Arabs are handsome, and have a certain hawk-like dignity and grace of carriage. The women are fair, and go about unveiled. Some of the children have brown or chestnut hair. The riverain Arab is noted for his teeming progeny. The sheikh with three or four wives can generally boast of a family of from forty to fifty. The Muntafik, the first

blight where he has governed is as certain as famine after drought.

Upstream of Kurna, on the Tigris and Euphrates, one passes through the country of the marsh Arabs. The land visible from the lower reaches of the Euphrates in the neighbourhood of the Hammar Lake and Nasrieh is the richest in Mesopotamia. In May and June all this land is inundated ; the highest ground in a village is not a foot above flood level, and most of the inhabitants take to their boats, leaving their reed huts standing in water. Higher up-stream the richness of the land becomes apparent in the broad, strong towers which lie like Saxon churches under the

tribal confederation one meets on leaving the Shat-el-Arab and following up the Tigris and Euphrates, a people spread over some fifty or sixty square miles, are believed to outnumber the Anazeh, the great Beduin tribe which peoples the desert from the borders of Syria to the sands of Central Arabia.

The riverain Arab, degenerate as he may be, judged by the Beduin code, is not unmanly. Under the Ottoman rule he consistently defied the Turk when opportunity offered. There is not a tribe on the Euphrates or Tigris that has not been in a state of rebellion at some time against the Osmanli. The attempts to collect the rice revenue from the Shamiah on the Euphrates were always the prelude to quite extensive autumn manoeuvres; the marsh Arabs lower down the river in the neighbourhood of the Hammar lake used to fire on the Turkish flag as a matter of principle, so that it was generally safer for the Ottoman official to conceal his insignia of office.

North of the Muntafik on the Tigris one meets the Abu Mohammed and the Beni-Lam, great rebels against the Ottoman Government before the Great War. The Beni-Lam have long had the reputation of being the most truculent and inhospitable of the Tigris Arabs, men who, according to Layard, neither respected the laws of hospitality nor behaved in any sort like good Mussulmans, who were as treacherous as they were savage and cruel, and who would cut the throat of a guest for a trifle. They joined the Turk against the British, but proved most uncomfortable allies, turning always with the tide

SILVER SPEECH BEGUILES THE TASK OF BEATING OUT THE GOLD

Conversation is a serious occupation in the East, and the dark little shops afford pleasantly shady recesses in which to carry it on. Here, in Mosul, a goldsmith, squatting on the floor amid all the paraphernalia of his trade, clinks his hammer on the metal held in the vice before him, entertained the while by a constant succession of garrulous neighbours

Photo, Major W. J. P. Rodd

"REVEALED THE SECRET STANDS OF NATURE'S WORK"

Blandishments of the photographer prevailed over the force of convention, and this Bagdad Jewess was induced to unveil before the camera the face on which none but her family was supposed to gaze. The wife of a wealthy man, her robe is of white silk of finest quality, fringed and lined with gold thread, and her long braids of hair are fastened at the ends with trinkets

Photo, Major W. J. P. Rodd

DARK EYES AND BRIGHT ROBES OF ARABY

Character and high intelligence as well as attraction are clearly marked in the pleasing features of this dignified lady of Irak, with her shawled head and gay ornaments, as she stands beneath the palm tree's shade. Her bare feet, accustomed to the lack of shoes, peep out beneath her dress as she stands, confidence in every line of her, to undergo the novelty of being photographed

Photo, Major W. J. P. Rodd

DINNER AND DEVOTION JOINTLY AIDING LABOUR

It would be surprising to see a gang of Roman Catholic navvies eating their dinner with their rosaries ready at hand for immediate use afterwards. These Arab coolies, devout followers of Mahomet, see nothing incongruous in eating their midday meal without tables or cloth, and spreading out their prayer mat whereon to turn towards Mecca and pray at the appointed hour

Photo, Harry Cox

of fortune and murdering and looting their Mahomedan brethren whenever opportunity delivered them into their hands. The Beni-Lam were not alone in this. It has been the privilege of the Arab in Mesopotamia for at least two thousand years to attack, pillage, and murder the losing side. They were "the Saracens" who hung on the flank of Julian's army and fell upon the stragglers by the way. Townshend's wounded were stripped and mutilated by them. They are frankly plunderers, and kill their prey before they strip it. They dig up graves and leave the dead stark.

On account of these practices the British and Indian troops in Mesopotamia formed a very low estimate of the Arab of the country, or only admired him as an expert rifle thief. The Turk has always had a contempt for his fighting qualities, while the proud Beduins of the inner desert, "the people of the camel," will not associate with him, and deny that he is capable of loyalty even among his own community. Nevertheless he is not wanting in a kind of straw-fire courage. If he has proved useless in war it is because he has never felt bound by any allegiance, but has played for his own hand, and therefore is found on the side of the strongest battalions. When he puts his person in jeopardy

PEACE IN A BACKWATER OF A PALM-FRINGED STREAM

It is only in a narrow belt lining the river beds that any vegetation, even remotely suggesting the
Paradise of tradition, exists in Irak. Here the date palms give a tropical appearance to the scene
and exclude thought of the arid waste behind. This pretty spot is a creek off the Shat-el-Arab,
near Basra, the mat-screened structures being a date-packing station

Photo, Harry Cox

he demands his quid pro quo. His adventures are frankly predatory, and his code, if ever he had one, has long since been forgotten.

The bulk of the Arab population of Mesopotamia are Shiahs, though the country has long been under the rule of the Turk, who is a Sunni. Under the Ottoman Government the Shiahs had no political status. Shiah religious bequests had no legal recognition. Nor was Shiah religious law, which differs from that of the Sunnis, included in the Ottoman code. The Sunni minority in the country has a political and social importance out of proportion to its numbers. It includes the Naquibs of Basra and Bagdad and the largest landowners and wealthiest merchants.

The Sunnis among the settled population are, with few exceptions, town-dwellers. The nomad Arab, too, like his brother of the Arabian desert, is generally a Sunni; but the Shiah sentiment in Irak, which is the birth-place of the religion, and contains the holy shrines of Kerbela and Najaf, is so strong that generation after generation of Sunni immigrants have adopted the faith of the country. In Bagdad there is a large Christian and Jewish population. The Armenian Bagdadis suffered less from the Turk in and before the Great War than their co-religionists in any other part of the Ottoman Empire, and escaped the general massacres. The Arabs of Mesopotamia are little infected with the fanaticism of Islam, while the Turks were a small community, confined more or less to the families of the officials. The Armenians in Bagdad were never regarded by them as an economic menace, or even as a cause of political uneasiness.

The Sabaeans, or Star Worshippers, of Mesopotamia, as they are sometimes called, are found scattered in the towns by the two rivers. Their religious observances make it incumbent upon them to live near running water. Suk-esh-Sheyukh is their headquarters on the Euphrates and Amara on the Tigris. They are a distinct people with many curious characteristics and beliefs, which they have inherited from Jews, Christians, Pagans, and Mahomedans. Their bible, the Sidra Rabba, a jumble of borrowed and contradictory doctrines, is a closed book to the profane. They observe the first day in the week, baptism, the Lord's Supper, and reverence for John the Baptist. Yet they are not Christians. Neither are they Jews, though their ritual of sacrifice and purification is

GERM-FEARLESS DRAWERS OF WATER FROM OLD TIGRIS

Water supply and drainage systems are matters of small concern to the Oriental. At Bagdad and other riverside towns in Irak the Arabs come down to the river to fetch water, the men with the goatskins in which they purvey it in the streets, the women with their ornamental pitchers, all regardless of the fact that it is contaminated by sewage leaking down from the towns

Photo, Harry Cox

range, to the far north, a persecuted non-Arab race, probably of Kurdish stock. The principle of evil which they propitiate is symbolised for them in the snake and the sacred peacock.

In the latitude of Bagdad the Tigris and Euphrates are within twenty-five miles of meeting. This means that the roads from the Mediterranean into Asia, the Tadmor-Deir-el-Zor route by the Euphrates, the road which crosses the Taurus by the Cilician Gates and follows the Tigris down from Mosul, all lead to Bagdad or Babylon. The convergence of the river routes has from time immemorial dictated the site of the metropolis of Mesopotamia. Bagdad, too, receives the commerce of the Gulf ; it is

peculiarly Semitic. Expert silversmiths, they were known to the British troops chiefly by their inlaid work of antimony on silver, probably the only form of modern indigenous handicraft worth taking away from the country. The community form an isolated guild, in which the secrets of their trade are preserved as jealously as their religious arcana.

Another strange obscurantist Mesopotamian cult is that practised by the Yezidis or devil-worshippers, who dwell in the Jebel Sinjar

"JUDGE THE WORLD BY THE WAY THEY TREAD"

In their queer little caverns in Bagdad, Arab shoemakers turn out scores of pairs of the heelless slippers affected by the population, and, like the old cobbler shown above, patch up soles worn threadbare on the ill-paved streets

Photos, R. Gorbold

MAMMON SETS HIS MARKET ALONGSIDE THE MOSQUE

Floods played havoc with Bagdad in the early part of the nineteenth century, and it is only in the solidly-built mosques that good examples of early Arab architecture remain. Outside these old brick buildings, variegated with peacock-blue and old gold, a cosmopolitan crowd is generally found, venders of bread, sweetmeats, and fruit welcoming the open spaces as a convenient market place for their wares

Photo, Major W. J. P. Rodd

PURSUING THEIR LAWFUL OCCASIONS IN LABYRINTHINE BAGDAD

Bagdad long ago lost the magnificence of architecture and ornament that made it famous in the days of Haroun Al Raschid. The town, as it now exists, lacks plan, and the unpaved, mostly narrow streets are flanked by uninviting houses of yellowish red brick taken from old ruins, with latticed windows on the first floor, and, below, only mean doors to break the monotony of the walls

Photo, Major W. J. P. Rodd

easy of access by river from the desert outposts on the Euphrates, where the caravans off-load from Central Arabia ; it is the ancient Babylon-Ecbatana (Hamadan) road which was the pathway of armies for centuries before the Chosroes, and it lies on the great pilgrim route from Persia to the holy Shiah shrines of Kazimain, Kerbela, and Najaf.

Thus, in the narrow barren strip of land between the Tigris and the

archaeologists have identified the crumbling monuments of succeeding dynasties of the Assyrian, neo-Babylonian, Persian, and Greco-Parthian periods.

Ctesiphon, eighteen miles from Bagdad, was the capital of the Sassanidae, and Seleucia, on the opposite bank of the Tigris, of the last Greek empire in Mesopotamia. Bagdad, in the time of the Abbasid Caliphs, was the centre of Islam, and in after years,

CROSSING THE TIGRIS TO MOSUL BY THE BRIDGE OF BOATS

Mosul, always important from its position on a great caravan route into North-West Persia, has acquired new importance from the oilfields in the vilayet of which it is the capital. It stands on the Tigris, here crossed by a bridge, partly of stone and partly of boats. The latter portion can be cut in time of flood, or to allow the passage of traffic

Photo, Major W. J. P. Rodd

Euphrates, three hundred and fifty miles inland from the Persian Gulf, the excavator has brought to light the relics of many buried civilizations. The buildings which are pointed out to the visitor at Babylon belong to the comparatively modern period of Nebuchadrezzar (561-504 B.C.), but there are traces in the ruins left by the first Babylonian kings (circa 2,500 B.C.), and deep down below the water level relics that point to a prehistoric city. In the strata superimposed

until General Maude entered the city in March, 1917, the southern capital of Asiatic Turkey. Since Aug. 23, 1921, the Emir Feisal has reigned there as king of the Arab confederation which, under British auspices, replaced the Turk.

Bagdad has probably always been cosmopolitan. In the arched and vaulted thoroughfares of the bazaars one meets a diversity of races, drawn as in old times along the old roads to the metropolis by motives of commerce or faith. The mosque of Abdul Kadr

MERCHANDISE AVAILABLE FOR EVERY TASTE AND NEED

Merchandise of all kinds is stacked in the dark little shops that line the arched and vaulted thorough-fares of Bagdad's bazaars, and the races represented among the buyers and sellers are as various. Flat projecting beams supporting roofs of dried leaves or branches of trees and grass, are common in the streets of the business quarter and afford grateful shelter from the sun

Photo, J. L. Mudd

CIVILIZED DESCENDANTS OF ANCIENT NOMAD STOCK

Exceptional dignity and grace, and beauty of no mean order, are displayed by these Arab women of Amara. The family belongs to the higher social class of the settled Arab population, engaged for the most part in business, and the man was in the service of the British Government as interpreter to the forces. Riverain Arab women are fair, and go unveiled

Photo, C. Kemp

Turks, Armenians, and Jews, and by all the hybrid flotsam and jetsam of the streets, from the Turkish official to the Chaldaean astrologer or Ethiopian slave. The precise-looking Persian merchant from Dizful or Ispahan is wearing the brown or black abas of the Arab, which flows from the shoulder like an undergraduate's gown. The kefieh, the headgear of the Arab, is a blue or red-spotted kerchief, bound round with the aagal, a twisted coil of black or brown camelhair rope. Many of the women wear black horsehair visors; one meets them coming up from the river bank carrying water in tapering copper vessels with fluted necks.

The dark taverns are crowded with Arabs, who squat on their high pew-like benches, gravely discussing the high politics of the desert, drinking coffee, and playing dominoes or dice. Wild-eyed Beduins, generally on horseback, pass distrustfully in the streets, which in many quarters are so narrow that the bags on the pack-animals rub the walls on either side, while the latticed and fretted bow-windows overhead almost meet. The massive iron-clinched doors, with their curious antique brass knockers, open into spacious courtyards planted with palms and orange trees and pomegranates. The houses are two-storeyed, the verandas on the four sides of the first floor overlooking the courtyard.

ONE OF "THE PEOPLE OF THE CAMEL"
Beduins of the inner desert are a fine, proud people, generally of commanding figure, erect, lithe, and taut as steel, with a stamp of nobility set on their features by generations of freedom
Photo, R. Gorbold

is frequented by Sunnis from all over the East; the Shiahs pour in from Persia and India to the shrine of Kazimain, many of them Seyyids, descendants of Ali, with their tarbushes wound round with the green turban. One may recognize the Kurds and Lurs by their high bulbous hats of rough felt, like elongated coal-scuttles, their smooth locks hanging free and clipped about their ears after the Afghan fashion; the Bakhtiari by his brimless top hat, the Tartar by his astrachan of the north. The fez, of course, is ubiquitous, and is worn by

In the dog-days the Bagdadi takes refuge in the serdab, a kind of vaulted cellar sunk some six feet under the ground level with ventilation shafts, which run up to the roof and end in

ITALY: TWO GAY RAGAZZI OF THE CAMPAGNA

The vivacity of these two sun-tanned lads of the Roman Campagna is drawn, like the love of colour displayed in their traditional costume, from the brightness of their own blue skies

Photo, Donald McLeish

hood-like cowls, all pointing the same way to catch the shamal, or prevailing north wind, which provides the only alleviation against the suffocating heat. The temperature in the serdab is generally from eight to ten degrees lower than in the rooms on the first floor.

From May to October the whole population of the city sleeps on the roof. In 1917 the shade temperature rose to 122.8 degrees in Bagdad, and 122 degrees in Basra. Bagdad has the advantage of a drier atmosphere and cooler nights than obtain in the lower part of the delta, where the humidity of the air is relaxing. Perhaps the climax of discomfort in Mesopotamia is reached in Basra during September, when " the date wind," under which the crops ripen, rolls up the moisture from the Gulf and then drops, leaving a clammy, humid film in the air as suffocating as a blanket.

The only broad thoroughfare in Bagdad was cut through the city in 1916, and named after Khalil Pasha, the Turkish commander, to whom General Townshend's garrison surrendered. By the irony of fate, the street which was built to commemorate the British reverse at Kut was completed just in time to admit the passage of the British troops, eleven months afterwards, through Bagdad. The architecture of the city is picturesque and distinctive, if not imposing. In colour the only relief to the dun monotony of the walls and roofs is the peacock-blue and old gold of the mosques and minarets.

Few of the buildings are old. The foundations of most of the houses gave way in the floods of the thirties of the nineteenth century, but the old bricks have been used again, some of them the debris of Babylon, and there is no air of modernity in the purlieus of the city. The mosques, with their solid foundations, escaped destruction by the flood, and have preserved some good examples of fourteenth-century Arab architecture. The most inspiring view of Bagdad is from the broad sweep of the river front. The chief houses and consulates

DEFT FINGERS SUPPLEMENTED BY PREHENSILE TOES

Revolving on spikes at either end, the piece of wood is revolved by a saw-like movement of the bow in the wood-turner's right hand, the string passing round the piece and thus supplying the rotary motion. The sunlight illumines the turner's work while a little Arab holds the bar on which he steadies the chisel that is held with both feet and one hand

Photo, R. Gorbold

ARAB BOYS PADDLING CANOES IN FRONT OF BAGDAD

As peculiar to the Tigris as the gufa and mahaila is the bellum, a light, rather graceful canoe-shaped boat, which is paddled or poled according to the depth of the water. At Basra they correspond to the gondola of Venice, being particularly convenient for navigating the numerous little tidal canals that intersect the town. These boys' canoes are small modified forms of the bellum

Photo, W. A. Harvey

are built on immensely solid revetments with their foundations deep in the water. Many of them have small gardens with steps running down to the river. The main city is on the left bank; the suburb on the right bank contains little of interest beyond Zobeide's tomb, a tall, tapering, crenellated minaret, like an inverted fir cone. The railway station lies in the desert beyond, a mile from the Tigris. The river is now crossed by two bridges of boats, admitting of traffic passing only one way.

The cauldron-like gufa described by Herodotus, a reed basket with wooden uprights, planted over with pitch from the bitumen wells of Hit, is still used as a ferry, and is probably the oldest type of vessel in the world. The long narrow canoe-shaped boat is the Arab bellum, the gondola of Basra, which is paddled or poled, according to the depth of the stream. The mahailas, with their high forward-sloping masts, huge rudder, lateen sail, cut-away barbed prow, and poop boarded over for the crew, are the indigenous cargo-

boats of the river, and carry anything from fifteen to seventy tons. Downstream on the Shat-el-Arab, the bold and sweeping curves of the river craft are even more reminiscent of illustrations of the sagas. At Basra one meets the Arab buggalow, with the penthouse roof astern, intricately carved, and windows through which one looks for the face of Sindbad, or the boom of Koweit with its sharp stern and nose of a swordfish.

The country around Bagdad is capable of great fertility. A single year of British administration sufficed to alter the face of the desert, and achieved more for the prosperity of the Arab than a century of Ottoman " reform." The settlement and development of the country kept pace, as the Expeditionary Force advanced, with the occupation. Under Ottoman rule, owing to the lack of control of the irrigation, and the vicious land revenue system with its fluctuating assessments, which left the cultivator at the mercy of the farmer of taxes, outlay and initiative were discouraged. The new system saw the lifting of the general blight.

The constructive energy of the British was visible in the railways, dykes, dams, and irrigation channels. Land which had lain fallow for years became rich and profitable. The great Euphrates Irrigation Scheme, designed by Sir William Willcocks and constructed by Sir John Jackson's firm, was actually finished before the Great War, but the Turk, by his supineness, neglected to profit by it. The digging of the new canals and the scouring out of the disused ones, essential to the working of the scheme, was left to the British. They occupied the district in June, 1917 ; three hundred thousand acres were at once brought under irrigation, and the summer of 1918 saw a blossoming of the desert which had no parallel in the memory of the Arab.

The mineral wealth of Mesopotamia is limited to the bitumen wells of Hit, the petroleum wells of Qaiyarah in the neighbourhood of Mosul, and a few stone quarries on the Euphrates. The undeveloped resources of the country are mainly agricultural. Its potential productivity has perhaps been exaggerated. Nevertheless, with capital, initiative, and a settled government it might yet become a considerable granary as in the past.

Under the Emir Feisal the Arabs have again become the dominant race. They are a homogeneous people, speaking one language. But any forecast of the future in which they figure as the regenerators of the soil that has been restored to them must be guided by considerations of their character and history. It would be unwise to count too much on the development of Mesopotamia by the Arab, whether fellah or Beduin, until he has proved himself strong enough with British support, unbacked by the necessary legions, to maintain his solidarity and independence.

Mesopotamia, with all its historic associations dating from the Sumerian

QUAINT BASKET BOATS USED FROM IMMEMORIAL TIMES

Probably the oldest type of vessel in the world, the gufa is still used, chiefly for ferrying purposes, on the Tigris. It is a large circular basket of reeds, plastered inside and out with pitch from the bitumen wells of Hit. Gufas vary considerably in size, and are used both for conveying passengers and for transporting fruit or other commodities

Photo, W. A. Harvey

FRESH FRUIT AND VEGETABLES FOR SALE IN MOSUL

Mosul's shops are mostly poor, and disproportionate grandeur is given to this fruit-seller's scantily furnished emporium by the good casement windows, topped by elaborate iron fan tracery. His stock includes some fine melons, which, with other gourds and vegetables, are grown to perfection in the islands and dry portions of the river-bed of the Tigris during the season of low water

Photo, Albert E. Cree

AMID THE CLINKING CANNIKINS OF THE TINSMITH'S SHOP

All is grist that comes to the mill of this Arab tinsmith, and the unusually tidily arranged shelves of his small workshop show a curious medley of wares—Eastern jars and lanterns rubbing shoulders with Western tankards and pot-bellied circular-wick lamps, while bully beef tins provide him with plenty of tin and solder for patching up old vessels and fashioning new

Photo, R. Gorbold

BEARDED WEAVER OF IRAK'S CHIEF CITY

With his twelve spindles swollen with thread this Bagdad weaver is holding them up for inspection against the ancient wall of time-worn bricks between whose interstices the mortar has long since begun to crumble

Photo, R. Gorbold

before he reached the age of twelve. The pilgrims who flock to the golden mosque near by Julian's tomb expect his advent there.

At Kerbela is the mosque of the martyred Hussein, the son of Ali, and at Najaf the mosque of Ali. These desert shrines, lying on the pilgrim route from Bagdad to Mecca, are a magnet for the faithful all over the East, for the religious sentiment of the fervent Shiah clings more closely to the tradition of Ali and Hussein than to the memory of the Prophet himself. It was at Kerbela, some twenty miles to the west of the Euphrates, that Hussein and his small band were overwhelmed. The Moharram festival, which is celebrated by the Shiahs with such frenzied beatings of the breast, weeping, and self-inflicted wounds, is a dramatisation of the scene at Kerbela. After twelve hundred years their anger and sorrow are so intense that the uninitiated spectator might think they were commemorating a tragedy of yesterday.

paradise, is singularly devoid of ancient monuments or relics, beyond brick and dust, of bygone civilizations. The only abiding monument of man's greatness that still stands on its foundations is Ctesiphon, the arch of the Chosroes.

Far more attractive than the Biblical or classic sites of Mesopotamia are the Shiah shrines of Najaf, Kerbela, Kazimain, and Samarra. Kazimain, four miles upstream from Bagdad, on the Tigris, is the burial-place of the seventh and ninth Imams. Samarra on the Tigris marks the spot where the twelfth and last of the Imams—the promised Mahdi—disappeared in a cave

It is the dearest wish of the Shiah's heart to be buried at Najaf or Kerbela that they may be near Ali or Hussein on the Day of Resurrection. Their Wadi-al-Salam, or Valley of Peace, is the fold in the desert outside the north wall of Najaf. Here one may meet the bodies of the faithful coming in from Merv or Bokhara, or Teheran, wrapped in wattle or silk or bundles of palm leaves, according to their condition. Some lie buried in the mosque itself where Ali lies, others in the houses of the city, or in rooms rented by relatives of the corpses, but most in the vast cemetery beyond the north wall, directly between Ali and Hussein, among crumbling monuments and humble slabs, where countless small domes, the colour and shape of thrushes' eggs, lend the only relief to the camel-coloured sand.

Najaf is far the most picturesque and impressive desert city in Mesopotamia. It stands on a high bluff six miles from Kufa, its river port on the Euphrates. The golden dome and minarets of Ali's tomb, dominating the earth-coloured walls of the city, are visible to pilgrims three marches from the shrine. Apart from its sanctity, Najaf is a great desert emporium where the caravans of Central Arabia bring in the raw material of the desert and return with rice and clothing, where Beduin middlemen exchange the silks and calicoes of Homs and Hama with grain, cattle, and merchandise from Basra or Bombay.

The city, but for the fact that it is approached by a tramline from the Euphrates, shows no trace of Western influences. The merchants and their clients probably differ little in dress, habit, or mind from those who frequented the dead cities of the Euphrates in the days of Pharaoh. One may watch the wild Beduin, who regards the door of a house as a trap and a roof over his head as a menace to his security, and the Persian pilgrim floating ecstatically in the crowd intoxicated with religious fervour. It is difficult to get a near view of the mosque. Only as one wanders in the bazaars one catches a glimpse of the rich mosaic of blue and green and gold glittering at the end of some covered avenue.

At Kerbela and Kazimain one may stand by the gate and peer into the courtyard, but at Najaf a near approach to the shrine by the infidel is resented, and the only way to gain a view of it is from the roof of some friendly Arab or Persian's house. The bazaars, an irregular and intricate warren of alleys and courtyards, preserve more of the ancient

WARP AND WEFT ON A SILK LOOM IN BAGDAD

Among the oldest of handicrafts is the weaving of fabric, and here we see an Arab hard at work making silk in a cellar, in whose cool atmosphere he can labour the more comfortably. The main principles of the machine before him are similar to those which have been in use generation after generation, for modern appliances make but slow progress with the native craftsman

Photo, R. Gorbold

ARABS AT EASE OUTSIDE A CAFÉ IN THE VALLEY OF THE TIGRIS

In the cool evening the men of the vicinity who have borne the day's burden and heat find pleasure in relaxation by the gliding river, whose changeless flow forms a soothing accompaniment to the murmur of easy conversation. On the veranda, with its rude seats and thick-thatched roof, the coffee, a delicacy of which the Arab never tires, and the fragrant fumes of tobacco have an added delicacy of flavour. Here, till night shuts the café's narrow doors, its turbaned patrons may enjoy a protracted prelude to their leisurely homecoming in discussing their own and their neighbours' business

GOOD ACCOMMODATION FOR PILGRIMS IN A CARAVANSERAI IN THE CITY OF KERBELA

Kerbela, some sixty miles south-west of Bagdad, where Hussein, son of Ali the fourth Caliph, was slain in A.D. 680, almost ranks with Mecca as a Moslem holy city. Something like a quarter of a million Shiah Moslems annually make pilgrimage to the great shrine with golden dome and gilded minarets that contains the martyr's remains. Like Mecca, Kerbela's material prosperity depends largely on the pilgrims, for whom caravanserais like this provide accommodation. They are built round the four sides of an open courtyard, with stables for animals on the ground floor and bare rooms for the travellers above

Photo, Major W. J. P. Rodd

PATIENT CUSTOMERS WAITING THEIR TURN IN THE OPEN-AIR ESTABLISHMENT OF A WAYSIDE BARBER OF IRAK

Here are no glass shelves laden with bottles of many-coloured unguents. Even the barber's chair is absent, and a rough mat laid upon the unkind surface of the mud wall must serve the purpose. Those who sit and wait have the benefit of a tree's welcome shade, and the passer-by is perhaps weighing his chances of a shave in the near future against their number. The little girl is determined to miss no detail of this fascinating operation, and the photograph admirably illustrates the leisureliness and the indifference to publicity that characterise the Oriental man in the conduct of his personal affairs

Photo T Slaves

BARBER-SURGEON OF IRAK: A MAN WITH TWO TRADES

The importance of his calling, combining surgery and shaving, may account for the smile on his Mephistophelean features. In Amara, where the photograph was taken, the practice of joining the two occupations still obtains, and this is the less surprising when the Arab's indifference to the curing of ailments and his readiness to leave all to Allah are considered

Photo, E. Kemp

East than one finds in other Arab cities. Those of Bagdad, Cairo, and Damascus appear modern and hybrid in comparison with them. The city is fabulously rich, for the profits of sanctity from endowments and the contributions of the faithful are great. Treasure in the form of gold and silver and jewels and precious stones, silks and shawls and pearled curtains is buried and sealed in the vaults of the mosque.

A large part of the population is dependent on religious charities. The city contains more than twenty ecclesiastical colleges and some 6,000 students of religious law. As the seat of the great Mujtahids, who have the power of promulgating religious orders and interpreting the Koran and the Law, Najaf has always exercised a predominant influence in Shiah Islam. In Persia especially, the home of Shiahism, this influence has been felt, and it was said in the past that the Mujtahids could make or unmake a Shah. Now that democracy has entered the East, the

![TO HEIGHTS OF LEARNING BRED]

TO HEIGHTS OF LEARNING BRED
Learned in both civil and ecclesiastical law, the Mullah is an influential personage among all Mahomedan peoples. In Irak he beats the drum ecclesiastic to less martial purpose than some of his brethren have done elsewhere
Photo, R. Gorbold

sanction of Najaf or Kerbela is sought by parties and factions where it used to be sought by kings, and the desert cities have become even more the seats of religious bigotry and fanaticism and the storm centres of political intrigue.

The Euphrates markets, of which Najaf is one, are the connecting links between the great nomad confederations and the settled population of the riverain tracts. The rulers of the inner desert are Ibn Rashid and Ibn Sa'ud, the Emirs of northern and southern Najd, and farther north, Fahad Beg, the chief of the Anazeh, who are spread over the desert from the Euphrates

to the Syrian border. These tribes were practically independent of the Sultan; the Turks did not attempt to impose military service on them.

In the absence of the Osmanli, sentiment points to the Emir Feisal, the popularly-elected sovereign of Irak, the son of the Sherif of Mecca, an Arab of the family of the Prophet, as their natural ruler. But the politics of the inner desert are as shifting as sand. The picture of a centralised Arab organization of tribal groups owing permanent fealty to an overlord is a chimerical vision. The proud Beduin has always been his own master, and probably always will be. The only hold the paramount power in Bagdad

ARAB WITCHERY UNVEILED
Her languorous eyes, pencilled brows, and the half-smile that just lifts a corner of her mocking mouth are eloquent of the torrid East
Photo, R. Gorbold

can have over the desert tribes is by closing the markets to them.

The Beduins are independent of everything but supplies. Guns, and pots and pans, corn and ammunition the desert cannot give them. They must come in to the frontier outposts for most

RELIGIOUS ECSTASY RUNNING RIOT IN THE FAST OF RAMADAN

Fanaticism goes to extremes among some Mahomedans, and extraordinary scenes are enacted on the occasion of certain religious ceremonies. The last ten days of the fasting month of Ramadan are specially sacred, and on the concluding day the wildest fanatics gash themselves with knives in token of mourning, and inflict the goriest tortures of flagellation on their own bodies

CARNAGE SELF-WROUGHT AT HILLA IN THE CAUSE OF HOLINESS

Parched with thirst and exhausted by their prolonged absolute fast, these misguided people persist in their self-torture even to death. Thus the swooning fanatic, in blood-saturated robes, shown supported in the background of this photograph, expired a few minutes later. These photographs give some idea of the fearful and unforgettable scene as it was enacted at Hilla in November, 1918

Photos, E. Kemp

AFTER THE FRUIT IN A GROVE OF DATE PALMS

Tension on the rope around the trunk enables the climber to maintain himself, and he is further aided
in this by the deep leaf-scars which afford a foothold. The date palm, a native of North Africa, is also
cultivated in the Levant and India, but there is a world of difference in the quality of the fresh-plucked
article and the dried remnant of export

Photo, J. L. Mudd

GATHERING THE FRUITS OF THE EARTH IN DUE SEASON

The date palm is the chief source of income to the riverain population of Irak, and its fruit is their staple food. Eaten fresh, it is delicious, sustaining but not satiating, despite its richness, and free from the heating property which it possesses when dried. These Arab women are collecting in their flat basket the fruit which is being picked by a man at the crown of the tree

Photo, Harry Cox

"WHAT THE EYE DOESN'T SEE THE HEART DOESN'T GRIEVE AT"

As dried and sold in Europe, the date is a very different article of food from the fruit newly gathered in its proper habitat. Part of the process of preparing dates for export consists in pressing them, and in Irak this is done as shown here, men pouring them into bags and treading them down with naked feet, as grapes are still trodden in some vineyards

Photo, J. L. Mudd

ACTIVITY ON ASHAR CREEK, BASRA, THE CENTRE OF TRANSHIPMENT BETWEEN IRAK AND THE OUTER WORLD

As the main seaport of Irak, with regular steamship communication with Europe and India, Basra is immensely important commercially. It stands at the head of navigation on Ashar Creek, by which all merchandise is brought by boats and mahailas from and to the big ships in the Gulf sixty miles below. Thus Ashar Creek is always humming with activity, Kurds and Arabs unloading grain, and cargoes of rice and coffee from India, and of manufactured articles from Europe, or loading outgoing mahailas with dates and other produce exported from Irak

of the necessaries of life. In the wilderness they may set up or depose their sheikhs, settle their own confederacies, but their dependence on the markets for provisions and clothing enforces on them, if not an exact observance of treaties, at least a certain respect for constituted government in the settled tracts and some limit to their depredations.

Beside the fellah of the delta the Beduin is generally a commanding figure, thin, erect, lithe, and taut as wire, with a certain stamp of nobility on his features, the imprint of generations of freedom and self-sufficiency. In the same way, the waste lands over which the children of the wilderness exercise their primitive sway are more inspiring than the disciplined tracts that have absorbed their degenerate kinsmen.

After the monotony of lower Mesopotamia it is a relief to come upon land with any features to it. The limits of the flat, uncompromising delta are reached on both rivers some sixty miles north of Bagdad. At Hit, on the Euphrates, one enters a new country, a land of limestone and gypseous clay, where the valley winds between low hills. Between Samarra and Tekrit, on the Tigris, one enters the broken desert steppes that stretch northward for 150 miles to Mosul, an arid, verdureless country, but very satisfying to the eye after the delta. The cultivation between the rivers is negligible. The Euphrates, along its whole course, is the more fertile of the two. The spring vegetation, though short-lived, is fresh and homelike, in

great contrast to the tracts farther south that are as flowerless as the deserts of Sind or the Punjab.

But the best antithesis to the dead, featureless land through which the British troops fought their way up the Tigris will be found in the Jebel Hamrin

WESTERN DEVICES FOR EASTERN DEVOTEES
Kazimain, four miles upstream from Bagdad on the Tigris, contains the burial places of the seventh and ninth Imams. For the convenience of pilgrims to these Shiah shrines, Midhat Pasha built a small tram line in 1870
Photo, K. N. Moyser

range and the Diala valley close to the Persian border. The broken ground here is the old sea margin; north and east the landscape becomes more varied, rocks and streams and meadows, which in spring are carpeted with wild flowers. One has left behind the flat alluvial silt

PRIDE OF POTTERY
This is the potter's daughter engaged in arranging the products of her father's craftsmanship, damp from the wheel, to dry in the sun

land intermittently along the banks of the two rivers.

No religious, intellectual, or Arab nationalist movement is likely to proceed from the soil of Irak. Arab regeneration, if it is to come, will be inspired by " the people of the camel," who alone have preserved the independence of character from which initiative springs. For centuries the Ottoman hand has laid its blight on the country, forbidding initiative, sterilising spirit and matter. British administration, which alone might have saved Mesopotamia, is out of the question. And it would be sanguine to hope that, under the Arabs, if, indeed, they are left in possession, the desert will ever be restored to its Babylonian fertility.

where flowers do not grow, or grow unwillingly.

Kurdistan, farther north, part of which also falls within the confines of Mesopotamia, is a land of streams and rolling downs and wide horizons bounded by the hills, a fertile, well-watered plateau, with abundant cornfields and pasture. Stripped of this fringe of foot-hills, valleys, and mountains, which really belong geographically to Persia on the east, and Asia Minor on the north, Mesopotamia is easy to describe : flat desert or undulating barren steppes, with strips of irrigated

SEMI-FINAL STAGE IN THE BIRTH OF A BOWL
Here the glazing mixture is being applied to the almost finished article, and behind the aged workman are rows of ready-fashioned crockery in process of drying before being taken to the kiln
Photos, Major W. J. P. Rodd

EARTHENWARE FACTORY IN THE POTTERY DISTRICT OF BAGDAD

Without the city wall is the potters' village, and the photograph shows some buyers in their astrakhan tarbushes about to inspect these products of native manufacture. On every hand are samples from which to choose, and one of the potters, evidently well pleased with his work and the situation in general, has taken up such a position that the camera shall miss nothing of his white-robed person

LAST STAGE OF ALL THAT ENDS THIS INDUSTRY

Passed down into the dark deep kiln for their completion, these pitchers are going to join their fellows on the shelves round the space hollowed out below. Brushwood will then be taken from the pile behind the pots, stacked in the kiln, ignited, and the man inside—invisible in the photograph—having climbed out, will close the entrance till the fire has done its work

Photos, Major W. I. P. Rodd

A HUMAN AIR PUMP	**FLOATING MADE EASY**
He is inflating a skin to serve as a float, a task for which he would find a bicycle pump better adapted than lips and lungs	With his goatskin filled, the native wades into the river, confident that however long its crossing takes he certainly will not sink

TAKING HIS CUSHIONED EASE ON TIGRIS STREAM

Goatskins filled with air are an ingenious device in common use for crossing the Tigris. Blowing one up, as shown above, the native rests his breast upon it and propels it forward by kicking out with his legs. A similar device in use on the river Sutlej in India is shown on page 2809

Photos, R. Gorbold

Irak

II. From Babylon's Empire to the Modern Arab State

By A. D. Innes, M.A.

Associate Editor of "Harmsworth's History of the World"

THE name of Mesopotamia signifies the land lying between and including the basins of the two great rivers, Euphrates and Tigris, which rise in the mountains of Armenia and in later historic times mingle their waters at some distance before they disembogue at the head of the Persian Gulf. In the earliest historic times the lower lands had not yet been raised above sea-level by the silt which the floods bring down year by year, and the rivers entered the Gulf separately some way above their modern point of confluence.

Lower Mesopotamia, or Irak (or Iraq) as it is now called, the region, roughly speaking, between Bagdad and the sea, shares with the Nile Valley the distinction of being one of the two areas in possession of a continuously recorded history extending over more than 5,000 years, unless we may credit China with being a third. The early records are either monumental carvings or inscriptions on clay in the cuneiform script which the Mesopotamians would seem to have invented. The area fell into the two divisions—Akkad the upper, and Sumer the lower. Sumer in this pristine stage was the land of the Sumerians, a people neither Aryan nor Semitic, but of a type suggesting kinship with the Dravidians of India, or possibly with the Chinese. Whence they came we do not know, but we do know that five thousand years ago they had learnt to use metal implements and were already dwellers in builded towns. The Sumerian records suggest that the dwellers in Akkad were Semites, and curiously enough, while they present their own gods as of Semitic type, those gods were clearly not the indigenous deities of the Semites themselves. When Semites dominated the Sumerians, it was the conquerors who definitely adopted the culture of the conquered, not vice versa.

The story of Mesopotamia down to the conquest by Cyrus the Persian is one mainly of periodical Semitic dominations, gradually or suddenly yielding to the Sumerian influences of Babylonia, which, except when the power of Assyria was at its greatest height, was the constant or recurring culture-centre of the whole region.

Either the Semites were indigenous in Upper Mesopotamia and the northern mountains, or they came thither from Arabia through Syria, across the western Euphrates. They appear actively about 3000 B.C. Till that time Sumerian towns or states—Lagash, Umma, Eridu—have the field to themselves. Then Semitic lords are found ruling in Akkad. Tradition elaborates a mighty monarch, Sargon of Agade, about 2700 B.C., who, like certain Egyptian kings, was probably a composite of two or three actual princes, who, with a successor, Naram Sin, subjugated Sumer, and led conquering armies to the

IRAK AND ITS PEOPLE

ONE MAN'S IGNORANCE IS ANOTHER MAN'S OPPORTUNITY

Many of the natives of Irak are unable to read or write. Profiting by this common illiteracy the professional scribe is a familiar figure in the towns. He sets up his table by any convenient wall and translates the halting thoughts of his clients into flowing periods, which he then reads aloud for the approval of his employer and the edification of any casual listener

Photo, W. A. Harvey

Mediterranean on the west and the hills of Elam (the later Susiana) on the east. Then the Sumerians recovered an ascendancy tempered by Elamite conquests, till, a little earlier than the twentieth century, the Semites again predominated.

In the twentieth century emerges the great figure of the Semite Hammurabi, king of Babylon (in the Hebrew record, Amraphel, king of Shinar), the contemporary of Abraham, the Semite Sheikh from whom sprang the Hebrew people. We find Amraphel in alliance with an Elamite, a Sumerian, and a Hittite king from the north-west. Hammurabi was a mighty prince, who codified the laws and customs of Babylonia. His code, in the cuneiform script, survives to this day, witness to a very advanced political and social organization, which regulated slavery, the relations of debtor and creditor, employer and employee, and shows that women enjoyed a notable freedom.

In the eighteenth century the power of Babylon was broken by a great Hittite incursion from beyond the Taurus mountains. The Hittites or Khatti retired, but the ruin they had wrought gave entry to a new people from the east, apparently Aryan predecessors of the Medes and Persians, who set up the dynasty called Kassite in Babylonia, and a kingdom known as Mitanni in north-west Mesopotamia, though they only provided their dominions with an Aryan aristocracy ruling over a Semite population with a Sumerian infusion in lower Mesopotamia. Somewhat later we find these Kassite and Mitannian monarchies in active diplomatic relations with the Egyptian Pharaohs, especially with Amenhotep III. and IV., which brings our story down to the fourteenth century.

Assyria now appears on the stage—a Semite power with its headquarters on the upper Tigris, pushing itself cautiously towards a front rank position by playing off Mitanni against Babylonia, each of which regarded the growing power as its own vassal and dependent. The Hittites, too, thrusting from Asia Minor, were aiming at an ascendancy in Syria. Mitanni during the century was crumbling away. In the thirteenth century the Hittites became the dominant power of the northwest, but in the middle of the century there began a period of chaos in which Assyria made her first bid for ascendancy; the Hittite dominion perished, apparently of inertia. Babylonia and Assyria strove against each other with alternating fortunes, and finally, early in the twelfth century, the Kassites were ejected from Babylon by a dynasty of native origin.

Names which were to become extremely familiar at a later date—the first Babylonian Nebuchadrezzar and the first Assyrian Tiglath-Pileser, both of them distinguished warriors—appear in the latter years of the century; but then there followed two hundred uneventful years before Assyria again arose portentous, and during that period there had arisen that group of Syrian powers, the records of one among which have given to all peoples nursed upon the Hebrew

Scriptures a sense of extreme if superficial intimacy with Babylon and Nineveh, the Chaldee and the Assyrian.

In the days of " Jeroboam the son of Nehbat, who made Israel to sin," began the revival of Assyria under Adad-Nirari. From the close of his reign (890 B.C.) the registering of annual magistracies (like that of the Roman consuls in later days) preserved a precise record of dates in Assyrian history. In 884 Adad-Nirari's grandson Ashur-nasir-pal succeeded to the sceptre of Nineveh, inaugurating the long and awful period of the Assyrian tyranny. Nineveh stood on the outskirts of the Mesopotamian civilization. The conqueror Ashur-nasir-pal organized the people of Asshur as a purely military state, existing for the purpose of conquest and adopting " frightfulness " as the guiding principle of the conqueror. The rude Assyrians were trained as a nation in arms, utterly merciless, lusting for blood, cruel from sheer delight in inflicting pain.

Ashur-nasir-pal's victories were accompanied by the most ruthless massacres on record. Sated after some years of campaigning, he passed the close of his reign in raising magnificent temples to Asshur

and the other gods of his people. He did not turn upon Babylonia ; the region of his conquests was in the north and the west. His son Shalmaneser, invading Syria, met with a check at the hands of Benhadad. The material success of his reign was the conquest of Babylonia, which he accomplished by effecting the restoration of a dethroned prince who necessarily received the crown as his vassal. In fact, the large mercantile community of Babylonia found greater security for its trade under the military sovereignty.

During the latter part of the ninth century Assyria was hard pressed by the expanding state of Urartu or Ararat in the northern mountains ; and then there followed half a century of disintegration, which was ended by the usurpation (745) of the military adventurer who took the name of Tiglath-Pileser IV.—just after Babylon had, apparently, recovered independence under Nabonassar—and a new era of devastating conquest began.

A military demonstration sufficed to convince Babylonia of the wisdom of submission. A short campaign taught the eastern mountaineers a similar lesson. Then it was the turn of Syria and Urartu.

LORDLY INDOLENCE BESIDE THE STREAM OF LIFE

Dignity of presence and of manner the Arab possesses in good measure, but of the dignity of labour he has no idea. He deems it more consistent with his masculine importance to sit in stately indolence among his peers, enjoying the soothing influence of tobacco smoke cooled in the hookah set before him where he watches the activity of the rest of the human swarm

Photo, W. A. Harvey

Northern Syria and Urartu were smitten. Then came southern Syria. The two Hebrew kingdoms were prompt in submission. Wherever resistance had been offered Tiglath-Pileser introduced the system most characteristic of Assyrian conquest—the populations were deported en masse, and other populations were imported to take their place.

When all Syria had been rendered tributary, the conqueror bestowed his attention on a disordered Babylonia where Chaldeans from the south-eastern borders were giving trouble, having overturned the reigning dynasty. The Assyrian subjugated the Chaldeans, and at last set on his own head the crown of " Sumer and Akkad " (729).

Assyria's Splendour and Extinction

A revolt in the south brought upon Samaria the vengeance of Tiglath-Pileser's short-lived heir Shalmaneser, who was succeeded in 722 by Sargon. Sargon completed the destruction of the kingdom of Israel. But he found himself ousted from Babylon by a Chaldean rebel, backed by the power of Elam. The south revolted again, and received support from Egypt. The Assyrian arms were completely victorious, but the conquest of Egypt was postponed. The empire was again being threatened from the north-west and north-east. Conquest was impracticable, but Sargon's return from the south brought a pacification of the borders, and the Chaldean Merodach Baladan was suppressed in Babylonia.

Sargon's successor Sennacherib lost Babylon to the Chaldeans and Elamites, but recovered it again. His unsuccessful expedition against Egypt and the destruction of his host is recorded in the Hebrew chronicle and by Herodotus, but not in the Assyrian register. The Egyptian conquest was actually effected by his son Esarhaddon, and completed by the next king, Ashurbanipal (Sardanapalus), who also waged war upon Elam, to the complete destruction of that power.

Empire follows Empire in the East

But when he died, in 626, the vast, unwieldy empire was hopelessly unmanageable, for the Assyrian never organized an imperial system like Darius a century later. Under feeble successors it broke up into its component parts. Babylon once more set up a Chaldean dynasty, and in conjunction with the newly-arisen power of Media fell upon Assyria. In 606 B.C. the tyrant power was blotted out for ever.

Babylon rose again on the ashes of Nineveh. Nebuchadrezzar, as a conqueror, continued the Assyrian practice of deportation. He was also a great military engineer, and the probable creator of those " hanging gardens " which were

counted among " the seven wonders of the world." But his reign ended in 562 ; his successors were incompetent, and in 539 Cyrus the Persian turned upon Babylon from his victories in the west, captured it, and absorbed it into the Persian empire of which he was the creator. From that time Mesopotamia was never anything but a province of one empire or another, until in the eighth century (A.D.) Bagdad rose to prominence as the headquarters of the Moslem Caliphate.

After Persia was overthrown by Alexander the Great the Macedonian empire fell to pieces. Mesopotamia went to the Seleucids, but in course of time, when the dominion of the Parthian nomads arose in the east, Irak, or Babylonia, was generally included in the Parthian empire. Rome never established a continuous authority beyond the Euphrates. In the early centuries of the Christian era Parthia gave way to a new Persian empire, which, in its turn, generally kept its hold upon Mesopotamia, though in perpetual conflict with the eastern Roman empire after Constantinople became its headquarters. The contest reached its climax at the beginning of the seventh century (A.D.), but was brought to an end by the sudden irruption of the followers of Mahomet.

Vicissitudes under Moslem Sway

In 632, the year of the Prophet's death, Persia had been greatly weakened by its struggle with the emperor Heraclius. It still kept its hold upon Irak proper, the old Babylonia ; Syria and the old Assyria were more or less subject to the empire. The first caliphs turned the arms of the Arabs upon Persia and Syria separately. Within ten years all that had ever formed part of the Assyrian or Babylonian empires was under Moslem sway.

Both Irak and Syria were mainly Semitic, but Irak was largely impregnated with what may be called cosmopolitan but especially Persian influences, and also by a hereditary hostility to the Syrians. During the next hundred years, while Islam was confused by sectarian antagonisms, the orthodox Caliphate, resting upon Syria and with its headquarters at Damascus, found Irak and Persia perpetual hotbeds of disaffection; and when, in the middle of the eighth century, the Ommiad caliphs were, in the east, overturned by the Abbasides (descendants of the Prophet's uncle), the Abbasid caliphs established their headquarters in Irak ; through which lay not only the road communications with the farther east, but also the sea communications by way of the newly-established Basra on the Shat-el-Arab at the head of the Persian Gulf.

Here a new court and a new city were established at Bagdad on the Tigris, which may be said to have taken the place of the ancient Babylon. Before the end of the century Bagdad had become the wealthiest, the most luxurious, and the most enlightened city in a world where enlightenment was as yet very much to seek, though the splendour of the great Haroun Al Raschid (786-809) is not without legendary elements, like that of his great contemporary Charlemagne.

Not only was Bagdad the centre of commerce, the terminus of the caravans from the east, it was the centre also of the most active literary and scientific culture of the middle " Middle Ages." Even the Hellenism which had perished in Western Europe was preserved or revived by the Bagdad Caliphate, and filtered into the west from Saracen more than from Byzantine sources. And it is curious to find that an infinitely wider toleration was permitted to diversities of religious opinion than in the Western world till many centuries later. The Arab might wage war on idols, but the infidel might go his own ignorant way, and the heretic might preach what he chose so long as his heresies were not politically subversive.

The Arabianised Irak was great as the seat of a powerful Arab Caliphate. Its political importance waned as the Abbasid dynasty found itself compelled to rely upon mercenary forces, instead of upon the traditional tribal system of levies, for the maintenance of its own authority. Islam spread into the Trans-Oxus regions, where it found fanatical adherents in the Turkish tribes ; the Turk mercenaries, called in by the caliphs, soon became their actual masters while nominally their servants. The Turkish ascendancy reduced Irak to impotence.

The devastating inroad of the Mongols in the thirteenth century completed its ruin. Persia broke away from Bagdad, and for some centuries Irak was alternately a province of the Turkish or the neo-Persian dominion till in the seventeenth century it was permanently incorporated in the Ottoman empire. As in all areas dominated by the Turk, not only did all

progress cease, retrogression took its place. Long before the nineteenth century Mesopotamia had reverted to the primitive Semitic tribal conditions which preceded Hammurabi, while Turkish rule meant little but the exaction of taxes for the benefit more of Turkish officials than of the government they were supposed to serve.

The available statistics at the beginning of the twentieth century gave about two-thirds of the population as Arabs (the prevalent language is Arabic), Kurds (the hillmen who troubled the Shalmanesers) and Turks making up almost another quarter, the miscellaneous remnant being chiefly congregated in the towns. The population of upper Mesopotamia is much more sparse than that of Irak proper.

In the latter part of the nineteenth century there set in a period of European competition for concessions, the British having already established a considerable trade and an appreciable influence which was jealously regarded in other quarters.

When in the first months of the Great War Turkey threw in her lot with Germany, Arabia, with the approval of the Allies, rejected the Turkish authority and recognized the King of Hejaz. The Turkish armies in Mesopotamia were finally shattered in the campaign of 1918. The Turk was ejected from Mesopotamia, of which the administration was temporarily assigned to Britain as mandatory of the Powers.

But it was by no means clear that the Arab tribes would accept a British protectorate even with Arab autonomy as an ultimate goal ; and in 1921 the Arab Emir Feisal, son of King Hussein of Hejaz, accepted the proffer of the crown of Irak upon certain understandings— generally presumed to mean that the British administration would carry on with his authority, pending the organization of the new State under British guardianship, of which the immediate withdrawal could only result in chaos. With the proclamation of King Feisal on August 23, 1921, our story closes.

IRAK: FACTS AND FIGURES

The Country
District between Kurdistan north, Syria and Palestine west, Arabia south, and Persia east. Total area estimated at 143,250 square miles. Includes vilayets of Bagdad, Basra, and Mosul. Population (1920), 2,849,282.

Government
After the Great War recognized as an independent State under a Mandatory Power (Great Britain). Emir Feisal, third son of King of Hejaz, proclaimed King of Irak by popular vote August 23, 1921, and a Cabinet was formed to succeed the provisional Council of State.

Defence
Except with consent of Mandatory, local forces to be employed solely for the maintenance of order and defence.

Commerce and Industries
Chief product, oil ; petroleum wells at Qaiyarah, near Mosul, and at Mandali. Bitumen deposits at Hit. Wheat, barley, cotton, dates, and ground nuts grown ; soil rich, and agriculture being developed by irrigation. Principal exports, carpets and grain. Railways link Basra, Samarra, Kefil, Hilla, Bagdad, Kuraitu, Kazimain, Kala Shergat, and Kut-el-Amara. Telegraph lines, 2,995 miles. Chief seaport, Basra.

Religion and Education
About 1,146,680 Sunni Mahomedans, 1,494,000 Shiahs, 87,488 Jews, 78,790 Christians. Numerous Government schools ; special attention given to secondary and technical education.

BAREFOOT BEAUTY STOOPS TO FILL HER BUCKET

Where the young stream bursts impetuously from the grassy hilltop, making before the black entrance of this stone-mouthed tunnel a frothy, bubble-flecked pool beneath the brambles, a sweet-featured colleen leans to swing her stout bucket down to the water. Her face she has draped demurely with a bright-hued handkerchief, but, against the background of rock, there are charms less effectually veiled

Photo, Horace W. Nicholls

Ireland

I. Life & Character in North & South

By Milton Kelly

Author, Lecturer, and Journalist

NO people has flowed into so many world-channels as the Irish, made its character so widely familiar, or, in proportion to its size, contributed more liberally to the number of the world's famous men. Wherever the English language is spoken, Irishmen are found in high positions, and in the ranks of the workers, influencing the course of events by their eloquence, their management of men, their industry, and their votes.

On the Continent of Europe, especially in France and in Spain, are many families of distinction descended from Irish " adventurers " who took service in foreign armies or settled abroad to make their fortunes during the centuries when their own country offered them small opportunity of distinguishing themselves, and when in England they were looked upon with suspicion and prejudice.

Genius Without Honour at Home

Irish wit, Irish learning, Irish military genius were known to the peoples of the Continent before they were appreciated in the British Isles. In the United States of America, in Canada, in Australia, it has been given to the Irish to take such a part in the building up of the new countries as they have not been able to play in their own old country. They were the first to pour in vast numbers into the United States, and they have profoundly influenced the development of that branch of the American nation. From the first they exhibited a positive genius for political control. They worked as they had never worked in the moist, soft climate of Ireland ; they rapidly became prosperous, and they soon established a political ascendancy in both local and national affairs from which they have not yet been ousted.

Everywhere in the civilized world the qualities of the Irish are known, and, though they are frequently made fun of, they are valued and respected. In general the character of the Irish is singularly misunderstood. They are apt to be reckoned among the light-hearted peoples. The deep strain of melancholy in their nature is overlooked because they are not inclined to parade it. Their Celtic origin is supposed to show itself in muddle-headedness, in rapid transition from one extreme of feeling to another, in facile mirth.

Subtlety Mistaken for Simplicity

The same mistake is made about the French, who are commonly supposed by those who do not know them to be a " gay " race. In truth, their Celtic ancestry has endowed them with a character not unlike that of the Irish ; at the base of it in both nations is a sceptical disinclination to take the world and mankind seriously, a whimsical conviction that a witty comment upon a difficulty is of as much use as a practical solution.

When the Englishman in Ireland finds that he is answered as the Irish think he will like to be answered, he is apt to set this down to simplicity on their part. It is, indeed, the result of a trait very far removed from simplicity. They speak to him as they would to a child. They understand that in mind he is, compared with them, childlike. His mental processes are straightforward. Black is black and white white. He believes in going directly towards whatever he desires. He has no doubt that the aims he sets before him are the aims which Heaven meant him to pursue. He cannot understand the detached attitude of the Irish towards much that he considers of the highest importance. No two peoples

GIRLS WHOSE NIMBLE FINGERS HELP TO MAKE BELFAST FAMOUS

Here are some happy Ulster girls from a linen factory of North Ireland's chief city. Irish linen long ago made a name for itself, and many of the finest handkerchiefs and lingerie come from this source. The flax fibre is derived from the stalk of the plant. Each girl in the photograph has round her waist a cord sustaining various implements used in her work

Photo, J. Johnson

could be farther apart in mind and sympathies than the Irish and the English who have ruled over them for nearly seven centuries Yet there is far more common to them in the way of racial stock than is generally believed. It is usual to speak of the Irish as Celts; as a rule both their good and less amiable qualities are attributed to the Celtic temperament. They pride themselves on this temperament, and they are accustomed to speak of the Irish civilization which flourished before that of England had taken shape as if it had been a purely Celtic development. But there is reason to suppose that both the elements of this Irish civilization and the Celtic language itself were introduced into the country by Scandinavian invaders of Teutonic origin, who arrived probably a hundred years or so before Christ.

It is clear from what remains of Irish literature that there was once a dominant race of fair-haired and long-limbed people, with a servile population who were dark-haired and short. These two separate stocks remained until the Norman kings of England began the struggle to hold Ireland under the English Crown by force—that is to say until the thirteenth century. After that the misfortunes which befell all classes drew the two races together, and ever since they have blended more and more, though it is still clear to everyone who has studied Irish types that there remain distinct traces of the ancient division.

There are dark, short people who plainly belong to the Mediterranean Celtic race which laid the foundations of Irish culture, and there are blue-eyed, fair-haired people who are quite as evidently of Scandinavian origin. It is often suggested that the dark-haired Irish with foreign grace in their movements and their manners are the result of the Armada being destroyed and many Spanish ships being driven ashore on the Irish coast in the sixteenth century. There is no need to look for the explanation so late in history. Such people are no doubt the descendants of the settlers in Ireland who came from the Mediterranean. They are the true Celts, if there are any left. The cast of appearance which is considered typically Irish—the blue eyes, the fair hair and complexion—cannot be reckoned Celtic at all, but is racially akin to the appearance of the English so far as they are descended from Scandinavian stocks.

There is an interesting proof that in the days when Ireland stood far above England in the arts and the knowledge which constitute civilization there existed an aristocracy of foreign origin and a population in servitude consisting of the former possessors of the land. There are two collections of ancient manuscripts dating from this period. One is called " The Book of the Dun Cow," the other " The Book of Leinster." In each of these all the

IRISH PEASANTS ENJOY THE SPORT OF KINGS

The sporting instinct is as strong in the Irishman as in the Englishman, and a race meeting draws the inhabitants of every cabin within measurable distance. This peasant has packed himself and his wife and his half-dozen children into the donkey-cart and brought them out for a day's pleasurable excitement at the Kildare and National Hunt races on the famous steeplechase course at Punchestown

DÁIL EIREANN, THE IRISH PARLIAMENT, SITS IN DUBLIN TO TREAT WITH GREAT BRITAIN

Members of the Dáil in their crowded rows, representatives of an American delegation, archbishops and bishops in the distinguished visitors' gallery around the statues, and those among the public fortunate enough to have gained access to the gallery above—all have eyes and attention fixed on one man, De Valera. He is seated in the high-backed chair behind the table beneath which the pencils of busy reporters keep pace with the momentous words. This is one of the historic sessions at the Dublin Mansion House in 1921 when, on August 23, the Assembly, under Republican influence, rejected the British peace offer

GUARDIANS OF NORTHERN POLITICS: ULSTER'S CABINET IN CONCLAVE

Under the Government of Ireland Act passed in 1920 the legislative powers over the six northern counties were entrusted to the Senate and House of Commons of Northern Ireland. The Ministry formed is here seen in deliberation under the presidency of Sir James Craig, the Ulster Premier, who is seated at the head of the table. The scene is an apartment in Stormount Castle, just outside Belfast

SOUTH IRELAND'S SENATE AT THE RATIFICATION OF THE TREATY

Upright at his desk in the centre of the oak room in the Dublin Mansion House is the Speaker of the House of Commons for Southern Ireland reading the momentous words at the final confirmation of the Peace Treaty. Michael Collins and Arthur Griffith were both present at this sitting which opened a new volume of Ireland's chequered history in which England was to share no part

characters held up to admiration for their bravery, their courtesy, their good faith, are men with flowing fair hair and of good height, while every person described as mean, untrustworthy, ill-natured, and unpleasant, has close-cropped dark hair, and is short of stature.

All of these manuscripts were written either by or for the aristocracy with the idea of impressing upon the overlords what a fine race they were, and how just was their rule over the baser folk. When the two stocks were amalgamated under English pressure, the dark-haired people, being the more

conversation. This gives a flavour and a zest to daily intercourse which are absent from the talk of more matter-of-fact peoples. The proverbs are wise as well as witty. Here are some examples :

The advice you pay for is worth more than the advice you get for nothing.

Don't say grace until you have got your dinner.

Don't speak good of yourself, nor ill either.

Don't show your teeth unless they can bite.

No one can be called wise until he has had misfortunes.

When you go to court leave your soul at home.

BARGES LADEN WITH MALT LIQUOR ON THE RIVER LIFFEY

For more than a hundred and fifty years Dublin stout and porter have been famous the world over, and their manufacture gives employment to thousands of hands in the Free State capital. Barges laden with casks of the popular liquor swarm on the Liffey in the neighbourhood of Kingsbridge, where the quays and stores of the greatest brewery are situated

numerous, had the greater influence on the appearance and the character of the resultant Irish nation. But it did not by any means succeed in washing out the Scandinavian traits, which have remained prominent to this day.

A characteristic which the Irish have in common with the Spaniards, and which dates back possibly to a common ancestry on the sunny Mediterranean shore, is the use of proverbs in

The same terseness of expression, combined with lyrical charm, is found in the Irish folksongs. There was no ballad literature to speak of until the songs of Tom Moore supplied something of the kind, but the intensity of imagination to be discovered in the poetry of the people transcends anything that has grown out of other parts of the United Kingdom. The Irish fairy tales have also a more poetic

BLESSING THE IRISH TRICOLOUR AT GORMANSTOWN CAMP

Much romance of history is concentrated in flags as symbols of the independence and honour of communities, and it is in accordance with natural instinct that the blessing of Heaven is invoked upon national flags flown for the first time. Great ceremonial attended the hoisting of the flag of the Irish Free State over official buildings and military centres handed over by the British Government

SHEDDING THE ARCHIEPISCOPAL BLESSING ON A NEW CHURCH

Lying about four miles north of Dublin, Finglas, the little village on the " clear stream " which gives it its name, has long been famous for its old church dating nearly from the time of S. Patrick and for its ancient Irish cross. Its religious associations were added to in 1922, when the Roman Catholic archbishop of Dublin consecrated a new church dedicated to S. Canice

ANNUAL PROCESSION OF ORANGEMEN IN BELFAST COMMEMORATING THE VICTORIES OF WILLIAM III.

In the year 1795 the Orange Society, taking its name from William of Orange, was formed in Armagh for the advancement of Protestant organization. It met with opposition from rival formations, notably the White Boys, who championed the religion of their country, and Wolfe Tone's Society of United Irishmen, which aimed at uniting Catholic and Protestant to oust the English. Orangery spread its ramifications over the United Kingdom and the British Empire, and, as seen above,

character than those of the English or the Germans; they are more akin to the Russian. A great many of them are concerned with the Little People or Good People who were supposed to inhabit the interiors of the hills.

It may be surmised that the origin of these supernatural beings is traceable to the disappearance of the race which held the country before the Celts from the Mediterranean drove them into remote mountains and inaccessible valleys. Who they were is uncertain; they were exterminated or chased into corners by the Milesians about ten centuries before Christ. Travellers catching sight of the fugitives may have spread the story that they lived under the earth, and so the legend of a race of immortals may have come into being. At first they were regarded as gods exercising divine power. Then they became national heroes; now they are thought of as tiny creatures, gnomes, or elves. Not even the power of the Church of Rome has been able to root out of the Irish peasant mind the lingering belief in these relics of a pagan mythology.

Imagination Preferred to Intellect

Superstition in some form or another holds sway over the imaginations of most Irish people. Second sight, warnings of death, banshees, curses laid on individuals or families, the interference of the fairies with mortal concerns, all these and numbers of other supernatural occurrences are stoutly defended as coming within fairly common experience. Protestantism, which bases itself upon reason and invites men to test their faith by the intellect, has never made much headway in Ireland. That is due not so much to any innate religious vein in the Irish nature as to the fact that their Church long ago became identified with their national feelings and desires. It was the attempt made to impose the Reformation upon Ireland which bound people and Church so closely together. Protestant became among them a synonym for "oppressor." The parish priest, who took a leading part in the struggle for

freedom, made the Church a rallying-point for all the national forces.

This had a hardening effect upon English opinion during the long period through which Roman Catholics were regarded as enemies of the State. The rival religions began then that disastrous contest which has so complicated and intensified the misfortunes of Ireland.

Protestantism and Oppression

If the Irish had not been induced to support James II. after he had been driven out of England for sound reasons, there would not be one-tenth of the bitterness between the north and the south which still corrodes the nation, there would not have been the same animosity in the English mind against it. The Irish stood for the Stuart because he was a Roman Catholic and they had orders from Rome. But they stood for him also because they had reason to fear the English Parliament which had driven him out, and had, not many years before, sent many of their people to the plantations in Virginia and Carolina.

Forgetful of history, many English people complain that the Irish are by nature a turbulent, dissatisfied race; that it is their restlessness which has been the cause of all their troubles; that they would never be contented, whatever form of government they lived under.

Sense and Sensibility

That is not a reading of the Irish character which receives any support from those who have attentively studied it without any preconceived opinions or any desire to make out a case against the Irish people. The view expressed by a French traveller (M. de Latocnaye) in the country towards the end of the eighteenth century is admitted by those who know Ireland well to come much nearer the truth:

Guided by capable men who are actuated by motives of public welfare, there is no people I have known so easily led for good. These frequent seditions prove nothing more than the sensibility of the race, and if the Government would only give up at once and absolutely the attempt to anglicise the Irish at any cost, and

SMILING AND PENSIVE SHYNESS

On their way home from gathering brushwood, perhaps for the pig's bedding, these two mites have been caught in a happy pose. Possibly they must choose between tam-o'-shanter and bare feet, or shoes and no hat

Photo, A. W. Cutler

the practical sense of the English would have persuaded them to desist from an undertaking in which success was clearly not to be won.

While the English pay too little heed to history, the Irish pay too much. They treasure the memory of the wounds inflicted on them. They will not let bygones be bygones or recognize the efforts that the English have made from time to time, especially during the period from about 1890 onwards, to mend the breach between them. All nations that have suffered persecution carry their recollections far back and harbour resentful thoughts; it would be unreasonable to expect that the Irish should let sporadic shoots of goodwill blot out the record of seven centuries of misgovernment and repression. But there certainly would have been more chance of reaching a happier state of relationship if the mass of moderate feeling in Ireland had triumphed at certain moments over the extreme sentiments of a few.

Here is revealed one of the defects of the Irish character. It has little of the sturdiness of conviction which is found among the northern English and the Scotch. Irishmen are fearful of public opinion. They will not express their disapproval of counsels they consider mistaken for lack of the courage or the obstinacy to speak out their view. They allow themselves to be swept along with a stream which they believe in their hearts is likely to lead to misfortune. So it is always the extreme of opinion that seems to prevail in Ireland. Thus it happens that every

would lead them through their prejudices and customs, it would be possible to do with them anything that could be wished. In that passage the French observer pointed to the cause which more than any other has kept Ireland disturbed, the " attempt to anglicise the Irish." No two peoples could be less alike, therefore the attempt was bound to miscarry. Every renewal of it has been met with more determined opposition. It might have been thought that its failure would have taught the rulers of the United Kingdom wisdom, and that

OULD PAT AND THE COSTUME THAT, LIKE HIMSELF, IS PASSING

With the improved circumstances of trade and communications prior to the Great War, much that was once considered characteristic in Irish dress and Irish manner had fast begun to disappear. But this white-haired ancient, on whose fine old face time has drawn the lines of age, is, with his blackthorn stick and knee-breeches, a concept of the Irishman that dies hard

Photo, A. W. Cutler, by permission of Messrs. Raphael Tuck & Sons, Ltd.

concession has been followed by demands for still further measures of independence, with the result that the English, taking fright, have withdrawn even what they had screwed themselves up to offer, and the contest has grown more envenomed by hatred on both sides.

The Irish contention is that the fault lies with the English, who always delay so long over their concessions that by the time they are granted the national spirit has gone forward and is eager for something more. If the Home Rule Bill had been passed within a few years of its first introduction by Mr. Gladstone it would certainly have been accepted, as an instalment at any rate. The thirty years which were spent in discussing it and in persuading the

WITH A RED FLANNEL PETTICOAT OVER HER HEAD

This is a peasants' cabin in Connemara, where the folk of the district, as exemplified by the woman on the right of the doorway, often wear a petticoat in place of the shawl, like that round the head of the younger woman seated with the baby. Behind are the rough thatched roof, white walls, and low floor on which struts a hen, picking up unconsidered trifles

Photo, A. W. Cutler, by permission of Messrs. Raphael Tuck & Sons, Ltd.

"THE RUDE INELEGANCE OF POVERTY REIGNS HERE ALONE"

Home comfort as realized in even the poorest English cottages is entirely lacking in the poorest Irish cabins, and this bare interior could be matched in far too many Connemara homes. Only the peat fire is never missing, with, hanging over it, the iron pot in which the potatoes and the water are boiled. For the rest, a few low stools often represent all the furniture

Photo, A. W. Cutler

English to make the experiment saw a wide development of the Irish ambition to govern themselves. The very agitation which went on over the measure was bound to leave that ambition broader and deeper than it had been before. And when, after the Home Rule Bill had been passed, its operation was suspended because the Liberal Party leaders in England could not bring themselves to trust the Irish during the Great War, it became certain that some advance towards independence much more alarming to the English mind would be demanded. This tendency, strong enough before, to

IRISH SCHOOLBOYS OF THE CONNEMARA COAST SAFELY SHELTERED BEHIND PETTICOATS

With the single exception of the biggest lad on the left all these schoolboys are wearing petticoats, one of the quaint customs prevailing in the Connemara district. The peasantry of this region are steeped in superstition, and still preserve a firm belief in good and bad fairies. It is said that bad fairies are liable to run away with little boys but will not touch little girls, and for this reason the boys are disguised as girls until they are old enough to take care of themselves

Photo, A. W. Cutler

WHERE SPECIAL VEHICLES ARE NEEDED FOR THE NARROW ROADS

This is an Irish jaunting-car from the Claddagh district of Galway. There is accommodation for four passengers besides the driver, who usually sits across the front of the "well" between the seats. This last not only provides a rest for the back, but has a lid, and can be used for carrying small luggage. The footboards can fold up over the seats, a device that is often necessary in the narrow country roads, and leaves the car no wider than the distance between the hubs of the wheels

Photo, A. W. Cutler, by permission of Messrs. Raphael Tuck & Sons, Ltd.

BURNING SEAWEED FOR KELP ON A STONE-STREWN SHORE OF THE ARAN ISLANDS

Kelp, the ash of burnt seaweed, was at one time produced in some quantity in both Scotland and Normandy as well as in Ireland. From it were derived soda salts, used in soap and glass making, salts of potash, and iodine. Cheaper processes were, however, discovered, and kelp-burning is gradually dying out. Above, some ragged coast-dwellers are seen about to throw some handfuls of seaweed on their fire, about twenty tons being required to produce one ton of kelp

Photo, A. W. Cutler

TWO RAGGED KELP-BURNERS OF THE ARAN ISLANDS AND A STACK OF DRYING SEAWEED

Before being fit to burn the seaweed used in kelp-making has to be dried in the sun for several months, and kelp stacks, as seen in the photograph, are piled near the shore, and in this case, perhaps, rather near the waves for safety. The top of the stack is secured by a kind of net with a very wide mesh, and at the bottom is a foundation of stones. These weather-beaten islanders depend largely for their livelihood on the dwindling kelp industry

Photo, A. W. Cutler

SMILING IRISH GOSSOONS ENGAGED IN STACKING SODS OF PEAT ON A MOUNTAIN BOG

About three million acres in Ireland are bog, yielding an inexhaustible supply of peat, a useful fuel. The vegetable tissues of aquatic plants are disintegrated by the combined effect of moist atmosphere and bacterial action, and the decomposing products sink to the bottom of water-filled depressions, where they become compressed and carbonised. The sods are removed layer by layer with long, narrow, very sharp spades, called slanes, and are stacked for about ten days to dry

Photo, A. W. Cutler

HAULING CUT PEAT HOME TO BARNA, ON THE COAST OF GALWAY

Mountain peat, composed mainly of sphagnum and andromeda mosses, makes better fuel than the lowland peat, which is principally hypnum moss. The top layers are used for moss litter, paper pulp, and textile fabrics, and only the compact dark peat obtained two feet and more below the surface is much good for fuel. The calorific value of pure peat is rather more than half that of a similar weight of black coal, and it is, of course, much easier to raise from the soil

Photo, A. W. Cutler

WHEN THE LOAD IS WELCOME THE BURDEN IS EASY

Clean to handle, cheap, and plentiful, peat is much appreciated by the Irish peasant women, two of whom, mother and daughter, are here shown bending willing shoulders to their well-filled baskets of fuel. It throws out a red and lurid flame, and fills the cabin interiors with an aromatic fragrance peculiarly its own that lingers in Irish memory as a true savour of home

Photo, A. W. Cutler

push forward with fresh proposals while previous ones hung in the balance, was reinforced by the adherence of the British and the Allied Governments generally to the principle of "self-determination" during the war. Ireland declined to forget that the right of Bohemia and of the Southern Slavs to insist upon being free from the yoke of Austrian domination had been championed eloquently by the heads of the British Government and by the English Press.

The Irish were now prosperous. They had managed by methods of agitation to secure Land Acts which enabled them to purchase at prices fixed by tribunals, and in defiance it might be of the wish of the owner, the land which had been taken from them over a long period of centuries and given or sold to English and Scottish settlers. Their agriculture was paying handsomely. For the first time since their industries were destroyed by English statesmen intent upon benefiting English trade, they seemed to have a fair prospect of seeing their manufactures revive and bring wealth with them. It was hoped by many in England who had not troubled to study the Irish character that these material advantages would put the idea of self-government out of their heads. The English regard the management of public affairs with quite unsentimental practicality. So long as they can transact their business and go about as they please in security they care little who exercise authority. They have had Danish kings, Norman kings, French kings, Scottish kings, a Dutch king, and German kings, and they have for the most part got along comfortably enough with them all. When they did not find comfort, they turned a king out or cut his head off, or forced him to accept a position of subordination to Parliament. They find it very hard indeed to understand why a people should make a fuss about governing themselves when they are well-off and can look forward to increasing their bank balances, living in better houses, seeing more food upon their tables, wearing better clothes.

Therefore it came as a shock to them that the Irish, instead of dropping their demand for the right to govern themselves, should still insist upon it, and even ask for more complete independence than had ever been formally suggested in the course of earlier agitation.

No leader of the Irish had yet put forward the proposal that Ireland should be free, if she chose, to become an independent republic. O'Connell had worked for repeal of the union. Parnell would have been content with an Irish legislature for local affairs, leaving a certain number of Irish members at Westminster. The new leaders, De Valera and Arthur Griffith, announced that they would be satisfied with nothing less than full national status, carrying with it the liberty to establish any form of government for which the people might declare.

That these new leaders had the support of the people seemed to be proved by the result of the general

OLD-FASHIONED WHEELS OUSTED BY NEWFANGLED MILLS

Though spinning-wheels, such as this Galway peasant proudly exhibits, are occasionally found in remote parts of Ireland, they are becoming ever more rare, and must be sought rather in the shops of dealers in antiques. Upon these simple machines all the native homespun cloth was fashioned, honest stuff that might make modern manufacturers blush for their shoddy products

Photo, A. W. Cutler, by permission of Messrs. Raphael Tuck & Sons, Ltd.

elections in 1918, when the old National-ist Party was almost entirely swept out and members were elected pledged to support the Irish Parliament (Dáil Eirann), and to have nothing to do with the one at Westminster. Now began the attempt to disregard the English occupation. Courts of justice were established under the " Republic," an Irish Republican Army was formed. Soon the Republicans came into collision with the authorities. There were assassinations on a scale more alarming than in any previous agitation. Repressive measures served no purpose save to blow up the fire of rebellion.

Leaders' Lack of Moral Courage

If the leaders had stood boldly out against murder, if they had announced that they did not want the help of assassins, they would not have lost the sympathy of so many in England and Scotland. But they, like Parnell, hesitated to follow the impulse of their hearts. They were afraid of losing support, of being thought lukewarm. Although Parnell disproved the charge of having encouraged murderers and was known to hate their vile deeds, he would not speak his mind plainly. He would not risk all for what he believed to be the right course, and say, " That is my opinion, and sooner than act against my conviction I will cease to be your leader." He was subject, in spite of his strength of character, to this weakness of the Irish nature. The Sinn Fein leaders suffered from the same disinclination to condemn acts which they detested. The violent party gained the power and the English hardened their hearts, saying they would not be intimidated, and that they would give as good as they got.

Military Rule and Civil War

So began what soon came to be regarded by both sides as civil war. The country was put under military rule. A new force, more military even than the Royal Irish Constabulary, was recruited, largely among young men in England who had been officers during the Great War and who had failed to find employment after demobilisation. A policy of "reprisals" was resolved upon, and the state of the unhappy land grew steadily worse. The peaceable folk who wanted to go about their business undisturbed were crushed between the upper and the nether millstones of the Republican bands and the forces of the Crown. Yet these peaceable folk, by far the greatest part of the population, made no definite move to end this wretched state of affairs.

In England it is always the moderate counsel which prevails. There is always a compromise ; each side abates something of its claims. But in Ireland the victory falls to extreme opinions and measures. Those who would prefer to be moderates are carried over to the more violent group. Sentiment is allowed to play more and more the principal part ; judgement, cool reckoning up of the possibilities of the situation, reason, common sense, are given no chance to seek for a solution.

Fatal Mutual Misunderstanding

In private affairs the Englishman and the Irishman usually hit it off well. The Irishman is apt to flare up and demand what the Englishman calls impossibilities and to threaten a complete breaking-off of relations. But the Englishman knows that if he keeps quiet and does nothing to stir up fresh flames of indignation the fury will subside in a little while, and the Irishman will smile at his own excitement and agree to some reasonable settlement. If only this method could have been followed in political affairs, both countries would have been spared many deplorable occurrences and the inflaming of ill-will to a dangerous point.

Unfortunately, the English in the mass have never at all understood the Irish. For centuries they were taught to think of the inhabitants of the island so close to them as savages, as " wild men." They were the " mere Irish ! " who did not count for anything when their interests clashed with those of the settlers among whom their lands had been divided. The English know nothing of the learning and art, the trade

AWAITING A BITE IN A LIKELY SPOT FOR ROCK-BREAM AND POLLOCK

Though the sea is eighty feet below these lichened cliffs, and the chances of losing a good fish in the process of elevation must be great, yet the tackle is stout, and this is no affair of finesse and fine casts. These are utilitarian anglers to whom the cooking-pot's future contents are naturally of more appeal than sport's uncertain chances, and to whom an empty creel means no dinner

Photo, A. W. Cutler

WAITING FOR THE DOCTOR IN REMOTE GALWAY

Family affection is very deep among the Irish peasantry, and the love which the parents lavish on their children is repaid in old age by the support ungrudgingly given to them by their offspring. There is poignant human interest in this photograph of a grandmother seeking assurance from her aged husband while rocking the cradle in which a sick grandchild has fallen into a troubled sleep

Photo, A. W. Cutler

and the industry, which flourished across the Irish Sea while they themselves were in a lower stage of civilization.

The Irish kept up regular intercourse with their kinsmen, the Gauls, which is another form of Gael, the ancient name for Irishman. They learned from them how to work gold and other metals, and applied their knowledge with originality of genius and an exquisite native skill. In the Dublin Museum there are some 500 golden ornaments belonging to ancient times, the result of searches and casual " finds " in graves and bogs and

the sites of old buildings. The weight of these ornaments is 570 ounces. In the British Museum a similar collection of English gold ornaments weighs only twenty ounces.

Ireland was a country rich in gold; there were deposits of silver and copper as well. From the Gauls the Irish learned designs for the shapes into which they fashioned metals; they learned also enamelling and the illumination of manuscripts. It was from Gaul that S. Patrick took ship to Ireland when he carried Christianity thither, and he

STUDY IN MATERNAL PRIDE AND FILIAL AFFECTION

Outside the low-roofed cabin, where she has spent most of her life, sits this aged Irish mother beside her long-limbed son. There is a dignity and beauty about her, and the wrinkled face whose eyes peer into the past, and the striped skirt that flutters beneath her apron, the crossed shawl and dingy cloth that binds her furrowed cheeks, each contribute to her fascination

Photo, A. W. Cutler

found himself, not in a land of "savages," but among scholars, who made fun of him for his lack of erudition in Latin and Greek.

The value of the Celtic literature in Ireland has been exaggerated. During the years in which the study of it revived all patriots were required to profess perfervid admiration for it. At the same time an effort was made to make Gaelic once more the language of the people. Many of them still spoke it in remote parts where it had never died out ; schools were set up for others to learn the old tongue as a means of strengthening Irish nationality. Another inducement offered to students of Gaelic was the charm and imaginative splendour of Celtic literature, but this soon proved to be rather a patriotic than a critical estimate. There is much beauty in the legends and the poems that have survived from the Celtic period, but the themes are limited in number ; there is monotony also in the expression, when they are considered as a whole.

Still, there is no doubt that had Ireland been allowed to develop her

NINETY-SEVEN AND THREE MAKE A HUNDRED

That poverty does not necessarily destroy good health is proved by these two natives of one of the most poverty-stricken corners of Connemara. The little maid, three years of age, has chubby cheeks and sturdy limbs, and the strong old gentleman, sitting so erect as he lights his pipe with a piece of glowing peat, is within three years of completing his century

Photo, A. W. Cutler, by permission of Messrs. Raphael Tuck & Sons, Ltd.

resources in her own way and to establish a civilization suited to the national character, she would have had a literature in later times worthy to compare with the literary output of England and Scotland. The number of Irish names in English literary history is large since the eighteenth century. Any Irishman who displayed talent crossed to England. In the reigns of the Georges the English contempt for the Irish was deepened by the experience

they had of numerous " swashbucklers," as they were called, attracted to London by the hope of making fortunes. Such " swaggering blades," full of bounce and stratagem, are frequently met with in eighteenth-century memoirs and novels. There was a saying at the time : " If one threw a naked Irishman over London Bridge he would come up at Westminster in a laced coat and a sword." That suggested, however, a greater knack of getting rich quickly than most of these Irish adventurers possessed. They lived, as a rule, upon the fringe of polite society. They were more often than not dependent upon the bounty of some patron, very likely a fellow-countryman who had fallen on his feet. They were ready to hire themselves out in any service that called for daring, impudence, eccentricity, or a quick wit.

Such men contributed liberally to make up the picture of the Irishman which was drawn by the English

imagination. They played the fool to please their patrons; they knew that oddity was expected of them, and they gave good measure of it. In speech, in manners, in dress, in his habits of life Edmund Burke resembled the Englishmen with whom he mixed, though he was superior to nearly all of them in parts and eloquence. But it was not he, nor the many like him, who was accepted by the English as typical of Irish character. The popular idea of the

IN THE FANTASTIC DRESS OF THE NOTORIOUS STRAW BOYS

During the early years of the nineteenth century sections of Ireland were overrun by one of the many terrorist gangs that have from time to time existed there, known, from their peculiar but effective grass masks, as the Straw Boys. Through these masks they could see without being recognized, and their habit of dressing as women added to their grotesque appearance

Photo, A. W. Cutler

FISHERMEN OF INISHMAAN CARRYING THEIR CURRAGHS DOWN TO THE WATER OF THE BAY

These canoes have been in use among the Aran Islanders for upwards of a thousand years. Although only something like one-eighth of an inch of stout sheet canvas saturated with tar separates the crew from the water, these light and fragile craft are very seaworthy, and the men who handle them are so skilful that they will venture out in rougher seas than the Galway steamer, which calls at the islands three times a week, cares to face

Irish was taken from the noisy, blustering, indigent fellows who posed deliberately as figures of fun in order to amuse those whose employment or charity kept them alive.

So the stage Irishman of the English theatre came into being, and the belief was firmly established in the English mind that the Irish were a jovial, lazy, improvident, dishonest lot, people who did not take themselves seriously nor expect anyone else to do so. A great deal of the blame for this misrepresentation must be laid on Irish authors. Sheridan parodied his countrymen when he drew Sir Lucius O'Trigger. Charles Lever's novels gave an altogether wrong idea of the Irish nature to the English readers who found them so amusing.

Mysticism and Philosophy

The first author of foremost position to make an attempt at showing how grotesquely the Irish character had been misconceived in England was Bernard Shaw. In " John Bull's Other Island " he drew attention to the melancholy tinge of that character, to the diffidence which marks off the Irish from the confident, practical English, to the mystical element in the Irish make-up which prevents it so often from accomplishing anything that the English mind can consider " definite."

The Irish aim in living is not accomplishment, but happiness ; and because happiness is so elusive, they are more often sad than merry, more inclined to pensive reflection than to jolly, self-satisfied talk. They would like to obey literally the command, " Take no thought for the morrow " ; the impossibility of obeying it literally they resent as a burden and an unnecessary complication of life. The Irishman does not save money, like the Scot, because he likes saving, but simply because he knows that if he does not save he will have no dowry to give his daughters and they will not get married, or because he must buy more cattle, or because one son must be sent to college so that there may be a priest in the family. The Scot thrives on economy, it seems to do him good, he has no wish to live

from hand to mouth. The Irishman has a feeling that he ought not to be expected to live in any more circumspect way.

Effect of Climate upon Character

Whether there may be, as many have surmised, some influence in the climate of Ireland which disinclines to steady industry is a question that has never been sufficiently discussed. It may be that the soft, damp, misty weather which is so prevalent over the western part of the island, and which affects the whole of it to a certain extent, is a deterrent to energy. But against this is set the example of the Ulster Irish who, though of Scottish origin, have been in Ireland long enough to be subjected to the influence of atmosphere, and who form one of the most tenacious and forcible populations in the whole of the British Empire.

A British ambassador in the United States, Sir Cecil Spring-Rice, hit off the characteristics of the Ulsterman in a remark he made about President Wilson, whose ancestry came from that part of Ireland. Someone said to him, in depreciation of the President : " What can you expect ? He is just a Scottish Presbyterian." To which the ambassador replied : " Ah, but from Ulster."

" What difference does that make ? " the American asked him.

" All the difference," he said, " between an alligator and a lizard."

Ulstermen are Irishmen

The Scots who were " planted " in the north of Ireland during the seventeenth century underwent a sea-change which has transformed their descendants into a race quite distinct from their blood-relations across the narrow water which divides Ulster from Scotland. Often the Ulster folk are spoken of by Englishmen who know nothing of them as if they were not Irish, as if they desired to stand apart from the Irish. But there is no quicker way to irritate an Ulsterman than to suggest that he is not Irish ; and, indeed, they have more in common with the rest of the people of the island than they have in opposition

SIMPLE INVENTIONS SUFFICE FOR SIMPLE NEEDS

Civilization progresses very slowly in the islands that fringe the west coast of Ireland, and implements are in use that show no improvement on mankind's earliest invented devices. There is no essential difference between this hand flourmill in use on Achill Island and the grinding-stones used by the early Chaldeans, and, to-day, by the natives of the Belgian Congo, as shown on page 391

Photo, A. W. Cutler, by permission of Messrs. Raphael Tuck & Sons, Ltd.

to southern traits. They are an emotional, excitable race, which the Lowland Scots certainly are not. They almost always have their eyes fixed on some end which, for all their success in business, is not altogether material.

Thus the wealthy merchants and manufacturers of Belfast took up the cause of " Ulster's liberty " with a fierce enthusiasm which equalled, and in truth surpassed, the Home Rule fervour of the south. They suddenly became attached to England and the Empire with a devotion which was all the more surprising when one recalled their attitude on many occasions towards the monarchy and the central government. A leader in British politics had spoken of their readiness to " kick the Crown into the Boyne " if they could not get exactly what they wanted. Now they were ready to die in the last ditch in order to prove their attachment to that Crown and to the Parliament which they had so roundly abused for neglect of their interests. Had they not been Irish they

WHERE THE CONNEMARA BOY HIDES HIS ILLICIT STILL

From their safe hiding-place beneath the water these very reprehensible Connemara men have fished up the tank, the connecting-arm, and the worm, or spiral copper tube, that compose the illicit still of which they are the proprietors. Having got the complete outfit safely stowed aboard, they are taking a last look round for lurking policemen before making for shore to begin operations

CRITICAL DISTILLERS SAMPLING THEIR ILLICIT POTHEEN

Having eluded the vigilance of peelers, the men set up their illicit still in some hollow or hedge well screened from observation. A rough fireplace is built, and directly over this the malt-filled still is set and connected with the worm enclosed in a cold chamber. The spirit vapour passing through the worm is condensed by the cold and trickles into the receiver in the form of potheen

Photos, A. W. Cutler

LAST JOURNEY BY DARRYNANE BAY'S SAD SHORE TO A LONG HOME BENEATH THE TURF

Leaning under their melancholy burden the bearers go, while behind come the mourners, the men hat in hand, and the women hooded in their shawls. The long chain of dark mountains, misty with the distance, gives a sombre frame to this picture of desolate sky and lonely water. Darrynane, on the wild Kerry coast, was the home of Daniel O'Connell, the Irish Liberator, who struggled so hardly for Catholic Emancipation. This arm of the vast Atlantic that has thrust into the hills is, for a while, at rest from the torment of the fierce westerly gales

Photo, C. Chichester

would never have treated politics so seriously (the Scots never have ; they know better) ; they would not have dramatised their opposition to Home Rule with such effective stage-management ; they would not have drilled an army and made ostentatious preparations for civil war. In England these preparations were laughed at. People could not believe them to be anything more than a very elaborate bluff. But the Ulster men were in earnest. They were carried away by the exuberance of their own bellicosity, to parody Disraeli's famous phrase about Gladstone. They marched and counter-marched, handled their rifles, went through their musketry instruction, engaged in laborious field operations, with a solemnity, with a total inability to see the humorous side of their proceedings, which were entirely and exclusively Irish.

Object-Lessons in Recalcitrancy

To everyone who took a calm survey of the situation it was obvious that in their first encounter with the regular troops, whom they expected to meet and drive from the field, they would be scattered, if not annihilated, by artillery, of which they possessed none. That prospect had not occurred to them, though it can hardly have escaped the attention of their leaders. These leaders, however, were politicians, unaccustomed to telling unpalatable truths. No doubt they reckoned on being able to gain their ends without bloodshed, and in a sense they did so. But it was the following of the Ulster example by the Home Rulers first, and then by the Sinn Feiners who formed the Irish Republican Army, that led to the worst period of violence in Ireland since the end of the eighteenth century. It would be contrary to the character of the English or the Scots to take up arms openly and with bravado in order to rebel against Imperial authority. By doing this the Ulstermen made good their claim to be counted as true Irishmen. They showed how completely the spirit of the country had entered into them.

The resemblance between north and south is seen again in the vindictive treasuring up of bitter memories and in the using of religion as a weapon for political purposes. In Ulster the Battle of the Boyne is spoken of as if it had been fought within the last year or two instead of in 1690. The southern people keep green their recollection of " old, unhappy far-off things " with the same inveterate hostility. Both cling to their forms of religious belief with fierce intolerance, for the reason that they are symbols of another kind of faith and hope from the company of which charity is jealously excluded.

Political for Religious Cleavage

The best judges of Irish character have always believed that if once an Irish Parliament were established the carefully-stoked flame of hatred between Roman Catholic and Protestant would die down. Another line of cleavage would be marked out. There would be a Conservative party and a Radical party. The latter would be formed by the working-men of the north acting in conjunction with their fellows in south and west. The Conservative strength would be drawn from the well-to-do in all parts supported by the priests and a large proportion of the peasantry.

Enterprise Responds to Encouragement

Irishmen are not more intolerant by nature than other men. Indeed, they show themselves in the countries they have adopted to be rather more inclined than most others to let everyone follow his own bent. The religious feelings of the Roman Catholics and the Presbyterians have been kept up in Ireland by artificial means, and the Irish people as a whole have not yet had the wit to see that they are being sacrificed and used as cats' paws in the old, old game of Beggar-my-Neighbour played for their own advantage by warring interests.

When the Ulster folk are contrasted with the southern people, they are held up to admiration for their industry and enterprise. Certainly they are entitled to the greatest credit for the prosperous trades they have established;

YOUNG IRELAND, TOUCHED TOO SOON BY EARTHLY CARE

Petticoats, as explained on page 2936, may protect him from wicked fairies, but they cannot conceal the masculine character of this stern-faced Connemara boy escorting his sister home from school. The faces of both these children are, indeed, stamped with unusual maturity, due, perhaps, to the hard struggle with poverty which the Connemara peasant has to wage from earliest infancy

Photo, A. W. Cutler

the linen trade, the shipbuilding trade, dairying, mineral water bottling, and others of less wide fame. But what is usually forgotten is that every encouragement has been given to these, while in the south and west the native industries were deliberately hampered by England in the past, and even Irish revenues were burdened by English exactions.

The changes which have been observable in Ireland since England ceased to interfere in such a persistent way with her industries for the benefit of English rivals, have proved that the character of the southern Irish is far from being so indolent and thriftless as most English people have supposed. While they had no inducement to work hard and to put by money and to improve their methods they remained in a stupor of hopeless lethargy. So long as his landlord could make every sign of prosperity an excuse for raising his rent the farmer preferred to live in a grimy, tumble-down-looking house with outbuildings apparently falling into ruins and to cultivate just enough to keep his family alive. As soon as he was established on his own land, as soon as he was free from the exactions of the agent employed to screw out of the tenants every penny they could be forced to part with, the Irish farmer's house began to look altogether different. He and his sons could be seen at work early and late, tilling and manuring, fencing and draining, adding to the value of the farmstead and the family acres. There was more food on the table and more variety. The boys and girls were sent to better schools. The shadow of poverty moved away and the sun of prosperity began to shine upon the place. The labourers shared in its beams. Their cottages were no longer hovels of mud, their wages rose, they cultivated their patches of garden to supply themselves with potatoes and other vegetables.

Irish farmers showed themselves readier to take up the cooperative

HERSELF AND HIMSELF OFF TO GALWAY MARKET

Having seen that her old man is decently arrayed this capable old lady slips one arm through her consort's and the other through the handle of the basket containing the eggs laid by her "trifle of poultry," and sallies forth to the market in quest of both pleasure and profit. Her clay pipe drawing easily serves the double purpose of keeping her nose warm and maintaining her equanimity

Photo, A. W. Cutler, by permission of Messrs. Raphael Tuck & Sons, Ltd.

THE DAY'S WORK DONE, PEACE RESTS LIKE A BLESSING ON RURAL DONEGAL

Throughout rural Ireland the peasants' dwellings are invariably one-storeyed, whitewashed, and straw-thatched. In Donegal they have a local peculiarity in the shape of netting spread over the thatch to prevent serious disarrangement by heavy winds. Chimneys are not common, a hole in one corner of the roof providing a way of escape for the peat smoke which spreads a warm incense over the interior and tinges the rafters an ever-deepening hue. The ancient spinning-wheel, at which a woman is here seen working, is still found in use in country districts

system than English farmers have ever been. When Sir Horace Plunkett first talked about it, and tried to spread an understanding of what its benefits might be to all who lived by the land, the usual question was asked: " What about my money if the new scheme fails ? " But very quickly the farmers and the poultry-keepers, the millers and bacon-curers, saw the advantages of the system that was offered to them. Thus the Irish Agricultural Organization Society established over a thousand branches, each of them independent and self-governing, with a membership of 120,000, and developed an annual trade of over £12,000,000 a year.

The I.A.O.S. quickened the life of the rural districts in all sorts of ways. It brought the farmers together, it suggested to them progressive methods. Men of different religious faiths and different political opinions met without any hostility, and worked together for the common benefit in the most amicable spirit, supplying the best possible answer to those who prophesied that such cooperation was inconceivable in Ireland, and that Irishmen were constitutionally incapable of managing their own affairs.

Revival of Irish Manufactures

In the industrial sphere the advance has not been so marked for the reason partly that the opportunities have been more restricted. Yet the possibility of reviving the Irish manufactures is eloquently pleaded by the prosperity which came to the district in which, just after the twentieth century had begun, a nun started the Foxford Woollen Mill. All around were small farmsteads, wretched almost beyond belief, miserably poor and squalid and hopeless. Gradually employment was found in the mill for more and more of the people on the barren hillsides and moors of the Moy Valley. Their houses became tidy without and within, the whole appearance of the place and population altered. The cloth woven by the Foxford looms has a high repute. Out of most unlikely materials a successful industry was built up.

Another enterprise in Donegal held out still brighter hope and encouragement. This was established by the peasants themselves. At first they had a cooperative store, which had to be resorted to by night because of the power of the " gombeen man," that is, the local shopkeeper and money-lender. The store grew and prospered. It was moved into the village of Dungloe, and there the making of hosiery was started. For a time all the work was done by hand. The villagers had no one to finance them, no one to advise them, even. However, they saved up until they could buy a machine, and they learned to use it. Soon they were able to buy more machines, and their enterprise was so firmly rooted by the time the Great War came that they undertook big contracts, one of them for the Belgian Army.

Pioneers of Peasant Industry

In 1919 they opened a new factory in which two hundred girls worked, some of them earning up to £5 a week. The whole fruit of their labour was reaped by the workers themselves. They were their own employers. The manager was one of themselves ; he often earned less in a week than some of those who were under him. All were paid according to their energy and skill. The factories were close to the ocean; health and vigour were blown into it by the salt breezes. The people looked well and seemed happy. They showed what enterprise and perseverance can do to remove poverty and discontent. They proved that workers can create an industry for themselves, something which has not yet been proved in England, Scotland, or Wales.

Adaptability to Environment

Those Irish who know the history of their nation protest indignantly against the belief that it has always been backward and opposed to new ideas. They point out that inoculation as a preventive of smallpox was adopted in Ireland before the English or the Scots practised it, and long before the Continent took it up. It is only in his own

FRIENDSHIP AND CONTENTMENT GROWN IN INISHMAAN

Good humour and kindly feeling play about the smiling mouths and eyes of these tall, broad-shouldered men of Inishmaan. Their trousers and cowhide slippers, or pampooties, have been worn to shreds in their hard life of fishing and burning seaweed, but they are comfortable enough in their warm homespun garments and are living pictures of healthy virility

Photo, A. W. Cutler

country that the Irishman has lacked heart to exert himself, and has let himself sink into a lethargic but grievance-full state of life. As soon as he found that he was in a country where the race was to the swift and the battle to the strong, he exerted himself to good purpose. The explanation must be looked for in the atmosphere of discouragement and pessimism which spread over the land during the dark centuries of Irish history. Only the very strongest souls could resist it, and most of these chose to emigrate rather

than fight against conditions so difficult at home.

This accounts for the melancholy of the mass of the people and for the spiritual gloom in which Irish literature is steeped. Neither is natural, one feels; neither, one learns after living with the Irish, is altogether real. They are acquired characteristics, and they are implanted in each generation, not by the process of heredity, but by inculcation. Almost every Irish child is taught " at its mother's knee " that the English are a nation of usurpers and despots. It learns all about Cromwell and 1798, and the Land League and Parnell. It grows up thinking of its race as one which had not been given a fair chance. If it has any knack of expression, it luxuriates in turning that thought into imaginative prose or verse. If a generation of Irish could be left free from all this bitter burden of memories the gloom would be lifted, the melancholy would disappear.

It is because their natural feelings of kindliness are warped at the recollection of what their forefathers suffered that the Irish can be cruel, not only to their fellow human beings, but to unfortunate animals. The ham-stringing was one of the most revolting features of the Land War. The absence of it from later warfare suggests that there has been a raising of the national sentiment. In later as in earlier struggles, however, there have been assassinations and

ambushes, the methods of the masked murderer hiding behind a wall. It is all the stranger that the Irish should have adhered to these methods, because they pride themselves, as they have a right to, on being a " nation of sportsmen." They are born judges of a horse. At any tiny race meeting in a country place in Ireland there is no less genuine delight in horses, no less appreciation of their qualities, no less knowledge of their points, than there is at Ascot or Epsom, or any English racecourse, excepting Newmarket, perhaps.

Men and boys who have attended Republican meetings and thrilled to denunciations of the gentry and cheered proposals to put a stop to hunting, will turn out when the hounds are heard, and run with them, enjoying the sport immensely and forgetting all their resolves to make an end of it. They will offer the huntsman advice, show him

LITTLE PITCHERS COLLECTED BY THE WELL-SPRING OF NEWS

Like the schoolboys shown on page 2936 these village lads outside Inishmaan post-office are wearing petticoats. The feminine garment imparts no air of effeminacy to its masculine wearers, perhaps because to a stranger it suggests the Scottish kilt—a suggestion carried further by the tam-o'-shanter worn with it. Certainly if there is one quality from which the Irish gossoon is free it is effeminacy

Photo, A. W. Cutler

SIX LITTLE PIGS GO TO MARKET AT GALWAY FROM INISHMAAN QUAY

Pigs' feet, though in themselves considered a table delicacy at some Irish fairs, are, by reason of their hoof-like nature, very out of place in the local canvas-covered curraghs, shown on page 2950, whose sides they could easily pierce. The steamer from Galway heaves to a mile off shore, and the market produce for the mainland has to be transported in canoes for that distance. Lively Irish pigs, resentful of the discomforts of sea voyaging, make bad canoeing companions, and their indignation has to be restrained with stout rope

" near ways," tell him where to draw coverts that certainly hold foxes. Should they be twitted with their inconsistency, they will turn off the subject with a witty remark or maybe a shamefaced grin. Where horses are concerned, all classes of Irishmen, and Irishwomen, too, adherents of all religious faiths, of all political groups, meet as friends and fellow-connoisseurs.

How is it possible, the Englishman asks, that after such cordial intercourse they can split up again into their different camps and so rancorously abuse one another and strive so fiercely for their separate ends ? He does not understand that all the striving and the abuse are to them more like part of a game.

An Article of Irish Faith

Many Irishmen who disapproved entirely of the Easter rebellion in 1916 were of opinion that it was treated too seriously, and that this mistake led to all the disastrous consequences which distressed men of goodwill for so long afterwards. The rebels, say these Irishmen, ought to have been left alone. They would soon have got tired of what they took up mainly for fun. Lack of opposition would have disconcerted them. Whatever their political views may be, almost all Irishmen agree that no Englishman knows how to govern Ireland. That is an article of faith even with those who are most rigidly opposed to any loosening of the tie which has bound their country to the British Empire. The only one among the numerous holders of high office in Ireland under the British Parliament who is spoken of with respect and affection as a man who did his best for the country is George Wyndham, and he is counted as an Irishman, not as an Englishman at all.

The usual attitude of the Irish towards the English is one of pitying belief that " they can't help themselves." There is less rancour than might be expected. There seems to be in the Irish nature so strong an impulse to be friendly, so little of the bad blood which breeds sullenness and the deliberate desire to wound in cold blood, that personal relations are seldom anything but agreeable. It is true that this readiness to make friends is usually no more than a surface manifestation. Hospitable as the Irish are, warm though their welcome of guests may be, they soon forget them, as a rule. Nowhere do strangers receive more kindness or feel more quickly that they are accepted as desirable acquaintances.

Feminine Beauty and Charm

But they must not suppose that this betokens anything deeper than the working of a national temperament inclined towards courtesy and eager to please. There is the same easy friendliness among the French, and it means just as little. But it ensures pleasant experiences to the visitor in France, and the same is true of Ireland.

A large part of the visitor's contentment springs from the charm of Irish women. There is among them a large proportion of beautiful faces ; even those which are not beautiful are almost always attractive by reason of bright eyes, clear complexions, and bewitching smiles. They are, for the most part, cool-blooded. The passionate type is rare. But they are faithful and kindly and forgiving ; they have often better heads for business than their husbands, and their children adore them.

Woman's Influence in Irish Life

It is a pity that the system of arranging marriages on a basis of bargaining for so much money or land on either side keeps many who would make the best of wives and mothers from finding mates. Here, again, the common ancestry of the Irish and the French has led to the prevalence of the same custom in both countries. In both, too, there exists an alternative occupation to marriage for a number of women— the convent. Irish nuns are famed all over the world, not alone for their piety, but for their resourcefulness, their ability as teachers, their skill in government when they are advanced to high positions of responsibility. It

SMOKING THE PIPE OF REMEMBRANCE ON A LONE TOMB OF WIND-SWEPT INISHMAAN

Bracken and cow-parsley and long, rank grass strive in tangled profusion to efface this rough stone monument to old mortality, where sleeps some bygone islander. Seated on the rugged slab is a relative who has been attending a funeral near by. Having been presented, according to Aran Island custom, with a clay pipe by the relations of the just-buried man, the recipient goes to the grave of an ancestor and smokes his present, the blue tobacco fumes going up, like incense, to old memories

SHIRT-SLEEVED MEN AND RED-HOODED WOMEN IN A FUNERAL PROCESSION ON INISHMAAN

Over the desolate landscape the ground is covered with stones piled together into walls more for the sake of collecting them and leaving some space for cultivation than for reasons of enclosure. In the foreground of this unkindly scene peasants are going to the Aharla, or burial ground, for the funeral of an islander. There is a custom among these peasants of going, not to the new grave but to the graves of their own departed, where they kneel and set up a mournful keening

Photo, A. W. Cutler

is mainly the women in Ireland, as elsewhere, who have kept up the authority of the priests. How forcible that still is can only be appreciated by those who have lived in small Irish towns and villages. Very often the parish priest is the only person of education or experience of the world in a village, even in a district. It is natural that his influence should be strong.

On the whole it is exercised with good results, though it can hardly be questioned that much more might have been done to educate the Irish peasantry if the Church had been interested in the matter, or that drink would be less of a curse if the priesthood generally had followed the lead of

Father Mathew, the apostle of temperance. In both these directions the unfortunate effects of the efforts to anglicise can be traced. Drinking was increased and made more harmful by the numberless illicit stills which were set up, largely out of bravado, to cheat the Government, and which distilled the most horrible stuff. The national schools were used for some time as instruments for the attempt to crush the national spirit. The school books were written from the purely English point of view. The efforts failed, as all others have done. " Ireland a nation " is a faith that has stood against every kind of destructive agency, and has grown stronger, instead of weaker, the more fiercely it was assailed.

CORACLES THAT CAN CARRY TWO MEN AND THAT A BOY CAN CARRY

Though many types of boats have evolved, flourished for a time, and then been replaced, the coracle, which Caesar described, and even adopted in his Iberian campaign, has remained practically unchanged in a thousand years. Made of split birch and a canvas skin, it is still used for fishing in the rapid-running rivers of West Ireland. It is the most portable of craft, as can be seen in the photograph

Photo, A. W. Cutler

HOME-MADE FOOTGEAR OF THE ARAN ISLANDERS

On the islands off the mouth of Galway Bay a special kind of footgear has been developed for negotiating the slabs of limestone with which the land is covered. Called the pampootie, it is contrived of raw cowhide, and in the photograph, taken on Inishmaan, an islander is seen making himself a pair of these novel shoes, what time a wild-haired daughter of the isle sits patiently by

Photo, A. W. Cutler

WENDING HER HOMEWARD WAY DOWN A WILD VALLEY ROAD OF ACHILL ISLAND

Through this grassy vale almost innocent of habitation the pony plods along under his double burden of loaded baskets and black-cloaked colleen. The hills, beyond the wide sweep of distance, darkening under the advance of night, rise gradually all round, helping to shut out the last of the day; meanwhile heavy clouds loom up from the Atlantic, holding the promise of wind and cold rain. Achill Island, an outpost of the mainland, lies off Mayo's broken seaboard on the north-west coast

Photo, A. W. Cutler

Ireland

II. Its Racial & Political History

By Stephen Gwynn

Author of " A History of Ireland," etc.

IRELAND from the earliest times of which we have any knowledge was inhabited by a mixed race. The Gaels, coming from the north of France or the Rhine countries, conquered it three or four centuries before Christ. The earlier inhabitants, whose work survives in megalithic monuments and in objects of wrought bronze, were reduced by them to servitude, and continued to exist for many centuries as distinct communities under tribute. Among them were the Picts. But though in Britain the Pictish speech survived till the time of Bede, we have no record of any language but Gaelic spoken in Ireland.

The Gaelic organization was tribal. The earliest cycle of Gaelic literature shows us a strong centre of rule at Armagh, another at Cruachan in county Roscommon. The country was so densely wooded that tracts had to be cleared for cultivation, and all building was done with wood, walls being of wattle and daub. But there was no town life ; the seats of power were little more than permanent camps. Literature and keeping of records appear to have been highly developed through the institution of bards specially trained to memorise.

Ireland was known early to the Greeks and Romans; but it was never reached by Roman conquest. Its first important contact with Roman civilization came on the introduction of Christianity early in the fifth century.

By this time a central power had grown up in the country. The kings of Connaught had secured control of the central plain, and had established rule at Tara, in Meath. Cormac MacArt, who conquered Tara, probably created the institution of the High Kingship, under which the king who ruled in Tara was entitled to tribute from all other kings in Ireland. He appears to have

possessed a standing army. In his time there existed the Fianna, a body of highly-trained fighting men, whose duty was to make war on the king's enemies in Ireland and to protect the coasts against invasion. Their leader was Finn MacCool.

A cycle of epic story centres about this force in the time of Cormac MacArt, as the earlier cycle about the heroes of the Red Branch in the reign of Conachar Mac-Nessa at Armagh. The warriors of the earlier cycle, of whom Cuchulain is the Achilles, were chariot-fighters ; the date assigned is about the lifetime of Christ. The Fianna, in English speech the Fenians, three centuries later, were foot soldiers. According to the chronicles the Fianna mutinied, and were destroyed in battle by Cormac MacArt's son and successor.

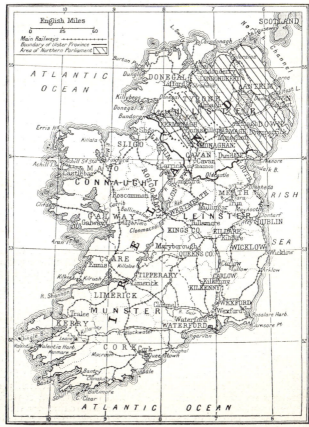

IRELAND: THE FREE STATE AND ULSTER

There was hereafter no regular army in Ireland; it was a country of warriors, not of soldiers. But the High Kingship increased in strength. Leinster was under tribute to Tara; Ulster was gradually subdued, and sons of the famous King Niall of the Nine Hostages established a principality in the extreme north, with its stronghold at Aileach, between Lough Swilly and Lough Foyle. The descendants of this king held the High Kingship for six centuries. But a singular usage grew up by which the sovereignty passed alternately between the southern branch of the Hy Neill (Niall's descendants) ruling in Meath, and the northern, who ruled at Aileach.

S. Patrick's Conversion of Ireland

Niall and his successors lived when the Roman Empire was being finally broken up, and they helped in the pillage. Niall was killed in the English Channel on board his own ship in 404; the next High King, Dathi, was struck by lightning when making war in southern France. Naturally, the British possessions of Rome were much harassed by these Scoti, as the Romans called the Irish.

In one raid a British youth, son of the deacon Calpurnius, was carried off, and sold into slavery. In his captivity he experienced spiritual conversion, and was filled with the desire to Christianise his captors. Having escaped, he took the name Patricius, and, after long training in France, was sent to Ireland in charge of a mission to the scattered Christians already existing there. Within thirty years from 432 he completed the conversion of the island, sweeping away the whole Druid organization, strong in Ireland as in all other Celtic countries. But he won to his side the whole native institution of traditional learning and poetry, accepting in so far as it could be reconciled to Christianity all the native law.

Scholars, Saints and Apostles

The High King Laoghaire, though he did not embrace Christianity, employed Patrick and his fellow missioners to assist in drawing up a written code. Wherever the saint went he brought the use of Latin letters and the Latin tongue. These were then the keys to knowledge and to civilization.

Patrick made Ireland part of Christendom, yet it remained very distinct. Throughout the Roman world Christian organization was based on the municipal system. In Ireland, where there was no town life, Patrick adapted it to the tribal organization, and bishoprics were enormously multiplied, so that the episcopal office came to be of little account. The new Church grouped itself about individuals of special sanctity who settled generally in some desert locality, such as the isles of Aran, or Clonmacnoise among vast bogs by the Shannon; and communities gathered about these saints, and grew to be centres of study as well as of religion.

Men with aptitude were employed to copy manuscripts, a beautiful art of penmanship developed, and Ireland became a manufactory and store of books while the whole apparatus of learning was being destroyed elsewhere in Europe. Armagh, which S. Patrick established as the central ecclesiastical settlement of Ireland, grew into a university with thousands of students, who came from all parts of Ireland and also "in fleetfuls" from Britain, and even from the Continent. Alfrid King of Northumbria, and Dagobert II. of France were trained in Ireland.

There was also a great missionary movement. S. Columba was its pioneer. Like most of the leading saints, he was a noble. A branch of his kindred, the northern Hy Neill, had in 470 founded a colony on the Scottish coast destined to develop into the kingdom of Scotland. From them the saint got a grant of the island of Iona, and founded there in 563 a monastery with a mission to the Picts.

Scandinavian Raiders and Traders

Its work was carried on by Irish monks, and in the seventh century appeal was made to Iona to undertake conversion of the Saxon. Aidan, sent from Iona, founded Lindisfarne in Northumbria, with such results that, in Lightfoot's words, "Augustine was the apostle of Kent, but Aidan was the apostle of England."

To the Continent also Irish monks carried not only religion but learning; the trace of their foundations is found in Italy, Switzerland, Germany, and France. Ferghail, or Virgil, the Geometer, taught about 750 at Salzburg, as he had taught in Ireland, that the earth was a sphere and that antipodes existed. Alcuin, the Northumbrian, chief adviser to Charlemagne, was trained in Ireland, and from Charlemagne's court corresponded with Colgu, chief professor at Clonmacnoise.

This period, perhaps the most important in Ireland's history, was ended by the inroads of Scandinavian seamen. The Norse conquest in Ireland was much less complete than in England or France, but, beginning with sporadic descents on the coast, they established permanent posts along the east and south of Ireland. At no time in their history, at all events from S. Patrick's coming onward, were the Irish a seafaring people; and the Norse came trading as well as raiding. They introduced also for the first time the life of towns. No Irish town is of Gaelic origin, though some are on the site of

Gaelic ecclesiastical communities. Dublin, Wicklow, Arklow, Wexford, Waterford, Cork, and Limerick are all Danish foundations; Kilkenny and Galway, Norman or English; Belfast and Derry (Londonderry) only began to be towns after Gaelic rule in Ireland was destroyed.

From their seaports the Norse or Danes (both peoples were represented) ravaged the country terribly, and destroyed the monastic seats of culture and learning. Yet a certain degree of fusion went on, especially between Dublin and the Irish of Leinster. After the battle of Brunanburg the Danes, being completely driven from power in England, began to attempt a complete conquest of Ireland. Dublin was now the centre of a Scandinavian kingdom which included the Isle of Man, portion of the Scottish coast, the Hebrides, Orkney, and Shetland.

Irish Schism England's Opportunity

But Irish resistance developed strongly from two centres. Malachy the Great, King of Meath and High King of Ireland, defeated the Danes of Dublin and rescued a host of enslaved Irish; ten years earlier, the King of Thomond, that is north-west Munster, had destroyed an army of the Danes of Limerick and captured their town. Brian, the hero of this victory, shortly after became King of Thomond and, soon growing supreme in Munster, challenged Malachy's power. At the close of the century the two combined to defeat the Danes of Dublin, allied with the Leinstermen; but in 1002 Brian forced Malachy to submit, was proclaimed High King, and for twelve years exercised real sovereignty over Ireland. In 1014 Danish forces with Irish allies made a last great effort at conquest; they were defeated at Clontarf, but after a desperate battle, in which Brian, his son, and his grandson were slain.

Brian had destroyed the traditional sovereignty of the Hy Neill; he was regarded as a usurper, and the power created by him did not last. For 150 years the sovereignty was disputed, till in 1166 Rory O'Conor, King of Connaught, was proclaimed High King without opposition. He used his power to banish Dermot MacMurrough, King of Leinster, who sought aid from Henry II. This great ruler had from the first thought of conquering Ireland, and had obtained a Bull from the Pope justifying him. He now authorised any of his subjects to assist MacMurrough.

Richard, Earl of Clare, known as Strongbow, promised help. The first expedition was only some 200 men, but their armament and skill made them the equivalent of European troops of to-day among native tribes in Africa; they captured the Danish town of Wexford,

and, joining an Irish force under Dermot MacMurrough, restored the king to his former position. In 1169 a large force under Strongbow himself landed near Waterford and carried the place by assault, and in the captured Danish city Strongbow was solemnly married to Aoife, or Eva, daughter of MacMurrough, with whose hand he received promise of succession to the kingdom of Leinster.

Strongbow's Conquest of the Island

The combined Norman and Irish forces then marched north to Dublin. A great Irish host was mustered under Rory O'Conor to resist them, but failed; Dublin fell into their hands. Shortly after MacMurrough died, and Strongbow, in breach of all Irish custom, became King of Leinster.

Henry now asserted his overlordship, and having received complete submission from Strongbow, came to Waterford with a great fleet, moved gradually to Dublin, and established himself there for the winter. He returned to England in the spring, leaving his barons to carry on the work of conquest, which they did by a widespread process of building castles at strategic points—a proceeding new to the Irish. In 1175 was signed the Treaty of Windsor, by which Rory O'Conor recognized Henry as overlord, and was in return recognized as High King. But Leinster, together with Dublin, Wexford, and Waterford, were specially excluded from his jurisdiction and placed directly under the English Crown.

Initial Mistakes of English Policy

Essentially, however, the conquest remained ineffectual because the conquerors refused to admit the conquered to rights of citizenship, and sought to destroy the laws under which the Irish lived without affording them the protection of their own. They persistently regarded the Irish as " natives," people of an inferior stock, not fitted for equality. Yet at the same time they intermarried, and by a continuous process Irish blood, Irish speech, and Irish customs spread themselves among the invaders and their descendants. This fusion, which had been encouraged in England, was resisted by all the power of the State. Edicts were passed to prohibit the use of Irish speech, Irish costume, Irish courts of law in the English settled territories; they were unavailing, but they kept wounds open. Briefly, it was the policy of England to claim all native Irishmen as subjects, yet to regard them all as enemies.

In the opening of the fourteenth century Edward Bruce, invited by the Irish princes, came to Ireland with an army of Scottish Gaels in 1315 and was accepted as King; his campaign was

THREE FISHERS OF ARAN COME BACK FROM THE WEST

Herring and mackerel abound off the west coast of Ireland, though the fishing industry has not been so sedulously cultivated as the resources of the Atlantic would have seemed to warrant. In the Aran Islands the inhabitants were handicapped by a dearth of suitable boats, having to rely on curraghs and small open boats, so that the scope of the available fishing grounds was limited by the size of the craft and the state of the weather. The Congested Districts Board, however, turned their attention to the problem and established facilities for

brilliantly successful. But after three years of war, in which Ireland was devastated, Bruce was slain. He had weakened English rule, but had not liberated Ireland. From this period onward Ireland passed more and more into the control of certain great earls, descended from the conquerors, yet become Irish rather than English.

The De Burgos, who before Bruce's coming were paramount, shook off English allegiance completely, and as MacWilliam Burkes ruled most of Connaught. Power, however, passed to the Earls of Desmond and Kildare, both descended from Maurice FitzGerald, one of the original band of invaders. The Geraldines of Desmond ruled Munster; the Geraldines of Kildare, with their seat at Maynooth, a few hours ride from Dublin, had less independence but more influence over the government. Between these two potentates lay the Earls of Ormonde, whose seat was at Kilkenny.

New Troubles Brought by the Reformation

By the end of the fifteenth century the Desmonds had become almost independent, while the Earls of Kildare were continuously the king's representatives and held great authority, reinforced by alliances with the leading Irish princes. The Pale, as that part of Ireland governed directly from Dublin was termed, had shrunk greatly.

With the growth of an absolute monarchy, which relied on ministers, not on vassals, the position of these Irish earls grew precarious. Three successive Kildares as deputies openly disregarded the laws which enjoined separation between the races. Finally, in 1534, the Earl of Kildare was impeached and brought to London to answer certain accusations; he left his son, a young man known as Silken Thomas, in his place; on rumour of Kildare's execution Silken Thomas went into revolt, and the rebellion was ended with his execution and that of all accessible males of the line. Yet after this Henry VIII.'s Lord Deputy, St. Leger, succeeded in bringing it to pass that all the Irish princes agreed to admit Henry's sovereignty, surrender their lordships, and accept titles at his hand. Nearly all attended a Parliament held in Dublin in 1541.

The conquest of Ireland may be said to have been completed at this point, after 370 years, most of the Gaelic rulers being left in occupation of their territories. There were still great difficulties, for under English law succession to title was by lineal descent; under Irish, the clan chose its ruler from among the adult men of a family group. The transition might have been effected, and was effected in Thomond, but a new dividing issue came

with the Reformation, which in England had sprung from a popular movement; in Ireland it was simply known as an order from the English Court. The counter-reformation, headed by the Jesuits, took strong hold and was inevitably allied with a crusade against English rule. Henceforward, Continental Catholic powers sought to strike at England in Ireland, and the Irish became doubly detested as the allies of Spain.

Conquest by Plantation and Starvation

Yet it was under the Catholic Queen Mary that England made a beginning in Ireland of the policy of plantation—that is, of driving out the Irish and replacing them by English—which was pursued with increasing savagery for more than a hundred years. All natives were expelled from Leix and Offaly, the region afterwards known as King's County and Queen's County; the process of extermination lasted through Elizabeth's reign. After the rebellion of the Earl of Desmond, virtually all Waterford, Cork, and Kerry were declared forfeit and distributed to English settlers, who undertook to plant the land with Englishmen.

Yet this Munster plantation was shortly after blotted out in the great war in which Hugh O'Neill, Earl of Tyrone, and Hugh O'Donnell, chief of Tyrconnell, overran all Ireland outside the walled towns. A considerable force of Spaniards landing at Kinsale to reinforce them in 1601 brought English rule into great danger; but the English won the battle of Kinsale. After prolonged resistance Hugh O'Neill surrendered before he knew of Elizabeth's death. Thus under Elizabeth the conquest of Ireland was made absolute. The main instrument of victory was famine produced by the destruction of all crops.

Persecution under Cromwell

James I. found Ireland prostrate, and a policy of conciliation was at first pursued. O'Donnell's brother was created Earl of Tyrconnell; O'Neill retained his earldom of Tyrone. But the greed for confiscations had been kindled, and accusations were brought against the two earls; fearing arrest, they fled, and the whole of their territory was declared forfeit. Then began the plantation of Ulster, carried out chiefly by Scots. Only the mountains and bogs were left to the natives.

When civil strife broke out in England, Ulster rose in 1641; there was a general expulsion of the planters. It is estimated that some ten thousand Protestants were killed. The authorities in command in Dublin used fearful reprisals, as also did the Scots in eastern Ulster. In the twelve years' war that followed the most distinguished figure was Owen Roe O'Neill

SIX OF IRELAND'S YOUNGER GENERATION OBEYING THE COMMAND TO LOOK PLEASANT

It must be rare to meet anywhere such a galaxy of grins as this. The shy little maid on the left, with her white shawl and bare feet, has summoned the courage for a covert smile; her neighbour, whose tam-o'-shanter was evidently made for wider brows, beams frankly; the next two are in a state of hardly-suppressed mirth, while the last boy makes no doubt about it. Finally comes the father with the smallest of this group that radiates homespun and happiness

Photo, A. W. Cutler

of the Tyrone house, who had already gained fame as a soldier in Flanders. But his genius failed to keep united the discordant elements.

Gaels and Anglo-Irish Catholics were both represented in the Catholic Confederation, whose assembly sat at Kilkenny. All parties in the Confederation represented themselves as acting for King Charles. When the Commonwealth was victorious Cromwell came to Ireland. Owen Roe was dead of illness, and the brutal measures which Cromwell adopted did not prevent the prolongation of resistance for two years more. At last the struggle ended, and the Commonwealth decreed that all Catholic Irish should be driven into the barren province of Connaught. The transference of an entire population proved impossible, but all Catholic property was confiscated.

While resettlement was still in progress the Restoration came, but except for a few individual landlords no Catholics were restored to their lands; the English Parliament confirmed Cromwell's policy in broad outline. Under Charles II. the Catholic religion, which had been completely persecuted by Cromwell, enjoyed a degree of toleration. James II., a Catholic, proceeded to reverse the policy of penalising his own religion, and sent Tyrconnell, a Catholic viceroy, to bring Ireland generally into Catholic hands. When the Revolution came, Catholic Ireland sided with James, but in the north the Ulster Protestants held Derry and Enniskillen.

Tyranny of the Penal Laws

A Parliament held in Dublin proceeded to reverse the confiscations of Cromwell's time and restore lands to their previous owners. Its laws decreed toleration for all creeds and allocation of tithes to the church of those who paid them. But none of this legislation took effect. William landed in Ulster and routed the inferior army of James on the Boyne. James fled, but the struggle was prolonged for two years, Louis XIV. reinforcing the Irish with troops and munitions. The battle of Aughrim was decisive, but Sarsfield, the ablest Irish leader, fell back on Limerick with a strong force, and further help from France was expected. A treaty was signed guaranteeing to Catholics who surrendered that they should not be disturbed in possession of their lands, and that all Catholics should enjoy such freedom as in the reign of Charles II. Soldiers were allowed if they chose to take service in France; and Sarsfield, with 11,000 men, left the country. The treaty was at once broken.

Catholics, who included practically all the old inhabitants of the island and a majority of the Anglo-Irish settled before the time of the Stuarts, were now, save for a few hundred persons, landless men and disarmed. The population had been reduced till it was little more than a million : a great immigration of Scots into Ulster increased the number of Protestants, so that the Catholics ceased entirely to be formidable. A system of penal laws was constructed by degrees, designed to make them poor and keep them poor, to prevent their acquiring land, to deny them education unless they abandoned their religion. Generally they were reduced to the condition of helots.

Fight for Freedom of Irish Trade

Most of the penal laws were passed by the Irish Parliament, which had existed since the beginning of the fourteenth century, but which had always represented only the settlers, and now represented only the Episcopalian Protestants. It was by origin co-ordinate with that of England ; but by laws passed, repealed, and passed again, under pressure from the English Government, it had conceded to the English Privy Council the right to veto or alter any law proposed in Ireland ; also, the English Parliament claimed the right to bind Ireland by its own legislation.

Through these powers the English Government, from the reign of William III. onwards, passed a system of legislation which debarred Irish manufacturers from competing in any respect with those of Great Britain. From the reign of George III. onwards the Irish Parliament showed increasing resentment of this interference. When America rebelled, Protestant Ireland showed much sympathy for it ; finally, in 1779, the coasts being threatened by French privateers and no force being available to defend them, volunteers were raised ; the force became very powerful, and, moved by the example of America, demanded freedom for Irish trade. It was conceded in 1779.

Union and Catholic Emancipation

The demand was pushed farther and, in 1782, under threat of rebellion, Ireland received for its Parliament complete freedom from control. This was still, however, a Parliament solely for one-tenth of the population ; attempts supported by Grattan to give equal freedom to Catholics and Dissenters failed ; the French Revolution affected all minds, and in 1798 a rising organized by Wolfe Tone broke out. Help from France came late, but there was much bloodshed ; the Protestant Parliament, fearing for its ascendancy and for the title of Protestants to confiscated lands, agreed, after much bribery, to pass an Act of Union in 1800.

Since then the ascendancy has been gradually destroyed, but by demoralising methods. Daniel O'Connell first succeeded in uniting the Catholic population as a political force, and in 1829 Catholic emancipation, which had been persistently refused to argument, was conceded to avoid civil war. But in 1843, when O'Connell tried to carry Repeal of the Union by the same threat, force was opposed to him and he yielded. A section of his following considered that he should have risked rebellion, and thenceforward there were two sections of Nationalist Ireland, one advocating, one rejecting, the use of physical force.

NOT SO OLD AS HER CLOAK

Blue cloaks serve for both hat and coat in West Cork, and are passed on from mother to daughter until the generations have outlasted the fabric

Photo, Rt. Hon. F. S. Wrench

The main event of Irish history in the nineteenth century was the great famine. Multitudes of Irish cottiers had no food but the potato. In 1845 the potato crop failed, and failed for four years in succession. The population fell from eight and a quarter millions in 1845 to six and a half millions in 1851. About a million had died, the rest had emigrated. From this point onward Ireland's population decreased rapidly, till by 1900 it was lower than in 1800; and in the United States an Irish population grew up, even more hostile to England than that in Ireland.

The abortive insurrection headed by Smith O'Brien in 1848 did not for long discourage rebellion, and men who had been concerned in it founded the Fenian organization in Ireland and America. Their attempt at a rising in 1867 was futile, but combined with certain acts of violence in Great Britain it drew attention to Irish affairs, and was followed by Mr. Gladstone's Act, which disestablished the Irish Church—though that institution was guaranteed by the Act of Union. His Land Act of 1870 recognized certain limitations of the landlord's power of eviction, which had been unsparingly used.

In 1876 Charles Stuart Parnell, elected to Parliament, began a policy of obstruction which threatened to block all business until Ireland's demand for self-government was attained. He linked this policy to one of agrarian agitation in Ireland, and by the help of Michael Davitt induced the Fenians to combine with those who regarded physical force as useless. After violent disorder and coercive measures in Ireland, the Land Act of 1881 was passed which established dual ownership by decreeing that all rents should be fixed by a legal tribunal, and that no tenant should be ejected while he paid the rent so fixed. This principle was altered later, as Parnell had desired, to that of State-aided land purchase, through which the British Government undertook to buy out those who had ruled Ireland under the Union.

Gladstone's first attempt to carry Home Rule through Parliament in 1886 failed, and Parnell's career, broken by a divorce case, ended by early death. But four-fifths of the Irish representation at all elections was for Home Rule, and by an Act of 1898 all local government was conceded to elective bodies. Ireland was still governed from Westminster, but the property and the power had passed back to the descendants of the dispossessed.

The first real obstacle to carrying Home Rule was the opposition of the House of Lords. This was removed by the Parliament Act carried in 1911. In 1912 a Home Rule Bill was introduced and carried through the Commons by a large majority. Protestant Ulster, the last line of defence, now made preparations to resist by force, and was encouraged by the English Tory party. This led to a counter organization of volunteers on the Nationalist side. In 1914 the Bill had passed the Commons for its third time when the Great War broke out.

Redmond, the Irish leader, pledged Ireland's support; the Home Rule Bill was passed into an Act on condition that it should not operate till a year after the war ended, and that Ulster should not be "coerced." Many thousand Irish Nationalists fulfilled Redmond's pledge by entering the Army, but a section of the volunteers split off and, as Germany's success increased, grew more menacing. A rising was planned for Easter, 1916; the German ship bringing arms was captured and attempts were made to stop the rising; but a body in Dublin, headed by Patrick Pearse, seized the Post Office and other points, and proclaimed the Irish Republic; after several days' fighting the rebellion was crushed. It was generally unpopular; but the execution of fifteen prisoners turned feeling the other way. Men in the Government of that day were known to have been deeply concerned in Ulster's preparations and even acts of rebellion.

The feeling gradually spread, and finally, when an attempt was made to apply conscription to Ireland, the whole country outside of Protestant Ulster became anti-British. At the general election after the Armistice in 1918, 73 members out of 103 were returned under pledge to go no more to Westminster and to support an Irish Republic. This body assembled in Dublin and, holding its proceedings in Irish, declared itself to be Dáil Eireann, the Parliament of Ireland, and elected a ministry with Mr. de Valera as President.

The British Government did not at first interfere. But Dáil Eireann issued orders and enforced them; policemen who interfered with this process were shot, and so conflict began which developed into a sort of guerrilla war of which there had been many previous examples in Irish history under the Union. In 1920 the Government attempted to quell it by enlisting a special police force from ex-soldiers, and employing them to dragoon neighbourhoods where violence was committed and conviction could not be obtained. But English public opinion turned against this, and as an alternative to complete concession or to a campaign of reconquest, Mr. Lloyd George, in July, 1921, offered terms of self-government similar to those enjoyed by the Dominions.

Abolition of the Union

After long parleying, a treaty was signed by representatives of the British Cabinet and representatives of Dáil Eireann, which abolished the Act of Union completely and gave Ireland complete legislative and fiscal freedom, with power to raise and control her own military forces, but insisted that Ireland should remain within the British Empire as the Irish Free State; and that the six counties of Northern Ireland should have power by vote of their local Parliament, established in 1920, to remain separate.

The treaty was generally accepted in Ireland, but Mr. de Valera repudiated it, and it was only carried in the Dáil by seven votes. De Valera resigned, Arthur Griffith replaced him as President, and a Provisional Government was formed with Michael Collins at its head. The British forces began their evacuation of the country, the old police force was disbanded, and the transfer of authority proceeded. But mutiny broke out in the ranks of the Irish Republican forces, and civil war followed.

The Free State and Ulster

Before order was fully restored in Dublin, Griffith died; and a few days later Collins was killed in a skirmish in county Cork. But the open resistance to the National troops was steadily got under, and Dáil Eireann met to appoint ministries and frame a constitution. Mr. William Cosgrave was chosen President. By Dec. 6, 1922, the Constitution adopted by the Dáil had been adopted also by the British Parliament. An Upper Chamber, the Senate of sixty members, was chosen; and for the first Governor-General, Mr. T. M. Healy, a prominent figure in the Land League of Parnell's day, was appointed.

The parliament of Northern Ireland, immediately after the passing of the Constitution, used the power given under the treaty to vote itself a separate State, having a distinct status, governed partly from Westminster and partly through its own parliament.

IRELAND: FACTS AND FIGURES

The Country

Second largest island of the British archipelago. Area, 32,586 square miles; greatest length, 302 miles; average breadth, 110 miles. Divided since April 1, 1922, into the Irish Free State and North Ireland (or Ulster). Geographical divisions: Four provinces of Ulster, Leinster, Munster, and Connaught, subdivided into thirty-two counties, twenty-six in the South, and six in the North. Estimated total population, 4,390,200 (South, 3,139,690; North, 1,250,500).

Government and Constitution

By the Government of Ireland Act of 1920, Parliaments were established for North and South. Under the Irish Free State Agreement Act of 1922 the Government of the Irish Free State has all the powers of the Dominion of Canada in relation to the Empire. Powers of Parliament and Government of Northern Ireland (parliamentary counties of Antrim, Down, Armagh, Fermanagh, Londonderry, and Tyrone, and parliamentary boroughs of Belfast and Londonderry) wholly domestic.

Commerce and Industries

In the South occupations are largely agricultural, oats, flax, potatoes, hay, butter-making, pig-breeding, horse-breeding being carried on. Cottage spinning encouraged. Brewing important in Dublin, Cork, Dundalk; distilling in Dublin, Belfast, and Cork. Great linen and shipbuilding industries centred in Belfast. Sea fisheries (mackerel and herring chiefly) fluctuate. Coal is worked in Kilkenny and Tyrone.

Communications

Chief railways: Great Southern and Western, 1,130 miles; Great Northern, 561 miles; Midland Great Western, 516 miles Several smaller lines and light railways; also 848 miles of canals and canalised waterways. River Shannon navigable for over 140 miles.

Chief Towns

Belfast (population 393,000), Cork (76,673), Dublin (399,000), Galway (13,250), Kilkenny (10,500), Limerick (47,000), Londonderry (41,000), Tralee (10,300), Waterford (28,900).

WHERE VENICE, THE QUEEN OF THE ADRIATIC, RISES IN STATE, THRONED ON HER HUNDRED ISLES

Venice, the glorious Republic which in past centuries engaged in incessant conflict with her rival, Genoa, for the sovereignty of the Mediterranean, is situated at the head of the Adriatic. Built mainly on piles in the Venetian Lagoon, the city differs from all other European cities in that—instead of streets—it has canals and water-passages, on which graceful gondolas glide and in which are reflected magnificent creations of architecture that are so many poems in stone

Photo, Donald McLeish

Italy

I. Italian Life in Town & Country

By Hamilton Fyfe

Special Correspondent in Italy of " The Daily Mail "

STRANGE are the trifling accidents which shape our opinions about our fellow - men. Because a certain number of Italians came to England as organ-grinders and ice-cream men, the whole of their fellow-countrymen were regarded by many English people with good-humoured tolerance. They were thought of as children. There was perhaps some excuse for this in the childlike demeanour of the Italian abroad. At home a shrewd and calculating and rather sceptical character, he was apt to be bewildered amid foreign surroundings. He did not learn English easily ; he seldom spoke it well when he had learned it.

At the same time the British drama and novel circulated among a different class the impression that Italians, especially titled Italians, were as a rule spies, like the Countess Zicka in "Diplomacy," or ruffians like Macari in " Called Back," adventuresses, blackmailers, thieves.

All this was the more surprising for the reason that ever since the sixteenth century Italy has been the land in which Englishmen have most travelled; the land, too, which has awakened more sympathy, more passionate devotion, than any other among men and women of British blood. At all times there have been a few English admirers of Italy who have known her and her people intimately. English colonies in Rome and Florence have existed for generations. The Italian manner of life has fascinated Englishmen from the days of Elizabeth, when the proverb said that " Inglese Italianato e diavolo incarnato " (an Italianised Englishman is the very devil). The best books on the country in our own time have been written by those who, like Mr. Richard Bagot, Miss Helen Zimmern, Mr. Edward Hutton, have made their homes there. They and others who have borne true witness have striven of late to give their countrymen a juster view of the Italian people, but much yet remains to be done before the old misconceptions can be wiped out.

There is this added difficulty facing them, that the Italian people appear to be changing more rapidly than any other, and that what might have been quite true even so lately as twenty years ago would be misleading, and colour the picture wrongly to-day. This change

DÉBUTANTE FROM CALABRIA

Her garments bright as her own eyes, and her fingers busy with her knitting, this demure maiden comes from the most southerly part of Italy

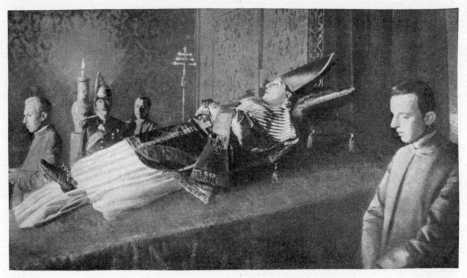

THE PASSING OF A PONTIFF OF ROME

Robed in full pontificals—the stole, the dalmatic, the gloves, the pallium, the ring, the chasuble, and the gold mitre—the body of Pope Benedict XV., the occupant of the Chair of S. Peter during the Great War, is here seen lying in the Throne Room of the Vatican preparatory to being borne to S. Peter's for the lying-in-state in the Chapel of the Blessed Sacrament

is not so wonderful if we recollect that it was only in 1870 that the Italians became one people. Up to the struggle for unity, which began to attract the world's attention in 1848, there had been many separate and distinct populations in Italy, so distinct that they spoke different languages, dialects so varied that a Roman could not understand the Venetian patois, nor a Sicilian find any medium of conversation with a Milanese.

When the union of the whole peninsula was completed, a famous Italian remarked with truth as well as humour, " Now that we have made Italy, we must set to work and make an Italian People." This the rulers of Italy, with the aid of the people, have done, and the achievement may be set off fairly against many things which, for the people's welfare, they had better not have done. Whether the individual is any better off for the unification is a question that has been exhaustively discussed. The discussion has not led to any agreement. There was a great deal of corruption and misgovernment in the states which were ruled by the Pope, the King of Naples, the Grand Duke of Tuscany, the Emperor of Austria. Yet

it may be that the peasant felt the burden of his obligations less then than he does to-day.

Some observers, among them those famous French writers the brothers De Goncourt, have even pitied the people for the loss of their old governments!

If, however, we would judge for ourselves we must look at the facts as they present themselves to the average observer. In every town and village in Italy one sees shops labelled " Tobacco, Salt, and Stamps." Why should salt be bought at a tobacco shop instead of at the grocer's ? The reason is that salt has to pay a heavy tax, and is also a Government monopoly, like tobacco. Both human beings and animals suffer from the high price of salt. Sugar is taxed heavily as well, which prevents Italian fruit from being made into jam and Italian oranges into marmalade in Italy. Large quantities of fruit are sent into Switzerland and turned into preserve there.

Then, besides the duties which are exacted at the frontier on all articles coming into the country from abroad, there is a tax on articles of food for household usage taken into any town. One consequence of this burdensome taxation is a great deal of fraud. There is a proverb which says in effect that " as soon as a law is passed, it is time to think how it can be evaded." For example, when the octroi officials come into a tram passing through a town gate all the passengers are ready to help those who have something to hide. A countrywoman will put her basket of eggs under the skirts of her well-dressed neighbour. A professor will conceal with his voluminous cloak a bottle of some local liqueur that a farmer is taking in as a present to his married daughter. The tax on wine shops is evaded by setting outside the house where wine is sold a board with white and black balls painted on it, indicating to those who understand " White and red wine sold here." (Red wine is called black in Italy—vino nero.)

In some parts the taxes on land are evaded by an ingenious but simple device. The cultivator finds that, hard as he may work, the land will not yield enough to satisfy both the needs of his family and the demands of the tax-collector. As for improving the land, that is altogether beyond him. So his little property is seized and put up to

HIS HOLINESS POPE PIUS XI. ON HIS WAY TO CHURCH

This unusual photograph was taken of Pius XI. when on his way to attend service at the Cathedral Church of S. Peter in Rome. On his election, and again after his coronation, he created a precedent by appearing on the balcony of S. Peter's, whence he blessed the crowd in the square below. He was the first Pope to be seen in public since the abolition of the temporal power in 1870

WOMEN FASCISTI ON PARADE WEARING THE FAMOUS BLACK SHIRTS

Fascismo, one of the most remarkable products of the Great War, had for its chief aim the securing for Italy of "the full moral and material fruits of victory." The movement, primarily a patriotic reaction of the youth of Italy against the menace of Bolshevism, was begun in Milan in 1919, and quickly spread through the community; a striking feature being the enthusiasm of women for the cause

Photo, Bartlett, Rome

AT AN INSPECTION OF THE PATRIOTIC REVOLUTIONARIES OF ITALY

Many able, patriotic men belong to the Fascisti movement, which brought the most rigid discipline into the national life of Italy. Benito Mussolini, its founder, the son of a blacksmith of the Romagna, has been termed the "strong man of Italy," and this resolute leader of a powerful organization became, as Prime Minister, intent on purging Italian politics and restoring the prestige of Government

Photo, Vaucker, Rome

STALWARTS OF ITALY'S HIGHLY EFFICIENT POLICE FORCE

The Carabinieri police are easily recognized by their gorgeous uniform of black, red, and gold, and their three-cornered plumed hats. A military force, recruited by selection from the army, they are fine and efficient men, who patrol the country day and night, some mounted, some on foot, and by their indomitable courage and thorough reliability have done much to make travelling safe in Italy

Photo, Donald McLeish

auction. There are no bids. The neighbours are afraid to buy. They know that a vendetta would follow. So the land becomes the property of the State, and then the original owner goes back to it and makes a better living than before, because now he is not asked for any taxes. He is a squatter, paying neither rent nor dues.

This general approval of fraud makes the people dishonest towards their neighbours as well as towards the Government. At the railway stations it used to be a regular practice for the ticket-clerk to give wrong change. I hit upon a method of meeting this. Instead of trying quickly to count over the change I received, I would stand at the booking-office window and continue to hold out my hand. I almost always got some more change. Sometimes, if I thought the ticket-clerk looked more villainous than most, I would wait for a third instalment, and even get that.

There is a good deal of fraud in the dealings with landlords by peasants who farm land on the sharing system.

PRIVATES OF THE BERSAGLIERI, A CRACK LIGHT INFANTRY REGIMENT

Besides the ordinary regiments of the Italian army there are several bodies of troops recruited for special purposes. Chief among these are the Bersaglieri, or riflemen, extremely mobile soldiers, with small, agile frames admirably adapted for skirmishing and scouting. A regiment of Bersaglieri, consisting of three battalions of infantry and one of cyclists, is usually attached to each army corps

Photo, Donald McLeish

ITALIAN DRAGOONS: THE PRIDE OF THE PEOPLE

In Italy, where conscription is in force, all who have reached the age of twenty are obliged to join either the army or the navy. Stalwart specimens of humanity, chiefly recruited from the peasantry, are to be found in the cavalry regiments, where smartness and a fine physique stamp each individual trooper, and the splendid horsemanship of the Italian cavalry is famous throughout Europe

Photo, Donald McLeish

Owner and cultivator are supposed to share the produce. But the owner has no means of knowing what the produce amounts to unless he is on the spot, or unless he employs an agent to look after his properties. What he often does in order to secure himself against robbery is to accept a certain yearly rent from a middle-man, who makes what he can over and above this rent out of the tenant. Thus the tenant is apt to be harshly treated, and the land suffers also from having more taken out of it than it can fairly yield. Sometimes both the tenant and the landlord are cheated by a greedy or underpaid agent. But, on the whole, this system gives good results. It leads to a valuable kind of mixed cropping. The tenant, having to supply his family's daily needs as well as to cultivate grapes and olives for the market—either selling them as they are or turning them into wine and oil—plants grain and vegetables in the vineyard and among the olive trees. As one travels through Tuscany one sees a great deal of this kind of cultivation, and notices that the people on the land are a contented-looking folk, with pleasant manners and comfortable houses and good clothes. Some of these " metayer " arrangements

FRUITFUL CORNER OF THE PLAIN THAT WAS BELOVED IN ANTIQUITY BY THE WEALTHY PATRICIANS OF ROME

The beautiful ruins of the towns and villas that cover the Roman Campagna attest its ancient splendour; even in its desolation the plain is an unforgettable sight, and many a visitor is of Ruskin's opinion that "perhaps there is no more impressive scene on earth than the solitary extent of the Campagna of Rome under evening light." But all is not ruin; where the volcanic nature of the soil is less virulent the vegetation is more luxuriant, and pasture-lands and pleasant groves of olive trees flourish on the ground that the patient peasant has reclaimed from the "wild and wasted plain."

have been in force between the same landlords and the same families of peasants for centuries. The owner provides not only the land, but everything necessary for the working of it—farm buildings, farmhouse, cattle, seed, manure. He pays the taxes, too. The produce is divided equally, or is supposed to be. To ensure a just division the grain is threshed all at once and the sacks are separated on the spot.

The size of these small holdings is from fifteen to twenty-five acres. Certainly the people who live on them are far better off than the agricultural labourers who work for big farmers.

Life on the Poverty Line

For two or three shillings a day, sometimes less than two, they are in the fields for very many hours. Often they have to live a long way off and to walk a long distance in the early morning and at night. Their work is seldom continuous. Their food is scanty and poor in quality. It is they who were the chief sufferers from pellagra, the wasting disease which used to be terribly common in Italy, but of which the ravages have been happily reduced by preventive measures. It is caused by lack of salt and by eating maize which is musty or damp, either from not having ripened properly before it is cut, or from being kept in a defective store.

On the whole, the Italian peasant is not so badly off as impassioned reformers are inclined to represent him. The condition of the day labourer is bad, but sometimes even he has alleviations of his hard lot when he works for a humane employer. He makes the most of small enjoyments, and as he is probably unable to read more than a very little, if at all, he is not tantalised by the thought of others who live in comfort and can work or not as they please.

One small enjoyment by which the labourer sets great store is his food. It is scanty enough, and would be found painfully monotonous by those who are accustomed to a pleasantly varied diet.

But over his breakfast of bread with a slice of rough cheese or a slice of sausage, over his dinner of beans with plenty of oil, and over the pasta (or macaroni) which he eats in the evening, with perhaps chestnuts cooked in some way to follow, he lingers with satisfaction, and eagerly gulps down his few mouthfuls of wine, and smokes his rank cigarette afterwards with the appreciation of a connoisseur.

Fatalists who Live for the Day

Italians certainly know how to live for the moment and to squeeze the best out of the everyday routine of life. This is what makes them so cheerful and even so gay. They are not introspective. They are simple-minded, though perhaps not altogether simple-hearted. Every time I see the little farms and cottages on the slopes of Vesuvius I am astonished by the refusal of the folks who live in them to be kept away by the eruptions which happen from time to time, throwing out streams of molten lava to rush down the mountain-side and consume all that stands in their path. When this disaster occurs the people flee and their dwellings are destroyed. But as soon as the lava has cooled and the volcano has settled down to another period of quiet, back they go, rebuild, and settle in the jaws of death again.

Organized Attempts at Betterment

Yet the Italian peasant, though he may not do much thinking, and though he is not imaginative, is not by any means a fool. " The man with the brains and the big boots " he has been called. Brains he has certainly, and since the Government decided that efforts must be made for the improvement of the soil and in the methods of tilling it, and the provincial authorities have tried to help cultivators, some betterment is to be marked. The landlords' agents are now often men who have studied agriculture. The small farmers of a district club together and buy agricultural machinery ; or gunpowder for the dispersal of the hail-clouds, which, if they discharge their ammunition upon the vineyards or the standing crops, ruin utterly the year's labour; or insect-killer to save the fruit trees from devastation. Land banks and rural credit institutes are also proving of value.

The owners of large estates have here and there done a good deal themselves to improve the raising of crops, the breeding of beasts, the making of wine. This is a healthy change. It used to be considered beneath the dignity of an old family that its members should do any work. The combined pressure of poverty and common sense has altered the ideas of the Italian aristocracy. It is far more rare than it was thirty years ago to find an old family living in the corners of a huge palace, eking out a tiny income, supporting its dignity at the expense of its back and belly by half starving itself and wearing the oldest clothes. Many landowners farm part of their fields themselves. Many sons of the noblest families become lawyers or doctors, or go into business.

There is still, however, a "high society" more exclusive, less mixed with the newly-rich, than any that can be found in London or Paris. If you want to make acquaintance with this, you must provide yourself with

PROFESSIONAL LETTER-WRITERS OF THE ITALIAN CAPITAL

In countries where the percentage of illiteracy is high, as in a few provinces of Italy, the professional writer of letters plays an important part in local life. Here a woman is seen seated at a stall in the Campo di Fiori, Rome, where a rag fair is held, anxiously watching her agent at work, while in the nearer booth the two proprietors wait for custom

Photo, C. Chichester

ON ONE OF THE NUMBERLESS ROADS LEADING TO ROME

A solemn majesty broods over the Roman Campagna, where on the green of the plain are scattered the magnificent arches of the Claudian Aqueduct and picturesque fragments of ruined villas and tombs. And silence reigns supreme in this immense space, broken only by the faint rumble of vehicles along its winding roads, or the far-away voices of shepherds guiding their sheep to some fresh pasturage

ROMAN IMPERIAL TRIUMPH IMMORTALISED IN STONE

Erected in A.D. 312 to commemorate the victory of Constantine the Great over Maxentius, this arch is one of the most imposing monuments of Rome. Under its trio of archways, with four fluted Corinthian columns on either front, passes many a Roman citizen with mind too engrossed with modern affairs to pay attention to the inscription and sculpture on this remnant of the ancient empire

Photo, Underwood Press Service

irreproachable introductions, and then, if you make yourself agreeable, you will find it kindly and simply hospitable. You will be invited to five o'clock teas, to small evening receptions, perhaps to one of the infrequent entertainments on a large scale in one of the vast and magnificent palaces of Rome, Florence, Naples, or Genoa. In the long, lofty rooms, hung with tapestries or with of the Third. It has struck out a line for itself. Modern Italy has tried to follow neither the skill in the art of government by the heavy-handed methods which the ancient Romans displayed, nor the pursuit of beauty which marked the Italy of Bellini and Titian, of Michelangelo and Della Robbia, of Cæsar Borgia, and of the bishop who ordered a tomb of jasper for

OIL AND WINE SHOP IN THE WRECKAGE OF ANCIENT POMPEII

Owing to the new methods of excavation employed in recent years many of Pompeii's hidden treasures have been brought to light in excellent condition. Two-storeyed houses, complete with balconies and windows, shrines still bearing the ashes of the last sacrifice, and various shops and public offices stand almost as they stood nineteen centuries ago before the city was overwhelmed

paintings by old masters, executed possibly to the order of the first owner, you understand why there is talk of " The Third Italy."

We all associate Rome with the Romans. That was the First Italy. But what Italy means to most of us derives rather from the art of the Quattrocento (the fourteenth century) and of the Renaissance than from the glories of Roman times. That was the Second Italy. Now we are watching the development his own remains. Its triumphs are in the mechanical direction, electricity, wireless telegraphy, motors ; in medical science and in surgery ; in the measuring of the skies. It has thrown its energy also into industrial expansion. The north has become a region of factories turning out silk and cotton fabrics in enormous quantities, and other manufactures in smaller bulk.

This enterprise and material prosperity have brought into prominence numbers

WORKGIRLS OF NAPLES AT THEIR MIDDAY MEAL

These gaily-dressed Neapolitans are taking advantage of the weather to eat their lunch in the open. Their black hair gleams in the sunlight as they consume their plates of raviuoli, a food made from a wheaten paste similar to that used for macaroni. The children crowd round in the hope of a spare morsel, and one worker has brought her baby and another her dog

POPULAR OPEN-AIR RESTAURANT ON THE QUAY OF NAPLES

The Neapolitan is primarily a democrat. With light-hearted irresponsibility he takes a share in the commercial activity of his sea-washed native town, then, hands in pockets, saunters along the quay and passes a few leisure moments at the alfresco restaurant presided over by a weather-beaten old sailor, whose voluble loquacity is sometimes even more attractive than his fare

of " new men." But there has not yet been so complete an obliteration of the old lines of social demarcation as took place in England during the later years of the nineteenth century. Those who have inherited their money, along with some name and title made familiar by the prowess or the crimes of a long line of ancestors, still, upon occasion, show that they feel themselves to be of finer clay than those whose fortunes are of recent growth. Italian society is a pleasant society, graciously welcoming strangers who can produce their cards of entry properly signed, more intelligent than what is still called Society in London. In many ways it is imitative of the English—the women by their

GRIZZLED FISHERMAN OF SALERNO
Wrinkled and weather-bitten by the salt sprays of the Tyrrhenian Sea, this old fisherman of Salerno has spent a long and healthy life catching tunny off the coasts of Sardinia, Sicily, and Elba

country clothes and efforts to take up open-air pastimes; the men by their clean-shaven faces, their studiously unobtrusive fashion of dress, their addiction to sports, such as fox-hunting,

which is practised on the Roman Campagna.

No better opportunity for seeing society in its English mood than a meet of the " Roman Society for the Hunting of the Fox." We have an invitation. Let us go. It is cold when the motor comes round after breakfast. A nip of frost in the air, welcome because invigorating. Just the ideal winter morning—ground white, sky blue, sunshine steady. We leave the city by the Gate of San Giovanni and speed along the new Appian Way.

At all hours, at all seasons of the year, the Campagna is serenely beautiful. In the charm which is nature's gift and in the warmth of human interest that history radiates, I know of no spot richer than this rolling plain of Rome, with the faintly pencilled Alban Hills against the skyline and the broken arches of the aqueduct across it; with its sheepfolds and pink-tiled farmhouses, its tombs and wayside inns, its dark, romantic groups of spreading pine. Sometimes the Campagna is a symphony stirring deep emotions; sometimes a sombre fugue, mysterious, even sinister. This morning, with every blade of grass a-glitter, it affects me like a gay ritornelle. Stop the car. Let us get out and walk, nay, run and jump fences. The air makes us feel like two-year-olds.

We have plenty of time. Here are the golf-links. We will tramp across them—the very thing. Two Italian enthusiasts are playing an early round, more from a sense of duty, I am inclined to believe, than from any enthusiasm for the game. It is

ITALIANS OF TO-DAY
In Ancient Rome & Venice

From shallow Venetian waters rises a small wooden shrine on which devout fisherfolk lay floral offerings in honour of the Blessed Virgin

All photos, except that on page 3000, by Donald McLeish

I X 4

*Architecture is prodigal in the City of the Sea, and the beautiful Scuola
di San Marco is but one of the many immortal " Stones of Venice "*

*In the labyrinth of narrow waterways only the soft splash of the
oar breaks the golden noonday hush of the silent city of Venice*

Even the prosaic calling of the vegetable merchant assumes an aspect of romance amid the winding waterways of the Doges' ancient city.

*With costly equipment and amid a wealth of flowers a Venetian
sets forth on his last voyage to the lone cemetery island outside the city*

*Carnations are sold for a few soldi in the streets of the Eternal City
by women and girls whose faces are as lovely as their flowers*

Swiss Guards, in their sixteenth-century parti-coloured uniforms, are always on duty at the entrance to the Vatican to preserve the Papal peace

*Youth and old age mingle in the monastery of Monte Oliveto Maggiore,
and the good works of the monks are known to the whole countryside*

From a niche in Aosta Cathedral a radiant Madonna looks down on a human mother who, spent with toil, pours out her heart in prayer

With heart at peace this white-robed monk views the beautiful world he has renounced for the cloistered solitudes of Certosa di Val d'Ema

In the colonnade of S. Peter's, the Mecca of half Christendom, this Roman mother loves to sit and listen to the soft prattle of her bambino

A venerable Roman in the old-time costume still to be seen among the humble inhabitants of the wide expanse of the sunburnt Campagna

3004

Dolce far niente!   In Roman sunshine a flower-girl stands, her nose-gays all but vanished, happy thoughts beguiling the hot, languid hours

Life still flows under Rimini's triumphal arch, an ancient monument full of memories, erected twenty-seven years before the birth of Christ

*Cased with varied coloured marbles, the magnificent Campanile of
Giotto in Florence is regarded as the finest existing work of its kind*

3007

*The straw-plaiting industry is centred in the old Etruscan city of
Fiesole, where lovely designs are fashioned with lightning rapidity*

"English," therefore it must be done. By the time we come on to the road again strings of led horses are passing. Motors and carriages have become numerous. It is nearing eleven, the hour of the meet.

A short run brings us to the meeting-place. The horses, still in their cloths, are standing in lines along the wooden fences or being walked briskly about. In a big tent there is drinking of coffee, munching of crisp little rolls with salami (sausage) sandwiched into them, tossing off of petits verres. Every moment more motors throb alongside, and swell the throng of women exquisitely dressed, who chatter of last night's dinners and dances, of the new play or the new novel, the latest gossip of "high society" in Rome.

Officers are conspicuous in trim uniforms. The master, Prince Gianbattista Rospigliosi, is in "pink," with several more whose coats make the picture gayer. Hat-boxes are brought out of the cars by servants for their masters, who have arrived in caps. Everyone is chatting vigorously, laughing. It is like a scene in a play, with the most perfect back-cloth imaginable and costumes by the most expensive firms.

Exactly at the right dramatic moment here come the hounds. The huntsman trots beside them. "Coom oop, lads!" he says, or seems to say. "Coom over, then!" Did he really say that? I ask myself. I listen again. Yes, I heard

ARTLESS NEAPOLITAN CHILDHOOD
Here and there in the crowded alleys of old Naples a young face of elusive beauty stands out in startling relief against the sordid surroundings
From a Kodak snapshot

aright. The huntsman has a fine North-country accent, which is natural enough seeing that he hails from Cheshire and that his name is Jim Brown.

Ladies gather round the hounds and pet them. Jim looks on with a curious curl of the lip. " Plenty of foxes ? " he repeats, in reply to a question. " No, they shoot 'em, to maak laadies' furs." No time to lose, therefore, in finding one. " Coom oop ! " cries Jim again ; and the hounds trot off, the riders following. Up a slope, then across the flat, over a stone wall, and away into the distance. Quickly they are lost to view.

The spectators clear off. Grooms and chauffeurs settle down to their lunch at tables spread in the sun-shine. Walk a little distance, a few hundred yards, and we can see no human being save an old shepherd, picturesquely ragged, and a small boy, like a red-faced lamb himself, helping the old man to look after the flock. Peace has settled down again on the Campagna. Insects whir in the hot noon.

The smartness of that meet is typical of the change that has come over Rome in less than a generation. The Roman season has developed from a half-hearted dowdy business into a rush of costly entertainments, at which every-thing must be dernier cri. The dinner parties, and even the dances, are more often given in the big new hotels of the cosmopolitan order than at home.

These hotels are signs of the times also. Gone is the old cheap Italy where an English family could spend a winter and spring for the double purpose of cultivating their artistic intelligence and saving money. The cost of living in the towns has increased to three times what it was.

The passing of the old custom of bargaining in shops has helped to make everything dearer. The shopkeeper used to mark his goods a hundred per cent. above what they were worth, and could be bargained down to something like a fair price. He expected this. Haggling was all in the day's work. It was no pleasure to do business with anyone who did not haggle. Such a person must be a fool. Now the goods are marked fifty per cent. above their value, and you have to pay it, for the system is " Fixed Prices." As usual, the consumer pays.

Once more let us mix with Roman society on the Pincian Hill, where all that is fashionable may be seen driving of an afternoon. The fact, learned by rote at school, that the city is built upon seven hills, is forced upon one's notice as one walks about it. There is no more tiring place. Yet the hills have their advantages as well as their drawbacks. For example, look from the Pincio at the surrounding country. Could any view be more refreshing ? Grander prospects I will show you, but none that I could be more grateful to look upon from the heart of a city, none that more persuasively whispers, " Peace, be still."

Close by, the fields are being tilled, the olive orchards tended, the sheep pastured. Hardly at all can this quiet, peaceful landscape have altered in two thousand years. It keeps Rome in touch with reality, with nature. Hard as the powers in Rome have tried in the past, and are trying still, to prevent

"SET EYES ON NAPLES AND THEN DIE CONTENT"

Naples lies along the northern shore of the superb, exquisitely azure Bay of Naples, at the foot of a range of luxuriantly vine-clad volcanic hills which culminate in Mount Vesuvius. Viewed, as here, from the harbour, the city is seen at its best, challenging consent to its claim to be, with the possible exception of Constantinople, the most beautifully situated city in Europe

THE INEXHAUSTIBLE MATCH OF THE NEAPOLITAN

The Neapolitan is not a practical person, and if left to his own devices would contentedly jog along in his old happy-go-lucky way and leave all innovations alone. But modern conveniences are breaking down his conservatism, and this indisputably useful public cigar-lighter, consisting of a lengthy rope that burns very slowly, is gradually being superseded by matches

Photo, Publishers' Photo Service

life from being natural and rational, there has always been a reminder of sanity and the true sweetness of existence in the country round about that can be seen from the Seven Hills. I think it still has an influence in saving even " society " in Rome from sinking into quite the same fever of folly and perpetual excitement which afflicts it incurably elsewhere.

However this may be, we can escape the disease by the simple expedient of quitting society and studying other classes of Italians. Let us leave the Pincio at once and go down by the Piazza di Spagna where, on the steps called after the church of the Trinita del Monti, there is a delicious winter flower market. Here the air is scented by roses, violets, stock, carnations, jonquils, mignonette. The women who

set them out vary these with daffodils and snow-white narcissi, anemones, pansies, delicate heaven-blue irises, and branches of white cherry-blossom waving over all

Then up another hill, the Montecitorio, to make the acquaintance of some members of Parliament and to see the Parliament buildings. In the House of Deputies lawyers predominate. It is no great distinction to be a deputy. It is, rather, a nuisance. For the idea prevails among the peasant and artisan classes that members of Parliament must be willing to do their constituents any little service that may be asked of them.

Crowds of voters or voters' wives wait while the House is sitting to see their deputy and lay their wants before him. Many of them ask for small appointments in the Post Office or the Customs Department. One will complain of the

SCENE PAINTERS' ARTISTRY OUTCLASSED IN REAL NAPLES

Garish Neapolitan life as represented by imaginative writers is actually to be seen in the Santa Lucia quarter. The tall white-fronted tenement houses, a-flutter with variegated garments hanging out to dry and gay with green jalousies and balconies look down upon a brilliant-hued crowd chaffering over fruit and macaroni, olives in round baskets, and wine in demi-johns

severity of a schoolmaster towards a child. Another will plead for the release of a son sentenced to hard labour. Here is a young fellow with his mother. He cannot pass some examination for a Government post. Cannot he get the post without passing? Here is a small contractor who seeks an order for a new bridge or a piece of road-making. This man, who is defendant in a debt action, wants his deputy to influence a judge in his favour. This woman pours out a voluble petition for assistance to get her husband a pension, to which he can put forward no valid claim.

Those who are better-dressed than the majority have most probably come to ask for a decoration. Titles and ribbons are sought after in Italy almost as eagerly as in England. A politician who had been Prime Minister, and knew how useful this kind of bribery could be, declared once that Italy was governed by decorations. A King of Italy said with bitter humour : " Knighthoods and

cigars are things you can't refuse to anyone." Italians of all classes are apt to consider that they have a right to get all they can out of their country. The prevailing conception of the State is that of a pump set up for the benefit of those who can work the handle.

The consequence is that those who either cannot get near the pump, or who do not care to prey upon the Government, speak contemptuously of members of Parliament and others who are supposed to be bent solely on advancing their own interests at the cost of their fellow-countrymen. Men of letters and men of science alike despise the " trade of politics." I have heard Italian doctors, who are both highly skilled in their profession and, as a rule, men of high general intelligence, declare that all politicians are " out for what they can get." It was the general disgust with politicians and the feeling that democracy had failed to give good results that made it possible for the Fascist leader, Mussolini, to make himself dictator. Begun as a reaction against Bolshevist doctrine, the Fascisti movement (called after the " fasces " carried by ancient Roman lictors and signifying unity) rapidly gained control of the country by reason of the wide-spread dissatisfaction with those who had misgoverned so long.

So now, having visited the scene of their misgovernment, let us leave Montecitorio and wander up and down the Eternal City in the sunshine. It is no use trying to " do " Rome tourist fashion, rushing from one " sight " to another. That will only result in tired feet and jumbled recollections and disappointment. Rome is a proud mistress and must be patiently wooed.

There is not really very much to " see " in the guide-book sense. The value you get out of your wanderings will be in the suggestions that the streets and buildings, the ruins and the sites of ancient greatness, will slip into your mind.

The way to see Rome is to let it soak in gradually. Take a trifling example. You are in what has been uncovered of the Forum. Hard to take it in. Can it be here that Mark Antony spoke Caesar's funeral oration ? You look round vaguely. Then your eye lights on a patch of metal clinging to a slab of grey stone. That you learn is molten money. The building in which that grey slab formed part of the pavement was burned down eighteen hundred years ago. It housed the tables of the

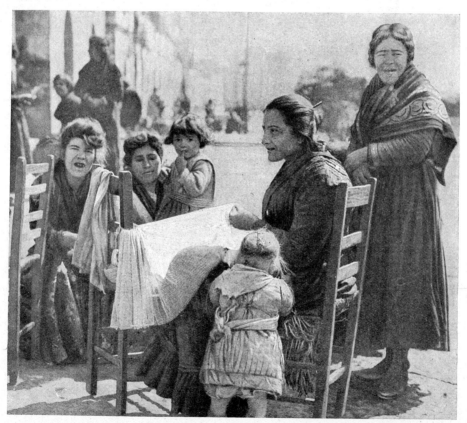

MOTHERS' MEETING IN THE PUBLIC THOROUGHFARE

Few cities in the world rival Naples in the animation of the streets, owing to the Neapolitans' entire indifference to publicity. It is the general custom for the women to do all their work, net-mending, sewing, and so forth, out of doors, and they have no objection to performing most private services for their children or making their own toilet in full public view

Photo, Publishers' Photo Service

FAVOURITE HAUNT OF THE POPULACE OF PALERMO

The word "maccheroni" exercises magical influence over the Sicilian no less than the Neapolitan. In this macaroni factory at Palermo a colossal quantity of flour is converted into paste which when forced through perforated presses has the appearance of string. This is cut into lengths and hung —regardless of dust—over rods in the open air to dry ; when stiff it is broken up, boxed, and sold

money-changers. Reconstruct the scene, the busy market-place, the alarm of fire, the rush to escape, the Roman soldiers keeping order — rather roughly — the money left behind soon melted. That is the money there.

S. Peter's, if you pay it a hurried visit, will haunt you for ever as one of the world's great disillusions. It is frankly a hideous place inside, all gilt and gewgaws ; like a railway station, with no more sense of devotion about it than the foyer of a music-hall. But think of the history which S. Peter's has seen made, think of the endless procession of the Popes ; study the vast Piazza which stretches before it with its satisfying semi-circular colonnade of heavy columns ; enjoy the sombre dignity of its severe rectilinear façade. Then you carry away with you

impressions which can distinguish between what is of permanent enduring value and that which bears merely the stamp of its own age.

Into which of these categories we are to place the men and women who kneel in S. Peter's, who kiss the images, who mutter as they turn with nimble fingers the beads of a rosary, I shall not offer to decide. Are the Italians who still hold to the Christian faith merely carrying out observances which they think it might be rash to neglect ; rash in the event of all that the priests teach proving to be true ; rash, too, because public opinion, in country districts at all events, is, on the whole, inclined to frown on "unbelievers"? Or are their souls lit up by divine radiance, the outward and visible signs being proof of an inward and spiritual grace? The Church has lost ground in Italy since education for the masses began the spread of modern ideas. But it would be very hard to say how much this loss amounts to.

There is, even among the intellectuals, a movement away from the materialism, the positivism, which was dominant during the nineteenth century, a movement in the direction which the mind of the novelist Butti has taken, and which was indicated by his story of a man of science forced to declare that "the narrow, dark prison provided with no way out in which science would confine us" cannot really represent the final truth about human existence. One thing is sure. Religion would be more honoured in Italy if the priests, speaking generally, were of a higher type, more like those of France, or of Belgium even. Exception must be made in favour of the Jesuits, who are men of education and decent habits, and many of them broad-minded, with a knowledge of the world and of human nature that few men in any of the professions can equal.

It is not surprising that in general the Italian priests win little respect. Yet the Church is, by the mass of the people, both respected and regarded

WOMEN MAKERS OF ITALY'S STAPLE ARTICLE OF FOOD

Italian macaroni manufacturers are ever sure of a market for their wares; nowhere is there such a demand for this farinaceous food as in Italy, where macaroni-eating may be said to be a business of the man in the street. The paste, prepared from a variety of hard wheat, can be made into macaroni, vermicelli, spaghetti, and into the various small fantastic shapes used in soups

VENERABLE INMATE OF THE CERTOSA MONASTERY NEAR FLORENCE

A short distance from Florence on a hill clothed with cypresses and olive trees stands the Certosa di Val d'Ema, an imposing old monastery founded in the fourteenth century. Very few monks now live within its walls, but this white-haired ascetic knows no other home, and is content to spend the evening of his days in quiet seclusion, the Holy Book his never-failing companion

Photo, Donald McLeish

FRANCISCAN FRIARS DISCUSS A DIFFERENCE OF INTERPRETATION

They belong to the Order of friars founded by S. Francis of Assisi in the early part of the thirteenth century. Under various names the order spread rapidly through Europe and many eminent men were enrolled among its members. The Franciscan Friars of Italy make very effective missionaries, and numberless good works are wrought by them among the poor and distressed

Photo, Donald McLeish

FLORENTINE BROTHER OF MERCY

One of the brethren of the Order of the Misericordia in Florence who frequently walk the streets in long black robes, the head closely covered with a cowl, their sad eyes, burning with ascetic light, the only facial feature visible

Photo, Donald McLeish

as an institution to be proud of. There is no feeling of this kind among the Socialist leaders or the more studious of the professional classes. But sometimes among the Socialist rank and file, and certainly in the middle classes, which neither practise religion with any fervour nor pretend to be influenced by it, one finds this attitude towards the Church. Italy is pleased that the Pope should be an Italian and live in Rome. It is pleased that the whole Catholic world should take its orders from Rome.

However contemptuous an Italian may be towards "miracles," or towards the doctrines of the Church, or even towards the claims of the Pope to speak with an infallible voice, he will nevertheless wish to keep up the Roman system. In this intelligent Italian men are mostly alike — the shrewd peasant, the clever doctor or lawyer, the successful manufacturer, and even those who devote themselves to applied science. They have no use for religion themselves, but they think it is a good thing for women. They cannot imagine what women would do without it. What would become of the odd ones who do not get married if there were no convents for them to enter? Therefore, Italians look upon the Church as useful and even necessary. This is an attitude of mind hard for the British to understand. It is not essentially Latin, as some say, for the French adopt it, and many of the Irish, too. How often have I heard farmers in Galway or Normandy joke about the priests and the ceremonies and the " miracles," and yet on a Sunday off they go to service with their women, and if they did not go they would have a vague apprehension that some ill might come of it. There are a great many Italian farmers like that.

In Rome one finds as little genuine devotion to the faith as anywhere. The outward signs of religion abound.

Troops of priests and young men preparing to be priests are seen continually·in the streets. The machinery of ecclesiasticism obtrudes itself everywhere. But of any fervent faith behind the machinery there is little evidence. " In Rome," an English Roman Catholic priest complained to me once, as we walked through the Vatican galleries, " it is very difficult to be a good Roman Catholic."

The Roman temperament is not ardent. It is lymphatic. It refuses to take much interest in anything. To find anything like real devotion in Italy you must go south—to Naples, to

BEARING A DEAD BROTHER TO HIS LAST RESTING-PLACE
Nearly six hundred years ago the Order of the Misericordia was founded for the succouring of the sick, poor, and injured. The splendid mission of this charitable fraternity has never swerved from its original purpose, and to this day in Florence the black-robed brethren—men from all classes of society anxious to devote their lives to good works—are ever ready to answer calls of distress

HONOURING THE HOLY VIRGIN IN AN ITALIAN ALPINE VILLAGE

In the grand mountainous region where Cogne is situated, life is lived very simply by the country folk, who retain many of the customs and costumes of the ancient Alpine peasantry. Scarcely a week passes but one may witness some quaint ceremony, in which all participate, whether it be secular festivity or, as shown above, a religious procession in honour of the Holy Virgin

Photo, Donald McLeish

Sicily. There everything is done with enthusiasm, with vigour. In the few hours that are occupied by the train journey from Rome to Naples you leave behind all classical associations, and almost all that binds one to medieval Italy. Pompeii is not classical. It is romantic. They were not Romans who built the houses which have been so marvellously laid bare again after so many centuries under the lava, nor had they anything in common with the Romans. The stern rulers of the world spoke of the south with an accent of contempt. Dallying at Capua was not worthy, they considered, of a man with a man's work to do in the world. They lived in a different atmosphere, an atmosphere morally as well as physically harder.

You may leave Rome on a winter's evening, nipped by an eager air. The same night you lean out of your window in Naples, listening to the little waves that splash playfully against the sea-wall. From the old, old houses on the rock of Santa Lucia faint gleams cast flickering reflections on the dark water. The curve towards Posilipo is marked by glittering lamps. The hills which rise from the bay are jewelled plenteously with points of light. The air is soft and truly southern. And somewhere near at hand a man's voice, flexible and resonant, begins to sing one of the old Neapolitan songs. True, there may be a sudden breath of the ice king; Naples may wake up shivering. I landed once from Sicily, and found the puddles on the quay all frozen. I never saw a population looking more miserable. By ten o'clock the sun was hot, and they had recovered their spirits.

These violent variations of temperature are discomposing even to a northerner. But they are infrequent. The prevailing condition of weather is sunshine hot and clear, sunshine which makes doing nothing a positive instead of a negative enjoyment. That is why the Neapolitans are supposed to be an idle race. They are not idle, far from it. But when they do nothing they do it with such complete abandonment to the delight of relaxation that the visitor from the north imagines they seldom do anything else.

The city, when you know it, gives the lie vehemently to this legend of Neapolitan indolence. It swarms with swarthy life. It is an astonishing human ant-heap, if one could imagine ants endowed with penetrating voices, and

COMELY PEASANT MAIDENS OF THE VAL DI COGNE

In North Italy where Teutonic influence has blended with Celtic, the Italians are of a much fairer skin than their southern kinsmen, a fact well illustrated by these girls of Cogne. The same foreign influence is observed in their dress, and it is noteworthy that the apron, without which their attire would be incomplete, is worn tied up on weekdays and let down only on Sundays

Photo, Donald McLeish

ON THE QUAYSIDE OF PALERMO, WHERE ACTIVITY AND INDOLENCE ARE INSEPARABLE COMPANIONS

Quay hands are numerous in Palermo where the willing worker is never at a loss for an occupation. But the indolence of the southerner is strong in the Sicilian, who loves nothing better than to spend his time in strolling aimlessly along the " smiling sea-shore." Many of these loafers are country peasants who, tired of the rough hill tracks, have come to the town, but they soon weary of the unhealthy tenements where they are huddled with their families and go back to their hills

DAY OF RELIGIOUS REJOICING WHEN THE HEARTS OF THE PEOPLE ARE KNIT TOGETHER BY A COMMON FAITH

Sicily's capital enters whole-heartedly into the celebration of all religious holidays, and there are many days in the year when the streets of Palermo are thronged with devout souls full of reverential regard for the "celestial patron," whose festa they are honouring. By far the greater number of the feste are devoted to the Madonna, for it is she who orders the goings and comings of the people and who, under every guise, is their patroness—no matter what their station in life

Photo. A. W. Cutler

WHERE STANDS THE ANCIENT FOUNTAIN IN TAORMINA'S MARKET PLACE
Natives of more northern climes find Taormina, a coast town of eastern Sicily, a warm and benign winter resort with its clear seas and skies. This fountain, that has assuaged the thirsty throats of man and beast for centuries, still gurgles with cool water ever pouring from the gaping mouths of the statuary at each corner. Above, like a sentinel, frowns the hill whose top bears a medieval castle

all using them as loudly as possible at once. The steep staircase streets are littered with humanity. On the shady side tailors, bootmakers, and other rude mechanicals stitch and hammer. The housewives are chaffering in the markets with a vigour that you find exhausting even to watch. In the broader streets of the new town the cab-drivers scream after strangers, the postcard sellers murmur hoarsely, the flower women and those who sell sweets at little stalls cry aloud their wares with smiling vehemence. No one talks of Neapolitan indolence who has heard the noisiest population in Europe doing business, haggling, quarrelling, swearing, swindling, love-making with all the force of its southern, deep-chested lung-power.

"Immoral" is another epithet flung at them. Well, if you are shown the innermost recesses of Pompeii, you know that a strict morality has never characterised the people of this shore. But are they so much worse than other people, or is it merely that they do not take the trouble to hide their faults? They do not count them faults in the cold northern way. I cannot feel that we have the right to judge them. It is best, I think, to leave it at that.

Better enjoy the spectacle of Naples than waste time in condemning its people. What a comic opera spectacle it is! Here we have the Italian of British tradition, black-eyed, with shiny black ringlets, earrings, and red neckerchief, and the most persuasively theatrical smile. He transacts all the business of life in the highest emotional key. If you tip him a halfpenny less than he expected, he beats his breast and calls Heaven to witness that injustice has been done. The most trivial discussion is carried on with gestures which lead the stranger to fear bloodshed.

Those who live among the Neapolitans —foreigners I mean, especially the

English—grow attached to them, and say they would not live anywhere else. I know an old poet who has spent the last forty years in the island of Capri, which you see from Naples as plainly as if it were only five miles distant instead of twenty. He would not shift his dwelling if you offered him a million a year. He went to the island, meaning to stay a few days. That was forty years ago. He has been there ever since, and has only paid one visit to England in all that time. He married there and brought up a family, half Italian, half English.

From the flat roof of his villa he showed me his garden, where roses in full bloom wreathed themselves on sunny pergolas amid groves of bay and orange (the month was January). Then he showed me the mountain which on one side towers above him, and after that the view across the blue sea to Ischia and the mainland. I had sometimes asked myself how he could stay there so contentedly. I did not wonder on that January day.

Poke about in Pompeii, and you will discover how little two thousand years have changed either the character of the southern Italian or the nature of mankind at large. I like to sit on one of the green mounds which command the full extent of the ruins, and muse upon the wonder of it, and moralise over the evidence that the viciousness of a great city found the same outlets then as now.

Pompeii is like nothing else in the world. I shall never forget my astonishment when I first saw how perfect it was. I had expected no more than a fragmentary ground plan, not much more definite than the lines traced amid heaps of rubble which mark the site of

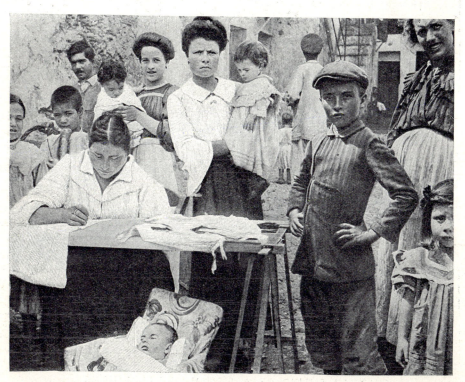

HOW THE SICILIAN WOMAN COMBINES BUSINESS, DUTY, AND GOSSIP

Between one domestic occupation and another this Palermo housewife usually finds time in which to ply her clever fingers at some remunerative work. Seated at the threshold of her cottage, though intent on her embroidery, she manages to carry on a glib conversation with her leisured neighbours and to keep a vigilant ear for her youngest-born, sleeping tranquilly beneath her table

GUARDIAN SHRINE OF A SICILIAN COTTAGE HOME

In this little whitewashed house everything is trim and neat, simplicity personified. A home blessed by good fortune, as would testify the pleasant, serene faces of its inmates, whose simple faith attributes all contentment to the holy saint enshrined within the wall to the portal's right, before whom at night a dim light burns and at whose feet tiny bunches of flowers lie in humble homage

Photo. A. W. Cutler

"THE PEALING ANTHEM SWELLS THE NOTE OF PRAISE"

Excellence of intention may excuse imperfection of performance, and true piety prompts this Sicilian squeezing the pigskin bag of his pipes and emitting weird noises from his drones and chaunter. For it is Christmas-time, and by custom the Sicilian piper visits every shrine and pipes in honour of the Madonna before proceeding to his neighbours' houses to entertain them with his music

Photo, A. W. Cutler

Ephesus. I found that I could walk along street after street on the same stones that were trodden by the feet of the Pompeiians, see the ruts indented by their chariot-wheels, look into their houses where they lived the luxurious life of the first century, study their wall-paintings, admire their little gardens, dive into their wine-bars, and even read upon walls the election addresses which had just been put up when the liquid fire swallowed up the city, as Sodom and Gomorrah were destroyed. From the number of drug-shops it is plain that the Pompeiians were as much addicted as we moderns are to pick-me-ups and patent medicines, antidotes against excess, and so forth. I have no doubt the drug-shops sold opiates, and that dope-parties were known.

Again, there is proof that in Pompeii they were furious gamblers, as the Italians are to-day. In Naples the drawings of the State lotteries cause a positive furore. Everyone who is credulous enough to believe that luck may bring him fortune is a regular buyer of lottery tickets. The aristocracy used to gamble heavily in their clubs, and there still goes on a good deal of that kind of " amusement."

The masses find their excitement provided for them by the Government. This seems to me a wise plan. It is certain that in cities the craving for some form of thrill which gives the possibility of making money without working for it, can only be repressed by raising the level of intelligence, and that will take a long time, even when we have hit upon such methods of education as are likely to raise it. Surely, therefore, if there is bound to be a profit for someone out of gambling, it is better that it should go towards the lightening of taxation than into the pockets of

WHEN THE ALMOND BLOSSOM FLOWERS IN SUNNY SICILY

Near Taormina in the early year the vivid colouring of the loveliest of all Mediterranean islands is seen to full advantage. Hill and dale are clothed with a tender green, delicate pink blossoms dance against a cloudless sky, Etna sleeps peacefully in the blue distance, everywhere beautiful, bountiful spring. Here, surely, one must rest awhile to drink in the rich beauty of the sunlit scene

AMID THE MOIL AND TOIL OF UNCONVENTIONAL SICILY

In the tangled alleys that intersect Sicily's capital, life is entirely free from affectation or adornment. A babble of voices is heard the livelong day from the throngs in these airless streets ; overhead hangs the family linen in variegated confusion, and piles of bedding and other lumber litter the cobbles where stray dogs and fowls wander at will. Simplicity is the keynote of the Sicilian character

individuals who are not merely undeserving, but usually pests of society.

The Italian Government makes its lotteries pay. The public has the satisfaction of knowing that they are honestly conducted, and there is the further advantage that those who regularly lose their money, as, of course, ninety-nine per cent. do, can console themselves by reflecting that they have contributed to public funds instead of handing over their money to bookmakers, and giving a particularly detestable class of sharps a comfortable living.

Once a week in the public squares of towns and villages the winning numbers are read out, and payment is made without delay. There are also private games of chance, known, like the State lotteries, as " Tombola." These are often got up for charitable objects and large sums are made. There is never any difficulty in attracting ticket-buyers. The Italians enjoy this mild

form of gambling immensely. They talk about their chances a great deal, and try to hit upon magical methods of discovering lucky numbers. I saw once in the cemetery at Naples a vast crowd, and I inquired what famous person had been buried. I was told that the crowd had gone to the cemetery to see a grave opened. It was the grave of a lottery tipster who had put five numbers into his sister's coffin some twelve months before. These, he, said would be the winning numbers of the week when her body was exhumed. It is the custom to dig up bodies after a certain interval and then rebury them. How long the period may be is uncertain to a few weeks, so here the element of chance came in. As soon as the numbers had been taken from the coffin and read out the people gathered at the graveside rushed off to back them without delay !

In Tuscany the countryfolk are quite different from the Neapolitans. They

TOY BEAST OF BURDEN FROM SARDINIA

The diminutiveness of this Sardinian donkey is accentuated by the height of its Sicilian owner who, while not over particular about taxing its miniature muscles, is bent on its cutting a handsome figure in the streets of Palermo. Indeed, bedecked with fine trappings, harnessed to a cart decorated with gaudily-painted allegorical pictures, its appearance is certainly calculated to call forth expressions of admiration

HIRSUTE PAYING GUESTS THAT LIVE WITH THE FAMILY

Deficiency of outside accommodation and precaution against thieves explain the Palerman goat-keeper's custom of installing his goats under his own roof. The goats occupy the ground floor and the family the upper storeys. The practice is no more unhygienic than that found elsewhere, of human beings living over horses, but it is more unpleasant, owing to the strong smell of the goat

Photos, A. W. Cutler

PRIESTLY DIGNITY PERCHED ON MONASTIC PROVISIONS

One of the chief diversions in the life of this Sicilian monk comes in the shape of periodical visits to
the neighbouring town, where he spends several hours in buying provisions to replenish the store-
cupboards of the monastery. Although the crucifix, seldom out of his hand, is a constant reminder
that worldly affairs are but transitory, asceticism does not appear to weigh too heavily on him

Photo, A. W. Cutler

have more dignity. They are not so hot-blooded. Round about Florence they are apt to prey a little upon the English visitor, but even so, they prey in such a charming, caressing manner that one quite enjoys it. Florence reveals far more than Rome can the Italy of English dreams. All through the Middle Ages Rome was of slight importance. It is only within the last half-century that she has become again a leading city of the world. Florence, though she cannot

well-worn stones, and whose fame or infamy is familiar. Here is where Dante paced beside the Arno, his spirit broken by the death of Beatrice. Here are chapels painted by Giotto's hand. That was Duke Cosimo's dwelling. There Savonarola was burned. Around us are the very buildings which saw history and literature and the great art of the Quattrocento made. Out over there on the way to picturesque, perched-up Fiesole, is the villa, with its

AT HOME WITH THE SICILIAN MOUNTAINEER

The inhabitants of the ancient mountain village of Mola, situated just above Taormina, are exceedingly poor ; nevertheless, they usually attain a ripe old age, despite the fact that poverty wrinkles and cripples them when scarce beyond the prime of life. The hooded cape worn by the master of the house is a homespun garment and an effective one against the keen winds of winter

Photo, A. W. Cutler

boast so antique a past, has a record which is more romantic, more vivid, more highly charged with drama.

As we walk through the tall, crooked, sometimes narrow, but always fascinating streets of Florence, with glimpses at every opening of frowning palaces and marble-fronted churches, and graceful loggias and soaring towers, we stumble at every turn upon reminders of the great men whose footsteps trod these same

cypresses and marble terrace overlooking the city, where Boccaccio laid the scene of the telling of his joyous Tales while the plague raged down below. In the same direction we see the monastery where Fra Angelico painted his mystically lovely Madonnas. In that grey-stone fortress with the slender tower of warm red brick Lorenzo the Magnificent planned his poisonings. In the shadow of that corner Benvenuto Cellini

TRANSPORT ALONG SICILY'S LEMON-SCENTED BRIDLE PATHS

Lemons, oranges, and other fruit trees grow luxuriantly all over the plain and encompassing hills of the Conca d'Oro, or Golden Shell, wherein Palermo is set. On the hills the tracks are so steep and rough that the fruit as gathered has to be put into crates and brought on ponies to the high roads, where it is transferred to carts for conveyance to Palermo

Photo, A. W. Cutler

THE EVENING HOUR THAT GIVES REST TO THE TOIL-WORN AND BRINGS THE LABOURER HOME FROM THE FIELDS

Small stone structures form the dwelling-places of a large proportion of the Sicilian peasantry, and in the decayed town of Taormina there are many such humble homesteads, like the one seen above, on which antiquity has laid none too light a hand. From their seat under the stone arch these peasants can see Mount Etna, " that proud and lofty head of Sicily," which in the eyes of many is an actual personality, its every grumble awakening the countryside to apprehension

Photo, A. W. Cutler

3034

STORY-TELLER OF CATANIA HOLDING A CROWD BY THE MAGIC SPELL OF IMAGINATIVE NARRATIVE

Professional story-tellers are quite a feature of Catanian life, and an able member of the profession gathers his audience with little difficulty, and from the appearance of the grown-up children—for such the Sicilians are ever at heart—judges with a shrewdness born of wide experience which of his abundant repertoire would be likely to excite interest and emotion. Anybody may join the circle and occupy a chair, but need not pay anything unless the story appeals to him

Photo, A. W. Cutler

RUNNING LIQUID SULPHUR FROM THE SMELTING FURNACE INTO MOULDS

The chief industry of any importance in Sicily is sulphur-mining. The miners have a desperately hard life ; gaunt and wrinkled, old before their time, the killing work in the tortuous underground tracks, where the air is suffocatingly hot and reeking with the poisonous fumes of the sulphur, has made them some of the most miserable and degraded men of poverty-stricken Sicily

DUMPING-GROUND OF LUMPS OF SULPHUR PRODUCED FROM THE MINE

The desolation of the sulphur districts of Sicily is difficult to describe. To the unaccustomed spectator the scene appears as a blasted region of yellow earth perforated with holes, over which a nauseating odour of sulphur hangs. The system of working the mines is, for the most part, of a very primitive nature, and the strenuous life quickly tells on the health of the miners

WEIGHING BAGS OF BROKEN SULPHUR AT THE DOCKYARD OF CATANIA

The sulphur trade was formerly the monopoly of Sicily, but in recent years the United States and Japan have become serious competitors, with the result that the Sicilian export figures have dwindled considerably. Several thousands of workers, chiefly drawn from the rural classes, are engaged in the various branches of the industry, but by far the most strenuous work is that performed by the miners

LOADING A STEAMER WITH SULPHUR FROM THE CALTANISSETTA MINES

There is a large sprinkling of boys among the sulphur workers at the Catanian docks. Although their burdens are far above their strength, they are infinitely better off than the carusi, boy miners, of Caltanissetta, who, from eight years of age, carry such crushing loads that one has not to search far to find the reason why one youth of every six in that district is undersized

PULPING SICILIAN TOMATOES FOR TABLE SAUCE

When the sorting process has been completed, tomatoes are taken to the pulping-room and emptied into huge vats. From these they are passed through a pulping machine and speedily reduced to a mash. The work requires little or no skill, and is carried out in a decidedly primitive manner; quite young boys being employed in this particular branch of the industry

COOKING TOMATO PULP IN THE FURNACE-ROOM

The tomatoes, having been reduced to a pulp, are then boiled. The furnace-room presents an interesting sight. The stone ovens form a high parapet on either side, on which the " cooks " stand to stir the seething mass of pulp in the cylindrical pans; while on the ground the stokers keep a vigilant eye on the fires that the boiling may continue without interruption

WOMEN WORKERS IN A TOMATO FACTORY SORTING THE FRUIT

Sicily is extraordinarily rich in fruits and vegetables, of which large quantities are exported each year to the Italian mainland and various countries in Europe and America. Several Sicilian factories are carrying on a thriving trade in preserving vegetables in tins. Tomato sauce is one of the principal products, and our photograph shows heaps of the fruit in the hands of the sorters of a tomato factory

TOMATO SAUCE IN THE LAST STAGE BEFORE TINNING

The final process is drying the pulp. Spread out on trays and lightly stirred, it soon stiffens in the open air, and is then dispatched to the packing-rooms where it is placed in tins and bottles and hermetically sealed. This sauce is very popular for culinary purposes, and a colossal number of tins, running into some millions, is annually exported from Sicily

waited for his enemy, to stab him, praying his patron saint to send the victim quickly because poor Benvenuto felt cold!

When we think of Florence we have in our minds the image of those stirring centuries when, amid battle, murder, and sudden death, there flowered suddenly and richly the greatest age of beauty that the world has known. Florence was governed by a succession of profligate, faithless, and cynically wicked rulers, who had, however, one redeeming quality. They loved beauty, and they paid for its creation with princely magnificence. While tumults were breaking out in the city every day, while the nobles from their fortress-palaces fought one another in the public streets, while the compounders of deadly draughts were busy, and the blades of hired assassins flickered privily in quiet spots, there were artists at work creating the most exquisite pictures, the most impressive churches, and the noblest sculpture the world has seen.

Art and religion then went hand in hand. In the thirteenth century happened that vigorous revival of faith which brought forth S. Dominic and S. Francis of Assisi, the one preaching

SICILIANS GATHERING EDIBLE FRUIT FROM THE PRICKLY PEAR

This succulent shrub is a native of the hot, dry regions of America, but flourishes abundantly in Sicily's beautiful climate. From the large, oval, spiny leaves, pale yellow flowers spring which are succeeded by egg-shaped fruits of a smooth, pulpy nature. These " figs," a plague in Australia, are prized by the poorer Sicilian peasants, for whom—with bread—they form the staple food

ITALY: WOODLAND BEAUTY FROM THE ABRUZZI

She is a native of Ciociaria, a region of forest and mountain in the Abruzzi, named from the peasant
custom of wearing sandals. The beauty of the women has made it a source of artists' models

From a Kodak snapshot

HARDY YOUNG COUPLE OF MOUNTAINOUS SARDINIA

Natives of Iglesias, Sardinia, these young married people, with their open faces and sturdy frames, are excellent representatives of the vigorous mountain race from which they have sprung. The bride's dress bespeaks European influence, but the bridegroom displays the silver buttons, voluminous trousers, and quaintly-shaped cap still in vogue among his conservative countrymen

sound doctrine, the other good works. No sooner were their two Brotherhoods established than both Franciscans and Dominicans resolved to build them each a great church in Florence, and to decorate these as gloriously as they could. Thus there arose Santa Maria Novella and Santa Croce, adorned by the noblest works of Cimabue, of his pupil Giotto, and of their followers, too many to be named. The swift Arno (which runs almost dry, though, in summer) ; the old bridge with its shops, one of the very last of its kind left to us ; the surrounding hills and valleys, add to Florentine art the delight of living, natural beauty. Come up to the hill of San Miniato at sunset and look down over the city. The Duomo (the cathedral) stands out hugely from the sea of red-roofed buildings jammed together without form or plan. The great dome, and beside it Giotto's Campanile, seems to brood over Florence in the softly gathering dusk. The order which the chief magistrate gave for this tower in 1334 was for a monument " which shall be so magnificent in its height and for the quality of the work as to excel all that was ever done of its kind by the Greeks or ancient Romans." That shows what sort of people the Florentines were. They still keep something

SARDINIAN GRACE AND GENIALITY

Her costume proclaims her a girl of the Sardinian peasantry, though her strong, sunburnt features, and the graceful poise of the earthenware amphora on her coiled white head-cloth, would suggest traces of her Arab antecedents

Photo, Clifton Adams

sunset the city had been blotted out and that the bell was tolling its funeral dirge. It is a relief to walk down quickly, to mingle with the cheerful, prattling throng, to read in the gaily-lit streets the notices of the evening's operas and plays, to join the rest of Florence in making game of the young men who lounge outside the Nobles' Club, looking out, so malicious gossip says, for rich and beautiful—but especially for rich—wives.

Of the theatre the Italians are all fond. Singing and acting are arts which come naturally to them. Neither in opera nor in drama is their taste hard to satisfy. The simpler the emotions expressed, the more familiar the plot, the better they seem to enjoy their entertainment. One does now and then see acting of a very moving quality in little towns or even villages. Occasionally one has the luck to hear a Caruso or a Tetrazzini before they have been

of the same large pride in their city. Now the veil of night falls quickly. The Duomo becomes grey and indistinct. Behind us the western sky still flames with a threatening sombre gorgeousness. There is a glory of deepest crimson above a band of palest green. Below that again are a lowering, leaden cloud-bank and the intense purple of the distant hills. From the city there rises one sound detaching itself from the vague murmur of the human hive. It is the clangour of a deep-toned Angelus bell. One might fancy that in the consuming fire of that blood-red

"discovered." But in general the standard of performance is not high. The audience love long speeches, turgid rhetoric, windy tirades. They can listen interminably while mouthing tragedians unpack their hearts in words. They want plenty of hot seasoning. The feelings and actions of the characters must be elemental. For the dissection of the finer shades of temperament they have no use.

They are severe critics of acting. When they are pleased they applaud. When they are dissatisfied they let the actors know it, even though these

SUNLIGHT AND SHADE UNDER THE ARCHES OF A PIEDMONTESE DWELLING

Thrown into lovely contrasts of light and shade is this portal of an old-world dwelling house in a Piedmontese hamlet. While the elder woman plies her knitting, the younger stands—a comely figure silhouetted against the bright background—chatting gaily in true neighbourly fashion. And their soft-sounding dialect echoes through the ancient stone archways

From a Kodak snapshot

may be old favourites. Thus they give proof both of their enjoyment and of their sincerity in expressing their feelings. These traits shine out in all that the Italians do, or say, or think.

To see Italian acting of the kind that is most popular we must go to Sicily, unless we could light upon a Sicilian company touring. But the fierce animal passions, the gusts of frenzied rage, jealousy, or devotion, which cause the actors' frames to tremble and their voices to come hoarse and thick from their heaving chests, are better appreciated in Sicily, where they seem to be less unreal than in more northerly surroundings.

One can believe anything of the Sicilians, though, indeed, in this age they are a more peaceful folk than ever they have been in all their long, eventful history. They have shaken off the reputation of being the least law-abiding race in Europe. Under a

HAPPY WAGONERS RETURNING FROM MARKET

In Piedmont many of the peasant-proprietors are fairly well off, their frugality and general shrewdness being chief factors in their prosperity. A highly-developed family affection exists among them, and this Piedmontese mother, occupied from morning till night with farm or house work, is rarely seen unaccompanied by her children, whose pleasures and pastimes she is ever ready to share

Photo, Donald McLeish

GLINTING COPPER AND GLEAMING TIN ON SALE IN AOSTA

She makes a bright picture, knitting in the sunshine among the pots and pans that are the stock of the dark little shop behind her. Metal-ware shops are numerous in Aosta, and this little maid can supply customers with copper cauldrons for cheese-making, saucepans and strainers, pails, and cow-bells for cattle in the Alpine pastures

Photo, Donald McLeish

stable government they quickly settled down. A stranger is as safe in Sicily as at Charing Cross. I once asked an old inhabitant, up in Mola, whether there were any briganti (brigands) left.

"Signor," he replied, quite seriously, with a gesture of appeal to Heaven to bear witness that he spoke the truth, "they have all emigrated to the United States." Yet in becoming more tolerant of law the Sicilians have lost little of their picturesqueness. Among the hill tracks it is nothing unusual to see women taking the upward way with big pitchers of traditional Greek shape balanced on their heads, their bare feet picking out the smoothest paths, hands on hips, their whole bearing indescribably

SMILING YOUNG SCIONS OF A STURDY PASTORAL STOCK

Hand in hand they are returning from a neighbouring market to their cottage home in the Strona Valley, one of the few valleys of Italy where the traditions of the natives still have their roots far back in bygone centuries, and where the peasant children do not consider it below their dignity to follow in the footsteps of their fathers as tillers of the soil

Photo, Donald McLeish

CONFIDENCE AND AFFECTION IN OLD-WORLD AOSTA

This white-haired peasant-woman is a native of Aosta, a town in the province of Turin. Ancient Roman influence can be traced in many other buildings apart from this handsome portico, under which this lowly old dame spends long hours in company with her pet rabbit and in tending her geraniums and sweet herbs which fill the air with their fresh fragrance

Photo, Donald McLeish

OLD-WORLD TREASURES IN THE HEART OF MODERN VENICE

The Church of S. Mark, a noble basilica glowing with mosaics, bronzes, and enamels, has received its full share of homage from European devotees of beauty. Its impressive piazzetta contains two ancient granite columns of Eastern origin, one crowned with the winged lion of S. Mark, the tutelary saint of Venice, the other with a statue of S. Theodore, the patron of the ancient republic

Photo, Donald McLeish

graceful. They are seldom beautiful in feature. There has been such a mixture of races in Sicily that the types are curiously indeterminate. But their eyes are dark, lustrous, inscrutable. There is an Arab dignity in their flexible bodies which lends them both distinction and charm.

Goatherds, too, we meet on the hills, clad in garments of goathide, looking like descendants of Dionysus, and through the streets of Taormina the flocks are driven to be milked at the door of every purchaser. Another quaint and pretty sight I saw one sunny December afternoon, a bagpipe-player, followed by a troop of children, for all the world like the Pied Piper of Hamelin, though, happily, without his tragic intent.

With sky and water of a blue that is unsurpassable in tenderness and depth, with a mixture of styles in architecture —Greek, Roman, Saracen, Norman,

FEEDING THE FEATHERED FLOCK OF S. MARK'S CATHEDRAL

On the trachyte and marble-paved Piazza of S. Mark's flocks of pigeons strut and flutter among the pedestrians, who reward their intrepidity with generous supplies of grain and peas. Towards evening the Piazza becomes a lively scene of whirling wings, as the doves cluster round the arches of S. Mark's, preparatory to nestling for the night in the nooks and crannies of the sacred building

Photo, Underwood Press Service

Gothic, Renaissance—with flowers and green foliage all the year round, Taormina attracts many winter visitors. The sun, from the moment of his rising, superb and splendid, until the time comes for him to sink in a crimson glory behind the ridge of Etna, sheds a glowing radiance over the panorama of sea and mountain. Yet there is shade if you know where to seek it, even at midday. The grey medieval street which runs round the top of the half cup, whose sides plunge sheer down to the sea hundreds of feet below, secretes a surprising coolness. In the ruins of the Greek theatre, which closes one end of the semicircle, we can escape the heat and gaze through Corinthian pillars at Etna, snowy, sinister, superb, dominating the landscape of Sicily as Fujiyama dominates that of Japan. In the clear golden atmosphere the villages, and even the single houses, which lie thick upon the fertile flanks of the volcano, stand out white and distinct. The shore is a gentle curve,

DARK-EYED DAUGHTER OF THE CITY OF LAGOONS
Full worthy of her beautiful birthplace is this handsome maid of Venice, whose vivacity, graceful physique, and refinement of manner are in such pleasant harmony with the natural beauties of her colourful surroundings
Photo, C. Naya

edged with a strip of pebbly beach. A vast green cultivated plain slopes quietly to the dream-like sea, which sleeps in the hot sun, still and shining like mother-o'-pearl and shot with opal hues, so that on the horizon it melts away imperceptibly into shimmering cloud.

They are a simple folk, the Sicilians. They love and hate fiercely. They live by their emotions. They delight in colour. Their very carts are painted in startling hues with scenes from history and legend. Their fruit stalls are gorgeous with the gold of oranges, the pink of prickly pears, the gay green of finocchio, and the deep red of a

vegetable strange to the English eye, deep purply-red like a plum. From the dusky recesses of Eastern-looking shops gleam suggestions of red copper vessels and garish stuffs. The churches glow with mosaic, and if we are lucky enough to see a religious procession winding its way along a white street in a blaze of sunshine, with the grey green-flecked mountains above, and the sea basking in sapphire splendour below, there will be colour enough to drive a painter crazy. Until you have seen Sicily you can hardly understand what colour is. It is this vivid, passionate nature that accounts for the Sicilian temperament.

Yet another distinct Italian type is to be found in Venice and the province of Venetia. The tourist knows it not. He scarcely notices that there are any Italians in Venice beyond hotel keepers, waiters, shopkeepers, guides, and gondoliers. These are mostly not the real inhabitants at all. To realize the genuine Venetian we must enter the city of the lagoons by boat, and not by train. The railway station made me think the first time I arrived in it that, by some infernal magic, I had been transported back to Charing Cross or Cannon Street. Far better cross the lagoon in the little steamer which plies from Mestre or San Giuliano. Then, as we puff into the canal which runs past the quay of S. Job, we are plunged at once into the real as opposed to the tourists' Venice.

These are the "mean streets." We smile as we compare them with the horrible slums of London, Paris, or

MIDDAY REFRESHMENT ON THE GLEAMING WATERS OF THE LAGOON

These Venetian fishermen are resting from their labours to partake of the midday meal. A net has been hauled up and slung over the willowy masts, where it trembles in the breeze like the frail gossamer wing of a butterfly. Then, with laden baskets, they will make for Venice and dispose of their wares near the famous Rialto Bridge, the central point for retail dealers

WATER-FRONT NEAR THE LOFTY DUCAL PALACE OF VENICE

Alongside the piazzetta of S. Mark the gondolas have their chief stand, and here the livelong day may be heard the stentorian cry of the sunburnt gondolier: "Comanda la Barca, Signore?" Overlooking the busy scene towers the majestic Palace of the Doges, the seat of Venetian secular authority, which in splendour is scarcely outrivalled by any one of Italy's numerous architectural masterpieces

SIMPLE FOLKS OF BURANO PRACTISING THEIR BEAUTIFUL CRAFT

The women of the small fishing town of Burano, situated on an island about six miles from Venice, have long been noted for their beautiful lace. After a busy day's work the housewife is never so tired but that she can spend an hour or two at her pillow, and under the light play of her fingers among the bobbins lovely lacework of exquisite design is produced

Photo, Donald McLeish

Chicago. They may be dirty. They certainly smell at times. But there is no degradation here, no squalid ugliness. Then we turn into the Grand Canal, and once more yield our imaginations captive to the charm and wonder of this incomparable city.

How penetrating the charm, how inexhaustible the wonder, I learned afresh by seeing Venice under stress of war. Those who had known her only as a city of pleasure and sightseeing found it hard to conceive a Venice without crowds on the Piazza, without innumerable gondolas, without pictures, without statues, with the glorious front of S. Mark hidden by sandbags and the delicious arcade which supports the Doges' Palace bricked up. But there were compensations. One could see the people of Venice. They owned their city, as they had once owned it before the tourist horde descended. Witty and sharp-tongued, the women sitting outside their houses with their needlework or peeling their potatoes, tossed back amusing replies to chaff. The ancient gondoliers had none of the jarring scraps of English that were picked up parrotwise by the young and handsome boatmen. They told the news of the day with mumbling garrulity in the Venetian patois, so hard to understand. The few guides who were left, made fierce by hunger, pursued the chance foreigner with desperate energy.

Most changed of all was the Piazza, usually the hub and centre of all movement, all activity. During the day it was deserted. At an hour when Florian's café used always to be crowded to overflowing, I saw a weary tramp sleeping at a table in the open. A few people sat under the arcade, but no waiter thought it worth while to shoo the poor old scarecrow away. Only the pigeons were as many and as friendly as ever. Not many bought the old man's bags of maize to feed them, but they were fat and well-looking. The city saw to that. Not

HUMBLE FOLLOWER OF THE REVERED INDUSTRY OF MURANO

The island of Murano has been the seat of the Venetian glass industry since the fourteenth century. Originally introduced by Byzantine glass-workers during the Crusades, the industry developed rapidly, and its followers were held in such high esteem as to be eligible for the highest posts in the Republic, the daughter of a glass-manufacturer inheriting her father's rank

Photo, Donald McLeish

VENETIAN HEARSE-BOAT, WITH ATTENDANT GONDOLAS, BEARING THE DEAD TO THE ISLAND OF REST

Gliding over the smooth surface of the half mile of water separating Venice from the Cemetery Island, draped funeral boats such as these are often to be seen. On the quiet islet, clearly defined in the background, the bodies of the dead are buried, and like all other Venetian ceremonies a funeral displays the romantic and gorgeous character that has always been associated with the doings of the Queen of the Adriatic, which still remains one of the most religious cities in Italy

Photo. Donald McLeish

until after dark did the Piazza regain any semblance of its old self. Even then it was "like, but oh, how different!" Venice had fewer lights than London at its blackest period. Frequent were the raids of Austrian airmen. One or two cafés had music still and could almost fill their tables. Up and down under the arcade passed an attenuated throng. In the centre, seeking air, and the refreshment of the starry depths of pale, velvety blue, walked just a handful.

Yet, for all the changes, Venice had not changed. The soul of her rose above them. She floated, as she floats always, in an ether of shining memories. Her stones were as lovely and enchanting as ever. On her canals the reign of ancient peace was undisturbed by the passing threats and tumult of war. Still the morning broke glorious, gilding the towers and palaces that lay reflected in the motionless lagoon. Still at evening the sun died in a mist of crimson glory behind the roofs and domes and campaniles, which, so long as they exist, will stand among the perfect works of man.

It was in Venetia one autumn that I saw the vintage, and thereby learned to know better the pleasant folk of Italy's great fertile plain. The first signs of wine-making were at Padua. Strolling through its arcaded streets and blessing the builder, for the September sun was burning hot, we came upon a large cart with three men in it dancing vigorously. Why they danced appeared from the thin stream of pale red fluid which ran out of the bottom of the cart

FRAGRANT FLOWERS FOR SALE

Although surrounded by the numberless beauties of Venice and the dazzling blue of sky and lagoon, the Venetian still keeps a corner in his heart for flowers, and the flower-girl is usually a smiling personification of contentment

Photo, Donald McLeish

into a tub set to catch it. When, at their invitation, I climbed on the wheel to peep into the cart, I saw a squelching mass of grapes in which the six bare feet went continually up and down.

"Ecco, signor," said one of the dancers, reaching out a leg purple with the blood of the vine, "ecco, vino."

Wine it was, indeed, though at that stage it was not tempting. One shrinks from the mere thought of drinking wine made by such a process, even after it has been fermented and clarified and brought into a state fit for the palate. You know that the fermentation carries off any unpleasant substances, and purifies the liquor which is to comfort man's heart. All the same, you do not fancy it. This simple method of wine-making, however, is only practised on a small scale. The farmer makes his own wine thus, and the humble innkeeper, and perhaps the poorer class of landed

FINE OLD SEAMAN OF THE ISLE OF CAPRI
Capri is a favourite resort for the tourist and artist on account of its romantic and bold scenery, and this old fisherman never tires of displaying to the multitudinous visitors the natural beauties of his island home

an exposition of relics and High Mass. We had seen them earlier in the day praying earnestly to the saint and kissing, in the ecstasy of their devotion, the marble of his stately tomb. Was this the twentieth century, or were we back in the age when Donatello's great statue outside the church (the finest statue of a man on horseback in the world, they say) had just been set up to keep in mind the deeds of the famous warrior whose methods of warfare were commemorated by his nickname, Gattamelata, the patient cat? The hard white sunlight and the cool grey stone cannot have looked any different then, and I make no doubt that the medieval wine-treaders were just such merry rogues as these, and made equally witty remarks about the appearance of pilgrims and the oddness and curiosity of strangers.

A few days later, as we walked through the smiling landscape which frames Verona, we found the operations of the grape harvest active on every side. In the hill villages the carpenters were hammering away at huge casks. The wine-presses were being scrubbed, having their screws and joints set in order. The whole available population had turned out into the vineyards to pick. At every turn of the road we met carts piled high with grapes, carts drawn by teams of patient oxen with satin hides and large, mild, wondering eyes, and curly formidable horns that set us marvelling they should bear the yoke so tamely. Not a hillside but had its terrace of

proprietor who is far from wine-presses and such like conveniences of later civilization. All the wine that the hotel-keeper sets before the Signor Inglese is pretty certain to have been made in modern fashion. But the more ancient method is the more picturesque.

That street scene in Padua brought back in a flash the Italy of the Middle Ages. We were close to the great church of S. Antony of Padua. A stream of pilgrims was pouring out after

ITALIAN HARMONIES
Of Life & Scenery

*For these Sicilian villagers who dwell under the shadow of Mount Etna
the charm of wild romantic nature is destroyed by the pinch of poverty*

Photos on pages 3057-3061 and 3072 by A. W. Cutler

Under his rags and tatters the heart of this Sicilian grandsire glows with pride as he gazes into the open, upturned face of his son's son

Weather-stained and worn as the ancient walls, this Sicilian Darby and Joan still keep happy home in the tumbledown village of Mola

The heyday of vitality and vigour has long since waned in the storm and stress of life, and now, in close fraternity, these old folks of Sicily spend the evening of their days in a hospice for the aged poor

" Laugh, and the world laughs with you !" Though poor as church mice, these care-free children of a mountain village of sunny Sicily enjoy two of the greatest blessings of life—good health and high spirits

Time presses lightly on the Benedictine monks of Catania, Sicily, as they ponder the wisdom of the Book of Books within their garden fastness

In a pinewood setting lies the old Sacro Eremo of Camaldoli, whose monks have long held a reputation for austere discipline and sanctity

Busy hands and lively chatter are the order of laundry day on the stone ledge skirting the placid stream in the old-world town of Omegna

Photo, Donald McLeish

In the centre of Lake Orta's sheet of shimmering blue is the Isle of
San Giulio, widely famed for its ancient church founded in A.D. 379

Photo, Donald McLeish

*From the quarries in this quiet neighbourhood near Lake Maggiore
has come the building stone of many cathedrals and churches of Italy*

*This simple scene on Maggiore is transfigured by a lowly woman's
maternal love, as was another humble shelter of a Mother and Child*

Photos, Donald McLeish

Justly called the Garden of Lombardy are the fair districts bordering Lake Como, on which Nature has lavished every gift of beauty

Their lines are fallen unto them in pleasant places; the glories of Como are a goodly heritage of which her children are justly proud

Photos, Donald McLeish

From the precarious perch at the extremity of this lofty wooden device the men of the Istrian coast watch for the shoals of tunny fish that flounder unawares into the traps set by these wily fisherfolk

Churchward bound are these Istrian peasants. This sylvan paradise, filled with the song of birds and the rippling laughter of streams, is surely a nobler temple wherein one may worship than any made with hands

*In the narrow alleys of the old town of San Remo mouldering houses,
gaunt and sombre, stretch up to the tortuous ribbon of blue sky*

Photo, Horace W. Nicholls

The Nativity of the Virgin is celebrated in Bellagio, a lovely resort on Lake Como, with solemn fervour and many time-honoured rites

Photo, Donald McLeish

Simple fare, suited to the simple life enjoined by monastic rule, is set before these monks of the highland village of Savoca, Sicily, who are here seen in the severe surroundings of their humble refectory

vines, not a cottage without its pergola, not a garden that lacked its burden of grape-bearing. Not a foot of cultivable space from which the bounty of nature had not brought forth gifts to add to this plenteous harvesting. The very railway stations were festooned with gracious trails; amid the leafage could be spied the ripe bunches which were to furnish afresh the station-master's modest cellar.

And with all this profusion there was a kindly carelessness on man's part which to a northern eye had a special charm. The vines were trellised even along the roadway. The purple clusters with their delicate bloom, the breath of autumn upon them, hung within reach of any hand that might think it worth while to pick them. It was their very profusion that kept them safe. After all, if a few bunches were picked, what matter? "It is but a spoonful out of the sea."

That was, at any rate, the view of a peasant proprietor who was working in the midst of his grape-gatherers, a band of laughing peasant girls, and who invited us, with the grace of an archduke, to enter and help ourselves. We were more interested in the pickers than in the fruit, but we took a handful, and delicious they were, warm from the sun and ripened in the soft air to a fragrant delicacy of flavour. Still, our aim was not the satisfaction of our palate, but the bettering of our acquaintance with the people. Would it incommode the signorine if we took their photographs? So far from incommoding, this would,

it appeared, delight the signorine beyond everything. Then might we presume so far as to ask the signor to invite the signorine to stand with their baskets, so; and next, scissors in hand under the large vine, giusto; and yet again, upon

SUGARED DRINKS FOR THE THIRSTY OF PALERMO
A cool draught on a sultry day never comes amiss, and honey-water, flavoured with lemon and slightly sweetened with sugar, is to the thirsty Sicilian in the sun-baked streets of Palermo not unlike what nectar was to the gods of old Olympus
Photo, Georg Haeckel

the ladder set against the tree which supports the trellis, exact. E fatto. Grazie tanto. (All over. Thank you very much). To which we receive in reply a chorus of " Niente, niente." (It is nothing at all).

All through Venetia, all through Italy, indeed, but I think especially in Venetia, this same gentle courtesy of manner smooths down the asperities of life. Mr. Howells, I seem to remember,

MODENA'S MEDIEVAL MASTERPIECE OVERLOOKS ITS MODERN MARKET

A beautiful touch of animation and colour is given to the grey old town of Modena by the fruit and vegetable market, which floods the Piazza Grande with its rich luxuriance. In the background, above the throng of busy buyers and sellers, the cathedral, Modena's pride, towers solemn and majestic, its austere Romanesque aspect contrasting pleasantly with the bustle and business of modern Modena

Photo, Donald McLeish

attributes the pleasing manners of the Italian to the ages upon ages of civilization that lie behind him. The Italian, says this writer in effect, is attractive because he has been polished by many centuries of polite intercourse. The Anglo-Saxon is a barbarian still; the savage traits in his nature are not yet eradicated. Thus Mr. Howells; but for my part I fancy the climate has a good deal to do with it. Hardships enough the peasants of Venetia endure, yet they are never brooding, harsh, or misanthropic.

How vastly better to bear, if you can, your troubles with a smile, than to groan and grumble as we should under like burdens of extortion and need. Perhaps, though, under the Italian sky, even northerners might learn to smile more readily. How it poured down upon those vineyards in October! The heat-haze which hid the far-off hills in a silvery mist would have done credit to July. The "baked cicala" (grass-hopper) filled the air with a deafening chirrup, the timid lizards rushed up walls at the sound of our footsteps. Farther south the sun had burned all colour out of the prospect—one could see nothing but the neutral tints of light-brown earth and grey-green olive leaf.

In Venetia the grass was green, the acacia still wore its vivid livery of spring. As we sat by the roadside, under the grudging shade of stunted olive trees, a handsome, brown-eyed, straight-featured peasant came along, and feeling the heat, stooped down and dashed water from a brook over his brown hands and face, and so, with a smile and a "buon giorno" went on his way refreshed.

From the pickers' hands to the baskets carried yoke-wise on the shoulder or else on the back, from the baskets to the huge tubs on the ox-wagons, from the tubs to the press or the treading-cart—these are the stages in the transformation of grapes into wine. White wine you get if you separate skins and stalks from fruit, red wine is the result of everything going into the press together.

The Italians are careless wine-makers. They are not so particular as the French about what the press crushes, therefore their wine is rougher, lacking the quality of silkiness that wine merchants extol. But Italian wine is real wine, and nearly always pure wine. It is mostly sold in casks, not in bottles. Unless you order an Asti spumante

PADUAN MARKET PLACE IN A JUDICIAL SETTING

An interesting medieval structure of Padua, a city famed throughout the Middle Ages as a centre of Italian literature and art, is the Palazzo della Ragione (called the Salone, after the great hall on its upper floor), begun in 1172 as a court of justice, and the stone pillory still exists on which debtors were exposed to the derision of the populace in the market place

or some other of the " fizzy " brands, you get your wine at hotel and restaurant straight from the cask. An elaborate show of cork-drawing, sometimes even a neatly arranged piece of tinfoil round the neck of the bottle, may deceive the inexperienced traveller, but he may rest assured that he is drinking " wine from the wood," as English public-houses used to call it.

Italians of all classes, knowing the difference between well-cooked and badly-cooked food, insist upon being properly nourished. Therefore, neither their palate nor their stomach craves for fiery stimulation. They are a temperate, eupeptic race.

While I was with the Italian Army in the field during the Great War, I had plenty of opportunities to see how much

HUCKSTERS BARTER WHERE MONTAGUE AND CAPULET BRAWLED

Once the forum of Verona, the Piazza delle Erbe is one of the most picturesque squares in Italy. Umbrella-protected stalls of fruit and vegetables now surround the canopied tribune where the Signori and the Podestà were elected in the fifteenth century. At the far end is the fine baroque Palazzo Trezza, with a column surmounted by the Lion of S. Mark before it

Photo, Donald McLeish

One effect of the honest character of Italian wine is that you very seldom see drunken men. A drunken Italian woman I have never seen. I do not know anyone who has. The shame and horror of it would be too acutely felt. The cafés are well filled. On Sunday evenings they are crowded. But there is in them no drinking in the harmful sense. Spirits do not make the same appeal to the Italians as they do to people in cold, damp climates. And

hard work the soldiers could do upon rations which an Englishman would have called " scarcely enough to feed a bird on." The officers fared wonderfully well. I have had dinners high up in the mountains, where all supplies had to be got up by " teleferica," which would have done credit to a restaurant in Rome or even Paris. Often I felt ashamed to sit down to a well-served table and eat luxuriously while the men were supping their pannikins of soup

PRACTISING THE INTRICATE STEPS OF THE TARANTELLA

Dancing is the delight of all Italians, and accompanies or terminates most of their entertainments in town or country. The tarantella, or Neapolitan dance, enjoys universal favour among the Italian peasantry. In triple time, it begins slowly and gradually increases in speed until the dancers, accompanied by tambourine or castanets, whirl rapidly in a veritable maze of lightning steps

and macaroni or rice, standing about outside the cook-house from which it was served out.

These telefericas in the mountain regions of the Italian front impressed all who used them as evidence of that mechanical ingenuity which in the Italy of to-day takes the place of that medieval passion for beauty of which Italian art was the child. The fighting in the Dolomites and the Julian Alps could not have been carried on without them. One summer morning I found myself at the top of one of the highest peaks in the Dolomite group. To reach the summit, ten thousand feet up, from Cortina, on foot, took even hardened climbers the best part of a day. Yet I arrived within less than two hours after leaving the Alpini officers' mess in the town.

I had climbed into a narrow box, like a coffin, with just enough room in it for two people, sitting snug, and this box, slung on a wire rope, had been tugged upward, sometimes at an angle approaching the perpendicular, swinging in mid-air hundreds of feet above rocks, loose stones, and snow. I caught myself wondering the first time I travelled by

WITHIN THE WALLS OF AN ITALIAN RELIGIOUS HOUSE

These nuns are inmates of a convent near Perugia, the picturesque old town built on a group of hills overlooking the valley of the Tiber. Besides religious duties, social work forms an important part of the daily routine, and these women, some of whom are from the upper classes, devote much time to teaching and nursing, and offer admirable examples of useful and charitable lives

Photo, C. Chichester

GOOD SAMARITANS OF THE PERILOUS ALPINE PASSES

By countless selfless deeds they have gained for themselves a name that arouses instant admiration
and enthusiasm in the hearts of all civilized peoples. The good monks of the hospice of S. Bernard!
Who has not heard of them and their daring exploits when, caring naught for personal safety, they
brave the elements to bring succour to travellers lost in the treacherous Alpine snows?

Photo, Donald McLeish

teleferica whether, if the rope broke, it would be better to fall on rock and be killed outright, or on snow, with the offchance of being alive when picked out.

The tugging upward of the box was done by powerful motors housed in sheds. There were occasional accidents, but wonderfully few considering the constant use of the wire-ropes and the necessity of sending up the carriers in all kinds of weather. To one part of the line I ascended by means of five telefericas, one after the other. Then we found dog-sleighs waiting for us; we had come to the region of perpetual snow.

In the sleighs we were pulled for some miles by the willing dogs. Then we had to walk for nearly an hour. Everything

QUAYSIDE OF TRIESTE, THE FORMER GREAT EMPORIUM FOR AUSTRIAN TRADE IN THE ADRIATIC

Trieste, the former chief seaport of Austria, stands on the Adriatic at the head of the Gulf of Trieste, and was assigned to Italy by the Treaty of St. Germain. The old town was a Roman colony under Vespasian, known as Tergeste, and still contains many precious Roman antiquities, among which a ruined amphitheatre and aqueduct attest its importance under the Caesars. The long, narrow streets wind up the steep slopes of the Castle Hill, and overlook the broad thoroughfares of fine houses of the modern town bordering on the sea

GLIMPSE OF THE GRAND CANAL OF TRIESTE, WITH THE CHURCH OF S. ANTONIO IN THE BACKGROUND

As an Austrian seaport the importance of Trieste was augmented by every possible political device. With its several moles and breakwaters, most of which have been constructed in recent years, the harbour is the centre of an immense maritime trade. The mouth of the Grand Canal is a very busy waterway, invariably filled with shipping. At the east end of the canal rises the Church of S. Antonio Nuovo, a handsome edifice in the Greek style, erected towards the middle of the nineteenth century, while to the right there is a glimpse of the Serbian church of S. Spiridione.

LATEST INHERITORS OF ISTRIA'S HISTORIC SEAPORT

Romans and Istrians, Venetians and Genoese, Austrians and Italians have all in turn been masters of Pola, with its fine harbour at the head of the Bay of Pola. This street, the Via Sergia, commemorates in its name the Sergii whose fine triumphal arch in the Corinthian style, erected soon after the battle of Actium in 31 B.C., is the oldest Roman relic in the town

FRIENDLY GREETINGS ON AN ISTRIAN COUNTRY ROAD NEAR POLA

The peninsula of Istria formerly belonged to the Austrian Küstenland, or Coastland, and is now under Italian suzerainty. Most of the inhabitants are Yugo-Slavs, mainly Croats and Slovenes, but large numbers of Italians are to be found in the cities and along the coast. The peasants, a thrifty, simple folk, are engaged chiefly in agriculture, and cultivate their small holdings with considerable success

WAYSIDE SCENE IN A ROCK-BOUND REGION OF ISTRIA

The bleak and barren aspect of this district, in the vicinity of Pola, is relieved by the old Roman well and water-trough, which must come as a refreshing sight to way-worn pedestrians and their four-footed companions. Relics of Roman ingenuity are numerous in and near Pola, which came under Roman power about 178 B.C, and still contains a remarkably fine amphitheatre and temple

ISTRIAN LAND LABOURER HOMEWARD BOUND FROM THE FIELDS

He is a native of Dignano, a town in Istria, the Italian peninsula at the head of the Adriatic Sea. Away in the hills is his small plot of land, a prized possession. Here, in the spring when the rain falls, and in the autumn when the dry sirocco blows, he works throughout the day, and as evening approaches leisurely wends his way towards his humble abode

HEALTHY SPECIMENS OF WOMANHOOD FROM ISTRIAN SOIL

The robust constitutions of these girls of a district of South Istria are due to the salt winds and the mountain air of their invigorating surroundings. Their Sunday best, consisting of a full silk skirt, tight bodice, and a light fringed shawl neatly draped over the shoulders, is the national costume of their people, and sets off their fine stature to a nicety

that the troops in this front line needed had to be brought up in this way. Not only their food and their ammunition, but every piece of firewood even. Up in the region of perpetual snow there was nothing.

In these high places of the earth the troops employed were nearly all Alpini, men from the Italian Alpine villages, accustomed to high altitudes from birth.

No other troops could have supported so easily, and even gaily, the conditions of life on rocky peaks and snowy ridges, far above the rest of mankind. I found the thin atmosphere trying even at midsummer. I suffered for a day or two from a form of mountain sickness. I had to wear snow-goggles to protect my eyes. My face became, in the beginning scarlet, and later on skinless, from the combined effect of sun and snow. I discovered for the first time, while I scrambled up an almost perpendicular rock-face, and clung with the desperate energy of a drowning man to a rope which dangled from the top, what it meant to be forty-seven years of age.

None of these things troubled the Alpini, though their ages ran up to fifty. The older men, I was told frequently, were among the best.

These Alpine soldiers were more like chamois than human beings. They leapt about in places where a slip meant

BRAVING THE BOISTEROUS BREEZE IN ADRIATIC WATERS

A fisherman from the island of Lussin, formerly an Austrian possession, but ceded to Italy, together with Istria, by the Treaty of St. Germain. Rough and uncouth as are many of its natives, they display unusual capacities as seafaring men, their muscles of whipcord and nerves of steel standing them in good stead as they ride the turbulent waters of the Adriatic

GIANT BLOCKS OF MARBLE ON THE WAY TO THE WORLD'S WORKSHOPS

Carrara has long been noted for its neighbouring marble quarries which produce most of the finer sorts of marble used by sculptors. Some 6,000 men are employed in these quarries, and their work consists chiefly in blasting the rocks, in hewing the great marble blocks into squares, and in dragging them by means of wooden rollers to the carts which are drawn by teams of oxen to the harbour

TRANSPORTING THE FAMOUS MARBLE FROM QUARRY TO QUAY

The long procession of carts with their burdens of glistening marble, drawn by oxen, four to ten pairs to each cart, presents a most remarkable sight as they wind down the steep and rugged mountain slopes to the small harbour near Carrara, whence they are shipped to all parts of the world. The drivers often sit on the yokes facing the rear, their sing-song cries urging the beasts onwards

destruction with, not merely a disregard, but a positive unconsciousness, of danger. They stood on pointed crags with eternity around and below them as if they were on a Canadian prairie or a Russian steppe. They ran down slopes, where their visitor sought most carefully each separate foothold, with an apparent longing to be dashed to pieces.

of rock and stones. Several times I was told to be quick across a sandy slope on the steep side of a mountain so as not to be caught by a rush from above. The Alpini seemed to me to possess a special sense which told them when peril was to be feared. Their ears may be sensitive to foreboding sounds which are not noticed by the people of the

FISHING-SMACK FROM POLA PORT: THE SKIPPER AND HIS CREW

On the peninsula of Istria, gained by Italy from Austria during the Great War, stands Pola harbour, once the chief base of the Austrian navy. Now these waters of the Northern Adriatic are scoured by fishermen instead of fleets, and this hoary old smacksman, though, like his craft, somewhat worn by wind and water, is still as sturdy as the staunch planks on which he sits

They took no more notice of the huge boards which said: " Beware of Avalanches ! " than a city-dweller takes of admonitions to be careful in crossing the road. Yet I saw spots where whole columns of men and parties of road-makers had been swept into annihilation, where wooden barracks had been torn off mountain-sides and hurled into space with all their occupants.

Even when there was respite from avalanches there was danger from falls

plain. They always knew when to "step lively," as a corporal who had lived in New York phrased it to me one day.

Of all the soldiers whose acquaintance I made during the war the Italians alone made any approach to gaiety of spirit. The British were cheerful in a cynical, Mark Tapley-ish kind of way. The French set their teeth and swore—how they swore ! The Russians were like children, now finding some enjoyment, now bewildered, now despairing, and

WHEN THE EVENING SHADOWS LENGTHEN ON THE TRANQUIL WATERS OF LAKE COMO

In Lombardy, near the Swiss border, lies one of the most beautiful of the Italian lakes, Lake Como. Surrounded by lofty hills, whose slopes are covered with flowering gardens and luxuriant groves, its shores studded with picturesque villages and villas, the lake resembles a shining jewel in a resplendent setting. All the bright day long the fisherfolk are busy at their labours, but when the sunlight fades they make for home, and set their nets for the night to the restful melody of evensong

Photo, Donald McLeish

BRIGHTLY GLEAMING BANNERS TROOPED TO RECEIVE THE BISHOP'S BLESSING AT AVRONA

Many travellers will remember the colossal bronze statue of S. Carlo Borromeo that stands on a height near Avrona at the southern end of Lake Maggiore. The burial-place of the Borromean family is in the Church of S. Maria at Avrona, to the porch of which all eyes are turned in this photograph. The occasion is a visit from the Bishop of Novara to bless the banners of the religious communities in the neighbouring villages, and the square of the little town is packed with a reverent crowd

Photo, Donald McLeish

AMONG THE GOATHERDS OF SOUTHERN ITALY

In these shaggy costumes they brave all weathers and fear none; nevertheless, the umbrella forms a part of their field equipment, for the open-air life of the goatherd is not all sunshine. Despite their rough-and-ready exterior, they are remarkably humane and devoted to their wards, and should there be a sickly member of the flock, they tend and care for it with exemplary skill

Photo, A. W. Cutler

the next hour filled with confidence. The Americans frankly hated the whole business of soldiering, but had made their minds up to see it through.

Only the Italians had the happy knack of forgetting their trouble and " living for the moment." They were at their best when they attacked. Appeals in fervid language to their patriotism scarcely ever failed. What they found most trying was to " stick it " in trenches, having hell rained upon them from the Austrian heavy guns. When they thought about the war they were anything but gay.

The Italian temperament is not reflective. Italians are not given to brooding. Their emotions flash out and are burned away by their own impetuosity. They keep their spiritual flues clean, do not let them get clogged. They are, therefore, able to be happy, good-tempered, gay.

Neither English nor French ever understood how hard were some of the tasks set to their Italian comrades in the Great War. Not only among the mountains. That hideous stony desolation, the Carso, was even worse ground to fight over. From a valley you went up and up through woods on to a plateau, which stretched as far as you could see every way. There was hardly any soil, only just enough to support a thin, harsh vegetation. The plateau is of rock, with loose stones covering it over the greater part of its area.

No trenches could be dug on the Carso. They had to be drilled and blasted out of the solid rock. How were the graves made in the pathetic little cemeteries one came across? They were hewn in the rock like the tomb which belonged to Joseph of Arimathea. And, of course, there was no water in this desert. Every drop the troops needed (and they needed a great deal under the burning sun) had to be carried up on to the plateau through pipes. More than once pursuit of the enemy had to stop for the reason that the pursuers were too parched to follow up their victory.

These and other difficulties the Italians overcame with obstinate patience. In many a fight their soldiers did well. Yet it may be doubted whether the war left behind good effects upon the Italian people. They were bitterly disillusioned when they found they were in for a long struggle. Their politicians had promised them that they would quickly recover from their old enemy Austria the territories they claimed on account of their Italian populations. The people suffered in many ways. Their feeling at the finish was one of resentment against those who had made them suffer.

This they may forget now they have got back to their work. Their natural carelessness and gaiety may reassert themselves. Whether these qualities could survive such a growth of industrialism as is gleefully foretold by those

BUSY BY-STREET IN A SMALL ADRIATIC FISHING-PORT

This is one of the several pleasant old thoroughfares in Grado, a quaintly-built fishing town at the head of the Adriatic. Genial, laughter-loving people are the inhabitants; busy as bees when the mood takes them; their intense fondness for social life drawing most of them to open-air occupations, and even the women manage to perform some of the household duties in the streets

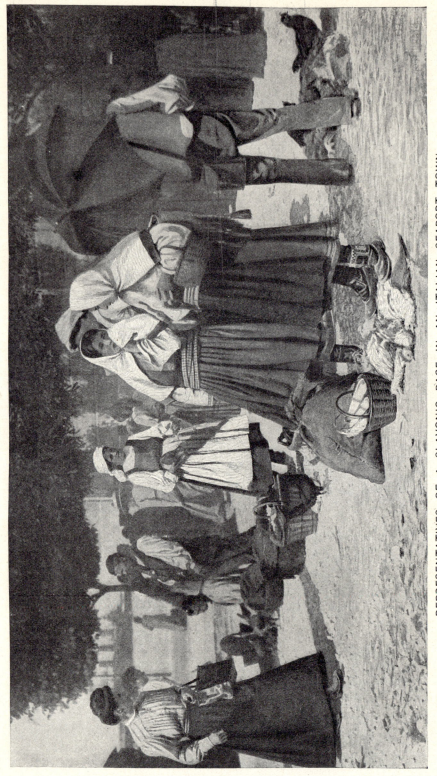

REPRESENTATIVES OF A SLAVONIC RACE IN AN ITALIAN SEAPORT TOWN

Even under Austrian rule, Zara, the Dalmatian seaport, was a town of thoroughly Italian character. Picturesquely situated on the Zara Canal, it is a lively place, teeming with busy movement. The country people, whose coloured costumes add to the interest of the town, are known as Morlaks, and belong to the Slavonic element of Dalmatia. These handsome women dominate among the peasant traders in the harbour market, to which they bring their poultry and supplies of grain.

FISHER FOLK OF NAPLES HAULING IN THEIR NET ON THE BEACH AT POSILIPO

Jutting out into the blue Mediterranean, the cape and village of Posilipo lie just west of Naples city, and form a suburb. The place is redolent of classic times, and among the vineyards stands the tomb of Virgil, while the ruined palace whose pierced and riddled shell is all that time has left, was once the residence of Donn' Anna Caraffa, a seventeenth-century duchess. Now, unawed by ducal authority, these fisher folk are bringing to shore to-morrow's breakfast for the people of the neighbouring town

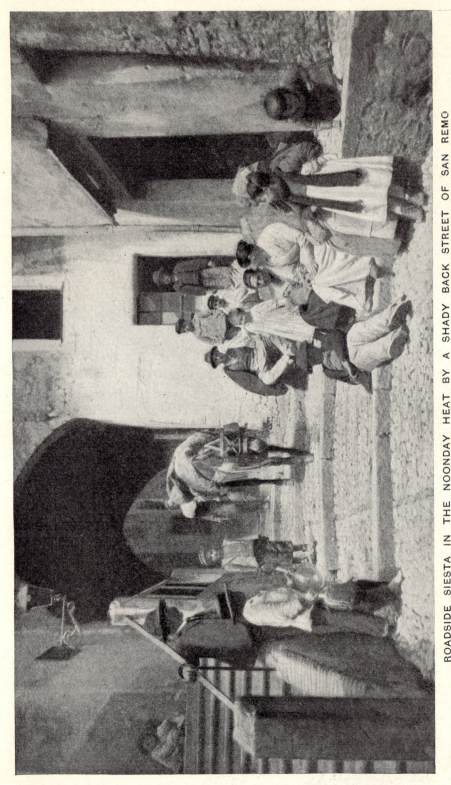

ROADSIDE SIESTA IN THE NOONDAY HEAT BY A SHADY BACK STREET OF SAN REMO

While thousands of visitors throng in languid flocks the gay promenades and bright villas of the new town of San Remo, the old city, wrapping with its twisted, sloping streets a steep hill, is yet one of the most attractive localities of the beautiful Italian Riviera. The wanderer who cares to lose himself awhile in these ways, may, any moment, light upon such a scene as this, with the smiling signore grouped about their doorways and perhaps just such a laden mule tapping the cobbles

ISTRIAN PIETY AND PROPRIETY PASSING THE TIME OF DAY AFTER THE MORNING SERVICE

A sober, darkly-clad throng has gathered outside the church at Dignano on this Sabbath morn. The women's costumes, especially, are conspicuous for their strange uniformity and lack of bright colouring. The men's attire is less sombre, and a couple of "blue-jackets" break the monotony of the scene. Istria is a rugged, sea-bound country, very hilly in the interior, which is inhabited chiefly by Yugo-Slav shepherds; most of the Istrian population dwell in the low coastlands

3095

PATIENCE SHELTERED IN BORDIGHERA'S ROMAN GATEWAY

Like the old town of San Remo, the old town or upper quarter of neighbouring Bordighera comprises
a maze of narrow streets built on steps up the hill slope, the tall houses being mutually supported
by overhead arches. Wheeled traffic is impracticable in these stepped causeways, and donkeys
patter up and down the cobbles bearing whatever loads the people cannot carry on their heads

Photo, Horace W. Nicholls

GOSSIP IN THE VIA SAN GIUSEPPE, IN OLD SAN REMO

Very different from the spacious promenades of the new town of San Remo are the labyrinthine alleys of the old town. Here the crowded houses rise, tall and rugged, sheer from the cobbled streets that form narrow stairways up the hill, linked overhead by arches for mutual support in time of earthquake. But though the houses lack external grace, they shelter cheery, amiable people

Photo, Horace W. Nicholls

whose shallow intelligence takes into account only material prosperity, I take leave to doubt. The industrialised Italian loses much of his national charm. His manners are still pleasanter than those of industrials in other countries. He takes a pride in keeping clean and in dressing well when he has done his work. But he is easily duped. He is credulous, easily influenced, fit for treasons, stratagems, and spoils, as was shown both by the short Socialist attempt at domination and by the dictatorship of the Fascisti which followed it.

Divorce the Italian from the soil and his character changes—not for the better, but for the worse.

BEAUTEOUS RUINS OF THE FORUM ROMANUM, THE CENTRE OF THE LIFE OF ANCIENT ROME

Rome, the city built on seven hills, was for many centuries the mistress of the world and was known as the Eternal City, so mighty and magnificent was this centre of the Roman Empire. But to-day little remains of that glorious epoch, the Forum being its most notable relic, which, as our photograph shows, is a mere mass of ruined temples and monuments, the great architectural beauty of which is eloquent of the splendour of the departed Empire

Photo, Donald McLeish

Italy

II. The Rise & Progress of Italian Nationhood

By Edward Hutton

Author of "Italy and the Italians," etc.

THERE could scarcely be found a better example of the modern energy and vitality of what we call nationality than the country whose history we are about to consider. The nineteenth century gives us two major examples of this energy, overwhelming in their force—the achievement of nationhood by the Germans and by the Italians. Of these the latter is not only the more complete and significant, but, rightly considered, is perhaps the most impressive and the most lasting political achievement of that great creative time.

That Italy should have been so late in achieving unity and nationhood might at first sight seem difficult to account for ; but on closer examination we shall easily discern the reasons for it, not only in her political history and in her geographical position, but especially in her spiritual relations to the rest of Europe.

These spiritual relations exist not only in a strictly religious sense, in which she appears as the seat of the Papacy and the source of the Catholic Faith, but also in the sense that she was the mother and the generous parent of all civilization and humanism : so that it was from her we learnt not only to plough, but to write, to paint, and to think ; and from her we learnt the story of the past, and even of our own past.

The great international position thus given her, obscured for many centuries, as it were, her own identity ; though that she was always passively aware of this is borne witness to by the fact that it would be impossible to find an Italian of to-day who would not claim that the first and complete impulse towards a realization of Italian nationality was expressed by Dante Alighieri at the beginning of the fourteenth century.

Italy Bound up with Rome

The history of Italy properly begins with the foundation of Rome (753 B.C.), and just as the history of Italy begins with that of Rome, so it has no existence apart from Rome. By 265 B.C. the whole peninsula south of the Apennines was in reality subject to Rome, though the genius of Roman diplomacy had, in nearly every case, known how to mask that subjection by infinitely various terms of agreement. The great test of this achievement came with the second Punic War (218-201 B.C.), in which the Semitic and essentially commercial power of Carthage, based on the command of the sea, was overthrown, and Rome was saved, and with her Italy and Europe and all that we value in life to-day.

This decision was achieved largely by the loyalty of the eighteen Italian colonies, and finally by the defeat of the Carthaginian armies at the Metaurus 207 B.C. The Roman energy was immediately directed to the subjection of that great continental province to the north of the Apennines, without the assistance of which Hannibal and his Carthaginian armies would have been helpless.

Collapse of the Imperial Authority

Cisalpine Gaul was subdued by 191 B.C., and during the ten following years it was brought into the Roman road system and the formal Roman administration ; but until the very end of the Republic it remained a separate province ; from 43 B.C. it became a part of Italy, which thus attained its natural confines.

The destruction of the Carthaginian power had other results besides the Roman conquest of Cisalpine Gaul. The whole of the Mediterranean was brought into the Roman system ; Corinth was occupied in the same decade as that which saw the destruction of Carthage ; Greece, Syria, Egypt were to follow ; the Mediterranean provinces of Spain, the corresponding belt of Southern Gaul, the fruitful littoral of Northern Africa fell into the hands of Rome.

It was a world in itself, but without con nes. It was to find these confines that Rome was compelled to conquer whole of Spain, and, most important of all for the future, Gaul and Britain, and to push into the Germanies, until the final frontier of that world was found—the lines of the Rhine and the Danube.

Thus was Italy established as the head and heart of Europe, with Rome as the soul thereof. In the moment of her maturity, as has been well said, she accepted the Catholic Faith as her religion.

Of the real causes of the decline of the Roman administration we are for the most part ignorant. The spectacle we see is that of a great and wealthy military State, gradually becoming inefficient and threatened with bankruptcy. In all this failure and consequent anarchy, Italy, though distracted by mutiny, by invasions, by conquest and re-conquest, remained the still beating heart of that universal thing, which was in paralysis; while Rome more and more appeared as its soul, as, little by little, the heir of that universal government appeared in the Catholic Church.

After a distracted century, which began with the invasion of the mutineer Alaric (A.D. 410) and the threat of the mere barbarian Attila, the imperial authority collapsed (476) in Italy, where the barbarian Odoacer, another mutinous soldier of the Roman service, established himself until overthrown by Theodoric, King of the Ostrogoths, at the re-conquest of Constantinople.

Light Appears Amid the Darkness

This great man and his great minister Cassiodorus, though they used Roman forms and Roman laws, for there were no other, were unable to establish a permanent State. Constantinople, under Justinian, finally cleared out the Ostrogoths in the bitter re-conquest of Italy by the armies of Belisarius and Narses (553), and Italy again entered the Imperial administration, being governed by an Exarch at Ravenna.

The country, however, was helpless before the new invaders that appeared in 568, when the Lombards overran Northern Italy, and in the following two hundred years practically extinguished the Imperial authority in the peninsula. Indeed, it may be said that only Rome remained, and was herself on the eve of falling into their hands when the new Latin authority at last declared itself, all this darkness and confusion was suddenly penetrated by a great light, and the Pope, Stephen II., crossed the Alps and persuaded Pepin to march upon Italy. Pepin was King of the Franks, and the Franks alone of all the barbarian peoples were Catholics. They came and they conquered; they took from the Lombards a great part of the Exarchate and gave it to the Roman Church.

Charlemagne Crowned by the Pope

Later, in 774, Pepin's son, Charlemagne, entered Italy again at the call of the Pope, Adrian I., broke the Lombard kingdom, and gave practically the whole of the Exarchate, the seat of the Imperial authority, to the Church. The new Latin authority in whose hands the future of Europe was to lie for so many hundred years had appeared. It was the Pope. And Italy and Rome were once more to be the seat of a universal authority in Europe. On Christmas Day, 800, the Pope re-established the Empire in the West by crowning Charlemagne as emperor.

This tremendous act, the crowning of Charlemagne by the Pope, followed though it was by enormous disaster, in which Europe was imperilled as never before or since, was the beginning of the resurrection of Latin power in Europe, of Latin thought and order and civilization. Upon it, rightly understood, stands the whole of the medieval and, therefore, of the modern world. The peculiar and special development of Italy, not on national but on universal lines, really depends upon it.

It involved enormous consequences, among others these : that the best energies of Italy, as of the Germanies, for the Imperial authority became German with the Ottos, were intent not upon a particular but upon a universal thing, and the dream of a universal authority in Europe faced, with an ever-decreasing chance of success, the passion of nationalism, which was to be its relentless foe.

Italy, when the Middle Age began to emerge from the Dark Age in the tenth and eleventh centuries, was the battlefield and the bone of contention of the two universal powers—the Papacy and the Empire. The donations of Pepin, of Charlemagne, and later of the Countess Matilda, had established the Papacy as a great Temporal Power in Italy, which endured until 1870 ; but its very existence as such was necessarily contested by the Empire.

Conflict of Papacy and Empire

To defeat the German Emperors the Popes successively used in Italy the Normans, the French, and the Spaniards, as they had called in Pepin and Charlemagne against the Lombards. Thus, in the earlier medieval Italy, with the exception of Venice, which was founded by the refugees from the mainland in the time of the barbarian invasions, and was by its geography inaccessible, and therefore independent, every city and every province of Italy was a fief of the Church or of the Empire, and later, more especially in the north and centre, became passionately Guelph — i.e., anti-imperial, or Ghibelline—i.e., pro-imperial.

The Papacy, which in Italy was certainly very much more national than the German Imperial Power could ever be, succeeded in finally ruining that power in Italy with the defeat and fall of the Hohenstaufen by means of the Angevin she had called into Italy. But long before then the burgher classes and the merchants had created the cities and the communes by their energy, and were busy, first in curbing and then in expelling the nobles, almost exclusively of Teutonic descent, who had been introduced into Italy as the representatives or the dependents of the Imperial power.

The rise, the splendour, and the decadence and disappearance of these city communes, especially in Lombardy and Tuscany, fills the Middle Age in Italy ; and though not a single one of them remained free beyond the middle of the fifteenth century, the world owes them more than it is ever likely to acknowledge on account of their enormous service to all that we mean by civilization, culture, and political freedom.

It is impossible here to put the reader in possession of the variety, the political confusion, and the energy of Italy, when, in these little cities, nothing less was accomplished than the resurrection of Roman law (Irnerius), and the formulation of canon law (Gratianus), the creation of modern art (Giotto, Donatello), of a vernacular literature which has influenced the entire world (Dante, Petrarch, Boccaccio), the revival of learning (the Humanists of the fifteenth century), the birth of natural science (the medical school of Salerno), the erection of the first European universities (Bologna and Padua), the inspiration and the energy of the mendicant orders (S. Francis, S. Thomas Aquinas, S. Catherine of Siena, S. Bernardine).

Meantime the Papacy, which with Gregory VII. had begun its great rôle of

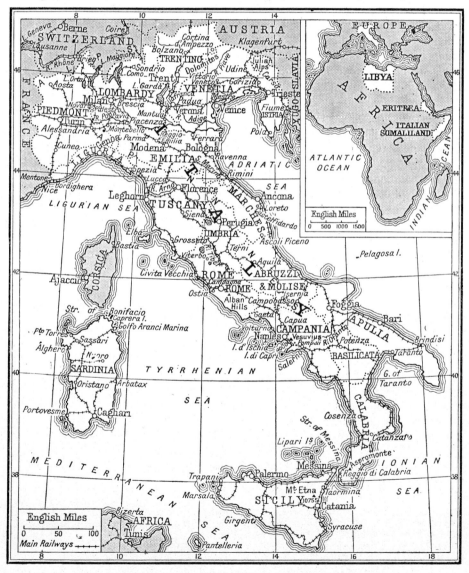

THE KINGDOM OF ITALY AND ITS DEPENDENCIES

arbiter of the world, and with Innocent III. (d. 1216) seemed to have reached its goal, became the creature of France with the death of Boniface VIII., and a few years later the Babylonian captivity in Avignon, which endured through the great part of the fourteenth century. But with the decadence of the Imperial power and the absence of the Papacy, Italy generally became subject to a host of despots, who without legitimacy of any sort seized power wherever they could.

Tyranny of the Great Families

Thus appeared the Sforza, first in Ancona and later in Milan, the Scaligers in Verona, the Baglioni in Perugia, the Malatesta in Rimini, and, indeed, though differently, the Medici in Florence, together with a host of others—individuals of great personal force, condottieri as in the case of Sforza and Malatesta, who seized what they could for their own personal benefit, and sometimes became, as in the case of the Medici especially (who rose from the merchant class to the rule of Florence, in which they preserved the outward aspect of a democracy), great patrons of the new learning and of art. One family of despots—the house of Este at Ferrara and Modena—stands apart by reason of ancient blood and long-established sovereignty.

In so far as the States of the Church (Umbria and the Marches) were concerned, the minor usurpers were cleared out by a great Spanish captain in the service of the absent Pope, Cardinal Gil d'Albornoz, who largely restored the Papal authority, which was not fully reinstated, however, till the end of the great schism and the election of Martin V. as Pope.

Emergence of the Italian States

The fifteenth century saw this work thoroughly achieved, and the emergence of five great States in Italy—namely, the Papacy, Naples, Milan, Florence, and Venice. Of these five States Venice was the most powerful. But this was not to endure. In 1494 Charles VIII. invaded Italy at the call of Milan, conquered Naples in the following year, but lost it in 1496. Three years later, Louis XII. joined Venice and conquered Milan ; but in less than ten years we see the League of Cambray formed against Venice, which temporarily loses its possessions on the mainland, and Spain, or rather the Emperor Charles V. and the King of France (Francis I.) from 1515 dispute the real mastery of the peninsula, till in 1525 Francis is taken prisoner at Pavia. The Treaty of Cateau-Cambresis (1559) established the Spanish predominance.

Thus by the end of the sixteenth century there remain but two great Powers in Italy, the Papacy and Spain, with Venice a bad third, and rapidly declining, but with the Duchy of Savoy, under Charles Emmanuel I., becoming an essential factor in Italian politics. All Tuscany had been formed in 1569 into a Grand Duchy under Cosimo de'Medici, the title of Grand Duke being granted him by Pius V.

The Protestant Reformation had largely no effect or influence at all within the peninsula, except in so far as it caused a reaction in the Catholic religion and policy. The genius of the people was against it.

It is usual to consider the seventeenth and eighteenth centuries in Italy as a period of repose, but the achievements of Galileo, Campanella, Tassoni, Vico, Muratori, Tiraboschi, Gravina, Paroni, and Alfieri, to name no others, are sufficient to expose the superficiality of this judgement. Politically Italy was still universalist, indifferent to the nationalism that was springing up more and more fiercely all round her. By the Treaty of Utrecht, 1713, Austria succeeded Spain in Milan and Mantua, and in 1737 obtained the Grand Duchy of Tuscany, and, later, the Spanish House of Bourbon entrenched itself in the kingdom of Naples.

Effects of the Congress of Vienna

It was upon this sleeping country, hardly aware of its own existence as a nation, and certainly unaware of the modern world, that the Soldier of the Revolution fell. The ancient Republic of Venice was extinguished by his guns in 1797, the greater part of Northern Italy became the short-lived Cisalpine Republic, the more ephemeral Ligurian (Genoa) Roman, and Parthenopean (Naples) Republics followed in 1798 and 1799. The Cisalpine Republic became the Italian Republic (1801), and ultimately was merged in the Napoleonic kingdom of Italy.

During the brief English protectorate of Sicily in 1812, that island had been given a constitution. It must be said, however, that of all the Italian States, Piedmont alone had developed any trace of national character. But the fall of Napoleon and the Congress of Vienna restored the old situation, save that it left Venice subject to Austria, which thus became really mistress of all Northern and Central Italy, except for the States of the Church.

Italy then appears as consisting of the following States : The Papal States, the Kingdom of the Two Sicilies (Naples, the South, and Sicily), the Kingdom of Sardinia (Piedmont and Sardinia), the Grand Duchy of Tuscany, the Duchies of

Modena, Parma, and Lucca (all with Austrian or Bourbon princes), and the Republic of San Marino. Lucca was a duchy under the Bourbons from 1817 to 1847. In 1847 the Duke of Lucca became Duke of Parma, and Lucca was annexed to the Grand Duchy of Tuscany. Lombardy, Venice, Trent and Trieste and Istria remained part of the Austrian Empire.

From a modern point of view a more artificial state of affairs could scarcely be imagined. Italy was, in fact, "a geographical expression." There was, indeed, but one independent national

was to be formed and to grow. The annexation of Genoa to Piedmont in 1814 was the first step towards the union of the States of Italy into one nation.

It is part of the irony of things that the first step in that glorious achievement, as the last, was taken by a people who, as Bersezio says, did not even know that they were Italian; while it was De Maistre, a Savoyard born at Chambéry, a man who regarded the Pope as the source of all earthly authority, who advised Piedmont to "cultivate the Italian tendencies, they are born of the Revolution. Your method of proceeding—timid, neutral,

MODEL FARM PREMISES OF A SANDSTONE-CUTTER OF SETTIGNANO
The homely little village of Settignano lying on the southern slope of the hill of Fiesole is famed as the birthplace of Desiderio da Settignano, the celebrated Italian sculptor, pupil of Donatello, of the fifteenth century. Large quarries of sandstone, of which the hill is formed, surround the village, and the inhabitants are still known by the name of "stone-cutters"

State in Italy—Piedmont, with Turin as its capital and the House of Savoy as hereditary ruler. It was round this State—and, as it proved, this House—that the unity of the whole country was to be formed. But this was by no means clear from the beginning.

It is true, however, that it is in Piedmont alone, the least Italian province in Italy, that any trace of national character capable of action was to be found at this time. Piedmont alone possessed the necessary independence, stability of institutions, scarcely touched by the Revolution, and tenacity, to be that nucleus upon which the modern nation

suspensive, balancing—is destructive. Let the King make himself head of the Italians. This is vital, essential; words fail me, but this is my last word, my last expression—if we stand uncertain and become an obstacle, requiem eternam."

The forty years that followed after the Congress of Vienna had thus apportioned Italy between the Pope, Austria, the Spanish Bourbon, and the House of Savoy, are full of a restless, if obscure, revolution, chiefly against Austrian rule; and this movement gradually forms itself under the banner of Piedmont, whose Prime Minister, Cavour, becomes the great brain of the new Italian unity, of which Mazzini is the voice and the prophet, and Garibaldi the soldier.

It is essentially of the Revolution, this movement—the Revolution is its impelling force, as we see in the figures of Mazzini and Garibaldi; but this force is controlled, used, and finally mastered by the brain of Cavour, who places Piedmont at the head of it, and assures its success. Thus the achievement of the unity of

CHRISTMAS PASTORALE PIPER OF CAPRI
He follows a hereditary calling and pipes before the shrines and in the houses of the islanders at Christmastide, for the shepherds played at the birth at Christ and he holds that this act of devotion should be annually repeated

Italy was an act of the Piedmontese Government, whose reigning House then ascended the new throne of Italy. Italy was created as a political reality by a force outside herself, and Massimo d'Azeglio realizes this when he says: "Having created Italy, it remained to create Italians."

The innumerable incidents of this revolution, with its conspiracies, assassinations, risings, guerrilla war and reprisals, cannot be followed here in detail. It must be enough to mark its stages.

The first of these stages may be said to be the formation of the Young Italian Party by Mazzini in 1831. There followed the insurrection in Lombardy and Venice in March, 1848, which was supported by Piedmont. But the army of Piedmont

was finally defeated at Novara, and the first war for Italian independence ended with the heroic defence of Rome against the French by Mazzini and Garibaldi, and of Venice against the Austrians by Daniele Manin in 1849.

The second stage is reached ten years later. In 1859 Cavour is in alliance with France; a second war of independence is declared, and, with the help of the French, the Austrians are defeated at Montebello (May 20), Palestro (May 31), Magenta (June 4), Marignano (June 8), and Solferino (June 24). Meantime, from Florence, Parma, and Modena the foreign princes had retired, and insurrection had broken out throughout the Papal States. The unity of Italy seemed to be within the grasp of Cavour, when suddenly he learned that, on July 8, Napoleon had deserted him and made an armistice with Austria.

There followed the "infamous treaty" of Villafranca, which the King of Sardinia was obliged to sign. By this treaty Lombardy was annexed to Piedmont, but Italy was left still in chains and still separated. The whole country was dismayed at such a peace; agitations arose in Milan, Florence, Modena, Parma, and other cities, and finally Count Cavour, enraged and disgusted, resigned.

Meantime, Garibaldi exhorted all Italy and all Italians to arms (July 19). The Grand Duke of Tuscany abdicated (July 21). In the following months Tuscany, Modena, Parma, and the Romagna entered into an alliance and declared for annexation to Piedmont, and by October economically they were one. That autumn was full of work.

In the following January Cavour was again called to office. In March annexation to Piedmont was voted by universal suffrage (plebiscite) in Parma, Modena, Romagna, the Marches, and Tuscany, and was accepted by the King. Meanwhile the French had been bought off by the surrender of Savoy and Nice, and their troops were withdrawn from Italy in May.

Far more glorious deeds were about to be accomplished. In November, 1859, Garibaldi had retired from the Piedmontese service. In May, 1860, he sailed with his Thousand from Genoa, landed at Marsala, in Sicily, assumed the office of Dictator, defeated the Bourbon army, and forced the Neapolitan Government to agree to evacuate the island. In August he landed at Reggio, in Calabria, and in September entered Naples, the King retiring to Gaeta. There followed the revolt of the Papal States and the entry into official action of Cavour.

Kingdom of Italy Established

On Sept. 11 the Piedmontese troops entered the States of the Church, defeated the Papal army at Castelfidardo on the 18th, and took Ancona on the 29th. On Oct. 4 Victor Emmanuel II. took command of the army of Piedmont. On the 15th he marched on Naples. Garibaldi had defeated the Neapolitans at Volturno on Oct. 1, the King defeating them at Isernia on the 17th; on the 26th King and captain met, and Garibaldi greeted Victor Emmanuel with the title " King of Italy."

On the 21st, by plebiscite, Naples and Sicily had voted for annexation to Piedmont. On Nov. 7 Victor Emmanuel entered Naples as King, and Garibaldi retired to Caprera. The fugitive King of Naples was besieged in Gaeta, which on Nov. 3 was attacked by sea ; but the attack was prevented by the French fleet, which did not retire till the following Jan. 19, when the fortress surrendered after heavy bombardment, and Francis II. retired to Rome.

On Feb. 18 the first Italian Parliament assembled at Turin, and declared Victor Emmanuel II. King of Italy. On March 31 following, Great Britain recognized the Italian kingdom and Italy as a nation. The French recognition followed on June 24, eighteen days after the death of Cavour (June 6).

Active Protest of the Papacy

The Pope not only protested against the new kingdom, but all Naples was unsettled by clerical intrigue. It was recognized that Italy was incomplete without Rome, its historic head and capital city. The next ten years, filled as they are by minor intrigues, are really a period of waiting for the opportunity to enter Rome—Florence, in 1864, being proclaimed the capital of Italy. Garibaldi, the great if impatient captain, moves across the scene a little tragically, enters Sicily, and at Marsala calls for volunteers and gives his watchword, " Roma o morte." The Italian Government was obliged to act, and presently at Aspromonte made him prisoner (Aug. 29), but on Oct. 5 he was pardoned.

All was going well, and the new kingdom gradually establishing itself, when war broke out between Prussia and Austria (June 18, 1866). With the former Italy had allied herself in the previous May. On June 23 the Italian army crossed the Mincio against Austria, and was defeated at Custozza on the next day. That was a year of defeats for Italy. In July the Italian fleet was utterly beaten by the Austrians at Lissa. But Prussia made up by her victories for the Italian failure, and by the Treaty of Vienna Venetia was freed and by plebiscite voted for annexation to Italy (Oct. 21, 1866).

In the following year Garibaldi was again busy, notwithstanding the defeats of the previous year, in organizing attacks upon and risings within the Roman territory. In spite of the efforts of the Italian Government he succeeded in crossing the frontier, in defeating the Papal troops, and in taking Monte Rotondo. Inevitably this brought in the French, whose army arrived in Civita Vecchia, two brigades entering Rome for defence of the Pope. There followed Garibaldi's defeat at the hands of the French and Papal troops at Mentana (Nov. 3).

Rome, the Capital of United Italy

Less than three years later the real opportunity for the occupation of Rome offered itself with the outbreak of the Franco-Prussian War (July, 1870). The Pope could no longer expect help from France, the French troops were withdrawn, and in September the Italians entered Papal territory, occupied Viterbo on Sept. 12, and Rome itself, after a formal resistance and attack, on Sept. 20, by a breach in the Aurelian Wall by Porta Pia.

By plebiscite the Papal territory voted for annexation to the Italian kingdom (Oct. 2). On Dec. 5 the King declared Rome to be the capital of Italy, and the city which had for nearly 2,000 years been the capital of the world became the capital of the new Italian kingdom.

Thus was Italy finally established as a nation in some fifty-five years from the Congress of Vienna which had divided her up as one divides a dead body. It was not too hard, one might think, to get rid of the petty Austrian or Spanish princelings or kings, or even, with the military assistance of the French, to turn Austria out. It was, however, a different thing to dispose of the Papacy—which, in fact, had an indefeasible right in history, and a citadel in the majority of Italian hearts.

Rome has become the " capital of Italy," but it will always remain the city of the Pope for the rest of the world. Nor is there any real danger of conflict. If the last thing the Pope desires is to leave Rome, the last thing Italy desires is to see him go. The first years of bitterness are over already, and the sweetness of the Italian temperament, as well as the historic sense and, indeed, the very acute sense of advantage of the Italian people, will easily accommodate and later welcome the presence of the Pontifex Maximus in the Eternal City. What danger of trouble there may be would arise from a situation in which the Italian Government and the Papacy were in too close accord, which might well be a source of suspicion to the rest of the world.

The last fifty years of the history of Italy, 1870-1920, have been chiefly complicated by the establishment of the country upon a sound financial basis, by certain Colonial adventures, and by the Great War of 1914-1918.

The protagonists of the long struggle gradually disappeared—the great Cavour had died in 1861 ; Mazzini passed away in 1872 ; Victor Emmanuel in 1878, and within a few days Pope Pius IX. followed him ; Garibaldi alone remained, to die at Caprera in 1882. A later figure, lesser, it is true, than these heroes, but one who had played a very great part in the financial problem of the kingdom, lingered on to die in 1884—Signor Sella, Minister of Finance.

Colonial and European Policy

The attempts of the Italians to colonise in Africa have not been very successful. In 1885, following a trading company, they were officially in Massawa, on the Red Sea, where they established a government. In 1888 Italy annexed the place. This was the beginning of the Colony of Eritrea. The colony of Italian Somaliland, which lies between British Somaliland, Abyssinia, and Kenya Colony, was another attempt to establish a successful colony in Africa. These colonial adventures involved Italy in a war with Abyssinia which, in 1896, culminated in the disastrous battle of Adowa, where 7,000 Italians fell and 1,500 were taken prisoner.

In 1912 Italy obtained the territories of Tripoli and Cyrenaica from Turkey. At Paris, in 1919, Italy was able to retain possession of the island of Rhodes which, with the rest of the Dodecanese, she had held since her war with Turkey, and to obtain certain territorial privileges in Asia Minor.

During the years between the final establishment of the Italian kingdom and the Great War, Italy had been well governed and administered, had become solvent and even well-to-do, and more and more had come to count for something in the councils of Europe. She ranked as a first-class Power, a position which the Great War showed to be a reality. The chief Ministers under whom she gradually

attained this position were Crispi, Giolitti, and Sonnino.

As Europe more and more came to be divided into two camps, Italy, who as an insurance against her old enemy Austria had joined the group known as the Triple Alliance (Germany-Austria-Italy) came to play a moderating part. She is believed to have made a Mediterranean agreement with Great Britain, and though it was never in her power to maintain a balance, she inclined steadily towards a central policy, leaning, as things grew worse, towards the group France - Russia - Great Britain, and at Algeciras played a very useful role.

Italy's Part in the Great War

When war broke out in August, 1914, Italy, though a member of the Triple Alliance, declared her neutrality because, as she claimed, the war was a wanton attack on France and Russia. Her neutrality had very great consequences. It gave France and her Allies the moral victory from the first, and it materially saved the situation, which would, to say the least, have been much more serious even than it was in the early weeks of the war had an Italian army attempted to outflank the French upon the south-east.

In May, 1915, after the signature of the Treaty of London, Italy entered the war on certain terms, most of which she was to forgo. For long, quite alone, she successfully faced and thrust back the larger Austrian army which opposed her, and was successful in entering Gorizia. Many of her heroic soldiers were for years fighting at such a height among the Alps that they were for long months amid the snow.

Victory—and After

In October, 1917, she suffered her first real setback. This was at Caporetto, and it developed into a serious defeat, in which her Second Army was destroyed and she lost 2,500 guns. Driven back on to the Tagliamento, she fell back on to the Piave, where she stood at bay. By this time English and French armies and guns were in support, though not in action, and they remained to assist her till the victory of Vittorio Veneto (October, 1918), on the eve of the German collapse. The marvellous and wholly Italian stand upon the Piave is one of the greatest glories in Italian history.

At Versailles, Italy played a far less brilliant part than might have been looked for. The countrymen of Machiavelli were quite overmatched and outplayed by the Americans, the French, and the English. Baron Sonnino, the Italian Foreign Minister, had, in fact, a case that circumstances, which the war had developed, made almost untenable ; he was a man who would have been in place rather at the Congress of Vienna, among gentlemen and diplomats, than at the Conference of Paris among the representatives of the American, French, and British democracies. They were far too well practised in the " new " diplomacy and the " new " politics for him to be able to cope with them, or even understand them.

Italy emerged from the war victorious, with her Allies ; but, like every country caught in that appalling catastrophe, she emerged enormously weakened in every department of life, the bonds of her society loosened, her finances in chaos, her lira worth about a quarter of its normal value, and burdened with huge foreign and internal debts.

Like France and Belgium and other countries, she beheld more than one of her provinces devastated and in ruin. Her loss in dead reached the awful total of six hundred thousand.

To balance this, she may be said to have gained at last her natural frontier of the Alps, with Istria, but not Fiume, within the kingdom. To-day, while yet reaping the aftermath of war, she faces an uncertain future, perhaps with more hopefulness than any of her late Allies.

ITALY : FACTS AND FIGURES

The Country

Central peninsula of southern Europe. Includes Sicily, Sardinia, and smaller islands ; also, since the Great War, the Trentino, Gorizia, Gradisca, Alto Adige, Carniola, Trieste, and Istria. Total area about 118,130 square miles ; population about 40,070,000.

Dependencies include (1) the Colony of Eritrea, on the coast of the Red Sea, area about 45,800 square miles, coastline 670 miles, population 405,700 ; (2) Italian Somaliland, East Africa, area 139,430 square miles, population about 650,000 ; (3) Tripolitania and Cyrenaica, or Libya Italiana, in North Africa, area about 406,000 square miles, total population estimated at about 1,000,000, of whom 30 per cent. are Arabs, 40 per cent. negroes, 20 per cent. Jews, and some 10 per cent. Europeans ; (4) Concession of Tientsin, area about one-fifth of a square mile, population about 10,000, mainly Chinese.

Government and Constitution

Limited hereditary monarchy. Legislative authority vested in King and Parliament of two Houses : Senate consisting of princes of the Royal blood and unlimited number of Senators nominated by the king for life, and a House of Deputies (535 in number). Universal suffrage for men and women twenty-one years of age, and for men less than twenty-one who performed military service during the Great War. Proportional representation and scrutin de liste introduced in 1919. The kingdom is divided into 508 electoral districts, subdivided into 19,508 sections. Duration of Parliament five years. Chief elective local administrative bodies are the communal and provincial councils, members of which are elected for four years.

Defence

Service in army or navy compulsory and universal for nineteen years from the age of twenty —two years in regular army, six years in reserve, four years in mobile militia, seven years in territorial militia. Active army establishment (1921), 250,000 men. Military police (Carabinieri) recruited by selection from army. Special African corps of 8,600 in Erythrea, and native corps of 4,700 in Italian Somaliland.

Navy includes five Dreadnoughts, three pre-Dreadnoughts, three armoured cruisers, eighteen light cruisers, scouts and flotilla leaders, two torpedo gunboats, sixty-five destroyers, ninety-one torpedo boats and forty-six submarines. Personnel of over 1,000 officers and 40,000 men.

Commerce and Industries

Of 71,652,592 acres, 65,995,000 are under crops. Chief products : Cereals, timber, wines, maize, olives, oil, beans, chestnuts, rice, potatoes, lentils, fruit, sugar-beet, hemp, flax, cotton, sugar-cane, and flowers. Principal industries are hemp, linen, silk and cotton spinning, silkworm rearing, fisheries, and the manufacture of straw and felt hats, pottery, glass, alabaster, mosaics, laces, and motor-cars.

Mining developed in Sicily, Tuscany, Sardinia, Lombardy, and Piedmont : sulphur in Sicily, zinc and lead in Sardinia, marble, iron, copper, lead and quicksilver in Tuscany, and iron in the Abruzzi and Elba. Over 46,000 employed in quarries, over 2,304,000 in industrial establishments, and about 162,760 in the fisheries. Imports in 1920 (wheat, coal, and coke, and raw cotton important), estimated at £634,485,437 ; exports (raw silk and cotton manufactures important), £312,151,668.

Mercantile marine, 603 vessels of 1,075,200 gross tons. Normal value of the lira, 25.22½ to £1 sterling ; in January, 1923, about 96 to the £.

Communications

Railway lines, 9,741 miles (8,761 State owned). Telegraph lines, 35,205 miles ; telephone lines, 19,374 miles.

Religion and Education

Religion mainly Roman Catholic, but freedom of worship general. Education regulated by the State, which maintains public schools of every grade ; religious instruction given where parents desire it ; only lower grade instruction compulsory. Various disabilities imposed on illiterates. There are seventeen State universities, four free universities, and three institutions of university rank, in addition to technical establishments and a national institute for the instruction of illiterate adults.

Chief Towns

Naples (population 697,900), Milan (663,000), Rome, capital (600,000), Turin (452,000), Palermo (346,000), Genoa (300,000), Florence (242,000), Catania (217,000), Bologna (189,800), Venice (168,000), Messina (150,000), Leghorn (108,600), Bari (109,000), Padua (105,000), Ferrara (102,500).

THE WATERMAN'S KNOCK IN TRIPOLI'S STREETS

Water supply in Libya is a problem which presents serious difficulties to the Italian engineers seeking to increase the productivity of the soil by irrigation and the health of the population by provision of pure water. Until Libya passed into Italian possession this vital matter was neglected, and even to-day water-sellers go from house to house distributing water of doubtful purity in their goatskin vessels

Italy

III. Peoples of Her Colonies in Africa

By L. J. S. Wood

Correspondent of " The Times " in Italy

OF the European States possessing direct or indirect control of the Dark Continent, Italy occupies a relatively subordinate position after Great Britain, France, Portugal, and Spain. Before her unification was completed she turned her eyes towards Tunisia, and for ten years after 1864 she cherished hopes of extending her influence over that part of North Africa.

Forestalled, however, by the French occupation of Tunisia in 1881, Italy adopted a forward policy in the Red Sea littoral. To-day, apart from the Tientsin Concession, all her overseas possessions are in Africa—Eritrea, the eastern portion of Somaliland, and Tripolitania and Cyrenaica (Libya Italiana).

The future of Italy's North African possessions lies in the land. As a trade outlet for products brought by caravan from the far interior they have yielded place to the Gulf of Guinea on the one hand and the Sudan railway on the other. Deposits—sulphur known, phosphates believed in, minerals guessed at— take second place to agriculture and pasturage. The climate is very similar to that of the drier parts of Southern Italy and Sicily, but favours the cultivation of such tropical products as the date palm.

Much, if not all, depends on water, in particular degree the much-argued question of the soil of the coastal plain of Tripolitania. In this plain of from sixty to seventy miles wide, between the sea and the mountainous tableland, with its spur to the sea near Homs, there are semi-nomad tribesmen, living in tents, with well-defined grazing ground and sowing barley regularly, but there is a large amount of land capable of cultivation, given water, though at first sight it may have an appearance of desert through having been out of cultivation for so many hundreds of years.

Except for one small stream at Derna there is no permanent river in the two provinces ; there are torrent-beds, filled in the rainy season but dry for more than half the year, and there are wells. Wherever a satisfactory supply of water has been found there is a fertile oasis, generally on the coast. The rainfall in Tripoli averages sixteen and a half inches, in Cyrenaica it ranges from eight to twenty-three and a half inches. To be made profitable, agriculture will depend on irrigation by reservoirs and conduits for the water from the hills and on raising water undoubtedly percolating underground at varying depths.

Cyrenaica holds more promise than Tripolitania ; the slopes of the hills approach the sea more closely ; its most fertile zone is the high ground extending from south of Benghazi as far as Bomba, called from its fertility and altitude, the " Green Mountain"—in comparison with the sandy steppes of the Great Libyan Desert,

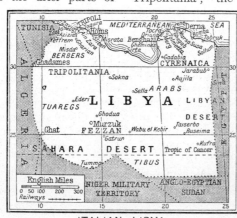

ITALIAN LIBYA

NATIVE VALOUR ENHANCED BY DISCIPLINE
A soldierly and dignified figure despite his bare feet, and a born fighting man, this is an Askari trooper of the squadron of native cavalry included in the special African corps in Eritrea that is a substantive part of the Italian army

proportion of this. The Berbers are a steadier race than the Arabs, contented with agricultural life, with less innate fighting tendencies. Nor is it correct now to look on the Arab of that district as nothing but a predatory fighter. He, too, now tends to settle down in a quiet life on his holding unless stirred up by some too-enterprising chief or instigator from outside.

In the region of Ghadames and Ghat the Tuareg element is strong, while the Fezzan is inhabited by a negroid population with some Arab and Berber admixture. Races have mixed, indeed, in an extraordinary manner, in the coastal towns and villages at least, the mixture of Arab, Berber, and negro from the interior producing "the bulky thick-lipped negroid, almost black, the slender thoroughbred of the pious legend, hook-nosed and bronzed, the white-faced degenerate that is not uncommon in the littoral, and intermediate types as well." The negro admixture follows naturally from the close connexion between the Barbary States and the regions of the Niger and Lake Chad. Many generations of slave-raiding in the interior have had their inevitable effect.

The ex-Turkish provinces of Tripolitania and Cyrenaica were gained by Italy as a result of the war with Turkey, under whose domination they had been for less than a hundred years after a long independent existence as one of the Barbary States. Economically and commercially Italian interests and

with its few oases, lying behind. The development of Libya Italiana has been retarded by the Great War, but the difficulties caused by restless and ambitious tribal chiefs are being eliminated methodically, and the natives—Berbers happily, Arabs with quite willing resignation—are settling down to the life of peace and gentle cultivation of the soil and pasturage with which they are contented if left undisturbed.

The word " Arab " is often used as a generic term in speaking of the population of Tripolitania and Cyrenaica, but the old Berber stock forms a very considerable

activity had been strong on the Libyan coast, and the region between French Tunis and British Egypt had long been regarded as Italy's sphere of influence. War was declared on Sept. 29, 1911. In November of that year the two provinces were formally annexed, and were surrendered by Turkey at the Peace of Lausanne, Oct. 15, 1912, but the resistance of the natives continued during 1913 and broke out again as a result of the Great War.

The native population of Tripolitania is prevalently Mussulman of Malechite rite; there are a fair number of Jews, a few Maltese, Greeks, Algerians, Moroccans, and Egyptians. Tripoli is the main port, and the centre from which the life of the country radiates; minor towns on the coast are Zuara, Zavia to the west, Homs, Tagiura, Misurata, Sliten, Sirte to the east, Azizia a short way inland but in the coastal zone, farther inland Cussabal in the Tarhuna, Garian, and minor settlements. Of the population of Tripoli itself two-thirds are natives and Jews. It has a fair harbour.

The life of the country is pastoral and agricultural in small holdings, producing

SPIRITUAL GUIDES FOR LIBYAN CHRISTIAN SOLDIERS
Bearded, stern-faced figures, whose native dignity is enhanced by their sombre robes and black turbans, these two Copts, priests of the ancient Coptic Church, are chaplains of an Askari regiment of the Italian army quartered at Benghazi. Seated between them is an army interpreter, whose bare feet are oddly incongruous with the khaki uniform and bandolier which he wears so proudly

FRIENDLY BLACKS AND KINDLY WHITES IN CONFERENCE
Their deliberations ended, these chiefs of the Middle Shebeli district of Italian Somaliland were gratified by being photographed with their benevolent governor. Well organized colonisation and scientific irrigation are turning their land into a prosperous agricultural region

grain, table grapes, henna, and olives, which now provide sufficient oil for home consumption ; sponge and tunny fishing are sound industries ; tobacco cultivation is progressing. Industry is growing for the preparation of local products for the market, hides, metals, wood, alfa, soaps. Native representatives have been granted a share in the parliamentary government.

Railways are open from Tripoli to Zuara, 80 miles ; Tagiura and Ain Zara, 17 miles ; Azizia, 32 miles ; and others are prospected. There are 1,000 miles of roads in addition to caravan routes, the two principal of which, one going due south through Murzuk, the other farther west through Ghadames and Ghat, and both, with interior derivations, cover many hundreds of miles to the heart of Africa. The caravans bring ivory, ostrich feathers, roughly cured sheep and goat skins, leather, woven fabrics from the Sudan ; they carry back cotton and silk fabrics, linen and woollen burnous, coral and glass objects, tea, coffee, sugar, mirrors, rough paper, colouring materials..

While the natives generally speak Arabic or Berber, Italian and other European languages are common in the chief centres. Corn, barley, and maize flour, rice, potatoes, dates, native butter, a moderate quantity of meat, tea, coffee, are the main articles of diet ; there is a great liking for sugar. Native clothing is universally maintained, some being manufactured at home, some imported.

The principal town and port of Cyrenaica is Benghazi. Smaller towns,

YOUNG MAIDS OF ITALY IN THE OLD TOWN OF TRIPOLI

There is plenty of colour and animation in Tripoli, the capital of the Tripolitania district of Italian Libya. It is an Oriental-looking town, with many arcaded streets, and, in the Turkish quarter, mosques and minarets breaking the monotony of the flat-roofed, whitewashed houses. The markets are thronged with a very mixed crowd of Arabs, Italians, Jews, Maltese, and negroes

WILD GRACE LEASHED IN SILKEN SCARVES

Very graceful posturing is the chief feature of the scarf dance of Libyan dancing girls, women of mixed blood, but often of prepossessing appearance. This girl adds variety to her performance by balancing a tray laden with tea-things on her head while sinking to and rising from her knees. The dance is performed to a monotonous accompaniment of drumming and clapping of hands

FROM TRIPOLI'S TOWER OF DARKNESS THE MUEZZIN CRIES

Every Mahomedan mosque has its muezzin, whose duty it is to proclaim the five daily hours of prayer—dawn, noon, four p.m., sunset, and midnight. The call, sounded from the minaret, comprises these sentences : " Allah is great " (thrice) ; " There is no God but Allah " (twice) ; " Mahomet is the Prophet of God " (twice) ; " Come to prayer " (twice) ; " There is no God but Allah " (twice)

with convenient harbours or anchorage, are found at intervals along the coast and in the immediate coast zone : Gadabia, Soluk, Ghemines, Driana, Tokra, Merg, Tolmeta, Marsa Susa, Cirene, Ghegab, Derna, with small but convenient harbour, Tobruk with large natural harbour. Sixteen miles of railway are open from Benghazi to Er Regina ; in addition sixteen miles of the extension to Merg are almost completed. There are over 1,000 miles of roads and caravan routes taking motor traffic.

Of caravan routes proper the principal is that running due south to the interior via Unjanga, but much of the caravan trade which used to come to Benghazi is attracted to the Sudan railway.

Arabic and Berber are the languages generally spoken, with Italian quite common in the towns. As in Tripolitania, native costume is still worn. The main industry is agriculture. In the year 1919-20 100,000 tons of barley alone, of excellent quality, were grown ; 31,000 tons of this were exported to

Italy and elsewhere for malt. There are promising signs of cooperation between Italians and native occupiers of the soil for improved cultivation of the fertile regions near the coast. Tunny fishing is a sound industry; sponges also realize a large monetary return. There are natural salt marshes and sulphur deposits, which leave a margin for export, mainly to Egypt, over the amount required at home for agricultural and medicinal purposes. A very promising industry is that of carpets and allied products from the wool abundant in the colony.

The colony of Eritrea lies along the African coast of the southern portion of the Red Sea from Ras Casar, where it touches Egypt, to Ras Duneira on the Straits of Bab-el-Mandeb, where the Red Sea merges into the Gulf of Aden and the Indian Ocean. Its beginnings go back to the purchase by the Rubattino

Company for a coaling-station of the port and district of Assab, almost at the southern end of the present coast-line of the colony, from the Sultan of Rahaita.

The province was formed in 1890, established on a civil basis in 1900, its boundaries defined in 1908 after negotiations with the countries interested— England and Egypt, Turkey, Abyssinia— and a short period of fighting with the last-named, which included the expedition to Adowa. On the north and north-west it touches the Anglo-Egyptian frontier, on the south and south-west Abyssinia, at its south-east point French Somaliland. It includes a number of small islands, principal among them the Dahlar group off Massawa.

The colony naturally divides itself into two parts, north and south, about equal in extent of coast-line but unequal in territory. In the northern part it extends inland in one part as far as

TRIPOLITAN MODESTY STEALING TO THE MOSQUE

Virtually the only excursion abroad that the town-dwelling Tripolitan women make is to the mosque, and even that is almost furtive, as heavily muffled, they steal along in the shadows of the walls to the screened portion of the building set apart for them. Decorum requires these harem women to enshawl themselves in the manner observed by the second lady in this procession

SWARTHY CHARMS FROM LIBYAN SANDS
This dark-eyed Beduin girl with her metal trinkets comes from Cyrenaica, one of the two administrative areas of the Italian colony of Libya that stretches from the southern shores of the Mediterranean far into the Sahara

maize are grown, but the people are mainly nomads, living in tents and pasturing large herds of cattle, sheep, goats, and camels, with a local trade of meat, hides, and butter. Here and in the valleys of the interior big game is found—lion, panther, elephant, leopard, hyena, jackal, giraffe, hippopotamus, caiman, and monkeys in infinite variety.

The nomad population of the south is peaceful, and the Abyssinian fighting-blood of the highland people is now tempered. That they can still fight, however, was seen in the gallantry of the Askari, the Eritrean regiments in the Italian campaign in Libya in 1911-1912. They are slimly built, of no great muscular development, but capable of bearing fatigue to an unlimited extent. Their colouring is bronze with paler shades, and here and there a darker strain, possibly negroid, though there are few traces of this or of Arab blood. They trace their origin back in tradition to the Queen of Sheba, and are, in fact, of Hamitic extraction. Their habitual dress is a pair of drawers, sometimes a shirt, always the draping sheet-like mantle.

340 miles from the coast ; the southern part, Dancalia, is a low-lying strip about thirty-six miles wide along the coast of the Red Sea.

Characteristics of the country and the life in it are dictated by climate, which in the low-lying ground on the coast and in the interior valleys is tropical, the temperature sometimes reaching 120° in the shade, and similarly in the valleys tropical vegetation is found. The Abyssinian plateau, however, which covers much of the northern part of the colony, has a temperate climate with regular rains between June and September, and is largely an agricultural district, grain, tobacco, cotton, and coffee being cultivated.

The southern strip is wild, with a few fertile oases interspersed. Durra and

The Askari are a simple people, their life, seen in such outward signs as agricultural implements, houses of rough stone and thatched roofs, cooking and other utensils, simple to the verge of primitive. If its inner signs are also simple, customs bear traces of a patriarchal civilization continuing throughout ages as regards marriage, birth, and death, respect for elders and social customs generally, and the Italian

السلام عليكم

HELMET AND MASK GUARDING BEAUTY'S FACE

Arabs, with a considerable admixture of Berber blood, are the dominant element of the coastal
population of Italian Libya. They have dark skin, oval face, aquiline features, and straight, black hair.
The women, many of whom are handsome, live secluded lives, and out of doors muffle themselves in
shawls, also concealing the lower part of the face with the thin dark covering here shown

authorities have wisely allowed administration in social matters to continue on old-established lines.

In religion the majority are Mahomedans or Coptic Christians, with a few Roman Catholics. They are generally a temperate people, drinking a mild beer made of durra grain, eating a little meat and various breads made from corn, maize, barley, durra, ground by women between two stones. The old Semitic language, Tigrai, is generally spoken. There are few Jews, and these isolated.

Mixed marriages between Europeans and natives are not recognized.

The development of the colony has proceeded slowly but surely. There are several ports with safe anchorage, principal among them Massawa, with over 1,000 feet length of quay space. There is a railway thence to the capital, Asmara, sixty-three miles inland, 7,600 feet above sea-level; railways are under construction from Asmara to Cheren and to Agordat. In addition to the numerous caravan routes to the interior

SONGS OF LAUD AND HONOUR AT JEWISH NUPTIALS

Jews of the Libyan coast towns are of finer type than those of Palestine and Egypt. They avoid fusion with other races, marrying only among themselves. At a Jewish wedding in Tripoli, the bride is brought to the synagogue heavily veiled, and two of her women friends sing a song praising her and her bridegroom's virtues, the children of both families accompanying it with hand-clapping

ARAB M.P.'S PLAY THEIR PART IN THE PARLIAMENT AT BENGHAZI

For administrative and military purposes Italian Libya is divided into two provinces—Tripolitania and Cyrenaica—each under a governor. A secretary-general organizes and supervises the civil administration in each, and in both provinces there is a small local parliament elected by all citizens, the natives having equal rights with the Italians. The Cyrenaican parliament sits at Benghazi

a number of roads radiate from Asmara, with a motor service on several, feeding the caravans.

The rivers of the colony generally have no great flow of water, though the Gash is utilised to irrigate nearly 4,000 acres in one spot and plans are on foot for storage reservoirs, whereby it is believed cotton can be grown largely and profitably even in the low-lying country on the coast.

Italian Somaliland is formed of a strip of territory running down the East African coast of the Indian Ocean from Cape Guardafui to the frontier with Kenya Colony near Port Durnford. On the land side it touches British Somaliland, Abyssinia, and Kenya.

The northern portion comprises the Italian Protectorate over the Sultanates of Obbia and the Migiurtini and the territory of Nogal by arrangement with Great Britain, Abyssinia, and the Sultan of Zanzibar in 1889. In 1905 the latter also sold to Italy his rights in the ports of Benadir, the southern part of the colony, the frontiers of which were defined in 1908 by agreements with

Great Britain and Abyssinia, and have been extended to include farther British East African territory.

In general it is a wild country with a rocky coast, especially in the north, where the hills rise directly from the sea. The towns—Alula, Illigh, Obbia the principal—are little more than coast settlements ; ports with reliable anchorage are lacking. Interspersed, however, in the prevailing sand dunes are many fertile oases with satisfactory pasturage ensured by rainfall and the percolation of the water from the hills. The southern portion, Benadir, holds out far better prospects. The country here rises slowly from the coast to the interior plateau, which is drained by two important rivers, the wealth of the colony : Webi Shebeli, which, after approaching the sea and running parallel to it for a hundred miles, finally spreads and loses itself in the dunes without finding direct outlet ; and the Juba, the outlet of which is just north of Kismayu.

The development of the fertile country on and between these two rivers has been in progress for some years ; a

3119